POSTCARDS FROM SOUTH FLORIDA

Every winter, millions of sunbathers head for the warm, pristine beaches of South Florida. See chapter 1 for a list of the best beaches in the region.
© Trevor Wood/Tony Stone Worldwide.

Stop in at Sloppy Joes, the quintessential Key West watering hole, where a lively crowd gossips the night away while downing martinis and smoking cigars. See chapter 11 for more on Key West's nightlife. © *Darrell Ray Jones/The Stock Market.*

Biscayne National Park and the Florida Keys offer some of the best snorkeling and scuba diving in South Florida. See chapters 10 and 11. © *Stephen Frink/Waterhouse Stock Photography.*

See the house where "Papa" Hemingway wrote some of his best works and check out other Hemingway haunts while in Key West. See chapter 11. © Michael Ventura Photography.

*Built alongside the ruins of oil magnate Henry Flagler's incredible Overseas Railroad, the Seven-mile Bridge is an excellent vantage point from which to view the stunning waters of the Keys. See chapter 11.
© Michael Ventura Photography.*

Take a boat tour through the wilds of Everglades National Park—you're almost guaranteed to glimpse a gator. See chapter 10. © D.E. Cox/Tony Stone Images.

It's hard to walk anywhere in Miami's South Beach without encountering magnificent examples of Art Deco architecture. See chapter 7 for information on walking tours of the Art Deco District. © Stuart Westmorland/Tony Stone Images.

*Sip cocktails at a hotel bar, see a show, or salsa the night away at a hot dance club; when the sun goes down, Miami just begins to heat up. See chapter 9 for more on Miami's nightlife.
© Catherine Karnow Photography.*

Miami Beach—home to a multitude of hotels, clubs and crowded beaches— offers a great nightlife, but if you're looking for peace and quiet, look elsewhere. See chapter 5 for information on accommodations in Miami. © Alan Schein/The Stock Market.

The oldest hotel in Coral Gables, the stately Biltmore is a National Historic Landmark—one of only two operating hotels in Florida so designated. See chapter 5.
© *Darrell Jones Photography.*

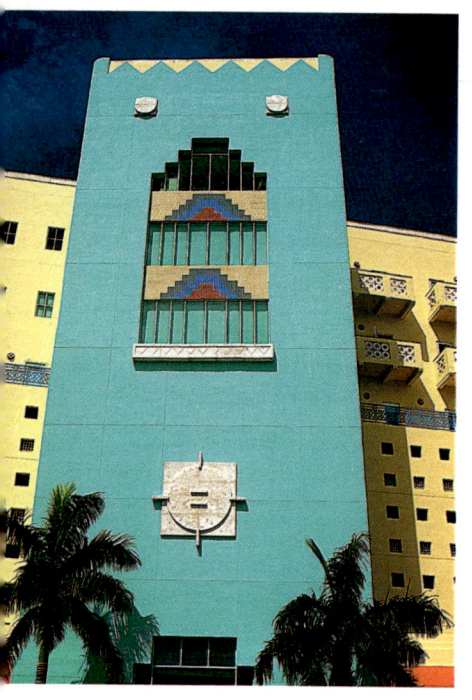

South Florida has the largest concentration of Art Deco architecture in the United States. © *Gail Mooney/Kelly/Mooney Photography.*

*You'll have no trouble renting a boat or hopping on a water taxi when you visit Fort Lauderdale's Isle of Venice, the "yachting capital of the world." See chapter 12.
© Jeff Greenberg/Silver Images.*

Tee up, or just practice your putting on Palm Beach's world-class golf courses. See chapter 12. © Allen Eyestone/Palm Beach Post/Silver Images.

Known as the "Taj Mahal of North America," The Flagler Museum features a 55-room Edwardian-style mansion and stunning grounds. See chapter 12. © M. Timothy O'Keefe Photography.

Taking a kayak trip down the Loxahatchee River is a great way to see the abundance of plant and animal life found on South Florida's Treasure Coast. See chapter 13. © Murry H. Sill/Silver Images.

When should I travel to get the best airfare?
Where do I go for answers to my travel questions?
What's the best and easiest way to plan and book my trip?

www.frommers.travelocity.com

Frommer's, the travel guide leader, has teamed up with **Travelocity.com**, the leader in online travel, to bring you an in-depth, easy-to-use resource designed to help you plan and book your trip online.

At **www.frommers.travelocity.com**, you'll find free online updates about your destination from the experts at Frommer's plus the outstanding travel planning and purchasing features of Travelocity.com. Travelocity.com provides reservations capabilities for 95 percent of all airline seats sold, more than 47,000 hotels, and over 50 car rental companies. In addition, Travelocity.com offers more than 2,000 exciting vacation and cruise packages. Travelocity.com puts you in complete control of your travel planning with these and other great features:

Expert travel guidance from Frommer's - over 150 writers reporting from around the world!

Best Fare Finder - an interactive calendar tells you when to travel to get the best airfare

Fare Watcher - we'll track airfare changes to your favorite destinations

Dream Maps - a mapping feature that suggests travel opportunities based on your budget

Shop Safe Guarantee - 24 hours a day / 7 days a week live customer service, and more!

Whether traveling on a tight budget, looking for a quick weekend getaway, or planning the trip of a lifetime, Frommer's guides and Travelocity.com will make your travel dreams a reality. You've bought the book, now book the trip!

Travelocity.com
A Sabre Company

Frommer's

Other Great Guides for Your Trip:

Frommer's Florida

Frommer's Florida from $70 a Day

Frommer's Portable Tampa Bay & St. Petersburg

Frommer's Walt Disney World & Orlando

Frommer's Caribbean Cruises & Ports of Call

Frommer's Caribbean Ports of Call

The Unofficial Guide to Miami & the Keys

The Unofficial Guide to Walt Disney World

Walt Disney World for Dummies

Florida for Dummies

Here's what the critics say about Frommer's:

"Amazingly easy to use. Very portable, very complete."
—*Booklist*

♦

"The only mainstream guide to list specific prices. The Walter Cronkite of guidebooks—with all that implies."
—*Travel & Leisure*

♦

"Complete, concise, and filled with useful information."
—*New York Daily News*

♦

"Hotel information is close to encyclopedic."
—*Des Moines Sunday Register*

♦

"Detailed, accurate and easy-to-read information for all price ranges."
—*Glamour Magazine*

Frommer's® 2001

South Florida

by Victoria Caldwell

IDG Books Worldwide, Inc.
An International Data Group Company
Foster City, CA • Chicago, IL • Indianapolis, IN • New York, NY

About the Author
Victoria Caldwell is a freelance journalist and a graduate of the Columbia University School of Journalism. When she isn't teaching classes in New York, the former Miami resident often heads back home to soak up the nightlife in South Beach. She is also a coauthor of *Frommer's Florida* and *Frommer's Florida from $70 a Day*.

IDG Books Worldwide, Inc.
An International Data Group Company
919 E. Hillsdale Blvd.
Suite 400
Foster City, CA 94404

Find us online at **www.frommers.com**

Copyright © 2000 by IDG Books Worldwide, Inc.
Maps copyright © 2000 by IDG Books Worldwide, Inc.

All rights reserved. No part of this book may be reproduced or transmitted in any form or by any means, electronic or mechanical, including photocopying, recording, or by any information storage and retrieval system, without permission in writing from the Publisher.

FROMMER'S is a registered trademark of Arthur Frommer. Used under license.

ISBN 0-7645-6090-5
ISSN 1530-8758

Editor: Naomi P. Kraus
Production Editor: Scott Barnes
Photo Editor: Richard Fox
Design by Michele Laseau
Staff Cartographers: John Decamillis, Elizabeth Puhl, and Roberta Stockwell
Page Creation by IDG Books Indianapolis Production Department

Special Sales
For general information on IDG Books Worldwide's books in the U.S., please call our Consumer Customer Service department at 1-800-762-2974. For reseller information, including discounts, bulk sales, customized editions, and premium sales, please call our Reseller Customer Service department at 1-800-434-3422.

Manufactured in the United States of America

5 4 3 2 1

Contents

List of Maps vii

1 The Best of Miami & South Florida 1

1 Frommer's Favorite South Florida Experiences 4
2 Best Hotel Bets 5
3 Best Dining Bets 7
   Catch a Rising Star 9

2 Planning a Trip to Miami & South Florida 10

1 Visitor Information & Money 10
   What Things Cost in Miami 12
2 When to Go 13
   South Florida Calendar of Events 13
3 Health & Insurance 20
4 Tips for Travelers with Special Needs 21
5 Getting There 23

Planning Your Trip: An Online Directory 28

3 For Foreign Visitors 42

1 Preparing for Your Trip 42
2 Getting to the United States 46
3 Getting Around the United States 46
Fast Facts: For the Foreign Traveler 47

4 Getting to Know Miami 52

1 Orientation 52
   The Neighborhoods in Brief 55
2 Getting Around 57
   Fast Facts: Miami 60

5 Miami Accommodations 64

1 South Beach 65
2 Miami Beach: Surfside, Bal Harbour & Sunny Isles 80
3 Key Biscayne 88
4 Downtown 90
5 West Miami/Airport Area 93
6 North Dade 95
7 Coral Gables 96
8 Coconut Grove 98

v

6 Miami Dining 101

1. Restaurants by Cuisine 102
2. South Beach 104
3. Miami Beach: Surfside, Bal Harbour & Sunny Isles 120
4. Key Biscayne 126
5. Downtown 128
6. Little Havana 132
   Cuban Coffee 133
   From Seviche to Picadillo: Latin Cuisine at a Glance 134
7. North Dade 135
   Family-Friendly Restaurants 137
8. Coral Gables & Environs 137
9. Coconut Grove 141
10. South Miami 144

7 What to See & Do in Miami 147

1. Miami's Beaches 147
2. The Art Deco District 151
3. Animal Parks 151
4. Miami's Museum & Art Scene 153
5. Worldly Wonders 157
6. Nature Preserves, Parks & Gardens 158
   Picnicking in the Park 160
7. Especially for Kids 161
8. Video Arcades & Entertainment Centers 162
9. Sightseeing Cruises & Organized Tours 162
10. Water Sports 164
11. More Ways to Play, Both Indoors & Out 166
    A Berry Good Time 167
12. Spectator Sports 170

8 Miami Shopping 173

1. The Shopping Scene 173
2. Shopping A to Z 175
   A Taste of Old Florida 181

9 Miami After Dark 187

1. Bars 188
2. The Club & Music Scene 190
   Breaking Through the Velvet Ropes 193
   Where to Learn to Salsa 197
3. The Performing Arts 198
4. Movies & More 201
5. Late-Night Bites 202

10 Side Trips from Miami 203

1. A Glimpse of Everglades National Park: The Southeast Portion 203
2. Biscayne National Park 214
3. Cruises & Other Caribbean Getaways 218

11 The Keys 220

1. The Upper & Middle Keys: Key Largo to Marathon 223
   The 10 "Keymandments" 226
2. The Lower Keys: Big Pine Key to Coppitt Key 240

The Truth About Keys Cuisine 245
3 Key West 246

Going, Going, Gone: Where to Catch the Famous Key West Sunset 251
4 The Dry Tortugas 266

12 The Gold Coast 268

1 Broward County: Hallandale & Hollywood to Fort Lauderdale 269
One If by Land, Taxi If by Sea 275
2 Boca Raton & Delray Beach 288

3 Palm Beach & West Palm Beach 297
The Sport of Kings 301
4 Jupiter & Northern Palm Beach County 310
Discovering a Remarkable Natural World 313

13 The Treasure Coast 317

1 Hobe Sound, Stuart & Jensen Beach 319
Wildlife Exploration: From Gators to Manatees to Turtles 321
2 Port St. Lucie, Fort Pierce & North Hutchinson Island 326

3 Vero Beach & Sebastian 330
4 A Side Trip Inland: Fishing at Lake Okeechobee 337
Going After the Big One 339

Appendix: Useful Toll-Free Numbers & Web Sites 341

Index 344

General Index 344
Accommodations Index 354

Restaurant Index 356

List of Maps

Florida 2
Miami at a Glance 53
South Beach Accommodations 67
Miami Beach Accommodations 81
Accommodations in Coral Gables, Coconut Grove, Downtown & Key Biscayne 89
South Beach Dining 107
Miami Beach Dining 121
Dining in Coral Gables, Coconut Grove, Downtown & Key Biscayne 127
Miami Area Attractions & Beaches 148

South Beach Attractions 155
Attractions in South Miami–Dade 159
South Beach After Dark 189
Everglades National Park 204
The Florida Keys 221
Key West 247
Fort Lauderdale Attractions & Accommodations 271
Palm Beach & Boca Raton 293
The Treasure Coast 319

AN INVITATION TO THE READER
In researching this book, we discovered many wonderful places—hotels, restaurants, shops, and more. We're sure you'll find others. Please tell us about them, so we can share the information with your fellow travelers in upcoming editions. If you were disappointed with a recommendation, we'd love to know that, too. Please write to:

Frommer's South Florida 2001
IDG Books Worldwide, Inc.
909 Third Avenue
New York, NY 10022

AN ADDITIONAL NOTE
Please be advised that travel information is subject to change at any time—and this is especially true of prices. We therefore suggest that you write or call ahead for confirmation when making your travel plans. The authors, editors, and publisher cannot be held responsible for the experiences of readers while traveling. Your safety is important to us, however, so we encourage you to stay alert and be aware of your surroundings. Keep a close eye on cameras, purses, and wallets, all favorite targets of thieves and pickpockets.

WHAT THE SYMBOLS MEAN
✪ Frommer's Favorites
Our favorite places and experiences—outstanding for quality, value, or both.

The following abbreviations are used for credit cards:

AE	American Express	EC	Eurocard
CB	Carte Blanche	JCB	Japan Credit Bank
DC	Diners Club	MC	MasterCard
DISC	Discover	V	Visa
ER	EnRoute		

FIND FROMMER'S ONLINE
www.frommers.com offers up-to-the-minute listings on almost 200 cities around the globe—including the latest bargains and candid, personal articles updated daily by Arthur Frommer himself. No other Web site offers such comprehensive and timely coverage of the world of travel.

The Best of Miami & South Florida

A friend of mine, upon arriving in Miami, once remarked, "You know what I like most about Miami? It's the closest thing to being in America." He wasn't too far off the mark. When you arrive in South Florida you'll immediately be taken by the vast array of ethnic groups from the Caribbean, South America, Europe, and Mexico that live here—it's a microcosm of America. Walk along almost any beach and you'll hear Spanish (in at least 10 dialects), Portuguese, Creole, French, and Italian almost as much as you hear English. It's easy to see why Miami has been called the "Capital of the Americas." The city is truly a kaleidoscope of colors, rhythms, scents, and accents.

Miami's history is marked by constant infusions of multilingual migrations (from the original Spanish occupation to the influx of Cubans, Nicaraguans, and Haitians in the last 30 years) and has become a gateway the United Nations can only dream of. Encompassing both the mainland and the barrier islands of Miami Beach, Greater Miami boasts about two million residents and hosts almost 10 million of the 20 million visitors that South Florida receives annually. It's also home to the international headquarters for hundreds of multinational corporations and serves as a hub for North, South, and Central American businesses and tourism.

Since the Spanish first colonized the area in the 16th century, South Florida has always been a magnet to the masses. The epitome of relaxation, it offers year-round warmth, exotic locales, and a truly international community! From the clubs of South Beach to the Gold Coast's beaches to the natural wonders of the Keys, South Florida offers an array of activities that will please even the most discriminating visitor.

Miami has an endless number of sporting and recreational activities to keep you entertained. Did I mention our sparkling beaches are beyond compare? Crystal clear waters span a turquoise horizon and sandy beaches are filled with palm fronds and seashells. And all these natural wonders are juxtaposed against pastel-colored hotels, exciting restaurants, excellent shopping, and a thriving nightlife that includes a ballet company, a symphony, and an opera house with national reputations.

Whether your idea of a night out on the town involves frolicking follies, a cabaret review, or waiting on line outside a hot nightclub, you'll find yourself in plenty of good company.

And though it is South Florida's crown jewel, Miami isn't all this area has to offer. While you're down here, take a day or two to explore

Florida

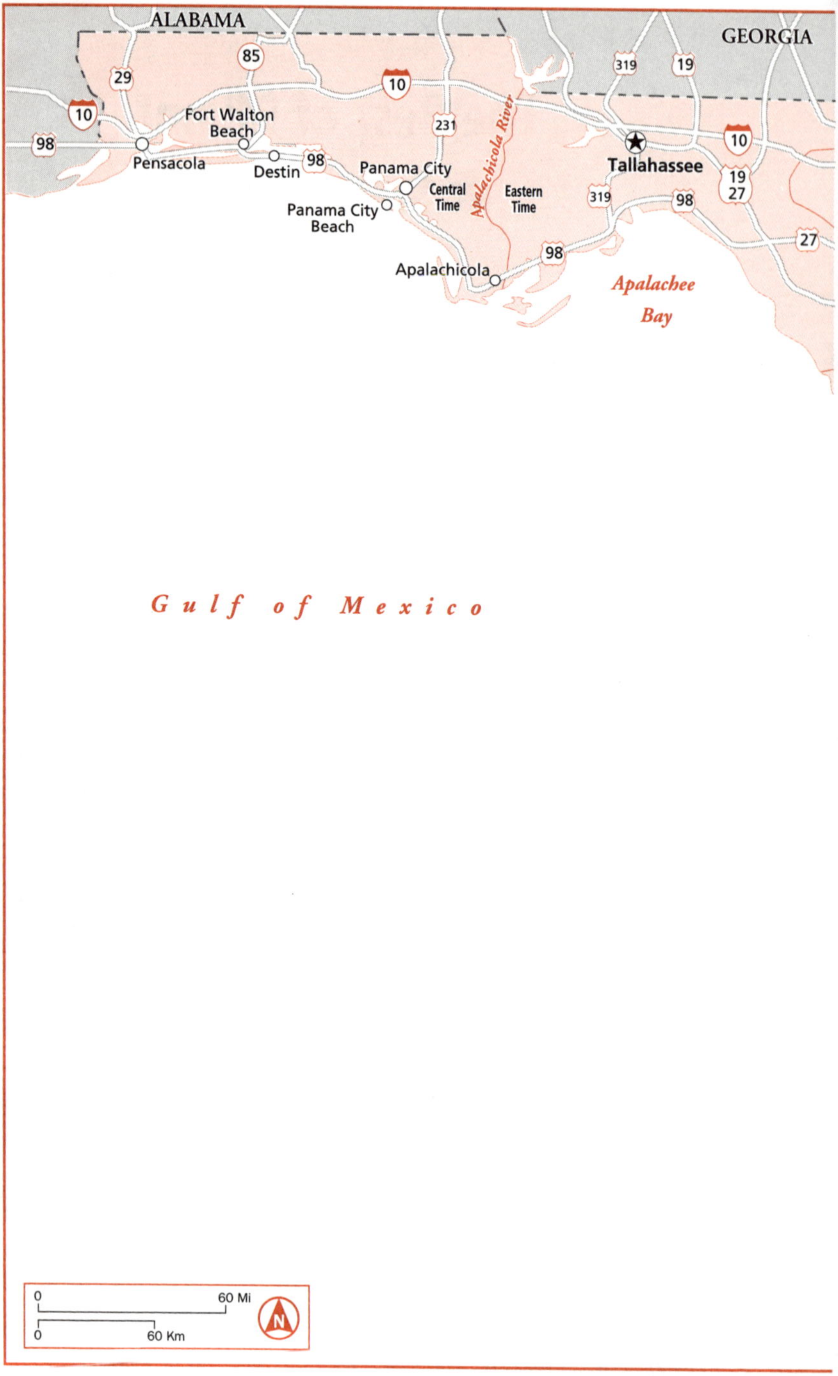

ATLANTIC OCEAN
Suwannee River
Amelia Island
Jacksonville Beach
Jacksonville
Ponte Vedera Beach
Lake City
St. Johns River
St. Augustine
St. Augustine Beach
Gainesville
Ocala National Forest
Ocala
Daytona Beach
Cedar Key
De Land
Homosassa Springs
Orlando
NASA-Kennedy Space Center
Cape Canaveral
Bee Line Expwy.
Tarpon Springs
Kissimmee
Cocoa Beach
Florida's Turnpike
Melbourne
Tampa
Lakeland
Winter Haven
Clearwater
Tampa Bay
St. Petersburg
Kissimmee River
Vero Beach
Anna Maria Island
Bradenton
Fort Pierce
Sarasota
Jensen Beach
Lake Okeechobee
Riviera Beach
West Palm Beach
Palm Beach
Caloosahatchee River
Fort Myers
Captiva Island
Delray Beach
Sanibel Island
Fort Myers Beach
Big Cypress Swamp
Boca Raton
Pompano Beach
Everglade Pkwy. (Alligator Alley)
Naples
Fort Lauderdale
Big Cypress National Preserve
Dania
Hollywood
Everglades City
Miami Beach
Marco Island
Miami
Ten Thousand Islands
Everglades National Park
Homestead
Flamingo
Florida Bay
Key Largo
Plantation
Florida Keys
Long Key
Marathon Key
Key West

the unique experiences of the Keys, the Gold Coast, and the Treasure Coast. In these spots, you can take in a spring baseball game, walk in the footsteps of Papa Hemingway, get up close and personal with the area's sea life, or just soak up the serenity of the unspoiled landscapes. From leisurely day cruises to exciting and culture-filled museums, the best can be found right here in South Florida, America's own backyard.

1 Frommer's Favorite South Florida Experiences

- **Boating off the Coast of Miami Beach.** Jump on a party boat, take a sightseeing cruise, or rent a skiff. A boat ride off the coast of Miami Beach is the best way to see the elegant waterfront mansions, dramatic skyline, and gorgeous coastline that make Miami so alluring.
- **Shopping.** One of South Florida's biggest draws is its incredible selection of stores and outlet malls. Many visitors from the Caribbean and Latin America come for the sole purpose of buying. From electronics to shoes and hardware to exotic grocery items, this is the place to shop. Bring the credit cards.
- **Cruising with the Top Down.** Driving in a convertible over the causeways to any of Miami's wonderful islands is one of my favorite things to do, especially in the mild winter months from December through March. Tune the radio to a Latin station, catch the warm sun on your bare shoulders, and watch the water glimmer around you.
- **Lunching in Little Havana.** Miami's Cuban center is the city's most distinctive ethnic enclave. Located just west of Downtown, Little Havana is centered around "Calle Ocho," SW 8th Street. Car-repair shops, tailors, electronics stores, and restaurants all hang signs in Spanish; salsa rhythms thump from the radios of passersby; and old men in guayaberas chain-smoke cigars over their daily games of dominoes. Stop for a big filling lunch, and top it off with a Cuban coffee to really get the day going.
- **Biking, Blading, or Walking Through the Art Deco District on Ocean Drive.** The beauty of South Beach's celebrated Art Deco District culminates on the 15-block beachfront strip known as Ocean Drive. Most of the buildings on this stretch are hotels built in the late 1930s and early 1940s. You'll appreciate the architecture and the colorful characters as you go down this street—by bike, by in-line skates, or on foot.
- **Relaxing on the Beaches.** Choose a spot on any of South Florida's many miles of white-sand beaches, edged with coconut palms on one side and a clear turquoise ocean on the other. Each beach boasts its own distinctive character. Don't forget your sunscreen.
- **Dancing Until Dawn.** Choose your dance floor, from salsa at the Latin clubs to techno and house at European-style places to jamming at outdoor reggae bars.
- **Enjoying New World Cuisine.** World-class chefs have discovered the richness of locally harvested ingredients, including tropical fruits and seafood. This culling of techniques and ingredients from the Cuban, Haitian, and Asian communities has created the now-famous "New World Cuisine."
- **Doing Whatever On, In, or Above the Water.** One of the best ways to appreciate South Florida is from the water—on it, in it, or above it. Options include parasailing, jet-skiing, kayaking, sailing, scuba diving, snorkeling, and windsurfing. Of course, you can always swim or ride the waves, as well.
- **Snorkeling in Biscayne National Park.** The thriving reef system at Biscayne National Park, a unique ecological preserve that's mostly underwater, attracts thousands of scuba divers and snorkelers every year.

> **Impressions**
>
> *They say Miami Beach will make a comeback, and who knows, maybe it will . . . for me, Miami Beach is still one of the most beautiful places in the world.*
> —Isaac Bashevis Singer, *My Love Affair with Miami Beach* (1986)

- **Canoeing Through the Everglades.** Paddling through the unique ecosystem that is the Everglades gives you a chance to slow down and appreciate the natural beauty of South Florida. You're sure to see an alligator or two, and maybe even a manatee.
- **Drumming on a Full Moon.** Barefoot drummers gather on the sands of Miami Beach each month to celebrate the full moon. Hundreds of locals circle the drummers and join in by dancing, clapping or simply sitting still in reverence to the celestial body. Just head down to the beach at 21st and Ocean Drive, and follow the beat of the drums.
- **Strolling Las Olas Boulevard.** Fort Lauderdale's premiere shopping, eating, and people-watching promenade is fun by day or night.
- **Barhopping on Duval Street.** From Mallory Square to the Atlantic Ocean you can walk or stumble (depending on how long you've been at it), to the dozens of bars and clubs that line this famously wild block of Key West. From Margaritaville to Sloppy Joe's and Louie's Backyard, there are bars for all types, whether you want to watch the sunset, feel a calm breeze, or listen to Jimmy Buffet wannabes.
- **Window Shopping Along Palm Beach's Worth Avenue.** It's been called "the Rodeo Drive of Palm Beach," and it's every bit as pricey. Check the Cartier display for a taste of opulence, or peek into Paper Treasures for an autograph of heroes such as Amelia Earhart, Joe DiMaggio, and even Honest Abe Lincoln.

2 Best Hotel Bets

- **Best Historic Hotel:** The **Biltmore Hotel** (☎ 800/727-1926 or 305/445-1926) is celebrating its 75th birthday and is Miami's oldest hotel. The founder of Coral Gables, George Merrick, built this grand old hotel in a Mediterranean style, with a huge bell tower based on the Giralda tower in Seville. It's now restored to its original 1926 splendor, and rooms are large and luxurious.
- **Best for Business Travelers:** The **Hotel Inter-Continental Miami** (☎ 800/327-0200 or 305/577-1000) wins for its amenities and convenient location—near the Metrorail and only a 10-minute drive from Miami International Airport. It features an extensive variety of well-appointed meeting rooms and every imaginable executive service on sight. The dining options are also superb.

    Business travelers heading to Fort Lauderdale will be thrilled to know about the four properties opened recently by **Extended Stay America/Crossland Economy Studios** (☎ 800-EXT-STAY). Year-round rates start as low as $49 a night and $159 per week, and long-term stays are even cheaper. The gleaming new studios include coffeemakers, irons and ironing boards, kitchens, and well-lighted desks. By dispensing with frills such as free shampoo and daily maid service, they are able to provide exceptional value.
- **Best for a Romantic Getaway:** The **Grove Isle Club and Resort** (☎ 800/88-GROVE or 305/858-8300), tucked just inside the Bay, is one of the most

romantic places in Miami. The huge mosquito-netted canopy beds are fit for kings and queens. A close second is the Honeymoon suite at the **Cardozo Hotel** (☎ **305/535-6500**) on South Beach. It's simply fabulous!

In the Keys, **Little Palm Island** (☎ **800/343-8567** or 305/872-2524), wins this designation not only because of its remote locale (on a private 5-acre island), but also because of the elegantly rustic accommodations and super pampering service.

- **Best Trendy Hotel:** With its Alice-in-Wonderlandesque interior designed by Philip Starck, the whimsical **Delano** (☎ **800/555-5001** or 305/672-2000), on South Beach, wins the vote for Miami's trendiest spot.

- **Best Hotel Lobby for Pretending You're Rich:** At the **Ritz-Carlton Palm Beach** in Manalpan (☎ **800/241-3333** or 561/533-6000), the valets won't flinch if you show up in a head-to-toe mink walking a pedigree poodle, and carrying an armload of packages from Tiffany's. Even without all that gear, though, you're likely to get the royal treatment. Find a spot near the lushly landscaped pool, and enjoy the opulence.

- **Best for Families:** The **Sonesta Beach Resort Key Biscayne** (☎ **800/SONESTA** or 305/361-2021) has family-friendly everything: restaurants, game rooms, gym, tennis courts, and a pool. Add to that the entertaining and educational programs, and you'll find your children will be coming back with their children. It's the perfect place for the entire family.

In Fort Lauderdale, **Lago Mar Resort and Club** (☎ **800/524-6627** or 954/523-6511), is another pricey selection, but one that guarantees a good time for the kids and parents. In addition to a game room, Ping-Pong tables, a small beach, and tennis courts, the hotel offers special events for kids during holidays. It might be a clown or an ice-cream party.

In Palm Beach, **The Breakers** (☎ **800/833-3141** or 561/655-6611) offers supervised programs for kids year-round.

- **Best Moderately Priced Hotels:** One of Miami's best-kept secrets is the **Miami River Inn** (☎ **305/325-0045**), hidden smack in the middle of downtown Miami. Every room is uniquely furnished with antiques dating back as far as 1908.

In the exclusive Bal Harbour area is the **Bay Harbor Inn** (☎ **305/868-4141**), an antique-laden hotel whose impeccable service and style make it so popular with discriminating budget-conscious travelers that it's booked a year in advance in season. In Key West, finding a hotel that is comfortable, conveniently located, and downright charming is nearly impossible. It does exist, however, in the form of **The Grand** (☎ **888/947-2630** or 305/294-0590), a two-story guest cottage less than 5 blocks from Duval Street.

- **Best Hotel Pool:** The **Fontainebleau Hilton**'s (☎ **800/548-8866** or 305/538-2000) incredible "Octopus" pool, with its dramatic grotto and waterfall is one of the most interesting and fun in the area. On the other hand, the pool at the **Biltmore Hotel Coral Gables** (☎ **800/228-3000** or 305/445-1926) is the nation's largest, graced with Italian statues and columns and beneath a huge Gothic tower.

- **Best Hotel Golf Courses:** In Miami, the **Biltmore** and the **Doral** share the distinction. At the Biltmore (☎ **800/448-8355** or 305/460-5364), you'll find one of South Florida's first courses with beautiful rolling hills and scenic vistas. The **Doral** (☎ **800/71-DORAL** or 305/592-2000), offers some of the country's most challenging courses, including a new course designed by The Shark, Greg Norman.

In Palm Beach, check out Florida's oldest 18-holer at **The Breakers** (☎ **800/833-3141** or 888/BREAKERS). This oceanfront, par-70 course was built in 1897.

- **Best Spas:** When you want to relax or be pampered, there's no better place to go than the world-famous **Doral Golf Resort and Spa** (☎ **800/22-DORAL**, 800/71-DORAL, or 305/592-2000). But then again, the graciousness of the spa at **Turnberry Isle Resort** (☎ **305/932-6200**), is matched only by its opulence and size—25,000 square ft. of everything you need to unwind. And the exclusive facilities at **Fisher Island Club** (☎ **305/535-6026**) are simply luxurious.

  In Fort Lauderdale, The **Wyndham Resort and Spa** (☎ **800/996-3426** or 954/389-3300) offers 23 acres of lush facilities, including golf, tennis, and spa. A $10 million renovation has brought it back as one of the area's premier resorts for exercise, facials, manicures, massages, and more.

3 Best Dining Bets

- **Best Spot for a Romantic Dinner:** The **Forge Restaurant,** 432 Arthur Godfrey Rd. (at 41st Street), Miami Beach (☎ **305/538-8533**), is where everyone's parents went in the 1950s for a really elegant meal. It's still the most romantic spot in town for black-tie service, stupendous food, and private conversation. For a truly intimate experience, reserve a booth in "The Library," perfect for popping the question. **Baleen's,** inside the Grove Isle Club & Resort (☎ **305/858-8300**), has the Bay as its backdrop and a cool evening breeze blowing white willowy curtains back and forth—you'll feel like you're dining in a dream.

- **Best Wine Lists:** The extensive and well-chosen wine list at **Smith & Wollensky,** at South Pointe Park, South Beach (☎ **305/673-2800**), beats other Miami restaurants hands-down. The wine list at **The Forge Restaurant** (see above), a tome really, encompasses more than 3,000 vintages and 250,000 bottles from all over the world.

- **Best for Kids: GameWorks** at the Shops at Sunset, (☎ **305/740-0417**), with it's almost endless supply of electronic amusements, is the best spot to take the kids.

  In Hollywood, the **Deli Den,** 2889 Stirling Rd. (☎ **954/961-4070**), offers a great deal for kids under 12. Every Thursday and Monday from 4 until 8pm, kids eat anything they want from the children's menu for free. Choices include chicken fingers, grilled cheese, and hot dogs.

- **Best Chinese Cuisine: Chrysanthemum,** 1248 Washington Ave., South Beach (☎ **305/531-5656**), has by far the beach's very finest Chinese food. The signature dish, chicken with crispy spinach, melts in your mouth while sparking a small flame. The Szechuan menu features lots of spicy favorites made of the very best quality ingredients.

- **Best Continental Cuisine:** The offerings at **Crystal Café,** 726 41st St., Miami Beach (☎ **305/673-8266**), have been dubbed "New Continental" by local food reviewers who rightfully consider it a shame to saddle the menu of this fantastic little spot with the pedestrian-sounding label of plain old "Continental."

- **Best Cuban Cuisine:** Cuban restaurants here range from take-out windows to diners to elegant establishments. The food comes in so many different styles that it's hard to choose a "best." If you're looking for a classic and filling Cuban meal, **Versailles,** 3555 SW 8th St. (☎ **305/444-0240**), or **La Esquina de Tejas,** 101 SW 12th Ave. (☎ **305/545-0337**), in Little Havana, are your two best bets. If you want a lighter, more expensive, nouvelle experience, **Yuca** is *el más sabroso* (the most delicious). You can find it in South Beach at 501 Lincoln Rd. (☎ 305/532-9822).

- **Best Italian Cuisine:** With so many good, cheap pasta joints, it's great to see Miami also knows how to enjoy the elegant Italian they have at **Escopazzo,** 1311 Washington Ave., South Beach (☎ 305/674-9450). Though prices are high, service and quality surpass all others.

  If you're craving Italian while in Palm Beach, try **Amici,** at 288 S. Country Rd. (☎ 561/832-0201).

- **Best Seafood:** For all-around good seafood, including tasty stews, seviche, and shellfish, the **Fishbone Grille,** 650 S. Miami Ave., Downtown (☎ 305/530-1915), is the place to go. They also have a location in Coral Gables at 1450 S. Dixie Highway (☎ 305/668-3033). A bonus: The prices are downright cheap.

- **Best Steakhouse:** There are suddenly dozens of steakhouses in Miami, but none is as popular as **Shula's,** at 7601 NW 154th St., Miami Lakes (☎ 305/820-8102), and in Miami Beach, at the Alexander Hotel, 5225 Collins Ave. (☎ 305/341-6565). **Capital Grille** in Downtown Miami (☎ 305/374-4500) has great ambience and incredibly huge portions. For a really delicious prime cut at a prime price, try **The Forge,** 432 Arthur Godfrey Rd., Miami Beach (☎ 305/538-8533).

  In Boca Raton, no place compares to **New York Prime,** 2350 Executive Center Dr. (☎ 561/998-3881), for huge meaty cuts and decadent side dishes like chopped salad, creamed spinach, and whipped potatoes.

- **Best Late-Night Dining:** You'll find dozens of good 24-hour spots, especially on South Beach, but I say, go to Little Havana, where **Casa Juancho,** 2436 SW 8th St. (☎ 305/642-2452), serves hearty good meals till all hours.

  Fort Lauderdale's late-night scene is best at **The Floridian Restaurant,** 1410 E. Las Olas Blvd (☎ 954/463-4041), where everything from steaks to eggs tastes good and costs very little.

- **Best People-Watching:** Nowhere will you find better people to watch than at the **Blue Door,** at the Delano Hotel, 1685 Collins Ave., South Beach (☎ 305/674-6400). From any seat in the house, you'll have a full parade of hipsters in view.

- **Best Pretheater Dinners: Franz and Joseph's,** 3145 Commodore Plaza (☎ 305/448-2282), is a popular spot for those on their way to the Coconut Grove theater. For an even more elegant experience, try the $28 special at **Norman's,** 21 Almera Ave., in the Gables (☎ 305/446-6767), offered between 5 and 7pm. Even if you don't have tickets to a show, it's a great way to eat cheap at this otherwise exorbitantly priced hot spot.

- **Best Fast Food: Mrs. Mendoza's Tacos al Carbon,** 1040 Alton Rd., South Beach (☎ 305/535-0808), is the best fast-food and Mexican in Miami. Time after time, this place turns out the tastiest burritos, tacos, and enchiladas with a superzingy salsa for the brave. There's another location at Doral Plaza, 9739 NW

Impressions

The first time I saw Miami, I experienced a series of emotions and was able to relive certain atmospheres, and breathe in the same imagination and creativity that was alive in the streets of Capri and St. Tropez' golden years. That is how I began my love affair with this city—with its people, its colors, and its surprisingly contagious vitality.

—Fashion designer Gianni Versace (1946–97)

Catch a Rising Star

Miami has become a popular backdrop on the large and small screen, with movie sets popping up in historic hotels, landmark homes, and along the city's fabulous stretches of white sand beach.

The city's image on film hasn't always been good. *Miami Vice,* one of the highest rated TV shows of the early '80s, made Miami infamous for its drug scene. Cocaine and profanity defined the city after Brian De Palma's gruesome action flick *Scarface* splattered the gritty city's drug culture across theaters everywhere in 1983.

But, in keeping with Miami's rejuvenation over the last 15 years, moviegoers now see more diverse and favorable views of Miami's hottest attractions and culture in a wide variety of films. The pictures themselves may not be classics, but the city looks grand in some of Hollywood's most recent releases, including: *There's Something About Mary,* starring Cameron Diaz and Matt Dillon; *The Birdcage,* starring Robin Williams and Nathan Lane; *Donnie Brasco,* starring Al Pacino and Johnny Depp; *and True Lies,* starring Jamie Lee Curtis and Arnold Schwarzenegger.

---

41 St. (☎ **305/477-5119**). **Pollo Tropical** ranks a close second with its superior rice and beans and roast chicken. Plus, it has drive-through windows at most locations for unbeatable speed and convenience. Check the phone book for locations throughout Dade and Broward counties.

- **Best Brunches:** The **Biltmore Hotel Coral Gables** (☎ **305/445-1926**) features the area's very best brunch for about $40 per person. A huge wraparound terrace is loaded with food stations offering sushi, omelettes, fresh carved lamb, roast beef, fresh shellfish, caviar and vodka, plus all the mimosas you can drink. There are a Spanish guitarist and harpist on hand to entertain. Children under 12 eat free. Reservations are required.

  In Boca Raton, **Boca Raton Resort and Club** (☎ **800/327-0101** or 561/447-3000) does a superb brunch daily for hotel guests or members. The price is $18.95 and includes all the usual dishes like made-to-order omelettes, carved meats, salads, and delectable desserts.

- **Best Happy Hours: Satchmo Blues Bar & Grill** (☎ **305/774-1883**) is the best happy hour spot in Miami. Hundreds of after-hour revelers crowd the sidewalks to get inside this blues and jazz spot. The food at **John Martin's,** 253 Miracle Mile, in Coral Gables (☎ **305/445-3777**), tastes even better when you've had one of their single-malt scotches or a pint of ale. Professionals and Irish nationals complete the scene at this weekday gala from 5 to 7pm. Drinkers can feast on hot pizza, chicken wings, cheeses, and fruits. Well drinks are usually 50¢ to 75¢ off. You'll also find a good deal at **Monty's Bayshore Restaurant,** downstairs at 400 Alton Rd. on South Beach (☎ **305/672-1148**). Not only are drinks half price between 4 and 8pm weekdays, but you can also get great deals on shellfish and raw bar items. Stone crab claws and shrimps are $2 each; oysters or clams are $3.

  In Palm Beach, the happy hour at **E. R. Bradley's Saloon** (☎ **561/833-3520**) is an institution. On weekdays between 4:30 and 6:30pm, an extensive hot buffet with pastas, chicken wings, veggies, and more attracts a diverse crowd. It's free with the purchase of two drinks.

2 Planning Your Trip: The Basics

South Florida, Miami especially, offers the perfect weekend getaway for the stressed and overworked, and the best week-long party for spring breakers. It's not unusual to find business travelers flying in to Miami by 9am and leaving by 7pm, but most visitors choose to stay a little longer to soak up as many rays as possible. Whether you choose spontaneity or the road most traveled, you are sure to enjoy your South Florida experience.

1 Visitor Information & Money

Note: For specific information on the Keys, Fort Lauderdale, Boca Raton, and other cities and towns on Florida's "Gold Coast," and the "Treasure Coast," refer to chapters 11 to 13.

VISITOR INFORMATION

The best source for any kind of specialized information about Miami is the **Greater Miami Convention and Visitors Bureau,** 701 Brickell Ave., Miami, FL 33131 (☎ **800/283-2707** or 305/539-3034; www.miamiandbeaches.com; e-mail: visitor@miamiandbeaches.com). Even if you don't have a specific question, call ahead to request its free magazine, *Destination Miami,* which includes several good, easy-to-use maps and other useful contact numbers. The office is open weekdays from 9am to 5pm.

For information on traveling in Florida, including a calendar of events, a guide to accommodations, and a list of useful Internet sites, contact **Visit Florida,** P.O. Box 1100, 66 E. Jefferson St., Tallahassee, FL 32302 (☎ **888-7-FLA-USA** or 850/488-5607; www.flausa.com). The office is open weekdays from 8am to 5pm. Europeans should note that this agency maintains an office in Great Britain at Roebuck House, Palace Street, London SW1 E 5BA (☎ **071/630-6602;** fax 071/630-7703).

In addition to information on some of South Beach's funkier hotels, the **Miami Design Preservation League,** 1234 Washington Ave., Ste. 207, Miami Beach, FL 33139 (☎ **305/672-2014**), offers an informative free guide to the Art Deco District as well as several books on the subject. It's open Monday through Saturday from 10am to 7pm.

Greater Miami's various chambers of commerce also send maps and information about their particular neighborhoods, including the following:

- **Coconut Grove Chamber of Commerce,** 2820 McFarlane Rd., Miami, FL 33133 (☎ **305/444-7270**).
- **Coral Gables Chamber of Commerce,** 50 Aragon Ave., Coral Gables, FL 33134 (☎ **305/446-1657**).
- **Florida Gold Coast Chamber of Commerce,** 1100 Kane Concourse (Bay Harbor Islands), Miami, FL 33154 (☎ **305/866-6020**)—this office represents Bal Harbour, Sunny Isles, Surfside, and other North Dade waterfront communities.
- **Tropical Everglades Visitor's Center,** 160 U.S. Hwy. 1, Florida City, FL 33034 (☎ **305/245-9180**); open daily 8:15am to 4:45pm.
- **Miami Beach Chamber of Commerce,** 420 Lincoln Rd, #20, Miami Beach, FL 33139 (☎ **305/672-1270**).

The following organizations represent dues-paying hotels, restaurants, and attractions in their specific areas. These associations can provide information about accommodations and tours: **Greater Miami and the Beaches Hotel Association,** 407 Lincoln Rd., Miami Beach, FL 33139 (☎ **800/531-3553** or 305/531-3553), and **Sunny Isles Beach Resort Association,** 17100 Collins Ave., Suite 208, Sunny Isles, FL 33160 (☎ **305/947-5826**).

If you are hooked into the Internet, surf over to **www.goflorida.com.** It provides a vast array of information on accommodations, dining, and entertainment options throughout Miami and South Florida.

MONEY

You never have to carry a lot of cash in Miami. Automated-teller machines (ATMs) are located at virtually every bank in the city, and credit cards are accepted by the vast majority of Miami's hotels, restaurants, attractions, shops, and nightspots. Traveler's checks are also widely accepted for goods and services and can be exchanged for cash at banks and check-issuing offices.

ATMs

Cirrus (☎ 800/424-7787; www.mastercard.com/atm/) and **Plus** (☎ 800/843-7587; www.visa.com/atms) are the two most popular ATM networks; check the back of your ATM card to see which one your bank belongs to. You won't have a problem finding an ATM in South Florida. **First Nationwide Bank,** 517 Arthur Godfrey Rd., in Miami accepts cards on Cirrus, Honor, and Metroteller networks. Be sure to check the daily withdrawal limit before you depart.

TRAVELER'S CHECKS

You can get traveler's checks at almost any bank. **American Express** offers various denominations at a service charge ranging from 1% to 4%. You can also get American Express traveler's checks over the phone by calling ☎ **800/221-7282**; by using this number, Amex gold and platinum cardholders are exempt from the 1% fee. AAA members can obtain checks without a fee at most AAA offices.

Visa offers traveler's checks at Citibank locations nationwide, as well as several other banks. The service charge ranges between 1.5% and 2%. **MasterCard** also offers traveler's checks. Call ☎ **800/223-9920** for a location near you.

CREDIT CARDS

Credit cards are a safe way to carry money while traveling. You can withdraw cash advances from your credit cards at any bank (though you'll start paying

What Things Cost in Miami	U.S. $	U.K. £
Taxi from Miami Airport to a downtown hotel	18.00–26.00	10.80–15.60
Local telephone call	.35	.21
Double room at the Sonesta Beach Resort (expensive)	285.00	171.00
Double room at the Coconut Grove Bed and Breakfast (moderate)	135.00	81.00
Double room at the Beachcomber Hotel (inexpensive)	65.00	39.00
Lunch for one at the News Café (moderate)	9.00	5.40
Lunch for one at Mrs. Mendoza's (inexpensive)	6.00	3.60
Dinner for one, without wine, at The Forge (very expensive)	40.00	24.00
Dinner for one, without wine at Van Dyke Café (moderate)	15.00	9.00
Dinner for one, without wine, at Versailles (inexpensive)	8.00	4.80
Pint of beer	3.50	2.10
Coca-Cola in a restaurant	1.50	.90
Cup of coffee	1.25	.75
Roll of ASA 100 film, 36 exposures	6.50	3.90
Admission to Miami Metrozoo, adult	8.00	4.80
Movie ticket	7.50	4.50

hefty interest on the advance the moment you receive the cash, and you won't receive frequent-flyer miles on an airline credit card). If you know your PIN number, you can get a cash advance at an ATM; if you've forgotten it or didn't even know you had one, call the phone number on the back of your credit card and ask the bank to send it to you.

THEFT If your wallet is stolen, immediately call your credit card company. They may be able to wire you a cash advance off your credit card immediately, and in many places, they can deliver an emergency credit card in a day or two. The toll-free information directory will provide the number if you dial ☎ **800/555-1212.** Citicorp **Visa's** U.S. emergency number is ☎ **800/336-8472. American Express** cardholders and traveler's check holders should call ☎ **800/221-7282** for all money emergencies. **MasterCard** holders should call ☎ **800/307-7309.**

If you opt to carry traveler's checks, be sure to keep a record of their serial numbers, separately from the checks of course, so you're ensured a refund in just such an emergency.

Odds are that if your wallet is gone, the police won't be able to recover it for you. However, after you realize that it's gone and you cancel your credit cards, it is still worth informing them. Your credit card company or insurer may require a police report number.

2 When to Go

Miami's tourist season, from November through April, is more reflective of the weather up north than it is of climatic changes in South Florida. It's always warm here. No matter what time of year you visit, you'll find that indoor spaces are always air-conditioned, cafes have tables out on the sidewalk, and the beaches are busy.

The tropical temperature has always been South Florida's main appeal, especially during the winter, when the rest of the country is shivering. When it's winter in Wisconsin, it's still summer in the Sunshine State.

South Florida's unique climate is extremely tropical. Hot, sometimes-muggy summers are counterbalanced by wonderfully warm winters. It's not uncommon for a sudden shower to be followed by several hours of intense sunshine. For natives, "winter" is too cold for swimming; however, for many visitors, 70°F January afternoons are great beach days. It isn't always perfect though—there are occasional cold snaps, and even one short tropical rain shower can ruin a day at the beach.

However, don't overlook traveling to South Florida during the "off" seasons, when the weather is warm, but hotel prices are significantly lower. In addition, restaurants, stores, and highways are less crowded.

Finally, a word about Florida's tropical storms and hurricanes. Most occur between August and November, and for local property owners, the tumultuous winds that sweep in from the Atlantic can be devastating. In August 1992, for example, Hurricane Andrew—one of the fiercest storms ever recorded in Florida—caused about $30 billion in damage to residential and business districts in Dade and Monroe counties. More than 250,000 people were left homeless. In 1999, a busy storm season caused enormous damage in the Florida Keys and resulted in a number of mass evacuations.

For visitors, high winds and incessant rains usually mean little more than a delayed vacation. Even Hurricane Andrew caused relatively little damage to most of Miami's hotels and major tourist attractions, all of which have been rebuilt.

Meteorologists know far in advance when a storm is brewing off the Atlantic Coast and can determine pretty accurately what force it will have; the information is then broadcast nationwide. With respect to Andrew, the National Hurricane Center, located in Coral Gables, gave due warning of the storm and tracked it closely as it approached Florida, although it couldn't predict the exact spot where the storm would make landfall, leaving the inland residents in Homestead unprepared for the hit. However, if there are reports of an impending storm before you leave for Florida, you may want to postpone your trip.

Miami's Average Temperatures & Rainfall

	Jan	Feb	Mar	Apr	May	June	July	Aug	Sept	Oct	Nov	Dec
Avg. High (°F)	75	76	79	82	85	87	89	90	88	84	80	76
Avg. Low (°F)	59	60	64	68	72	75	76	77	76	72	66	61
Avg. Rain (in.)	2.0	2.0	2.3	3.6	6.3	8.6	6.7	7.2	8.6	6.9	2.9	1.9

South Florida Calendar of Events

January

- **Orange BowFl,** Miami. Two of the year's college football teams do battle at Pro Player Stadium, preceded by the King Orange Jamboree Parade (see December listing, below). Tickets are available starting March 1 of the previous year through the Orange Bowl Committee. Call ☎ 305/371-4600 for details. Usually January 1 (but note that dates of this and the other college bowl games mentioned below may vary to accommodate TV schedules).

- **Art Miami,** Miami. This annual fine arts fair attracts more than 100 galleries from all over the world. International, modern, and contemporary works are featured here, attracting thousands of visitors and buyers. For information and ticket prices, call ☎ **561/220-2690.** Early January.

- **Three Kings Parade,** Miami. Since Cuban Pres. Fidel Castro outlawed this religious celebration more than 25 years ago, Cuban Americans in Little Havana have put on a bacchanalian parade winding through Calle Ocho from 4th Avenue to 27th Avenue, with horse-drawn carriages, native costumes, and marching bands. Call ☎ **305/447-1140** for the exact date during the first week of January.

- ✪ **Art Deco Weekend,** South Beach, Miami. Held along the beach between 5th and 15th streets, this festival—with bands, food stands, antique vendors, artists, tours, and other festivities—celebrates the whimsical architecture that has made South Beach one of America's most unique neighborhoods. Call ☎ **305/672-2014** for details. Usually held on Martin Luther King weekend.

- **Martin Luther King Day Parade,** Miami. This parade concludes a week of festivities, lectures, and concerts in honor of Dr. King's birthday. The parade takes place in Liberty City along NW 54th Street, between NW 12th and 32nd avenues. For information, call ☎ **305/636-1924.**

- ✪ **Royal Caribbean Golf Classic,** Key Biscayne. World-renowned golfers compete for more than $1 million in prize money at Crandon Park Golf Course, formerly known as The Links. Lee Trevino has won this tournament twice. Call ☎ **305/374-6180** for more information. Late January.

- **Winter Antique Show,** Miami Beach. Antique glasswork, coins, jewelry, furniture, and more fills 800 booths and two halls at the mammoth Miami Beach Convention Center. Call ☎ **305/754-4931** for details. Late January to early February.

- **Taste of the Grove Food and Music Festival,** Coconut Grove. This fundraiser in the Grove's Peacock Park is an excellent chance for visitors to sample menu items from some of the city's top restaurants and sounds from international and local performers. Call ☎ **305/444-7270** for details. Mid-January.

- **The Key Biscayne Art Festival,** Key Biscayne. One of the finest in the country, this high-quality, juried fine art show, held in Cape Florida State Park, brings hundreds of artists, some crafts makers, and lots of great international food together for charity. Call ☎ **305/361-5207** for details. Last weekend in January.

- ✪ **Key West Literary Seminar.** This 3-day festival attracts the biggest names in literature. Some past participants included Joyce Carol Oates, Amy, and Jamaica Kincaid. This event sells out months in advance. Call ☎ **888/293-9291** for details or check out the Web site at www.KeyWestLiterarySeminar.org. Early to mid-January.

February

- **Homestead Rodeo.** Bucking broncos, clowns, and competition mark this family event out in horse country. Call ☎ **305/247-3515** for details. Early February (the first weekend after the Super Bowl).

- **Everglades Seafood Festival,** Florida City. As many as 75,000 people show up each year for this 2-day eating festival in the quaint old town of Florida City. Florida delicacies like stone crab and gator tails are dished up from shacks and food booths on the outskirts of town. Friday night is family night where a carnival and craft fair attract the youngsters. No admission charge. Call ☎ 941/695-4100 for more details. First full weekend in February.
- **Miami Film Festival,** Miami. This 10-day festival has made an impact as an important screening opportunity for Latin American cinema and American independents. It's relatively small, well priced, and easily accessible to the general public. Contact the Film Society of Miami at ☎ 305/377-FILM. Early February.
- **The Palm Beach International Art and Antiques Fair,** West Palm Beach. This relatively new event features top dealers from New York galleries and around the world. It has quickly gained a national reputation since its inception in 1997. For details, call ☎ 561/220-2690.
- Palm Beach Seafood Festival, West Palm Beach. This festival at Currie Park features arts and crafts, kiddie rides, and of course, stone crabs, lobster, and more. Call ☎ 561/832-6397 for the word on the day's catch. Mid-February.
- **Coconut Grove Art Festival,** Coconut Grove. This is the state's largest art festival and the favorite annual event of many locals. More than 300 artists are selected from thousands of entries to show their works at this prestigious outdoor festival. Almost every medium is represented, including the culinary arts. Call ☎ 305/447-0401 for details. Presidents' Day weekend.
- **Miami International Boat Show,** Miami. This show draws almost a quarter of a million boat enthusiasts to the Miami Beach Convention Center and surrounding locations to see the megayachts, sailboats, dinghies, and accessories. It's the biggest anywhere. Call ☎ 305/531-8410 for more information and ticket prices. Mid-February.
- Doral Ryder Golf Open, West Miami. One of the country's most prestigious annual tournaments. Call ☎ 305/477-GOLF for more information. Late February to early March.
- Hatusume Fair, Delray Beach. Popular with residents and visitors alike for more than 20 years, this 2-day fair features art, music, food, plants, and martial arts performances to celebrate the first buds of spring. The elegant Morikami Japanese museum and garden hosts more than 15,000 visitors at this annual festival, which is also a great choice for families (☎ 561/495-0233). Last weekend of February.

March

- Winter Party, Miami. The Dade Human Rights Foundation hosts this gay and lesbian weekend-long party, which features several activities at clubs around town and culminates in a huge all-day dance fest on the beach on Sunday. Travel reservations can be made through Different Roads Travel—the official travel company of the event—at ☎ 888/ROADS-55, ext. 510. For more information on specific events and ticket prices, call ☎ 305/538-5908 or check out their Web site at www.winterparty.com. Early March.
- The Italian Renaissance Festival, Miami. Stage plays, music, and period costumes complement Villa Vizcaya's neo-Italianate architectural style. Call ☎ 305/250-9133 for more information. Mid-March.

- **Miami Gay & Lesbian Film Festival,** Miami. A 10-day festival of short and feature-length films and videos by gay filmmakers is presented at South Beach's Colony Theater on Lincoln Road and other smaller venues. For details, call Robert Rosenberg ☎ **305/532-7256.** Mid-March.
- **Grand Prix of Miami,** Homestead. This high-purse, high-profile auto race rivals the big ones in Daytona. It attracts the top Indy car drivers and large crowds. For information and tickets, contact Homestead Motorsports Complex at ☎ **305/230-5200.** Sometime in March.
- ✪ **Calle Ocho Festival,** Miami. This salsa-filled blowout marks the end of a 10-day extravaganza called Carnival Miami. It's one of the world's biggest block parties, held along 23 blocks of Little Havana's Southwest 8th Street between 4th and 27th avenues. Call ☎ **305/644-8888** for more information. Early to mid-March.
- **Ericsson Open (formerly the Lipton Championship),** Miami. One of the world's largest tennis events is hosted at the lush Tennis Center at Crandon Park on Key Biscayne. Call ☎ **305/446-2200** for details. Mid- to late March.

April

- **The Little Acorns International Kite Festival,** South Beach. Thousands of kite masters come from all over the world to display their flying works of art, filling up a mile of sky from 5th to 15th streets. Kids can build their own kites and scramble for candy during the candy drop at one of the country's largest festivals of its kind. Food and drinks, and of course, kites are sold to benefit this nonprofit educational organization. For more information on this free event, call ☎ **888/298-9815.** Third weekend of April.
- **PGA Seniors Golf Championship,** Palm Beach Gardens. Held at the PGA National Resort & Spa, it's the oldest and most prestigious of the senior tournaments. Call ☎ **561/624-8400** for the lineup. Mid-April.
- **World Cup Polo Tournament,** Palm Beach. Join royalty at the Palm Beach Polo and Country Club to see the best in international polo circles as the season closes. Call ☎ **561/793-1440** for details. Mid-April.
- **Sunfest,** West Palm Beach. A huge party happens on Flagler Drive in the downtown area with four stages of continuous music, a craft marketplace, a juried art show, a youth park, and fireworks. Call ☎ **561/659-5992** for details. Late April to early May.
- **Texaco Key West Classic,** Key West. Hailed as the top fishing tournament in Florida, this catch-and-release competition offers $50,000 in prizes to be divided between the top anglers in three divisions: sailfish, marlin, and light tackle. Call ☎ **305/294-4042** for more information. Late April to mid-May.

May

- **Arabian Nights Festival,** Opa-Locka. This yearly event commemorates the distinctive Moorish architecture in the heart of Opa-Locka. Historical tours, street festivals, live music, and food booths are part of the fun. For details, call ☎ **305/688-4611.** Early May.
- **Coconut Grove Bed Race,** downtown Coconut Grove. A colorful event in which local participants race hand-rigged beds to raise money for the Muscular Dystrophy Association (☎ **305/717-9937**). Usually the Sunday after Mother's Day.

- **Coconuts Dolphin Tournament,** Key Largo. This is the largest fishing tournament in the Keys, offering $5,000 and a Dodge Ram pickup truck to the person who breaks the record for the largest fish caught. The competition is fierce! Call ☎ **305/451-4107** for details. Mid-May, usually the weekend before Memorial Day.
- **The Great Sunrise Balloon Race & Festival,** Homestead. Every Memorial Day weekend, dozens of multicolored balloons rise up over Homestead Air Reserve Station as sky divers fall from the sky and other aircraft perform. The race is celebrated on the ground with a variety of food, music, arts, and crafts. For information, call ☎ **305/275-3317.**
- **Cajun/Zydeco Crawfish Festival,** Fort Lauderdale. Spend 3 days at Fort Lauderdale stadium dancing to Cajun music—if you don't know how, sign up for free lessons. Can you peel? If so, enter the crawfish-eating contest. Call the Crazee Crawfish 24-hour hot line at ☎ **954/761-5934.** Second weekend of May.
- **Shell Air and Sea Show,** Fort Lauderdale. A spectacular display of aeronautics featuring the Blue Angels and aquatic demonstrations by the navy guaranteed to evoke oohs and aahs. Call ☎ **954/527-5600** for details. Early May.

June

- **Super Boat Racing Series,** Key West. This event features 3 days of food, fun, and powerboat racing around downtown Key West. Call ☎ **305/296-6166** for details. Early June.
- ✪ **Coconut Grove Goombay Festival,** Miami. This bash, one of the country's largest black-heritage festivals, features Bahamian bacchanalia with dancing in the streets of Coconut Grove and music from the Royal Bahamian Police marching band. The food and music draw thousands to an all-day celebration of Miami's Caribbean connection. It's lots of fun—if the weather isn't scorching. Call ☎ **305/372-9966** for festival details. Early June.

July

- **Independence Day,** Miami. Celebrate July 4th on the beach, where parties, barbecues, and fireworks flare all day and night. For a weekend's worth of events on Key Biscayne, call ☎ **305/361-5207.** You can also find one of the wildest parties around—complete with fireworks and top-notch festivities—at Bayfront Park, 301 N. Biscayne Blvd. For more on this free event, call ☎ **305/358-7550.** It's a good idea, though, to check local papers for a more detailed list of events.
- **Miccosukee Everglades Festivals,** Miami. Native American rock, Razz (reservation jazz), and folk bands perform while visitors gorge themselves on exotic treats like pumpkin bread and fritters. Watch alligator wrestling and craft demonstrations. Call ☎ **305/223-8380** for prices and details. One in early and one in late July.
- ✪ **Lower Keys Underwater Music Fest,** Looe Key. At this outrageous celebration, boaters go out to the underwater reef of Looe Key Marine Sanctuary off Big Pine Key, drop speakers into the water, and pipe in music. It's entertainment for the fish and swimmers alike! A snorkeling Elvis can usually be spotted. Call ☎ **800/872-3722** for details. Usually second Saturday of July.
- ✪ **Hemingway Days Festival,** Key West. After years of controversy with Hemingway's heirs, this blowout is still going strong. Topped off by a

humorous look-alike contest. Call ☎ 305/294-4440 for details. Mid- to late July.

- **Wine and All That Jazz,** Boca Raton. A great way to quench your thirst on a sweltering summer day. It's one of the largest wine-tasting parties in the state; sample your choice from more than 100 wines and vintages while listening to a little live jazz. For details, call ☎ 561/395-4433. Friday night at the end of July or beginning of August.
- ✪ **Fourth of July Festivities,** Delray Beach. You can attend a celebration featuring art and jazz on Atlantic Avenue and Fla. A1A and enter a sand-sculpting contest, fly a kite, and sample fare from Delray's neighborhood restaurants. Call ☎ 561/278-0424 for more information. July 4.

August

- **Miami Reggae Festival,** Miami. Jamaica's best dance-hall and reggae artists turn out for this 2-day festival. Burning Spear, Steel Pulse, Spragga Benz, and Jigsy King have participated recently. Call Jamaica Awareness at ☎ 305/891-2944 for more details. Early August.

September

- **Festival Miami,** Miami. A 4-week program of performing arts, featuring local and invited musical guests. Based in the University of Miami School of Music and Maurice Gusman Concert Hall. For a schedule of events, call ☎ 305/284-4940. Mid-September to mid-October.

October

- ✪ **Columbus Day Regatta,** Miami. Find anything that can float—from an inner tube to a 100-foot yacht—and you'll fit right in. Yes, there actually is a race, but how can you keep track when you're partying with a bunch of seminaked psychos in the middle of Biscayne Bay? It's free and it's wild. Rent a boat, jet-ski, or sailboard to get up close. Be sure to secure a vessel early, though—everyone wants to be there. Check local newspapers for exact date and time. Columbus Day weekend.
- **SunTrust Sunday Jazz Brunch at Riverwalk,** Fort Lauderdale. This year-long music and food gig kicks off on the banks of the historic New River, promising leisurely afternoons of great live jazz and tasty food in the company of fellow music lovers. Call ☎ 954/761-5363 for details. First Sunday of every month.
- ✪ **Fort Lauderdale International Boat Show,** Fort Lauderdale. Your chance to meet fellow boating enthusiasts and look over more than 1,400 boats and every imaginable variety of marine paraphernalia. Call ☎ 800/940-7642 for details. Late October to early November.
- **Caribbean Carnival,** Miami. Thousands of Caribbean natives from islands such as Trinidad, Jamaica, Haiti, St. Vincent, Barbados, and St. Croix "play mas" in a masquerade parade while wearing traditional Mardi Gras costumes and windin' to the sounds of Calypso and Soca rhythms. It's a wonderful display of the diversity and beauty of West Indian culture. Contact the Carnival Hotline at ☎ 305/653-1877. Second week in October.
- **Lincoln-Mercury American Music Festival,** Fort Lauderdale. An impressive lineup of folk, country, and Native American musicians shows up for this lively show at the baseball stadium off Commercial Boulevard. Dates vary, so call ☎ 954/761-5934 for details.
- **Oktoberfest,** Miami. They close the streets for this German beer and food festival thrown by the Mozart Stub Restaurant in Coral Gables.

You'll find loads of great music and dancing at this wild party. Call Harald Neuweg (☎ 305/446-1600) to find out where and when.

✪ **Fantasy Fest,** Key West. It might feel as though the rest of the world is joining you if you're in Key West for this world-famous Halloween festival, Florida's version of Mardi Gras. Crazy costumes, wild parades, and even wilder revelers gather for an opportunity to do things Mom said not to. Definitely leave the kids at home! Call ☎ **305/296-1817.** Last week of October.

✪ **Goombay Festival,** Key West. Sample Caribbean dishes and purchase art and ethnic clothing in this celebration with a Jamaican flair that coincides with Fantasy Fest (see above).

November

- **Blues Festival at Riverwalk,** downtown Fort Lauderdale. This huge corporate-sponsored music event attracts big name performers to various venues in and around Ft. Lauderdale. Call the blues hot line ☎ **954/761-5934** for info. First weekend of November.
- **South Florida International Auto Show,** Miami Beach. An impressive collection of the latest models is on display in the vast halls of the Convention Center. For details call ☎ **305/947-5950.** Early November.
- **The Jiffy Lube Miami 300 Weekend of NASCAR,** Homestead. Here's more world-class racing at a recently constructed 344-acre motor sports complex. For information and tickets, contact Homestead Motorsports Complex, One Speedway Blvd., Homestead (☎ **305/230-5200**). Mid-November.

✪ **Miami Book Fair International,** Miami. An event that draws hundreds of thousands of visitors, including foreign and domestic publishers and authors from around the world, with great lectures and readings by world-renowned authors. Call ☎ **305/237-3258.** Mid-November.

- **Super Boat World Championship,** Key West. More than a week of high-speed fun and competition around downtown Key West. Call ☎ **305/296-6166** for details. Mid-November.

✪ **The Ramble,** Miami. Old-time Floridians love this yearly event at the Fairchild Tropical Gardens. Here you can buy antiques, exotic orchids, or vintage clothes. If you're not shopping, it's still worth strolling around the lush park where you can see an impressive array of botanical miracles. For more information, call ☎ **305/667-1651.** Mid-November.

- **Mercury Outboards Cheeca/Redbone Celebrity Tournament,** Islamorada, in the Upper Keys. Curt Gowdy from *American Sportsman* hosts this fishing tournament, the proceeds of which go to finding a cure for cystic fibrosis. The likes of Wade Boggs, actor James B. Sikking, and Gen. Norman Schwartzkopf compete most years. Call ☎ **305/664-2002** for more information. Second and third weekends of November. This event is followed by the George Bush Cheeca Lodge Bonefish Tournament. Call ☎ **305/664-4651,** ext. 556, for details.

✪ **White Party Week,** Miami. This weeklong AIDS fundraiser begins with a series of events in Miami Beach nightclubs and leads up to the Sunday night gala, where more than 10,000 gay men and women from around the country come out to celebrate at Vizcaya, the Renaissance mansion. Since the gala always sells out, make sure to buy your tickets as soon as they go on sale October 1. Call ☎ **305/667-9296** for details; www.whitepartyweek.com. Thanksgiving week.

December

- **Winterfest Boat Parade,** Fort Lauderdale waterways. For more than 25 years this festival has showcased some of the most extravagant boats in the area. Outfitted in holiday decorations, the vessels ply the local waterways to celebrate the winter season. The best view is from the water aboard your own boat or at one of the waterfront restaurants. For details, call ☎ 954/767-0686.
- **King Mango Strut,** Coconut Grove, Miami. This fun-filled march encourages everyone to wear wacky costumes and join the floats in a spoof of the King Orange Jamboree Parade, held the following night. Runs from Commodore Plaza to Peacock Park in Coconut Grove. Comedians and musical entertainment follow in the park. Call ☎ 305/444-7270 for details. December 30.
- ✪ **King Orange Jamboree Parade,** Miami. The world's largest nighttime parade is followed by a long night of festivities leading up to the Orange Bowl football game (see January listing, above). Runs along Biscayne Boulevard. For information and tickets (which cost $7.50 to $13), contact the Greater Miami Convention and Visitors Bureau at ☎ 305/539-3000. Usually December 31.
- ✪ **Santa's Enchanted Forest,** west of Coral Gables. The world's largest Christmas theme park includes rides, games, and food. A family tradition for years, this seasonal event is especially popular with teenagers. For details and ticket prices, call ☎ 305/893-0090. Late November to mid-January.
- **First Night,** Miami Beach. One of many nationwide New Year's Eve celebrations that are offered for families, this event starts in the late afternoon and offers dance, theater, art, poetry, and story reading. With no alcohol and lots of kid-friendly events, this is sure to become a big draw. Buttons for admission to all events cost $10 for New Year's 2000. Call ☎ 305/573-6477 for info.

3 Health & Insurance

STAYING HEALTHY

Be sure to use sunscreen, even on breezy, overcast days—the sun's rays in South Florida are always powerful, and there's nothing like a third-degree sunburn to ruin a trip. During the hurricane season, listen to radio and television broadcasts, which will describe evacuation routes. Better hotels will arrange transportation for their guests to safe areas.

WHAT TO DO IF YOU GET SICK AWAY FROM HOME

It can be hard to find a doctor you can trust when you're in an unfamiliar place. Try to take proper precautions the week before you depart, to avoid falling ill while you're away from home. Amid the last minute frenzy that often precede a vacation break, make an extra effort to eat and sleep well—especially if you feel an illness coming on.

If you worry about getting sick away from home, you may want to consider **medical travel insurance** (for suppliers, see below). In most cases, however, your existing health plan will provide all the coverage you need. Be sure to carry your identification card in your wallet.

If you suffer from a chronic illness, consult your doctor before your departure. For conditions like epilepsy, diabetes, or heart problems, wear a **Medic**

Alert Identification Tag (☎ 800/825-3785; www.medicalert.org), which will immediately alert doctors to your condition and give them a hot line. Membership is $35, plus a $15 annual fee. If you have dental problems, a nationwide referral service known as **1-800-DENTIST** (☎ 800/336-8478) will provide the name of a nearby dentist or clinic. If you need a doctor, ask your hotel concierge for a recommendation, or go to the local hospital emergency room.

Pack prescription medications in your carry-on luggage. Carry written prescriptions in generic, not brand-name form, and dispense all prescription medications from their original labeled vials. Also bring along copies of your prescriptions in case you lose your pills or run out.

INSURANCE

There are three kinds of travel insurance: trip cancellation, medical, and lost luggage coverage. **Trip cancellation insurance** is a good idea if you have paid a large portion of your vacation expenses up front. The other two types of insurance, however, don't make sense for most travelers. Rule number one: check your existing policies before you buy any additional coverage.

Your homeowner's insurance should cover stolen luggage. The airlines are responsible for $2,500 on domestic flights if they lose your luggage; if you plan to carry anything more valuable than that, keep it in your carry-on bag.

If you do require additional insurance, try one of the companies listed below. But don't pay for more than you need. For example, if you need only trip cancellation insurance, don't purchase coverage for lost or stolen property. Trip cancellation insurance costs approximately 6% to 8% of the total value of your vacation.

Among the reputable issuers of travel insurance are:

Access America, 6600 W. Broad St., Richmond, VA 23230 (☎ 800/284-8300); **Travel Guard International,** 1145 Clark St., Stevens Point, WI 54481 (☎ 800/826-1300); **Travel Insured International, Inc.,** P.O. Box 280568, East Hartford, CT 06128 (☎ 800/243-3174); or **Travelex Insurance Services,** P.O. Box 9408, Garden City, NY 11530-9408 (☎ 800/228-9792).

4 Tips for Travelers with Special Needs

Note: Again, for specific information on the Keys and cities on the "Gold Coast" and "Treasure Coast," please refer to chapters 11 to 13.

FOR TRAVELERS WITH DISABILITIES Many hotels offer special accommodations and services for wheelchair-bound visitors and travelers with disabilities, including large bathrooms, ramps, and telecommunication devices for the deaf. The Greater Miami Convention and Visitors Bureau (see "Visitor Information," above) has the most up-to-date information.

The **City of Miami Department of Parks and Recreation,** 2600 S. Bayshore Dr. (Coconut Grove), Miami, FL 33133 (☎ **305/860-3800;** TTY 305/860-3803), maintains quite a few programs for people with disabilities at parks and beaches throughout the city. Call or write for a listing of special services. The office is open weekdays from 8am to 5pm. The **Metro-Dade County Parks & Recreation Department** also runs hundreds of programs from swimming to sailing for visitors with disabilities. For a complete listing, call the department (☎ **305/755-7848**) weekdays from 9am to 5pm.

Primarily a referral service, the **Deaf Services Bureau,** 4800 W. Flagler St., Suite 213, Miami, FL 33134 (☎ **305/668-4407;** TTY 305/668-3323), may be contacted for any special concerns you have about traveling in and around Miami. They're available from 9am to 5pm. The **Division of Blind Services,** 401 NW 2nd Ave., Suite 700, Miami, FL 33128 (☎ **305/377-5339**), offers services to those with visual impairments. The office is open weekdays from 8am to 5pm.

Many of the major car-rental companies now offer hand-controlled cars for disabled drivers. **Avis** can supply such a vehicle at any of its locations in the United States with 48-hour advance notice; **Hertz** requires between 24 and 72 hours of advance reservation at most of its locations. **Wheelchair Getaways** (☎ **800/873-4973;** www.blvd.com/wg.htm) rents specialized vans with wheelchair lifts and other features for people with disabilities throughout the United States.

FOR GAY & LESBIAN TRAVELERS Miami, particularly South Beach, has a large gay community, supported by a wide range of services. There are many gay-oriented publications with information, up-to-date calendars, and listings of gay-friendly businesses and services. *TWN* is the only local gay newspaper in town; you'll find it in lavender boxes throughout the city and at bookstores and gay bars. Other local publications include *WIRE, Miamigo, Out Pages,* and *Scoop.*

The **Lambda Passages/Gay Community Bookstore,** 7545 Biscayne Blvd. (☎ **305/754-6900**), features quality literature, newspapers, videos, music, cards, and information on local businesses. It's open Monday to Saturday from 11am to 9pm and Sunday from noon to 6pm.

For a map and directory of gay businesses or a copy of the gay and lesbian community calendar (sponsored by the Dade Human Rights Foundation), call ☎ **305/572-1841.** For a copy of the calendar and other information, you can also log on to the foundation's Web site at **www.dhrf.com**.

For information on gay-friendly businesses in the area, contact the **South Beach Business Guild** at ☎ **305/534-3336.**

FOR SENIORS Miami is well versed in catering to seniors. Ask for discounts everywhere, at hotels, movie theaters, museums, restaurants, and attractions—you'll be surprised how often you're offered reduced rates. Many restaurants offer early bird specials and honor AARP memberships.

FOR STUDENTS A valid high school or college ID often entitles you to discounts at attractions (particularly museums) and sometimes to reduced rates at bars during "college nights." You're most likely to find these discounts at places near local colleges, in downtown Miami and Coral Gables.

You'll find lots of students at the large main campus of the **University of Miami** in south Coral Gables. In addition to the academic buildings, this campus encompasses a huge athletic field, a large lake, a museum, a hospital, and more. For general information, call the university (☎ **305/284-2211**). The school's main student building is the Whitten University Center, 1306 Stanford Dr. Social events are often scheduled here, and important information on area activities is always posted. The building houses a recreation area, a pool, a snack shop, and a Ticketmaster outlet.

For tickets to Miami Hurricanes basketball, football, and baseball home games, call the **U of M Athletic Department** (☎ **800/GO-CANES** in Florida, or 305/284-3822).

5 Getting There

BY PLANE

Miami is one of American's biggest hubs, and most major domestic airlines fly to and from many Florida cities, including **American** (☎ 800/433-7300; www.americanair.com), **Continental** (☎ 800/525-0280; www.flycontinental.com), **Delta** (☎ 800/221-1212; www.delta-air.com), **Northwest/KLM** (☎ 800/225-2525; www.nwa.com), **TWA** (☎ 800/221-2000; www.twa.com), **United** (☎ 800/241-6522; www.ual.com), and **US Airways** (☎ 800/428-4322; www.usair.com).

Several so-called no-frills airlines—offering low fares but no meals or other amenities—fly to Florida. The biggest is ✪ **Southwest Airlines** (☎ **800/435-9792;** www.iflyswa.com), which has flights from many U.S. cities to Fort Lauderdale (plus Jacksonville, Orlando, and Tampa).

Others flying to Florida include **AirTran** (☎ 800/AIR-TRAN); **Delta Express,** a branch of Delta Airlines (☎ **800/ 325-5205**); **MetroJet,** an arm of US Airways (☎ 800/428-4322); **Midway** (☎ 800/44-MIDWAY); **Midwest Express** (☎ **800/452-2022**); **Spirit** (☎ 800/772-7117); **SunJet** (☎ 407/328-8440); and **Vanguard** (☎ 800/826-4827).

If you're planning to visit Florida from another country, see chapter 3, "For Foreign Visitors," for information on which international carriers serve the Miami area.

FINDING THE BEST AIRFARE

There's no shortage of **discounted and promotional fares** to Florida. November, December, and January often see fare wars that can result in savings of 50% or more. Watch for advertisements in your local newspaper and on TV, call the airlines and do some comparison shopping, or surf for bargains on the Web (see Planning Your Trip: An Online Directory for more information).

Consolidators, also known as bucket shops, are a good place to find low fares, often below even the airlines' discounted rates. There's nothing shady about the reliable ones—basically, they're just big travel agents that get discounts for buying in bulk and pass some of the savings on to you. Before you pay, however, ask for a confirmation number from the consolidator and then call the airline itself to confirm your seat. Be prepared to book your ticket with a different consolidator—there are many to choose from—if the airline can't confirm your reservation. Also be aware that consolidator tickets are usually nonrefundable or come with stiff cancellation penalties.

Small ads for consolidators usually run in the Sunday travel section at the bottom of the page. But we recommend going with one of these reliable companies: Lots of folks on our staff have gotten great deals on a number of occasions from **Cheap Tickets** (☎ **800/377-1000** or 212/570-1179; www.cheaptickets.com). **Council Travel** (☎ **800/226-8624;** www.counciltravel.com) and **STA Travel** (☎ **800/781-4040;** www.sta.travel.com) cater especially to young travelers, but their bargain-basement prices are available to people of all ages. **Travel Bargains** (☎ **800/AIR-FARE;** www.1800airfare.com) was formerly owned by TWA but now offers the deepest discounts on many other airlines, with a four-day advance purchase. Other reliable consolidators include **1-800-FLY-4-LESS; Cheap Seats** (☎ **800/451-7200;** www.cheapseatstravel.com); **1-800-FLY-CHEAP** (www.1800flycheap.com); or "rebators" such as **Travel Avenue** (☎ **800/333-3335** or 312/876-1116).

Search the **Internet** for cheap fares—though it's still best to compare your findings with the research of a dedicated travel agent, if you're lucky enough

> **Money-Saving Tip**
>
> If your schedule is flexible, you can almost always secure a cheaper fare by staying over a Saturday night or by flying midweek. Many airlines won't volunteer this information, so be sure to ask.

to have one, especially when you're booking more than just a flight. See "Planning Your Trip: An Online Directory" after this chapter to learn how to use the Web to your best advantage.

A few of the better-respected virtual travel agents are **Travelocity** (www.travelocity.com) and **Microsoft Expedia** (www.expedia.com). Each has its own little quirks—Travelocity and Expedia both require you to register with them—but they all provide variations of the same service. Just enter the dates you want to fly and the cities you want to visit, and the computer roots out the lowest fares. Expedia's site will e-mail you the best airfare deal once a week if you so choose. Travelocity uses the SABRE computer reservations system that most travel agents use, and has a "Last Minute Deals" database that advertises really cheap fares for those who can get away at a moment's notice. Another good bet is **Arthur Frommer's Budget Travel** (www.frommers.com), which offers detailed information on 200 destinations around the world, plus ways to save on flights, hotels, car reservations, and cruises. Book an entire vacation online, or direct travel questions to Arthur himself. The newsletter is updated daily to keep you abreast of the latest breaking ways to save.

Great last-minute deals are also available through **E-savers,** free e-mail services provided directly by the airlines. Each week, the airline sends you a list of discounted flights, usually leaving the upcoming Friday or Saturday and returning the following Monday or Tuesday. You can sign up at each airline's Web site (see above for Web addresses).

Better yet, save yourself the headache and register with **Smarter Living** (www.smarterliving.com). Every week you'll get a customized e-mail summarizing the discount fares available from your departure city. Smarter Living tracks more than 15 different airlines, so it's a worthwhile time-saver. The site also features concise lists of links to hotel, car rental, and other hot travel deals.

MONEY-SAVING PACKAGE DEALS

Before you start your search for the lowest airfare, you may want to consider booking your flight as part of a travel package.

Package tours are not the same as escorted tours. They are simply a way to buy airfare and accommodations (and sometimes rental cars) at the same time. For Miami and many other destinations in South Florida, a package can be a smart way to go. In many cases, one that includes airfare, hotel, and car rental will cost you less than the hotel alone would have had you booked it yourself. That's because packages are sold in bulk to tour operators, who resell them to the public at a cost that drastically undercuts standard rates.

Packages, however, vary widely. Some offer a better class of hotels than others. Some offer the same hotels for lower prices. With some packagers, your choice of accommodations and travel days may be limited. Which package is right for you depends entirely on what you want.

Here are a few tips to help you tell one from the other, and figure out which one is right for you:

- **Read this guide.** Do a little homework; read up on the region. Compare the rack rates that we've published to the discounted rates being offered by the packagers to see what kinds of deals they're offering—if you're actually being offered a substantial savings, or if they've just gussied up the rack rates to make their offer *sound* like a deal. If you're being offered a stay in a hotel I haven't recommended, do more research to learn about it, especially if it isn't a reliable brand name like Holiday Inn or Hyatt. It's not a deal if you end up at a dump.

- **Read the fine print.** Make sure you know *exactly* what's included in the price you're being quoted, and what's not. Are hotel taxes and airport transfers included, or will you have to pay extra? Before you commit to a package, make sure you know how much flexibility you have, say, if your kid gets sick or your boss suddenly asks you to adjust your vacation schedule. Some packagers require iron-clad commitments, while others will go with the flow, charging minimal fees for changes or cancellations.

- **Use your best judgment.** Stay away from fly-by-nights and shady packagers. If a deal appears to be too good to be true, it probably is. Go with a reputable firm with a proven track record. This is where your travel agent can come in handy; he or she should be knowledgeable about different packagers, the deals they offer, and the general rate of satisfaction among their customers.

So how do you find a package deal?

The best place to start your search is the travel section of your local Sunday newspaper. Also check the ads in the back of national travel magazines like *Travel & Leisure, National Geographic Traveler,* and *Condé Nast Traveller.*

The major airlines package their flights to Florida together with accommodations. These include **America West Vacations** (☎ 800/356-6611), **American Airlines Vacations** (☎ 800/321-2121; www.americanair.com), **Continental Airlines Vacations** (☎ 800/634-5555; www.flycontinental.com), **Delta Vacations** (☎ 800/367-9112; www.deltavacations.com), **Midwest Express Vacations** (☎ 800/444-4479), **Northwest WorldVacations** (☎ 800/727-1111; www.nwa.com), **Southwest Airlines Vacations** (☎ 800/524-6442; www.iflyswa.com), and **US Airways Vacations** (☎ 800/455-0123).

Another option is the old reliable **American Express Vacations** (☎ 800/241-1700; fax 954/357-4682; www.leisureweb.com). Check out its **Last Minute Travel Bargains** Web site, offered in conjunction with **Continental Airlines** (www6.americanexpress.com/travel/lastminutetravel/default.asp), with deeply discounted vacations packages and reduced airline fares that differ from the E-savers bargains that Continental e-mails weekly to subscribers.

One of the biggest packagers in the Northeast, **Liberty Travel** (☎ 888/271-1584; www.libertytravel.com) boasts a full-page ad in many Sunday papers. You won't get much in the way of service, but you will get a good deal.

For one-stop shopping on the Web, go to **www.vacationpackager.com**, a search engine that will link you to many different package-tour operators, often with a company profile summarizing the company's basic booking and cancellation terms.

In addition to these all-inclusive tours, many Florida hotels and resorts and even some motels offer **golf and tennis packages,** which bundle the cost of room, greens and court fees, and sometimes equipment into one price. These deals usually don't include airfare, but they do represent savings over paying for the room and golf or tennis separately. See the accommodations sections in the destination chapters for resorts offering special packages to their guests.

A few words of **caution** are in order.

Given the propensity of discounted airfares to South Florida, and the number of hotels here offering various room-and-activities packages, especially during the off-seasons, you could save just as much by making your own arrangements. This is particularly true if you're renting a car and don't need transportation from and to the airport, a cost often included in package plans.

Second, think twice before buying a package that includes meals. Many hotels include breakfasts in their rates anyway, as indicated at the top of the listings in this book. Florida has a multitude of good restaurants in all price ranges, and prepaying for a dinner package could mean shelling out twice if you decide to dine out.

Third, the least expensive tours may put you up at a bottom-end hotel. And since the lower costs depend on volume, some more expensive tours could send you to a large, impersonal property. And because the tour prices are based on double occupancy, the single traveler is almost invariably penalized.

BY CAR

Although four major roads run to and through Miami—I-95, S.R. 826, S.R. 836 and U.S.1—chances are you'll reach Miami by way of I-95. This north-south interstate is the city's lifeline and an integral part of the region. The highway connects all of Miami's different neighborhoods, the airport, and the beach, and it connects all of South Florida to the rest of America. Unfortunately, many of Miami's road signs are completely confusing and notably absent when you need them. Take time out to study I-95's placement on the map. You will use it as a reference point time and again.

Other major highways that will get you to Florida include I-10, which originates in Los Angeles and terminates in Jacksonville, and I-75, which begins in North Michigan and runs through the center of Florida.

Before you set out on a long car trip, you might want to join the **American Automobile Association (AAA; ☎ 800/596-2227)**, which has hundreds of offices nationwide. Members receive excellent maps (they'll even help you plan an exact itinerary) and emergency road service. Other auto clubs include the **Allstate Motor Club,** 1500 Shure Dr., Arlington Heights, IL 60004 (☎ **847/253-4800**), and the **Motor Club,** P.O. Box 9046, Des Moines, IA 50309 (☎ **800/334-3300**).

For information on car-rental companies with offices in Miami, see "Getting Around" in chapter 4.

Arranging Car Rentals on the Web   Internet resources can make comparison shopping easier. **Microsoft Expedia** (www.expedia.com) and **Travelocity** (www.travelocity.com) help you compare prices and locate car-rental bargains from various companies nationwide. They will even make your reservation for you once you've found the best deal.

Demystifying Renter's Insurance   Before you drive off in a rental car, be sure you're insured. Hasty assumptions could cost you tens of thousands of dollars—even if you are involved in an accident that was clearly the fault of another driver.

If you already hold a **private auto insurance** policy, you are most likely covered in the United States for loss of or damage to a rental car, and liability, in case of injury to any other party involved in an accident. Be sure to find out whether you are covered in the area you are visiting, whether your policy extends to all persons who will be driving the rental car, how much liability is covered in case an outside party is injured in an accident, and whether the type of vehicle you are renting is included under your contract. (Rental trucks, sports utility vehicles, and luxury vehicles such as Jaguars may not be covered.)

Most **major credit cards** provide some degree of coverage, as well—provided they were used to pay for the rental. Terms vary widely, however, so be sure to call your credit card company directly before you rent.

If you are **uninsured,** your credit card provides primary coverage as long as you decline the rental agency's insurance. This means that the credit card will cover damage or theft of a rental car for the full cost of the vehicle. If you already have insurance, your credit card will provide secondary coverage—which basically covers your deductible.

Credit cards **will not cover liability,** or the cost of injury to an outside party and/or damage to an outside party's vehicle. If you do not hold an insurance policy, you may seriously want to consider purchasing additional liability insurance from your rental company. Be sure to check the terms, however: Some rental agencies only cover liability if the renter is not at fault; even then, the rental company's obligation varies from state to state.

Bear in mind that each credit card company has its own peculiarities. Most American Express Optima cards, for instance, do not provide any insurance. American Express does not cover vehicles valued at over $50,000 when new, luxury vehicles such as Porsches, or vehicles built on a truck chassis. MasterCard does not provide coverage for loss, theft, or fire damage, and only covers collision if the rental period does not exceed 15 days. Call your own credit card company for details.

The basic insurance coverage offered by most car rental companies, known as the **Loss/Damage Waiver (LDW)** or **Collision Damage Waiver (CDW),** can cost as much as $20 per day. It usually covers the full value of the vehicle with no deductible if an outside party causes an accident or other damage to the rental car. In all states but California, you will probably be covered in case of theft as well. Liability coverage varies according to the company policy and state law, but the minimum is usually at least $15,000. If you are at fault in an accident, however, you will be covered for the full replacement value of the car but not for liability. Most rental companies will require a police report in order to process any claims you file, but your private insurer will not be notified of the accident.

BY TRAIN

Amtrak (☎ 800/USA-RAIL; www.amtrak.com) may be a good option. Two trains leave daily from New York—the Silver Meteor at 7:05pm and the Silver Star at 11:50am. They both take from 26$\frac{1}{2}$ to 29 hours to complete the journey to Miami. At press time, the lowest-priced round-trip ticket from New York to Miami cost $146 for a coach seat, climbing to a whopping $417 for a sleeper (based on double occupancy).

If you are planning to stay in South Florida for some time, you might consider taking your car on Amtrak's East Coast Auto Train. The 16$\frac{1}{2}$-hour ride, connecting Lorton, Virginia (near Washington, D.C.), with Sanford, Florida (near Orlando), has a glass-domed viewing car and includes breakfast and dinner in the ticket price. Round-trip fares are only a few dollars higher than one way—about $170 for adults, $85 for children under 12, and $300 for your car. One-way fares are discounted as much as 50% when most traffic is going in the opposite direction.

You'll pull into Amtrak's Miami terminal at 8303 NW 37th Ave. Unfortunately, none of the major car-rental companies have an office at the train station; you'll have to go to the airport, just over 5 miles away, to rent a car.

Taxis meet each Amtrak arrival. The fare to downtown will cost about $22; the ride takes less than 20 minutes.

Planning Your Trip: An Online Directory

By Lynne Bairstow

Lynne Bairstow is the co-author of *Frommer's Mexico*, and the editorial director of *e-com* magazine.

Day by day, the Internet becomes more integrated into our lives, including the way we plan and book our travel. By early 2000, one in every 10 trips was being booked online, a trend that's sure to accelerate.

The Internet not only provides a wealth of destination information, it also gives you the chance to compare experiences with fellow travelers, ask experts for pretrip advice, seek out discounted fares once only accessible to travel industry insiders, and stay in touch via e-mail while you're away.

The Frommer's Online Directory will help you take better advantage of the travel planning information available online, and it's best used in conjunction with this book. Part 1 lists general Internet resources that can make any trip easier, such as sites for obtaining the best possible prices on airline tickets. In part 2 you'll find some top online guides for **South Florida and Miami**, organized by **category**.

Please keep in mind that this is not a comprehensive list, but rather a discriminating selection to get you started. Recognition is given to sites based on their content value and ease of use and are not paid for—unlike some Web-site rankings, which are based on payment. Finally, remember this is a press-time snapshot of leading Web sites—some undoubtedly will have evolved, changed, or moved by the time you read this.

1 Top Travel Planning Web Sites

While the Internet was once a conglomerate of sites for researching places to visit, several key companies have emerged that offer comprehensive travel planning and booking. In addition to the Frommer's Online (see box, above), we list the other top online travel agencies below, along with some more specialized services.

WHY BOOK ONLINE?

Online agencies have come a long way in the past few years; they now provide tips for finding the best fare, and will give you suggested dates or times to travel that yield the lowest price if your plans are at all flexible. Some sites even allow you to establish the price you're willing to pay, and will check the airlines' willingness to accept your bid. However, in some cases, these sites may not always yield the best price. Unlike a travel agent, for example, they may not have access to charter flights offered by wholesalers.

Editor's Note:
What You'll Find at the Frommer's Site

We highly recommend **Arthur Frommer's Budget Travel Online** (**www.frommers.com**) as an excellent travel planning resource. Of course we're a little biased, but you'll find indispensable travel tips, reviews, monthly vacation giveaways, and online booking. Among the most popular features of this site is the regular "Ask the Expert" bulletin board, which features one of the Frommer's authors answering your questions via online postings.

Subscribe to Arthur Frommer's Daily Newsletter (**www.frommers.com/newsletters**) to receive the latest travel bargains and inside travel secrets in your e-mailbox every day. You'll read daily headlines and articles from the dean of travel himself, highlighting last-minute deals on airfares, accommodations, cruises, and package vacations. You'll also find great travel advice by checking our Tip of the Day or Hot Spot of the Month.

Search our Destinations archive (**www.frommers.com/destinations**) of more than 200 domestic and international destinations for great places to stay, tips for traveling there, and what to do while you're there. Once you've researched your trip, the online reservation system (**www.frommers.com/booktravelnow**) takes you to Frommer's favorite sites for booking your vacation at affordable prices.

Online booking sites aren't the only places to reserve airline tickets—all major airlines have their own Web sites and often offer incentives—bonus frequent flyer miles or net-only discounts, for example—when you buy online or buy an e-ticket.

The new trend is toward conglomerated booking sites. A consortium of U.S. and European-based airlines are planning to launch an as-yet unnamed Web site in mid-2000 that will offer fares lower than those available through travel agents. United, Delta, Northwest, and Continental have initiated this effort, spurred on by their success at selling airline seats on their own online sites.

The best of the travel planning sites are now highly personalized; they store your seating preferences, meal preferences, tentative itineraries, and credit-card information, allowing you to quickly plan trips or check agendas.

In many cases, booking your trip online can be better than working with a travel agent. You'll get the widest variety of choices, control, and the 24-hour convenience of planning your trip when you choose to. All you need is some time—and often a little patience—and you're likely to find the fun of online travel research will greatly enhance your trip.

WHO SHOULD BOOK ONLINE?

Online booking is best for travelers who want to know as much as possible about their travel options, those who have flexibility in their travel dates and are looking for the best price, and for bargain hunters driven by a good value, who are open-minded about where they travel.

One of the biggest benefits of online booking, for both passengers and airlines, is the offering of last-minute specials, such as American Airlines' weekend deals or other Internet-only fares that must be purchased online. Another advantage of is that you can cash in on incentives for booking online, such as rebates or bonus frequent-flyer miles.

Business and other frequent travelers have also found numerous benefits in online booking, as the advances in mobile technology provide them with the ability to check flight status, change plans, or get specific directions from handheld computing devices, mobile phones and pagers. Some sites will even e-mail or page a passenger if their flight is delayed.

Online booking sites are increasingly able to accommodate complex itineraries, even for international travel. The pace of evolution on the Net is rapid, so you'll probably find additional features and advancements by the time you visit these sites. What the future holds for online travelers is ever-increasing personalization, customization, and reaching out to you.

TRAVEL PLANNING & BOOKING SITES

Below are listings for the top sites for planning and booking travel. The following sites offer domestic and international flight, hotel, and rental car bookings, plus news, destination information, and deals on cruises and vacation packages. Free (one-time) registration is required for booking.

✪ Expedia. expedia.com

Expedia is known as the fastest and most flexible online travel planner for booking flights, hotels, and rental cars. It offers several ways of obtaining the best possible fares: The **Flight Price Matcher** service allows your preferred airline to match an available fare with a competitor's; a comprehensive **Fare Compare** area shows the differences in fare categories among the airlines; and **Fare Calendar** helps you plan your trip around the best possible fares. The site's main limitation is that, like many online databases, Expedia focuses on the major airlines and hotel chains, so don't expect to find too many budget airlines or one-of-a-kind B&Bs here.

Personalized features allow you to store your itineraries, and receive weekly fare reports on favorite cities. You can also check on the status of flight arrivals and departures, and through MileageMiner, track all of your frequent-flyer accounts.

Expedia also offers vacation packages, cruises, information on specialized travel (such as family vacations, casino destinations, and adventure, ski, and golf travel). There are also special features for travelers accessing information on mobile devices.

(*Note:* In early 2000, Expedia bought travelscape.com and vacationspot.com, and incorporated these sites into expedia.com.)

Travelocity (incorporates Preview Travel). www.travelocity.com; www.previewtravel.com

Travelocity uses the SABRE system to offer reservations and tickets for more than 400 airlines, plus reservations and purchase capabilities for more than

Staying Secure

More people still look online than book online, partly due to fear of putting their credit card numbers out on the Net. Secure encryption, and increased experience in buying online, has removed this fear for most travelers. You can find a flight online and then book it by calling a toll-free number or contacting your travel agent, though this is somewhat less efficient. To be sure you're in secure mode when you book online, look for a little icon of a key (in Netscape) or a padlock (in Internet Explorer) at the bottom of your Web browser.

Airline Web Sites

Below are the Web sites for the major airlines. These sites offer schedules, flight booking and most have pages where you can sign up for e-mail alerts for weekend deals and other late-breaking bargains.

Alaska Airlines. www.alaskaair.com
America West. www.americawest.com
American Airlines. www.aa.com
ATA. www.ata.com
Continental Airlines. www.continental.com
Delta. www.delta-air.com
Northwest Airlines. www.nwa.com
Southwest. www.southwest.com
United Airlines. www.ual.com
US Airways. www.usairways.com

45,000 hotels and 50 car-rental companies. An exclusive feature of the SABRE system is their **Low Fare Search Engine,** which automatically searches for the three lowest-priced itineraries based on a traveler's criteria. Last-minute deals and consolidator fares (provided by Travel Information Software Systems, or TISS) are included in each search. If you book with Travelocity, you can select specific seats for your flights with online seat maps, and also view diagrams of the most popular commercial aircraft. Their hotel finder provides street-level location maps and photos of selected hotels.

Travelocity features an inviting interface for booking trips, though the wealth of graphics involved can make the site somewhat slow to load, and any adjustment in desired trip planning means you'll need to completely start over.

This site also has some very cool tools. With the **Fare Watcher** e-mail feature, you can select up to five routes and you'll receive e-mail notices when a fare changes by $25 or more. If you own an e-mail-capable alphanumeric pager with national access, Travelocity's **Flight Paging** can alert you if your flight is delayed. You can also access real-time departure and arrival information on any flight within the SABRE system.

Note to AOL Users: You can book flights, hotels, rental cars, and cruises on AOL at keyword: Travel. The booking software is provided by Travelocity/Preview Travel and is similar to the Internet site. Use the AOL "Travelers Advantage" program to earn a 5% rebate on flights, hotel rooms, and car rentals.

TRIP.com. www.trip.com
TRIP.com began as a site geared to business travelers, but its innovative features and highly personalized approach have broadened its appeal to leisure travelers as well. It is the leading travel site for those using mobile devices to access Internet travel information.

TRIP.com includes a trip-planning function that provides the average and lowest fare for the route requested, in addition to the current available fare. An on-site "newsstand" features breaking news on airfare sales and other travel specials. Among its most popular features are Flight TRACKER and intelliTRIP. **Flight TRACKER** allows users to track any commercial flight en route to its destination anywhere in the United States, while accessing real-time FAA-based flight monitoring data. **intelliTRIP** is a travel search tool that allows users to identify the best airline, hotel, and rental car fares in less than 90 seconds.

In addition, they offer e-mail notification of flight delays, plus, city resource guides, currency converters, and a weekly e-mail newsletter of fare updates, travel tips, and traveler forums.

Yahoo Travel. www.travel.yahoo.com
Yahoo is currently the most popular of the Internet information portals, and their travel site is a comprehensive mix of online booking, daily travel news, and destination information. Their **Best Fares** area offers what it promises, and provides feedback on refining your search if you have flexibility in your travel dates or times. There are also active message boards for discussions on travel in general, and to specific destinations.

SPECIALTY TRAVEL SITES

Although the sites listed above provide the most comprehensive services, some travelers have specialized needs that are best met by a site that caters specifically to them.

"Have Kids, Still Travel!" is the motto of the **Family Travel Forum (FTF)** (www.familytravelforum.com), a site dedicated to the ideals, promotion, and support of travel with children. FTF is supported by memberships, which are available in flexible prices ranging from a $2.95 monthly fee, to a heftier annual fee for more comprehensive services. Since no advertising is accepted, FTF provides its members with honest, unbiased information, informed advice and practical tips designed to make traveling with children a healthier, safer, hassle-free experience, not to mention a better value.

TOP VACATION PACKAGE SITES

Both **Expedia** and **Travelocity** (see above) offer excellent search engines for complete vacation packages. Travelers can search by destination and desired dates, coupled with how much they are willing to spend. Travelocity has a valuable "Cruise Critic" function, to help would-be cruisers obtain first-hand accounts of the quality and details of a cruise from recent passengers.

Travel wholesalers, such as **Apple Vacations** (www.applevacations.com) and **Funjet** (www.funjet.com) are also good starting points, but still require that the final booking be handled through a travel agent.

As travel agents tend to be more expert at sorting through the values in vacation packages, you might find **Vacation.com** (www.vacation.com) helpful in previewing packages and finding an appropriate agent to help you book the deal. This site represents a nationwide network of 9,800 local travel agencies that specialize in finding the best values in cruises, vacation packages, tours, and other leisure travel services. To find a Vacation.com member agency, enter your zip code and the Vacation.com Agency Finder will locate a nearby office.

LAST-MINUTE DEALS & OTHER ONLINE BARGAINS

There's nothing airlines hate more than flying with lots of empty seats. The Net has enabled airlines to offer last-minute bargains to entice travelers to fill those seats. Most of these are announced on Tuesday or Wednesday and are valid for travel the following weekend, but some can be booked weeks or months in advance. You can sign up for weekly e-mail alerts at airlines' sites (For Web sites of airlines, see "Airline Web Sites," above) or check sites that compile lists of these bargains, such as **Smarter Living** or **WebFlyer** (see below). To make it easier, visit a site that will round up all the deals and send them in one convenient weekly e-mail. But last-minute deals aren't the only online bargains; other sites can help you find value even if you haven't waited until the eleventh hour. Increasingly popular are services that let you name the price you're willing to pay for an airline seat or vacation package, and travel auction sites.

Cheap Tickets. www.cheaptickets.com
Cheap Tickets has exclusive deals that aren't available through more mainstream channels. One caveat about the Cheap Tickets site is that it will offer fare quotes for a route, and later show this fare is not valid for your dates of travel—most other Web sites, such as Expedia, consider your dates of travel before showing what fares are available. Despite its problems, Cheap Tickets can be worth the effort because its fares can be lower than those offered by its competitors.

✪ **1travel.com.** www.1travel.com
Here you'll find deals on domestic and international flights, cruises, hotels, and all-inclusive resorts such as Club Med. 1travel.com's **Saving Alert** compiles last-minute air deals so you don't have to scroll through multiple e-mail alerts. A feature called "Drive a little using low-fare airlines" helps map out strategies for using alternate airports to find lower fares. And **Farebeater** searches a database that includes published fares, consolidator bargains and special deals exclusive to 1travel.com. *Note:* The travel agencies listed by 1travel.com have paid for placement.

Bid for Travel. www.bidfortravel.com
Bid for Travel is another of the travel auction sites, similar to Priceline (see below), which are growing in popularity. In addition to airfares, Internet users can place a bid for vacation packages and hotels.

Go4less.com. www.go4less.com
Specializing in last-minute cruise and package deals, Go4less has some excellent offers. The **Hot Deals** section gives an alphabetical listing by destination of super discounted packages.

LastMinuteTravel.com. www.lastminutetravel.com
Suppliers with excess inventory come to this online agency to distribute unsold airline seats, hotel rooms, cruises, and vacation packages. It's got great deals, but you have to put up with an excess of advertisements and slow-loading graphics.

Moment's Notice. www.moments-notice.com
As the name suggests, Moment's Notice specializes in last-minute vacation and cruise deals. You can browse for free, but if you want to purchase a trip you have to join Moment's Notice, which costs $25. Go to **World Wide Hot Deals** for a complete list of special deals in international destinations.

✪ **Priceline.com.** travel.priceline.com
Even people who aren't familiar with many Web sites have heard about Priceline.com. Launched in 1998 with a $10 million ad campaign featuring William Shatner, Priceline lets you "name your price" for domestic and international airline tickets and hotel rooms. In other words, you select a route and dates, guarantee with a credit card, and make a bid for what you're willing to pay. If one of the airlines in Priceline's database has a fare lower than your bid, your credit card will automatically be charged for a ticket.

But you can't say when you want to fly—you have to accept any flight leaving between 6am and 10pm on the dates you selected, and you may have to make a stopover. No frequent flyer miles are awarded, and tickets are nonrefundable and can't be exchanged for another flight. So if your plans change,

Know When the Sales Start

Because last-minute weekend deals are limited, they can vanish within hours—sometimes even minutes—so it pays to log on as soon as they're available. Check the pages devoted to these deals on airlines' Web pages to get the info. An example: Southwest's specials are posted at 12:01am Tuesdays (Central Time). So if you're looking for a cheap flight, stay up late and check Southwest's site to grab the best new deals.

---

you're out of luck. Priceline can be good for travelers who have to take off on short notice (and who are thus unable to qualify for advance purchase discounts). But be sure to shop around first, because if you overbid, you'll be required to purchase the ticket—and Priceline will pocket the difference between what it paid for the ticket and what you bid.

Priceline says that more than 35% of all reasonable offers for domestic flights are being filled on the first try, with much higher fill rates on popular routes (New York to San Francisco, for example). They define "reasonable" as not more than 30% below the lowest generally available advance-purchase fare for the same route.

Smarter Living. www.smarterliving.com
Best known for its e-mail dispatch of weekend deals on 20 airlines, Smarter Living also keeps you posted about last-minute bargains on everything from Windjammer Cruises to flights to Iceland.

SkyAuction.com. www.skyauction.com
An auction site with categories for airfare, travel deals, hotels, and much more.

Travelzoo.com. www.travelzoo.com
At this Internet portal, more than 150 travel companies post special deals. It features a Top 20 list of the best deals on the site, selected by its editorial staff each Wednesday night. This list is also available via an e-mail list, free to those who sign up.

WebFlyer. www.webflyer.com
WebFlyer is a comprehensive online resource for frequent flyers and also has an excellent listing of last-minute air deals. Click on "Deal Watch" for a roundup of weekend deals on flights, hotels, and rental cars from domestic and international suppliers.

ONLINE TRAVELER'S TOOLBOX

Veteran travelers usually carry some essential items to make their trips easier. Following is a selection of online tools to smooth your journey.

Visa ATM Locator. www.visa.com/pd/atm/

MasterCard ATM Locator. www.mastercard.com/atm
Find ATMs in hundreds of cities in the United States and around the world. Both include maps for some locations and both list airport ATM locations, some with maps.

Intellicast. www.intellicast.com
Weather forecasts for all 50 states and cities around the world. Note that temperatures are in Celsius for many international destinations, so don't think you'll need that winter coat for your next trip to Athens.

✪ Mapquest. www.mapquest.com
The best of the mapping sites, it lets you choose a specific address or destination, and in seconds, will return back a map and detailed directions. It really is easier than calling, asking, and writing down directions. The site also has links to special travel deals and helpful sites.

Net Café Guide. www.netcafeguide.com/mapindex.htm
Locate Internet cafes at hundreds of locations around the globe. Catch up on your e-mail, log onto the Web, and stay in touch with the home front, usually for just a few dollars per hour.

Travelers' Tales. www.travelerstales.com
Considered the best in compilations of travel literature, Travelers' Tales are an award-winning series of books grouped by destination (Mexico, Italy, France, China) or by theme (Love and Romance, The Ultimate Journey, Women in the Wild, The Adventure of Food). It's a new kind of travel book that offers a description of a place or type of journey through the experiences of many travelers. It makes for a perfect traveling companion.

The Travelite FAQ. www.travelite.org
Tips on packing light, choosing luggage, and selecting appropriate travel wear—helpful if you always tend to pack too much, or are a compulsive list maker.

Universal Currency Converter. www.xe.net/currency
See what your dollar or pound is worth in more than 100 other countries.

U.S. Customs Service Traveler Information.
www.customs.ustreas.gov/travel/index.htm
Wondering what you're allowed to bring in to the United States? Check at this thorough site, which includes maximum allowance and duty fees.

Web Travel Secrets. www.web-travel-secrets.com
If this list leaves you yearning for more travel-oriented sites, Web Travel Secrets offers one of the best compilations around. One section offers advice and tips on how to find the lowest prices for airlines, hotels, and cruises. The other section provides a comprehensive listing of Web travel links for airfare deals, airlines, booking engines, cars, cruise lines, discount travel and best deals, general travel resources, hotels and hotel discounters, search engines, and travel magazines and newsletters.

Travel Discussion Sites

One of the best sources of travel information is the word-of-mouth from someone who has just been there. Internet discussion groups are offering an unprecedented way for travelers around the globe to connect and share experiences. The **Frommer's Online** site (www.frommers.com) offers these message boards, and their section "Ask the Expert" is an area where you can pose questions to the guidebook writers themselves. **Yahoo Travel, Expedia,** and **Travelocity** are other good sources of online travel discussion groups.

The granddaddy of specialized discussions on particular topics, is **Usenet,** a collection of more than 50,000 newsgroups. You'll find a comprehensive listing at **Deja News (www.dejanews.com/usenet/)** or at **www.liszt.com**.

Check E-mail at Internet Cafes While Traveling

Until a few years ago, most travelers who checked their e-mail while on the road carried a laptop—an expensive and often technologically problematic option. Thankfully, Web-based free e-mail programs have made it much easier to check your mail.

Just open an account at any one of the numerous "freemail" providers—the original leaders continue to be **Hotmail** (hotmail.com), **Excite** (www.excite.com), and **Yahoo! Mail** (mail.yahoo.com), though many are available. AOL users should check out **AOL Netmail,** and USA.NET (**www.usa.net**) comes highly recommended for functionality and security. You can find hints, tips, and a mile-long list of freemail providers at **www.emailaddresses.com.**

Then, all you'll need to check your mail is a Web connection, easily available at Net cafes and copy shops around the world. After logging on, just call up your freemail's Internet address, enter your username and password and you'll have access to your mail. From these sites, you can download all of your e-mail—even from office accounts—or your local or national Internet Service Provider address. There will be a section generally called "check other mail" that allows you to add the names of other e-mail servers.

The downside is that most Web-based e-mail sites only allow a maximum of 3 megabytes capacity per mail account, which can fill up quickly. Also, message sending and receiving is not immediate; some messages may be delayed by several hours, or even days.

2 The Top Web Sites for Miami & South Florida

GENERAL SOUTH FLORIDA SITES

Digital City South Florida on AOL. Keyword: South Florida
Click here for entertainment, dining, sports, and festival information produced in cooperation with the *Sun-Sentinel.* This site includes a lively forum, where you can read comments from others or post a question of your own. Digital City is also available on the Web at southflorida.digitalcity.com.

✪ FLA USA. www.flausa.com
A product of Florida's official tourism bureau, this extensive Web site includes information on attractions, beaches, golfing, and water sports, as well as airport information, weather, and maps. The beach guide is nicely organized by region, and there's advice on Florida's natural attractions in the Activities section.

Florida Association of Convention and Visitors Bureaus.
 www.facvb.org
Links to more than a dozen bureaus throughout the state, including several in South Florida. Most of the sites include information on attractions, dining, lodging, and shopping.

Florida State Parks. www.dep.state.fl.us/parks
Though the home page is awkwardly designed (this is a government site after all), you can find parks by clicking on "Parks Map" or "Park Index." From

there, you can learn about camping at each park, including information on fees, nearby attractions, and facilities.

Just Go: South Florida. www.justgo.com/southflorida
Dining, music, theater, and movies are listed and reviewed on this site. Just Go does a nice job in spotlighting upcoming concerts and makes it easy to find restaurants by cuisine and neighborhood.

See Florida. www.see-florida.com
A nicely organized guide to theme parks, marine attractions, museums, boating, fishing, and much more. See Florida includes guides to many of South Florida cities and has advice for first-time visitors to the Sunshine State.

CITY GUIDES & ENTERTAINMENT SITES

City guides are a good way to get acquainted with what's going on in Miami. While some are geared toward residents, they are still excellent resources for travelers who want to get the local scoop on nightlife, restaurants, and places to shop.

About.com: Miami for Visitors. gomiami.about.com
Primarily a collection of Web sites for travelers to Miami, you'll find sections on culture, fishing, and shopping, among many others. While you won't find in-depth stories here, the site does include some short features on Miami, such as one on what to do if it's too cold for the beach. All these features are rich with links to other relevant Web sites.

✪ CitySearch: Miami. miami.citysearch.com
This site offers listings and reviews for Miami arts and entertainment events, restaurants, shopping, and attractions. CitySearch is part of a national network of city guides, and has editorial reviews as well as Web pages paid for by restaurants and other businesses. CitySearch clearly labels its pages as either "editorial profile" or advertiser's "Web site." Click on the calendar link for events recommended by the editors. The extensive shopping listings range from clothing to specialty stores and include updates on sales. Along with Sidewalk, CitySearch is a leading directory for arts and dining in Miami.

Discover: Key West. key-west.com
A well-rounded guide to Key West, including an events calendar and extensive listings for attractions, sightseeing and ecotours, theater, and art galleries. You'll also find a dining guide, lodging options, and sections on dining, fishing, and shopping.

Gay Key West Travel Guide. www.gaykeywestfl.com
A guide to gay-friendly lodgings, restaurants, and clubs.

Metroguide: Miami. miami.metroguide.net
This site offers listings for arts and entertainment, restaurants, shopping, and attractions. Wading through Metroguide after visiting CitySearch or Sidewalk is like watching home movies after seeing the latest Star Wars epic. But it's still worth visiting for its relatively deep events listings (though you'll have to click down three pages to get these). The dining, hotel, and shopping listings appear to include only businesses that have paid for pages on Metroguide. These can still be valuable, provided you realize you're not getting the whole enchilada.

Time Out: Miami. www.timeout.com/miami
This site offers reviews and listings for attractions, entertainment, restaurants, hotels, and shopping, and includes categories for kids and gays and lesbians.

Time Out is a lively guide with a youthful approach, but has features for everyone, including festival previews. Unlike some other city guides, Time Out Miami makes a concerted effort to cater to tourists as well as locals. The listings appear uninfluenced by ads, because there are no ads visible here. Plus, the site's clean design makes it a pleasure to navigate.

Tropicool Miami (Miami Convention & Visitors Bureau).
www.miamiandbeaches.com
This nice site will provide you with a good overview of Miami and its beckoning beaches. Sure, the content is a bit sales-heavy, but it's still informative. You won't find detailed listings for restaurants and hotels, but there is general information about Miami's dining and arts scene, as well as advice about shopping and lodging in various districts. If you want more, you can order the print guide through the Web site or by calling a toll-free number.

NEWSPAPERS & MAGAZINES

One of the best ways to take a city's pulse is to browse through the virtual pages of its newspapers and magazines. Now, you no longer have to go to a newsstand to browse through Miami's news sources, which also contain entertainment information.

Miami Herald. www.herald.com
Miami's leading news source can give you a sense of what's going on in the city, but don't expect extensive entertainment listings.

Miami New Times. www.miaminewtimes.com
Miami's leading alternative weekly includes features and listings for music, theater, film, and more. Click on Music and then Concerts This Week to see listings ranging from the Florida Philharmonic to the Blues Festival.

Sun-Sentinel: Showtime. www.sun-sentinel.com/showtime
Here's a nice roundup of music, theater, sports, and dining choices in South Florida, with coverage of local festivals and events. For hard news and weather, see www.sun-sentinel.com.

DINING GUIDES

Get a taste of Miami's restaurants with online reviews. You can also find extensive restaurant listings at Sidewalk, CitySearch, and some other city guides (see above).

CuisineNet. www.cuisinenet.com
Listings and reviews for Miami and 15 other U.S. cities. Each restaurant has a capsule review compiled by CuisineNet and ratings based on surveys received from site users. For many restaurants, only two or three people have bothered to submit ratings, so they may not be statistically significant. However, comments can be instructive, as CuisineNet's readers discuss service, parking, free birthday desserts, and a host of other insightful topics.

Zagat Restaurant Survey. www.zagat.com
Reviews of top restaurants for Miami and many other U.S. cities. Zagat has made a name for itself as the people's choice, as its listings are based on extensive surveys.

ATTRACTIONS

Though there's absolutely nothing wrong with just lying on a beach, Miami offers much more for visitors. Here's a sampling.

Bayside Waterfront. www.baysidemarketplace.com
You'll find tourism information, a searchable directory and calendar of events for this downtown shopping, dining, and entertainment complex. There's even a coupon on the Web site that you can print and redeem at Bayside.

Biltmore Hotel. www.biltmorehotel.com
Even if you don't stay at the Biltmore, you can enjoy its opulence and events, which include historic tours, opera nights, and afternoon tea.

Biscayne National Park. www.nps.gov/bisc
Just a hop, skip, and jump across Biscayne Bay, this park is a terrific place for recreation and is home to mangrove shorelines, a shallow bay, undeveloped islands, and living coral reefs. The site includes basic information on activities, attractions, and nearby lodgings.

✪ **Everglades National Park.** www.nps.gov/ever
This fairly comprehensive guide from the National Park Service includes everything you'd expect—information on attractions, activities, lodging, camping, fishing, and climate for this remarkable park. You'll also find superb features on the Everglades at GORP—visit **www.gorp.com** and search for "Everglades."

The Everglades and 10,000 Islands. www.florida-everglades.com
Sponsored by the Everglades Area Chamber of Commerce, this site offers maps, fishing tips, and dining advice. You'll also find event listings, a wildlife photo gallery, and a guide to southwest Florida. It's not the cleanest site ever designed, but it does have some valuable information.

Fairchild Tropical Garden. www.ftg.org
Visitor information, events, and historical information for this lush botanical garden of rare tropical plants, flowering trees, and vines.

Historical Museum of Southern Florida. www.historical-museum.org
Tracing human history in South Florida back 10,000 years, the Historical Museum site lets you preview the exhibition online. Perhaps most interesting to tourists are the Historic Tours—by foot, bus, boat, metrorail, and bicycle. A schedule is available at the site.

Jungle Queen. www.junglequeen.com
Schedule, fares, and online reservations for this riverboat, which cruises between Miami and Fort Lauderdale.

Miami-Dade County Online. www.co.miami-dade.fl.us
At Dade County's official government site, you'll find up-to-date information on county parks, sports, attractions such as the Miami Metrozoo, and cultural events.

Miami Film Festival. www.miamifilmfestival.com
If you'll be in Miami during the latter half of February, the film festival could be just the thing to wake up your mind. The site offers information about the films, events, and show times.

Miami International Boat Show.
www.boatshows.com/miami2000/images/home.html
One of the largest boat shows anywhere. Check this site for a schedule, an overview, a list of exhibitors, and ticket information. *Note:* The Web address above was for the 2000 show—if it doesn't roll over to the current site, try replacing the "2000" with "01" or "2001."

Miami Museum of Science. www.miamisci.org
Visitor information, exhibit previews, and a look inside the museum's Space Transit Planetarium, where you can lean back and search the night sky during the brightest Miami day.

Miami Seaquarium. miamiseaquarium.com
Featuring dolphins, whales, manatees, and alligators, Seaquarium is fascinating for the entire family. The site includes general park information (admission prices, hours), and a virtual tour of the attractions.

Parrot Jungle. www.parrotjungle.com
Homo sapiens aren't the only species that go to Florida to retire—some colorful parrots and macaws spend their golden years at this south Miami park. The site includes park information, a $2 coupon, and audio samples of a park tour. *Note:* RealAudio software is required to hear this audio sample—the software is available for free from **www.real.com.**

Venetian Pool. www.venetianpool.com
From humble beginnings as a rock quarry, the 820,000-gallon Venetian Pool today features two waterfalls, coral caves, and grottoes. The site includes a tour, maps, photos, history, programs, and other visitor information.

LOCAL SPORTS TEAMS

Miami is home to some of the best professional and college teams in the country. You can learn more about them and make plans to catch a game during your next trip.

Florida Marlins. www.flamarlins.com
Despite a fire sale by then-owner Wayne Huizenga, which left the Marlins practically starless after the team won the World Series several years ago, the team is rebuilding under new ownership and can be entertaining at times. You'll find schedules, tickets, and game coverage here.

Florida Panthers. www.flpanthers.com
Though hockey seems like a sport more suited to northern climes, tropical South Florida has caught hockey fever. The Panthers' site includes arena and ticket information, schedules, and player profiles.

Miami Dolphins. www.miamidolphins.com
Tickets, schedules, and news for the NFL team that spawned such legends as Bob Griese, Larry Csonka, and coach Don Shula.

Miami Heat. www.nba.com/heat
Scores and schedules, player profiles, and tickets for this NBA team that has become a perennial playoff contender.

University of Miami Hurricanes. www.hurricanesports.com
Schedule, tickets, and arena information, and game stories for the 'Canes, who are usually at or near the top of college football polls.

TICKETS

If you want to purchase concert, theater, or sporting event tickets, try the following online services.

TicketMaster. www.ticketmaster.com
A national outlet, TicketMaster sells tickets for sports, theater, and concerts—and tacks on a hefty service charge. You can also buy tickets through Culturefinder. com and reach TicketMaster through CitySearch.

TicketWeb. www.ticketweb.com
TicketWeb sells theater and concert tickets, usually for a much lower service charge than TicketMaster. TicketWeb is best for events at smaller venues—many of the larger arenas and halls are locked into exclusive deals with large ticket sellers and do not sell through other outlets.

GETTING AROUND

Get acquainted with the airport, check options for getting from the airport to your hotel, and learn how the locals get around at a fraction of the cost of a cab.

Miami-Dade Transit. www.co.miami-dade.fl.us/mdta/
Though this is a terribly slow-loading site, it does have basic information on bus and rail lines in and around Miami.

Miami International Airport. www.miami-airport.com
This site features a terminal map, airline counter locations, car-rental information, taxi and van advice, and other services to help you get around this labyrinthine airport.

Supershuttle: Miami. www.supershuttle.com/mia.htm
For single travelers this shuttle can be considerably cheaper than taking a cab. The site includes sample fares and toll-free reservations lines.

3 For Foreign Visitors

The pervasiveness of American culture around the world may make you feel that you know the USA pretty well, but leaving your own country still requires an additional degree of planning. This chapter will help prepare you for the more common problems that visitors may face. And don't despair if you encounter a problem while on your trip, South Floridians are usually quite willing to help out tourists in need.

1 Preparing for Your Trip

ENTRY REQUIREMENTS

The U.S. State Department has a **Visa Waiver Pilot Program** allowing citizens of certain countries to enter the United States without a visa for stays of up to 90 days. At press time these included Andorra, Argentina, Australia, Austria, Belgium, Brunei, Denmark, Finland, France, Germany, Iceland, Ireland, Italy, Japan, Liechtenstein, Luxembourg, Monaco, the Netherlands, New Zealand, Norway, San Marino, Slovenia, Spain, Sweden, Switzerland, and the United Kingdom. Citizens of these countries need only a valid passport and a round-trip air or cruise ticket in their possession upon arrival. If they first enter the United States, they may also visit Mexico, Canada, Bermuda, and/or the Caribbean islands and return to the United States without a visa. Further information is available from any U.S. embassy or consulate. Canadian citizens may enter the United States without visas; they need only proof of residence.

Citizens of all other countries must have (1) a valid passport that expires at least 6 months later than the scheduled end of their visit to the United States, and (2) a tourist visa, which may be obtained without charge from any U.S. consulate.

OBTAINING A VISA To obtain a visa, the traveler must submit a completed application form (either in person or by mail) with a 1 1/2-inch-square photo, and must demonstrate binding ties to a residence abroad. Usually you can obtain a visa at once or within 24 hours, but it may take longer during the summer rush from June through August. If you cannot go in person, contact the nearest U.S. embassy or consulate for directions on applying by mail. Your travel agent or airline office may also be able to provide you with visa applications and instructions. The U.S. consulate or embassy that issues your visa will determine whether you will be issued a multiple- or single-entry visa and any restrictions regarding the length of your stay.

British subjects can obtain up-to-date passport and visa information by calling the **U.S. Embassy Visa Information Line** (☎ **0891/200-290**) or the **London Passport Office** (☎ **0990/210-410** for recorded information).

IMMIGRATION QUESTIONS   Telephone operators will answer your inquiries regarding U.S. immigration policies or laws at the **Immigration and Naturalization Service's Customer Information Center** (☎ **800/375-5283**). Representatives are available from 9am to 3pm, Monday through Friday. The INS also runs a 24-hour automated information service, for commonly asked questions, at ☎ **800/755-0777.**

MEDICAL REQUIREMENTS   Unless you're arriving from an area known to be suffering from an epidemic (particularly cholera or yellow fever), inoculations or vaccinations are not required for entry into the United States. If you have a disease that requires treatment with narcotics or syringe-administered medications, carry a valid signed prescription from your physician to allay any suspicions that you may be smuggling narcotics (a serious offense that carries severe penalties in the United States).

For HIV-positive visitors, requirements for entering the United States are somewhat vague and change frequently. For up-to-the-minute information concerning HIV-positive travelers, contact the Centers for Disease Control's **National Center for HIV** (☎ **404/332-4559;** www.hivatis.org) or the **Gay Men's Health Crisis** (☎ **212/367-1000;** www.gmhc.org).

CUSTOMS   Every visitor over 21 years of age may bring in, free of duty, the following: (1) 1 liter of wine or hard liquor; (2) 200 cigarettes, 100 cigars (but not from Cuba), or 3 pounds of smoking tobacco; and (3) $100 worth of gifts. These exemptions are offered to travelers who spend at least 72 hours in the United States and who have not claimed them within the preceding 6 months. It is altogether forbidden to bring into the country foodstuffs (particularly fruit, cooked meats, and canned goods) and plants (vegetables, seeds, tropical plants, and the like). Foreign tourists may bring in or take out up to $10,000 in U.S. or foreign currency with no formalities; larger sums must be declared to U.S. Customs on entering or leaving, which includes filing form CM 4790. For more specific information regarding U.S. Customs, call your nearest U.S. embassy or consulate, the U.S. Customs office at ☎ **202/927-1770,** or point your Web browser to **www.customs.ustreas.gov**.

INSURANCE

Although it's not required of travelers, health insurance is highly recommended. Unlike many European countries, the United States does not usually offer free or low-cost medical care to its citizens or visitors. Doctors and hospitals are expensive, and in most cases will require advance payment or proof of coverage before they render their services. See "Health & Insurance," in chapter 2, for more information. Packages such as **Europ Assistance** in Europe are sold by automobile clubs and travel agencies at attractive rates. **Worldwide Assistance Services,** Inc. (☎ **800/821-2828**), is the agent for Europ Assistance in the United States.

Though a lack of health insurance may prevent you from being admitted to a hospital in nonemergencies, don't worry about being left on a street corner to die: The American way is to fix you now and bill the living daylights out of you later.

Insurance for British Travelers   Britain's Consumers' Association recommends that you insist on seeing a policy and reading the fine print before buying travel insurance. **The Association of British Insurers** (☎ **0171/600-3333**) gives advice by phone and publishes the free *Holiday Insurance*, a guide to policy provisions and prices. You might also shop around for better deals: Try **Columbus Travel Insurance Ltd.** (☎ 0171/375-0011) or, for students, **Campus Travel** (☎ 0171/730-2101).

Insurance for Canadian Travelers Canadians should check with their provincial health plan offices or call **HealthCanada** (☎ 613/957-2991) to find out the extent of their coverage and what documentation and receipts they must take home in case they are treated in the United States.

MONEY

CURRENCY The U.S. monetary system is painfully simple: The most common bills (all ugly, all green) are the $1 (colloquially, a "buck"), $5, $10, and $20 denominations. There are also $2 bills (seldom encountered), $50 bills, and $100 bills (the last two are usually not welcome as payment for small purchases). Note that a newly redesigned $100 and $50 bill were introduced in 1996, and a redesigned $20 bill in 1998. Expect to see redesigned $10 and $5 notes in the year 2000. Despite rumors to the contrary, the old-style bills are still legal tender.

There are six denominations of coins: 1¢ (1 cent, or a penny); 5¢ (5 cents, or a nickel); 10¢ (10 cents, or a dime); 25¢ (25 cents, or a quarter); 50¢ (50 cents, or a half dollar); and, prized by collectors, the rare $1 piece (the older, large silver dollar and the newer, small Susan B. Anthony coin). A new gold $1 piece was introduced in the year 2000.

Note: The "foreign-exchange bureaus" so common in Europe are rare even at airports in the United States, and nonexistent outside major cities. It's best not to change foreign money (or traveler's checks denominated in a currency other than U.S. dollars) at a small-town bank, or even a branch in a big city; in fact, you're better off leaving any currency other than U.S. dollars at home.

TRAVELER'S CHECKS Though traveler's checks are widely accepted, make sure that they're denominated in U.S. dollars, as foreign-currency checks are often difficult to exchange. The two traveler's checks that are most widely recognized—and least likely to be denied—are **Visa** and **American Express.** Be sure to record the numbers of the checks, and keep that information separately in case they get lost or stolen. Most businesses are pretty good about taking traveler's checks, but you're better off cashing them in at a bank (in small amounts, of course) and paying in cash. *Remember:* You'll need identification, such as a driver's license or passport, to change a traveler's check.

CREDIT CARDS & ATMs Credit cards are the most widely used form of payment in the United States: Visa (BarclayCard in Britain), **MasterCard** (Eurocard in Europe, Access in Britain, Chargex in Canada), **American Express, Diners Club, Discover,** and **Carte Blanche.** You must have a credit or charge card to rent a car. There are, however, a handful of stores and restaurants that do not take credit cards, so be sure to ask in advance. Most businesses display a sticker near their entrance to let you know which cards they accept. (*Note:* Often businesses require a minimum purchase price, usually around $10, to use a credit card.)

It is strongly recommended that you bring at least one major credit card. Hotels, car-rental companies, and airlines usually require a credit-card imprint as a deposit against expenses, and in an emergency, a credit card can be priceless.

You'll find automated-teller machines (ATMs) just about everywhere in South Florida. Some ATMs will allow you to draw U.S. currency against your bank and credit cards. Check with your bank before leaving home, and remember that you will need your personal identification number (PIN) to do so. Most accept Visa, MasterCard, and American Express, as well as ATM cards from other U.S. banks. Expect to be charged a fee, however, if you're not using your own bank's ATM.

Impressions

As we rode over the causeway, I could hardly believe my eyes. It was almost unimaginable that in Miami Beach it was 80 degrees while in New York it was 20. Everything—the buildings, the water, the pavement—had an indescribable glow to it. The palm trees especially made a great impression on me.
          —Isaac Bashevis Singer, describing his first visit to Miami in 1948

One way around these fees is to ask for cash back at grocery stores that accept ATM cards and don't charge usage fees. Of course, you'll have to purchase something first.

SAFETY

GENERAL SAFETY SUGGESTIONS While tourist areas are generally safe, crime is on the increase everywhere, and U.S. urban areas tend to be less safe than those in Europe or Japan. You should always stay alert. Avoid deserted areas, especially at night, and don't go into public parks at night unless there's a concert or similar occasion that will attract a crowd.

Avoid carrying valuables with you on the street, and don't display expensive cameras or electronic equipment. If you are using a map, consult it inconspicuously—or better yet, try to study it before you leave your room. Hold onto your pocketbook, and place your billfold in an inside pocket. In theaters, restaurants, and other public places, keep your possessions in sight.

Remember also that hotels are open to the public, and in a large hotel, security may not be able to screen everyone entering. Always lock your room door—don't assume that once inside your hotel you are automatically safe and no longer need to be aware of your surroundings.

DRIVING SAFETY Driving safety is important too, especially given the highly publicized carjackings of foreign tourists in Florida a few years back. South Florida's local and state governments have taken steps to help protect visitors against crimes particularly targeted against tourists. These measures include special, highly visible police units patrolling the airport and surrounding neighborhoods and better signs on the state's most tourist-traveled routes. Still, especially in Miami, the signs can be extremely confusing. If you are staying on South Beach, you might want to consider skipping a car for the time you are on the island. Taxis are plentiful and relatively inexpensive (see "Getting Around," in chapter 4).

Question your rental agency about personal safety and ask for a traveler-safety brochure when you pick up your car. Obtain written directions—or a map with the route clearly marked—from the agency showing how to get to your destination. And, if possible, arrive and depart during daylight hours.

If you drive off a highway into a doubtful neighborhood, leave the area as quickly as possible. If you have an accident, even on the highway, stay in your car with the doors locked until you assess the situation or until the police arrive. If you're bumped from behind on the street or are involved in a minor accident with no injuries and the situation appears to be suspicious, motion to the other driver to follow you. Never get out of your car in such situations. Go directly to the nearest police precinct, well-lit service station, or 24-hour store.

Always try to park in well-lit and well-traveled areas if possible. Never leave any packages or valuables in sight. If someone attempts to rob you or steal your car, don't try to resist the thief/carjacker—report the incident to the police department immediately by calling ☎ **911.**

2 Getting to the United States

The idea of traveling abroad on a budget is something of an oxymoron, but travelers can reduce the price of a plane ticket by several hundred dollars if they take the time to shop around. Travelers from overseas can take advantage of the APEX (Advance Purchase Excursion) fares offered by all the major U.S. and European carriers. **British Airways** (☎ 081/897-4000 from within the U.K.) offers direct flights from London to Miami and Orlando, as does **Virgin Atlantic** (☎ 02/937-47747 from within the U.K.). Canadian readers might book flights with **Air Canada** (☎ 800/776-3000), which offers service from Toronto and Montreal to Miami and Tampa.

Miami International Airport is a hub for flights to and from Latin America. Carriers include **Aerolineas Argentinas** (☎ 800/333-0276), **Aeroméxico** (☎ 800/245-8585), **American Airlines** (☎ 800/433-7300), **Avianca** (☎ 800/284-2622), **Lan Chile Airlines** (☎ 800/735-5526), and **Varig Brazilian Airlines** (☎ 800/468-2744).

The visitor arriving by air, no matter what the port of entry, should cultivate patience and resignation before setting foot on U.S. soil. Getting through Immigration control could take as long as 2 hours on some days, especially summer weekends, so have your guidebook or something else to read handy. Add the time it takes to clear Customs, and you will see you should make a very generous allowance for delay in planning connections between international and domestic flights—figure on 2 to 3 hours at least.

Air travelers from Canada, Bermuda, and some places in the Caribbean can sometimes go through Customs and Immigration at the point of departure, which is much quicker.

For further information about getting to Miami, see "Getting There," in chapter 2.

3 Getting Around the United States

BY AIR   Some large airlines (for example, Northwest and Delta) offer travelers on their transatlantic or transpacific flights special discount tickets under the name **Visit USA,** allowing mostly one-way travel from one U.S. destination to another at very low prices. These discount tickets are not on sale in the United States and must be purchased abroad in conjunction with your international ticket. This system is the best, easiest, and fastest way to see the United States at low cost. You should obtain information well in advance from your travel agent or the office of the airline concerned, since the conditions attached to these discount tickets can be changed without advance notice.

BY RAIL   International visitors can buy the **USA Railpass**—good for 15 or 30 days of unlimited travel on **Amtrak's** trains (☎ 800/872-7245). You can get it through many non-U.S. travel agents and buy passes for a region, such as the Southeast, or for the entire United States. Prices in 2000 for a pass to travel the country were as follows: A 15-day pass costs $285 off-peak (January to May), $425 peak (June to December); a 30-day pass costs $375 off-peak, $535 peak. With a foreign passport, you can also buy passes at some Amtrak offices in the United States, including the one in Miami. Reservations are generally required and should be made for each part of your trip as early as possible.

Visitors should be aware of the limitations of long-distance rail travel in the United States. With a few notable exceptions, service is rarely up to European standards: Delays are common, routes are limited and often infrequently served, and fares are rarely significantly lower than discount airfares. Thus, cross-country train travel should be approached with caution.

BY BUS Although bus travel is often the most economical form of public transit for short hops between U.S. cities, it can also be slow and uncomfortable. **Greyhound/ Trailways** (☎ **800/231-2222;** www.greyhound.com), the sole nationwide bus line, offers an **International Ameripass** that must be purchased before coming to the United States, or at the Greyhound International Office at the Port Authority Bus Terminal in New York City. The pass can be obtained from foreign travel agents and costs less than the domestic version. The 2000 rates ran from $149 (7 days) to $429 (60 days). For more information call ☎ **212/971-0492** or ☎ **402/330-8552.** In addition, special rates are available for senior citizens and students.

BY CAR South Florida does not have an extensive public transportation network, but it does have an excellent highway system. The most economical and convenient way to tour Miami and the other destinations in South Florida, is by car. To rent a car, you need a major credit card and a driver's license (sometimes a hefty cash deposit can be used instead of a credit card). You must also be at least 25 years old. Some companies rent to younger people but usually add a high daily surcharge. Be sure to return your car with the same amount of gas (petrol) you start with; rental companies charge excessive prices for gasoline. All the major car-rental companies are represented in South Florida (see "Getting Around," in chapter 4, for a list).

Fast Facts: For the Foreign Traveler

Automobile Organizations Auto clubs will supply maps, suggested routes, guidebooks, accident and bail-bond insurance, and emergency road service. The major auto club in the United States, with 983 offices nationwide, is the **American Automobile Association** (AAA). Members of some foreign auto clubs have reciprocal arrangements with the AAA and enjoy its services at no charge, so inquire about AAA reciprocity before you leave. The AAA can give you an International Driving Permit validating your foreign license, although drivers with valid licenses from most home countries don't really need this permit. You may be able to join the AAA even if you are not a member of a reciprocal club. To inquire, call ☎ **800/926-4222.** In addition, some car-rental agencies now provide these services, so ask when you rent your car.

Business Hours Banks are open weekdays from 9am to 3pm or later and sometimes Saturday morning. There's daily 24-hour access to the automated-teller machines (ATMs) at most banks and other outlets. Business offices are usually open weekdays from 9am to 5pm. Shops, especially department stores and those in shopping complexes, tend to stay open late—until about 9pm weekdays and until 6pm weekends.

Climate See "When to Go," in chapter 2.

Currency See "Money," in "Preparing for Your Trip," earlier in this chapter.

Currency Exchange The "foreign-exchange bureaus" so common in Europe are rare in the United States.

At Miami Airport you'll find several **Miami Currency Exchanges** (☎ **305/ 876-0040**). The main one is at the lower level of concourse E. Another, **Abbot Foreign Exchange,** 230 NE 1st St. (☎ **305/374-2336**), is open weekdays from 8am to 5pm and Saturday from 8am to 2pm.

Drinking Laws The legal age for purchase and consumption of alcoholic beverages is 21; proof of age is required and often requested at bars, nightclubs, and restaurants, so it's always a good idea to bring ID when you go out.

Do not carry open containers of alcohol in your car or any public area that isn't zoned for alcohol consumption. The police can, and probably will, fine you on the spot. And nothing will ruin your trip faster than getting a citation for DUI ("driving under the influence"), so don't even think about driving while intoxicated.

Electricity Like Canada, the United States uses 110 to 120 volts AC (60 cycles), compared to 220 to 240 volts AC (50 cycles) in most of Europe, Australia, and New Zealand. If your small appliances use 220 to 240 volts, you'll need a 110-volt transformer and a plug adapter with two flat parallel pins to operate them here. Downward converters that change 220 to 240 volts to 110 to 120 volts are difficult to find in the United States, so bring one with you.

Embassies/Consulates All embassies are located in the national capital, Washington, D.C.; some consulates are located in Miami. Travelers from other countries can get telephone numbers for their embassies and consulates by calling "**Information**" in Washington, D.C. (☎ 202/555-1212).

Brazil's Consulate General is in Coconut Grove at 2601 S. Bayshore Dr., Suite 800, Miami, FL 33133 (☎ 305/285-6200); the **British Consulate** is also located in Coconut Grove at the Brickell Bay Tower, Suite 2110, 1001 S. Bayshore Dr., Miami, FL 33131 (☎ 305/374-1522); a **Canadian Consulate** is at 200 S. Biscayne Blvd., Suite 1600, Miami, FL 33132 (☎ 305/579-1600); **Germany's Consulate General** is at 100 N. Biscayne Blvd., Miami, FL 33132 (☎ 305/358-0290); the **Italian Consulate** is at 1200 Brickell Ave., Miami, FL 33131 (☎ 305/374-6322); and the **Portuguese Consulate** is in Coral Gables at 1901 Ponce de León Blvd., Miami, FL (☎ 305/444-6311).

Emergencies Call ☎ 911 for fire, police, and ambulance. If you encounter such traveler's problems as sickness, accidents, or lost or stolen baggage, call **Advocates for Victims** (☎ 305/758-2546), an organization that specializes in helping distressed travelers.

U.S. hospitals have emergency rooms, with a special entrance where you will be admitted for quick attention. **Health South Doctors' Hospital,** 5000 University Dr., Coral Gables (☎ 305/666-2111), is a 285-bed acute-care hospital with a 24-hour physician-staffed emergency department.

Gasoline (Petrol) One U.S. gallon equals 3.75 liters, while 1.2 U.S. gallons equal one Imperial gallon. A gallon of unleaded "gas" (short for "gasoline"), which most rental cars require, costs about $1.60 if you fill your own tanks (it's called "self-serve"), and 10¢ more if the station attendant does it (called "full-service"). Most Miami gas stations are self-serve, with credit-card processors right on the pump.

Holidays On the following legal national holidays, banks, government offices, post offices, and many stores, restaurants, and museums are closed: **January 1** (New Year's Day); **third Monday in January** (Martin Luther King Day); **third Monday in February** (Presidents' Day, Washington's Birthday); **last Monday in May** (Memorial Day); **July 4** (Independence Day); **first Monday in September** (Labor Day); **second Monday in October** (Columbus Day); **November 11** (Veterans Day/Armistice Day); **fourth Thursday in November** (Thanksgiving);

and **December 25** (Christmas). The Tuesday following the first Monday in November is **Election Day.**

Languages Most hotels in Greater Miami have bilingual employees (Spanish and English). Unless your language is very obscure, they can usually supply a translator on request. Because more than half of Miami residents speak Spanish fluently, most signs and brochures are printed in both English and Spanish. In addition, since a large number of French, Canadian, Italian, and German tourists visit Miami, most visitor information is available in their languages.

Legal Aid The foreign tourist will probably never become involved with the American legal system. If you are "pulled over" for a minor infraction (for example, of the highway code, such as speeding), never attempt to pay the fine directly to a police officer; this could be construed as attempted bribery, a much more serious crime. Pay fines by mail, or directly into the hands of the clerk of the court. If accused of a more serious offense, say and do nothing before consulting a lawyer. Here, the burden is on the state to prove a person's guilt beyond a reasonable doubt, and everyone has the right to remain silent, whether he or she is suspected of a crime or actually arrested. Once arrested, a person can make one telephone call to a party of his or her choice. Call your embassy or consulate.

Mail You'll find the **Main Post Office,** 2200 Milam Dairy Rd., Miami, FL 33152 (☎ **305/639-4280**), just west of Miami International Airport. Letters addressed to you and marked "c/o General Delivery" can be picked up at 500 NW 2nd Ave., Miami, FL 33101. Mail delivery takes at least 30 days. The addressee must pick it up in person and produce proof of identity (driver's license, credit card, passport, or the like). Mailboxes are generally blue with a red-and-white logo, and carry the inscription "U.S. Mail."

Within the United States, it costs 20¢ to mail a standard-size postcard and 33¢ to send an oversize postcard (larger than 4^1/$_4$ by 6 inches, or 10.8 by 15.4 centimeters). Letters that weigh up to 1 ounce (that's about five pages, 8^1/$_2$ by 11 inches, or 20.5 by 28.2 centimeters) cost 33¢, plus 22¢ for each additional ounce. A postcard to Mexico or Canada costs 40¢, a ^{1}/$_2$-ounce letter 46¢. A postcard to Europe, Australia, New Zealand, the Far East, South America, and elsewhere costs 50¢, while a ^{1}/$_2$-ounce letter is 60¢, and a 1-ounce letter is $1.

Newspapers/Magazines The *Miami Herald* and the magazines *Newsweek* and *Time* cover world news and are available at newsstands. Most magazine racks at drugstores, airports, and hotels include a good selection of foreign periodicals, such as *Stern, The Economist,* and *Le Monde. El Herald* and *Diarios Las Americas* are Spanish-language newspapers. Spanish-language magazines are particularly abundant.

Taxes In the United States, there is no VAT (value-added tax), or other indirect tax at a national level. There is a $10 Customs tax, payable on entry to the United States, and a $6 departure tax.

A 6% state sales tax (plus .5% local tax, for a total of 6.5% in Miami) is added on at the register for all goods and services purchased in Florida. These taxes are not refundable. In addition, most municipalities levy special taxes on restaurants and hotels. In Surfside, hotel taxes total 10.5%; in Bal Harbour, 9.5%; in Miami Beach (including South Beach), 11.5%; and in the rest of Dade County, a whopping 12.5%. In Miami Beach, Surfside, and Bal Harbour, the resort (hotel) tax also applies to hotel restaurants and restaurants with liquor licenses.

Telephone/Fax   The telephone system in the United States is run by private corporations, so rates, especially for long-distance service and operator-assisted calls, can vary widely. Generally, hotel surcharges on long-distance and local calls are astronomical, so you're usually better off using a **public pay telephone.** Look for pay phones on street corners, as well as in bars, restaurants, public buildings, stores, and at service stations. In most areas, local calls cost 35¢. Within Miami you must dial the area code, either 305 or 786, before the seven-digit number.

For long-distance or international calls from a pay phone, it's most economical to charge the call to a telephone charge card or a credit card, or you can use a lot of change. The pay phone operator will instruct you how much to deposit and when to deposit it into the slot on the telephone box.

For local directory assistance ("information"), dial 411; for long-distance information, dial 1, then the appropriate area code, and then 555-1212.

Most long-distance and international calls can be dialed directly from any phone. **For calls within the United States and to Canada,** dial 1 followed by the area code and the seven-digit number. **For other international calls,** dial 011 followed by the country code, city code, and the telephone number of the person you are calling.

Calls to area codes **800, 888,** and **877** are toll-free. However, calls to numbers in area codes **700** and **900** (chat lines, bulletin boards, "dating" services, and so on) can be very expensive—usually a charge of 95¢ to $3 or more per minute, and they sometimes have minimum charges that can run as high as $15 or more.

For **reversed-charge or collect calls,** and for person-to-person calls, dial 0 (zero, not the letter O) followed by the area code and number you want; an operator will then come on the line, and you should specify that you are calling collect, or person-to-person, or both. If your operator-assisted call is international, ask for the overseas operator.

Before calling from a hotel room, always ask the hotel phone operator if there are any telephone surcharges. There almost always are, often as much as 75¢ or $1, even for a local call. Some hotels even charge a per-minute rate in addition to the surcharge.

In the past few years, many American companies have installed voice-mail systems. Listen carefully to the instructions (you'll probably be asked to dial 1, 2, or 3 or wait for an operator to pick up); if you can't understand, sometimes dialing zero will put you in touch with a company operator. It's frustrating even for locals!

Many car-rental companies also rent cellular phones, a wise and convenient option when traveling in unfamiliar territory.

Telegraph and telex services are provided primarily by Western Union. You can bring your telegram into the nearest Western Union office (there are hundreds across the country) or dictate it over the phone (☎ **800/325-6000**). You can also telegraph money or have it telegraphed to you, very quickly over the Western Union system, but this service can cost as much as 15% to 20% of the amount sent.

Most hotels have **fax machines** available for guest use (be sure to ask about the charge to use it), and many hotel rooms are even wired for guests' fax machines. A less expensive way to send and receive faxes may be at stores such as Mail Boxes Etc., a national chain of packing service shops (look in the Yellow Pages directory under "Packing Services").

There are two kinds of telephone directories in the United States. The so-called White Pages list private households and business subscribers in alphabetical order. The inside front cover lists emergency numbers for police, fire, ambulance, the Coast Guard, poison-control center, crime-victims hot line, and so on. The first few pages will tell you how to make long-distance and international calls, complete with country codes and area codes. Government numbers are usually printed on blue paper within the White Pages. Printed on yellow paper, the so-called Yellow Pages list all local services, businesses, industries, and houses of worship according to activity with an index at the front or back. (Drugstores/pharmacies and restaurants are also listed by geographic location.) The Yellow Pages also include city plans or detailed area maps, postal ZIP codes, and public transportation routes.

Time The United States is divided into six time zones. Miami, like New York, is in the Eastern Standard Time zone. America's eastern seaboard is 5 hours behind Greenwich mean time. Between April and October, daylight saving time is adopted, and clocks are set 1 hour ahead. To find out what time it is, call ☎ 305/324-8811.

Tipping Tipping is so ingrained in the American way of life that the annual income tax of tip-earning service personnel is based on how much they should have received in light of their employers' gross revenues. Accordingly, they may have to pay tax on a tip you didn't actually give them.

In hotels, tip **bellhops** at least $1 per bag ($2 to $3 if you have a lot of luggage) and tip the **chamber staff** $1 to $2 per day (more if you've left a disaster area for him or her to clean up, or if you're traveling with kids and/or pets). Tip the **doorman** or **concierge** only if he or she has provided you with some specific service (for example, calling a cab for you or obtaining difficult-to-get theater tickets). Tip the **valet-parking attendant** $1 every time you get your car.

In restaurants, bars, and nightclubs, tip **service staff** 15% to 20% of the check, tip **bartenders** 10% to 15%, tip **checkroom attendants** $1 per garment, and tip **valet-parking attendants** $1 per vehicle. Tip the **doorman** only if he has provided you with some specific service (such as calling a cab for you).

Tip **cab drivers** 15% of the fare.

As for other service personnel, tip **skycaps** at airports at least $1 per bag ($2 to $3 if you have a lot of luggage) and tip **hairdressers** and **barbers** 15% to 20%.

Tipping ushers at movies and theaters, and gas-station attendants, is not expected.

Toilets You won't find public toilets or "rest rooms" on the streets in most U.S. cities, but they can be found in hotel lobbies, bars, restaurants, museums, department stores, railway and bus stations, or service stations. Note, however, that restaurants and bars in resorts or heavily visited areas may reserve their rest rooms for the use of their patrons. Some establishments display a notice that toilets are for the use of patrons only. You can ignore this sign or, better yet, avoid arguments by paying for a cup of coffee or a soft drink, which will qualify you as a patron. If possible, avoid the toilets at parks and beaches, which tend to be dirty.

4 Getting to Know Miami

It's really not that difficult to learn the lay of the land in the magic city. Miami is a little less than 2,000 square miles and is comprised of unique and densely populated neighborhoods.

1 Orientation

ARRIVING
Originally carved out of scrubland in 1928 by Pan American Airlines, **Miami International Airport (MIA)** has become second in the United States for international passenger traffic and 10th in the world for total passengers. Like most airports, signs clearly point the way down to the baggage-claim area. And unlike most airports, you'll even find signs written in both Spanish and English. You can change money or use your Honor or Plus System ATM card at Barnett Bank of South Florida, located near the exit. Visitor information is available 24 hours a day at the **Miami International Airport Main Visitor Counter,** Concourse E, 2nd level (☎ **305/876-7000**). Information is also available at **www.miami-airport.com**.

GETTING INTO TOWN
The airport is located about 6 miles west of Downtown and about 10 miles from the beaches, so it's likely you can get from the plane to your hotel room in less than half an hour. Of course, if you're arriving from an international destination, it will take more time to go through Customs and Immigration.

BY CAR All the major car-rental firms operate off-site branches reached via shuttle from the terminals. See "Getting Around," later in this chapter, for a list of major rental companies. Signs at the airport's exit clearly point the way to various parts of the city. If you're arriving late at night, you might want to take a taxi to your hotel and have the car-rental firm deliver a car to your hotel the next day.

BY TAXI Taxis line up in front of a dispatcher's desk outside the airport's arrivals terminals. Most cabs are metered, though some have flat rates to popular destinations. The fare should be about $20 to Coral Gables, $18 to Downtown, and $24 to South Beach, plus tip, which should be at least 10% and more for each bag the driver handles. Depending on traffic, the ride to Coral Gables or Downtown takes about 15 to 20 minutes, and to South Beach, 20 to 25 minutes. One

Miami at a Glance

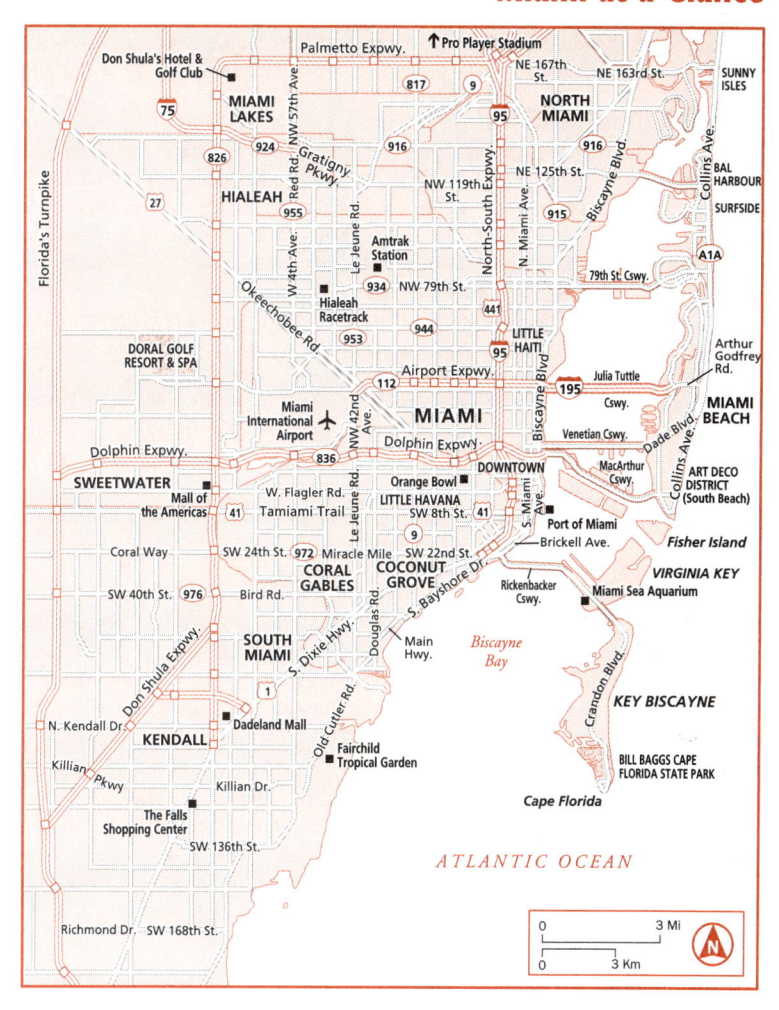

of the more reliable companies in the city (with an easy-to-remember number) is **Yellow Cab** (☎ 305/444-4444).

BY LIMO OR VAN Group limousines (multipassenger vans) circle the arrivals area looking for fares. Destinations are posted on the front of each van, and a flat rate is charged for door-to-door service to the area marked.

SuperShuttle (☎ 305/871-2000; www.supershuttle.com/mia.htm) is one of the largest airport operators, charging between $10 and $20 per person for a ride within the County. Its vans operate 24 hours a day and accept American Express, MasterCard, and Visa. This is a much better alternative than taking a cab.

Private limousine arrangements can be made in advance through your local travel agent. A one-way meet-and-greet service should cost about $50.

BY PUBLIC TRANSPORTATION I do not recommend taking public transportation to get from the airport to your hotel. Buses heading downtown leave the airport only once per hour (from the arrivals level), and connections are spotty at best. It could take about an hour and a half to get to South Beach. Journeys to downtown and Coral Gables are more direct. The fare is $1.25, plus an additional 25¢ for a transfer.

VISITOR INFORMATION

The best up-to-date information is provided by the **Greater Miami Convention and Visitors Bureau,** 701 Brickell Ave., Suite 700, Miami, FL 33131 (☎ **800/283-2707** or 305/539-3034; fax 305/530-4276; www.miamiandbeaches.com; e-mail: media@miamiandbeaches.com). Several chambers of commerce in Greater Miami will send out information on their particular neighborhoods; for addresses and numbers, please see "Visitor Information & Money" in chapter 2.

When you arrive at the Miami International Airport, you can pick up visitor information at the airport's main visitor counter on the second floor of Concourse E. It's open 24 hours a day.

Always check local newspapers for special things to do during your visit. The city's only daily, the *Miami Herald,* is a good source for current-events listings, particularly the "Weekend" section in Friday's edition. Even better is the weekly giveaway, *New Times,* available in bright red boxes throughout the city.

Information on everything from dining to entertainment in Miami is available on the Internet at **www.miami.citysearch.com**.

CITY LAYOUT

Miami may seem confusing at first, but it quickly becomes easy to negotiate. The small cluster of buildings that make up the Downtown area is at the geographical heart of the city. In relation to Downtown, the airport is northwest, the beaches are east, Coconut Grove is south, Coral Gables is west, and the rest of the city is north.

FINDING AN ADDRESS Miami is divided into dozens of areas with official and unofficial boundaries. Street numbering in the city of Miami is fairly straightforward, but you must first be familiar with the numbering system. The mainland is divided into four sections—NE, NW, SE, and SW—by the intersection of Flagler Street and Miami Avenue. Flagler divides Miami from North to South and Miami Avenue divides the city from east to west. Street numbers (First Street, Second Street, and so forth) start from here and increase as you go further out, as do numbers of avenues, places, courts, terraces, and lanes. Streets in Hialeah are the exceptions to this pattern; they are listed separately in map indexes.

Numerical addresses are descriptive with the first digits giving the cross streets. For example, 12301 Biscayne Blvd. is located at 123rd Street and 501 Ocean Dr. is at 5th Street. It's also helpful to remember that avenues generally run north-south, while streets go east-west.

Getting around the barrier islands that make up Miami Beach is somewhat easier than moving around the mainland. Street numbering starts with First Street, near Miami Beach's southern tip, and increases to 192nd Street, in the northern part of Sunny Isles. Collins Avenue makes the entire journey from head to toe. As in the city of Miami, some streets in Miami Beach have numbers as well as names. When they are part of listings in this book, both names and numbers are given.

You should know that the numbered streets in Miami Beach are not the geographical equivalents of those on the mainland, but they are close. For example, the 79th Street Causeway runs into 71st Street on Miami Beach.

STREET MAPS It's easy to get lost in sprawling Miami, so a reliable map is essential. If you are not planning on moving around too much, the tourist board's maps, located inside its free publication, "Destination Miami," should be adequate. If you really want to get to know the city, it pays to invest in one of the large accordion-fold maps, available at most gas stations and bookstores. The Trakker Map of Miami ($2.50) is a four-color accordion map that encompasses all of Dade County.

Some maps of Miami list streets according to area, so you'll have to know which part of the city you are looking for before the street can be found. All the listings in this book include area information for just this reason.

The Neighborhoods in Brief

Miami's many neighborhoods are occupied by a globe-spanning variety of ethnic groups. In fact, aside from the warm climate, the city's diversity is what attracts almost 10 million visitors each year. Every neighborhood is uniquely designed and takes on the characteristics of its residents. The lines that separate each minicity are thickly drawn, but the borders are easy to cross. Visit them all!

South Beach—The Art Deco District Without a doubt, South Beach is the heart of Miami. Long known as "America's Riviera," these 15 blocks and 10 miles of beach attract South American bankers, European investors, Canadian snowbirds, gay and lesbian club-goers, and common folks just looking to catch some rays. The thriving Art Deco District within South Beach contains the largest concentration of art deco architecture in the world. The outdoor cafes lining Ocean Drive are filled with model types, striving to be actors by day and waiters by night. It is a major playground for photographers snapping glimpses of the ocean, musicians plucking guitar strings, and artists splashing paints on canvases dripping with oil. The ambience is surreal. This area is definitely "Livin' La Vida Loca."

Miami Beach To tourists in the 1950s, Miami Beach *was* Miami. Its huge self-contained resort hotels were vacations unto themselves, providing a full day's worth of meals, activities, and entertainment. Then, in the 1960s and 1970s, people who fell in love with Miami began to buy apartments rather than rent hotel rooms. Tourism declined, and many area hotels fell into disrepair.

However, since the late 1980s, Miami Beach has experienced a tide of revitalization. Huge beach hotels are finding their niche with new, international tourist markets and are attracting large convention crowds. The **Miami Beach Convention Center,** 1901 Convention Center Dr., Miami Beach, FL 33139 (☎ **305/673-7311**), has more than 1 million square feet of exhibition space. New generations of Americans have discovered the qualities that originally made Miami Beach so popular, and they are finding out that the sand and surf now come with a thriving international city.

Surfside, Bal Harbour, and **Sunny Isles** make up the north part of the beach. Hotels, motels, restaurants, and beaches line Collins Avenue. For visitors, it seems that, with some outstanding exceptions, the farther north one goes, the cheaper lodging becomes. All told, excellent prices, location, and facilities make Surfside and Sunny Isles, although a little rough around the edges, attractive places to stay. Keep in mind, beachfront properties are at a premium, so many of the area's moderately priced hotels have been converted to condominiums, leaving fewer and fewer affordable places to stay.

In exclusive Bal Harbour, an upscale mall attracts savvy shoppers. A few elegant hotels remain amid the many beachfront condominium towers. Fancy homes, tucked away on the bay, hide behind gated communities.

Note that **North Miami Beach,** a residential area near the Dade–Broward County line, is a misnomer. It is actually northwest of Miami Beach on the mainland and has no beaches. North Miami Beach is part of North Dade County and has some of Miami's better restaurants and shops. Also, South Beach, the historic Art Deco District, is treated as a separate neighborhood.

Key Biscayne   Miami's forested and fancy Key Biscayne is technically one of the first islands in the Florida Keys. However, this luxurious island is nothing like its southern neighbors. Located south of Miami Beach, off the shores of Coconut Grove, Key Biscayne is protected from the troubles of the mainland by the long Rickenbacker Causeway and a $1 toll. Key Biscayne is largely an exclusive residential community, with million-dollar homes and sweeping water views, although it also offers visitors great beaches, some top resort hotels, and several good restaurants. Hobie Beach, adjacent to the causeway, is the city's premier spot for sailboarding and jet-skiing (see "Water Sports" in chapter 7). On the island's southern tip, Bill Baggs State Park has great beaches, bike paths, and dense forests for picnicking and partying.

Downtown   Miami's Downtown boasts one of the world's most beautiful cityscapes. If you do nothing else in Miami, make sure you take your time studying the area's inspired architectural designs. During the day, a vibrant community of students, businesspeople, and merchants make their way through the bustling streets. Vendors sell fresh-cut pineapples and mangos while young Latin American consumers on shopping sprees lug bags and boxes. The Downtown area has a mall (Bayside Marketplace, where many cruise passengers come to browse), culture (Metro-Dade Cultural Center), and a number of good restaurants (listed in chapter 6, "Dining") and the new American Airlines Arena.

Design District   With restaurants springing up between galleries and furniture stores galore, the Design District is fast becoming a spot to see and be seen. The District, which is a treasure trove of furniture import companies, interior designers, architects and more, has also banded together to create an up-to-date Web site, **www.designdistrict.com**, which includes a calendar of events and is chock-full of information. The district is loosely defined as the area bounded by NE 2nd Avenue, NE 5th Avenue East and West, and NW 36th Street to the South.

Biscayne Corridor   From Downtown near Bayside to the 70s, where trendy curio shops and upscale restaurants are slowly opening, Biscayne Boulevard is reclaiming itself as a safe thoroughfare where tourists can wine, dine, and shop. Previously known for dilapidated 1950s- and '60s-era hotels that had fallen on hard times, residents fleeing the high prices of the beaches in search of affordable housing are renovating Biscayne block by block, making this once again famous boulevard worth a Sunday drive. With the trendy Design District immediately west of 36th and Biscayne by 2 blocks, the area is assured a slow but steady recovery.

Little Haiti   During a brief period in the late 1970s and early '80s, almost 35,000 Haitians arrived in Miami. Most of the new refugees settled in a 200-square-block area north of Downtown. Extending from 41st to 83rd streets and bordered by I-95 and Biscayne Boulevard, Little Haiti is a neighborhood with at least 60,000 residents, more than half of whom were born in Haiti.

Little Havana   If you've never been to Cuba, just come to this small section of Miami and you'll come pretty close. The sounds, tastes, and rhythms all remind you of Cuba's capital city. Some even jokingly say you don't have to speak a word of English to live an independent life here. Street signs are in Spanish and English. Cuban coffee shops, tailor and furniture stores, and inexpensive restaurants line "Calle Ocho" (pronounced *Ka*-yey *O*-choh), SW Eighth Street, the region's main thoroughfare. Salsa and Merengue beats ring loudly from old record stores while old men in *guayaberas* smoke cigars over their daily game of dominoes.

Coral Gables "The City Beautiful," created by George Merrick in the early 1920s, is one of Miami's first planned developments. The houses here were built in a Mediterranean style along lush tree-lined streets that open onto beautifully carved plazas, many with centerpiece fountains. The best architectural examples of the era have Spanish-style tiled roofs and are built from Miami oolite, a native limestone commonly called "coral rock." The Gables's commerce center is home to many thriving corporations. Some of the city's best restaurants, headed by world-renowned chefs, are located here. You'll also find landmark hotels, great golfing, and upscale shopping.

Coconut Grove There was a time when Coconut Grove was inhabited by artists, intellectuals, hippies, and radicals, but times have changed. Gentrification has pushed most alternative types out, leaving in their place a multitude of cafes, boutiques, and nightspots. The intersection of Grand Avenue, Main Highway, and McFarlane Road pierces the area's heart. Right in the center of it all is CocoWalk and the MayFair, filled with lovely boutiques, eateries, and bars. Sidewalks here are often crowded, especially at night, when it really begins to sizzle. The Grove is a great alternative to squeezing by the people crowding South Beach.

Coconut Grove's link to The Bahamas dates from before the turn of the century, when islanders came to the area to work in a newly opened hotel called the Peacock Inn. Bahamian-style wooden homes, built by these early settlers, still stand on Charles Street. Goombay, the lively annual Bahamian festival, celebrates the Grove's Caribbean link and has become one of the largest black-heritage street festivals in America (see "South Florida Calendar of Events," in chapter 2).

Southern Miami–Dade County To locals, South Miami is both a specific area, southwest of Coral Gables, and a general region that encompasses all of southern Dade County and includes Kendall, Perrine, Cutler Ridge, and Homestead. For the purposes of clarity, this book has grouped all these southern suburbs under the rubric "Southern Miami–Dade County." Similar attributes unite the communities: They are heavily residential, and all are packed with shopping malls amidst a few remaining plots of farmland. Tourists don't usually stay in these parts, unless they are on their way to the Everglades or Keys, However, Southern Miami–Dade County does contain many of the city's top attractions (see chapter 7, "What to See & Do in Miami"), making it likely you'll spend some time during the day here.

2 Getting Around

Officially, Dade County has opted for a "unified, multimodal transportation network," which basically means you can get around the city by train, bus, and taxi. However, in practice, the network doesn't work too well. Things may improve when the city completes its transportation center in 2005, but until then, unless you are going from downtown Miami to a not-too-distant spot, you are better off in a rented car or a taxi.

With the exception of downtown Coconut Grove and South Beach, Miami is not a walker's city. Because it is so spread out, most attractions are too far apart to make walking between them feasible. In fact, most Miamians are so used to driving that they do so even when going just a few blocks.

BY PUBLIC TRANSPORTATION

BY RAIL Two rail lines, operated by the **Metro-Dade Transit Agency** (☎ 305/770-3131 for information; www.co.miami-dade.fl.us/mdta/), run in concert with each other.

Metrorail, the city's modern high-speed commuter train, is a 21-mile elevated line that travels north-south, between downtown Miami and the southern suburbs. If you are staying in Coral Gables or Coconut Grove, you can park your car at a nearby station and ride the rails Downtown. Unfortunately for visitors, the line's usefulness is limited. The first addition to the system, scheduled for completion in mid-2001, will only extend the rail from the Okeechobee station to just west of the Palmetto Expressway. There are plans to extend the system to service Miami International Airport, but until those tracks are built, these trains don't go most places tourists go, with the exception of Vizcaya in Coconut Grove. Metrorail operates daily from about 6am to midnight. The fare is $1.25.

Metromover, a 4.4-mile elevated line, connects with Metrorail at the Government Center stop and circles Downtown. This is a good way to get to Bayside if you don't have a car. Riding on rubber tires, the single-train car winds past many of the area's most important attractions and shopping and business districts. Metromover offers a fun, futuristic ride that you might want to take to complement your Downtown tour. You get a beautiful perspective from the towering height of the suspended rails. System hours are daily from about 6am to midnight. The fare is 25¢.

BY BUS Miami's suburban layout is not conducive to getting around by bus. Lines operate, and maps are available, but instead of getting to know the city, you'll find that relying on bus transportation will acquaint you only with how it feels to wait at bus stops. You can get a bus map by mail, either from the Greater Miami Convention and Visitors Bureau (see "Visitor Information" in chapter 2) or by writing the Metro-Dade Transit System, 3300 NW 32nd Ave., Miami, FL 33142. In Miami, call ☎ 305/770-3131 for public-transit information. The fare is $1.25.

BY CAR

Tales circulate about vacationers who have visited Miami without a car, but they are very few indeed. If you are counting on exploring the city, even to a modest degree, a car is essential. Miami's restaurants, attractions, and sights are far from one another, so any other form of transportation is impractical. You won't need a car, however, if you are spending your entire vacation at a resort, are traveling directly to the Port of Miami for a cruise, or are here for a short stay centered in one area of the city, such as South Beach.

When driving across a causeway or through Downtown, allow extra time to reach your destination because of frequent drawbridge openings. Some bridges open about every half hour for large sailing vessels to make their way through the wide bays and canals that crisscross the city, stalling traffic for several minutes. Don't get frustrated by the wait. It's all part of the easy pace of South Florida life.

RENTALS It seems as though every car-rental company, big and small, has at least one office in Miami. Consequently, the city is one of the cheapest places in the world to rent a car. Many firms regularly advertise prices in the neighborhood of $140 per week for their economy car. You should also check first with the airline you have chosen. There are often special discounts when you book a flight and reserve your rental car simultaneously. A minimum age, generally 25, is usually required of renters. Some rental agencies have also set maximum ages. A national car-rental broker, **A Car**

Rental Referral Service (☎ 800/404-4482), can often find companies willing to rent to drivers over the age of 21 and can also get discounts from major companies as well as some regional ones.

National car-rental companies with toll-free numbers include **Alamo** (☎ 800/327-9633), **Avis** (☎ 800/331-1212), **Budget** (☎ 800/527-0700), **Dollar** (☎ 800/800-4000 or 800/327-7607), **Hertz** (☎ 800/654-3131), **National** (☎ 800/328-4567), and **Thrifty** (☎ 800/367-2277). One excellent company that has offices in every conceivable part of town and offers extremely competitive rates is **Enterprise** (☎ 800/325-8007). Just make sure that you call several companies and comparison shop. Car-rental prices can fluctuate more than airfares. For information on car-rental insurance, see "Getting There" in chapter 2.

Many companies offer cellular phones or electronic map rental. It might be wise to opt for these additional safety features, although the cost can be exorbitant; the phone especially can come in handy if you get disoriented. There is nothing worse than being lost in an unfamiliar city in a questionable area with no one to turn to.

Finally, think about splurging on a convertible. Few things in life can match the feeling of cruising along warm Florida highways with the sun smiling on your shoulders and the wind whipping through your hair. At most companies, the price is only about 20% more.

PARKING   Always keep plenty of quarters on hand to feed hungry meters. Or, on Miami Beach, stop by the chamber of commerce at 1920 Meridian Ave. or any Publix grocery store to buy a magnetic **parking card** in denominations of $10, $20, or $25. Parking is usually plentiful (except on South Beach and Coconut Grove), but when it's not, be careful: Fines for illegal parking can be stiff.

In addition to parking garages, valet services are commonplace and often used. Expect to pay from $5 to $15 for parking in Coconut Grove and on South Beach's Ocean Drive on busy weekend nights.

LOCAL DRIVING RULES   Florida law allows drivers to make a right turn on a red light after a complete stop, unless otherwise indicated. In addition, all passengers are required to wear seat belts, and children under 3 must be securely fastened in government-approved car seats.

BY TAXI

If you're not planning on traveling much within the city, an occasional taxi is a good alternative to renting a car. If you plan on spending your vacation within the confines of South Beach's Art Deco District, you might also want to avoid the parking hassles that come with renting your own car. Taxi meters start at $1.50 for the first $1/4$ mile and 25¢ for each $1/8$ mile. There are standard flat-rate charges for frequently traveled routes—for example, Miami Beach's Convention Center to Coconut Grove would cost about $16.

Major cab companies include **Metro** (☎ 305/888-8888), **Yellow** (☎ 305/444-4444), and, on Miami Beach, **Central** (☎ 305/532-5555).

BY BICYCLE

Miami has several interesting areas to bike, including most of Miami Beach, where the hard-packed sand and boardwalks make it an easy and scenic route. However, unless you are a former New York City bicycle messenger, you won't want to use a bicycle as your main means of transportation.

For more information on bicycles, including where to rent the best ones, see chapter 7, "What to See & Do in Miami."

Fast Facts: Miami

Airport See "Orientation," earlier in this chapter.

American Express You'll find American Express offices in downtown Miami at 330 Biscayne Blvd. (☎ 305/358-7350); 9700 Collins Ave., Bal Harbour (☎ 305/865-5959); and 32 Miracle Mile, Coral Gables (☎ 305/446-3381). Offices are open weekdays from 9am to 5pm and Saturday from 10am to 4pm. The Bal Harbour office is also open on Sunday from noon to 6pm. To report lost or stolen traveler's checks, call ☎ 800/221-7282.

Area Code The original area code for Miami and all of Dade County was 305. That is still the code for older phone numbers, but all phone numbers assigned since July 1998 have the area code 786 (SUN). For all local calls, even if you're calling across the street, you must dial the area code (305) or (786) first. Even though the Keys still share the Dade County area code of 305, calls to there from Miami are considered long distance and must be preceded by 1-305. Within the Keys, simply dial the seven-digit number. The area code for Fort Lauderdale is 954; for Palm Beach, Boca Raton, Vero Beach, and Port St. Lucie it's 561.

Business Hours Banking hours vary, but most banks are open weekdays from 9am to 3pm. Several stay open until 5pm or so at least 1 day during the week, and many banks feature automated-teller machines (ATMs) for 24-hour banking. Most stores are open daily from 10am to 6pm; however, there are many exceptions. Shops in the Bayside Marketplace are usually open until 9 or 10pm, as are the boutiques in Coconut Grove. Stores in Bal Harbour and other malls are usually open an extra hour one night during the week (usually Thursday). As far as business offices are concerned, Miami is generally a 9am to 5pm town.

Car Rentals See "Getting Around," earlier in this chapter.

Climate See "When to Go," in chapter 2.

Curfew Although not strictly enforced, there is a curfew in effect for minors after 11pm on weeknights and midnight on weekends in all of Miami–Dade County. After those hours, children under 17 cannot be out on the streets or driving unless accompanied by a parent or on their way to work.

Dentists **A&E Dental,** 11400 N. Kendall Dr., Mega Bank Building (☎ 305/271-7777), also offers round-the-clock care and accepts MasterCard and Visa.

Doctors In an emergency, call an ambulance by dialing 911 from any phone. The Dade County Medical Association sponsors a **Physician Referral Service** (☎ 305/324-8717) weekdays from 9am to 5pm. **Health South Doctors' Hospital,** 5000 University Dr., Coral Gables (☎ 305/666-2111), is a 285-bed acute-care hospital with a 24-hour physician-staffed emergency department.

Driving Rules See "Getting Around," above.

Drugstores See "Pharmacies," below.

Embassies/Consulates See chapter 3, "For Foreign Visitors."

Emergencies To reach the police, ambulance, or fire department, dial ☎ 911 from any phone. No coins are needed. Emergency hot lines include **Crisis Intervention** (☎ 305/358-HELP or 305/358-4357) and **Poison Information Center** (☎ 800/282-3171).

Eyeglasses **Pearle Vision Center,** 7901 Biscayne Blvd. (☎ 305/754-5144), in Miami, can usually fill prescriptions in about an hour.

Hospitals See "Doctors," above.

Information See "Visitor Information," above.

Laundry/Dry Cleaning For dry-cleaning, self-service machines, and a wash-and-fold service by the pound call **All Laundry Service,** 5701 NW 7th St. (☎ **305/261-8175** west of Downtown); it's open daily from 7am to 10pm. **Clean Machine Laundry,** 226 12th St., South Beach (☎ **305/534-9429**), is convenient to South Beach's art deco hotels; it's open 24 hours. **Coral Gables Laundry & Dry Cleaning,** 250 Minorca Ave., Coral Gables (☎ **305/446-6458**), has been dry-cleaning, altering, and laundering since 1930. It offers a lifesaving same-day service and is open weekdays from 7am to 7pm and Saturday from 8am to 3pm.

Massage There are some great spa packages at some of the more ritzy hotels, but if you're on South Beach, "The White Salon" located at 900 Collins Ave. will give you a 30-minute facial, 30-minute massage, and a manicure for $78.

Liquor Laws Only adults 21 or older may legally purchase or consume alcohol in the state of Florida. Minors are usually permitted in bars that serve food. Liquor laws are strictly enforced; if you look young, carry identification. Beer and wine are sold in most supermarkets and convenience stores. The city of Miami's liquor stores are closed on Sunday. Liquor stores in the city of Miami Beach are open all week.

Lost Property If you lost it at the airport, call the **Airport Lost and Found** office (☎ **305/876-7377**). If you lost it on the bus, Metrorail, or Metromover, call **Metro-Dade Transit Agency** (☎ **305/770-3131**). If you lost it somewhere else, phone the **Dade County Police Lost and Found** (☎ **305/375-3366**). You may also want to fill out a police report for insurance purposes.

Luggage Storage/Lockers In addition to the baggage check at Miami International Airport, most hotels offer luggage-storage facilities. If you are taking a cruise from the Port of Miami (see "Cruises and Other Caribbean Getaways," in chapter 10, "Side Trips from Miami"), bags can be stored in your ship's departure terminal.

Newspapers/Magazines The *Miami Herald* is the city's only English-language daily. It is especially known for its Latin American coverage and its excellent Friday "Weekend" entertainment guide. The most respected alternative weekly is the give-away tabloid called ***New Times,*** which contains up-to-date listings and reviews of food, films, theater, music, and whatever else is happening in town. Also free if you can find it is ***Ocean Drive,*** a gorgeous oversized glossy magazine, available at a number of chic South Beach boutiques and restaurants. It is also available on newsstands.

For a large selection of foreign-language newspapers and magazines, check with any of the large bookstores (see chapter 8, "Miami Shopping") or try **News Café** at 800 Ocean Dr., South Beach (☎ **305/538-6397**), or in Coconut Grove at 2901 Florida Ave. (☎ 305/774-6397); **Eddie's Normandy,** 1096 Normandy Dr., Miami Beach (☎ **305/866-2026**); and **Worldwide News,** 1629 NE 163rd St., North Miami Beach (☎ **305/940-4090**).

Pharmacies **Walgreens Pharmacy** has dozens of locations all over town, including 8550 Coral Way (☎ **305/221-9271**), in Coral Gables; 1845 Alton Rd. (☎ 305/531-8868), in South Beach; and 6700 Collins Ave. (☎ **305/861-6742**), in Miami Beach. The branch at 5731 Bird Rd. at SW 40th Street

(☎ 305/666-0757) is open 24 hours, as is **Eckerd Drugs,** 1825 Miami Gardens Dr. NE, at 185th Street, North Miami Beach (☎ **305/932-5740**).

Photographic Needs One of the more expensive places to have your film developed is **One Hour Photo** in the Bayside Marketplace (☎ **305/377-FOTO**). They charge $17 to develop and print a roll of 36 pictures, and they're open Monday to Saturday from 10am to 10pm and Sunday from noon to 8pm. **Coconut Grove Camera,** 3317 Virginia St. (☎ **305/445-0521**), features 30-minute color processing and maintains a huge selection of cameras and equipment. It rents, too. Walgreens or Eckerd's will develop film for the next day for about $6 or $7.

Police For emergencies, dial ☎ **911** from any phone. No coins are needed. For other matters, call ☎ **305/595-6263**.

Post Office The **Main Post Office,** 2200 Milam Dairy Rd., Miami, FL 33152 (☎ **305/639-4280**), is located west of Miami International Airport. Letters addressed to you and marked "c/o General Delivery" can be picked up at 500 NW 2nd Ave. Conveniently located post offices include 1300 Washington Ave. in South Beach, and 3191 Grand Ave. in Coconut Grove. There is one central number for all post offices ☎ **800/275-8777**.

Radio About 5 dozen radio stations can be heard in the Greater Miami area. On the AM dial, 610 (WIOD), 790 (WNWS), 1230 (WJNO), and 1340 (WPBR) are all talk. There is no all-news station in town, although 940 (WINZ) does give traffic updates and headline news in between its talk shows. WDBF (1420) is a good big-band station and WPBG (1290) features golden oldies. The two most popular R&B stations are WEDR or 99 Jams (99.1) and Hot 105 (105.1). The best rock stations on the FM dial are WZTA (94.9) and the progressive-rock station WVUM (90.5). WKIS (99.9) is the top country station. Public radio can be heard either on WXEL (90.7) or WLRN (91.3). WGTR (97.3) plays easy listening. WDNA (88.9) has the best Latin jazz and multi-ethnic sounds.

Religious Services Miami houses of worship are as varied as the city's population and include St. Patrick Catholic Church, 3716 Garden Ave., Miami Beach (☎ **305/531-1124**); Coral Gables Baptist Church, 5501 Granada Blvd. (☎ **305/665-4072**); Temple Judea, 5500 Granada Blvd., Coral Gables (☎ **305/667-5657**); Coconut Grove United Methodist, 2850 SW 27th Ave. (☎ **305/443-0880**); Christ Episcopal Church, 3481 Hibiscus St. (☎ **305/442-8542**); and Plymouth Congregational Church, 3400 Devon Rd., at Main Highway (☎ **305/444-6521**).

Rest Rooms Stores rarely let customers use the rest rooms, and many restaurants offer their facilities for customers only. Most malls have bathrooms, as do many fast-food restaurants. Many public beaches and large parks provide toilets, though in some places you have to pay or tip an attendant. Most large hotels have clean rest rooms in their lobbies.

Safety As always, use your common sense and be aware of your surroundings at all times. Don't walk alone at night, and be extra wary when walking or driving though Downtown Miami and surrounding areas.

Reacting to several highly publicized crimes against tourists several years ago, both local and state governments have taken steps to help protect visitors. These measures include special, highly visible police units patrolling the airport and surrounding neighborhoods, and better signs on the state's most tourist-traveled routes. Also, look for bright orange sunbursts on highway exit signs that point the way to tourist-friendly zones.

When driving around Miami, always keep a good map handy, keep the doors locked, and stay alert. Never stop on a highway—if you get a flat tire, drive to the nearest well-lighted, populated place. If you are renting a car, you may consider additional safety features in the car, such as cellular telephones or electronic maps.

Taxes A 6% state sales tax (plus .5% local tax, for a total of 6.5% in Miami) is added on at the register for all goods and services purchased in Florida. In addition, most municipalities levy special taxes on restaurants and hotels. In Surfside, hotel taxes total 10.5%; in Bal Harbour, 9.5%; in Miami Beach (including South Beach), 11.5%; and in the rest of Dade County, a whopping 12.5%. In Miami Beach, Surfside, and Bal Harbour, the resort (hotel) tax also applies to hotel restaurants and restaurants with liquor licenses.

Taxis See "Getting Around," earlier in this chapter.

Television The local stations are Channel 6, WTVJ (NBC); Channel 4, WCIX (CBS); Channel 7, WSVN (Fox); Channel 10, WPLG (ABC); Channel 17, WLRN (PBS); Channel 23, WLTV (independent); and Channel 33, WBFS (independent).

Time Zone Miami, like New York, is in the Eastern Standard Time zone. Between April and October, daylight saving time is adopted, and clocks are set 1 hour ahead. America's eastern seaboard is 5 hours behind Greenwich mean time. To find out what time it is, call ☎ **305/324-8811.**

Transit Information For Metrorail or Metromover schedule information, phone ☎ **305/770-3131** or surf over to **www.co.miami-dade.fl.us/mdta/**.

Weather Hurricane season runs from July through November. For an up-to-date recording of current weather conditions and forecast reports, call ☎ **305/229-4522.**

5 Miami Accommodations

Miami's great economic boom has given rise to an ever increasing number of upscale hotels that give savvy, yet price-conscious travelers more choices for their money. No place in Miami has seen a greater increase in construction than Miami Beach. Since the renaissance that began in the early 1980s, the Beach has turned what used to be a vacation spot for the rich and famous into a bikini-clad, in-line skating paradise for the young at heart. You can't look in any direction without seeing a sea of sand and emerald waters luring you away from your home away from home.

Unfortunately, although there are a lot more choices in and around the beach, the increasing demand means increasing costs. But not to worry, the smart vacationer can almost name his price if he's willing to live without a few luxuries, like an oceanfront view. Always remember to ask about packages, since it's often possible to get a better deal than the published rates.

Many of the old hotels from the 1930s, 1940s, and 1950s have been totally renovated, giving way to dozens of "boutique" hotels. Keep in mind that when a hotel claims that it was just renovated, that can mean they've completely gutted out the entire building—or just added a few coats of fresh paint. Always ask what specific changes were made during a renovation, and be sure to ask if a hotel will be undergoing construction while you're there. You should also find out how near your room will be to the beats and rhythms of the nightlife crowd; trying to sleep directly on Ocean Drive, especially over the weekend is next to impossible.

I've included the best hotel options for their price as well as those that have been fully upgraded recently. Exceptions are noted. Also, keep in mind that along South Beach's Collins Avenue are dozens of hotels and motels—in all price categories—so there's bound to be a vacancy. If you do try the walk-in routine, don't forget to ask to see one of the rooms first. A few dollars could mean the difference between sleeping in a comfortable bed or being greeted by creepy crawlers.

SEASONS & RATES   South Florida's tourist season is well defined, beginning in mid-November and lasting until Easter. Hotel prices escalate until about March, after which they begin to decline. During the off-season, hotel rates are typically 30% to 50% lower than their winter highs.

But timing isn't everything. In many cases, rates also depend on your hotel's proximity to the beach and how much ocean you can see from your window. Small motels a block or two from the water can be up to 40% cheaper than similar properties right on the sand.

Rates below have been broken down into two broad categories: winter (generally, Thanksgiving through Easter) and off-season (about mid-May through August). The months in between, the shoulder season, should fall somewhere in between the highs and lows. Rates always go up on holidays. Remember too, that state and city taxes can add as much as 12.5% to your bill in some parts of Miami. Some hotels, especially those in South Beach, also tack on additional service charges. And parking is pricey.

PRICE CATEGORIES The hotels below are divided first by area, then by price, using the following guidelines: **very expensive,** over $250; **expensive,** over $180; **moderate,** $99 to $180; and **inexpensive,** below $99. Prices are based on published rates (or rack rates) for a standard double room during the high season. Check with the reservations agent since many rooms are also available above and below the category ranges listed. And always ask about packages, since it's often possible to get a better deal than these "official" rates. Most important, *always call the hotel to confirm rates, which may be subject to change without notice because of special events, holidays, or blackout dates.*

LONG-TERM STAYS If you plan to visit Miami for a month, a season, or more, think about renting a room in a long-term hotel or condominium apartment. Long-term accommodations exist in every price category, from budget to deluxe, and in general are extremely reasonable, especially during the off-season. Check with the reservation services below, or write a short note to the chamber of commerce in the area where you plan to stay. In addition, many local real estate agents also handle short-term rentals (meaning less than a year).

RESERVATION SERVICES Central Reservations (☎ 800/950-0232 or 305/274-6832; www.reservation-services.com; e-mail: rooms@america.com) works with many of Miami's hotels and can often secure discounts of up to 40%. It also gives advice on specific locales, especially in Miami Beach and Downtown.

The **South Florida Hotel Network** (☎ 800/538-3616 or 305/538-3616) lists more than 300 hotels throughout the area, from Palm Beach to Miami and down to the Keys.

1 South Beach

Most of the art deco hotels on South Beach were built in the late 1930s, just after the Depression, in an area originally planned as an affordable destination for middle-class northeasterners. My how things have changed. After many years of transition, South Beach has become South Florida's number-one tourist destination and is home to models, writers, producers, glitterati, fashion directors, outdoor cafes (to see and be seen), nightlife that beats incessantly, and of course, miles of sandy beach and crystal blue waters.

Outside cafes line Ocean Drive filled with model types striving to be actors by day and waiters by night. It has truly become a playground for photographers snapping glimpses of the ocean, musicians plucking guitar strings, and artists splashing paints on canvases dripping with oil. The ambience is surreal. This is truly "Livin' La Vida Loca."

VERY EXPENSIVE

✪ **The Bentley Hotel.** 510 Ocean Dr. South Beach, FL 33139. ☎ **800/236-8510** or 305/538-1700. Fax 305/532-4865. www.thebentley.com. 53 units. A/C TV TEL. Winter $290 junior suite; $390 one bedroom; $540 ocean view; $1,100 penthouse suite. Off-season $210 junior suite; $290 one bedroom; $375 ocean view; $625 penthouse suite. AE, CB, DC, DISC, MC, V.

The Bentley Hotel is an exquisite gem located on Ocean Drive in the area that is the heart of Sobe. With a private front entrance that leads, via elevator, to the main lobby, the entire hotel—from the architecture to the staff—exudes an old world charm that seasoned travelers will find reminiscent of Monaco or Biarritz. Casa Salsa (owned by the swivel-hipped Ricky Martin), TGI Fridays (on the other side of the hotel), and the Strand at the Savoy (one block down), will keep hungry guests happy.

The hotel's 53 suites are similar to those of the Alexander in that they are both hotel rooms and condos; some of them can be rented year-round through exclusive real estate agents. The hotel is blessed with a small intimate courtyard and each room comes with a complete kitchen that will rival the one in your own home. Try not to get a corner room, or you'll hear your neighbor's every move.

✪ **Casa Grande Suite Hotel.** 834 Ocean Dr., South Beach, FL 33139. ☎ **800/OUTPOST** or 305/672-7003. Fax 305/673669. www.islandlife.com. 34 units. A/C MINIBAR TV TEL. Winter $295 junior suite; $315 one bedroom suite; $525 two bedroom suite; $1,500 three-bedroom suite. Off-season $250 junior suite; $295 one bedroom suite; $425 two bedroom suite; $750 three-bedroom suite. Additional person $15 extra. AE, CB, DC, DISC, MC, V. Valet parking $14.

Europeans and vacationing celebs looking for privacy enjoy the casual elegance and thoughtful service of this hotel right on "Deco Drive." Here, you'll feel as though you're staying in a very stylish apartment, not in a cookie-cutter hotel room. Every room is outfitted in a slightly different style with fully equipped kitchenettes, beautifully tiled bathrooms, reed rugs, mahogany beds, handmade batik prints, and antiques from all over the world, particularly Indonesia. There's no pool on the property, but considering that you can see the ocean, stock your own fridge, and veg out with a good stereo and VCR, this is one of the most desirable hotels on South Beach. Some rooms facing the ocean can be noisy, especially on weekend nights.

Amenities: Room service, overnight dry cleaning and laundry, complimentary newspaper and evening turndown with chocolates, twice-daily maid service, express checkout, baby-sitting arrangements. VCRs and videos are available to rent. Full kitchens, CD/cassette stereo, conference rooms, car rental, activities desk, access to a nearby health club.

Loews Hotel. 1601 Collins Ave., South Beach, FL 33139. ☎ **800/23-LOEWS** or 305/604-1601. www.loewshotels.com. 800 units. A/C MINIBAR TV TEL. Winter from $309 double. Off-season from $250 double. $2,500–$5,000 presidential suite. AE, DC, DISC, MC, V. Valet parking $19.

The Loews Hotel is one of the largest hotels to grace South Beach in almost 30 years. This 800-room hotel is truly one of the most dynamic properties to crown the white sands of Miami Beach. The Loews makes a great effort to maintain the intimacy of an art deco hotel while still trying to accommodate business travelers who come to the nearby convention center. Each luxurious guest room offers dedicated data ports, two-line telephones, a minibar, coffeemaker, bathrobes and a hair dryer. The hotel is also linked to the original art deco structure, the St. Moritz, which holds 100 of the Loews's 800 rooms and several of the 57 presentation rooms, which are ideal for business meetings.

South Beach Accommodations

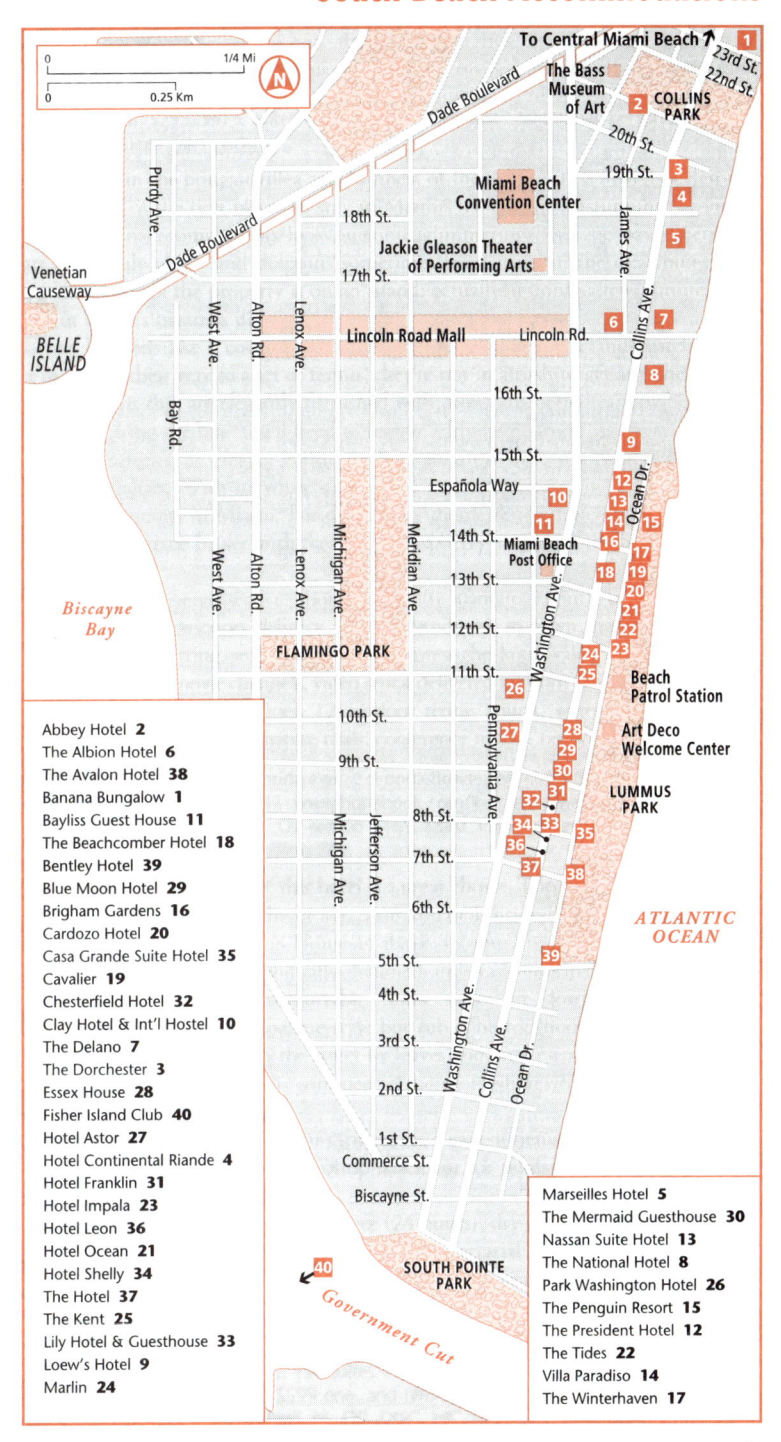

Abbey Hotel **2**
The Albion Hotel **6**
The Avalon Hotel **38**
Banana Bungalow **1**
Bayliss Guest House **11**
The Beachcomber Hotel **18**
Bentley Hotel **39**
Blue Moon Hotel **29**
Brigham Gardens **16**
Cardozo Hotel **20**
Casa Grande Suite Hotel **35**
Cavalier **19**
Chesterfield Hotel **32**
Clay Hotel & Int'l Hostel **10**
The Delano **7**
The Dorchester **3**
Essex House **28**
Fisher Island Club **40**
Hotel Astor **27**
Hotel Continental Riande **4**
Hotel Franklin **31**
Hotel Impala **23**
Hotel Leon **36**
Hotel Ocean **21**
Hotel Shelly **34**
The Hotel **37**
The Kent **25**
Lily Hotel & Guesthouse **33**
Loew's Hotel **9**
Marlin **24**

Marseilles Hotel **5**
The Mermaid Guesthouse **30**
Nassan Suite Hotel **13**
The National Hotel **8**
Park Washington Hotel **26**
The Penguin Resort **15**
The President Hotel **12**
The Tides **22**
Villa Paradiso **14**
The Winterhaven **17**

67

Dining/Diversions: Six different restaurants and lounges offer American, Argentinean, and casual bar food. A sleek martini bar and coffee shop round out the offerings making it possible to spend your entire time in this impressive new resort.

Amenities: Full-service beachfront resort, 24-hour concierge service, meeting rooms, ballrooms, room service, two phones in each room, dry cleaning, laundry, newspaper delivery, in-room massage, twice-daily maid service, baby-sitting, secretarial service, express checkout. VCRs available on request, video rental, 900 feet of beachside property, complete with 20 cabanas, outdoor pool with jet streams, access to nearby health club.

✪ **The Delano.** 1685 Collins Ave., South Beach, FL 33139. ☎ **800/555-5001** or 305/672-2000. Fax 305/532-0099. 209 units, 1 penthouse. A/C MINIBAR TV TEL. Winter $375–$2,600. Off-season $220–$2600. Additional person $35 extra. AE, DC, DISC, MC, V. Valet parking $20.

The Delano—pronounced like FDR's middle name—has become one of the hottest hotels on South Beach. The all-white elegantly styled hotel is known for its extravagant decor and deco architecture. Look for a huge hedge with a simple blue arched door in its center, or look up for a rocketlike fin (an original 1947 detail) sprouting from the top of the deco building. New York's Ian Shrager, of Studio 54 fame, brought in designer Philippe Starck, who went wild with the decor, including 40-foot sheer white curtains hanging outside, mirrors everywhere, white billowing curtains, Adirondack chairs, and fur-covered beds. The guest rooms are all white; a perfectly crisp green Granny Smith apple in each one is the only dose of color. It may sound antiseptic, but it actually comes across as sexy and sophisticated. The poolside cabanas are the most desirable rooms because of their huge size, but they can be noisy, since they're on an active poolside walkway.

The location is ideal; it's just north of the Art Deco District strip of bars and restaurants, away from the noisy street traffic but close enough to walk to hopping Lincoln Road Mall. And of course, it's right on the ocean with plenty of in-house activity to keep you busy.

Dining/Diversions: An elegant bar attracts curious and beautiful people nightly. The Blue Door (owned in part by Madonna) is known as a place to be seen and for great cuisine, but the service is full of attitude. The thatched Beach Bar restaurant serves fantastic sandwiches and salads. Another good choice is Blue Seas, an Asian seafood restaurant with communal seating offering, among other things, sushi, stone crabs, lobster, and caviar.

Amenities: Concierge, room service, same-day dry cleaning and laundry, newspaper delivery, evening turndown, in-room massage, executive business services, express checkout. VCRs, video rentals, children's movie theater and child activity programs, large outdoor pool, wide guarded beach, business center, conference rooms, rooftop solarium, extensive water-sports recreation, funky gift shop, 24-hour state-of-the-art David Barton gym with sauna. The rooftop Aqua Spa is $10 for hotel guests; open for women 9am to 7pm, men 7:30 to 11pm, and closed Tuesday night. Offers facials and a plethora of massages and water treatments.

Fisher Island Club. One Fisher Island Dr., Fisher Island, FL 33190. ☎ **800/537-3708** or 305/535-6020. Fax 305/535-6003. www.fisherisland-florida.com. 60 units. A/C TV TEL. Winter $385–$625 double; $750–$1,350 suite or cottage. Off-season $330–$415 double; $525–$1,200 suite or cottage. Golf, tennis, and spa packages available seasonally. 20% gratuity added to all food and beverages. AE, DC, MC, V.

This exclusive island just off Miami Beach epitomizes the height of luxury. Luciano Pavarotti, Oprah Winfrey, and other celebrities keep condos here, and many other celebs come here for R&R. To get to the resort, visitors and residents take a private ferry, which shuttles guests to and from the mainland every 15 to 20 minutes. Don't worry if you are car-less—on this exclusive island, golf carts will get you anywhere you need to go.

As for location, you're only minutes from the airport, South Beach, Coral Gables, and The Grove (not counting ferry time). Still, considering the pampering you'll receive in this former Vanderbilt mansion turned resort extraordinaire, you probably won't want to leave the island. Rooms vary in size and shape, and cottages come with hot tubs. A world-class spa and club offer all the amenities you could possibly imagine.

Dining/Diversions: The elegant Vanderbilt Club offers continental cuisine. The Beach Club and Golfer's Grill serve basic but expensive sandwiches and salads. An Italian Cafe prepares exceptional pastas and seafood. A dinner theater features live music.

Amenities: Concierge, room service (7am to 10pm), dry cleaning, laundry, national newspaper delivery, nightly turndown, twice-daily maid service, baby-sitting, secretarial service, valet parking, airport transportation, world-class spa, P. B. Dye Golf Course, 18 tennis courts, two deep-water marinas, boutiques, huge corporate board room, helipad, seaplane ramp, auto-ferry system, beach.

The National Hotel. 1677 Collins Ave., South Beach, FL. 33139. ☎ **800/327-8370** or 305/532-2311. Fax 305/534-1426. www.nationalhotel.com. 152 units. A/C MINIBAR TV TEL. Winter $295–$425 double; $700–$1,000 suite. Off-season from $225–$325 double; $500–$750 suite. AE, DC, JCB, MC, V. Valet parking $16.

Only 3 years old, this elegant newcomer has joined the ranks of South Beach's particular brand of luxury resorts. With its towering ceilings, sultry furnishings, and massive gilded mirrors, the elegant 1940s lobby ought to be the backdrop for a gangster flick. At 11 stories, the main building stands taller than most of its neighbors and offers grand views of the beach and ocean below. Rooms in the garden wing are slightly larger and have balconies but all are comfortable and pretty spacious.

Dining/Diversions: The Oval Room is an elegant and formal dining room offering decent fare from an eclectic menu. Two outside dining spots overlook the pools and serve drinks, light meals, snacks, and sandwiches. There are three bars, including The Deco Lounge, which features a lively happy hour with live jazz in season.

Amenities: Concierge, room service (6am to midnight), dry-cleaning and laundry service, newspaper delivery, evening turndown, twice-daily maid service, baby-sitting, express checkout. Stereos and two TVs in suites, VCRs, video rental, two outdoor pools, large beach, small fitness room, small business center, water-sports concession (including scuba and sailing).

○ **The Tides.** 1220 Ocean Dr., South Beach, FL 33139. ☎ **800/OUTPOST** or 305/604-5000. Fax 305/672-6288. www.islandoutpost.com. 45 units. A/C MINIBAR TV TEL. Winter $450–$525 double; $1,100–$2,000 penthouse. Off-season $350–$450 double; $900–$2,000 penthouse. Additional person $20 extra. Rates include continental breakfast. AE, CB, DC, JCB, MC, V. Valet parking $15.

This 12-story art deco masterpiece is one of the tallest buildings on the strip of Ocean Drive. Rooms are starkly white but luxurious. The welcoming staff and central location are its definite strong points. Also, all rooms are at least twice the size of a typical South Beach hotel room and have a view of the ocean. They feature king beds, spacious closets, and large bathrooms. Although small, the freshwater pool on the rear mezzanine is a welcome plus for those who have had enough of the wild beach scene across the street.

Dining/Diversions: Twelve Twenty is the hotel's fine restaurant. It serves dinner nightly 6pm to midnight. The Terrace, a gorgeous outdoor cafe overlooking the ocean, does a fine job of breakfast and lunch. There's also a lobby lounge with live entertainment.

Amenities: Concierge, room service (24 hour), dry cleaning, laundry service, newspaper delivery, in-room massage, twice-daily maid service, baby-sitting, secretarial services, express checkout. Stereos with cassette and CD player and a selection of CDs in each room, VCRs, video rentals, heated outdoor pool, small health club and discount at large nearby health club, conference rooms.

EXPENSIVE

Albion Hotel. 1650 James Ave. (at Lincoln Rd.) South Beach, Fl 33139. ☎ **888/665-0008** or 305/913-1000. Fax 305/674-0507. www.rubellhotels.com. 100 units. A/C MINIBAR TV TEL. Winter $250–$325 double; $375–$700 suite. Off-season $200–$225 double; $299–$600 suite. AE, CB, DC, DISC, MC, V. Valet parking $17.

An architectural masterpiece originally designed in 1939 by internationally acclaimed architect Igor Polivitzky, this large streamline modern building looks like a cruise ship with portholes, smokestack, and sleek curved lines. It was totally renovated under the guidance of the hip New York family, the Rubell's. Although you have to walk a few blocks to find beach access, you may not want to. A huge pool and artificial beach are original features at this unusual resort. Rooms have wonderful modern furnishings custom-designed for the space. The hotel is popular with those in the music and modeling industry and often serves as the backdrop for parties and shoots. If you plan to stay on a Friday night, be sure to go down to the "Magic Garden Party," where you'll be surrounded by a young hip crowd perusing through on their way to one of the other hot clubs on the beach. But don't plan on getting any sleep until 4am when the music finally dies down to a low murmur.

The Rubell family owns a second hotel just around the corner, The Greenview, with rates about 40% lower. Rooms are just as comfortable but amenities are slightly more limited—you won't find a pool, restaurant, or bar, for example—but it's a great alternative if you want to save a little spending money for shopping on nearby Lincoln Road.

Dining/Diversions: Mayya, an elegant Mexican restaurant, serves more than the typical taco or burrito. (See listing under "South Beach" in chapter 6, "Miami Dining.")

Amenities: Concierge, room service, dry cleaning, evening turndown, in-room massage, newspaper delivery, twice-daily maid service, baby-sitting, executive business services, valet parking, airport limo service. VCRs available on request, large outdoor heated pool with adjacent artificial sand beach, workout room, business services on request, small conference and production rooms, stereos with CD and cassette player (but no CDs), state-of-the-art phones with data port and voice mail.

The Blue Moon Hotel. 945 Collins, South Beach, FL 33139. ☎ **305/673-2262.** Fax 305/534-5399. E-mail: blmoon@bellsouth.net. 75 units. A/C TV TEL. Winter $199–$275 single or double. Off-season $85–$275 single or double. AE, CB, DC, MC, V.

The Blue Moon is steps away from the legendary nightlife and energetic shopping that define South Beach. This **Merv Griffin** hotel excels in luxury and splendor. If you're looking for a charming, intimate oasis of serenity (and security) amid the South Beach Deco madness, a stay at The Blue Moon is mandatory. Several tasteful patios are sprinkled throughout the hotel and encourage, in the property's own words, "the art of lingering." There is also a refreshing pool on the premises, fresh flowers abound in rooms, and soothing fountains decorate hallways. It's an ideal location for a small business retreat.

Dining: The Cheeky Monkey is open 7 days a week (see chapter 6, "South Beach Dining").

✪ **Cardozo Hotel.** 1300 Ocean Dr. South Beach, FL. 33139. ☎ **305/535-6500.** Fax 305/532-3563. 44 units. TV TEL. Winter $195–$225 double; $400–$1,200 suite. Off-season $150–$180 double; $300–$920 suite. AE, DC, MC, V. Valet parking $17; public parking (behind hotel) $4–$6.

Owned by musical couple Gloria and Emilio Estefan, this sexy, extravagantly restored 1939 art deco landmark is a true gem. The terra-cotta walls, wrought-iron and leopard-printed chairs, cherry wood floors, and the dimly lit lamp shades create an ambience that's so soothing, you'll wish you didn't have to go home. All the rooms are spacious, featuring handcrafted furnishings and a host of amenities. The Honeymoon Suite is exceptionally luxurious. The mosquito-netted canopy bed with African prints, a full-size Jacuzzi and a view of the ocean add to its charm. If it hasn't been booked, ask to see it.

Dining/Diversions: At press time, the Cardozo Café & Bar had closed, and the News Café on South Beach was slated to move in its place.

Amenities: Entertainment center with TV, VCR, CD/cassette stereo; fully stocked minibar; bathrobes; paper delivery; hair dryer; iron and ironing board; telephones with data port and voice mail; laundry and dry-cleaning service; 24-hour concierge services with a multilingual staff; Jacuzzi tubs in specialty suites; in-room safe; business services available. Access to nearby gym at a discounted rate.

The Hotel. 801 Collins Ave., South Beach, FL 33139. ☎ **305/531-2222** or 877/843-4683. Fax 305/531-2222. www.thehotelofsouthbeach.com. 52 units. A/C TV TEL. Year-round rates range from $195–$345 double occupancy. Rates include 12.5% hotel tax. AE, DC, DISC, MC, V.

The Hotel, formerly The Tiffany Hotel, was named one of 50 top new hotels worldwide by *Condé Nast Traveller* in 1999. Fashion designer Todd Oldham amazingly restored this 1939 gem without destroying its timeless beauty. Laced with lush, cool colors, artisan detailing, terrazzo floors, and porthole windows, the hotel will make you feel like you're a captive on a luxury cruise liner smack in the middle of the ocean. The small, soundproof rooms are very comfortable and stylish. There's no need to pay more for an oceanfront view, go up to the rooftop and you'll see the most amazing view of the Atlantic without having to get sand in your toes.

Dining: Wish offers a wide selection of delightful dishes, from blue corn tortilla soup to marinated grilled rack of lamb at (see chapter 6).

Amenities: All rooms have Kiehl's products, remote TV and VCR, video library, CD/cassette/stereo system, minibar, two-line telephone with data port and voice mail, rooftop pool and patio, pool bar, poolside cabanas, fitness center, concierge, room service, valet, small meeting/banquet facilities, business center, and an off-site gift shop.

Hotel Astor. 956 Washington Ave., South Beach, FL 33139. ☎ **800/270-4981** or 305/531-8081. Fax 305/531-3193. www.hotelastor.com. 40 units. A/C MINIBAR TV TEL. Winter $165–$400 suite; $1,000 Astor suite. Off-season $155–$340 suite; $800 Astor suite. Additional person $30 extra. AE, MC, V. Valet parking $14.

A small but elegant and modern hotel, the Astor attracts many loyal return guests. Originally built in 1936, a renovation in 1995 greatly improved on the original design of this simple three-story gem. There is a small lap pool and a beautiful waterfall outside the sleek lobby bar area. All the details—swivel stands for the large-screen TVs, Belgian linens and towels, funky custom lighting with dimmer switches, and more—are pure luxury. The hotel staff is known for bending over backward. This low-profile hotel is definitely a place for those in the know.

Dining: Astor Place is one of Miami's best restaurants. The Florida-style menu is diverse and delicious (see listing under "South Beach" in chapter 6, "Miami Dining"). Sunday brunch is one of the best in town.

Amenities: 24-hour concierge service, room service, dry cleaning, laundry, newspaper delivery, in-room massage, twice-daily maid service, baby-sitting, secretarial service, express checkout. VCRs available on request, video rental, outdoor pool with jet streams, access to nearby health club, two phones in suites.

The Hotel Impala. 1228 Collins Ave., South Beach, FL 33139. ☎ **800/646-7252** or 305/673-2021. Fax 305/673-5984. E-mail: HTIMPALA@aol.com. 17 units. A/C TV TEL. Winter $225–$450 double. Off-season $200–$350 double. AE, CB, DC, MC, V. Valet parking $18.

During the heyday of 1990s excess, the Beach was known for the fabulous parties thrown by the eclectic designer Gianni Versace. The late Versace desired an intimate European-styled guest house that would please well-seasoned travelers, and the Impala is the result. His personal touch on this renovated Mediterranean inn is still evident, from the Greco-Roman frescos and friezes to an intimate garden that is perfumed with the scents from carefully hanging lilies and gardenias. Each comfortable room offers Internet connections and in-room safes; the sheets are of imported cotton, the bathrooms and showers are oversized and the cotton towels are sumptuous to the point of being sinful. The staff is multilingual, and a 24-hour concierge service is available. Though the hotel does not have its own restaurant, guests may charge room service from the restaurant, Spiga that is adjacent to the hotel.

Hotel Ocean. 1230 Ocean Dr., Miami Beach, FL 33139. ☎ **800/783-1725** or 305/672-2579. Fax 305/672-7665. 27 units. A/C TV TEL. Winter $215–$515. Off-season $199–$475. Superior suites $390. Penthouse suites $550. Rates include continental breakfast. AE, DC, DISC, MC, V.

This lovely French boutique hotel lies directly on the ocean. The rooms are Mediterranean in style and elegantly furnished with art deco collectibles from the 1930s. The comfortable rooms feature two-line telephones, an in-room safe, a wet bar, and an iron and ironing board. Each room is soundproof, a must on the noisy Ocean drive. The spacious bathrooms have bathrobes, a hair dryer, and French toiletries. For a particularly fabulous experience, stay in the Penthouse suite, where a 1-night stay ($550) includes a bottle of champagne, a basket of fruits, and breakfast for two. Spring for 2 nights and you'll also get 30-minute massages for two. As long as your pet can fit in the elevator, it is welcome here, too.

Dining/Diversions: Le Deux Fontaines is an exquisite seafood restaurant with an extensive wine list. The "Speak Easy" bar provides happy-hour drink specials and entertainment; a variety of jazz and Dixie bands perform here nightly.

Amenities: Copy and fax services, meeting facilities, laundry service, gift shop, VIP pass at Crunch Fitness, newspaper delivery.

Marlin. 1200 Collins Ave., Miami Beach, FL 33139. ☎ **305/672-5254**. Fax 305/672-6288 www.islandoutpost.com. 13 units. A/C TV TEL. Winter $195–$450 one bedroom suite. Off-season $150–$325 one bedroom suite. AE, DC, DISC, MC, V.

Don't be surprised if you hear guitar sounds as you enter, because this "rock and roll" hotel houses South Beach Studios, a recording and mixing facility. It has also hosted well-known celebrities and entertainers such as Johnny Depp and Mick Jagger. And don't be taken back if you see beautiful models strolling by—the Elite Modeling Agency also calls the Marlin home. The rooms here sport a sleek, Afro-urban decor, with soft earth tones, custom-made furniture, and hardwood floors; they almost feel like individual bungalows. No two rooms are alike and each one is distinctively designed with a kiss of class and style. You'll find all the creature comforts—Internet access, two-line telephones, bathrobes, coffeemakers, full-stocked refrigerators, hair dryers, and a microwave—in every room.

Dining: The Marlin Bar offers appetizers with a Jamaican accent, and a full selection of wines, beer, and liquor.

Amenities: Concierge, laundry service, baby-sitting, secretarial services, reduced rates at Crunch Fitness, VIP access to local clubs. The Tides hotel (see above) provides room service.

The Winterhaven Hotel. 1400 Ocean Dr., Miami Beach, FL 33139. ☎ **800/395-2322** or 305/531-5571. Fax 305/538-6387. 71 units. A/C TV TEL. Winter $189–$725 double. Off-season $139–$499 double. AE, CB, DC, DISC, MC, V. Valet parking $18.

The Winterhaven is one of South Beach's newest renovations, situated in a quiet area (yes, there is one) on Ocean Drive. This historic art deco property—it was built in 1938—is right near all the cafes, restaurants, clubs, and boutiques to make your stay as pleasant as possible. You should definitely check out the exquisitely decorated mezzanine, which often hosts receptions and business meetings. Most of the 71 spacious rooms have ocean views; all of them have two-line telephones with voice mail, Internet access, in-room safes, hair dryers, and ironing boards. There's also a 50-seat lounge and bar in the lobby. This hotel is a proud member of the Coral Collection of Fine Hotels and Resorts, and when you pass by or stay, you'll realize why.

MODERATE

Abbey Hotel. 300 21st Street Miami Beach, FL 33139. ☎ **305/531-0031.** Fax 305/672-1663. www.abbeyhotel.com. 50 units. A/C TV TEL. Winter $135–$195 double. Off-season $99–$140 double. Rates include breakfast. AE, DC, DISC, MC, V. Off-site parking $15 per day.

This lovely boutique hotel is within walking distance of the Jackie Gleason Theater, the Convention Center, the Bass Museum of Art, the Miami City Ballet, and is only 1 block from the beach. The hotel recently underwent a complete makeover, adding soft white-covered chairs and candles in the lobby, and the rooftop sundeck is being restored to its 1940s glamour. Suites here are equipped with CD stereos, VCRs, T-1 Internet access lines, in-room safety deposit boxes, and minibars.

Dining/Diversions: Full-service restaurant and bar.

Amenities: Fitness room, concierge, laundry and dry cleaning; photocopying, typing, faxing, and computer rental; room service. The solarium (still undergoing renovations) will offer semiprivate nude sunbathing, outdoor showers, and spa services.

Avalon Majestic Hotel. 700 Ocean Dr. (at 7th St.), South Beach, FL 33139. ☎ **800/933-3306** or 305/538-0133. Fax 305/534-0258. www.southbeachhotels.com. 103 units. A/C TV TEL. Winter $120–$210 double. Off-season $89–$175 double. Rates include continental breakfast. 10% discount for stays of 7 days or more. AE, CB, DC, DISC, MC, V. Valet parking $14.

This striking hotel offers classic art deco digs right on the beach at even more attractive prices. The simple rooms, decorated in traditional 1930s style, are nothing fancy but are comfortable if a bit on the small side. The modest lobby holds a casual restaurant, best for lunch either inside or on the breezy outdoor patio.

Room service, free coffee, refreshments, and breakfast are also available. If the Avalon is full, don't hesitate to accept a room in its companion property, the South Seas on 17th and Collins. You can also use the pool there.

Cavalier. 1320 Ocean Dr., South Beach, FL 33139. ☎ **800/OUTPOST** or 305/604-5064. Fax 305/531-5543. www.islandoutpost.com. 45 units. A/C MINIBAR TV TEL. Winter $170–$195 double; $300–$375 suite. Off-season $130–$160 double; $250–$275 suite. Additional person $15 extra. AE, DC, DISC, MC, V. Valet parking $16; self-parking $6.

This island getaway is right here at home. You can't beat its oceanfront location, adjacent to shops and restaurants. Palm trees brush the ceilings of the modest lobby, where young trendy guests make their way to their rooms. Funky prints cover the walls, which are the colors of a tequila sunrise. African fabrics cover cozy couches. A young, competent staff waits on guests and offers lots of good advice about local clubs, restaurants, and shopping. Rooms come equipped with CD players and CDs. You can also use a VCR and rent videos. Despite the Ocean Drive location, most rooms are relatively quiet.

Chesterfield Hotel. 855 Collins Ave., South Beach, FL 33139. ☎ **800/244-6023** or 305/531-5831. Fax 305/672-4900. www.southbeachgroup.com. A/C TV TEL. Winter $99–$249 double. Off season $69–$179 double. AE, MC, V.

The Chesterfield Hotel is the kitchiest property in the South Beach Hotel Group, and has enough drama in its Zimbabwe meets Baroque lobby to titillate any would-be author. The Chesterfield is located in the heart of South Beach's Deco District, just a skip away from all the restaurants on Ocean or the nightclubs on Washington. This original 1930s art deco hotel was recently renovated with modern-day amenities. The 50 unique rooms are finished with Zebra or Leopard prints, and adorned with faux renditions of fabulous Euro art. The hotel's Safari Bar/Café caters to both a European and an alternative crowd with impunity. The bar turns into a spot for a quaint Euro continental breakfast in the morning. There's also a happy hour each evening from 4 to 8pm with two-for-one cocktails. The hotel's proximity to area clubs and modeling agencies, and its ability to create its own eclectic nightlife, make the Chesterfield an award-winning locale for people watching.

The Dorchester Hotel. 1850 Collins Ave., Miami Beach, FL 33139. ☎ **800/327-4739** or 305/531-5745. Fax 305/673-1006. 100 units. A/C TV TEL. Winter $199–$250 one bedroom suite. Off-season $175–$205 one bedroom suite. AE, DC, DISC, MC, V.

Located in Miami Beach's famous Historic Art Deco District, this hotel is one street away from the Miami Beach Convention Center and the Theater of the Performing Arts. Each guest room has a refrigerator, and some suites come with kitchenettes. The swimming pool has a private pool deck lounge, along with a spacious tropical patio garden where a summer poolside barbecue is not an uncommon occurrence. There is parking on the premises (a plus on busy Collins Avenue) and a small entertainment room with billiards and table tennis. In the morning, the Dorchester Café serves fresh breakfast (not included in the room rate) on the tropical garden patio. Water sports are available at the Dorchester's sister hotel, the Marseilles, across the street.

Essex House Hotel and Suites. 1001 Collins Ave., Miami Beach, FL 33139. ☎ **800/553-7739** or 305/534-2700. Winter $169–$379 single or double. Off-season $119–$300 single or double. Rates include breakfast. AE, DC, DISC, MC, V.

The Essex House Hotel and Suites was awarded the title "Best of South Florida in 1999" by *Miami Metro Magazine*. This art deco gem was created by Henry Hohauser in 1938 and has received numerous awards for its authentic restoration. The hotel's whimsically created shiplike architecture rises from the shore with decks that are designed to take in succulent ocean breezes. The sleek Bauhaus interiors add to the distinct charm of the place. All suites feature solid-oak furnishings and have a fridge, wet bar, and Jacuzzi. Although the hotel is right on the pulse of South Beach's constant activity, the new double-glazed, sound-absorbing windows provide an acoustical barrier to the street noise.

A spa pool graces the south patio and gardens. In an area where the infamous Al Capone used to play cards with cronies now rests an intimate dining area where a complimentary breakfast is served and in the evening cocktails are enjoyed.

Hotel Continental Riande. 1825 Collins Ave., South Beach, FL 33139. ☎ **800/RIANDE-1** or 305/531-3503. Fax 305/531-2803. E-mail: riande@iconnect.net. 251 units. A/C MINIBAR TV TEL. Winter $170–$550 double. Off-season $150–$480 double. Additional person $10 extra. Frommer's readers get a 20% discount. AE, DC, DISC, MC, V. Valet parking $8.

The Riande is just the ticket if you want value and convenience right on South Beach. Catering to a largely Latin and European clientele, this hotel overlooking the ocean has become quite well known. It's just 2 blocks from The Delano and the best of South Beach. The rooms and lobby areas are clean and well maintained, but not too fussy. A large outdoor pool and sundeck are just out back. There's also a restaurant/coffee shop with both buffet and menu service. Room service is available daily for breakfast and dinner.

Hotel Franklin. 860 Collins Ave., South Beach, FL 33139. ☎ **305/531-5541.** Fax 305/673-4112. 48 units. A/C TV TEL. Winter $149–$299 double. Off season $69–$99 double. Rates include continental breakfast (excluding holidays). AE, DC, DISC, MC, V. Valet parking $16.

Centrally located in the heart of South Beach's Art Deco District, the Hotel Franklin enables you to indulge yourself at one of Miami Beach's most exciting places to stay. You will be in the middle of the best the Beach has to offer: the glamour, the nightlife, and the world's most beautiful beaches. It's just a moment's walk to dozens of unique bars, excellent restaurants, designer shops, and wonderfully wild nightclubs. The hotel's accommodations include uniquely decorated rooms with wood floors, refrigerators, and in-room safes. The lobby has a friendly, intimate bar, and since a small European Hostel is located across the street, don't be surprised to find it crowded most evenings with effervescent young tourists downing beers while spouting Kierkegaard and Kant. It's really a quaint moment in the heart of South Beach's hustle and bustle.

✪ **Hotel Leon.** 841 Collins Ave., South Beach, FL 33139. ☎ **305/673-3767.** Fax 305/673-5866. www.hotelleon.com. 18 units. A/C TV TEL. Winter $135–$235 suite; $395 penthouse. Off-season $110–$195 suite; $335 penthouse. Additional person $10 extra. AE, DC, MC, V. Valet parking $16.

A true value, this stylish sliver of a property has won the loyalty of fashion industrialists and romantics alike. The very central location, 1 block from the sea and in the heart of shopping and dining, means a car isn't necessary. The spacious well-renovated rooms are sparkling clean and warmly appointed. Gleaming wood floors and simple pale furnishings are appreciated in a neighborhood where many others overdo the art deco motif. Each room has two phones, sunken oval tubs, robes, CD players, and CDs. Unfortunately, there's no pool or sundeck but the beach is only a 2-minute walk away. A meeting room and business center make it a fine choice for business trips. In the standard rooms, there are no minibars or fridges, but you can order room service. In the morning, enjoy a moderately priced breakfast ($8.50) of croissants, fresh rolls, ham, cheese, and eggs cooked to order. The owners, a young German couple, have made a commitment to providing excellent service with a distinctly personal touch, and they have succeeded.

Miami Accommodations

Hotel Shelley. 844 Collins Ave., South Beach, FL 33139. ☎ **800/414-0612** or 305/531-3341. Fax 305/672-4900. A/C TV TEL. Winter $119–$179 double. Off-season $79–$149 double. Rates include breakfast. AE, MC, V.

Serious shoppers will appreciate the Hotel Shelley's location on Collins Avenue, a block away from the lush white sands of South Beach and right in the heart South Beach's fashion district. It's just doors away from such world-famous shops as Versace, Nicole Miller, Kenneth Cole, Benetton, Banana Republic, and Betsy Johnson. Restored and renovated to its 1930 art deco luster, the hotel's interior is designed with rustic European period antiques. The rooms have wood and terra-cotta floors, and sponge-painted walls separated by high arched doorways. In the morning, the hotel provides a complimentary breakfast. If you're looking for a place to party, the multilingual staff seems well connected to the club and restaurant scene.

The Kent. 1131 Collins Ave., South Beach, FL 33139. ☎ **800/OUTPOST** or 305/604-5000. Fax 305/531-0720. www.islandlife.com. 54 units. A/C MINIBAR TV TEL. Winter $130–$275 suite. Off-season $100–$250 suite. Additional person $15 extra. AE, DC, DISC, MC, V. Valet parking $14; self-parking $6.

This is an excellent value right in South Beach's active center. Even if the other Island Outpost hotels are full, you're likely to find a spot here. The prices are the same as the group's beachside hotels, the Cavalier and the Leslie, but the rooms tend to be less noisy. The staff is eager to please and the clientele comes largely from the fashion industry. Frequent shoots are coordinated in the lobby and conference room, where full office services are available. Thanks to a vacant lot in the backyard (for now), some rooms in the rear offer nice views of the ocean. The decor is modest but tasteful. CD players are standard, as are bright and whimsical furnishings. VCRs and video rentals are available. There's no pool or sundeck, but you're only 1 block from the beach.

Lily Guest House. 835 Collins Ave., South Beach, FL 33139. ☎ **888/742-6600** or 305/535-9900. Fax 305/535-0077. www.southbeachgroup.com. 19 units. A/C TV TEL. Winter $159 single; $179 superior; $209 one-bedroom suite; $259 two-bedroom suite. Off-season $109 single; $129 superior; $159 one-bedroom suite; $209 two-bedroom suite. AE, MC, V.

The Lily is one of the premier hotels on the beach, maintaining a quiet simplicity amid some of the wildest action in America's Riviera. This hotel has proven to be popular with production companies and movie industry glitterati so don't be surprised to find yourself bunking near a cover girl or Mr. Beautiful. The all-suite property has just 19 guest rooms, all featuring wrought-iron and wood furnishings, hardwood floors, and marble bathrooms. While not all rooms are decorated exactly alike, some would probably be described in *Architectural Digest* as a "vision in white," with plush oversized furniture, plusher pillows, and gauzy white curtains that move in synch with an ocean breeze that tastes of sun and sea salt. Very relaxing, the rooms seem to deflect the noise outside. All guests have access to a private sundeck.

Marseilles Hotel. 1741 Collins Ave., South Beach, Fl 33139. ☎ **800/327-4739** or 305/538-5711. Fax 305/673-1006. www.marseilleshotel.com. 124 units. A/C TV TEL. Winter $125–$150 double; $200 suite. Off-season $99–$109 double; $155 suite. Frommer's readers get 10% discount. AE, DC, DISC, MC, V. Self-parking $9.

Reminiscent of the sunbaked shores of St. Tropez or the cosmopolitan "je ne sais quois" of Nice, South Beach has deservedly been dubbed America's Riviera, and the Marseilles is one of its secret jewels. A stay here will allow you to romp in the surf by day, and hop around famous clubs and trendy eateries by night. Its location, minutes away from the galleries and designer boutiques of Ocean Drive, Lincoln Road, and Collins Avenue, can't be beat. Business travelers need only walk around the corner to get to the Miami Beach Convention Center. The resort offers newly decorated rooms, 3 studio suites (each with a charming Jacuzzi), an intimate restaurant, a fitness center, ballroom and meeting facilities, and a sidewalk cafe. The Marseilles is more intimate than the larger and similarly priced Riande, a few doors away. The bar and restaurant here are popular with budget-seeking locals.

✪ The Mermaid Guesthouse. 909 Collins Ave., Miami Beach, FL 33140. ☎ **305/ 538-5324.** 8 units. A/C TEL. Winter $115–$280 single or double. Off-season $95–$215 single or double. Additional person $10 extra. Discounts available for longer stays. AE, MC, V.

There's something magical about this little hideaway tucked behind tropical gardens in the very heart of South Beach. You won't find the amenities of the larger hotels here, but the charm and hospitality at this one-story guest house keeps people coming back. Plus, it's smack in the middle of the hottest part of South Beach and less than 2 blocks from the ocean.

Owners Ana and Gonzalo Torres did a thorough clean-up, adding new brightly colored fretwork around the doors and windows and installing phones in each room. Also, the wood floors have been stripped or covered in straw matting, one of the many Caribbean touches that make this place so cheery. There are no TVs, so guests tend to congregate in the lush garden in the evenings. The owners sometimes host free impromptu dinners for their guests and friends. Ask if they've scheduled any live Latin music during your stay; you won't want to miss it.

The Nassau Suite Hotel. 1414 Collins Ave., South Beach, FL 33139. ☎ **305/534-2354.** 22 units. A/C TV TEL. Winter $150 studio suite; $190 one-bedroom suite. Off-season $99 studio suite; $149 one-bedroom suite. AE, DC, DISC, JCB, MC, V. Parking $8.

Here you'll find premium modernity and space, all in South Beach, for a remarkably reasonable price. The Nassau Suite Hotel was built in 1937 as a 50-room hotel but was recently renovated and the room count was pared down to 22 large and spacious studios and one-bedroom units. This is tropical luxury at its finest, with beautiful white linens, gauzy curtains, and rattan chairs. Wooden floors and blinds, and the use of wicker and rattan throughout the property create the continued feeling of comfort and relaxation. Each unit has a king bed, a sitting area (many have sofa beds), a dining table, open kitchens, data ports, voice mail, and large closets. The property advertises itself as gay-friendly, so don't be surprised to see the colorful gay standard of the rainbow flag, blowing gently outside in the ocean breeze.

The Penguin Resort. 1418 Ocean Dr., South Beach, FL 33139. ☎ **305/534-9334.** E-mail: Penguinhotel@sprynet.com. 40 units. A/C TV TEL. Winter $129 double; $189 oceanfront penthouse. Off-season $99 double; $149 oceanfront penthouse. Deluxe room rates include continental breakfast. AE, MC, V.

You'll be able to walk everything that South Beach has to offer from this hotel, located in the heart of the Historic Art Deco District. The hotel may be only a 10-minute walk from the Lincoln Road Shopping District, but it's located on the quiet side of the Ocean Drive community, near the new Loews Hotel. The comfortable rooms have data port connections, and safety deposit boxes are available gratis at the front desk. Several rooms have been designed to meet the needs of travelers with disabilities. The Penguin is also home to the Front Porch Café, a nice local hangout with good food at economic prices.

The President Hotel. 1423 Collins Ave., South Beach, FL 33139. ☎ **305/538-2882.** Fax 305/674-7809. 64 units. A/C TV TEL. Winter $150–$280 single or double. Off-season $105–$175 single or double. AE, MC, V.

The President boasts a location near a multitude of exclusive boutiques and shops offering everything from the latest fashions by world-renowned designers to art deco posters from the 1930s. Hoping to attract tech-savvy guests, all of the hotel's rooms have data port connections, satellite TV, and voice-mail service. There is room service and the hotel is handicapped-accessible. At press time, the President was preparing to open a full business center equipped with everything a business traveler could need. The President Hotel is also scheduled to open the President Sidewalk Café on trendy Collins.

INEXPENSIVE

The Bayliss Guest House. 504 14th St., South Beach, FL 33139. ☎ **888/305-4863** or 305/531-3755. Fax: 305/673-8609. 20 units. A/C TV TEL. Winter $75 standard room; $95 efficiency. Off-season $45 standard room; $60 efficiency. AE, DC, DISC, MC, V.

The Bayliss Guest House is the smallest of three jointly owned properties that cater to a European and gay clientele. Built in 1939 in the tropical art deco style, rounded corners, glass blocks, neon, and a lobby floor of fancy terrazzo give the Bayliss a definite '40s feel. The Bayliss offers hotel rooms, large efficiencies, and one-bedroom apartments. All accommodations are equipped with ceiling fans, a refrigerator, and voice mail. The property is a bit off the beaten path, but this quiet residential spot is an added amenity—you will rarely hear the raucous noise that defines Collins and Washington.

Banana Bungalow. 2360 Collins Ave., Miami Beach, FL 33139. ☎ **800/7-HOSTEL** or 305/538-1951. Fax 305/531-3217. www.bananabungalow.com. 90 units. A/C TV TEL. Winter $13–$16 per person in shared units; $70–$80 double. Off-season $12–$14 per person in shared units; $50–$60 double. MC, V. Free parking.

This youth hostel-like hotel is a bright spot on the South Beach budget scene. Across the street is a popular beach; the best shops, clubs, and restaurants are only 6 or 7 blocks away. A redone 1950s two-story newcomer surrounds a pool and deck complete with shuffleboard, a small alfresco cafe serving cheap meals, and a tiki bar where young European travelers hang out.

The best rooms face a narrow canal where motorboats and kayaks are available for a small charge. In general, rooms are clean and well kept, despite a few rusty faucets and chipped Formica furnishings. Guests in shared rooms need to bring their own towels. This is one of the only hotels in this price range with a private pool. Guests can also take advantage of free coffee and refreshments each morning, a communal kitchen, access to a nearby health club, a coin laundry, free movies, sightseeing tours, discounts at local clubs, and a great community spirit.

The Beachcomber Hotel. 1340 Collins Ave., South Beach, FL 33139. ☎ **888/305-4683** or 305/531-3755. Fax: 305/673-8609. 29 units. A/C TV TEL. Winter $90–$145. Off-season $70–$125. AE, DC, DISC, MC, V.

Built in 1937, The Beachcomber Hotel was renovated in 1997. The rooms are decorated in a colorful art deco style, and all have a private bathroom and shower. A deco terrace on Collins Avenue provides the perfect place for sipping a cocktail. The hotel's restaurant serves breakfast, lunch and dinner. Check before arrival if a continental breakfast is included in your rate. The property's location couldn't be better, since it's away from the noise but near the action. Two doors down is the saucy Café Des Artes, and around that corner lies the (in)famous Club Deuce and all the assorted taco stands, sandwich huts, and tattoo parlors you'd expect in glitzy South Beach.

✪ **Brigham Gardens.** 1411 Collins Ave., South Beach, FL 33139. ☎ **305/531-1331.** Fax 305/538-9898. A/C TV TEL. www.brighamgardens.com. 20 units. Winter $95–$145 one-bedroom. Off-season $60–$110 one-bedroom. Additional person $5 extra. 10% discount on stays of 7 days or longer. AE, MC, V. Pets stay for $6 a night.

This funky place is a homey and affordable oasis in the midst of high prices and commercialization. Also, the location is prime. Because most rooms have full kitchens, you'll find many people staying for longer than a weekend. You may, too. All rooms have microwaves and coffeemakers. You can barbecue in the garden.

When you enter the tropically landscaped garden, you'll hear macaws and parrots chirping and see cats and lizards running through the bougainvillea. The tiny but lush grounds are framed by quaint Mediterranean buildings—they're pleasant, although in need of some sprucing up. At press time, a rooftop sundeck with a view of the ocean was being installed.

Clay Hotel & International Hostel. 1438 Washington Ave. (at Española Way), South Beach, FL 33139. ☎ **305/534-2988.** Fax 305/673-0346. www.clayhotel.com. 350 beds in doubles and dorm rooms. $45–75 double; $14–$16 dorm beds. Sheets $2 extra. During the off-season, pay for 6 nights in advance and get 7th night free. JCB, MC, V.

A member of the International Youth Hostel Federation (IYHF), the Clay occupies a beautiful 1920s-style Spanish Mediterranean building at the corner of historic Española Way. Like other IYHF members, this hostel is open to all ages and is a great place to meet people. The usual smattering of Australians, Europeans, and other budget travelers makes it Miami's best clearinghouse of "insider" travel information. Even if you don't stay here, you might want to check out the ride board or mingle with fellow travelers over a beer at the sidewalk cafe.

Although a thorough renovation in 1996 made this hostel an incredible value and a step above any others in town, don't expect nightly turndown service or chocolates. You will find a self-serve Laundromat, occasional movie nights, and a tour desk with car rental available. Reservations for private rooms are essential in season and recommended year-round. In summer, be sure to ask for a room with air-conditioning. Don't bother with a car in this congested area.

Park Washington Hotel. 1020 Washington Ave., South Beach, FL 33139. ☎ **305/532-1930.** Fax 305/672-6706. www.parkwashingtonresort.com. 36 units. A/C TV TEL. Winter $129–$159 suite. Off-season $69 double; $99 suite. Rates include self-serve coffee and Danish. Additional person $20 extra. AE, MC, V.

The Park Washington is a large, refurbished hotel just 2 blocks from the ocean that offers some of the best values in South Beach—good rooms at incredible prices. Designed in the 1930s by Henry Hohauser, one of the beach's most prolific architects, the Park Washington reopened in 1989. Most of the rooms have original furnishings and well-kept interiors, and some have kitchenettes. Guests also enjoy a decent-sized outdoor heated pool with a sundeck, bikes for rent, and access to a nearby health club.

The same owners run the adjacent Taft House and Kenmore hotels. All three attract a large gay clientele, and all offer privacy, lush landscaping, a great pool and sundeck, consistent quality, and a value-oriented philosophy. You can't park on the premises, but there's a public garage at 7th Street, less than 3 blocks away.

Villa Paradiso. 1415 Collins Ave., Miami Beach, FL 33139. ☎ **305/532-0616.** Fax 305/673-5874. www.sobe.com/villaparadiso. 17 units. A/C TV TEL. Winter $100–$145 apt. Off-season $69–$105 apt. Weekly rates are 10% less. Additional person $5–$10 extra. AE, DC, MC, V. Parking nearby $12 a day.

This guest house, like Brigham Gardens, is more like a cozy apartment house than a hotel. There's no elegant lobby or restaurant, but the amicable hosts, Lisa and Pascal Nicolle, are happy to give you a room key and advice on what to do. The apartments are simple, but perfect for the beach, since you'll be spending most of your time outside anyway. Plus, the spacious apartments are quiet considering their location, a few blocks from Lincoln Road and all of South Beach's best clubs. Most have full kitchens or at least a fridge, and Murphy beds or foldout couches for extra friends. Bathrooms have recently been renovated with marble tile. There are also laundry facilities on the premises and free local phone service. Parking is available at a nearby city lot for about $12 a day.

2 Miami Beach: Surfside, Bal Harbour & Sunny Isles

The area just north of South Beach encompasses Surfside, Bal Harbour, and Sunny Isles. Unrestricted by zoning codes throughout the 1950s, 1960s, and especially the 1970s, area developers went nuts, building ever-bigger and more brazen structures, especially north of 41st Street, which is now known as "Condo Canyon." Consequently, there's now a glut of medium-quality condos, with a few scattered holdouts of older hotels and motels casting shadows over the beach by afternoon.

Miami Beach, as described here, runs from 24th Street to 192nd Street, a long strip that varies slightly from end to end. Staying in the southern section, from 24th to 42nd streets, can be a good deal—it's still close to the South Beach scene but the rates are more affordable. Bal Harbour and Bay Harbor are at the center of Miami Beach and retain their exclusivity and character. The neighborhoods north and south of here, like Surfside and Sunny Isles, have nice beaches and some shops, but are a little worn around the edges.

Just north of South Beach is the **Days Inn** (☎ 800/325-2525 or 305/673-1513) at 42nd Street and Collins Avenue. It's well kept and right on the ocean. Rates in season start at about $99. The **Howard Johnson** (☎ 800/446-4656 or 305/532-4411) at 4000 Alton Rd., just off the Julia Tuttle Causeway (I-95), is a generic eight-story building on a strip of land near a busy road, but it's convenient to the beach, by car or bike. Rooms, renovated in 1995, are clean and spacious, and some have pretty views of the city and the Intracoastal Waterway. Winter rates start at $100.

VERY EXPENSIVE

✪ **Alexander All-Suite Luxury Hotel.** 5225 Collins Ave., Miami Beach, FL 33140. ☎ 800/327-6121 or 305/865-6500. Fax 305/341-6553. www.alexanderhotel.com. 150 units. A/C TV TEL. Winter $325 one-bedroom suite; $470 two-bedroom suite. Off-season $250 one-bedroom suite; $370 two-bedroom suite. Additional person $35 extra. Packages available. AE, CB, DC, DISC, MC, V. Valet parking $18.

This stunning hotel is a great luxury option and just a few miles from happening South Beach or ritzy Bal Harbour. It's expensive, but worth it for the service and attention. The Alexander features spacious one- and two-bedroom miniapartments with private balconies overlooking the Atlantic Ocean and Miami's Intracoastal Waterway. Each contains a living room, a fully equipped kitchen, two bathrooms, and a balcony. The rooms are elegant without being pretentious and have every convenience you could want, including hair dryers, coffeemakers, VCRs upon request, and cable TVs. The hotel itself is well decorated, with sculptures, paintings, antiques, and tapestries, most of which were garnered from the Cornelius Vanderbilt mansion. The two oceanfront pools are surrounded by lush vegetation; one of these "lagoons" is fed by a cascading waterfall.

Dining/Diversions: Shula's Steakhouse, owned by former Dolphins football coach Don Shula, is open for lunch and dinner daily. A more casual garden restaurant, a piano lounge, and a pool bar are also available.

Amenities: Concierge, room service (24 hours), dry-cleaning and laundry service, newspaper delivery, evening turndown on request, in-room massage on request, twice-daily maid service, secretarial services, express checkout. Two large outdoor pools,

Miami Beach Accommodations

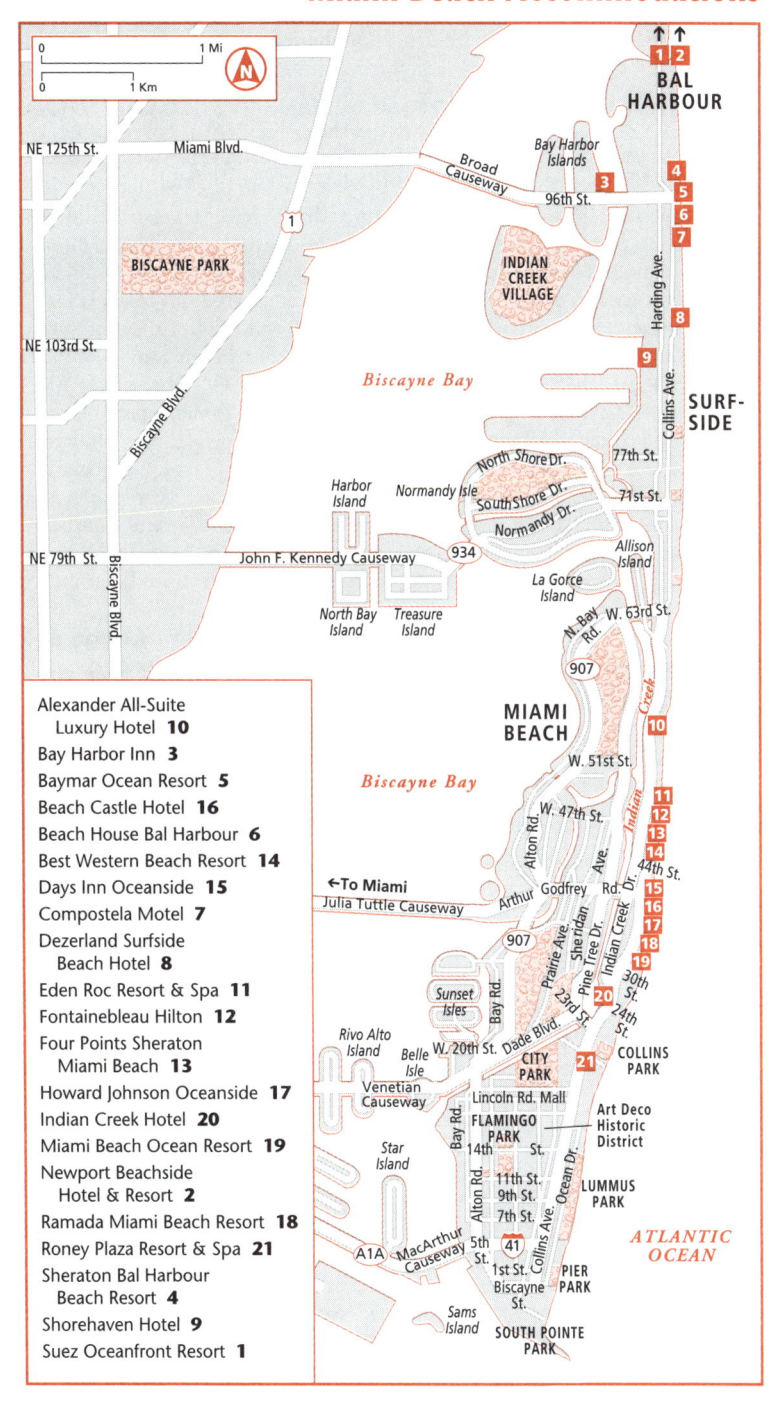

Alexander All-Suite Luxury Hotel **10**
Bay Harbor Inn **3**
Baymar Ocean Resort **5**
Beach Castle Hotel **16**
Beach House Bal Harbour **6**
Best Western Beach Resort **14**
Days Inn Oceanside **15**
Compostela Motel **7**
Dezerland Surfside Beach Hotel **8**
Eden Roc Resort & Spa **11**
Fontainebleau Hilton **12**
Four Points Sheraton Miami Beach **13**
Howard Johnson Oceanside **17**
Indian Creek Hotel **20**
Miami Beach Ocean Resort **19**
Newport Beachside Hotel & Resort **2**
Ramada Miami Beach Resort **18**
Roney Plaza Resort & Spa **21**
Sheraton Bal Harbour Beach Resort **4**
Shorehaven Hotel **9**
Suez Oceanfront Resort **1**

81

Miami Accommodations

beach, small fitness center, four Jacuzzis, sauna, business center and conference rooms, car rental through concierge, sundeck, water-sports equipment, beauty salon.

○ **Beach House Bal Harbour.** 9449 Collins Ave., Surfside, Fl. 33154. ☎ **877/782-3557** or 305/865-3551. Fax: 305/861-6596. www.rubellhotels.com. 170 units. A/C TV TEL. Winter $215–$315 standard; junior suite $245–$305. Off-season $180–210 standard; junior suite $230–$270. $800 one-bedroom suite all year-round. AE, DC, DISC, MC, V.

The Rubells have done it again. What began with the already successful Albion hotel on South Beach has now spread north to the oceanfront resort Beach House. The hotel's attention to detail, and its ability to make you feel like you're someone special and not just another guest is a Rubbell signature touch. And this touch is found all over the Beach House, from the screened-in porch with turn-of-the-century-wicker collectibles to the Bamboo Room with Asian antiques and giant bamboo trees. Each room has Ralph Lauren furnishings and linens, remote TV, alarm clock, AM/FM stereo with CD player, a refrigerator, in-room movies and games, a portable two-line telephone with voice mail and modem link, iron and ironing board, a hair dryer, and bathrobes. No matter what your needs are, they'll be taken care of. Guaranteed.

Dining: The Atlantic Restaurant offers a little of Nantucket right here in Miami. Sheila Lukins, author of the best-selling *Silver Palate* cookbook, creates some delicious feasts, such as her buttermilk fried chicken, with Austin baked beans and homemade cornbread. The Atlantic is open from 7am until 11pm, 7 days a week, for breakfast, lunch, and dinner.

Amenities: The Beach House has a private beach with water sports, topiary garden, heated pool, poolside spa, children's playground, exercise facility, business center, banquet and meeting rooms, and a 24-hour pantry.

○ **Eden Roc Resort and Spa.** 4525 Collins Ave., Miami Beach, FL 33140. ☎ **800/327-8337** or 305/531-0000. Fax 305/674-5568. www.edenrocresort.com. 349 units. A/C MINIBAR TV TEL. Winter $309–$459 double; $820–$1,700 suite. Off-season $185–$335 double; $620–$1,500 suite. Additional person $15 extra. Packages available. AE, CB, DC, DISC, MC, V. Valet parking $20–$25.

Just next door to the mammoth Fontainebleau, this large, flamboyant hotel, opened in 1956, seems almost intimate by comparison. The hotel completed a top-to-bottom $24 million renovation in late 1999. The accommodations here are a bit gaudy, but this is Miami Beach after all. The amenities by far make up for the ostentation. The huge, modern spa has excellent facilities and exercise classes, including yoga. The popular pool deck overlooking the ocean is a great place to spend the afternoon.

The big, open, and airy lobby is often full of name-tagged conventioneers. The rooms, uniformly outfitted with purple and aquatic-colored interiors and retouched 1930s furnishings, are unusually spacious. Because of the hotel's size, you should be able to negotiate a good rate unless there's a big event going on.

Dining/Diversions: The main restaurant serves northern Italian cuisine. From Jimmy Johnson's, the poolside sports bar, patrons can watch swimmers through an underwater "porthole" window. A lobby lounge and bar has occasional jazz.

Amenities: Concierge, room service, dry cleaning and laundry, newspaper delivery, in-room massage, nightly turndown, baby-sitting, secretarial services, express checkout, valet parking. Kitchenettes in suites and penthouses, VCRs for rent, two outdoor pools, beach, full-service spa and health club with sauna, business center and conference rooms, car-rental desk, sundeck, squash, racquetball and basketball courts as well as a rock-climbing arena, water-sports equipment, tour desk, beauty salon, sundries shop.

Fontainebleau Hilton. 4441 Collins Ave., Miami Beach, FL 33140. ☎ **800/HILTONS** or 305/538-2000. Fax 305/674-4607. www.fontainebleau.hilton.com. 1,206 units. A/C TV TEL. Winter $289–$459 double. Off-season $209–$329 double. $525–$1,240 suite year-round. Additional person $30 extra. Packages available. AE, CB, DC, DISC, MC, V. Overnight valet parking $13.

This is, in many ways, the quintessential Miami hotel. Designed by famed architect Morris Lapidus, who is overseeing an expansion, this grand monolith has symbolized Miami decadence. Since its opening in 1954, the Fountainbleau has hosted presidents, pageants, and movie productions, including the James Bond thriller *Goldfinger*. This is where all the greats, including Sinatra and his buddies, performed in their prime.

Adding to the Fountainebleau's opulence is the new 7,000-square-foot Octopus pool designed to bring splashes of fun-filled adventure to families and children. Eight huge tentacles stretch across a children's wading pool and they rain, squirt, spray, and mist water in every direction. There's also a river raft ride and a 24-foot water slide. The waterfalls and fountains in the shape of dolphins, shells and a seahorse will make you believe you've escaped to Splash Mountain.

Dining/Diversions: The Steak House serves dinner until 11pm. A continental restaurant offers a huge Sunday buffet brunch. There are five other cafes and coffee shops (including two by the pool), as well as a number of cocktail lounges, such as the Poodle Lounge, which offers live entertainment and dancing nightly. Another lounge features a Las Vegas–style floor show with dozens of performers and two orchestras.

Amenities: Concierge, room service, dry cleaning and laundry, newspaper delivery, nightly turndown on request, in-room massage, baby-sitting, secretarial services, valet parking. VCRs, two large outdoor pools, beach, large state-of-the-art health club, three whirlpool baths, sauna, game rooms, special year-round activities for children and adults, elaborate business center, conference rooms, car-rental and tour desks, sundeck, seven lighted tennis courts, water-sports equipment rental, beauty salon, boutique, large shopping arcade.

Roney Palace Resort & Spa. 2399 Collins Ave., Miami Beach, FL 33139. ☎ **305/604-1000.** Fax 305/538-7141. www.roney-palace.com. 585 units. A/C TV TEL. Year-round $300–$450 executive suite; $400–$750 one-bedroom suite; $600–$800 two-bedroom suite; $1,275–$2,950 penthouse suite. AE, DC, MC, V. Valet parking $10.

This luxury hotel, built in 1926, hosted such celebrities as Rita Hayworth, Orson Welles, and the duke and duchess of Windsor back in its heyday, and just completed $25 million worth of renovations. The outdated pink and green flamingo furnishings have been replaced with an ultra modern decor and natural woods. All suites include two-line speaker phones with data ports, Internet and voice mail connections, mini-bars, safes, TV and VCR; radio/alarm clocks, a hair dryer, robes, microwave, coffeemaker, and an iron and ironing board. Located directly on the ocean, the hotel offers its guests a private beach club, an indoor-outdoor cafe, and water-sport rentals. Don't want to get sand on your feet? Well, take in the sun by sitting at the fantasy pool deck with cabanas and attendants waiting to satisfy your every desire. Catering to both the business and leisure traveler, one of the hotel's greatest attractions is the Larry North Fitness Center of South Beach, a 10,000-square-foot fitness center and spa.

Dining: There's a 24-hour restaurant serving breakfast, lunch, and dinner. There's also a pool bar and grill overlooking the beach.

Amenities: Dry-cleaning and laundry service, nightly turndown, in-suite spa services, baby-sitting and cellular phones on request, child-care center, playroom and game room, on-site shopping, grand ballrooms, meeting rooms, business and conference center, concierge, room service, airport pickup and drop-off service, and covered valet parking.

⊙ **Sheraton Bal Harbour Beach Resort.** 9701 Collins Ave., Bal Harbour, FL 33154. ☎ **800/999-9898** or 305/865-7511. Fax 305/864-2601. 642 units. A/C MINIBAR TV TEL. Winter $349–$449 double. Off-season $129–$449 double. $650–$1,500 suite or villa year-round. Additional person $25 extra. Weekend and other packages and senior discounts available. Lowest rates reflect bookings made at least 14 days in advance for rooms without ocean views. AE, CB, DC, DISC, JCB, MC, V. Valet parking $12.

This hotel has the best location in Bal Harbour, on the ocean and just across from the swanky Bal Harbour Shops. Bill and Hillary Clinton have stayed here, and Bill even jogged along the beach with local fitness enthusiasts. It's one of the nicest Sheratons I've seen, with a glass-enclosed two-story atrium lobby that's especially welcoming. A spectacular staircase wraps itself around a cascading fountain full of wished-on pennies. The large, well-decorated rooms include convenient extras such as voice mail, coffeemakers, and hair dryers. One side of the hotel caters to corporations and comes complete with ballrooms and meeting facilities, but the main sections are relatively uncongested and removed from the convention crowd. Serious shoppers will enjoy the hotel's location, right across from the ritzy Bal Harbour Shops.

Dining/Diversions: Guests have their choice of four restaurants and lounges. An Argentinean steak house serves good, heavy meals with live Latin music nightly. The other less formal spots serve Mediterranean-influenced beach food, pizzas, and gourmet coffees. A lounge serves good tropical drinks.

Amenities: Concierge, room service (24 hours), laundry and dry cleaning, valet, newspaper delivery, nightly turndown, in-room massage, twice-daily maid service on request, baby-sitting, secretarial services, express checkout, valet parking. VCRs in some rooms, water sports, outdoor heated pool, sundeck, large state-of-the-art fitness center and spa (with aerobics, Jacuzzi, sauna, and sundeck), two outdoor tennis courts, jogging track, game room, children's programs, large business center, conference rooms, tour desk, gift shop and shopping arcade, nearby golf course.

EXPENSIVE

Miami Beach Ocean Resort. 3025 Collins Ave., Miami Beach, FL 33140. ☎ **800/550-0505** or 305/534-0505. Fax 305/534-0515. www.mbo.com. 243 units. A/C TV TEL. Winter $170–$210, 1 to 4 people; $240–$650 suite. Off-season $150–$180, 1 to 4 people; $220–$550 suite. AE, DC, MC, V. Valet parking $6.

Popular with tour groups and Europeans, this oceanfront resort is a great choice for those who want a quiet place on the ocean in close proximity to South Beach and the mainland. It's priced like many other chains on the oceanfront, but it's got more character. The vast lobby is done up in Mexican tile, wood fretwork, and attractive furnishings. Rooms are basic but very tastefully decorated with wicker and rattan furnishings and new carpeting. Rooms also include coffeemakers and hair dryers. A huge outdoor area is landscaped with palms and hibiscus and has a large heated pool as its centerpiece. It faces a popular boardwalk for runners and strollers as well as a large beach where water-sports equipment is available.

Dining/Diversions: The recommendable restaurant serves a breakfast and dinner buffet of simple but good Caribbean and international cuisine to many who choose the meal programs. À la carte offerings and lunch are also available. A patio garden offers cake and coffee, a pool bar serves snacks and drinks, and a colorful indoor/outdoor lounge features cocktails and live music most nights.

Amenities: Concierge, room service, valet parking, laundry and dry-cleaning services, baby-sitting. Outdoor heated pool, beach, sundeck, bicycle rental, game room, self-service Laundromat, currency exchange, tour desk, conference rooms, car-rental desk, beauty salon, boutique.

MODERATE

✪ **Bay Harbor Inn.** 9660 E. Bay Harbor Dr., Bay Harbor Island, FL 33154. ☎ **305/868-4141.** Fax 305/867-9094. www.bayharborinn.com. 45 units. A/C MINIBAR TV TEL. Winter $149–$239 double; $159–$279 suite. Off-season $80–$159 double; $95–$179 suite. Additional person $35 extra. Rates include continental breakfast. AE, MC, V. Free parking.

Under the management of Johnson & Wales University, this thoroughly renovated inn is just moments from the beach, fine restaurants, and Bal Harbour Shops, Miami's ritziest shopping mall. The inn comes in two parts. The more modern section sits squarely on a little river and overlooks a heated outdoor pool and a boat named Celeste where guests eat a complimentary breakfast buffet. On the other side of the street, "townside" is the cozier, antique-filled portion, where glass-covered bookshelves hold good beach reading. The rooms have a hodgepodge of wood furnishings (mostly Victorian replicas). Suites boast an extra half bathroom. You can sometimes smell the aroma of cooking from the restaurant below, but you might find that this only adds to the charm of this homey inn.

Adjacent to the hotel is The Palm, a clubby steak-and-lobster house. Students from the Johnson & Wales Culinary Institute run a superb restaurant, The Island Cafe, and bar across the street.

Baymar Ocean Resort. 9401 Collins Ave., Miami Beach, FL 33154. ☎ **800/8-BAYMAR** or 305/866-5446. Fax 305/866-8053. www.baymar.com. 96 units. A/C TV TEL. Winter $115–$125 double; $125–$135 efficiency; $150–$235 suite. Off-season $85–$95 double; $95–$105 efficiency; $125–$185 suite. Additional person $10 extra. AE, CB, DC, DISC, MC, V. Parking $5.

Depending on what you're looking for, this hotel could be one of the beach's best buys. It's just south of Bal Harbour, right on the ocean, with a low-key beach that attracts few other tourists. It offers all the modern conveniences, including some kitchenettes and large closets. You won't flip over the decor, but it's pleasant enough and all brand-new. A recent renovation has done wonders. The location is close enough to walk to tennis courts, some shopping and dining and just a few minutes drive to the larger attractions. It may not be worth it to pay more for the oceanfront rooms since they tend to be smaller than the others. Rooms overlooking the large pool and sundeck area can get loud on busy days. The first-floor ocean-view rooms have a nice shared balcony space. This hotel is popular with budget travelers and conservative religious groups.

A small restaurant serving basic American fare and a tiki bar are popular with guests.

Beach Castle Hotel. 4210 Collins Ave., Miami Beach, FL 33140. ☎ **305/531-3399.** Fax 305/531-4454. www.beachcastlehotel.com. E-mail: bchcastle@aol.com. 28 units. A/C TV TEL. Winter $59–$109 suite. Off-season $49–$99 suite. MC, V.

The Beach Castle is a kitty walk away from the 41st street area and is a bargain for your buck. Not ones to settle for "you get what you pay for," the friendly Iranian owners are anxious to please, and their continued renovations make the reduced room rates well worth the investment for vacationers looking for an extended stay in a nice room that isn't overpriced. The personalized service here is outstanding. The lobby is scheduled to be renovated and expanded, and the Prego Pizzeria (which offers pick-up service) expects to have an expanded Persian oriented menu that's also gentle on your budget.

86 Miami Accommodations

Best Western Beach Resort. 4333 Collins Ave., Mid Miami Beach, FL 33140. ☎ **800/832-8332** or 305/532-3311. Fax 305/531-5296. 290 units. A/C TV TEL. Winter $115 standard; $125 bay view; $145 oceanfront; $195 penthouse suite. Off-season $85 standard, $95 bay view; $105 oceanfront; $150 penthouse suite. AE, MC, V.

Located on the world-famous Miami Beach boardwalk and 5 to 10 minutes in either direction (north or south) to South Beach or Bal Harbour, this refurbished resort is a nice inexpensive getaway spot for just the right price. A full service restaurant and lounge, in-room safes, a gift shop, valet parking, and an outdoor pool just a short walk from the ocean are some of the many amenities this Best Western tries to offer its valued guests—and it succeeds in every way. The resort is perched atop 375 feet of white sandy beachfront, where the ocean kisses the sky in a tranquil vista that extends as far as the eye can see.

Dezerland Beach Resort Hotel. 8701 Collins Ave., Miami Beach, FL 33154. ☎ **800/331-9346** in the U.S., 800/331-9347 in Canada, or 305/865-6661. Fax 305/866-2630. www.dezerhotels.com. 227 units. A/C TV TEL. Winter $99–$139 double. Off-season $69–$99 double. Additional person $10 extra. Special packages and group rates available. AE, CB, DC, DISC, MC, V.

Designed by car enthusiast Michael Dezer, the Dezerland is one-of-a-kind—part hotel and part 1950s automobile wonderland. Visitors, many of them German tourists, are welcomed by a 1959 Cadillac stationed by the front door, one of a dozen mint-condition classics around the grounds and lobby. The pleasant beachfront hotel recently underwent a $2 million renovation of its guest rooms, lobby, and public areas. Look for the mosaic of a pink Cadillac at the bottom of its surfside pool.

Other amenities here include a Jacuzzi, adjacent tennis courts and jogging track, Windsurfer and jet-ski rental, game room, laundry, car-rental and tour services desk, and an antiques shop featuring 1950s memorabilia. Some rooms contain fully equipped kitchenettes. There's also a restaurant and a lobby lounge with all-you-can-eat buffets and nightly entertainment.

Four Points Sheraton Miami Beach. 4343 Collins Ave., Miami Beach, FL 33140. ☎ **800/5254-6994** or 305/531-7494. Fax 305/532-2490. 216 units. A/C TV TEL. Winter $169 standard; $199 superior; $229 junior suite; $269 one-bedroom suite. Off-season $119 standard; $139 superior; $159 junior suite; $199 one-bedroom suite. AE, DC, DISC, MC, V.

Right on the Miami Beach Boardwalk, this elegantly appointed hotel features interiors inspired by the grandeur of ancient Greece. A lush lobby of marble and rich mahogany provides a fitting prelude to the hotel's luxurious spacious rooms and suites. Designed with both business and leisure travelers in mind, every guest room features a full range of amenities, including coffeemakers, data ports, voice mail, and in-room safes. Suites offer the added luxury of a Jacuzzi tub, microwave, and fridge. The additional convenience of valet parking, same-day dry cleaning, and an excellent concierge rounds out a hassle free stay. There's a full-service restaurant and lobby bar.

Indian Creek Hotel. 2727 Indian Creek Dr. (1 block west of Collins Ave.), Miami Beach, FL 33140. ☎ **800/491-2772** or 305/531-2727. Fax 305/531-5651. www.indiancreekhotelmb.com. 61 units. A/C TV TEL. Winter from $140–$160 double; from $240 suite. Off-season $90 double; $150 suite. Additional person $10 extra. Group packages available. Summer specials. 18% gratuity added to room service. AE, CB, DC, DISC, JCB, MC, V. Limited parking available on street.

Although there isn't much in the way of views or amenities, this small hotel just north of South Beach is pleasant and not too far from the action. Every detail of the 1936 building has been meticulously restored, from one of the beach's first operating elevators to the period steamer trunk in the lobby. The modest rooms are outfitted in art deco furnishings, with pretty tropical prints and all the modern amenities. They are used to hosting production crews and therefore provide things like data ports and voice mail in all rooms. Just 1 short block from a good stretch of sand, the hotel is also within walking distance of shops and inexpensive restaurants. A landscaped pool area is a great place to lounge in the sun. There's a small fitness center and conference facilities. A tiny restaurant serves continental breakfast and dinner.

Newport Beachside Hotel & Resort. 16701 Collins Ave., Miami, FL 33160. ☎ **800/327-5476** or 305/949-1300. Fax 305/947-5873. 300 units. A/C TV TEL. Winter $129 standard; $169 one bedroom suite; $299 two bedroom suite. Off-season $95 standard; $149 one bedroom suite; $250 two bedroom suite. AE, CB, DC, JCB, MC, V. Valet parking $5.

Formerly called the Newport Crowne Plaza, this 300-suite hotel is just minutes away from the Aventura Mall and Bal Harbour Shops. Though major renovations have been completed to improve the hotel's overall appeal, its decor is still reminiscent of its pink and green Miami Vice days. This is definitely a child-friendly place, as evidenced by the many kids running about in the lobby. The hotel staff is very hospitable and helpful. The guest rooms are comfortable and spacious, and most rooms have ocean views and balconies. All rooms are equipped with a safe, minirefrigerator, microwave, ironing board, hair dryer, and a radio alarm clock. There are several restaurants on the premises, including a fully stocked sports bar. Guests will find all of the amenities associated with a higher-priced hotel—from a concierge to baby-sitting to a full business center—for a much more reasonable rate.

Ramada Miami Beach Resort. 4041 Collins Ave., Miami Beach, FL 33140. ☎ **305/531-5771.** Fax 305/673-1612. 254 units. A/C TV TEL. Winter $109–$139. Off-season $95–$105. AE, MC, V.

Situated in the heart of Miami Beach—it's within minutes of the 41st Street Shopping area, the Convention Center, the Art Deco District, and the Bal Harbour Shops—the Ramada is ensconced in a very nice location. Formerly the kosher Crowne Hotel, the Ramada has revamped this lush property and then some. The rooms have been refurbished and a complimentary fitness center has been added. The outdoor pool and tiki bars are relaxing, the inside bar and cafe are quaint and intimate. This is one property that is no secret—in the off-season its was operating at 85% capacity and in season it was almost booked solid—but when you add its proximity to the Fontainebleau and Eden Roc with its reasonable rates, that's no wonder. Book early!

INEXPENSIVE

Days Inn Oceanside. 4299 Collins Ave., Miami Beach, FL 33140. ☎ **800/356-3017** or 305/673-1513. Fax 305/538-0727. 143 units. A/C TV TEL. Winter $99 standard; $119 ocean front. Off-season $79 standard; $99 ocean front. AE, MC, V.

The Days Inn Oceanside is still home to a kosher Chinese restaurant, a throwback to the days when the area was inundated with Brooklyn's elderly Jewish population during the season. The western section of the neighborhood still maintains a religious preference, but visiting tourists, replete with Speedos and thongs, from Argentina to Germany have replaced the yarmulke-and-caftan crowd hands down. One of the most economical choices for travelers, this hotel has been refurbished in splashy pastels and bright lavenders that hearken to its sister property farther south. Waterskiing, parasailing, and scuba diving are available nearby, check with the front desk. Guests have access to a laundry room, and there is fax and copier service as well. Big plus—pets are allowed (deposit required).

Shorehaven Hotel. 8505 Harding Ave. (1 block west of Collins Ave.), Miami Beach, FL 33141. ☎ **888/775-0346** or 305/867-1906. Fax 305/867-1716. E-mail: Infor@shorehaven.com. 15 units. A/C TV TEL. Winter $89–$129 1 to 3 people. Off-season $69–$79 1 to 3 people. Additional person $10 extra. AE, DISC, MC, V. Free street parking.

Located in up-and-coming North Beach, this funky one-story motel was thoroughly made over with style and charm by Sabrina and Scott Barnett. She is a former model who has graced the pages of major magazines, and he is a developer. The large rooms, outfitted in bright tropical prints, offer full kitchens and spacious bathrooms. Each has its own theme, like the Lemon Twist room, which has huge murals of bright yellow lemons on the walls and wood floors painted a glossy royal blue. Other rooms have romantic canopies of mosquito netting or other creative touches. There's also a holistic day spa providing aromatherapy, facials, massages, and Reiki treatment. All offer a real bargain just 1 block from the beach and less than a 10-minute drive to the hip and much pricier South Beach.

Suez Oceanfront Resort. 18215 Collins Ave., Sunny Isles Beach, FL 33160. ☎ **800/327-5278** or 305/932-0661. Fax 305/937-0058. www.suezresort.com. 200 units. A/C TEL. Winter $85–$99 double; $101–$118 suite. Off-season $65–$98 double; $83–$100 suite. Kitchenettes $10–$15 extra. AE, DC, MC, V. Free parking.

Guarded by an undersize replica of Egypt's famed Sphinx, the campy Suez offers newly renovated rooms on the beach, where most of the other old hotels have turned condo. Its Sunny Isles location is actually closer to Hallandale in Broward County than to South Beach but the area has got plenty to offer.

The strict orange-and-yellow motif makes the Suez look more like a Las Vegas attraction than anything in ancient Egypt. There are several convenient pluses, however, like a low-priced restaurant, fully equipped kitchenettes in some rooms, a large heated outdoor pool, a kiddie pool, an exercise room with saunas, lighted tennis courts, and a Laundromat. A kitschy but pleasant and inexpensive lounge reminds you that you are indeed in a tropical paradise. For the price, it's a great choice, and you can say you saw the pyramids.

3 Key Biscayne

There are only a couple of hotels here, not counting the superluxurious Grand Bay Resort, currently under construction. All are on the beach, and room rates are uniformly high. If you can afford it, Key Biscayne is a great place to stay. The island is far enough from the mainland to make it feel like a secluded tropical paradise, yet close enough to Downtown to take advantage of everything Miami has to offer.

Silver Sands Beach Resort. 301 Ocean Dr., Key Biscayne, FL 33149. ☎ **305/361-5441.** Fax 305/361-5477. 56 units. A/C TV TEL. Winter $149–$349 oceanfront suite. Off-season $129–$309 oceanfront suite. Additional person $30 extra. Weekly rates available. AE, DC, MC, V. Free parking.

If Key Biscayne is where you want to be and you don't want to pay the prices of the next-door Sonesta, consider this quaint, one-story motel. Everything is crisp and clean, and the pleasant staff will help with anything you may need, including babysitting. But despite the name, it's certainly no resort. Except for the beach and pool, you'll have to leave the premises for almost everything, including food. The well-appointed rooms are very beachy, sporting a tropical motif and simple furnishings; extras include microwaves, refrigerators, and coffeemakers. Oceanfront suites have the added convenience of full kitchens with stoves and pantries. You'll sit poolside with an

Accommodations in Coral Gables, Coconut Grove, Downtown & Key Biscayne

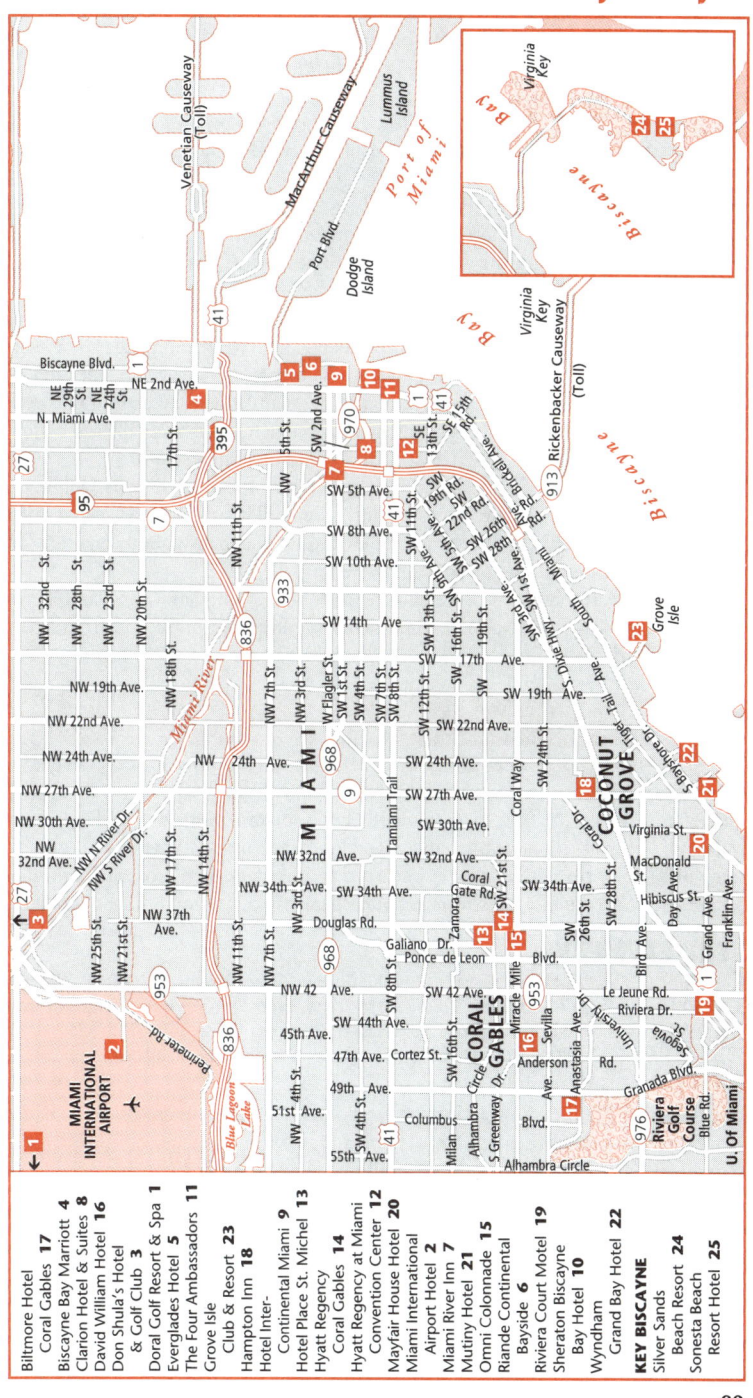

Biltmore Hotel
Coral Gables **17**
Biscayne Bay Marriott **4**
Clarion Hotel & Suites **8**
David William Hotel **16**
Don Shula's Hotel
& Golf Club **3**
Doral Golf Resort & Spa **1**
Everglades Hotel **5**
The Four Ambassadors **11**
Grove Isle
Club & Resort **23**
Hampton Inn **18**
Hotel Inter-
Continental Miami **9**
Hotel Place St. Michel **13**
Hyatt Regency
Coral Gables **14**
Hyatt Regency at Miami
Convention Center **12**
Mayfair House Hotel **20**
Miami International
Airport Hotel **2**
Miami River Inn **7**
Mutiny Hotel **21**
Omni Colonnade **15**
Riande Continental
Bayside **6**
Riviera Court Motel **19**
Sheraton Biscayne
Bay Hotel **10**
Wyndham
Grand Bay Hotel **22**

KEY BISCAYNE
Silver Sands
Beach Resort **24**
Sonesta Beach
Resort Hotel **25**

89

unpretentious set of Latin American families and Europeans who have come for a long and simple vacation—and get it.

Amenities include secretarial services, twice-daily maid service, VCRs in some rooms, medium-sized outdoor pool, beach, kitchenettes, and a coin laundry.

✪ **Sonesta Beach Resort Key Biscayne.** 350 Ocean Dr., Key Biscayne, FL 33149. ☎ **800/SONESTA** or 305/361-2021. Fax 305/361-3096. www.sonesta.com. 300 units. A/C MINIBAR TV TEL. Winter $285–$465 double; $600–$1,650 suite or villa. Off-season $190–$310 double; $525–$1,325 suite or villa. 15% gratuity added to food and beverage bills. Special packages available. AE, CB, DC, DISC, EURO, JCB, MC, V. Valet parking $12.

One of South Florida's most private and luxurious resorts, the Sonesta is an ideal retreat. From the moment the valets, clad in tropical prints, take your car, you'll know you've entered a world of no concern. Each of the 300 rooms has a private balcony or terrace. Sports, from tennis to jet-skiing, are available all around you. Although you may not want to leave the lush grounds, Bill Baggs State Recreation Area and the area's best beaches are right at hand, and if you choose to venture out, you're only about 15 minutes from Miami Beach and even closer to the mainland and Coconut Grove. The vacation homes have fully equipped kitchenettes. The resort is scheduled to complete a $7 million overhaul of its guest rooms by the end of summer 2000.

Dining/Diversions: The hotel has four restaurants, including Purple Dolphin, for "New World" cuisine, and Two Dragons, for Chinese. There's also an excellent seafood restaurant with a terrace, and several lounges and bars. The restaurants regularly draw locals, who have few dining options on "The Key."

Amenities: A full business center, a slate of children's programs, a spa, an Olympic-size pool, access to a beach, and complimentary transportation to and from Miami's shopping districts.

4 Downtown

Most Downtown hotels cater primarily to business travelers, but tourists can get well-located, good-quality accommodations, too. Although business hotels are expensive, quality and service are of a high standard. Look for discounts and packages for the weekend, when offices are closed and rooms often go empty. Downtown is closest to some of Miami's best shopping. Be warned that after dark there's virtually nothing to do outside of the hotels; the streets are often deserted and crime can be a problem.

VERY EXPENSIVE

✪ **Hotel Inter-Continental Miami.** 100 Chopin Plaza, Miami, FL 33131. ☎ **800/327-3005** or 305/577-1000. Fax 305/577-0384. www.interconti.com. 615 units. A/C MINIBAR TV TEL. Winter $229–$289 double; $325–$450 suite. Off-season $149–$259 double; $325–$450 suite. Additional person $20 extra. Weekend and other packages available. AE, CB, DC, DISC, MC, V. Valet parking $12.

If you want to see the most fascinating view of all of Miami Beach, Biscayne Bay, the Miami River and the Atlantic Ocean, book a room with a panoramic view. Trust me, it's worth it. Especially since the $5 million renovation of all its guest rooms and some common areas (further improvements are planned), the Inter-Continental is downtown's swankiest hotel. It boasts more marble than a mausoleum (both inside and out), but it's warmed by colorful, homey touches. The five-story lobby features a marble centerpiece sculpture by Henry Moore and is topped by a pleasing skylight. Plenty of plants, palm trees, and brightly colored wicker chairs also add charm and enliven the otherwise stark space. Perfectly designed for business travelers, each room is outfitted with a desk and Internet-ready telephone lines. Some suites have fully equipped kitchenettes. If the presidential suite isn't booked, ask to see it. Only the likes of Bill Gates could afford to stay there, but you'll be amazed by its sheer opulence.

Dining/Diversions: Three restaurants cover all price ranges and are complemented by two full-service lounges.

Amenities: Concierge, room service, dry cleaning and laundry, newspaper delivery, twice-daily maid service, express checkout, free refreshments in lobby. Olympic-size heated outdoor pool, health spa, sundeck, jogging track, large business center, 15 conference rooms, self-service Laundromat, car-rental desk, travel-agency/tour desk, beauty salon and barbershop, shopping arcade, access to nearby golf course.

EXPENSIVE

Hyatt Regency at Miami Convention Center. 400 S.E. Second Ave., Miami, FL 33131. ☎ **305/358-1234.** Fax 305/374-1728. 612 units. A/C TV. Winter $229–$254 single or double; Off-season $139–$179 single or double. AE, DC, DISC, MC, V. Valet parking $17.

The Hyatt Regency is located just off the Miami River in the heart of downtown Miami. It shares space with the Miami Convention Center, the James L. Knight Convention Center Theater, an exhibition hall, and a 5,000-seat auditorium and concert hall. The University of Miami even holds classes here. This hotel is perfect for large groups or the business traveler on the go. The spacious guest rooms are equipped with data ports, voice mail, in-room safes, hairdryers, and coffeemakers. Most rooms have a balcony with either a view of the city or the bay. No matter what your needs or interests, they will be met by the Hyatt's massive facilities and knowledgeable staff.

Dining: At press time, the hotel's main restaurant, Hamilton's, was closed for renovations. There is room service.

Amenities: Business center with computer stations, printers, word processing services, copying, faxing and express mail; outdoor pool and gym. The People Mover and Metrorail are just blocks away and water taxis are available at the front steps.

MODERATE

Biscayne Bay Marriott. 1633 North Bayshore Drive. Miami, FL 33132. ☎ **305/374-3900.** Fax 305/375-0108. 600 units. A/C TV TEL. Winter $194–$250 single or double. Off-season $124–$204 single or double. AE, DISC, MC, V. Valet parking $15.

Just 7 miles east of the airport, the Biscayne Bay Marriott Hotel and Marina is just minutes from downtown Miami, yet it manages to create a world unto itself of tranquility and entertainment. The 603-room hotel is equipped with a 220-slip full-service marina. Parasailing and Waverunner and jet-ski rentals are available nearby. There's also 24-hour on-site security and valet parking. Each guest room has a mini bar, an iron and ironing board, and a safe. Some rooms face the Bay, and some have balconies. A skywalk connects the hotel with the 85-store Omni Mall (currently undergoing renovations), where the Metrorail can scoot you into downtown, or to Bayside's shopping—all for a quarter!

Diners can choose from the Bayview Grille Restaurant, the Bayview Lounge, the Venetia Lounge, the Coastal Café, or La Playa.

The Four Ambassadors. 801 Brickell Bay Dr., Miami, FL 33131. ☎ **305/371-6500.** Fax 305/789-2900. A/C TV TEL. 180 units. Winter $125–$175. Off-season $110–$150. AE, MC, V. Valet parking.

The Four Ambassadors is one of downtown Miami's best-kept secrets; both apartments and rental condominiums are available, but the rentals are limited to only 130 rooms. The rooms come complete with safety deposit boxes, daily maid service, laundry and dry cleaning, as well as valet parking. Elegant banquet and meeting facilities are also available. With a splendid view of Biscayne Bay and easy access to the banking world of Brickell and beyond, the Four Ambassadors is best known for its two highly acclaimed restaurants: Sushi Siam and Porcão Churrascaria. There are two Olympic-size swimming pools and a Jacuzzi, and a yacht marina is available. An in-house beauty salon, travel agency, grocery store/deli, and dry cleaners are additional amenities, but perhaps their best is the new Lord's Body 2000—the Brickell version of the Kendall gym that has everything from saunas to personal trainers.

○ **Miami River Inn.** 118 SW South River Dr., Miami, FL 33130. ☎ **305/325-0045.** Fax 305/325-9227. A/C TV TEL. E-mail: miamihotels@aol.com. 40 units. Winter $99–$145 double. Off-season $69–$89 double. Rates include continental breakfast. Additional person $15 extra. AE, CB, DC, DISC, MC, V. Free parking.

The Miami River Inn, listed on the National Register of Historic Places, is a quaint, country-style hideaway smack in the middle of downtown Miami. Every room is uniquely furnished with antiques dating from 1908. In one room, you might find a hand-painted bathtub, a Singer sewing machine, and an armoire from the turn of the century restored to perfection. In the foyer you can peruse through a library filled with books about old Miami, with histories of this land's former owners: Julia Tuttle, William Brickell, and Henry Flagler. It's close to public transportation, restaurants, and museums, and only five minutes from the business district. Extras include a small outdoor pool, Jacuzzi, and complimentary coffee and wine in the lobby. Yes, you'll need to obey all the rules of safety in this neighborhood, but for all you get for the price, you really can't beat the tranquillity and coziness of these country cottages.

Riande Continental Bayside. 146 Biscayne Blvd., Miami, FL 33132. ☎ **800/RIANDE-1** or 305/358-4555. Fax 305/371-5253. 250 units. A/C MINIBAR TV TEL. Winter $95–$110 double. Off-season $85–$90 double. Frommer's readers get a 20% discount year-round. AE, DC, MC, V. Parking $8.

Like its sister hotel in South Beach, this Riande caters to a Latin American crowd that descends on Downtown in droves to shop for clothes and electronics. The location is ideal, only steps away from a Bayside shopping center, many great ethnic restaurants, and a Metrorail stop. The reasonable prices and helpful staff are reason enough to consider staying here, if you want to be right in downtown Miami.

○ **Sheraton Biscayne Bay Hotel.** 495 Brickell Ave., Miami, FL 33131. ☎ **800/284-2000** or 305/373-6000. Fax 305/374-2279. www.sheraton.com. 598 units. A/C TV TEL. Winter $199–$209 double; $225–$305 suite. Off-season $149–$175 double; $200–$250 suite. Additional person $10 extra. Senior discounts and weekend and other packages available. AE, CB, DC, DISC, MC, V. Parking $11.

This Downtown hotel's waterfront location is its greatest asset. Nestled between Brickell Park and Biscayne Bay, the Sheraton is set back from the main road and surrounded by a pleasant bay-front walkway. Since a recent $14 million renovation, this Sheraton is especially recommendable. Its identical rooms are well furnished and comfortable. There isn't much to do in the area, but you're within a short drive to anything Miami has to offer.

The Regatta Bar and Grille serves American cuisine and a buffet with made-to-order pastas too. A huge bar has happy hours and occasional live music.

INEXPENSIVE

The Clarion Hotel & Suites. 100 SE 4th St., Miami, FL 33131. ☎ **305/374-5100.** Fax 305/381-9826. A/C TV TEL. 149 units. Year-round $99–$169. AE, DC, DISC, MC, V. Valet parking $15.

This hotel is specially designed for the seasoned business traveler. Its ideal location in downtown Miami (right on the river) makes it perfect for the person who is going to visit either the commercial world of nearby Brickell Avenue, or the legal precincts in downtown. Due to its position adjoining the Hyatt, a Metromover station, and some major parking lots, this hotel does, however, lack a room with a view and might be disheartening to those looking for an idyllic vista. The spacious and elegantly appointed guest rooms and suites offer a complimentary USA Today (weekdays), a speaker phone with voice mail and data port, an ironing board, a hair dryer, and a coffeemaker. The two-room apartment suites are ideal for extended stays. A cocktail lounge is on the premises, and the River View Café serves breakfast, lunch, and dinner. Laundry/valet services are available and there is also a small fitness center.

Everglades Hotel. 244 Biscayne Blvd., Miami, FL 33132. ☎ **800/327-5700** or 305/379-5461. Fax 305/577-8445. www.miamigate.com/everglades. 376 units. A/C TV TEL. Year-round $95 double; $120 suite. Extra person $10. AE, CB, DC, DISC, MC, V. Parking $8.

This hotel has been around almost forever on Downtown's active Biscayne Boulevard. Many traveling business types and Latin American families stay here because of its convenient, safe location, low rates, and many services, which include a bank in the building. It's also one of the only Downtown properties with a pool. The hotel will provide overnight cruise package rates on request. It's near the highways and Metrorail, and there's great shopping across the street at Bayside Marketplace. It may not be the most extravagant choice, but it's definitely one of the least expensive.

5 West Miami/Airport Area

As Miami continues to grow at a rapid pace, expansion has begun westward, where land is plentiful. Several resorts have taken advantage of the space to build world-class tennis and golf courses. While there's no sea to swim in, a plethora of facilities makes up for the lack of an ocean view.

EXPENSIVE

✪ **Doral Golf Resort and Spa.** 4400 NW 87th Ave., Miami, FL 33178. ☎ **800/22-DORAL,** 800/71-DORAL, or 305/592-2000. Fax 305/594-4682. www.doralgolf.com. 623 units (plus an additional 58 suites at the spa). A/C MINIBAR TV TEL. Winter $225–$315 double; $325–$1,280 spa suite. Off-season $95–$275 double; $155–$825 spa suite. Additional person $35 extra. 18% service charge added. Golf and spa packages available. AE, CB, DC, DISC, MC, V. Valet parking $8.50.

The Doral epitomizes the luxury resort in Florida. While the pamperings in the spa attract worldwide attention, the next-door golf resort hosts world-class tournaments and just opened the Great White Course—the Southeast's first desert-scape course, designed by The Shark himself, Greg Norman. The season is usually booked well in advance by those who have been here before or have just read about the fantastic offerings on this 650-acre, fully self-contained resort. There's also a new Blue Lagoon—an adventurous water recreation area featuring two 80,000-gallon pools with cascading waterfalls, a rock facade, and the 125-foot Blue Monster water slide. The hotel is just moments from the Miami airport.

The spacious lobbies and dining areas shimmer with polished marble, mirrors, and gold. The rooms, too, are luxuriously large and tastefully decorated; big windows allow views of the tropical gardens or golf courses below. The resort itself is surrounded by warehouses and office buildings.

The Spa restaurant serves delicious low-fat cuisine, including reduced-calorie desserts. Other options include a cafe with super Italian sandwiches, salads, and pasta. A sports bar at the golf club offers excellent club fare.

Miccosukee Resort and Convention Center. 500 S.W. 177 Ave., Miami, FL 33194 (intersection of SW 8th St. and 177th Ave.). ☎ **877/242-6464** or 305/221-8623. Fax 305/221-8309. 256 units. A/C TV TEL. Winter $99 standard room; $135 suite. $325 presidential year-round. (All rooms sleep 1 to 4 persons.) AE, DC, DISC, V, MC. Free parking.

Located on the edge of the Everglades, the Miccosukee Resort is one of Miami's newest and hottest attractions. The history lesson alone is worth the trip to this resort, located about 30 to 40 minutes west of the airport. The Miccosukee tribe was originally part of the lower Creek Nation and lived in areas now known as Alabama and Georgia. Following the final Seminole War in 1858, the last of the Miccosukees settled in the Everglades. Following the lead set recently by many other American Indian tribes, they built the resort to accumulate gambling revenue. Although many tourists go out to the resort solely to gamble, the resort also has expansive meeting and banquet facilities, spa services, great children's programs, entertainment, and excursions to the Florida Everglades. Guest rooms come equipped with all the usual amenities, plus a hair dryer, robes, slippers, and an in-room safe. The rooms are elegantly designed with custom-made furniture, created especially for the resort.

Dining: Empeeke Aaweeke, Empeeke Aya, and the Empeek Cheke offer everything from sandwiches and burgers to Native American delicacies such as venison, frog legs, boar, buffalo, snook, and Indian fry bread. Empeeke Cheke also offers an extensive wine list, after-dinner drinks, and cigars.

Amenities: Some suites have a whirlpool and wet bars. 24-hour room service, dry cleaning, laundry service, and shoe shine.

MODERATE

Don Shula's Hotel and Golf Club. Main St., Miami Lakes, FL 33014. ☎ **800/24-SHULA** or 305/821-1150. Fax 305/820-8190. 330 units. A/C TV TEL. Winter from $129–$289 suite. Off-season $99–$209 suite. Additional person $10 extra. Business packages available. AE, DC, MC, V.

Guests come to Shula's mostly for the golf, but there's plenty here to keep nongolfers busy, too. Opened in 1992 to much fanfare from the sports and business community, Shula's resort is an all-encompassing oasis in the middle of a highly planned residential neighborhood, complete with a Main Street and nearby shopping facilities—a good thing, since the site is more than a 20-minute drive on the highways from anything. The guest rooms, located in the main building or surrounding the golf course, are plain but pretty, and come with VCRs (on request).

The award-winning Shula's Steak House and the more casual Steak House Two rank in the top 10 nationwide. They serve huge Angus beef steaks and seafood. Another restaurant on the premises serves natural food.

Miami International Airport Hotel. P.O. Box 997510, NW 20th St. and LeJeune Rd., Airport Terminal Concourse E., Miami, FL 33299-7510. ☎ **800/327-1276** or 305/871-4100. Fax 305/871-0800. www.miahotel.com. 260 units. A/C TV TEL. Winter $149–$199 double; $275–$650 suite. Off-season $130–$175 double; $250–$270 suite. Additional person $10 extra. AE, CB, DC, EURO, JCB, MC, V. Parking $10.

If you need to be at the airport and want excellent service, this is your best bet. I don't know of a nicer airport hotel, and you can't beat the convenience—it's actually in the airport at Concourse E. You'll find every amenity of a first-class tourist hotel here, including a large rooftop pool, health club, Jacuzzi, sauna, sundeck, racquetball courts, jogging track, small business center, conference room, beauty salon, tour desk, boutiques, and several cocktail lounges and restaurants. The rooms are modern, clean, and spacious, with industrial-grade carpeting. The furnishings are nondescript but tasteful. You might think you'd be deafened by the roar of the planes, but all of the rooms have been soundproofed and actually allow very little noise. In addition, the hotel has modern security systems and is extremely safe. The restaurants are decent, but many of Miami's best are just a short cab drive away.

BARGAIN CHAINS

If you must stay near the airport, consider any of the dozens of moderately priced chain hotels. You'll find one of the cheapest and most recommendable options at either of the **Days Inn** at 7250 NW 11th St. or 4767 NW 36th St. (☎ 800/329-7466 or 305/888-3661), each about 2 miles from the airport. Rates range from $47 to $69.

The larger property on 36th Street offers slightly cheaper rates with singles starting as low as $49. The 11th Street locale may charge more for weekends, but prices usually start at $70. Prices include free transportation from the airport.

A more luxurious option is the **Wyndham** at 3900 NW 21st St. (☎ 800/933-1100) with rates from $100 to $225. There's also another location in downtown Miami at 1601 Biscayne Blvd,(☎ **800/WYNDHAM** or 305/374-0000). Rates there run from a high of $238 in season to $158 during the summer.

6 North Dade

✪ **Turnberry Isle Resort and Club.** 19999 W. Country Club Dr., Aventura, FL 33180. ☎ **800/223-6800** or 305/936-2929. Fax 305/933-6550. www.turnberryisle.com. 395 units. A/C MINIBAR TV TEL. Winter $395–$3,500 resort room or suite. Off-season $175–$3,500 resort room or suite. $175–$495 yacht club room or suite year-round. AE, DC, DISC, MC, V. Valet parking $10; free self-parking.

A top-rated resort, this gorgeous 300-acre compound has every possible facility for active guests, particularly golfers. You'll pay a lot to stay here—but it's worth it. The main attractions are two newly renovated Trent Jones courses, available only to members and guests of the hotel. A new seven-story Jasmine wing looks like a Mediterranean-style village surrounded by tropical gardens that are joined by covered marble walkways to the other wings. While there, treat yourself to a "Turnberry Retreat" at the Turnberry Spa, which has been renovated to the tune of $10 million. The spa consists of three levels of deluxe pampering and includes aerobics and fitness classes, stress reductions, massage therapy, and a juice bar designed for complete rejuvenation. Impeccable service from check-in to checkout brings loyal fans back to this resort for more. The North Miami Beach location means you'll find excellent shopping and some of the best dining in Miami right in the neighborhood.

Unless you're into boating, the higher-priced resort rooms are where you'll want to stay; you'll be steps from the spa facilities and the renowned Veranda restaurant. The well-proportioned rooms are gorgeously tiled to match the Mediterranean-style architecture. The bathrooms even have a color TV mounted within reach of the whirlpool bathtubs.

There are six restaurants, including the Veranda, which serves healthful and tropical New World cuisine in an elegant dining room. The resort's numerous bars and lounges, including a popular disco also have enough entertainment and local flavor to keep anyone busy for weeks.

7 Coral Gables

Coconut Grove eases into Coral Gables, which extends north toward Miami International Airport. "The Gables," as it's affectionately known, was one of Miami's original planned communities and is still among the city's prettiest neighborhoods. It's close to the shops along the Miracle Mile and the University of Miami.

If you're looking for luxury, Coral Gables has a number of wonderful hotels, but if you're on a tight budget, you may be better off elsewhere. Two popular and well-priced chain hotels in the area are a **Holiday Inn** (☎ **800/327-5476** or 305/667-5611), at 1350 S. Dixie Hwy, with rates between $75 and $125, and a **Howard Johnson** (☎ **800/446-4656** or 305/665-7501) at 1430 S. Dixie Hwy. Rates range from $65 to $95. Both are located directly across the street from the University of Miami and are popular with families and friends of students.

VERY EXPENSIVE

✪ **Biltmore Hotel.** 1200 Anastasia Ave., Coral Gables, FL 33134. ☎ **800/727-1926**, 305/445-1926, or Westin at 800/228-3000. Fax 305/442-9496. www.biltmorehotel.com. 275 units. A/C TV TEL. Winter from $319–$489. Off-season from $259–$409. Additional person $20 extra. Special packages available. AE, CB, DC, DISC, MC, V. Valet parking $9.

The Biltmore, which was built in 1926, is the oldest Coral Gables hotel and a National Historical Landmark—one of only two operating hotels in Florida to receive the designation. It's also one of the only four-star rated hotels in the area. Always a popular destination for golfers, including President Clinton, the Biltmore is situated on a lush rolling 18-hole course that is as challenging as it is beautiful. The hotel is surrounded by a pretty residential area, 5 minutes from the airport and excellent dining and shopping selections, and about 20 minutes from Miami Beach. It is a wonderful option for those seeking a luxurious getaway in a quiet setting. I especially recommend a visit to the huge, beautiful spa.

Now under the management of the Westin Hotel group, the hotel boasts large rooms decorated with tasteful period reproductions and some high-tech amenities. The enormous lobby, with its 45-foot ceilings, serves as an entry point for hundreds of weddings and business meetings each year. Rising above the Spanish-style estate is a majestic 300-foot copper-clad tower, modeled after the Giralda bell tower in Seville and visible throughout the city. Over the years, the Biltmore has passed through many incarnations (for example, it was used as a VA hospital after World War II), but is now back to its original 1926 splendor.

Dining/Diversions: An elegant European restaurant serves excellent French/Italian cuisine nightly and champagne brunch on Sunday. An impressive wine cellar and cigar room are popular with local connoisseurs. The more casual Courtyard Café and Poolside Grille both serve three meals daily. There's also a lounge and piano bar where drinks are accompanied by live music nightly.

Amenities: Concierge, room service (24 hours), laundry and dry cleaning, newspaper delivery, nightly turndown on request, twice-daily maid service, baby-sitting, secretarial services, express checkout. Kitchenettes in tower suite, VCR and video rentals, 21,000-square-foot swimming pool surrounded by arched walkways and classical sculptures, state-of-the-art health club, full-service spa, sauna, 18-hole golf course, elaborate business center, conference rooms, car rental through concierge, sundeck, 10 lighted tennis courts, beauty salon, boutiques.

Hyatt Regency Coral Gables. 50 Alhambra Plaza, Coral Gables, FL 33134. ☎ **800/233-1234** or 305/441-1234. Fax 305/441-0520. www.hyatt.com. 242 units. A/C MINIBAR

TV TEL. Winter $224–$1,800 suite. Off-season from $164–$1,800 suite. Additional person $25 extra. Packages and senior discounts available. AE, CB, DC, DISC, MC, V. Valet parking $10; self-parking $9.

High on style, comfort, and price, this Hyatt is part of Coral Gables' Alhambra, an office-hotel complex with a Mediterranean motif. The building itself is gorgeous, designed with pink stone, arched entrances, grand courtyards, and tile roofs. Inside you'll find overstuffed chairs on marble floors, surrounded by opulent antiques and chandeliers. The large guest rooms feature in-room safes, coffeemakers, hair dryers, bathrobes, irons and ironing boards, 2-line telephones, and voice mail. A few rooms have balconies. The hotel opened in 1987, but like many historical buildings in the neighborhood, the Alhambra attempts to mimic something much older and much farther away.

Dining/Diversions: A good New-World cuisine restaurant serves a varied menu with many local specialties.

Amenities: Full concierge services, room service (6am to midnight), same-day laundry and dry-cleaning services, newspaper delivery, nightly turndown on request, in-room massage, baby-sitting arrangements available, secretarial services, express checkout, valet parking. Large outdoor heated pool, health club with Nautilus equipment, Jacuzzi, two saunas, nearby golf course, basic business center, conference rooms, small gift shop.

EXPENSIVE

✪ **David William Hotel.** 700 Biltmore Way, Coral Gables, Fl 33134. ☎ **800/757-8073** or 305/445-7821. 116 units. A/C TV TEL. Winter $139–$319 one bedroom; $339–$439 two bedroom. Off-season $129–$249 one bedroom; $319–$389 two bedroom. AE, DISC, MC, V.

This "sister" hotel to the Biltmore shares many of the same amenities without the Biltmore's price. You can even take a shuttle to the Biltmore to play a round of golf, enjoy the health club and spa, play tennis or take a dip in the pool. The David William is truly a home away from home. The luxurious one- and two-bedroom suites are extremely spacious and all have eat-in kitchens for extended stays. If you plan to bring the kids, you won't be screaming for space, there's plenty of room for everyone. If you really want a time-out from the kids, go up to the roof and have a drink by the pool, there's a spectacular view of Miami. The hotel also caters to business travelers and is located just a few blocks away from the commerce district. It's directly across the street from the Granada Golf Course, less than 5 miles away from the airport and only 20 minutes to Miami Beach. If you want luxury without the price, this is your best alternative in the Gables.

Dining: Donna's Bistro & Bar is truly a hidden jewel. Executive chef, Donna Wynter was the Chef de Cuisine at the Biltmore Hotel and has worked as a chef in New York at Tavern on the Green and Toscana Ristorante. Wynter infuses various flavors from the Caribbean (especially her native country of Jamaica), Asia, France, Italy, Japan, and Thailand in her dishes. Her signature dish is the Jamaican jerk chicken with potato timbale, which she has perfected.

Amenities: Executive rooms equipped with refrigerators, microwaves, coffeemakers, and toaster ovens. Fully-stocked refrigerator and minibar; bookstore; coffee shop and lounge; gourmet market and sundry shop; rooftop pool and sundeck. Four meeting rooms and catering facilities. Billing privileges when making purchases at the Biltmore and a free shuttle service between hotels.

✪ **Hotel Place St. Michel.** 162 Alcazar Ave., Coral Gables, FL 33134. ☎ **800/848-HOTEL** or 305/444-1666. Fax 305/529-0074. www.hotelplacestmichel.com. 27 units. A/C TV TEL. Winter $165 double; $200 suite. Off-season $125 double; $160 suite. Additional person $10 extra. Rates include continental breakfast. AE, DC, MC, V. Self-parking $7.

This unusual little hotel in the heart of Coral Gables is one of the city's most romantic options. The accommodations and hospitality are straight out of Old-World Europe, complete with dark wood-paneled walls, cozy beds, beautiful antiques, and a quiet elegance that seems startlingly out of place in trendy Miami. Everything here is charming—from the parquet floors to the paddle fans. One-of-a-kind furnishings make each room special. Guests are treated to fresh fruit baskets upon arrival and enjoy every imaginable service throughout their stay.

Dining/Diversions: The Restaurant St. Michel is a very romantic and elegant dining choice. A lounge and deli complete the hotel options.

Amenities: Concierge, room service, laundry and dry cleaning, newspaper delivery, evening turndown, in-room massage, twice-daily maid service, complimentary continental breakfast.

The Omni Colonnade Hotel. 180 Aragon Ave. (at Ponce de León and Miracle Mile), Coral Gables, FL 33134. ☎ **800/THE-OMNI** or 305/441-2600. Fax 305/445-3929. 157 units. A/C MINIBAR TV TEL. Winter $215–$289 double; $405 suite. Off-season $165–$265 double; $365 suite. Packages available. AE, CB, DC, DISC, MC, V. Valet parking $10.

The Colonnade occupies part of a large historic building, originally built by Coral Gables's founder George Merrick in 1926. Faithful to its original style, the hotel is a successful amalgam of new and old, with an emphasis on modern conveniences. The structure stands 14 elegant stories high, although guest rooms occupy only four floors. It's popular with business travelers.

The oversized rooms are worthy of the hotel's rates. They feature sitting areas, historic photographs, marble counters, gold-finished faucets, and solid wood furnishings. Thoughtful extras include complimentary shoe shines and champagne upon arrival.

Dining/Diversions: Doc Dammers Saloon and restaurant offers a good happy hour for the 30-something crowd. There's live entertainment on weekends.

Amenities: 24-hour concierge and room service, same-day laundry and dry-cleaning service, newspaper delivery, evening turndown on request, in-room massage, twice-daily maid service on request, baby-sitting, express checkout, valet parking, free morning coffee and tea in the lobby. Heated outdoor pool on rooftop, small modern rooftop fitness center, Jacuzzi, sundeck, large conference centers and meeting rooms, Laundromat, car-rental and tour desks, gift shop and shopping arcade.

INEXPENSIVE

Riviera Court Motel. 5100 Riviera Dr. (on U.S. 1), Coral Gables, FL 33146. ☎ **800/368-8602** or 305/665-3528. 30 units. A/C TV TEL. Winter from $70 double; $82 efficiencies. Off-season from $61 double; $73 efficiencies. 10% discount for seniors and AAA members. AE, CB, DC, DISC, MC, V.

Besides the Holiday Inn down the road, this family-owned motel is the best discount option in the area. The comfortable and clean two-story property, dating from 1954, has a small pool and is set back from the road, so that the rooms are all relatively quiet. Vending machines are the only choice for refreshments, but guests are near many great dining spots. You can also choose to stay in one of the efficiencies, which all have fully stocked kitchens.

8 Coconut Grove

This intimate enclave hugs the shores of Biscayne Bay, just south of U.S. 1 and about 10 minutes from the beaches. The Grove is a great place to stay, offering ample nightlife, excellent restaurants, and beautiful surroundings, and the hotel rates are reflective of the high style of living found here.

VERY EXPENSIVE

✪ **Grove Isle Club and Resort.** Four Grove Isle Dr., Coconut Grove, FL 33133. ☎ **800/88-GROVE** or 305/858-8300. Fax 305/854-6702. 49 units. A/C TV TEL. Winter $350–$495 suite. Off-season $295–$475 suite. Rates include breakfast. Additional person $20 extra. AE, DC, MC, V. Free valet parking.

Hidden away in the bougainvillea and lushness of the Grove, the Grove Isle Resort is definitely one of the best places to stay in Miami. Its location is stunning. From the lobby and many rooms, guests look out onto glimmering Biscayne Bay, where sailboats drift lazily about and dolphins sometimes leap circles in the clear blue water. You'd almost think the property is on an island; actually, it's only a few minutes from Coconut Grove's business district.

Grove Isle feels like a country club. Everyone dresses in white and pastels, and if they're not on their way to a set of tennis, they're not in a rush to get anywhere. You'll step into rooms that are elegantly furnished with mosquito-netted canopy beds and a patio overlooking the bay. You'll need to reserve early here—rooms go very fast.

Dining: Baleen's, an elegant continental restaurant, serves fresh seafood and other regional specialties. With its white drapes and intimate setting, it's one of the most romantic restaurants in Miami. For dessert, try the dessert sampler. You won't find a more delicious crème brûlée with flavors like raspberry, mango, and chocolate, just to name a few.

Amenities: Concierge service, room service (6:30am to 10pm), laundry and dry-cleaning services, newspaper delivery, nightly turndown, in-room massage, twice-daily maid service, baby-sitting, secretarial services, express checkout, valet parking, free coffee in the lobby. VCRs, movie channels, video rental delivered to room ($5), large heated outdoor pool, deluxe fitness facilities, 12 outdoor tennis courts, water-sports equipment rental available, jogging track, nature trails, conference rooms, beauty salon.

Mayfair House Hotel. 3000 Florida Ave., Coconut Grove, FL 33133. ☎ **800/433-4555** or 305/441-0000. Fax 305/441-1647. www.hotelbook.com/live/welcome. 179 units. A/C MINI-BAR TV TEL. Winter $249–$800. Off-season $169–$800. Packages available. AE, DC, DISC, MC, V. Valet parking $15; self-parking $6.

If you want to be in the Grove, this hotel is a great choice. Though very expensive and more than 20 minutes from the beach—it is situated inside the posh Mayfair Shops complex—the all-suite Mayfair House is about as centrally located as you can get. Each guest unit has been individually designed and was renovated in 1998. All have terraces and are extremely comfortable. Some suites are downright opulent and include a private, outdoor, Japanese-style hot tub. The top-floor terraces offer good views, and all are hidden from the street by leaves and latticework. Since the lobby is in a shopping mall, recreation is confined to the roof, where you'll find a small pool, sauna, and snack bar.

Dining/Diversions: The Mayfair Grill serves a varied menu with particularly good steaks and seafood. There's also a rooftop snack bar for poolside snacks and a private nightclub open late.

Amenities: Concierge and room service (24 hours), dry cleaning, newspaper delivery, nightly turndown, twice-daily maid service, secretarial services, express checkout. VCRs and video rentals, outdoor pool, access to nearby health club, Jacuzzi, elaborate business center, conference rooms.

Mutiny Hotel. 2951 South Bayshore Dr., Coconut Grove, FL 33133. ☎ **888/868-8469** or 305/441-2100. Fax 305/441-2822. 120 suites. A/C TV TEL. Winter $249–$799 one- and two-bedroom suite. Off-season $199–$599 one- and two-bedroom suite. $799–$1,799 one- and two-bedroom penthouse year-round. AE, DC, DISC, MC, V. Valet parking $16.

In the center of the Grove, docked along the marina, lies this simply elegant hotel. The newly converted condos promise to be the best-kept secret in the Grove. The suites' soft drapes, comfortable mattresses, and regal Old-English furnishings are charming. Each suite comes with a full kitchen, complete with china and complimentary coffee, and has all the usual amenities associated with this class of hotel. The Mutiny is just a few blocks away from CocoWalk and the shops at MayFair.

Dining: The Pirates Bar and Grill serves great salads, hot and cold sandwiches, gourmet pizzas, and desserts. Pirates also has a full bar and an extensive wine list. Breakfast, lunch, and dinner are served daily and room service is available from 7am to midnight.

Wyndham Grand Bay Hotel. 2669 S. Bayshore Dr., Coconut Grove, FL 33133. ☎ **800/ 996-3426** or 305/858-9600. Fax 305/859-2026. www.grandbay.com. 178 units. A/C MINI-BAR TV TEL. Winter $365–$1,525. Off-season $285–$1,525 suite. Additional person $20 extra. Packages available. AE, CB, DC, MC, V. Valet parking $13.

The Grand Bay opened in 1983 and immediately won praise as one of the most elegant hotels in the world. This stunning pyramid-shaped hotel—which Wyndham acquired in February 2000 and was upgrading at press time—is a masterpiece both inside and out. The rooms are luxurious, each featuring high-quality linens, comfortable overstuffed love seats and chairs, a large writing desk, and all the amenities you'd expect in deluxe accommodations, including VCRs and video rentals. It has recently added ironing boards, irons, and voice mail to all the rooms as well. Original art and armfuls of fresh flowers are generously displayed throughout.

The Grand Bay consistently attracts wealthy, high-profile people, and it basks in its image as a rendezvous for royalty, socialites, and superstars. Guests come here to be pampered and to see and be seen.

Dining/Diversions: Opened in late 1998, the hotel's main restaurant, Bice (pronounced *Bee*-chey), serves classic northern Italian cuisine in an elegant setting. Drinks are served in the Ciga Bar, and the Lobby Lounge offers a traditional afternoon tea.

Amenities: Concierge, room service (24 hours), same-day laundry and dry cleaning, newspaper delivery, evening turndown, masseuse on call, twice-daily maid service, baby-sitting, secretarial services, express checkout, courtesy limousine service to Cocowalk, free refreshments in the lobby. Heated indoor pool, small health club, access to nearby health club, Jacuzzi, sauna, VCR and video rentals, sundeck, watersports equipment rental, bicycle rental, business center, conference rooms, car-rental and activities desks, beauty salon, gift shop, nearby golf course.

MODERATE

Hampton Inn. 2800 SW 28th Terrace (at U.S. 1 and SW 27th Ave.), Coconut Grove, FL 33133. ☎ **888/287-3390** or 305/448-2800. Fax 305/442-8655. www.Hampton-inn.com. 137 units. A/C TV TEL. Winter $134–$154 double. Off-season $104–$124 double. Rates include continental breakfast buffet. AE, CB, DC, DISC, MC, V. Free parking and free local calls.

This very standard chain hotel is a welcome reprieve in an area otherwise known for having only very pricey accommodations. The rooms are nothing exciting, but the freebies, like local phone calls, parking, in-room movies, breakfast buffet, and hot drinks around the clock make this a real steal. Although there is no restaurant or bar, it is close to lots of both—only about half a mile to the heart of the Grove's shopping and retail area and about as far from Coral Gables. Rooms are brand new and have large televisions, voice mail phones, and refrigerators and microwaves upon request. A workout room, large outdoor pool, and Jacuzzi are added bonuses in this generic but recommendable hotel.

Miami Dining 6

Few things bring as much pleasure to Florida visitors as exploring and enjoying the city's cavalcade of culinary delights. We excel when it comes to food; in fact our world-renowned chefs have fused Californian-Asian with Caribbean and Latin elements to create a world-class flavor all its own: *Floribbean*. So break out the mango chutneys over fresh swordfish and spill the sushi sauce alongside the Peruvian seviche—it's eating time in the magic city!

It should come as no surprise that a population that spends so much of its time outdoors not only looks good, they eat well too. The carnivorous among you, however, will not go hungry. We do have sumptuous steak houses, from Morton's downtown to Ruth's Chris in the Gables; and who could ignore the heavenly feasts served up at Tuscan on the Beach?

Nevertheless, a visit to the "New World" of Miami will evoke plentiful meals that are actually good for you too! Exotic vegetarian dishes and healthy fruit platters comprise ample parts of many restaurant's menus when dining in this tropical citadel.

In addition to enjoying the world-class chefs who now call Miami home, we also enjoy the fruits of our own food university: Johnson & Wales College in North Miami. And many of our premier restaurants also take advantage of being able to reap what we sow in our own back yard; there are so many fruits and vegetables raised locally (in western Miami-Dade and Broward, large citrus and vegetable plantations abound) that the "u-pick-it" season becomes a carnival.

Of course sitting pretty on America's Gold Coast, we can't talk about food if we can't talk about the fish! Try Cuban-styled *camarones* in salsa (that's jumbo shrimp for those in the know), a seared tuna steak at one of our fine American bistros, or Spanish paella—a mix of mussels, meats, and shrimp in a food mélange that takes jambalaya to task! Other South Florida specialties include Jamaican jerk sea bass, conch, swordfish, continental mahimahi, deli-style lox, and of course our crowning jewel: the stone crab (which, with a little bit of effort, you don't have to loose an arm over to sample). This is the tropics, so don't just slather that fish in butter, puree it in coconut oil or slap on some fresh key lime juice—even Gilligan never had it so good.

Miami is all grown up now and ready to share its cooking expertise with the rest of the world. Asian cuisine and Pacific Rim fare have all blended in quite well with the local Caribbean mix and have created

Miami Dining

food fusions that will make Miami a dining capital for years to come. So when you plan to visit South Florida, bring a healthy appetite.

Many restaurants keep extended hours in season (roughly December to April), and may close for lunch and/or dinner on Monday, when the traffic is slower. Always call ahead, since schedules do change. If you want to picnic on the beach or pick up some dessert, check out the gourmet food shops, green markets, and bakeries listed in chapter 8.

1 Restaurants by Cuisine

AMERICAN
Biscayne Miracle Mile Cafeteria (Coral Gables, *I*)
Blue Door (South Beach, *VE*)
Christy's (Coral Gables, *VE*)
Curry's (Miami Beach, *I*)
The Forge Restaurant (Miami Beach, *VE*)
The Front Porch (Miami Beach, *I*)
Gables Diner (Coral Gables, *M*)
Granny Feelgood's (Downtown, *I*)
Here Comes the Sun (North Dade, *I*)
Joe Allen's (South Beach, *M*)
Kaleidoscope (Coconut Grove, *M*)
Lou's Philly Cheesesteak (South Beach, *I*)
News Café (South Beach, *I*)
News Café in the Grove (Coconut Grove, *I*)
Nexxt Café (South Beach, *M*)
Ruth Chris (Coral Gables, *E*)
S&S Restaurant (Downtown, *I*)
Sergio's (Coral Gables, *I*)
Sheldon's Drugs (Miami Beach, *I*)
Shula's Steak House (Miami Beach, *E*)
Soyka (Miami, *M*)
Sundays on the Bay (Key Biscayne, *E*)
Wilderness Grill (South Dade *M*)
Van Dyke Cafe (South Beach, *I*)

ASIAN
Bambu (South Beach, *VE*)
Emerald Coast (Sunny Isles, *I*)
NOA (Noodles of Asia) (South Beach, *M*)
Pacific Time (South Beach, *VE*)

BARBECUE
Shorty's (South Miami, *I*)

BISTRO
Jeffrey's (South Beach, *M*)

CANTONESE
The Red Lantern (Coconut Grove, *M*)

COLOMBIAN
El Habito (Miami Beach, *M*)
Mama Vieja (South Beach, *M*)

CONTINENTAL
Aura (South Beach, *E*)
Cafe Hammock (South Miami, *M*)
Cheeky Monkey (South Beach, *E*)
Crystal Café (Miami Beach, *E*)
Green Street Cafe (Coconut Grove, *M*)
Indigo Lounge (Downtown, *M*)
Jeffrey's (South Beach, *M*)
The Lagoon (North Dade, *M*)
The Palm (Miami Beach, *E*)
Rusty Pelican (Key Biscayne, *E*)
Strand Restaurant (South Beach, *E*)

CREPES
The Crepe Maker Cafe (South Miami, *I*)

CUBAN/LATIN FARE
Casa Salsa (South Beach, *E*)
Conga Room (Downtown, *I*)
Gaucho Room (South Beach, *VE*)
La Carreta (Little Havana, *I*)
La Cibeles Cafe (Downtown, *I*)

Key to Abbreviations: *VE* = Very Expensive; *E* = Expensive; *M* = Moderate; *I* = Inexpensive

La Esquina de Tejas
(Little Havana, *I*)
Larios on the Beach
(South Beach, *M*)
Macarena (South Beach, *M*)
Mayya (South Beach, *VE*)
The Oasis (Key Biscayne, *I*)
Pollo Tropical (South Miami, *I*)
Puerto Sagua (South Beach, *I*)
Sergio's (Coral Gables, *I*)
Versailles (Little Havana, *I*)
Yuca (South Beach, *VE*)

DELI

Bagel Factory (South Beach, *I*)
Stephan's Gourmet Market & Cafe
(South Beach, *I*)
Wolfie Cohen's Rascal House
(Miami Beach, *M*)

DINER FARE

S&S Restaurant (Downtown, *I*)

ENGLISH TEA

The Tea Room (South Miami, *I*)

FAST FOOD

Mrs. Mendoza's Tacos al Carbon
(South Beach, *I*)
Pollo Tropical (South Miami, *I*)
Raja's (Downtown, *I*)

FONDUE

The Melting Pot (North Dade, *M*)

FRENCH

BED (South Beach, *VE*)
Brasserie Les Halles
(Coral Gables, *M*)
Café des Artes (South Beach, *I*)
The Crepe Maker Cafe
(South Miami, *I*)
The Gourmet Diner
(North Dade, *M*)
La Boulangerie (Key Biscayne, *I*)
La Fontaine (Coconut Grove, *M*)
La Sandwicherie (South Beach, *I*)
Le Bouchondu (Coconut Grove, *E*)
Le Festival (Coral Gables, *E*)
L'Entrecote de Paris
(South Beach, *M*)
Lemon Twist (Miami Beach, *M*)

Provence Grill (Downtown, *M*)
Tantra (South Beach, *VE*)

GREEK

The Daily Bread Marketplace
(Coral Gables, *I*)
The Greek Place (Miami Beach, *I*)

HAITIAN

Tap Tap (South Beach, *M*)

HEALTH FOOD

Amos' Juice Bar (North Dade, *I*)
Granny Feelgood's (Downtown, *I*)
Here Comes the Sun
(North Dade, *I*)

INDIAN

House of India (Coral Gables, *I*)
Raja's (Downtown, *I*)

INTERNATIONAL

Balans (South Beach, *M*)
Cafe Tu Tu Tango
(Coconut Grove, *I*)
The Globe (Coral Gables, *M*)
John Martin's (Coral Gables, *M*)

ITALIAN

Anacapri (South Miami, *M*)
Bice (Coconut Grove, *E*)
Bocca di Rosa (Coconut Grove, *E*)
Cafe Prima Pasta (Miami Beach, *M*)
Cafe Ragazzi (Miami Beach, *M*)
Café Tabac (South Beach, *VE*)
Caffe Abbracci (Coral Gables, *E*)
Caffe Da Vinci (Bal Harbour, *M*)
Carpaccio (Miami Beach, *E*)
Coco Pazzo (South Miami, *E*)
Escopazzo (South Beach, *VE*)
Franz & Joseph (Coconut Grove, *M*)
Joia (South Beach, *VE*)
Laurenzo's Cafe (North Dade, *I*)
Macaluso's (South Beach, *M*)
Miami Beach Place (Miami Beach, *I*)
Oggi Caffe (Miami Beach, *M*)
Osteria del Teatro (South Beach, *VE*)
Perricone's Marketplace
(Downtown, *I*)
Pauloluigi's (Coconut Grove, *M*)
Rosinella
(South Beach and Downtown, *M*)

Sport Cafe (South Beach, *I*)
Stefano's (Key Biscayne, *E*)
Stephan's Gourmet Market & Cafe (South Beach, *I*)
Tuscan Steak (South Beach, *VE*)
Wish (South Beach, *E*)

JAMAICAN
Caribbean Delite (Downtown, *I*)
Norma's (South Beach, *E*)
Ortanique (Coral Gables, *M*)

JAPANESE
Toni's (South Beach, *M*)

MEXICAN
Mrs. Mendoza's Tacos al Carbon (South Beach, *I*)
Mayya (South Beach, *VE*)
Señor Frogs (Coconut Grove, *M*)

NEW WORLD CUISINE
Astor Place in the Astor Hotel (South Beach, *VE*)
Blue Door (South Beach, *VE*)
Chef Allen's (North Dade, *VE*)
Crystal Café (Miami Beach, *E*)
Nemo's (South Beach, *E*)
Norman's (Coral Gables, *VE*)
Ortanique (Coral Gables, *M*)
Pacific Time (South Beach, *VE*)

PIZZA
Miami Beach Place (Miami Beach, *I*)

SEAFOOD
Bayside Seafood Restaurant and Hidden Cove Bar (Key Biscayne, *I*)

Café Tabac (South Beach, *VE*)
East Coast Fisheries (Downtown, *M*)
Fishbone Grille (Downtown, *M*)
Grillfish (South Beach, *M*)
Joe's Stone Crab Restaurant (South Beach, *VE*)
The Lagoon (North Dade, *M*)
Monty's Stone Crab/Seafood House (South Beach, *E*)

SPANISH
Cafe Tu Tu Tango (Coconut Grove, *I*)
Casa Juancho (Little Havana, *M*)
Gaucho Room (South Beach, *VE*)
Macarena (South Beach, *M*)
Puerto Sagua (South Beach, *I*)

STEAK HOUSE
Ruth Chris (Coral Gables, *E*)
Shula's Steak House (Miami Beach, *VE*)
Smith & Wollensky (South Beach, *VE*)
Tuscan Steak (South Beach, *E*)

SUSHI
Toni's (South Beach, *M*)

SZECHUAN/PEKINESE
Chrysanthemum (South Beach, *M*)

VIETNAMESE
Hy-Vong (Little Havana, *I*)

WRAPS
Wrapido (South Miami, *I*)

2 South Beach

The renaissance of South Beach has spawned dozens of first-rate restaurants. In fact, big names from across the country have decided to capitalize on South Beach's international appeal and have begun to open branches here with great success. A few old standbys remain from the *Miami Vice* days, but the flock of newcomers dominates the scene, with places going in and out of style as quickly as the tides. The listings below represent the restaurants that have (or should have) quickly gained national attention.

The Lincoln Road area is packed with places offering good food and great atmosphere. Since it's impossible to list them all, I recommend strolling and browsing. Most restaurants post a copy of their menu outside, and staff members are happy to chat with curious passersby.

South Beach Dining

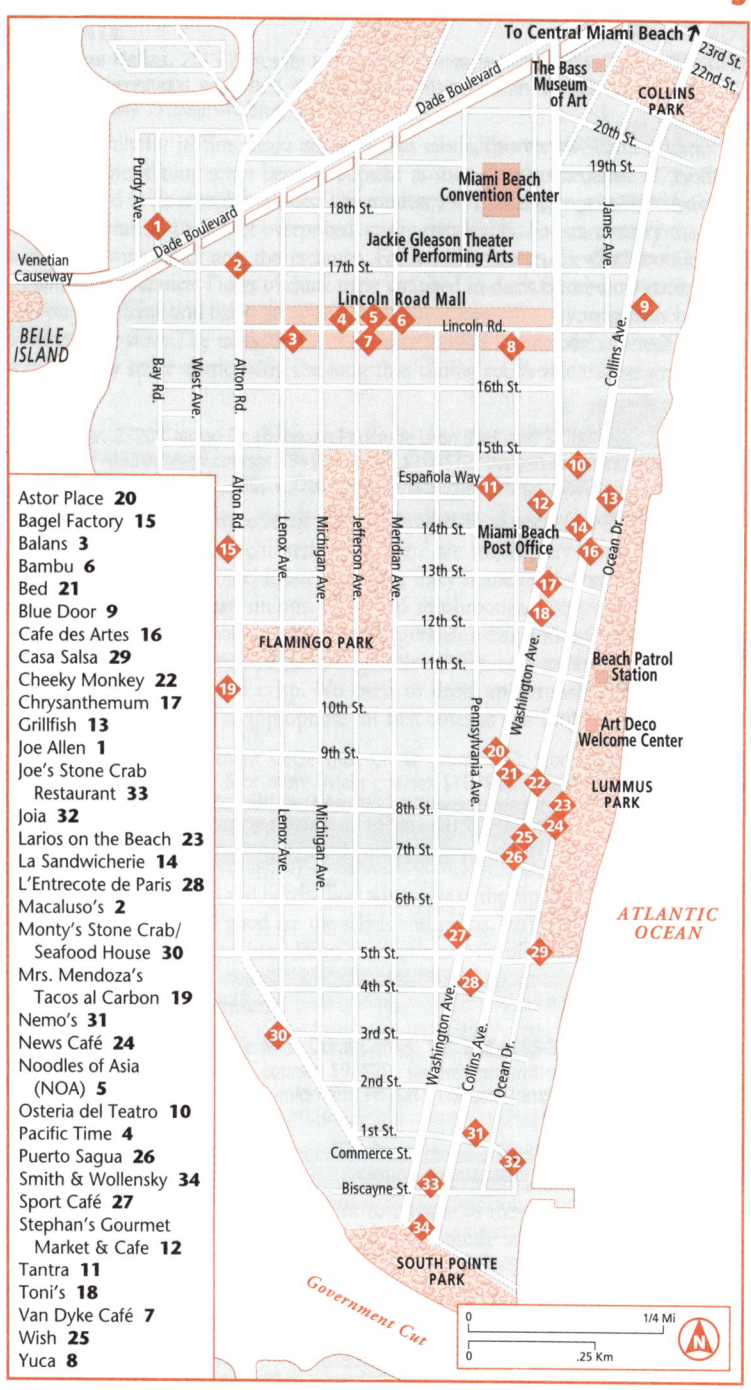

Astor Place **20**
Bagel Factory **15**
Balans **3**
Bambu **6**
Bed **21**
Blue Door **9**
Cafe des Artes **16**
Casa Salsa **29**
Cheeky Monkey **22**
Chrysanthemum **17**
Grillfish **13**
Joe Allen **1**
Joe's Stone Crab
 Restaurant **33**
Joia **32**
Larios on the Beach **23**
La Sandwicherie **14**
L'Entrecote de Paris **28**
Macaluso's **2**
Monty's Stone Crab/
 Seafood House **30**
Mrs. Mendoza's
 Tacos al Carbon **19**
Nemo's **31**
News Café **24**
Noodles of Asia
 (NOA) **5**
Osteria del Teatro **10**
Pacific Time **4**
Puerto Sagua **26**
Smith & Wollensky **34**
Sport Café **27**
Stephan's Gourmet
 Market & Cafe **12**
Tantra **11**
Toni's **18**
Van Dyke Café **7**
Wish **25**
Yuca **8**

107

When you walk in, you won't be sure whether to sit on the fine dining side (white tablecloths and all) or the cafe and bar side. The Mayya Café offers more traditional Mexican foods. You can choose from *taquitos* (rolled tortillas filled with beef tenderloin, spicy avocado, and queso fresco), *quesadillas* (an oversized flour tortilla with your choice of pulled chicken or grilled vegetables); enchiladas filled with roasted mushrooms or chorizo, or a choice of three kinds of tacos.

The Mayya is a lot pricier. You can sample a tasting menu of creative Mexican mixtures for $70 per guest or $100 per guest with wine. From the tasting menu you can choose from such delights as the truffle scented potato soup with diver scallops and ancho-honey puree; *Salpicon de Jaiba*, an enchilada with caramelized onions and black trumpet mushrooms; or the beef tenderloin with black beans and spicy chorizo-potato cake. For dessert, the chilled mango soup with Meyer lemon sorbet is wonderful. But my favorite is the chipotle and chocolate ganache with caramelized bananas. À la carte selections change daily. The cuisine at Mayya is exquisite and each entree is cooked to perfection, but don't come here if you're starving. An average entree costs around $34, but the portions will leave you wanting more for your money.

Osteria del Teatro. 1443 Washington Ave. (at Española Way), South Beach. ☎ **305/538-7850.** Reservations recommended. Main courses $13–$34; appetizers $9–$24. AE, CB, DC, JCB, MC, V. Mon–Thurs 6–11pm; Fri–Sat 6pm–midnight. Closed Sun and for 3 weeks in Sept. ITALIAN.

The curved entryway of this well-established enclave of reliable, if slightly overpriced, Italian cuisine is abuzz nightly. Reams of locals and tourists wait for a seat at one of the small tables. Move the fresh orchid aside to make room for a big basket of lightly toasted chunks of real Italian bread and then wait for your very knowledgeable server to recommend a daily special.

Start with any of the grilled vegetables, such as portobello mushrooms with fontina or the garlic-infused peppers. All the pastas are handmade and done to perfection. The risotto al'aragosta is a creamy rice dish with a decadent lobster and shrimp sauce full of tasty morsels of seafood. Of the five or so entrees offered nightly, usually at least three are seafood. The tuna loin is served with a rich mushroom sauce with just a hint of rosemary. The duck breast, doused in a sweet balsamic honey sauce and fanned over a bed of wilted radicchio leaves, is rightfully very popular. Each slice of duck is perfectly seared on the outside and tender throughout without even a hint of gamey flavor.

✪ **Pacific Time.** 915 Lincoln Rd. (between Jefferson and Michigan aves.), South Beach. ☎ **305/534-5979.** Reservations recommended. Main courses $20–$32. AE, DC, MC, V. Sun–Thurs 6–11pm; Fri–Sat 6pm–midnight. ASIAN/NEW WORLD CUISINE.

Chef and co-owner Jonathan Eismann was awarded the Robert Mondavi Award for Culinary Excellence in June 1994 and his restaurant, Pacific Time has been recognized by *Bon Appétit* and Esquire magazines as one of America's "Best New Restaurants." Eismann's dishes infuse elements of Chinese, Japanese, Korean, Vietnamese, Korean, Mongolian, and Indonesian flavors. One of the best dishes for meat-eaters is the Mongolian lamb salad, which has a lightly sweet, earthy taste with a crunchy kick of onion. For a main course, the ever-changing menu offers many locally caught fish specialties, including grouper served on a bed of shredded shallots, and ginger with a sweet sake-infused sauce and tempura-dunked sweet potato slivers on the side. Under the midnight-blue sky ceiling and against the pale yellow distressed walls, you'll probably see stars. The famous chocolate bomb is every bit as decadent as they've said, with hot bittersweet chocolate bursting from the cupcakelike center. The wine list is quite extensive and includes red and white wines from Italy, France, the Napa Valley, Australia, Argentina, New Zealand, and South Africa.

✪ **Smith & Wollensky.** 1 Washington Ave. (in South Pointe Park), South Beach. ☎ **305/673-2800.** Reservations recommended. Main courses $20–$35; lobster $38. AE, CB, DC, DISC, MC, V. Daily noon–midnight. The Grill 5pm–2am. STEAK HOUSE.

This pricey New York import opened its doors in late 1997 and was packed from the start. The handsome clubby atmosphere is enhanced by views of the Intercoastal Waterway that leads to the Port of Miami. The menu, like the setting, is basic, almost austere, with a few chicken and fish choices and beef served about a dozen ways. The classic is the sirloin seared lightly and served naked. Also good is the thick and buttery filet mignon. Delicious side dishes such as asparagus, baked potato, onion rings, creamed spinach, and hash browns are sold à la carte. Ask for advice from the wine steward, since the vast and impressive menu can be overwhelming. Service here, unlike so many other South Beach restaurants, is usually professional and polite. Desserts are superb, too. Just hope someone else is paying.

To avoid the clanking bustle of the main dining rooms, ask for a seat upstairs or, better yet, in The Grill, where you can order from a more casual and less expensive menu. You'll find meat entrees at about 30% less than in the regular restaurant. Portions in here are a bit smaller, too, eliminating the need for doggie bags.

✪ **Tantra.** 1445 Pennsylvania Ave. (at Española Way), South Beach. ☎ **305/672-4765.** Reservations required. Main courses $26–$46; appetizers $12–$34. AE, MC, V, D. Daily 7pm–1am. Late-night menu 1am to closing. FRENCH.

Forget the fact that it's the hottest stargazing spot on the beach and the likes of Jennifer Lopez, Leonardo Dicaprio, Will Smith, and Robert De Niro have all become captivated by its spell. Tantra is the most alluring and mesmerizing haven of sensuality to hit Miami in a very long time. The ambience could come right out of a scene from the Kama Sutra. Take your shoes off and tippy-toe across the thatched lawn as you listen to sounds of cascading waterfalls and Middle Eastern chants. Smell the Egyptian musk incense. Indulge in the tantalizing dishes, each of them tempting you to let all your inhibitions free. The cuisine borrows properties from aphrodisiacs from all over the globe and along with every object in the place, is founded on the ancient Tantric philosophy that every sense organ must be used to its greatest potential. So your first order should be the Tantra Plate, a blending of the most potent aphrodisiacs of the sea including oysters, shrimp, yellow-fin tuna over sushi rice, barbecued eel, and bay scallop seviche. The best dish on the menu for its price is the Saffron Scented Bouillabaisse. You won't find this sambuca-scented seafood stew anywhere else, not even a cheap imitation. Tantra's proprietors believe that "cooking is like love, it should be entered into with abandon or not at all." With that premise in mind, enter at your own risk.

Wish. In The Hotel, 801 Collins Ave., South Beach. ☎ **305/531-2222.** Reservations recommended. Main courses $16–$32; appetizers $8–$18. AE, DC, DISC, MC, V. Tues–Sun 6–11pm; Fri–Sat 6pm–midnight. ITALIAN.

Wish is both colorful and playful, with a light and airy feel that will appeal to diners seeking a calm evening out. This romantic restaurant, with hand-blown Venetian lamps, Persian red banquettes, and a beautiful mosaic fountain in the garden, whispers for attention. The chef, Andrea Curto, borrows ingredients that are imported from Asia, Italy, the Caribbean, and the U.S. Southwest. Try the ginger Fresno tuna tartare with taro root chips, tobiko, and caviar to start. My favorite entree is the crispy-skinned yellow eye snapper, served with grilled shrimp, sweet corn, and poblano risotto, baby bok choy, and cilantro butter sauce. There's also an extensive wine list and a full-service bar.

○ **Yuca.** 501 Lincoln Rd. (corner of Drexel), South Beach. ☎ **305/532-9822.** Reservations required. Main courses $22–$40; appetizers $7–$16. AE, DC, DISC, MC, V. Mon–Sat noon–3pm; 6–11pm; Sun noon–3pm; 5–10pm Closed summer for weekday lunches. CUBAN.

This is the place to take out-of-towners you want to impress with a dose of upscale Latin culture. The menu is large and exotic. Unfortunately, it's also badly translated, so don't be shy about asking for a waiter who is proficient in English (most are) if you don't *habla español*. By the way, don't give yourself away as a gringo by pronouncing it "Yucka." It's "*Yoo*-ka," and is a play on words, being the name of a staple root vegetable and an acronym for young upscale Cuban Americans.

To enjoy your meal, insist on being seated in the front of the restaurant, facing Lincoln Road; otherwise, you'll be in the hectic path of the kitchen and too close to the very talented but loud salsa band that plays on weekends. Start with the lobster medallions with sautéed spinach and a portobello mushroom stuffed with vegetarian paella. The pieces of lobster tail are expertly grilled, with a touch of oil over just-wilted greens. The mushrooms are good, but the paella can be a bit pasty. For a main course, the pork tenderloin is a favorite—I thought it must have marinated for days, because I could cut it with a butter knife. The hearty *congri*, a mash of red beans and rice, and a green apple and mango salsa make a perfect balance. The veal loin, the menu's most expensive entree, has a rich, meaty flavor, but can be a bit dry. A full selection of traditional and exotic dessert choices is available, as well as some of the best coffee in town.

Go on the weekend for a late dinner and then head upstairs for live music. If Cuban diva Albita is playing, you're in for a real experience. It's pricey but well worth it.

EXPENSIVE

Aura. 613 Lincoln Rd., Miami Beach. ☎ **305/695-1100.** Reservations recommended. Main courses $15–$21. AE, MC, V. Tues–Sun 11am–3pm and 6pm–midnight. Closed Mon. CONTINENTAL.

Under the direction of French Moroccan chef Kamel Dahmani, this delightful restaurant offers a fusion of Mediterranean, Asian, African, and continental European cuisine. Rivaling the food for attention is the interior of the restaurant, which was designed by legendary Miami architect Morris Lapidus, who at 97, proved that he hadn't lost his touch when it came to eclectic interior design. Try the shish kebab of lamb, chicken, or beef (served with a barley semolina gallete) or the spicy mussels salad with saffron mayonnaise during lunch. Dinners include delightful appetizers (foie gras with polenta and truffle sauce or a pâté of the day) and main courses that focus on meat and fish with Dahmani's signature touch. The tuna fillet served with a basil, olive, and bouillabaisse sauce is great, as is the peppered filet mignon, with polenta, ratatouille, and veal stock reduction. Check for daily specials; the fresh seafood runs out rather quickly, but for lunch we also recommend the pizza-oriented dishes made with phyllo dough.

Casa Salsa. 524 Ocean Dr., South Beach. ☎ **305/604-5959.** Reservations recommended. Main courses $16–$29; appetizers $7–$9. AE, MC, V. Daily noon–4pm; Sun–Thurs 6–11pm; Fri–Sat 6pm–1am. PUERTO RICAN.

Move over Gloria Estefan, Ricky Martin is the new Latin sensation bringing his name and talents to South Beach in the form of Casa Salsa. The ambience here takes you back to old San Juan with the carved mahogany wood pedestals and the red glass candlelight lamps. This is the finest in Puerto Rican cuisine, but there's plenty more on the menu that's not from that Caribbean nation. Wild savory dishes mixed with rice, beans, plantains, cassava, and white yams make up typical Puerto Rican fare, but Casa Salsa does it gourmet style. For an appetizer start off with the grilled beefsteak sandwich made of two large *tostones* served with fried cassava. Or, you might opt for the puff pastry roll filled with lobster, both for $10.95. The *Monfongo en pilon,* green plantain dough filled with your choice of pork chunks, chicken, shrimp, or lobster, is the most requested dish. You could also have the *monfongo* stuffed with Cornish hen baked with Bacardi Rum and mushroom sauce. My favorite is the grilled tuna fillet served in molasses and Don Q 151 rum sauce for $21.95. It's well worth the price.

Every Friday night is Salsa Night, when the tables and chairs get pushed to the side and the live band, Pina Colada, rocks while couples sweat and gyrate until the wee hours of the morning. Don't be surprised if Ricky stops by to swivel his hips in ways only a hula-hoop champion could match.

Cheeky Monkey. 944 Collins Ave., Miami Beach. ☎ **305/534-2650.** Reservations recommended on weekends. Main courses $19–$28; appetizers $8–$12. AE, DC, DISC, MC, V. Daily 8am–2:30pm and 5:30–11pm. Bar open until 3:30am. INTERNATIONAL.

Tucked Inside Of Merv Griffin's Blue Moon Hotel, Cheeky Monkey's jungle-filled environment, with playful monkeys splattered everywhere, will alert you that you're in for a wild ride. The great bar and back patio make for a perfect setting for the huge happy-hour crowd that saunters through on Friday evenings. The menu is an eclectic mixture of cuisines from Asia, Africa, and the Americas. The chef, Steven Marsella, mixes in an influence of French, Italian, and New Orleans dishes. For starters, sample the Maine lobster and saffron brioche with a sherry and roasted corn sauce and heirloom tomato essence. The crispy calamari with lemon sambal chile garlic sauce is also a good choice. For the main course you should definitely try the wild Louisiana catfish with an almond crust and meunière sauce served with braised collard greens and creole mashed potatoes—you'll swear you're in Cajun country. If you have room left for dessert, try the banana beignets with double chocolate ice cream and dark rum caramel sauce. Yum!

Gaucho Room. In the Loews Hotel, 1601 Collins Ave. (St. Moritz Bldg.), South Beach. ☎ **305/604-5290.** Reservations recommended. Main courses $22–$52. AE, MC, V. Daily 7pm–1am. ARGENTINEAN STEAK HOUSE.

This restaurant will set you back *mucho dinero,* but the delicate renditions of a variety of recipes makes it well worth the expense for the traveler with cash clout or for a local who'd like to wine and dine someone in romantic bliss. The Gaucho Room is a hip Argentinean dining room serving prime aged meats, as well as local seafood. The Chilean sea bass with whipped roasted poblano potatoes and a sweet-sake reduction sauce is wonderful, and the Grilled marinated Colorado Lamb Loin with truffle wild mushroom tamale is exquisite. *Warning:* Those with lighter palates should probably request light seasoning on their food. The Gaucho Bar is an intimate lounge, with a wine list and selection of scotches and ports that would make a European count envious.

Joia Restaurant and Bar. 150 Ocean Dr., Miami Beach. ☎ **305/674-8871.** Reservations recommended. Main courses $15–$30. AE, DC, DISC, MC, V. Daily 6pm–1am. HAUTE ITALIAN.

Dining at Joia isn't easy on the wallet, but it can guarantee you a club card to gain entrance later to either Liquid or the Bar Room. So, if you're interested in doing some high-caliber celebrity sighting—diners here include Madonna, Al Pacino, and Cameron Diaz—while dining, and don't wish to wait in line later, this is the place to be. This is not the spot for beer or bottled plain water; nearly everything on the menu ends with an apostrophized vowel, so price yourself accordingly to enjoy the best this decadent, yet delicious, menu has to offer. The wine list is exquisite; there are Italian whites and robust reds from Italy, France, and California that run from $25 to $150. There is a laundry list of appetizers, salads, and pastas in every conceivable shape, from penne to farfalle, covered with delightful toppings such as *tagliolini al moscardini* (baby octopus). Recommended dishes include the *rigatoni al funghi*, a mushroom-lover's delight, with large tube pasta filled with shiitake and porcini mushrooms; the *crema di porri e patate*, a puree of leeks and potatoes; and the *bauletti di pollo al funghi*, a folded chicken breast stuffed with Fontina cheese, mushrooms, and sage.

✪ **Monty's Stone Crab/Seafood House.** 300 Alton Rd., South Beach. ☎ **305/673-3444.** Reservations recommended. Main courses $20–$40. AE, DC, MC, V. Sun–Thurs 5:30–11pm; Fri–Sat 5:30pm–midnight. SEAFOOD.

Seafood fans, long enamored of Monty's various menus in the Grove and in Boca, have taken to its South Beach location as well. Opened only a couple of years ago, the restaurant has a rustic oak floor and a raw bar set outside around a large swimming pool. The best deal in town is still the all-you-can-eat stone crabs—about $40 for the large ones and $35 for the mediums. That's about the same price that Joe's, located 2 blocks away, charges for just three or four claws. (But don't order stone crabs in summer—they aren't as fresh.) Enjoy the incredible views and off-season fish specialties, including the Maryland she-crab soup, rich and creamy without too much thickener. Year-round, you can enjoy the saffron and tomato-based bouillabaisse, and the key lime pie is the real deal.

✪ **Nemo.** 100 Collins Ave., South Beach. ☎ **305/532-4550.** Reservations recommended. Main courses $22–$36; appetizers $8–$18; Sun brunch $26. AE, MC, V. Mon–Fri noon–3pm and 7pm–midnight; Sun 11am–3pm and 6–11pm. Valet parking $10. NEW WORLD CUISINE.

This dark and superstylish hotspot is an oasis in a hip area of South Beach below 5th Street. Here models and celebrities rub elbows—literally, since the tables are so close together. Ask to be seated in the more private back room, which has a pleasant garden and is the only place where you can hear your dining companions or your server. The staff here is professional, personable, and efficient.

Nemo has a great raw bar that offers a variety of oysters as well as stone crabs, lobster, clams, seviche, caviar, and shellfish platters. One of the most popular fish dishes is the charred salmon. The flash-cooking in a wok gives it a unique flavor, slightly blackened outside and tender and sweet inside. If you're in the mood for something light, try the grilled portobello mushroom appetizer, served with a rich, creamy garlic polenta. The spicy Vietnamese beef salad is indeed very spicy, but it's too small a portion. You can never go wrong choosing one of the daily specials. An exotic and delicious choice for dessert is the California figs soaked in port syrup and surrounded with balls of tamarind (said to be an aphrodisiac) ice cream.

✪ **The Strand Restaurant and Beach Grill.** In the Savoy Hotel, 455 Ocean Dr., South Beach. ☎ **305/535-8882.** Reservations required. Main courses $18–$36. AE, CB, DC, MC, V. Mon–Sun 12–4pm; Sun–Thurs 7pm–12am; Fri and Sat 7pm–1am. FRENCH

Under the direction of nationally recognized Chef Michelle Bernstein, this restaurant offers classic French cuisine that has been brilliantly fused with Mediterranean and Caribbean elements. In addition to the main restaurant, there is also a beach grill, an outside verandah that overlooks the ocean and is primarily a lunch locale, but available for soirees. For those who aren't in the know, The Strand was the restaurant on Miami Beach that truly started the revolution that created the new infusion of cuisines in Sobe. Lunch ranges from light items such as salads ($8 to $11) to goodies such as prosciutto and mozzarella on a baguette ($11) or house-cured salmon with juniper, citrus, and warm St. Marcelin cheese on French bread ($9). New Yorkers will take to the kosher dogs with sauerkraut and fries for $6. Dinner is the real tour de force of Bernstein's extravagant culinary creations. Try her original Caribbean Bouillabaisse finished with chilies and fresh lime juice dashed by cilantro, or the whole boneless Squab stuffed with duck meat and pate and served over Israeli couscous, dried apricots, and figs—it's a steal at $27.

Tuscan Steak. 433 Washington Ave. South Beach, Fl. 33139. ☎ **305/534-2233.** Reservations strongly recommended on weekends. Main courses $20–$65; family-style meals $50 per person, including appetizer and main course. AE, CB, DISC, MC, V. Sun–Thurs 6pm–midnight; Fri–Sat 6pm–1am. ITALIAN/STEAK.

The real reason for coming to this restaurant is the meat—the place is a carnivore's delight. For an exceptional meal, start off with the garlic bread, drizzled in white truffle butter. You can't go wrong ordering the Tuscan grilled prime Florentine T-bone, which can easily be shared with others. The Oven Roasted New York Strip Steak, served with a Parmesan crust and black peppercorn sauce, is another excellent choice. The restaurant's rendition of lamb chops, it comes with smoked onion mashed potatoes, amaretto-infused sweet potatoes, and sautéed spinach is simply marvelous. And if you're watching your cholesterol, the seared rare tuna with white bean salad is a gastronomic feat. There is a sumptuous wine list; the servers are all trained to literally wait hand and foot upon you, and can recommend selections for your meal.

MODERATE

Balan's. 1022 Lincoln Rd. (between Lenox and Michigan), South Beach. ☎ **305/534-9191.** Reservations not accepted. Main courses $6–$16; appetizers $3.50–$8.50. AE, DISC, MC, V. Daily 8am–midnight. INTERNATIONAL.

This well-run sidewalk cafe, a London import, is a good value, especially when the weather is right. It's a favorite hangout for the gay community, and is right at home on fabulous Lincoln Road. Dinners here are a bargain, with winning entrees like a hearty lobster club sandwich served with bacon, lettuce, and tomato on toasted onion bread, and a hoisin Port fillet nestled over baby bok choy and crisp leek spring rolls. The tempting starters are relatively small, so you can try a few. Try Thai soup, as well as the concoction of goat, cheese, and lightly breaded fried mushrooms. A large herb salad with a mix of more than five types of baby greens is a great way to start any meal. The tahini chicken salad, however, is sadly lacking in spice. The menu, with lots of healthful salads and sandwiches, seems to please a wide audience.

Café Des Artes. 1360 Collins Ave., Miami Beach. ☎ **305/535-8247.** Reservations necessary only during holidays. Main courses $8–$20; appetizers $4–$7. MC, V. Daily 8am–1am. FRENCH.

French Chef Vincent Thilloy is one of South Beach's hidden stars. He believes in being "all about the art," so his interiors will often have some very eclectic pieces that fit only because they are so altruistically thrown together. He enjoys musicians too, and promoted his place so well that Brazilian maestro Gilberto Gil now calls the Café home. Don't be surprised to see a group of musicians from different genres go at it a capella at the bar. The menu doesn't excel at presentation so much as it sparkles with subtlety and affordability. A continental breakfast, priced at $5.50 will get you croissants, bread, tea, coffee, and juice. The dinner menu has some lovely salads (an absolutely heaping pile of fresh greenery with edible goodies), including Vincent's take on a salad Niçoise. For seafood, I recommend the steamed snapper fillet putanesca, served with shallots and tomato sauce for only $14.50. Finding a good steak dinner for under $20 at the beach is both a shock and a delight; it underlines Vincent's approach to service—let the customer enjoy a good meal without having to sell the house. There's a small but delightful wine list as well as cigars and after-dinner ports.

✪ Café Tabac. 136 Collins Ave., Miami Beach. ☎ **305/695-8411.** Reservations highly recommended. Main courses $7–$14; appetizers $5–$12. AE, DC, MC, V. Daily 11am–2am. MEDITERRANEAN.

This restaurant is a favorite among the hip Sobe crowd—an eclectic mix of locals, fashion industry types, and celebrities—that knows instinctively what's hot and what's not. Live DJs spin a mix of sounds guaranteed to put diners in the mood for a lively evening. For those who want to investigate their inner child, we suggest the rope swing located just inside the main entrance—it's perfect for pics! Burger fans will enjoy the ones here, which can be mounted with goodies ranging from blue cheese to mushrooms, onions, and fresh bacon. A Eurofavorite in the sandwich department is the *Pan bagnot* (tuna, onion, tomato, anchovies, eggs, lettuce, olives, and dressing), or, if you're not calorie counting, check out the *croque monsieur* (French grilled ham and cheese sandwich). Appetizers range from soup du jour to steamed stuffed mussels. The dinner menu, is both refreshing and light. There are a number of moderately priced chicken and fresh fish dishes. If you like pasta, try the penne alla vodka or the fusilli vesuvio, which is truly volcanic.

✪ Chrysanthemum. 1256 Washington Ave., South Beach. ☎ **305/531-5656.** Main courses $14–$23; appetizers $3.95–$9.95. AE, CB, DC, MC, V. Tues–Sun 6–11pm. Closed Mon. SZECHUAN/PEKINESE.

At first, the unpretentious atmosphere may be a surprise in glitzy South Beach, but after you've tried the tasty dishes in Chrysanthemum, you'll want to come back. Count on the service to be prompt but not solicitous. The many vegetarian specialties include spicy eggplant strips in a rich balsamic vinegar sauce and black mushrooms sautéed with tiny Shanghai lettuce hearts. Start with the Chinese salad, which comes heaped with a fresh mix of greens, vermicelli, bean sprouts, and cilantro. The steamed whole fish is best with the ginger and scallions. It comes with bones, but ask the waiter to remove them; he will gladly and expertly oblige.

Grillfish. 1444 Collins Ave. (corner of Española Way), South Beach. ☎ **305/538-9908.** Reservations recommended on weekends. Main courses $8–$15. AE, DISC, DC, MC, V. Winter Sun–Thurs 6–11pm; Fri–Sat 6pm–midnight. Off-season daily 6–11pm. SEAFOOD.

From the beautiful Byzantine-style mural and the gleaming oak bar, you'd think you were eating in a much more expensive restaurant. Grillfish manages to pay the exorbitant South Beach rent because the restaurant has a loyal following of locals who come for fresh, simple seafood in a relaxed but upscale atmosphere. As the name implies, fish, fish, and fish are what you'll get.

The servers are friendly and know the menu well. The barroom seafood chowder is full of chunks of shellfish, as well as some fresh white fish fillets in a tomato broth. The small ear of corn, included with each entree, is about as close as you'll get to any type of vegetable offering besides the pedestrian salad. Still, at these prices, it's worth a visit to try some local fare including mako shark, swordfish, tuna, marlin, and wahoo (they'll either grill or sauté it). Also, I recommend the spicy red pasta sauce as a great complement to this rustic, Italian-inspired seafood fare.

Jeffrey's. 1629 Michigan Ave. (half block south of Lincoln Rd.), South Beach. ☎ **305/673-0690.** Reservations highly recommended. Main courses $12–$24; appetizers $7–$11. AE, CB, DC, MC, V. Tues–Sat 6–11pm; Sun 5–10pm. Closed Sept. CONTINENTAL/BISTRO.

Jeffrey's is a real find on South Beach—the genuinely concerned and doting owner, Jeffrey Landsman, treats everyone as a regular and calls grandmothers and children alike "kids." Some say this is the most romantic restaurant on the beach, and South Beach's gay crowd certainly seems to agree. Old-fashioned lace curtains and candlelight are a welcome repast from the glitz and chrome of the rest of the island.

You can choose a succulent ¾-pound burger or try a hearty chicken breast marinated in a balsamic sauce and served with freshly mashed sweet potatoes over spinach, on white lace tablecloths. Some of the better seafood options include the conch fritters and the crab cakes. Jeffrey's is known for its perfectly dressed Caesar salad, which could use some more anchovies for my taste, but is nonetheless delicious. Most desserts are tasty, but the homemade tarte Tatin, a caramelly deep-dish apple tart, is superb. Go early before it sells out.

Joe Allen. 1787 Purdy Ave. (3 blocks west of Alton Rd.), South Beach. ☎ **305/531-7007.** Reservations recommended, especially on weekends. Main courses $13–$24. MC, V. Mon–Fri 11:30am–11:45pm. AMERICAN.

There's no need to wonder why this spot is still considered to be the "locals" place. The food, which ranges from old-fashioned meat loaf to rigatoni with goat cheese, is reliably good. The service can be a bit sluggish, especially when the place is busy. Especially good here are the many inventive pizzas and salads.

Larios on the Beach. 820 Ocean Dr., South Beach. ☎ **305/532-9577.** Reservations recommended. Main courses $8–$24. AE, MC, V. Sun–Thurs 11:30am–midnight; Fri–Sat 11:30am–2am. CUBAN.

Gloria and Emilio Estefan brought in their favorite chef to create this ultrastylish restaurant in the heart of the South Beach hustle. Enjoy a few appetizers at the handsome chrome and wood bar while you wait for a seat amid the sea of Spanish-speaking regulars.

Portions are large and prices are reasonable. The menu runs the gamut, from diner-style *medianoches* (Cuban sandwiches with pork and cheese) to a tangy and tender *serrucho en escabeche* (pickled kingfish) with just enough citrus to mellow the fishiness but not enough to cause a pucker. You could get away with ordering three or four *aperitivos* and *ensaladas* (appetizers and salads) for two people. If you're still hungry, try the *camarones al ajillo* (shrimp in garlic sauce), *fabada asturiana* (hearty soup of black beans and sausage), or *palomilla* (thinly sliced beef served with onions and parsley). Save room for the rich custard desserts, which include a few stunning variations on the standard flan. A spoonful of pumpkin or coffee-accented custard with a cup of *cortadito* (espresso-style coffee with milk and sugar) will get you prepped for a full night of dancing.

L'Entrecote de Paris. 413 Washington Ave., South Beach. ☎ **305/673-1002.** Reservations suggested on weekends. Fixed-price dinner $14–$21. DC, MC, V. Daily 6pm–1am. FRENCH.

Everything in this classy little bistro is simple. For dinner, you choose between salmon or steak, and beyond a few salads, that's it—but both are great. The salmon looks like spa cuisine, served with a pile of bald steamed potatoes and a salad with pedestrian greens and an unmatchable vinaigrette. The steak, on the other hand, is the stuff cravings are made of, even if you're not a die-hard carnivore. Its salty sharp sauce is rich but not thick, and full of the beef's natural flavor. The slices are served on top of your own little hibachi, which also keeps the accompanying fries warm.

Most diners are very Euro and pack a petit attitude. Tables and booths are squeezed tight together. On the other hand, the servers are superquick and professional, and almost friendly in a French kind of way. The short and very French wine list includes several well-priced bottles for under $20. Even if you are on a diet or have forsaken chocolate, try the *profiteroles au chocolat,* a perfect puff pastry filled with vanilla ice cream and topped with a dark bittersweet chocolate sauce.

Macaluso's. 1747 Alton Rd., Miami Beach. ☎ **305/604-1811.** Main courses $9–$23; pizza $9–$11. AE, MC, V. Tues–Sat noon–3pm and 6pm–midnight; Sun 6–11pm; after 10:30pm only pies are served. Closed Mon. ITALIAN.

At this star-studded spot, it's all about Frank (that's Sinatra, kids), but don't be surprised to hear the groovy sounds of Lauryn Hill or Barry White to make the folks at Ally McBeal feel quite welcome! Art lovers will also enjoy a rotating minigallery that has featured the works of Romero Britto and Shirley Henderson. Of course, you must try one of the many pizza pies (perfect for two people or as appetizers for four to six). Catch the fantastic clam pie when in season—the portions are huge. Expensive items fluctuate throughout season, but will likely be fresh fish products that Chef Michael hand picks. Repeat customers, and locally that means everyone, will recommend perennial favorites such as the rigatoni and broccoli rabe, which can be bitter to the untrained palate, but for food connoisseurs is heaven. There are delicious desserts that range from Chef Michael's homemade anisette cookies to Patricia Scott's pastries. There's a wonderful wine list. The French Beaujolais George Duboeufat at $22 a bottle is a steal, when you consider it comes nicely chilled with slices of luscious Georgia peaches—which make a great, and affordable, dessert by themselves.

✪ **Macarena.** 1334 Washington Ave., South Beach. ☎ **305/531-3440.** Reservations suggested on weekends. Main courses $12–$20; tapas $5–$8. AE, DC, MC, V. Mon–Fri noon–3pm; daily 8pm–midnight (later on Fri–Sat) SPANISH.

This South Beach gem is a great place to eat and enjoy. It's looked after by a young crew of Spanish imports whose families own several popular restaurants in Madrid. Show up before 10pm and you're sure to get a table. After that time, especially on weekends, it's standing room only.

The gorgeous Euro crowd shows up for foot-stomping flamenco (every Wednesday, Friday, and Saturday) and an outrageous selection of tapas, as well as Miami's very best paella. Order a large portion and share it among at least four people. The garlic shrimp is tasty and aromatic, and the yellow squash stuffed with seafood and cheese is especially delicious. All the seafood, such as mussels in marinara sauce and clams in green sauce, is worth sampling. With such reasonable prices, you can taste lots of dishes and leave satisfied. Try some of the terrific sangria made with slices of fresh fruit and a subtle tinge of sweet soda.

Nexxt Cafe. 700 Lincoln Rd. (off Euclid Ave.), South Beach. ☎ **305/532-6643.** Reservations accepted, however, your credit card will be charged $15 per seat if you don't show up. Main courses $12–$23. AE, MC, V. Daily 9am–1am. AMERICAN.

Set on Lincoln Road between two coffee shops—gay favorite Jeoffrey's and a ubiquitous Starbuck's, is the newest cafe to take light dining to a new (and pricier) level. Nexxt has made quite a splash on South Beach, attracting an evening crowd looking for nighttime revelry and a morning crowd on the weekends for a standing-room-only brunch sensation. The fresh food comes in lavish portions that could easily feed two; the salads are an especially good bargain. Start off your meal with the calamari fritti, they're a lot fresher here than at most other local restaurants, and the Popcorn shrimp are pretty sizable. The burgers and sandwiches are similarly big, and the steaks are well worth a taste. They have coffees in tall, grande, and "maxxi" (which range from $1.75 to $4.35, the latter for "iceberg" coffees). Coffee cocktails, mixed drinks, frozen beverages and a reasonable wine list abound, which is why this cafe is none too shabby as a bar either. The only drawback here is the wait—so peruse the menu as quickly as possible to get your order in the first time your server swings by.

NOA (Noodles of Asia). 801 Lincoln Rd., South Beach. ☎ **305/925-0050.** Main courses $16–$20; noodles $10–$15; appetizers $4–$8. AE, MC, V. Sun–Thurs noon–midnight; Fri–Sat until 1am. ASIAN.

A relative newcomer to Lincoln Road, and the latest outpost in China Grill's growing empire, this Asian-inspired noodle shop attracts a trendy, good-looking crowd that comes for a variety of noodle dishes served in a stylish but uncomfortable setting. The appetizers, especially the delicate pork dumplings and the sautéed vegetables, are first-rate. Some main courses still need fine-tuning. Prices are not outrageous, but a bit high for what you get. With some work, the place could become a favorite hangout, especially thanks to an extensive and exotic selection of drinks and outrageous desserts.

Tap Tap. 819 Fifth St. (between Jefferson and Meridian aves. next to the Shell station), South Beach. ☎ **305/672-2898.** Reservations recommended in season and for special events. Main courses $9–$16. AE, MC, V. Sun–Thurs 6pm–midnight; Fri–Sat 6pm–2am. Closed Aug. HAITIAN.

The whole place looks like an overgrown tap tap, a brightly painted jitney common in Haiti. Every inch of the place is painted a neon blue, pink, or purple and every color in between, and the atmosphere is always fun. It's where the Haiti-philes and Haitians, from journalists to politicians, hang out. Even Manno Charlemagne, the mayor of Port-au-Prince, shows up when he has the time to play his brand of protest music and drink some Rhum Barbancourt.

The *Lanbi nan citron,* a tart, marinated conch salad, is perfect with a tall tropical drink and maybe some lightly grilled goat tidbits, which are served in a savory brown sauce and are less stringy than a typical goat dish. Another supersatisfying choice is the pumpkin soup, a rich brick-colored puree of subtly seasoned pumpkin with a dash of pepper. An excellent salad of avocado, mango, and watercress is a great finish. Even if you don't stay for a full meal, try the pumpkin flan with coconut caramel sauce, an ultra-Caribbean sweet treat. *Warning:* This place gets very crowded on weekends.

✪ **Toni's Sushi.** 1208 Washington Ave., South Beach. ☎ **305/673-9368.** Reservations recommended. Main courses $13–$25; rolls $3.50–$10.50. AE, MC, V. Daily 6pm–midnight; Fri–Sat 6pm–1am. JAPANESE/SUSHI.

One of Washington Avenue's first tenants, Toni's has withstood the test of time on fickle South Beach. By serving local fish caught daily and some imports from the Pacific and beyond, Toni has created a vast menu with options from teriyaki to hand rolls. The atmosphere is comfortable and even allows for quiet conversation—a rarity in this neighborhood. The hundreds of appetizers and rolls you can order make it a fun place to go with a group.

Consider the seaweed salad, a crunchy, salty green plant dressed with a light sesame sauce. The miso soup is hearty and a bit sweet. A good appetizer from the sushi bar is Miami Heat, which contains slabs of tuna with bits of scallion in a peppery sesame oil. I suggest skipping the entrees unless you are somehow still hungry after all the warm-ups. Many of the main dishes are good, however, like the lobster teriyaki in a dark sweet sauce over white rice.

✪ **Van Dyke Cafe.** 846 Lincoln Rd., South Beach. ☎ **305/534-3600.** Reservations recommended for evenings. Main courses $8–$17; appetizers $3–$9. AE, DC, MC, V. Daily 8am–1am; Fri–Sat 8am–3am. AMERICAN.

Owned by the same group that owns the successful News Café, the Van Dyke has used the same formula to guarantee its longevity on Lincoln Road. The smart, upscale decor inside and the European sidewalk cafe outside are always crowded because of the dinerlike prices and fast, friendly service. There is nothing too ambitious on the menu, which offers basic sandwiches, salads and, best of all, breakfast all day long. The pastas are decent, although not too exciting. House specialties include an excellent smoked salmon on thick black bread and a smooth, lemony hummus with pita chips. Also, since you're in Miami Beach, you may want to consider a nice hot bowl of cure-all chicken soup with matzo balls. In the evenings, the sounds of a talented jazz band waft down from the dark elegant club upstairs.

MODERATE/INEXPENSIVE

Front Porch Café. In the Penguin Hotel, 1418 Ocean Dr., South Beach. ☎ **305/531-8300.** Reservations recommended for weekend brunch. Main courses $10–$16; salads and sandwiches $4–$8. AE, MC, V. Open daily 8:30am–10:30pm. AMERICAN.

The Front Porch Café, a local fixture since 1990, is a spot favored by locals who still like to call a piece of Ocean Drive their own (the southern end of the highly touted drive being populated by tourist droves). When I recently stopped in for a late lunch, there were more than 10 local celebs and well-known Sobe residents dining there. The fresh and sumptuous portions served at the Front Porch are just as famous as the crowd that eats them, and they won't bust your budget. Omelettes are fluffy and filled with goodies, and the breakfast burritos and the Front Porch Feature (three scrambled eggs, fresh fruit, potatoes, toast, and your choice of meat—all for only $5.95) easily establish this as the hot spot for brunch, or as one local diva explained, "a quick recovery meal to make it through the next two days." Sandwiches range from the exotic, brie and prosciutto on croissants or sourdough, to a simple bagel with the usual toppings. Small pizzas are scrumptious, and dinner items such as sesame chicken ($10.95) or roasted leg of lamb ($12.95) are a real bargain.

Lou's Philly Cheesesteak and South Street BBQ. 805 Lincoln Rd. (near Lincoln and Meridian), South Beach. ☎ **305/534-0609.** Reservations not accepted. Main courses $10–$16; salads and sandwiches $4–$8. MC, V. Sun–Thurs 10am–11pm; Fri–Sat 10am–1am. AMERICAN.

Lou's Philly Cheesesteak, safely ensconced on the busy corner of Lincoln and Meridian, proves you don't have to skimp on quality to provide a bargain bite. Word to the diet conscious—unless you're an Atkins fan, this place is not for you! Burger lovers should definitely try Lou's signature version: $1/2$ pound of choice beef, which usually comes drizzled with bacon, creamy cheeses, and all the usual works. But why stop there when such gastronomic delights as the scrumptious rack of baby back ribs—sliding in on Lou's famous and tasty fries—and coleslaw await you. At $6.75, Lou's Famous Cheesesteak sandwich is one of the city's best dining bargains and as tasty as they come. There's also a beer bar that comes with fresh frosted mugs, and Lou has his own brew too. It's a fun place for everyone—just don't let your trainer or nutritionist know you've been.

INEXPENSIVE

Bagel Factory. 1427 Alton Rd., South Beach. ☎ **305/674-1577.** Sandwiches $2–$7. No credit cards. Daily 5:30am–3pm. DELI.

There are bagel joints all over South Beach, but this narrow storefront on Alton Road is one of the best. The Rishty family makes the city's finest hand-rolled bagels in every imaginable flavor, from sunflower to banana raisin to sun-dried tomato. The bagels are deliciously chewy, but not too doughy. Add to that the phenomenal salads, including a range of decent fat-free options, and you'll understand why every weekend, the line of customers snakes out the door. Grab a spot at one of the three small inside tables or take the order to go, as most loyal patrons do.

✪ **La Sandwicherie.** 229 14th St. (behind the Amoco station), South Beach. ☎ **305/532-8934.** Sandwiches and salads $5–$10. No credit cards. Daily 9:30am–5am. Delivery 9:30am–10pm. FRENCH.

For the most incredible gourmet sandwich you've ever tasted, stop by the green-and-white awning that hides this fabulously French lunch counter. Choose pâté, saucisson, salami, prosciutto, turkey, tuna, ham, roast beef, or any of the perfect cheeses (Swiss, mozzarella, cheddar, or provolone). Vegetarians can make a meal out of the optional sandwich toppings, which include black olives, pickles, cucumbers, lettuce, onions, green or hot peppers, or tomatoes. You can have your sandwich made on delicious fresh French bread or on a relatively uninspired croissant.

If the six or so wooden stools are all taken, don't despair; you can stand and watch the tattoo artist do his work through the glass wall next door. Or douse your creation with the light tangy vinaigrette and bring lunch to the beach—that is, if you can make it 2 blocks without eating the whole thing. In addition to the cans and bottles of teas, sodas, juices, and waters, you can get coffees, fresh juices, and smoothies here.

✪ **Mrs. Mendoza's Tacos al Carbon.** 1040 Alton Rd., South Beach. ☎ **305/535-0808.** Main courses $3–$5; side dishes 80¢–$3. No credit cards. Mon–Sat 11am–9pm; Sun noon–10pm. FAST FOOD/MEXICAN.

This hard-to-spot storefront is a godsend—it's the only fresh California-style Mexican place around. The steak and chicken are grilled as you wait and then stuffed into homemade flour or corn wrappings. You order at the tile counter and pick up your dish on a plastic tray in minutes. This is a popular spot for locals.

The vegetarian offerings are huge and hearty. One of my favorites is the veggie burrito, which includes rice, black beans, cheese, lettuce, and guacamole doused in tomato salsa. They offer three types of salsa, from mild to superhot. You can see the fresh-cut cilantro and taste the superhot chiles. The chips are hand-cut and flavorful, but a bit too coarse. Skip them and enjoy an order of the rich chunky guacamole with a fork. By the way, there's another location at Doral Plaza, 9739 NW 41st St.

News Café. 800 Ocean Dr., South Beach. ☎ **305/538-6397.** Main courses $7–$17; salads $4–$8; sandwiches $5–$10. AE, MC, V. Daily 24 hours. Valet parking $10. AMERICAN.

This is absolutely one of the best people-watching spots on the beach. Of all the outdoor cafes on trendy South Beach, News Café has been around the longest. Inexpensive breakfasts and cafe fare are served at about 20 perpetually congested tables. Most of the seating is outdoors, and terrace tables are most coveted. Ocean Drive's multitude of fashion photography crews and their models meet here regularly to get the international newspapers and magazines.

The menu is heavy on health-oriented dishes, and includes yogurt with fruit salad, various green salads, imported cheese and meat sandwiches, and a choice of quiches.

Puerto Sagua. 700 Collins Ave., South Beach. ☎ **305/673-1115.** Main courses $8–$24; sandwiches and salads $5–$10. AE, DC, MC, V. Daily 7:30am–2am. CUBAN/SPANISH.

This brown-walled diner is one of the only old holdouts on South Beach. Its steady stream of regulars range from *abuelitos* (little old grandfathers) to hipsters who stop in after clubbing. It has endured because the food is good, if a little greasy. Some of the less heavy dishes are a superchunky fish soup with pieces of whole flaky grouper, the chicken and seafood paella, or the marinated kingfish. Also good are most of the shrimp dishes, especially the shrimp in garlic sauce served with white rice and salad.

This is one of the most reasonably priced places left on the beach for simple, hearty fare. Don't be intimidated by the hunched older waiters in their white button shirts and black pants. Even if you don't speak Spanish, they're usually willing to do charades. Anyway, the extensive menu, which ranges from BLTs to grilled lobsters to yummy fried plantains, is translated into English. Hurry, before another boutique goes up in its place.

Sport Cafe. 560 Washington Ave., South Beach. ☎ **305/674-9700.** Reservations accepted for 4 or more. Main courses $8–$14; sandwiches and pizzas $6–$9. AE, MC, V. Daily noon–1am; sometimes earlier for coffee. ITALIAN.

Don't expect to see the latest football or baseball games at this Sports Cafe; instead, you're more likely to find a soccer match or bicycle race on the television. The Sport Cafe's owners, brothers Tonino and Paolo Doino, hail from Rome. They've put together an authentic Italian menu, listing only half a dozen entrees and a few pizzas. It can be a challenge placing your order, but definitely request a plate of fresh crushed garlic when they bring your bread and oil. I recommend asking for the day's specials and ordering one of them. Always good is the perfectly al dente penne with salmon served with a pink sauce. The eggplant parmigiano, almost always available though not on the menu, is the best in the county. For dessert, try the tiramisu, which, unlike the more common cake or pudding style, is served partially frozen, like an ice cream.

The atmosphere is rustic and young and the prices so reasonable that on some nights you may have to wait for a seat, especially for sidewalk tables.

Stephan's Gourmet Market & Cafe. 1430 Washington Ave. (at Española Way), South Beach. ☎ **305/674-1760.** Main courses $6–$19; dinner special for 2 with salad and a bottle of wine $24.95. AE, MC, V. Sun–Thurs 8am–midnight; Fri–Sat 8am–2am; dinner special served daily 5:30–11pm. DELI/ITALIAN.

This deli, which could be in New York's Little Italy, sells a huge assortment of fresh pastas, breads, and salads, as well as cold cuts, cheeses, and grocery items. Upstairs, however, in a tiny loft used to store wine bottles, you'll find a cozy dining room with space for about 10 couples. Dinner is also served out on the sidewalk or delivered to your hotel.

A chalkboard displays the chef's special, usually a pasta dish with some kind of chicken or fish. One of my favorites is the linguini Alfredo with tender pieces of chicken breast mixed into the light cheesy sauce. While you wait, you'll want to eat baskets and baskets of the very garlicky garlic bread and get started on the bottle of wine that comes with the daily special. The red is an excellent full-bodied Italian Merlot. (The Pinot Grigio, however, I found undrinkable.) If the special doesn't strike you, consider any of the other moderately priced dishes, such as rotisserie chicken with potatoes and vegetables, ziti, sausage and peppers, or eggplant parmigiano. Choose whatever looks good to you from the glass case downstairs or see what else the chef is dishing out. Other locations: 2 NE 40th St. (☎ **305/571-4070**) and 19495 Biscayne Blvd., One Turnberry Pl. (☎ **305/932-8885**).

3 Miami Beach: Surfside, Bal Harbour & Sunny Isles

The area north of the Art Deco District—from about 21st Street to 163rd Street—had its heyday in the 1950s when its huge hotels and gambling halls blocked the view of the ocean. Now, many of the old hotels have been converted into condos or budget lodgings and the bay-front mansions renovated by and for wealthy entrepreneurs,

You Paid What?

47,000 hotels, 700 airlines, 50 rental car companies. And a few million ways to save money.

Travelocity.com
A Sabre Company

Go Virtually Anywhere.

AOL Keyword: Travel

Travelocity™ and Travelocity.com are trademarks of Travelocity.com LP and Sabre™ is a trademark of an affiliate of Sabre Inc. © 2000 Travelocity.com LP. All rights reserved.

Will you have enough stories to tell your grandchildren?

Yahoo! Travel

Do You YAHOO!?

Miami Beach Dining

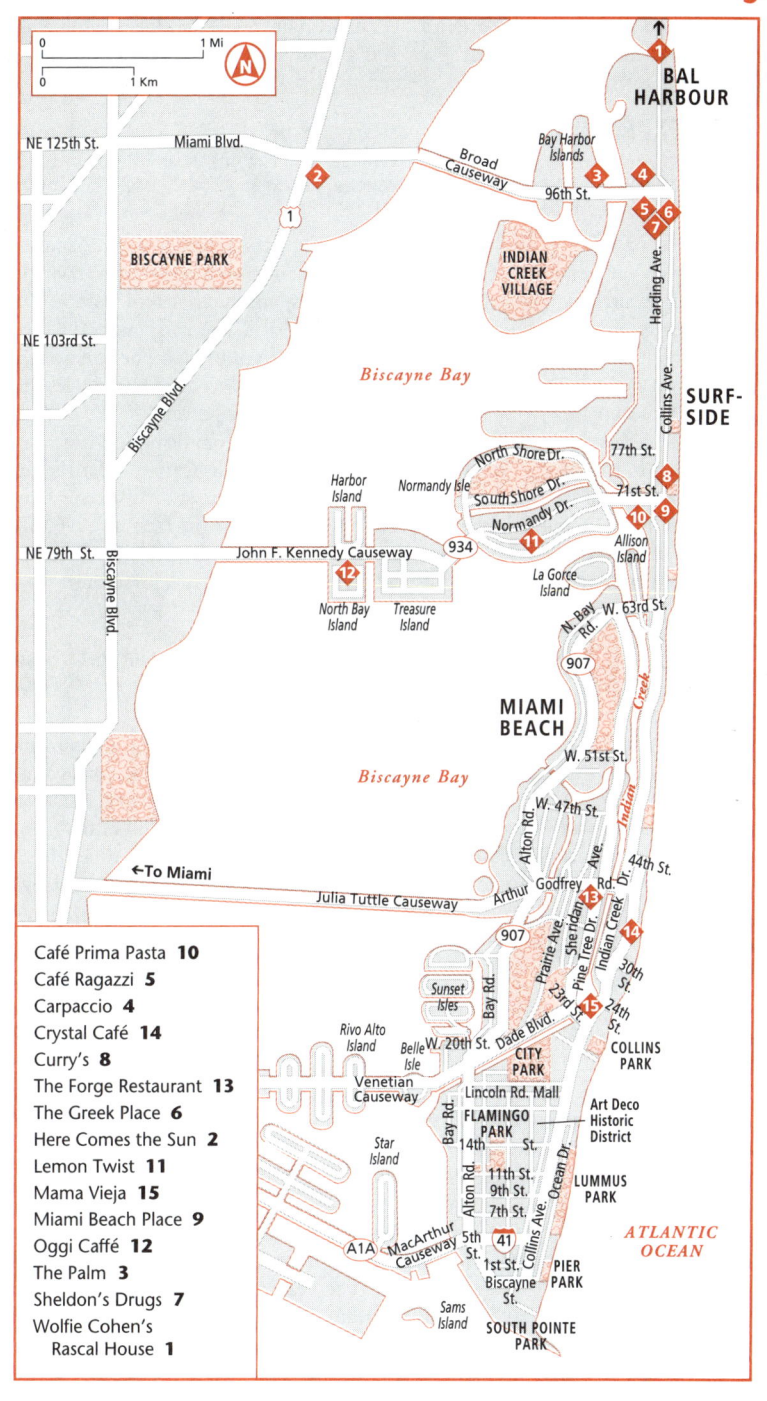

Café Prima Pasta **10**
Café Ragazzi **5**
Carpaccio **4**
Crystal Café **14**
Curry's **8**
The Forge Restaurant **13**
The Greek Place **6**
Here Comes the Sun **2**
Lemon Twist **11**
Mama Vieja **15**
Miami Beach Place **9**
Oggi Caffé **12**
The Palm **3**
Sheldon's Drugs **7**
Wolfie Cohen's Rascal House **1**

families, and speculators. The area now has many more residents, albeit seasonal, than visitors. On the culinary front, the result is a handful of super-expensive, traditional restaurants and a number of value-oriented spots.

VERY EXPENSIVE

✪ **The Forge Restaurant.** 432 Arthur Godfrey Rd. (41st St.), Miami Beach. ☎ **305/538-8533.** Reservations required. Main courses $21–$55. AE, DC, MC, V. Sun–Thurs 6pm–midnight; Fri–Sat 6pm–1am. AMERICAN.

English oak paneling and Tiffany glass suggest high prices and haute cuisine, and that's exactly what you get at The Forge. Each elegant dining room possesses its own character and features high ceilings, ornate chandeliers, and high-quality European artwork. The most intimate room is the library in the back. The Forge attracts a mix of young, moneyed Miamians, well-dressed Euros, and Saudi royalty. The atmosphere is elegant but not too stuffy, especially on Wednesday night, when the singles scene shows up for mingling at the bar and dancing next door at Jimmy's.

Like the rest of the menu, appetizers are mostly classics, from Beluga caviar to baked onion soup to shrimp cocktail and escargot. When they're in season, order the stone crabs. For the main course, any of the seafood, chicken, or veal dishes are recommendable, but The Forge is especially known for its steaks. In fact, in 1996, *Wine Spectator* magazine voted the Super Steak the "Best in America." Finally, The Forge still has one of Miami's best wine lists and an extensive cellar. Ask for a tour.

EXPENSIVE

Carpaccio. 9700 Collins Ave. (97th St., in Bal Harbour shops), Bal Harbour. ☎ **305/867-7777.** Reservations suggested. Main courses $15–$25; pastas $12–$15. AE, MC, V. Daily 11:30am–11pm. ITALIAN.

Serving up some of the best northern Italian cuisine in Miami's ritziest shopping mall, this pricey and elegant cafe packs them in for elegant handmade pastas, pizzas and, of course, carpaccio in a dozen variations. Service is better than at most area restaurants, though when it's really busy, you'll find it hard to attract the attention of the friendly waiters who are scurrying amid the crowds. The feel is casual though diners tend to dress in designer outfits. Some of them actually deign to wait in line on the sidewalk for a table—imagine that!

✪ **Crystal Café.** 726 41st St., Miami Beach. ☎ **305/673-8266.** Reservations recommended on weekends. Main courses $11–$25. AE, CB, DC, DISC, MC, V. Tues–Thurs 5–10pm; Fri–Sat 5–11pm. CONTINENTAL/NEW WORLD.

The setting is sparse, with Lucite salt and pepper grinders and a bottle of wine as the only centerpiece on each of the 15 or so tables. I promise you won't need the seasoning. Chef Klime has done it all with the help of his affable wife and a superb wait staff. Enjoy his unique sparkle at this little-known hideaway, which attracts stars like Julio Iglesias and other discriminating guests.

With approximately 30 entrees, including a few nightly specials, I can't figure out how each appears so perfectly prepared and beautifully presented. The shrimp-cake appetizer, for example, is the size of a bread plate and rests on top of a small mound of lightly sautéed watercress and mushrooms. Surrounding the delicately breaded disc are concentric circles of beautiful sauces. The veal marsala is served in a luscious brown sauce thickened not with heavy cream or flour but with delicate vegetable broth and a hearty mix of mushrooms. Most main courses come with a choice of three side dishes, such as zucchini, carrots, mashed potatoes, or pasta. The osso buco is a masterpiece.

The Palm. 9650 E. Bay Harbor Dr., Bay Harbor Island. ☎ **305/868-7256.** Reservations highly recommended. Main courses $18–$29. AE, CB, DC, MC, V. Daily 5–11pm. From Collins Ave., turn west onto 96th St.; at Bal Harbour Shops, go over a small bridge, and turn right onto East Bay Harbor Dr. The restaurant is half a block down on the left. CONTINENTAL.

You'll feel like you're in New York at this dark clubby steak house known for enormous sirloins and jumbo Maine lobsters. The same celebrity caricatures and photos adorn the walls as in the other Palms in Los Angeles and New York. There are currently more than a dozen branches throughout the country, all known for pleasing a demanding corporate and tourist clientele.

You can't go wrong with the limited, simple menu filled with old standbys, such as Caesar salad, shrimp cocktail, clams oreganata, salmon, broiled chicken, and veal. A selection of steak ranges from chopped to filet mignon. The prices are as big as the portions. You'll find more martini drinkers than health-conscious types here.

Shula's Steak House. In the Alexander Hotel, 5225 Collins Ave., Miami Beach. ☎ **305/531-8300.** Reservations recommended. Main courses $18–$58. AE, DISC, CB, MC, V. Daily 11:00am–3:30pm and 6–11pm. Free valet parking. AMERICAN/STEAK.

Climb a sweeping staircase in the Alexander All Suites Ocean Front Resort and go through the glass hallway—designed like an atrium so exotic flora and fauna beckon both within and without—and you'll find yourself in this magnificent restaurant that has been acclaimed as one of the greatest steak houses in all of North America. If you're feeling adventurous, try the 48-ounce club (you can get your name engraved on a gold plaque if you can finish this absolutely *huge* piece of meat) or settle for the 20-ounce Kansas City strip or the 12-ounce filet mignon. Fresh seafood abounds when in season, and the oysters Rockefeller are a particularly good choice. Each dinner menu is presented with a signed (by Coach Shula of course) NFL Football. The entertaining staff is very knowledgeable, and there's a sizable and reasonably priced wine list. The restaurant also has the "No Name Lounge," where live piano music, premium spirits, and cigar smoking are available.

There's another branch of Shula's at 7601 NW 154th St. (in Don Shula's Golf Club off the Palmetto Expressway; ☎ **305/820-8102**) in West Dade.

MODERATE

Cafe Prima Pasta. 414 71st St. (half a block east of the Byron movie theater), Miami Beach. ☎ **305/867-0106.** Reservations not accepted. Main courses $9–$17; pastas $7–$9. No credit cards. Mon–Thurs noon–midnight; Fri noon–1am; Sat 1pm–1am; Sun 5pm–midnight. ITALIAN.

Here's another tiny pasta joint that serves phenomenal homemade noodles with good old-Italian sauces, such as carbonara, dioliva, putanesca, and pomodoro. There are only 30 seats, so you might feel a bit cramped, but the crowd is generally a pleasant, young, laid-back set. The stuffed agnolotti, with tomato or pesto sauce, spinach, and ricotta are so delicate and flavorful that you'll think you're eating dessert. Speaking of which, you'll want to try the apple tart with a pale golden caramel sauce. Ask for it à la mode and plan to come back again for more.

Its location, closer to Collins Avenue, makes this place more popular than the superior Oggi just a few miles west. Be prepared to stand in line.

Cafe Ragazzi. 9500 Harding Ave. (on corner of 95th St.), Surfside. ☎ **305/866-4495.** Reservations accepted for 4 or more. Main courses $9–$18. MC, V. Mon–Fri 11:30am–3pm and 5:30–11pm; Sat–Sun 5:30–11pm. ITALIAN.

A relative newcomer in a neighborhood of old-time delis and diners, this little Italian cafe, with its rustic decor and a handsome wait staff, enjoys great success for its tasty simple pastas. The spicy putanesca sauce with a subtle hint of fish is perfectly prepared, with just enough bits of tomato to give it some weight. Also recommended is the salmon with radicchio. You can choose from many decent salads and carpacci, too. Lunch specials are a real steal at $7, including soup, salad, and daily pasta. The mostly Italian/Argentinean staff is efficient, although sometimes limited in their ability to communicate. Expect a wait on weekend nights.

Caffe Da Vinci. 1009 Kane Concourse (96th St.), Bay Harbor Islands. ☎ **305/861-8166.** Reservations recommended. Main courses $10–$20; appetizers $7–$9. AE, MC, V. Daily 11:30am–2:30pm and 5:30–11:30pm. ITALIAN.

Caffe Da Vinci is owned by the same brothers who put the 79th Street Causeway on the map with Oggi Caffe—both spots have cuisine that appeals to the cultured palate. Specials vary, but the *ossobuco milanese* served with Risotto, and the homemade black linguine, with calamari, mussels, shrimp, and crabs are seasonal favorites. The wine list is a special treat—this has to be one of the few restaurant groups that serves wine by the glass, from a variety of at least a dozen bottles, which range from an Australian Shiraz ($18.50 per bottle) to a California Cabernet Sauvignon at ($23 per bottle). Clearly the mark-up is slight and reflects an honest attempt to keep the customers pleased and coming back—which they do.

Lemon Twist. 908 71st St. (on 79th St. Causeway), Miami Beach/Normandy Isle. ☎ **305/868-2075.** Reservations suggested on weekends. Main courses $9–$18; pastas $9.50–$14.50; appetizers $4–$10.50. AE, MC, V. Winter daily 6pm–midnight. Off-season Tues–Sun 6pm–midnight. FRENCH BISTRO.

This hip little French bar and restaurant in a burgeoning neighborhood is certainly worth a visit. The house specialties are salads and seafood. Both are quite good, but even better is the cozy atmosphere both inside and on the outside patio. The lamb shank and the chicken with lemon and cream sauce are two of the tastier dishes, and my favorite salad here features a mound of herbed goat cheese in a puff pastry shell over a bed of fresh baby greens dressed in a delicate but spicy vinaigrette. The pastas, on the other hand, are not even worth a try—most are overcooked and others underseasoned. An original touch: Complimentary lemon vodka shots are offered after each meal.

✪ **Mama Vieja.** 235 23rd St. (just west of Collins Ave.), South Beach. ☎ **305/538-2400.** Main courses $9–$30. AE, CB, DC, DISC, MC, V. Daily noon–midnight. COLOMBIAN.

This funky Colombian hangout is a real find. It serves supremely fresh national specialties in a setting that might well be the backdrop for a Latin American spaghetti Western. Brightly painted walls and elevated porches look out onto a large-screen TV showing music videos from the old country. The walls and ceilings are decorated with hundreds of hats that have been donated by customers and signed in exchange for a free meal. Bring in an interesting hat and mention it to the server before placing your order so they can bring you to the attention of the owner.

Start with an avocado salad and rich meat-filled empanadas served with spicy sauce or a creamy fish soup and green plantains stuffed with mixed seafood with large chunks of shellfish and fresh fillets. The best dishes are seafood selections—one outrageous dish is called *pargo rojo estofado a la mama vieja,* a red snapper stuffed with a super creamy and delicate seafood sauce in a rice base. It's made for two ($29.95), but if you order the *corvina a la mama vieja* for one ($12.95), you can try the same rich stuffing in a slightly smaller fish for much less money. All the dishes here are worth trying and so reasonably priced, it's easy to order a lot. Try to save room for the milky sweet desserts and a good strong coffee—you'll need it if you want to dance all night. Next door is a popular disco and nightclub, Studio 23.

✪ **Oggi Caffe.** 1740 79th St. Causeway (in the White Star shopping center next to the Bagel Cafe), North Bay Village. ☎ **305/866-1238.** Reservations recommended. Main courses $14–$25; pastas $9–$13. AE, CB, DC, MC, V. Mon–Fri 11:30am–2:30pm; daily 6–11pm. ITALIAN.

Tucked away in a tiny strip mall on the 79th Street Causeway, this neighborhood favorite makes fresh pastas daily. Each one, from the agnolotti stuffed with fresh spinach and ricotta to the wire-thin spaghettini, is tender and tasty. A hearty *pasta e fagiola* is filled with beans and vegetables and could almost be a meal. I also recommend the daily soups, especially the creamy spinach soup, when it's on the menu. Though you could fill up on the starters, the entrees, especially the grilled dishes, are superb. The salmon is served on a bed of spinach with a light lemon-butter sauce. The place is small and a bit rushed, but it's well worth the slight discomfort for this authentic, moderately priced food.

Wolfie Cohen's Rascal House. 17190 Collins Ave., Sunny Isles. ☎ **305/947-4581.** Main courses $8–$30. AE, MC, V. Daily 24 hours. DELI.

Open since 1954 and still going strong, this historic, nostalgic culinary extravaganza is one of Miami Beach's greatest traditions. Simple tables and booths, as well as plenty of patrons, fill the airy 425-seat dining room. The menu is as huge as the portions; try the corned beef, schmaltz herring, brisket, kreplach, chicken soup, or other authentic Jewish staples. Take-out service is available.

INEXPENSIVE

Curry's. 7433 Collins Ave., Miami Beach. ☎ **305/866-1571.** Reservations accepted. Main courses (including appetizer and dessert) $9–$20. MC, V. Daily 4–10pm. AMERICAN.

Established in 1937, this large dining room on the ocean side of Collins Avenue is one of Miami Beach's oldest restaurants. Neither the restaurant's name nor the Polynesian wall decorations are indicative of its offerings, which are straightforwardly American and reminiscent of the area's heyday. Broiled and fried fish dishes are available, but the best selections, including steak, chicken, and ribs, come off the open charcoal grill perched by the front window. Prices are incredibly reasonable here, and include an appetizer, soup, or salad, as well as a potato or vegetable, dessert, and coffee or tea.

Emerald Coast. 16850 Collins Ave. (RK Center South), Aventura. ☎ **305/787-1530.** Reservations accepted. Main courses $14–$17. AE, MC, V. Daily noon–2:30pm and 4:30–9pm; Sat–Sun until 10pm. ASIAN.

Sporting a sumptuous Asian buffet featuring items prepared with no MSG, Emerald Coast has become a haven for everyone from busloads of tourists to carloads of gray-haired hipsters to vans filled with hungry kids. Florida's largest Chinese Gourmet Buffet was voted the number-one Chinese Restaurant by the *Sun-Sentinel*, and rightly so. The buffet includes a sushi bar, four soup tureens, a meat carving station, and a dessert bar, in addition to a full Asian food bar. All items can be ordered separately by parties of 10 to 12. There's a nice selection of vegetarian fare. Seafood is the priciest cuisine here, with 16 pieces of Szechuan shrimp costing the most at $10.95. There's another location in Sunrise at 4519 North Pine Island Rd. (☎ 954/572-3822.)

✪ **The Greek Place.** 233 95th St. (between Collins and Harding aves.), Surfside. ☎ **305/866-9628.** Main courses $6–$7. No credit cards. Mon–Fri 10am–5:30pm; Sat 11am–3pm. GREEK.

It's a little hole-in-the-wall diner with sparkling white walls and about 10 wooden stools that serves fantastic Greek and American diner-style food. Daily specials like pastitsio, chicken alcyone, and roast turkey with all the fixings are big lunchtime draws for locals working in the area. Typical Greek dishes like shish kebab, souvlakis, and gyros are cooked to perfection as you wait. Even the hamburger, prime ground beef delicately spiced and freshly grilled, is exemplary.

Miami Beach Place. 6954 Collins Ave., Miami Beach. ☎ **305/866-8661.** Main courses $10–$13; pizzas and pastas $7–$16. MC, V. Sun–Fri 6pm–midnight; Sat 1pm–midnight. ITALIAN/PIZZA.

This Brazilian-owned pizza parlor is full most weekends, not only because of its good inexpensive pastas and pizzas, but also because of the fun Brazilian bands that play most weekend nights after 9pm. By midnight, the place is packed with Portuguese-speaking dancers who enjoy a late-night buffet and lots of wine and beer. I think the light garlicky rolls wrapped in golden twists are addictive. While the pizza tends to be too cheesy for my taste, its toppings are fresh instead of the canned variety offered at other places. If you've never tasted the ubiquitous Brazilian soda, Guaraná, I suggest trying a sip; it's like a rich ginger ale with not as much zing.

Sheldon's Drugs. 9501 Harding Ave., Surfside. ☎ **305/866-6251.** Main courses $4–$8; soups and sandwiches $2–$5. AE, DISC, MC, V. Mon–Sat 7am–9pm; Sun 7am–4pm. AMERICAN.

This typical old-fashioned drugstore counter was a favorite breakfast spot of Isaac Bashevis Singer. Consider stopping into this historic site for a good piece of pie and a side of history. According to legend, the legendary author was sitting at Sheldon's, eating a bagel and eggs, when his wife got the call in 1978 that he had won the Nobel Prize for Literature. The menu hasn't changed much since then. You can get eggs and oatmeal and a good tuna melt. A blue-plate special might be generic spaghetti and meatballs or grilled frankfurters. The food is pretty basic, but you can't beat the prices.

4 Key Biscayne

Key Biscayne has some of the world's nicest beaches, hotels, and parks, yet it's not known for great food. Most visitors eat at the island's largest hotel, where the food is reliable if not outstanding. Locals, or "Key rats" as they're known, tend to go off-island for meals or take-out, but here are some of the best on-the-island choices.

EXPENSIVE

Rusty Pelican. 3201 Rickenbacker Causeway, Key Biscayne. ☎ **305/361-3818.** Reservations recommended. Main courses $16–$20. AE, CB, DC, MC, V. Daily 11:30am–4pm; Sun–Thurs 5–11pm; Fri–Sat 5pm–midnight. CONTINENTAL.

The Pelican's private tropical walkway leads over a lush waterfall into one of the most romantic dining rooms in the city, located right on beautiful blue-green Biscayne Bay. The restaurant's windows look out over the water onto the sparkling stalagmites of Miami's magnificent downtown. Inside, quiet wicker paddle fans whirl overhead and saltwater fish swim in pretty tableside aquariums.

    The restaurant's surf-and-turf menu features conservatively prepared prime steaks, veal, shrimp, and lobster. The food is good, but the atmosphere is even better, especially at sunset, when the view over the city is magical.

Stefano's. 24 Crandon Blvd., Key Biscayne. ☎ **305/361-7007.** Reservations recommended on weekends. Main courses $11–$29; appetizers $8–$12. AE, DC, MC, V. Mon–Fri 11:30am–2:30pm; Sun–Thurs 6–11pm; Fri–Sat 6pm–12:30am. Disco open later. ITALIAN.

For retro-elegance, Stefano's has no match. Its restaurant and disco share the same strobe-lit atmosphere. Food is traditional and reliable, if a little pricey. You'll find an

Dining in Coral Gables, Coconut Grove, Downtown & Key Biscayne

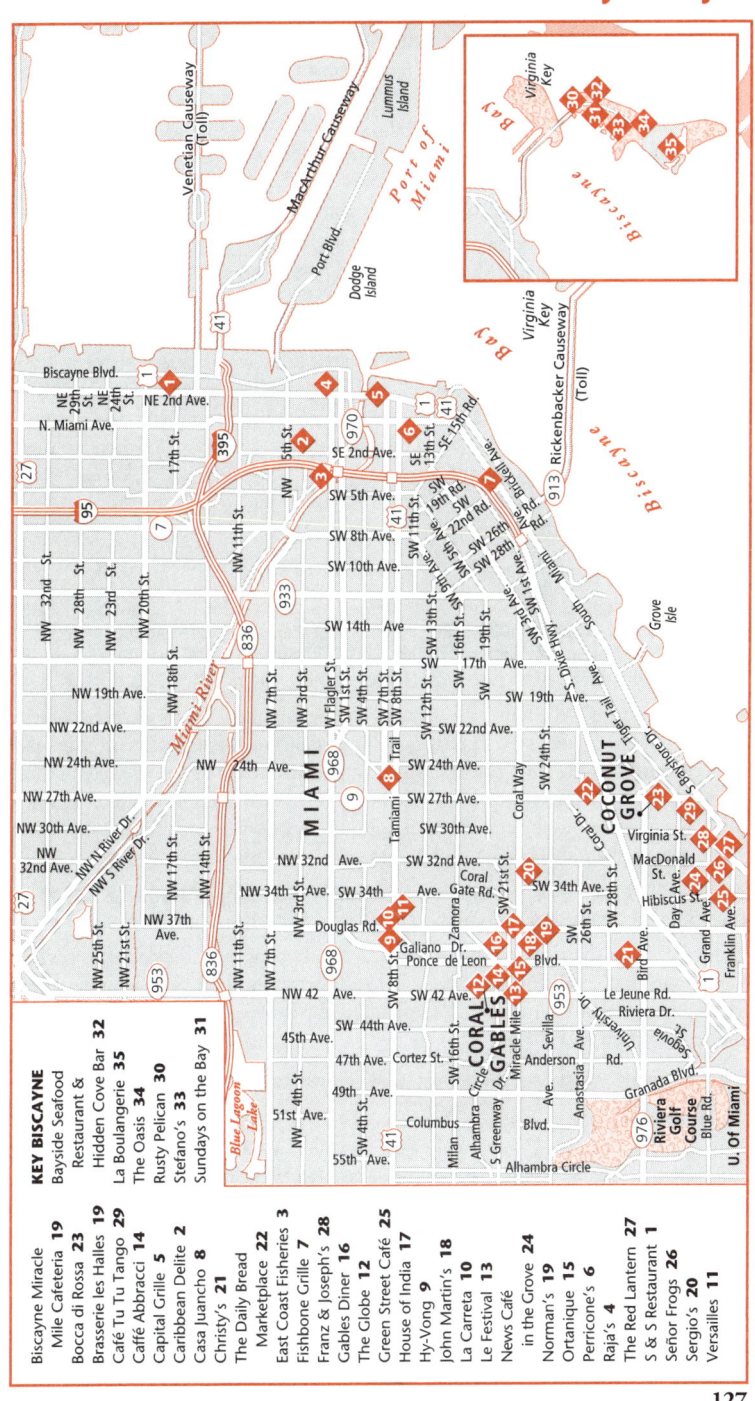

KEY BISCAYNE
Bayside Seafood Restaurant & Hidden Cove Bar 32
La Boulangerie 35
The Oasis 34
Rusty Pelican 30
Stefano's 33
Sundays on the Bay 31

Biscayne Miracle Mile Cafeteria 19
Bocca di Rossa 23
Brasserie les Halles 19
Café Tu Tu Tango 29
Caffé Abbracci 14
Capital Grille 5
Caribbean Delite 2
Casa Juancho 8
Christy's 21
The Daily Bread Marketplace 22
East Coast Fisheries 3
Fishbone Grille 7
Franz & Joseph's 28
Gables Diner 16
The Globe 12
Green Street Café 25
House of India 17
Hy-Vong 9
John Martin's 18
La Carreta 10
Le Festival 13
News Café in the Grove 24
Norman's 19
Ortanique 15
Perricone's 6
Raja's 4
The Red Lantern 27
S & S Restaurant 1
Señor Frogs 26
Sergio's 20
Versailles 11

127

older country club crowd here in the evenings, enjoying steaks, pastas, and seafood. One of the best entrees is the Delfino Livornese, a dolphin (not Flipper—a type of saltwater fish) sautéed with a spicy sauce of tomato, olives, capers, and onions. Stefano's also serves some rare game, such as guinea hen in wine sauce and quail wrapped in pancetta. I recommend sticking with the pastas and fish.

After 7:30pm, the band starts playing American pop and Latin favorites. Some nights you feel as if you accidentally happened upon your long-lost cousin's wedding, as you watch the parade of taffeta dresses and tipsy uncles. Stefano's has continued to do well over time because of its dependable service and kitchen.

Sundays on the Bay. 5420 Crandon Blvd., Key Biscayne. ☎ **305/361-6777.** Reservations recommended for Sun brunch. Main courses $15–$24; Sun brunch $18.95. AE, CB, DC, MC, V. Daily 11:30am–11:45pm; Sun brunch 11am–4pm. AMERICAN.

Although its food is fine, Sundays is really a fun tropical bar that features an unbeatable view of Downtown, Coconut Grove, and the Sunday's marina. The menu features local favorites—grouper, tuna, snapper, and good shellfish in season. Competent renditions of such classic dishes as oysters Rockefeller, shrimp scampi, and *lobster fra diablo* are recommendable. Particularly popular is the Sunday brunch, when a buffet the size of Bimini attracts the city's in-crowd.

The lively bar stays open all week until midnight and weekends until 2am, with a DJ spinning most nights from 9pm.

INEXPENSIVE

✪ **Bayside Seafood Restaurant and Hidden Cove Bar.** 3501 Rickenbacker Causeway, Key Biscayne. ☎ **305/361-0808.** Reservations accepted for 15 or more. Appetizers, salads, and sandwiches $4.50–$8; platters $7–$13. AE, MC, V. Sun–Thurs 11:30am–10:30pm; Fri–Sat 11:30am–midnight; disco on weekends ($5 cover) 11pm–4am. SEAFOOD.

Known by locals as "the Hut," this ramshackle restaurant and bar is a laid-back outdoor tiki hut and terrace that serves pretty good sandwiches and fish platters on paper plates. A blackboard lists the latest catches, which can be prepared blackened, fried, broiled, or in a garlic sauce. I prefer the blackened, which is supercrusty, spicy, and dark. The fish dip is wonderfully smoky and moist, if a little heavy on mayonnaise. Local fishers and yacht owners share this rustic outpost with equal enthusiasm and loyalty.

The Oasis. 19 Harbor Dr. (on corner of Crandon), Key Biscayne. ☎ **305/361-5709.** Main courses $4–$12; sandwiches $3–$4. No credit cards. Daily 6am–9pm. CUBAN.

Everyone, from the city's mayor to the local handymen, meet for delicious paella and Cuban sandwiches at this little shack. They gather around the little window or inside at the few tables for superpowerful *cafesitos* and rich *croquetas*. It's slightly dingy, but the food is good and cheap.

5 Downtown

Downtown Miami is a large sprawling area divided by the Brickell bridge into two distinct areas: Brickell Avenue and the bay-front area near Biscayne Boulevard. You shouldn't walk from one to the other—it's quite a distance and unsafe at night. Convenient Metromover stops do adjoin the areas, so for a quarter, it's better to hop on the scenic sky-tram (closed after midnight).

EXPENSIVE

✪ **Capital Grille.** 444 Brickell Ave., Miami, ☎ **305/374-4500.** Reservations recommended. Main courses $17–$46; appetizers $10–$30. AE, D, CB, MC, V. Mon–Fri 11:30am–3pm; Sun–Thurs 5–10pm; Fri–Sat 5–11pm. STEAK HOUSE.

This is elegant dining at its best. Here you'll find dark wood-paneled walls, wine cellars filled with high-end classics, pristine white tablecloths, chandeliers, marble floors, and stuffed game heads that look like they came right out of an Australian backyard. While the porterhouse steak is a mighty contender, I have yet to find a lobster as huge and succulent as theirs. To say it's mouth-watering is an understatement. Even the baby lobster is a giant. For an appetizer start with the lobster and crab cakes—you'd have to go to Maryland or Maine to find anything close to their equal. If you're not in the mood for beef or lobster, try the pan-seared red snapper and asparagus covered with Hollandaise. As you dine, look around, you're surrounded by cellars filled with about 5,000 bottles of wines—too extensive and rare to list. There are private dining rooms for large parties and smaller ones for more intimate settings.

Indigo Restaurant and Bar. In the Hotel Inter-Continental, 100 Chopin Plaza, Miami. ☎ **305/577-1000**, ext. 65. Reservations recommended. Main courses $9–$26; daily lunch buffet $19 per person; Sun brunch (features live jazz) $38. AE, DISC, MC, V. Daily 7am–11pm. CONTINENTAL.

The Indigo Restaurant and Bar is more than a splash of deep blue and canary yellow in the heart of the elegant Hotel Inter-Continental, it's a welcome place to meet friends or have a tasty repast. Their lunch buffet cycles through a different array of dishes from a variety of countries (once it was Italy, then Brazil, and you can expect India to take center stage soon) every 12 weeks. The dinner menu has some of the finest (albeit pricey) selections of steak, wines (in fact their wine list is as extensive as that in any of the other leading restaurants in the city), and seafood. The restaurant excels in producing international delights such as Moroccan tagines and contemporary fondues, as well as tasty appetizers such as tarragon gnocchis, stir-fried green vegetables, and orzo "risotto." For dessert, try the golden pineapple and star anise chimichanga—an exotic piece of heaven.

MODERATE

Bubba Gump Shrimp Co. In Bayside Marketplace, 401 Biscayne Blvd, Miami. ☎ **305/379-8866**. Main courses $12–18; appetizers $3–$12. AE, DC, DISC, MC, V. Sun–Thurs 11am–10pm; Fri–Sat 11am–midnight. SEAFOOD.

This is what Forrest Gump's place would probably have looked like had he really gone into the shrimpin' business. Located right on the water, Bubba Gump Shrimp Co. offers some of the best shrimp specials in town. For starters, try the "Run Across America Sampler." It includes Bubba's Far Out Dip and Chips, New Orleans Peel n' Eat Shrimp, Texas Wild Wings, and Alabama Fried Shrimp for only $12. The "Dumb Luck" coconut shrimp is my favorite, served with Cajun marmalade, coleslaw and fries for only $15.30. If you're not a coconut fan, try the crab legs served with a Cajun or garlic spice blend. There are also a number of salads to choose from. It's a fun place to bring the kids on a sunny afternoon. You can watch boats float lazily by, listen to a live band or watch salsa dancers perform at the Bayside Grandstand.

✪ **East Coast Fisheries.** 360 W. Flagler St., Miami. ☎ **305/372-1300**. Reservations recommended. Main courses $17–$24. AE, MC, V. Daily 11am–10pm. From I-95 South, exit at N.W. 8th St. (Exit 5A). Drive straight to N.W. 3rd St. and turn right. The next block is North River Dr. Turn left, and you'll see the restaurant 3 blocks down on the right side.

East Coast Fisheries is a no-nonsense retail market and restaurant offering a terrific variety of the freshest fish available. The dozen or so plain wood tables are surrounded by refrigerated glass cases filled with snapper, salmon, mahimahi, trout, tuna, crabs, oysters, lobsters, and the like. The absolutely huge menu features every fish imaginable, cooked the way you want it—grilled, fried, stuffed, Cajun-style, Florentine, hollandaise, or blackened. However, the smell of frying grease detracts from the otherwise quaint old Miami feel right on the riverfront. Service is fast, but good prices and good food can mean long lines on weekends.

✪ Fishbone Grille. 650 S. Miami Ave. (SW 7th Ave., next to Tobacco Rd.), Miami. ☎ **305/530-1915.** Reservations recommended for 6 or more. Main courses $9–$20. AE, CB, DC, DISC, MC, V. Mon–Thurs 11:30am–10pm; Fri 11:30am–11pm; Sat 5–11pm. SEAFOOD.

This is by far Miami's best and most reasonably priced seafood restaurant. Located in a small strip mall it shares with Tobacco Road, this sensational fish shop prepares dozens of outstanding specials daily. The atmosphere is nothing to speak of, although at one cool table you can stare into a fish tank.

Try the excellent seviche, which has just enough spice to give it a zing, yet doesn't overwhelm the fresh fish flavor. The stews, crab cakes, and all the starters are superb. If you like a nice Caribbean flavor, try the *jerk Covina* (the Biblical fish) or one of the excellent dolphin specialties. There's another Fishbone Grille in Coral Gables at 1450 S. Dixie Highway (☎ **305/668-3033**).

Provence Grill. 1001 South Miami Ave., Miami. ☎ **305/373-1940.** Reservations accepted. Main courses $13.95–$21.95; appetizers $4.95–$6.95. AE, V, MC. Mon–Fri 11am–3pm and 5–11:00pm; Sat–Sun 5–10pm. FRENCH.

This restaurant serves some of the best French meals this side of Toulouse. The brothers Cormouls-Houles use their prodigious culinary skills to assemble an affordable menu that allows the rest of us to know just how the French really live—and they do it, dare we say, with incredible panache. The grilled specialties, from chicken to salmon, are imbued with only the best seasonings and sauces. The 12 oz. rib-eye, served with a veal demiglace and fresh foie gras, is scrumptious and worth every bit of its $21.95. Canard lovers will enjoy the grilled duck fillet in a red port sauce. Real culinary adventurers should try the dessert menu—a crème brûlée spiced with lavender (a local French favorite) is just one selection—which is truly a delight.

Soyka Restaurant & Café. 5556 N.E. 4th Court (Design District), Miami. ☎ **305/759-3117.** Reservations recommended. Main courses $10.75–$24. AE, MC, V. Daily 11am–5pm and 5–11pm (bar open until midnight); Fri–Sat open until midnight (bar open until 1am). Happy hour Mon–Fri 4–7pm. AMERICAN.

Soyka is a much-needed addition to the area known as the Biscayne Corridor. The sleek interior design is a chic setting for power lunches or sumptuous dinners that can last well into an evening. Lunches focus on burgers, sandwiches, and wood-fired oven pizzas. Executive chef Gabrielle Hakman truly excels during the dinner hours when her starters of crispy calamari or polenta with sautéed mushrooms prepare the palate for some of the best-grilled steaks in the city. The turkey Salisbury steak ragout ($13.50) is a steal, and all the other steaks are excellent. The bar has a variety of sample drinks and desserts, from brie and fruit to lemon pound cake, to round out the succinct and successful menu. A children's menu is available for both lunch and dinner.

INEXPENSIVE

✪ Caribbean Delite. 236 NE First Ave. (across the street from Miami Dade Community College), Miami. ☎ **305/381-9254.** Main courses $5–$10. AE, MC, V. Mon–Sat 8:30am–7pm; Sun 8:30am–4pm. JAMAICAN.

You'd never spot this tiny storefront diner if you weren't looking for it, but you might smell it from the sidewalk. The aroma of succulent jerk chicken or pork beckons regulars back over and over again. Try the Jamaican specialties, such as the oxtail stew or the curried goat, tender tasty pieces of meat on the bone in a spicy yellow sauce. The kitchen can be stingy with its spectacular sauces, leaving the dishes a bit dry, so ask for an extra helping on the side, and they are happy to oblige. Also, if you come early in the day, you can get a taste of Jamaica's national dish, salt fish and ackee (usually served for breakfast). Ask chef-owner Carol Whyte to tell you the story of the national dish of her homeland made with "brain fruit," or quiz one of the many Jamaicans who stop in while they are in port off the cruise ships a few blocks away.

Conga Bar/Lombardi's. Bayside Marketplace, 401 Biscayne Blvd., Miami. ☎ **305/381-9580.** Reservations suggested. Pastas $15; pizzas $10.50; appetizers $7–$9. AE, MC, V. Daily 11am–1am; Thurs–Sat until 2am. LATIN/ITALIAN.

Bayside—the broad pedestrian shopping mall that straddles the bay front park of Miami's scenic downtown—is a must-visit for every new traveler to the city, and newcomers and locals alike will truly enjoy the newest addition to the Italian eatery Lombardi's, the Conga Bar. Like all good bars, the Conga Bar comes replete with every mixed drink this side of Havana. The catch is there's a two-drink minimum to enjoy what becomes a very lively and fun floorshow by experienced singers and dancers. Don't be surprised to find yourself climbing out of your seat to rumba or salsa alongside scantily clad lasses and swivel-hipped young lads. The restaurant also has a great raw bar, delicious pastas and pizzas, and some lovely desserts courtesy of chef Joe Monteiro (the double rich chocolate cake is a devilish must).

Granny Feelgoods. 25 W. Flagler St., Miami. ☎ **305/377-9600.** Reservations not accepted. Main courses $9–$12. AE, MC, V. Mon–Fri 7am–5pm. AMERICAN.

Owner Irving Fields has been in the business of serving healthful food for more than 28 years, and his flagship store's offerings are priced right. Due to its proximity to the courthouse, there's a lot of legal eagle traffic and networking going on here. Locals love Granny's for the fresh fish and poultry specials, a line of salads that define greenery and good health, and the always-impeccable service by a family oriented staff that likes to get to know its clientele. Tourists swinging through downtown on the Metromover or just spinning by can munch healthily on anything from a Brown Rice and Steamed Vegetable Plate to Granny's Famous Tuna Salad Platter. The chef's identity is a secret, but I happen to know he was trained under local extraordinaire Chef Allen, and also did a stint at Fisher Island, so the cuisine here will most definitely please the palate. Granny Feelgood's even sells its own line of vitamins and herbal products, and is available for evening functions and parties.

La Cibeles Cafe. 105 NE 3rd Ave. (1 block west of Biscayne Blvd.), Miami. ☎ **305/577-3454.** Main courses $5–$9. No credit cards. Mon–Sat 7:30am–7:30pm. CUBAN.

This typical Latin diner serves some of the best food in town. Just by looking at the line that runs out the door every afternoon between noon and 2pm, you can see that you're not the first to discover it. For about $5, you can have a huge and filling meal. Pay attention to the daily lunch specials and go with them. A pounded, tender chicken breast (*pechuga*) is smothered in sautéed onions and served with rice and beans and a salad. The trout and the roast pork are both very good. When available, try the *ropa vieja*, a shredded beef dish delicately spiced and served with peas and rice.

Perricone's Marketplace. 15 SE 10th St. (corner of S. Miami Ave.), Miami. ☎ **305/374-9693.** Sandwiches $6.95–$8.25; pastas $11.50–$16.95. AE, MC, V. Sun–Mon 7:30am–10:30pm, Tues–Sat until midnight. ITALIAN.

A large selection of groceries and wine, plus an outdoor porch for dining, makes this one of the most welcoming spots downtown. Sundays offer buffet brunches and all-you-can-eat dinners, too. But, it's most popular weekdays at noon, when the suit-types show up for delectable sandwiches, quick and delicious pastas, and hearty salads.

Raja's. 243 E. Flagler St. (in the Galeria International mall), Miami. ☎ **305/539-9551.** Menu items $3–$6; specials, including salad, rice, and vegetable side dishes $5. No credit cards. Thurs–Tues 9am–6:30pm; Sun 9am–4:30pm. INDIAN/FAST FOOD.

Nearly impossible to find, this tiny counter in the hustling Downtown food court serves some of the feistiest chicken stews and vegetarian dishes in Miami. It's surrounded by mostly Brazilian fast-food places packed with tour groups on shopping sprees.

If you like it spicy, try the rich masala spicy chile chicken. For vegetarians, the heaping platters of dal, cauliflower, eggplant, broccoli, and chickpeas are a valuable find. For those who know to request them, there are half a dozen tasty condiments, including lemon chutney with fresh orange rinds, bright green cilantro sauce, and glistening gold mango chutney that will complement the rough stews and tasty soups. The *masala dosa* (rice crepes stuffed with vegetable mash) is a filling lunch or dinner made to order.

S&S Restaurant. 1757 N.E. Second Ave., Miami. ☎ **305/373-4291.** Main courses $5–$11. No credit cards. Mon–Fri 6am–4pm; Sat–Sun 6am–2 or 2:30pm (later on Heat game nights). AMERICAN/DINER FARE.

This tiny chrome-and-linoleum-counter restaurant in the middle of Downtown looks like a truck stop. But locals have been coming back since it opened in 1938. Expect a wait at lunchtime while the mostly male clientele, from lawyers to linemen, wait patiently for huge quantities of old-fashioned fast food.

You'll get a slice of Miami history along with your pie at S&S. Although the neighborhood has become pretty undesirable, the food—basic diner fare with some excellent stews and soups—hasn't changed in years. It's one of the only places in town I know that serves creamed chicken on toast. Also good when it's on the specials' board is the stuffed cabbage roll in a pale brown sauce. In addition to cheap breakfasts, the diner serves up some of the most comfortable food in Miami.

6 Little Havana

The main artery of Little Havana is a busy commercial strip called Southwest 8th Street, or Calle Ocho. Auto body shops, cigar factories, and furniture stores line this street, and on every corner there seems to be a pass-through window serving super-strong Cuban coffee and snacks. In addition, many of the Cuban, Dominican, Nicaraguan, Peruvian, and other Latin American immigrants have opened full-scale restaurants ranging from intimate candlelit establishments to bustling stand-up lunch counters.

MODERATE

✪ **Casa Juancho.** 2436 SW 8th St. (just east of S.W. 27th Ave.), Little Havana. ☎ **305/642-2452.** Reservations recommended, but not accepted Fri–Sat after 8pm. Main courses $15–$34; tapas $6–$8. AE, CB, DC, DISC, MC, V. Sun–Thurs noon–midnight; Fri–Sat noon–1am. SPANISH.

One of Miami's finest Hispanic restaurants, Casa Juancho offers an ambitious menu of excellently prepared main dishes and tapas. The numerous dining rooms are decorated with traditional Spanish furnishings and enlivened nightly by strolling Spanish musicians. Try not to be frustrated with the older staff that doesn't speak English or respond quickly to your subtle glance. They are used to an aggressive clientele.

Cuban Coffee

Despite the more than dozen Starbucks that dot the Miami landscape, locals still rely on the many Cuban cafeterias for their daily caffeine fix.

Cuban coffee is a long-standing tradition in Miami. You'll find it served from the take-out windows of hundreds of *cafeterías* or *luncherías* around town, especially in Little Havana, Downtown, Hialeah, and the beaches. Depending on where you are and what you want, you'll spend between 40¢ and $1.50 per cup.

The best *cafe cubano* has a rich layer of foam on top formed when the hot espresso shoots from the machine into the sugar below. The result is the caramelly, sweet, potent concoction that's a favorite of locals of all nationalities.

To partake, you've just got to learn how to ask for it *en español*.

I suggest ordering lots of *tapas*, small dishes of Spanish "finger food." Some of the best include mixed seafood vinaigrette, fresh shrimp in hot garlic sauce, and fried calamari rings. A few entrees stand out, like roast suckling pig, baby eels in garlic and olive oil, and Iberian-style snapper.

INEXPENSIVE

La Carreta. 3632 SW 8th St., Little Havana. ☎ **305/444-7501.** Main courses $5–$22. AE, CB, DISC, DC, MC, V. Daily 24 hours. CUBAN.

This cavernous family style restaurant is filled with relics of an old farm and college kids eating *medianoches* (midnight sandwiches with ham, cheese, and pickles) after partying all night. Waitresses are brusque but efficient and will help Anglos along who may not know all the lingo. The menu is vast and very authentic. Try the *sopa de pollo*, a rich golden stock loaded with chunks of chicken and fresh vegetables or the *ropa vieja*, a shredded beef stew in a thick brown sauce.

Because of its immense popularity and low prices, La Carreta has opened several branches throughout Miami, including a counter in the Miami airport. Check the white pages for other locations.

✪ **La Esquina de Tejas.** 101 S.W. 12th Ave., Little Havana. ☎ **305/545-0337.** Daily specials $4–$12; appetizers 75¢–$5.50. AE, MC, V. Daily 8am–9pm. CUBAN.

Best known as the diner where Ronald Reagan ate during his 1983 campaign in Miami, La Esquina de Tejas has gained a national reputation for its great food and low prices. There's a shrine dedicated to the former president in the "Presidential Quarters," and the menu even has his signed autograph and the presidential seal of approval. This is Cuban food at its best. You must try the *arroz a la marinera*, the Cuban version of Spanish paella. It's filled with clams, oysters, mussels, lobster, shrimp, squid, snapper, stone crab, and scallops cooked in a fresh seafood broth. If you're not in the mood for seafood (after all this is a Cuban joint), try the *vaca frita*, a grilled, shredded flank steak served with moro rice (black beans cooked with white rice) and *maduros*—sweet, fried plantains. Another house specialty is the *masas de puerco fritas*, a pork tenderloin cut in chunks, roasted, and then quickly deep-fried and served with mojo, grilled onions, garlic, olive oil and bitter orange. You won't regret a trip here.

✪ **Hy-Vong.** 3458 S.W. 8th St. (between 34th and 35th aves.), Little Havana. ☎ **305/ 446-3674.** Reservations not accepted. Main courses $8–$15. No credit cards. Wed–Sun 6–11pm. Closed 2 weeks in Aug. VIETNAMESE.

From Seviche to Picadillo: Latin Cuisine at a Glance

In Little Havana and wondering what to eat? Many restaurants list menu items in English for the benefit of *norteamericano* diners. In case you're wondering what to eat, though, here are translations and suggestions for filling and delicious meals:

Arroz con pollo   Roast chicken served with saffron-seasoned yellow rice and diced vegetables.

Café cubano   Very strong black coffee, served in thimble-size cups with lots of sugar. It's a real eye-opener.

Camarones   Shrimp.

Ceviche   Raw fish seasoned with spice and vegetables and marinated in vinegar and citrus to "cook" it.

Croquetas   Golden-fried croquettes of ham, chicken, or fish.

Paella   A Spanish dish of chicken, sausage, seafood, and pork mixed with saffron rice and peas.

Palomilla   Thinly sliced beef, similar to American minute steak, usually served with onions, parsley, and a mountain of french fries.

Pan cubano   Long, white crusty Cuban bread. Ask for it tostada, toasted and flattened on a grill with lots of butter.

Picadillo   A rich stew of ground meat, brown gravy, peas, pimientos, raisins, and olives.

Plátano   A deep-fried, soft, mildly sweet banana.

Pollo asado   Roasted chicken with onions and a crispy skin.

Ropa vieja   A delicious shredded beef stew, whose name literally means "old clothes."

Sopa de pollo   Chicken soup, usually with noodles or rice.

Tapas   A general name for Spanish-style hors d'oeuvres, served in grazing-size portions.

Expect to wait hours for a table, and don't even think of mumbling a complaint—despite the poor service, it's worth it. Vietnamese cuisine combines the best of Asian and French cooking with spectacular results. Food at Hy-Vong is elegantly simple and superspicy. Appetizers include small, tightly packed Vietnamese spring rolls, and *kimchee*, a spicy, fermented cabbage. Star entrees include pastry-enclosed chicken with watercress cream-cheese sauce and fish in tangy mango sauce.

Enjoy the wait with a traditional Vietnamese beer and lots of company. Outside this tiny storefront restaurant, you'll meet interesting students, musicians, and foodies who come for the large delicious portions.

✪ **Versailles.** 3555 SW 8th St., Little Havana. ☎ **305/444-0240.** Soup and salad $2–$10; main courses $5–$8. DC, DISC, MC, V. Mon–Thurs 8am–2am; Fri 8am–3:30am; Sat 8am–4:30am; Sun 9am–2am. CUBAN.

Versailles is the meeting place of Miami's Cuban power brokers, who meet daily over *café con leche* to discuss the future of the exiles' fate. A glorified diner, the place sparkles with glass, chandeliers, murals, and mirrors meant to evoke the French palace. There's nothing fancy here—nothing French, either—just straightforward food from the home country. The menu is a veritable survey of Cuban cooking and includes specialties such as *Moors and Christians* (flavorful black beans with white rice), ropa vieja, and fried whole fish.

7 North Dade

Although there aren't many hotels in North Dade, the population in the winter months explodes due to the onslaught of seasonal residents from the Northeast. A number of exclusive condominiums and country clubs, including William's Island, Turnberry, and The Jockey Club, breed a demanding clientele, many of whom dine out nightly. That's good news for visitors, who can find superior service and cuisine at value prices.

VERY EXPENSIVE

✪ Chef Allen's. 19088 NE 29th Ave. (at Biscayne Blvd.), North Miami Beach. ☎ **305/935-2900.** Reservations suggested. Main courses $26–$35. AE, DC, MC, V. Sun–Thurs 6–10:30pm; Fri–Sat 6–11pm. NEW WORLD CUISINE.

For one of South Florida's finest dining experiences, Chef Allen's is a must. There simply isn't better food to be found in the county. Owner-chef Allen Susser, of New York's *Le Cirque* fame, has built a classy yet relaxed restaurant with art deco furnishings, a glass-enclosed kitchen, and a hot-pink swirl of neon surrounding the dining room's ceiling. It's more than a little kitschy, but this is Miami, after all. In a town of flash-in-the-pan restaurants, this 14-year-old spot has become an institution, helped by a young, energetic staff.

Appetizers are alluring and may include lobster-and-crab cakes served with strawberry-ginger chutneys, or baked brie with spinach, sun-dried tomatoes, and pine nuts. Favorite main dishes include crisp roast duck with cranberry sauce, and mesquite-grilled Norwegian salmon with champagne grapes, green onions, and basil spaetzle. Local fish dishes, in various delectable guises, and homemade pastas are always on the menu. The extensive wine list is well chosen and features several good buys. Handmade desserts are works of art and sinfully delicious.

MODERATE

The Gourmet Diner. 13951 Biscayne Blvd. (between N.E. 139th and 140th sts.), North Miami Beach. ☎ **305/947-2255.** Reservations not accepted. Main courses $11–$16. MC, V. Mon–Fri 11am–11pm; Sat 8am–11:30pm; Sun 8am–10:30pm. FRENCH.

This retro 1950s-style diner serves plain old French fare without pretensions. The lines are often out the door so you'll want to get there early to taste some of the house specialties, such as beef Burgundy, the trout amandine, and frog legs Provençale—these dishes tend to sell out quickly.

Check the blackboard, which, depending on where you are seated, can be hard to see. The salads and soups are all prepared to order. Even a simple hearts of palm becomes a gourmet treat under the basic, tangy vinaigrette. A well-rounded wine list with reasonable prices makes this place a standout and a great deal. The homemade pastries are also delicious.

The Lagoon. 488 Sunny Isles Blvd. (163rd St.), North Miami Beach. ☎ **305/947-6661.** Reservations accepted. Main courses $12–$40; appetizers $6–$14. AE, CB, MC, V. Daily 4:30–11pm; early-bird dinner 4:30–6pm. SEAFOOD/CONTINENTAL.

This old bay-front fish house has been around since 1936. Major road construction nearby should have guaranteed its doom years ago, but the excellent view and incredible specials make it a worthwhile stop. If you can disregard the somewhat dirty bathrooms and nonchalant service, you'll find the best-priced juicy Maine lobsters around.

Yes, it's true! Lobster lovers can get two $1^{1}/_{4}$ pounders for $22.95. Try them broiled with a light buttery seasoned coating. This dish is not only inexpensive but incredibly succulent, too. Side dishes include fresh vegetables, like broccoli or asparagus, as well as a huge baked potato, stuffed or plain.

The Melting Pot. In Sunny Isles Plaza shopping center, 3143 NE 163rd St. (between U.S. 1 and Collins Ave.), North Miami Beach. ☎ **305/947-2228.** Reservations recommended on weekends. Appetizers $7.95 for 2; fondues $11–$8. AE, DISC, MC, V. Sun–Thurs 5:30–10:30pm; Fri–Sat 5:30pm–midnight. FONDUE.

Traditional fondue is supplemented by combination meat-and-fish dinners, which are served with one of almost a dozen different sauces. The place, with its lace curtains and cozy booths, was voted most romantic restaurant in a local alternative paper several years ago.

As more diners become health conscious, the owners have introduced a more healthful version of fondue, in which you cook vegetables and meats in a low-fat broth. It tastes good, although this version is less fun than watching drippy cheese flow from the hot pot. Best of all, perhaps, is dessert: chunks of pineapple, bananas, apples, and cherries you dip into a creamy chocolate fondue. No liquor is served here, but the wine list is extensive, and beer is available.

A second Melting Pot is located at 9835 SW 72nd St. (Sunset Drive) in Kendall (☎ **305/279-8816**).

INEXPENSIVE

Amos' Juice Bar. 18315 W. Dixie Hwy. (1 block west of Biscayne Blvd.), North Miami Beach. ☎ **305/935-9544.** Sandwiches and salads $4–$6. No credit cards. Mon–Sat 8:30am–6:30pm. HEALTH FOOD.

This brightly painted stand in the middle of a busy road attracts a varied crowd, from young pony-tailed Europeans to bikers. If you don't mind a bit of car exhaust with your snapper sandwich, consider this landmark in North Dade.

The food is made on the premises and includes one of the most unusual tuna salads I've ever run across, served in a pita with tons of crisp vegetables, including alfalfa sprouts, tomato, and lettuce. The hummus is also superb, although garlic lovers might want a hint more spark. You can also get a fresh smoothie or vegetable juice made on the spot.

Here Comes the Sun. 2188 NE 123rd St. (west of the Broad Causeway), North Miami Beach. ☎ **305/893-5711.** Reservations recommended in season. Main courses $8–$14; early-bird special $7.95; sandwiches and salads $5–$11. AE, DC, DISC, MC, V. Mon–Sat 11am–8:30pm. AMERICAN/HEALTH FOOD.

One of Miami's first health-food spots, this bustling grocery-store-turned-diner serves hundreds of plates a night, mostly to blue-haired locals. It's noisy and hectic but worth it. In season, all types pack the place for a $7.95 special, served between 4 and 6:30pm, which includes one of more than 20 choices of entrees, soup or salad, coffee or tea, and a small frozen yogurt. Fresh grilled fish and chicken entrees are reliable and served with a nice array of vegetables. The miso burgers with "sun sauce" are a vegetarian's dream.

Laurenzo's Cafe. 16385 West Dixie Hwy. (at the corner of 163rd St.), North Miami Beach. ☎ **305/945-6381.** Main courses $4–$12; salads $2–$5. No credit cards. Mon–Sat 11am–7pm; Sun 11am–4pm. ITALIAN.

This little lunch counter in the middle of a chaotic grocery store has been serving delicious buffet lunches to the *paesanos* for years. A meeting place for the growing Italian population in Miami, the store has been open for more than 40 years. Daily specials usually include a lasagna or eggplant parmigiano and two or three salad options. Also good are the rustic pizzas.

> ### Family-Friendly Restaurants
>
> **Bubba Gump Shrimp Co.** *(see p. 129)* Named after the character from the motion picture *Forrest Gump,* this is a great place to bring the entire family on a lazy Sunday afternoon. You get to eat some good moderately priced seafood, watch ships sail by on the bay and can shop at the Bayside Marketplace afterwards. There's a gift shop where you can buy Forrest Gump souvenirs, T-shirts, and caps.
>
> **Van Dyke Café** *(see p. 117)* One of South Beach's only family-friendly sit-down restaurants, Van Dyke is a large indoor/outdoor cafe whose whole menu is seemingly designed to please children. From PB and Js to grilled cheese to burgers, this is the spot for kids of all ages.
>
> **Wilderness Grill** *(see p. 145)* Located in the Shops at Sunset, this delightful Australian paradise has a huge aquarium and all sorts of wild beasts from the land "down under." Ask about the children's menu and desserts.

Choose a wine from the vast selection and take your meal to go, or sit in the trellis-covered seating area amid busy shoppers buying their evening's groceries. You'll get to eavesdrop on some great conversations over your plastic tray of real southern Italian–style cooking.

8 Coral Gables & Environs

VERY EXPENSIVE

Christy's. 3101 Ponce de León Blvd., Coral Gables. ☎ **305/446-1400.** Reservations recommended. Main courses $19.50–$35. AE, CB, DC, MC, V. Mon–Thurs 11:30am–4pm; Fri 4–11pm; Sat 5–11pm; Sun 5–10pm. AMERICAN.

Arrive famished. One of the Gables' most expensive and elegant establishments, Christy's is known primarily for its generous cuts of thick, juicy steaks and ribs, despite its demure Victorian style. Some say it's one of the most romantic spots in Miami. I say it's just fine for serious carnivores.

The prime rib is so thick that even a small cut weighs about a pound. New York strip, filet mignon, and chateaubriand are all on the menu here, and all steaks are fully aged without chemicals or freezing. Each entree is served with a jumbo Caesar salad and a baked potato. Seafood, veal, and chicken dishes are also available, but ordering anything except a steak at this pricey little candlelit spot would be a disappointment.

✪ **Norman's.** 21 Almeria Ave. (between Douglas and Ponce de León), Coral Gables. ☎ **305/446-6767.** Reservations highly recommended. Main courses $25–$32. AE, DC, MC, V. Mon–Thurs 11:30am–2pm and 6–10:30pm; Fri 11:30am–2pm and 6–11pm; Sat 6–11pm. Closed Sun. NEW WORLD CUISINE.

Master chef Norman Van Aken, one of the originators of New World Cuisine, reemerged after a 2-year break from restauranting to open what he has called his "culmination." The result is an open kitchen, surrounded by well-dressed diners, where a handful of silent industrious chefs prepare Asian and Caribbean-inspired dishes.

The food is the main focus of attention. Some think the exotic-sounding menu is pretentious or overwrought. I think there's plenty to enjoy, like pizzas and pastas with a good glass of wine and a hunk of bread. The fish, too, is out of this world. The *rhum*-and-pepper-painted grouper on mango-Habanero Mojo is an exotic-tasting dark-fleshed fish with an explosion of sauces to complement its heavy flavor.

The staff is adoring and professional and the atmosphere tasteful without being too formal. The portions are realistic, but still, be careful not to overdo it. You'll want to try some of the wacky desserts, such as mango ice cream served with Asian pears and crushed red pepper (the pepper really just adds color to the plate).

EXPENSIVE

✪ **Caffe Abbracci.** 318 Aragon Ave. (between LeJeune Rd. and Miracle Mile), Coral Gables. ☎ **305/441-0700.** Reservations recommended for dinner. Main courses $16–$25; pasta $15–$20. AE, CB, DC, MC, V. Mon–Fri 11:30am–3pm; Sun–Thurs 6pm–11pm; Fri–Sat 6pm–midnight. ITALIAN.

You'll be greeted with a hug by the owner and maître d' Nino, who oversees this remarkable spot as only an Italian could. The food is remarkable, yet the restaurant is not known to many outside of the Gables. Still, it's packed on weekends by those in the know. You are guaranteed perfect service in a pretty wood and marble setting, with the only drawback being the unfortunately loud dining room.

It's hard to get beyond the appetizers here, which are all so good that you could order a few and be satisfied. My favorite is the shrimp with a bright pesto sauce that has just enough garlic to give it a kick, but not so much you won't get a kiss later. The excellent risottos are served in half portions so that you'll have room for the indescribable fish dishes.

Le Festival. 2120 Salzedo St. (5 blocks north of Miracle Mile), Coral Gables. ☎ **305/442-8545.** Reservations required for dinner. Main courses $16–$25. AE, CB, DC, DISC, MC, V. Mon–Fri 11:45am–2:30pm; Mon–Thurs 6–10:30pm; Fri–Sat 6–11pm. FRENCH.

Le Festival's contemporary pink awning hangs over one of Miami's most traditional Spanish-style buildings, hinting at the unusual combination of cuisine and decor that awaits inside. The modern dining rooms, enlivened with New French features and furnishings, belie the traditional highlights of a well-planned menu.

Shrimp and crab cocktails, fresh pâtés, and an unusual cheese soufflé are star starters. Both meat and fish are either simply seared with herbs and spices or doused in wine and cream sauces. Dessert can be a delight if you plan ahead: Grand Marnier and chocolate soufflés are individually prepared and must be ordered at the same time as the entrees. There's also a wide selection of other homemade sweets.

✪ **Ruth's Chris Steak House.** 2320 Salzedo St., Coral Gables. ☎ **305/461-8360.** Reservations recommended. Main courses $23–$32; appetizers $4–$17. AE, MC, V, D. Daily 11:30am–2:30pm and 5:30–11:30pm. STEAK HOUSE.

With more than 70 restaurants nationwide, Ruth's Chris continues to make waves since it manages to make each dining experience—no matter what location you're in—feel like it has been your finest. Founded in 1965 in New Orleans, Ruth's Chris found a welcome home early on in the dining capitol of South Florida—the cushy world of Coral Gables. Today Ruth's Chris serves more than 1,200 steaks daily! Portions are large—12 to 22 ounces—because Ruth believes a larger cut of meat retains its natural juices during cooking. The beef is never frozen, so it is always exceptionally tender and flavorful. The barbecued shrimp is a local favorite, and for dessert, the crème brûlée is a great choice. There's a very user-friendly and extensive wine list. *Note:* Light eaters can share main courses without additional fees.

MODERATE

Brasserie Les Halles. 2415 Ponce de León Blvd. (at Miracle Mile), Coral Gables. ☎ **305/461-1099.** Reservations suggested on weekends. Main courses $12.50–$22.50. AE, DC, DISC, MC, V. Daily 11:30am–midnight. FRENCH.

Known especially for its fine steaks and delicious salads, this very welcome addition to the Coral Gables dining scene became popular as soon as it opened in 1997 and has since continued to do a brisk business. The modest and moderately priced menu is particularly welcome in an area of overpriced, stuffy restaurants. For starters, try the mussels in white wine sauce and the escargot. For a main course, the duck confit is an unusual and rich choice. Pieces of duck meat wrapped in duck fat are slow-cooked and served on salad frissé and baby potatoes with garlic. Service by the young French staff is polite but a bit slow. The tables tend to be a little too close, although there is a lovely private balcony space overlooking the long thin dining room where large groups can gather.

Gables Diner. 2320 Galiano Dr. (between Ponce de León Blvd. and 37th Ave.), Coral Gables. ☎ **305/567-0330.** Main courses $9–$16; pasta $10–$12; burgers and sandwiches $7–$9; salads $8–$10. AE, DC, DISC, MC, V. Daily 8am–10pm; Fri–Sat until 10:30pm. AMERICAN.

This upscale diner serves an eclectic mix of comfort food and nouvelle health food. From meat loaf to Chinese chicken salad, there are moderately priced options for everyone. My favorite is the chicken pot pie, a flaky homemade crust filled with big chunks of white meat, pearl onions, peas, and mushrooms. Also good are the large burgers with every imaginable condiment. Vegetarians can find a few good choices, including pastas, bean soups, pizzas, a vegetable stir-fry, and some hearty salads. All the ingredients are fresh and crisp. No need to dress up here, although the clean, almost romantic setting is as appropriate for first dates as it is for families.

✪ **The Globe.** 377 Alhambra Circle (just off Le Jeune Rd.), Coral Gables. ☎ **305/445-3555.** Reservations for 6 or more. Main courses $10–$22; salads $6–$10; pizzas and sandwiches $7–$11. AE, DISC, MC, V. Mon–Fri 11:30am–midnight; Sat 6:30pm–2am; Sun 10:30am–10:30pm. INTERNATIONAL.

This funky coffee shop/travel agency is an odd but welcome choice in a neighborhood dominated by fancy eateries and hotels. Take advantage of the hip surroundings and enjoy the decent food. Especially good are the salads and pizzas, particularly the chicken and blue cheese pizza, my favorite. In addition to an extensive list of wines and specialty beers, there are many interesting nonalcoholic choices. More important, sample some of the excellent live music every weekend.

✪ **John Martin's.** 253 Miracle Mile, Coral Gables. ☎ **305/445-3777.** Reservations recommended on weekends. Main courses $9–$20; sandwiches and salads $5–$16. AE, DC, DISC, MC, V. Mon–Thurs 11:30am–midnight; Fri–Sat 11:30am–1am; Sun noon–10pm. IRISH PUB.

Food at this pub is a step above average. The basic menu is loaded with fried bar snacks, as well as some British specialties, such as bangers and mash and shepherd's pie.

Of course to wash it down, you'll want to try one of the ales on tap or one of the more than 20 single-malt scotches. The crowd is upscale and chatty, as is the young wait staff. Check out happy hour on weeknights, plus the Sunday brunch with loads of hand-carved meats and seafood.

✪ **Ortanique on the Mile.** 278 Miracle Mile (next to Actor's Playhouse), Coral Gables. ☎ **305/446-7710.** Reservations requested. Main courses $14–$26; appetizers $6–$11. AE, MC, V. Mon–Fri 11:30am–2:30pm and 5:30–10pm; Sat to 11pm. Closed Sun. NEW WORLD CARIBBEAN.

Ortanique is as unique to the Gables as this orangelike fruit is to Jamaica. You'll be greeted as you walk in by soft spiderlike lights and canopied mosquito netting that will make you wonder whether you're on a secluded island or inside one of King Tut's temples. A friendly host greets you at the door and glides you past simple canvas oils hanging from papaya and mango-colored walls, and hand-painted columns laced with ortaniques. The dynamic duo of Cindy Hutson and Delius Shirley have remarkably reinvented the highly successful "Norma's" on South Beach here.

Though almost impossible, chef Hutson has truly perfected her tantalizing New World Caribbean menu. For starters, an absolute must is the pumpkin bisque with a hint of pepper sherry. Afterwards, move on to the tropical mango salad with fresh marinated Sable hearts of palm, julienne mango, baby field greens, toasted Caribbean candied pecans and passion fruit vinaigrette. For an entree I recommend the pan sautéed Bahamian black grouper marinated in teriyaki and sesame oil. It's served with an Ortanique orange liqueur sauce and topped with steamed seasoned chayote, zucchini, and carrots on a lemon-orange boniato sweet plantain mash. For dessert, my favorite is the chocolate mango tower—layers of brownie, chocolate mango mousse, meringue, and sponge cake, accompanied by a mango sorbet and tropical fruit salsa. It's certainly nice to know that someone is trying to spice up the stale variety of cuisine in the Gables.

INEXPENSIVE

Biscayne Miracle Mile Cafeteria. 147 Miracle Mile, Coral Gables. ☎ **305/444-9005.** Main courses $3.50–$4.50. MC, V. Daily 11am–8:30pm. AMERICAN.

Here, you'll find no bar, no music, and no flowers on the tables—just great Southern-style cooking at unbelievably low prices. The menu changes, but roast beef, baked fish, and barbecued ribs are typical entrees, few of which exceed $5.

Food is picked up cafeteria-style and brought to one of the many unadorned Formica tables. The restaurant is always busy. The kitschy 1950s decor is an asset in this last of the old-fashioned cafeterias, where the gold-clad staff is proud and attentive. Enjoy it while it lasts.

The Daily Bread Marketplace. 2400 SW 27th St. (off U.S. 1 under the monorail), Coral Gables. ☎ **305/856-0363** or 305/856-0366. Sandwiches and salads $3–$6. MC, V. Mon–Sat 8am–8pm; Sun 11am–5pm. GREEK.

Not only is there great take-out food and homemade breads, but you'll also find backgammon boards and water pipes for sale. The falafel and gyro sandwiches are large, fresh, and filling. The spinach pie for less than $1 is also recommended, though it's short on spinach and heavy on pastry. Salads, including luscious tabouli, hummus, and eggplant are also worth a go. To take in or eat out, the Middle Eastern fare here is a real treat, especially in an area so filled with fancy French and Cuban fare. Plus, you can pick up hard-to-find groceries such as grape leaves, fresh olives, couscous, fresh nuts, and pita bread.

House of India. 22 Merrick Way (near Douglas and Coral Way, a block north of Miracle Mile), Coral Gables. ☎ **305/444-2348.** Reservations recommended. Main courses $8–$17. AE, DC, DISC, MC, V. Daily 11:30am–3pm; Sun–Thurs 5–10pm; Fri–Sat 5–11pm. INDIAN.

House of India's curries, kormas, and kabobs are very good, but the restaurant's well-priced all-you-can-eat lunch buffet is unsurpassed. All the favorites are on display, including tandoori chicken, nan, various meat and vegetarian curries, as well as rice and dal (lentils). This place isn't fancy and could use a good scrub-down (in fact, I've heard it described as a "greasy spoon"), but it is nicely decorated with hanging batik prints.

Sergio's. 3252 Coral Way, Coral Gables. ☎ **305/529-0047.** Reservations not accepted. Main courses $5–$8. AE, DC, MC, V. Sun–Thurs 6am–midnight; Fri–Sat 24 hours. AMERICAN/CUBAN.

Located across from Coral Gables' Paseos Mall, Sergio's stands out like a Latin-inspired International House of Pancakes, with red-clothed tables, neon signs in the windows, and video games along the back wall. The family style restaurant serves everything from ham-and-eggs breakfasts to grilled-steak sandwich lunches and dinners, but it specializes in native Cuban-style dishes, as well as grilled chicken, fajitas, and a variety of sandwiches. Low prices and late-night dining keep it popular with locals.

9 Coconut Grove

Coconut Grove was long known as the artists' haven of Miami, but the rush of developers trying to cash in on the laid-back charm of this old settlement has turned it into something of an overgrown mall. Still, there are several great dining spots both in and out of the confines of Mayfair or Cocowalk.

EXPENSIVE

Bice. 2669 South Bayshore Drive (in the Grand Bay Hotel), Coconut Grove. ☎ **305/860-0960.** Reservations recommended. Main courses $13–$34. AE, MC, V. Daily 7–11am; 11:30am–3pm; 6–11pm. ITALIAN.

Bice is an elegant dining experience that can turn a business lunch into a successful close or a warm romantic evening into a special moment to hear "I do." Part of a unique chain of Italian restaurants scattered across several select cities (Singapore, Amsterdam, Milan, and Chicago to name a few) the restaurant's arrival a few years ago was proof of Miami's ascendancy as an international draw. The two-tone wood floors and the fresh roses in open bloom are just a few of the subtle hallmarks of class and taste that make up this establishment's more than satisfactory trademark. Executive Chef Antonello Fornasari has recreated some of Italy's best, and his version of Maryland crab cakes (*insalata di cetrioli e vinaigrette alla papaya*) shows he has adapted to Floribbean styles quite well. You will truly enjoy the *tagliata di manzo con rucola, radiocchio, e indivia belga*—steak served with several varieties of lettuce—an Atkins must! Adding a touch of class to the already sumptuous Grand Bay Hotel—the high tea served here in the early afternoon from 3 to 6pm, Monday through Saturday, offers savory tea sandwiches, a spot of sherry, and of course enough teas to make Lord Earl Grey feel at home.

Bocca di Rosa. 2833 Bird Ave. (between S.W. 27th and Virginia sts.), Coconut Grove. ☎ **305/444-4222.** Reservations recommended. Main courses $16–$24; pastas $11–$17. AE, DC, DISC, MC, V. Sun–Thurs 6–11pm; Fri–Sat 6pm–midnight. ITALIAN.

This elegant restaurant is nestled in a cozy corner of the Grove, but from the smells and tastes here you might as well be in Roma or Sicily. With dishes like *coniglio all contadina* (rabbit stew with white beans and polenta) and *penne cons salsa di sarde* (a sardine and fennel pasta), the menu touches all points on "the boot." On any day, there may be as many as 15 specials. The remarkably fresh seafood is especially recommended. My favorites are a savory bowl of steamed mussels in a white wine broth and a delicately seared swordfish. Frankly, whatever Chef Giorgio is cooking up is bound to be good.

Le Bouchondu. 3430 Main Highway, Coconut Grove. ☎ **305/448-6060.** Reservations recommended. Main courses $16–$22; appetizers $4–$12. AE, MC, V. Mon–Fri 10am–3pm; Mon–Thurs 5:30–11pm; Fri 5:30pm–midnight; Sat 8am–midnight; Sun 8am–11pm. FRENCH.

Le Bouchondu is an absolute delight—why pay airfare when a little piece of France awaits you in the Heart of the Grove? This spot is ideal for an intimate romantic encounter or a group of friends knocking about for a nice meal and a bottle of wine. Chef Georges is an adept pupil of Paul Bocuse (famous for his renditions of country cooking in Troisagros, near Lyon) and he has brought both family members and talent to the tables of this intimate cafe. From a wonderful *gratiné Lyonnaise* (traditional French onion soup) to a selection of appetizers and salads that warm both the heart and palate, the food is exceptional. Fish is brought in fresh daily; try the Chilean sea bass when in season (*filet de loup poele*), though is slightly heavy on the oil, it is delivered with succulent artichokes, a tomato comfit, and seasoned roasted garlic that is a gastronomic delight. The *carre d'agneau roti* (roasted rack of lamb with Provence herbs) is served warm and tender, with an excellent amount of seasoning. There is an excellent selection of pricey, but doable French and American red and white wines. Try the St. Emilion 1996 Baron Rothschild ($34, or $7 per glass) which compliments nearly the entire menu. The staff knows their food, it's history, and what goes best with what, so don't be afraid to broach the language barrier and ask. If you want proof that this place is a winner, ask the owners of other Miami restaurants who regularly diner here.

MODERATE

✪ Franz & Joseph's in the Grove. 3145 Commodore Plaza, Coconut Grove. ☎ **305/448-2282**. Reservations highly recommended. Main courses $15–$20; appetizers $6–$9. AE, MC, V. Tues–Sun 11:30am–2:30pm and 6–10:30pm. Closed Mon. CONTINENTAL.

This is a favorite restaurant of theatergoers and stars—Kathleen Turner and Jean Stapleton, to name a few—alike. Franz or Joseph, the gracious owners of this romantic restaurant that is chock full of Old-World charm, will personally greet you at the door. Before you sit down to dine, try a glass of Chardonnay, Cabernet, or Merlot at the intimate bar. It's a great place to unwind and enjoy the atmosphere. Give in to the European ambience here and start with the escargot in Roquefort butter with grilled herb bread. A local favorite is the stuffed avocado with marinated sea scallops, mussels, and shrimp; it's absolutely fresh. Try the soup du jour, whatever it is; soup lovers will think they've gone to heaven. Don't be afraid to order pasta, either. The penne with spicy grilled chicken, plum tomatoes, spinach, and feta cheese is wonderful. If you come to Florida for the seafood, you can't go wrong with the restaurant's fillet of snapper, pan-seared with mango chutney and glazed banana over rice. Well-prepared steaks and exotic chicken dishes are a specialty here, too. Their delicious desserts are made on premises. The kitchen is small, so the food is consistently fresh and cooked to order. The last thing the chef does each night before going home, is order for the next day's menu.

Green Street Cafe. 3110 Commodore Plaza, Coconut Grove. ☎ **305/567-0662**. Reservations not accepted. Main courses $10–$15. AE, MC, V. Sun–Thurs 7am–11:30pm; Fri–Sat 7am–1am. CONTINENTAL.

Green Street is located at the "100% corner"—the Coconut Grove intersection of Main Highway and Commodore Plaza that almost 100% of all tourists visit. The location and the loads of outdoor seating (great for people-watching) relieve Green Street of the pressure to turn out fine meals, but the food is still well above average. Continental-style breakfasts include fresh croissants and rolls, cinnamon toast, and cereal. Heartier American-style offerings include eggs and omelettes, pancakes, waffles, and French toast. Soup, salad, and sandwich lunches are overstuffed chicken, turkey, and tuna-based meals. Dinners are more elaborate, with several decent pasta entrees as well as fresh fish, chicken, and burgers, including one made of lamb.

La Fontaine. At MayFair Shops, 3390 Mary St., Coconut Grove. ☎ **305/447-0553** or 305/447-0796. Main courses $9.95–$26.95; appetizers $6–$10. AE, DISC, MC, V. Sun–Thurs 11:30am–midnight; Fri–Sat 11:30am–1am. FRENCH BISTRO.

La Fontaine serves up great, moderately priced French cuisine right in the Grove. On a lovely day, sit outside and sample the *escargot bourguignonne,* imported French snails baked in an herbs and garlic butter sauce, and sip the finest Merlots and Cabernet Sauvignons. Another great appetizer is *le champignon buphoria,* sautéed portobello mushrooms topped with roasted peppers, basil, garlic, and olive oil. For an entree, the *le rouger Caribbean* is a wonderful Florribean and French combination. It's a pan-seared snapper fillet served over a mango sauce and fruit julienne salsa with rice. For dessert, try the *dulce de leche* crepe with strawberries and chocolate; you're in for a real treat. There are also great tropical drinks and Martini selections. Ask about weekly lunch specials; you can get pasta and chicken for only $8.95 and fish for $9.95, including a soup or salad.

Pauloluigi's Ristorante Italiana. 3324 Virginia St., Coconut Grove. ☎ **305/445-9000.** Reservations recommended. Main courses $9–$17. AE, MC, V. Daily noon–4pm and 5–11pm; Fri–Sat 5pm–1am. ITALIAN.

Pauloluigi's serves rich dishes that include cold and hot appetizers, homemade soups and salads, pastas, and pizzas. Owners Paul and Lola Shalaj, restaurant entrepreneurs for the past 26 years, have gained and kept a large devoted clientele with their tasty light Italian cuisine, generous portions, and a friendly environment that has served as the perfect fine-dining hide away for both local and national customers alike (including celebrities).

A favorite is the *jumbo rigatti rubino,* a chicken dish with a side of sausages, asparagus, and portobello mushrooms, in a light marinara sauce. There's also *chicken marsala, linguine al fruitti di mare* (for poultry and seafood lovers), and a special children's menu. Sample a wine from their excellent list with your meal.

The Red Lantern. 3176 Commodore Plaza (Grand Ave.), Coconut Grove. ☎ **305/529-9998.** Reservations accepted. Main courses $8–$25. AE, MC, V. Mon–Thurs 11:30am–11pm; Fri 11:30am–midnight; Sat 4pm–midnight; Sun 4–11pm. CANTONESE.

This popular Chinese spot is better than most. Specialties include shark's fin with chicken, and steamed whole snapper with black-bean sauce. There's also an assortment of vegetarian dishes and some excellent soups. My favorite is the clay-pot stew of chicken in a ginger broth. Although the atmosphere is nothing to speak of, the varied menu and interesting preparation keep locals happy and make a meal here worthwhile.

Señor Frogs. 3480 Main Hwy., Coconut Grove. ☎ **305/448-0999.** Reservations not accepted. Main courses $12–$17. AE, CB, DC, DISC, MC, V. Mon–Sat 11:30am–2am; Sun 11:30am–1am. MEXICAN.

Filled with a college-student crowd, this restaurant is known for a raucous good time, its mariachi band, and its powerful margaritas. The food at this rocking cantina is a bit too cheesy, but it's tasty, if not exactly authentic. The mole enchiladas, with 14 different kinds of mild chiles mixed with chocolate, is as flavorful as any I've tasted. Almost everything is served with rice and beans in quantities so large that few diners are able to finish.

INEXPENSIVE

Cafe Tu Tu Tango. 3015 Grand Ave. (on the 2nd floor of CocoWalk), Coconut Grove. ☎ **305/529-2222.** Reservations not accepted. Main courses $4–$10. AE, MC, V. Sun–Wed 11:30am–midnight; Thurs 11:30am–1am; Fri–Sat 11:30am–2am. SPANISH/INTERNATIONAL.

This second-floor restaurant in the bustling CocoWalk is designed to look like a disheveled artist's loft. Dozens of original paintings—some only half-finished—hang on the walls and on studio easels. Seating at sturdy wooden tables and chairs is either inside, on wooden floors among the clutter, or outdoors, overlooking the Grove's main drag.

Flamenco and other Latin-inspired tunes complement a menu with a decidedly Spanish flare. Hummus spread on rosemary flat bread and baked goat cheese in marinara sauce are two good starters. Entrees include roast duck with dried cranberries, toasted pine nuts, and goat cheese, plus Cajun chicken egg rolls filled with corn, cheddar cheese, and tomato salsa. Pastas, ribs, fish, and pizzas round out the eclectic offerings, and several visits have proved each consistently good. Try the sweet, potent sangria and enjoy the warm lively atmosphere from a seat with a view. Especially when the rest of the Grove has shut down, Tu Tu Tango is an oasis.

Another Cafe Tu Tu Tango is located at 19501 Biscayne Blvd., (in Aventura Mall), 2nd Floor, Aventura. (☎ **305/932-2222**).

News Cafe in the Grove. 2901 Florida Ave. (behind Mayfair), Coconut Grove. ☎ **305/774-6397.** Main courses $12–$19. AE, DC, MC, V. Daily 24 hours. AMERICAN.

Like its predecessor in South Beach, this big modern diner offers everything from Caesar salads to hummus to burgers to omelets to ice cream sundaes. The food is predictably good and the service lively and pleasant. The best part is that it's open around the clock to serve the after-movie crowd from CocoWalk and Mayfair, as well as the real late-night club-goers.

10 South Miami

This mostly residential area has some very good dining spots scattered mostly along U.S. 1.

MODERATE

Anacapri. In the South Park Center (at 128th St. and U.S. 1), 12669 S. Dixie Hwy., South Miami. ☎ **305/232-8001.** Reservations recommended. Main courses $15–$27; pastas $10–$15. AE, DC, DISC, MC, V. Daily 11:30am–2:30pm; Mon–Thurs 5–10:30pm; Fri–Sat 5–11:30pm; Sun 5–9pm. ITALIAN.

Neighborhood fans happily wait in line here with a glass of wine and pleasant company for somewhat heavy but flavorful Italian cuisine. Prices are reasonable and everyone is treated like a member of the family. If you're in the area, check it out. Stick with the basics, such as pastas with red sauce, which are all flavorful, although a bit heavy on the garlic and oil. An antipasto with thinly cut meats and cheeses and some good green peppers is a great start to a hearty meal.

Cafe Hammock. 500 SW 177th Ave. (in the Miccosukee Indian Gaming site on Krome Ave. and Tamiami Trail), South Miami. ☎ **305/222-4600.** DISC, MC, V. Reservations recommended. Main courses $10–$22; dinner specials $5–$6. Daily 24 hours. CONTINENTAL.

In the clanging environs of the Native American gaming village way down south, you can dine on stone crab claws and decent steak for a few bucks while overlooking hundreds of fanatical bingo players. If you can keep away from the dealers and slots and don't mind a bit of smoke, you'll be amazed at the excellent service and phenomenal specials it runs to entice gamblers to this bizarre outpost. Don't expect Native Americans in native dress; you'll find servers from New Jersey and California before you see a Miccosukee serving burgers here.

◯ **Coco Pazzo.** Inside the Shops at Sunset, 5701 Sunset Dr., South Miami. ☎ **305/665-6055.** Reservations accepted weekdays only. Main courses $14–$25; lunch menu $4.50–$14; appetizers $4.50–$11. AE, DC, MC, V. Sun–Thurs 11:30am–10pm; Fri–Sat 11:30am–midnight. ITALIAN.

The atmosphere here depends on where you choose to sit: the outside cafe, with a full view of all the shopping frenzy and active children, or the more serene, airy lushness of the Tuscan dining room inside. The hand-painted murals of the ocean and the wide-open kitchen invite you in to the dining area. Owner Pino Luongo, who owns 14 other Coco Pazzos nationwide, strives to combine the best of Tuscan cuisine with accents of Latin and Caribbean favorites. One of the restaurant's signature dishes is the *focaccia alla robiola*, a thin-crusted focaccia stuffed with robiola cheese and drizzled with white truffle oil. Another great choice is the *calamari alla griglia* or grilled calamari stuffed with oxtails in a red wine sauce. My favorite is the *salmone con insalata estiva*, which is grilled salmon with mesclun lettuce, asparagus, mango and balsamic reduction. For dessert try the tiramisu with mascarpone cream and ladyfingers soaked in espresso. It's delightful.

Wilderness Grill. Shops at Sunset (57th and U.S. 1), 5701 Sunset Dr., #114, South Miami. ☎ **305/740-3033.** Main courses $8–$21. AE, MC, V. Daily 11:30am–midnight. Bar open until 1am on weekends. AMERICAN.

This unique restaurant really caters to kids of all ages, with sound effects, rolling lights simulating lightning in the outback, and aquariums and terrariums that abound with exotic flora and fauna. The real special for parents is the delicious menu, which has everything from salads to emu steak. Another added bonus is the individualized attention the staff provides. Try the Adelaide BBQ Chicken; it's slow roasted in a tasty sauce and a bargain at $12.95. The New York steak, accompanied by heavenly mashed potatoes (freshly whipped), is another good choice. Children's menus (which double as coloring books) are also available. *Note:* If you are an adult and attend without children, don't be surprised to find them a part of the wilderness wildlife.

INEXPENSIVE

The Crepe Maker Cafe. 8269 SW 124th St., South Miami. ☎ **305/233-4458** or 305/233-1113. Crepes $3–$7.50. No credit cards. Sun, Tues–Thurs 10:30am–8:30pm; Fri–Sat 10:30am–10:30pm. Crepe cart in CocoWalk Tues–Wed 4–10pm; Thurs 11am–11pm; Fri–Sat 11am–1am; Sun 11am–11pm. CREPES/FRENCH.

Create your own delicious crepes at this little French cafe. You can choose from ham, tuna, black olives, red peppers, capers, artichoke hearts, and pine nuts. Some of the best combinations include a Philly cheese steak with mushrooms and a classic cordon bleu. Delicious desert crepes have ice cream, strawberries, peaches, walnuts, and pineapples. Enjoy your crepe fresh off the griddle at the counter or on a bar stool. The soups are also delicious. Kids can run around in a small play area, too.

◯ **Pollo Tropical.** 18700 SW 40th St., South Miami. ☎ **305/225-7858.** Main courses $3–$6. No credit cards. Sun–Thurs 11am–10pm; Fri–Sat 11am–11pm. CUBAN/FAST FOOD.

This Miami-based chain is putting up new terra-cotta–arched, fast-food places so fast you can hardly finish your meal before another one has taken root.

This is lucky for Miamians and the Southeast, where dozens of these restaurants provide hot tender chicken with a variety of healthful side dishes, such as fresh chunks of carrots, onions, zucchini, and squash on wooden skewers and a variety of salads. The chicken is marinated in a seriously secret sauce and served with well-seasoned black beans and rice. The menu, although Latin inspired, is clearly spelled out in English. Pollo Tropical is a good place to get an education in Latin *sabor* (taste).

Other locations include 1454 Alton Rd., Miami Beach (☎ **305/672-8888**), and 11806 Biscayne Blvd., North Miami (☎ **305/895-0274**). Check the phone book for others.

✪ **Shorty's.** 9200 S. Dixie Hwy. (between U.S. 1 and Dadeland Blvd.), South Miami. ☎ **305/670-7732.** Main courses $5–$9. DISC, MC, V. Mon–Thurs 11am–10pm; Fri–Sat 11am–11pm. BARBECUE.

A Miami tradition since 1951, this hokey log cabin is still serving some of the best ribs and chicken in South Florida. People line up for the smoke-flavored, slow-cooked meat that's so tender it seems to jump off the bone into your mouth. The secret, however, is to ask for your order with sweet sauce. The regular stuff tastes bland and bottled. All the side dishes, including the cole slaw, corn on the cob, and baked beans, look commercial, but are necessary to complete the experience. This is Barbecue, with a neon capital *B*.

A second Shorty's is located in Davie at 5989 S. University Dr. (☎ **305/944-0348**).

The Tea Room. 12310 SW 224th St. (at Cauley Square), South Miami. ☎ **305/258-0044.** Sandwiches and salads $7–$12; soups $3–$4. AE, DISC, MC, V. Mon–Sat 11am–4pm. ENGLISH TEA.

Do stop in for a spot of tea at this recently rebuilt tearoom in historic Cauley Square off U.S. 1. The little lace-curtained room is an unusual site in this heavily industrial area better known for its warehouses than its doilies.

Try one of the simple sandwiches, such as the turkey club with potato salad and a small lettuce garnish or onion soup full of rich brown broth and stringy cheese. Daily specials, such as spinach-and-mushroom quiche, and delectable desserts are a must before beginning your explorations of the old antiques and art shops in this little enclave of civility down south.

Wrapido. 5812 Sunset Dr. (near 58th St.), South Miami. ☎ **305/662-7999.** Wraps and salads $5–$6. AE, MC, V. Sun–Thurs 10:30am–10pm; Fri–Sat 10:30am–midnight. WRAPS.

This trendy, fast-paced shop sells an impressive variety of wraps from Thai chicken to teriyaki tofu. All ingredients are superfresh and the sauces are fantastic, too. The sides reflect the ethnic mix of the city, with choices like black beans and rice, sweet plantains, or tortillas with guacamole and salsa. More than a dozen smoothies make choosing one difficult, though I like the Maui Dream with peach juice, passion fruit, strawberries, bananas, coconut, and frozen yogurt.

Another location is in Coral Gables at 2334 Ponce De León Blvd. (☎ **305/443-1884**).

What to See & Do in Miami

Miami is fast-becoming an international cultural magnet, attracting world-renowned musicians, dancers, and artists—from Ricky Martin and Will Smith to the cast of the hit Broadway musical *Rent*. As the number of visitors to Miami has grown, so has the city's capacity to provide world-class art and entertainment. There was a time when our beaches alone were enough to attract the average traveler to the city, but world class resorts throughout the state, not to mention in nearly every Caribbean country, have made Miami have to fight for its right to stay at the top. No longer branded solely as a haven for immigrants fleeing oppression or the elderly fleeing cold northern winters (our "snowbirds" as we fondly call them), travelers flock to Miami year-round in search of fun, sun, and pleasure.

If sightseeing is your cup of tea, the city is overflowing with museums, parks, and botanical exhibits. The young, and young at heart, will delight in touring the Seaquarium, Metrozoo, the Vizcaya Estate, Fairchild Tropical Gardens, the Spanish Monastery, and a unique Police Museum. And you'll have plenty of fun sampling the numerous nightclubs, theaters, and cultural activities that make Miami's nightlife the most vibrant in the country. When it comes time to fill your days and nights with things to do in Miami, you may not know where to begin because we have enough to keep you busy every day of the year.

And do try to remember that the most wonderful and peaceful things to do in Miami are provided by nature. Very few things compare to basking in the sun with the ocean breeze kissing your face while watching waves crash against the sand.

Take your pick from the many suggestions below. There is plenty to keep you busy for a day or a month.

1 Miami's Beaches

Perhaps Miami's most popular attraction is its incredible 35-mile stretch of beachfront, which runs from the tip of South Beach north to Sunny Isles and circles Key Biscayne and the numerous other pristine islands dotted throughout the Atlantic. The characteristics of Miami's many beaches are as varied as the city's population; some are shaded by towering palm trees, while others are darkened by huge condominiums. Some attract families or old-timers, others a gay singles scene, but basically, there are two distinct beach areas: Miami Beach and Key Biscayne.

Miami Area Attractions & Beaches

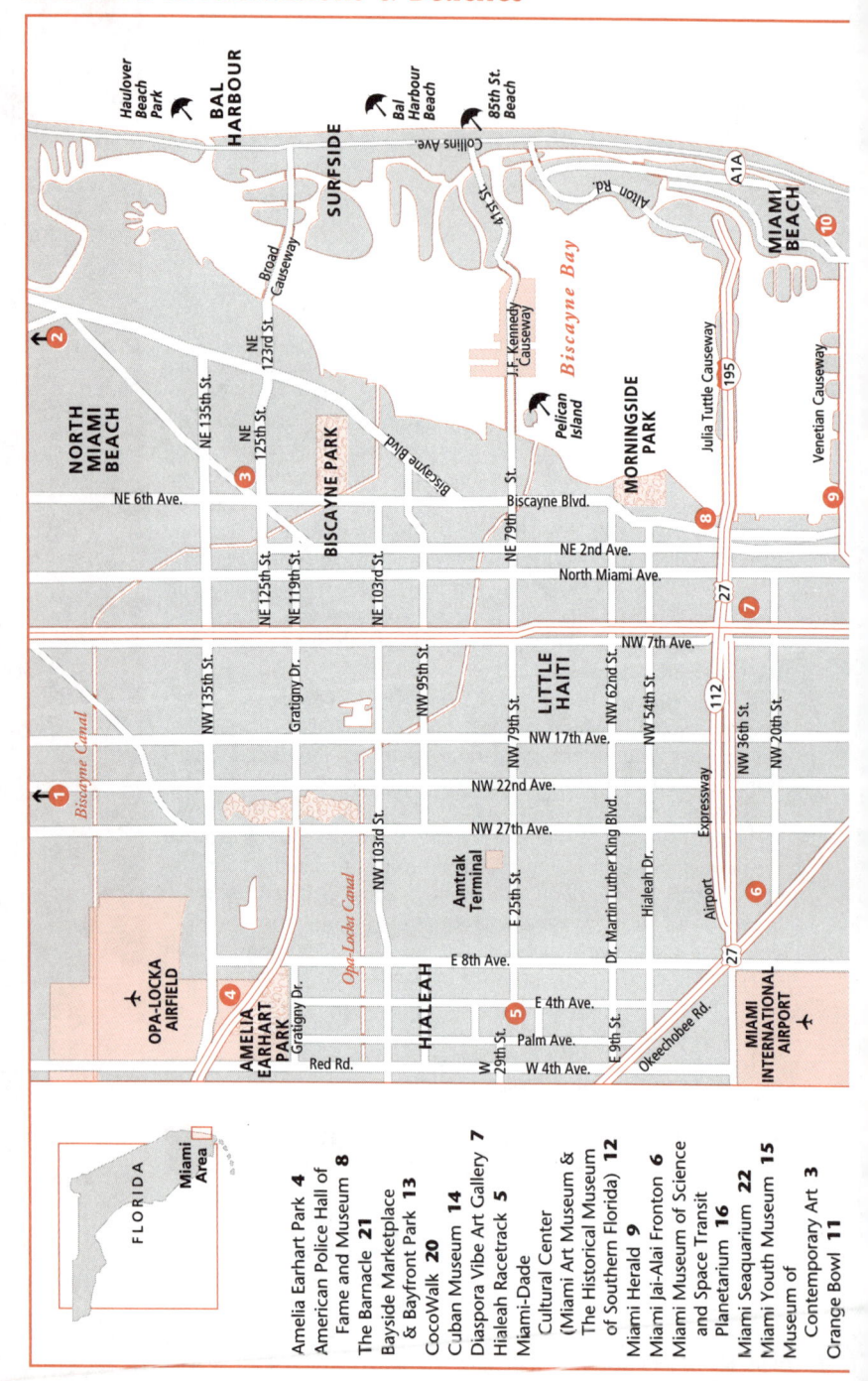

Amelia Earhart Park **4**
American Police Hall of Fame and Museum **8**
The Barnacle **21**
Bayside Marketplace & Bayfront Park **13**
CocoWalk **20**
Cuban Museum **14**
Diaspora Vibe Art Gallery **7**
Hialeah Racetrack **5**
Miami-Dade Cultural Center (Miami Art Museum & The Historical Museum of Southern Florida) **12**
Miami Herald **9**
Miami Jai-Alai Fronton **6**
Miami Museum of Science and Space Transit Planetarium **16**
Miami Seaquarium **22**
Miami Youth Museum **15**
Museum of Contemporary Art **3**
Orange Bowl **11**

Miami-Dade County, **Haulover Beach,** just north of the Bal Harbour border, attracts nudists from around the world and has created quite a boom for area businesses that cater to them.
- **Best Surfing Beach: Haulover Beach/Harbor House,** just north of Miami Beach, seems to get Miami's biggest swells. Go early to avoid the rush of young locals prepping for Maui.

2 The Art Deco District

The best single attraction in Miami is not a museum or an amusement park, but a piece of the city itself. Located in South Beach, the Art Deco District is a whole community made up of outrageous and fanciful 1920s and 1930s architecture. The district is roughly bounded by the Atlantic Ocean on the east, Alton Road on the west, 6th Street to the south, and Dade Boulevard (along the Collins Canal) to the north.

Most of the finest examples of the whimsical art deco style are concentrated along three parallel streets—Ocean Drive, Collins Avenue, and Washington Avenue—from about 6th to 23rd streets.

After years of neglect and calls for the wholesale demolition of its buildings, South Beach got a new lease on life in 1979. Under the leadership of Barbara Baer Capitman, a dedicated crusader for the art deco region and the Miami Design Preservation League, an area made up of an estimated 800 buildings was granted a listing on the National Register of Historic Places. Designers then began highlighting long-lost architectural details with soft sherbet shades of peach, periwinkle, turquoise, and purple. Developers soon moved in, and the full-scale refurbishment of the area's hotels was under way.

Today, hundreds of new hotels, restaurants, and nightclubs have been renovated or are in the process, and South Beach is on the cutting edge of Miami's cultural and nightlife scene.

EXPLORING THE AREA

If you're touring this unique neighborhood on your own, start at the **Art Deco Welcome Center,** 1001 Ocean Dr. (☎ **305/531-3484**), the only beachside building across from the Clevelander Hotel and bar. They give away lots of informational material including maps and pamphlets. Art deco books (including *The Art Deco Guide,* an informative compendium of all the buildings here), T-shirts, postcards, mugs, and other paraphernalia are for sale. It's open Monday to Saturday from 9am to 6pm, sometimes later.

Take a stroll along **Ocean Drive** for the best view of sidewalk cafes, bars, colorful hotels, and even more colorful people. Another great place for a walk is **Lincoln Road,** which is lined with galleries, cafes, and funky art and antique stores. The Community Church, at the corner of Lincoln Road and Drexel Avenue, is the neighborhood's first church and one of its oldest surviving buildings, dating from 1921.

For details on guided tours read "Sightseeing Cruises & Organized Tours," below.

3 Animal Parks

Kids of all ages will enjoy Miami's animal parks, which feature everything from dolphins to lions to parrots. Of course, there are plenty of alligators, too. Call to inquire about discount packages or coupons, which may be offered at area retail stores or in local papers.

152   What to See & Do in Miami

◯ **Miami Metrozoo.** 12400 SW 152nd St., South Miami. ☎ **305/251-0400.** www.miamimetrozoo.org. Admission $8 adults, $4 children 3–12. Daily 9:30am–5:30pm (ticket booth closes at 4pm). Free self-parking. From U.S. 1 south, turn right on SW 152nd St. and follow signs about 3 miles to the entrance.

This impressive 290-acre complex is completely cageless—animals are kept at bay by cleverly designed moats. This is a fantastic spot to take the kids; there's a wonderful petting zoo and play area, and the zoo offers several daily programs designed to both educate and entertain. Mufasa and Simba (of Disney fame) were modeled on a couple of Metrozoo's lions. Other residents include two rare white Bengal tigers, a Komodo dragon, rare koala bears, a number of kangaroos, and an African meerkat. The air-conditioned Zoofari Monorail tour offers visitors a nice overview of the park. A new Andean Condor exhibit opened in 2000 and the zoo is always upgrading its facilities. *Note:* The distance between animal habitats can be quite large, so you'll be doing *a lot* of walking here. Young children and the elderly, especially in summer, should take several rest breaks during the day (there are benches and shaded gazebos strategically positioned throughout the zoo).

◯ **Miami Seaquarium.** 4400 Rickenbacker Causeway (south side), en route to Key Biscayne. ☎ **305/361-5705.** Admission $23 adults, $18 children 3–9. Daily 9:30am–6pm (ticket booth closes at 4:30pm).

You'll want to arrive early to experience this fun and educational attraction. You'll need at least 3 hours to tour the 35-acre oceanarium and see all four daily shows starring a number of talented ocean mammals, although you can do it in about 2 if you're on a tight schedule. Trained dolphins, killer whales, and frolicking sea lions play with trainers and visitors. The Water and Dolphin Exploration Program (W.A.D.E.) allows visitors to touch and swim with dolphins in the Flipper Lagoon. The program costs $125 per person and is offered twice daily, Wednesday through Sunday. Children must be at least 52 inches tall to participate. Call ☎ **305/365-2501** in advance for reservations.

◯ **Monkey Jungle.** 14805 SW 216th St., South Miami. ☎ **305/235-1611.** Admission $13.50 adults, $10.50 seniors and active-duty military, $8 children 4–12. Daily 9:30am–5pm (tickets sold until 4pm). Take U.S. 1 south to SW 216th St. or from Florida Turnpike, take Exit 11 and follow the signs.

See rare Brazilian golden lion tamarins and watch the "skin-diving" Asian macaques. Yes, it's primate paradise! There are no cages to restrain the antics of the monkeys as they swing, chatter, and play their way into your heart. Screened-in trails wind through acres of "jungle," and daily shows feature the talents of the park's most progressive pupils. *Slight warning:* You've got to love primates to get over the heavy smell of the jungle; it's been here for more than 60 years.

Parrot Jungle and Gardens. 11000 SW 57th Ave., Southern Miami–Dade County. ☎ **305/666-7834.** www.parrotjungle.com. Admission $14.95 adults, $13.95 seniors, $9.95 children 3–10. Daily 9:30am–6pm. Cafe opens at 8am. Take U.S. 1 south and turn left at SW 57th Ave., or exit Kendall Dr. from the Florida Turnpike and turn right on SW 57th Ave.

This silly but fun Miami institution is expected to move to a new $46 million home along the McArthur Causeway in April 2001 (call before you go, since delays have been known to happen). The 18.6-acre park will feature an Everglades exhibit, a petting zoo, and several theaters, jungle trails, and aviaries. If it follows in the steps of its predecessor, you'll see hundreds of parrots, macaws, peacocks, cockatoos, and flamingos. Continuous shows star roller-skating cockatoos, card-playing macaws, and numerous stunt-happy parrots. There are also tortoises, iguanas, and a rare albino alligator on

Get Away For Less.

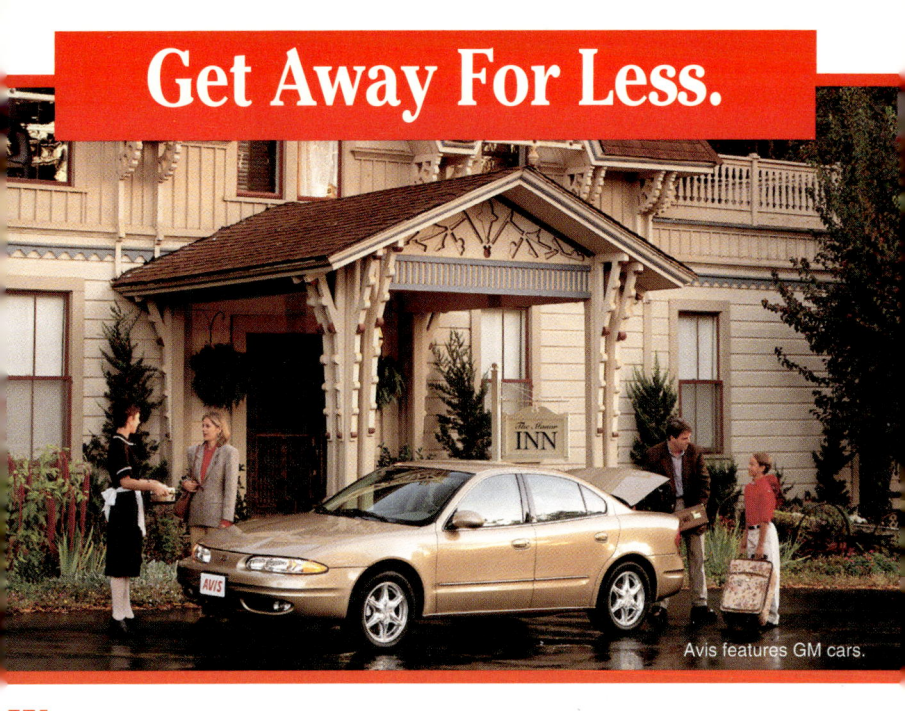

Avis features GM cars.

With great offers and services from Avis, you'll get more out of your vacation! And now you can **save $20 on a weekly rental**. All the information you need is on the coupon below. Plus most rentals come with free unlimited mileage to save you even more.

As an added touch you can count on our famous "We try harder." service for a fast, hassle-free rental. Because speed and personal service is what everyone at Avis is dedicated to delivering.

For more information and reservations, call your travel agent or Avis toll free at **1-800-831-8000**.

AVIS
We try harder.
For You.

Save $20 On A Weekly Rental

Reserve an Avis Intermediate through Full Size 4-Door car for a minimum of five consecutive days. At time of rental, present this coupon at the Avis counter and you can save $20. **An advance reservation is required**. Subject to complete Terms and Conditions below. Rental must begin by 06/30/01.

For reservations and information, call your travel consultant or Avis toll free at **1-800-831-8000**.

Terms and Conditions: Coupon valid on an Intermediate (Group C) through a Full Size 4-Door (Group E) car. Dollars off applies to the cost of the total rental with a minimum of 5 days. A Saturday night overstay is required. Coupon must be surrendered at time of rental; one per rental. Coupon valid at Avis participating locations in the U.S. An advance reservation is required. Cars subject to availability. Taxes, local government surcharges, vehicle licensing and an airport recruitment fee at some locations, optional items such as LDW, additional driver fee and refueling fee are extra. Renter must meet Avis driver and credit requirements. Minimum age is 25 but may vary by location. Rental must begin by 6/30/01.

Coupon #: **MUNA002**

Rental Sales Agent Instructions
At checkout:
In AWD, enter AWD number.
In CPN, enter **MUNA002**.
Complete this information:
RA # _____
Rental location _____
Attach to COUPON tape.

©1999 Avis Rent A Car System, Inc.

www.avis.com

11/99 DTPP

It's a Whole New World with

Frommer's

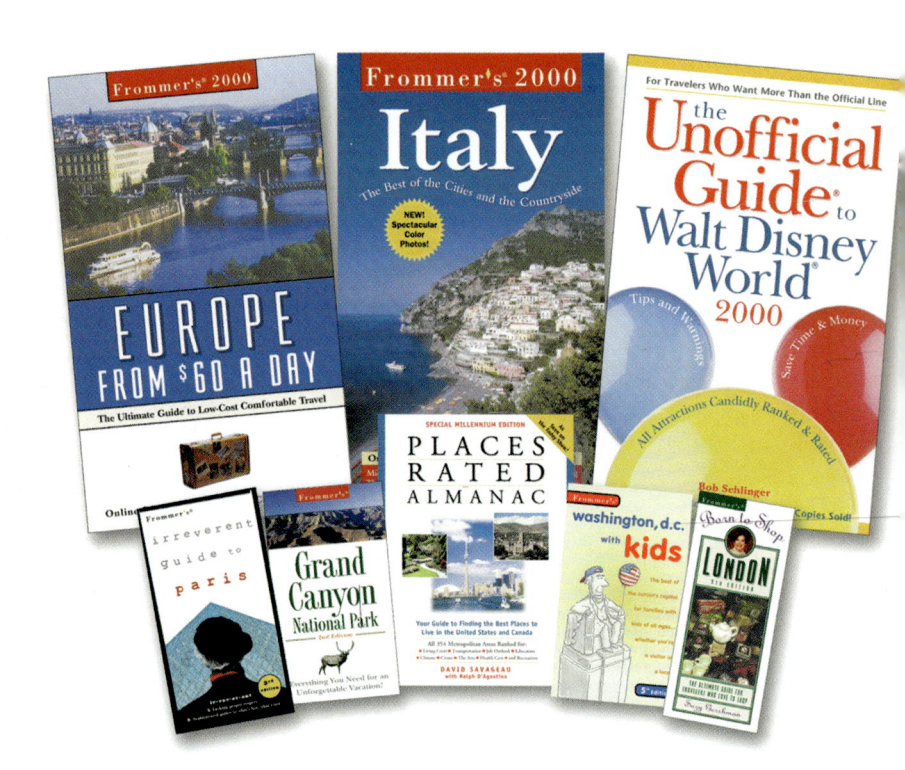

Available at bookstores everywhere.

exhibit. Parrot Jungle's current incarnation occasionally feels too commercial and has an overly high price tag; hopefully, the move will change this because the park does make for an enjoyable excursion. The park's Web site sometimes offers downloadable discount coupons, so if you have Internet access, take a look before you come.

4 Miami's Museum & Art Scene

Miami's museum scene has always been quirky, interesting, and inconsistent at best. Though several exhibition spaces have made forays into collecting nationally acclaimed work, limited support and political infighting have made it a difficult proposition. Recently, with the reinvention of the Wolfsonian, the reincarnation of MOCA, and the increased daring of the Miami Art Museum, the scene has improved dramatically. It's now safe to say that world-class exhibitions start here. Listed below is an excellent cross-section of the valuable treasures that have become a part of the city's cultural heritage, and as such, are as diverse as the city itself.

For gallery lovers, see "Specialized Tours," below, for scheduled gallery walks.

IN SOUTH BEACH

Bass Museum of Art. 2121 Park Ave. (1 block west of Collins Ave.), South Beach. ☎ **305/673-7530.** Admission $5 adults, $3 students and seniors, free for children 6 and under; 2nd and 4th Wed of the month by donation from 5–9pm. Tues–Sat 10am–5pm; Sun 1–5pm (every 2nd and 4th Wed open 1–9pm). Closed major holidays.

An important and growing visual arts museum in Miami Beach, Bass displays European paintings, sculptures, and tapestries from the Renaissance, baroque, rococo, and modern periods as part of their small permanent collection. Temporary exhibitions alternate between traveling shows and rotations of the Bass's stock, with themes ranging from 17th-century Dutch art to contemporary architecture. Built in 1930 from coral rock, the Bass is undergoing an $8.1 million renovation that will add a media center, a research section, new exhibition space, and a cafe by the end of 2000.

The Wolfsonian. 1001 Washington Ave., South Beach. ☎ **305/531-1001.** Admission $5 adults; $3.50 senior citizens, students, and children 6–12; $5 tour-group members; free on Thurs evenings. Members, children under 6, and students or faculty of Florida Universities are admitted free. Mon–Tues, Fri–Sat 11am–6pm; Thurs 11am–9pm; Sun noon–5pm.

Mitchell Wolfson Jr., an eccentric collector of late 19th- and 20th-century art and other paraphernalia, was spending so much money storing his booty that he decided to buy the warehouse that was housing it. It ultimately held more than 70,000 of his items, including glass, ceramics, sculptures, paintings, and photographs. He then gave this incredibly diverse and controversial collection to Florida International University. The former storage facility has been retrofitted with such painstaking detail that it's the envy of curators around the world.

✪ **Holocaust Memorial.** 1933 Meridian Ave. (at Dade Blvd.), South Beach. ☎ **305/538-1663.** Free admission. Daily 9am–9pm.

This heart-wrenching memorial is hard to miss and would be a shame to overlook. The powerful centerpiece is a bronze statue by Kenneth Treister that depicts thousands of victims crawling into an open hand to freedom. You can walk through an open hallway lined with photographs and the names of concentration camps and their victims. From the street, you'll see the outstretched arm, but do stop and tour the sculpture at ground level—what's hidden behind the beautiful stone facade is extremely moving.

IN & NEAR DOWNTOWN

✪ **Diaspora Vibe Art Gallery.** 561 NW 32nd St., Studio 48 (Bakehouse Art Complex), Miami. ☎ **305/759-1110.** www.diasporavibe.com. "Final Fridays" admission $15. Mon–Fri by appointment only; Sat–Sun 1–6pm; May–Oct last Fri of the month 7–11pm.

The Diaspora Vibe Art Gallery is one of the latest and hippest art galleries in Miami. It is home to some of the greatest art works of Miami's diverse Caribbean and Latin American cultures. Rosie Gordon-Wallace, the curator, connects art lovers to the artwork of emerging artists at art exhibitions throughout South Florida, Europe, and Africa.

Gordon-Wallace hosts "Final Fridays" at the Bakehouse Art Complex on the last Friday of every month from May through October. Each month a new artist's work is spotlighted and can be purchased. (*Hint:* These one-of-a-kind originals go pretty fast, so you must act quickly if you want to nab one). After perusing the halls to view these great works, you can go outside to the courtyard to listen to the sounds of a great R&B, jazz, or steel band, or to enjoy West Indian folk tales and poems during open mike. If that isn't enough to hold you, you can also nibble on delectable Caribbean dishes such as peas and rice, jerk chicken, curry goat, stew beef and Mama G's famous rock buns. You'll enjoy amazing art, great food and a jammin' live band for the low price of $15. You can't beat this deal anywhere else in Miami on a Friday night.

Rubell Family Art Collection. 95 NW 29th St. (near the Design District), Miami. ☎ **305/573-6090**. Free admission. Thurs–Sat 11am– 4pm, and by appointment.

If you're in Miami for the weekend, tour this private collection, which belongs to four famous New Yorkers: Mera and Don Rubell, and their adult children, Jennifer and Jason, who also own the Albion, Greenview, and the Beach House Bal Harbour hotels. The Rubells own a priceless collection of more than a thousand works of contemporary art, by the likes of Paul McCarthy, Keith Haring, Jean-Michel Basquiat, Charles Ray, and Cindy Sherman. These pieces are now on view in a former Drug Enforcement Agency warehouse in downtown Miami. They include McCarthy's Cultural Gothic (1992–93), a motorized sculpture of a man coaxing a young boy into an act of bestiality, and Beverly Semme's Blue Gowns (1993), three giant gowns flowing from a neck-craning height onto the floor. This is not the family-friendliest attraction; there's no avoiding nudity, erotica, and themes that some may find offensive—bring the kids at your discretion.

Florida Museum of Hispanic and Latin American Art. 4006 Aurora St. (between Altara St. and Bird Rd.), Coral Gables. ☎ **305/444-7060.** Free admission. Tues–Fri 11am–5pm; Sat 11am–4pm. Closed Aug and major holidays.

In addition to the permanent collection of contemporary artists from Spain and Latin America, this 3,500-square-foot museum hosts monthly exhibitions of works from Latin America and the Caribbean Basin. Usually, the exhibitions focus on a theme, such as international women or surrealism. It's not a major attraction, but definitely worth a stop if you're an art lover. On the same block, you'll find great design stores and a few other galleries.

✪ **Miami Art Museum at the Miami-Dade Cultural Center.** 101 W. Flagler St., Miami. ☎ **305/375-3000.** Admission $5 adults, $2.50 senior and students, free for children under 12, by contribution on Tues. Tues–Fri 10am–5pm; third Thurs of each month 10am–9pm; Sat–Sun noon–5pm. Closed major holidays. From I-95 south, exit at Orange Bowl–NW 8th St. and continue south to NW 2nd St.; turn left at NW 2nd St. and go 1¹/₂ blocks to NW 2nd Ave.; turn right.

The Miami Art Museum (MAM) features an eclectic mix of modern and contemporary works by such artists as Eric Fischl, Max Beckman, Jim Dine, and Stuart Davis.

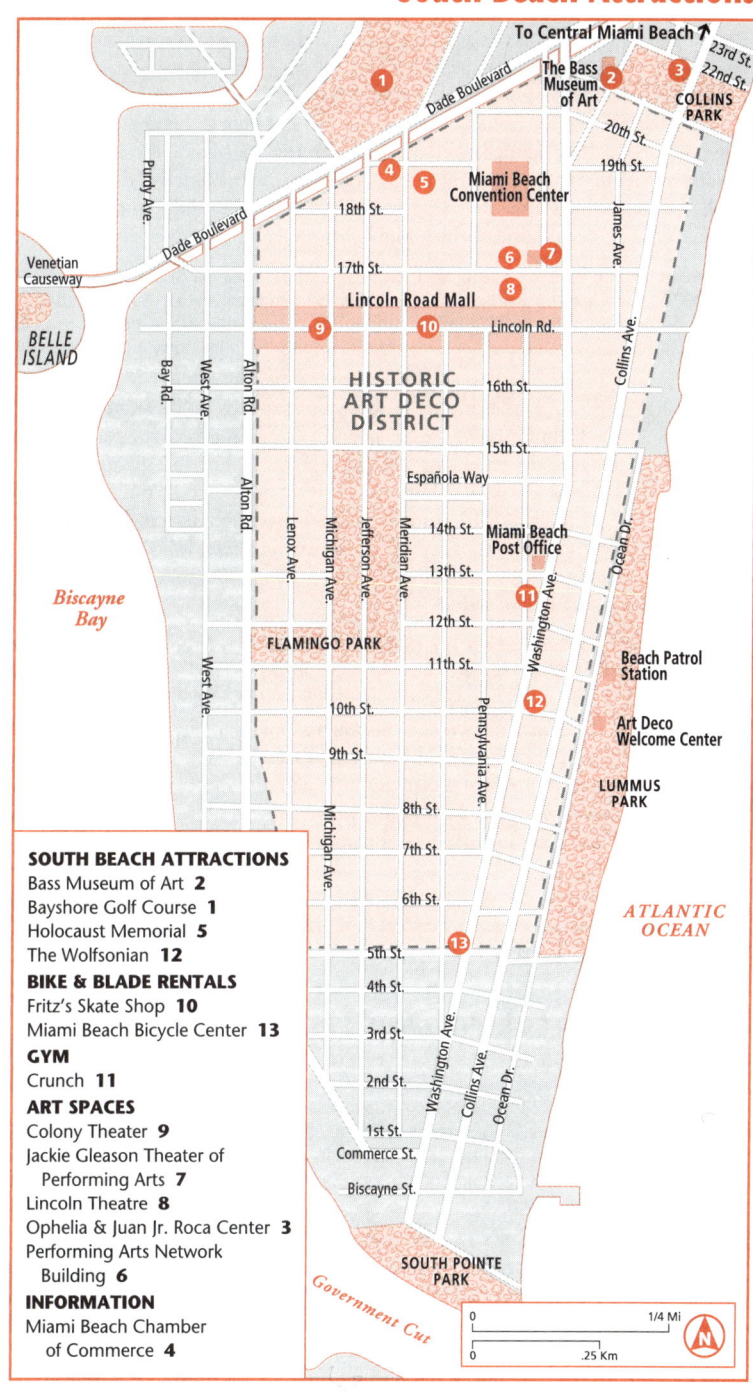

South Beach Attractions

SOUTH BEACH ATTRACTIONS
Bass Museum of Art **2**
Bayshore Golf Course **1**
Holocaust Memorial **5**
The Wolfsonian **12**

BIKE & BLADE RENTALS
Fritz's Skate Shop **10**
Miami Beach Bicycle Center **13**

GYM
Crunch **11**

ART SPACES
Colony Theater **9**
Jackie Gleason Theater of Performing Arts **7**
Lincoln Theatre **8**
Ophelia & Juan Jr. Roca Center **3**
Performing Arts Network Building **6**

INFORMATION
Miami Beach Chamber of Commerce **4**

155

Rotating exhibitions span the ages and styles, and often focus on Latin American or Caribbean artists. The shows are almost always superbly curated and installed, and sometimes subject to controversy from the ultrapolitical Cuban community.

The Miami-Dade Cultural Center, where the museum is housed, is an oasis for those seeking cultural enrichment during their trip to Miami. In addition to the acclaimed Miami Art Museum, the center houses the main branch of the Miami-Dade Public Library, which sometimes features art and cultural exhibits, and the Historical Museum of Southern Florida, which highlights the fascinating history of the area.

American Police Hall of Fame and Museum. 3801 Biscayne Blvd., Miami. ☎ **305/ 573-0070.** www.aphf.org. Admission $6 adults, $4 seniors over 61, $3 children 11 and under, $1 police officers. 50% off coupons often available from hotel racks. Daily 10am–5:30pm. Go north on U.S. 1 from downtown, it's the building with police car affixed to its side.

This strange museum appeals mostly to those fascinated by police and their gadgetry. Once inside, you'll find a combination of reality and fantasy that's part thoughtful tribute, part Hollywood-style drama. Just past the car featured in the motion picture *Blade Runner* is a mock prison cell, in which visitors can take pictures of themselves pretending they're doing 5 to 10. Also on hand are execution devices, including a guillotine and an electric chair (whose controversial use was recently abolished in Florida). In the entry is a touching memorial to the more than 3,000 police officers who have lost their lives in the line of duty.

✪ **Museum of Contemporary Art (MOCA).** 770 NE 125th St., North Miami. ☎ **305/ 893-6211.** Fax 305/ 891-1472. Admission $5 adults, $3 seniors and students with ID, free for children 12 and under. Tues–Sat 11am–5pm; Sun noon–5pm. Closed major holidays.

MOCA recently acquired a new 23,000-square-foot space in which to display its impressive collection of internationally acclaimed art with a local flavor. An impressive screening facility allows for film presentations to complement the exhibitions. You can see works by Jasper Johns, Roy Lichtenstein, Larry Rivers, Duane Michaels, and Claes Oldenberg. Guided tours are offered in English, Spanish, French, Creole, Portuguese, German, and Italian.

MOCA also hosts a series of monthly concerts, called "**Jazz at Moca,**" featuring big band jazz musicians. All concerts begin at 8:00pm. For more information call ☎ **305/ 893-6211.** MOCA is definitely worth the drive to view important contemporary art in South Florida.

IN CORAL GABLES & COCONUT GROVE
Miami Museum of Science and Space Transit Planetarium. 3280 S. Miami Ave. (just south of the Rickenbacker Causeway), Coconut Grove. ☎ **305/646-4200** for general information, or 305/854-2222 for planetarium show times. www.miamisci.org. $9 adults, $7 students, seniors and children 3–12, free for children 2 and under. Planetarium $5 adults, $2.50 children and seniors. Combination ticket $9 adults, $5.50 children and seniors. Half-price 4:30–6pm weekdays. 25% discount for AAA members. Museum of Science, daily 10am–6pm; call for planetarium show times.

The Museum of Science features more than 140 hands-on exhibits that explore the mysteries of the universe. Live demonstrations and collections of rare natural history specimens make a visit here fun and informative. A joint exhibit with the Smithsonian Institution on Latin America is currently on display, and a separate exhibit on sharks will run from February to September of 2001. There is also a Wildlife Center with more than 175 live reptiles and birds of prey. The adjacent Space Transit Planetarium projects astronomy and laser shows as well as interactive demonstrations of upcoming computer technology and cyberspace features.

Weeks Air Museum. 14710 SW 28th St. (south of 120th St. and west of the Florida Turnpike at the Kendall-Tamiami Airport), Miami. ☎ **305/233-5197.** Admission $6.95 adults, $5.95 seniors, $4.95 children under 12. Daily 10am–5pm.

This well-maintained museum is a must-see for aeronautic buffs, who will enjoy talking to the thoroughly dedicated staff who are always eager to answer questions from fellow enthusiasts. Exhibitions include a dramatic portrait of the Tuskeegee Airmen, who tell of their experiences on video. Also on display are dozens of airplanes dating from the turn of the 20th century and an intriguing display of planes damaged by Hurricane Andrew in 1992. Other highlights include a collection of propellers throughout the ages; a J47 jet engine; an aerobatic plane, the "Little Stinker" Soviet bombers; and lots of war memorabilia.

5 Worldly Wonders

South Beach may reign as the place to see and be seen, particularly with its well-touted Deco scene, but it's only one of many colorful neighborhoods that can boast architecture that dazzles the eye. The rediscovery of the entire Biscayne Corridor (from downtown to the eighties) has given light to a host of ancillary neighborhoods on either side that are filled with Mediterranean style homes and Frank Lloyd Wright gems. Coral Gables is home to many large and beautiful homes, mansions, and churches that reflect architecture from the 1920s, '30s, and '40s. Some of the homes, or portions of their structure, have been created from coral rock and shells. Even if you don't stay at the Biltmore Hotel, definitely take a tour of it. Call ☎ **305/445-1926** for more information.

Villa Vizcaya. 3251 S. Miami Ave. (just south of Rickenbacker Causeway), North Coconut Grove. ☎ **305/250-9133.** Admission $10 adults, $5 children 6–12, free for children 5 and under. Villa daily 9:30am–5pm (ticket booth closes at 4:30pm); gardens daily 9:30am–5:30pm.

Sometimes referred to as the "Hearst Castle of the East," this magnificent villa is the setting for many society weddings and galas. It was built in 1916 as a winter retreat for James Deering, cofounder and former vice president of International Harvester. The industrialist was fascinated by 16th-century art and architecture, and his ornate mansion—which took 1,000 artisans 5 years to build—became a celebration of that period. Most of the original furnishings, including dishes and paintings, are still intact.

The spectacularly opulent villa wraps itself around a central courtyard. Outside, lush formal gardens, accented with statuary, balustrades, and decorative urns, front an enormous swath of Biscayne Bay.

The Barnacle State Historic Site. 3485 Main Hwy. (1 block south of Commodore Plaza), Coconut Grove. ☎ **305/448-9445.** Fax 305/448-7484. Admission $1. Tours Fri–Sun at 10am, 11:30am, 1pm, and 2:30pm. Group tours Mon–Thurs with 2-week advance reservations. From downtown Miami, take U.S. 1 south to 27th Ave., make a left, and continue to South Bayshore Dr.; then make a right, follow to the intersection of Main Hwy. and turn left.

The former home of naval architect and early settler Ralph Middleton Munroe is now a museum in the heart of Coconut Grove. The house's quiet surroundings, wide porches, and period furnishings illustrate how Miami's privileged class lived in the days before skyscrapers and luxury hotels. Enthusiastic and knowledgeable state park employees offer a wealth of historical information to those interested in quiet, low-tech attractions like this one. Call for details on monthly moonlight concerts during which folk, blues, or classical music are presented. Cost is $5 per person, free for children under 10.

What to See & Do in Miami

Coral Castle. 28655 S. Dixie Hwy., Homestead. ☎ **305/248-6344.** www.coralcastle.com. Admission $7.75 adults, $6.50 seniors, $5 children 7–12. Daily 9am–6pm. Take U.S. 1 south to SW 286th St.

There's plenty of competition, but Coral Castle is probably the strangest attraction in Florida. In 1923, the story goes, a crazed Latvian, suffering from unrequited love, immigrated to South Miami and spent the next 25 years of his life carving huge boulders into a prehistoric-looking, roofless "castle." It seems impossible that one rather short man could have done all this, but there are scores of affidavits on display from neighbors who swear it happened. Apparently, experts have studied this phenomenon to help figure out how the Great Pyramids and Stonehenge were built.

Listen to the audio tour to learn about this bizarre spot, now in the National Register of Historic Places. The commentary lasts about 25 minutes and is available in four languages. Although Coral Castle is overpriced and undermaintained, it's worth a visit when in the area.

✪ **Spanish Monastery Cloisters.** 16711 W. Dixie Hwy. (at NE 167th St.), North Miami Beach. ☎ **305/945-1461.** Admission $4.50 adults, $2.50 seniors, $1 children 11 and under. Mon–Sat 10am–4pm; Sun 1:30pm–5:30pm.

Did you know that the oldest building in the Western Hemisphere dates from 1133 and is located in Miami? The Spanish Monastery Cloisters were first erected in Segovia, Spain. Centuries later, newspaper magnate William Randolph Hearst purchased and brought them to America in pieces. The carefully numbered stones were quarantined for years until they were finally reassembled on the present site in 1954.

Today, it has often been used as a backdrop for movies and commercials and is a very popular tourist attraction.

Venetian Pool. 2701 DeSoto Blvd. (at Toledo St.), Coral Gables. ☎ **305/460-5356.** www.venetianpool.com. Admission and hours vary seasonally. Nov–Mar $5 13 and older, $2 children under 13; April–Oct $8 13 and older, $4 under 13. Children must be 3 years old or 38 inches tall to enter.

Miami's most beautiful and unusual swimming pool, dating from 1924, is hidden behind pastel stucco walls and is honored with a listing in the National Register of Historic Places. Underground artesian wells feed the free-form lagoon, which is shaded by three-story Spanish porticos and features both fountains and waterfalls. It can be cold in the winter months. During summer, the pool's 800,000 gallons of water are drained and refilled nightly, ensuring a cool, clean swim. Visitors are free to swim and sunbathe here, just as Esther Williams and Johnny Weissmuller did decades ago. For a modest fee, you or your children can learn to swim during special summer programs.

6 Nature Preserves, Parks & Gardens

The Miami area is a great place for outdoors-minded visitors, with beaches, parks, and gardens galore. Plus, South Florida has two national parks; see chapter 10, "Side Trips from Miami," for coverage of the Everglades and Biscayne National Park.

BOTANICAL GARDENS & A SPICE PARK

Fairchild Tropical Garden, 10901 Old Cutler Rd. (☎ **305/667-1651;** www.ftg. org), is the largest of its kind in the continental United States. A veritable rain forest of both rare and exotic plants, as well as 11 lakes and countless meadows, are spread across 83 acres. Palmettos, vine pergola, palm glades, and other unique species create a scenic, lush environment. More than 100 species of bird have been spotted at the garden (ask for a checklist at the front gate), and it's home to a variety of animals. You

Attractions in South Miami–Dade County

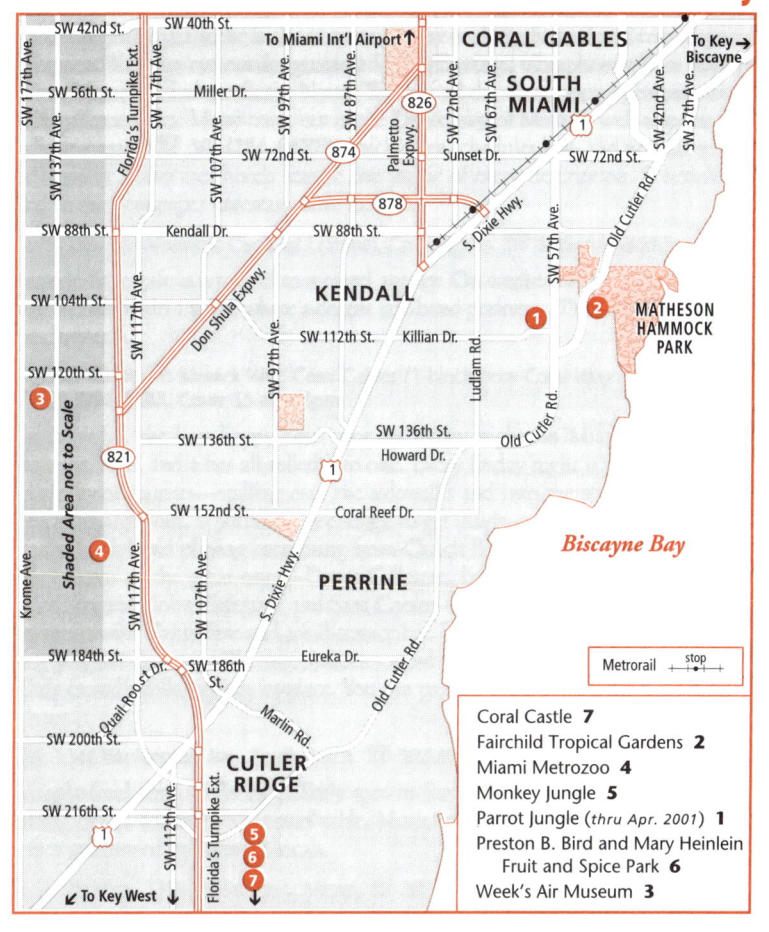

Map Legend:
- Coral Castle **7**
- Fairchild Tropical Gardens **2**
- Miami Metrozoo **4**
- Monkey Jungle **5**
- Parrot Jungle (*thru Apr. 2001*) **1**
- Preston B. Bird and Mary Heinlein Fruit and Spice Park **6**
- Week's Air Museum **3**

should definitely take the 30-minute narrated tram tour (tours leave on the hour) to learn about the various flowers and trees on the grounds. There is also a museum, a cafe, a picnic area, and a gift shop with fantastic books on gardening and cooking and edible gifts. The garden broke ground on a new 2-acre rain forest exhibit in January 2000, which should be up and running by mid-2001.

Admission is $8 for adults, and free for children 12 and under accompanied by an adult. Open daily, except Christmas, from 9:30am to 4:30pm. Take I-95 south to U.S. 1, turn left onto Le Jeune Road, and follow it straight to the traffic circle; from there, take Old Cutler Road 2 miles to the park.

A testament to Miami's unusual climate, the **Preston B. Bird and Mary Heinlein Fruit and Spice Park,** 24801 SW 187th Ave., Homestead (☎ **305/247-5727**), harbors rare fruit trees that cannot survive elsewhere in the country. Definitely ask for a guide. If a volunteer is available, you'll learn some fascinating things about this 30-acre living plant museum, where the most exotic varieties of fruits and spices—ackee, mango, ugly fruits, carambola, and breadfruit—grow on strange-looking trees with unpronounceable names.

Picnicking in the Park

Miami-Dade is home to literally dozens of small-, medium-, and large-sized parks, including many that line the bay and beaches, offering magnificent opportunities for recreation, sunbathing, or that favorite of any creative lover of culinary delights—a picnic! South Beach itself is home to several intimate restaurants, cafes, boutiques, and even supermarkets that can cater to your picnic needs, or just cater your picnic; it depends how much you're willing to spend and how far off the beaten path you want to explore.

Alton Road is the major beach thoroughfare that runs north-south on the most western end of the island. Dotted by high-rises that sprouted up in the '50s and still exist today, it doesn't contain the architectural charm of its deco counterpart to the immediate east, but it is home to many residents, as well as the numerous stores and restaurants they frequent. If you follow the ever-popular Lincoln Road due West (where it is capped by Alton as if creating a large T) you will run right into three specialty shops that just scream picnic!

On 1710 Alton Rd. (at the corner of 17th and Alton), is a little known cafe called **Crocante**. It is home to quite a number of little Spanish/French confections, including fresh loaves of French bread that are not only inexpensive (running $1 to $2), but whose piping hot smell is enough to start mouths a'salivatin'! Specialties here include champagne chicken breast at $6 a pop or salads for $4.25. Sizable fresh fruit tortes—they can easily feed 10—cost $18. Just around the corner at 1201 17th St. is the tiny Russian Deli known as **From Russia With Food,** which offers such sumptuous treats as specialty sausages, imported cheeses (the dill havarti is a must), and of course salmon and caviar. It's a nice spot to get exotic eastern European teas, jams, and hard crusty bagels. Down the street, on the corner of Alton and Lincoln, is the ubiquitous **Epicure**, a gourmet market for serious foodies. The store will prepare sandwiches for you on the spot, has a huge selection of deli items (turkey, pastrami, French and Italian hams), as well as wine and fresh produce from all over the world. *Warning:* This is not a market for the faint of wallet; a few fresh croissants and some Chilean peaches can set you back an easy $8 and you'll have only gotten started! However, if it can't be found at Epicure Market, it probably isn't edible.

The store with the best bang for your picnic buck is the **blu dog café** on 412 Española Way, a street dotted with so many shopping gems it's a must-walk on its own. Before heading over to the beach, stop in at this specialty picnic store, where a call ahead (☎ **305/534-9495**) can guarantee you a picnic basket designed to suit your needs and pocketbook. Basket items range from phyllo triangles of greens and feta to panko crusted chicken with honey mustard, melons, and prosciutto to assorted little quiches, and that's just for starters. It's a great spot to stock up on supplies for a romantic tête-à-tête on the beach. Enjoy!

The best part? You're free to take anything that falls to the ground. You'll also find samples of interesting fruits and jellies made from the park's bounty in the gift store. Cooks who like to experiment must visit the park store, which carries a number of exotic ingredients and cookbooks.

Admission to the spice park is $3.50 for adults and $1 for children under 12, and is open daily from 10am to 5pm; closed major holidays. Tours are included in the price of admission and are offered 11am, 1pm, and 2:30pm. Take U.S. 1 south, turn right on SW 248th Street, and go straight for 5 miles to SW 187th Avenue. Hours: 10am–5pm, 7 days a week.

MORE MIAMI PARKS

The **Amelia Earhart Park,** 401 E. 65th St., Hialeah (☎ **305/685-8389**), has five lakes stocked with bass and bream for fishing; playgrounds; picnic facilities; and a big red barn that houses cows, sheep, and goats for petting, and ponies for riding. There's also a country store and dozens of old-time farm activities like horseshoeing, sugarcane processing, and more. Parking is free on weekdays and $3.50 per car on weekends. Open daily from 9am to sunset. To drive here, take I-95 north to the NW 103rd Street exit, go west to East 4th Avenue, and then turn right. Parking is 1 1/2 miles down the street.

At the historic **Bill Baggs Cape Florida State Recreation Area,** 1200 Crandon Blvd. (☎ **305/361-5811**), at the tip of Key Biscayne, you can explore the unfettered wilds and enjoy some of the most secluded beaches in Miami. There's also a recently reopened lighthouse. A rental shack rents bikes, hydrobikes, kayaks, and many more water toys. It's a great place to picnic, and a newly constructed restaurant serves homemade Latin food, including great fish soups and sandwiches. Just be careful that the raccoons don't get your lunch, because the furry black-eyed beasts are everywhere. Admission is $4 per car with up to eight people. Open daily from 8am to sunset. Tours of the recently renovated lighthouse are available every day at 10am and 1pm, except Tuesday and Wednesday. Arrive at least half an hour early to sign up—there is only room for 10 people on each.

Tropical Park, 7900 SW 40th St. (☎ **305/226-8315**), has it all. Enjoy a game of tennis and racquetball for a minimal fee, or swim and sun yourself on the secluded little lake. You can use the fishing pond for free, and they'll even supply you with the rods and bait. If you catch anything, however, you're on your own. Open daily from sunrise to sunset.

Named after the now deceased champion of the Everglades, **Marjory Stoneman Douglas Biscayne Nature Center** offers hands-on marine exploration, hikes through coastal hammocks, bike trips, and beach walks. Local environmentalists and historians lead intriguing trips through the local habitat. Be sure to wear comfortable closed-toe shoes for hikes through wet or rocky terrain. The center is located in Crandon Park in Key Biscayne. Call (☎ **305/642-9600**) for tour schedules and prices.

7 Especially for Kids

The **Scott Rakow Youth Center,** 2700 Sheridan Ave. (☎ **305/673-7767**), is a hidden treasure on Miami Beach. This two-story facility boasts an ice-skating rink, bowling alleys, a basketball court, gymnasium equipment, and full-time supervision for kids. Call for a complete schedule of organized events. The only drag is that it's not open to adults (except on Sunday, which is family day). Admission is $1.50 per day for visiting children 9 to 17. Open daily from 2 to 8:30pm.

The following is a roundup of other attractions kids will especially enjoy. Details on each one can be found earlier in the chapter.

AMELIA EARHART PARK (see above) This is the best park in Miami for kids. They'll like the petting zoos, pony rides, and a private island with hidden tunnels.

MARJORY STONEMAN DOUGLAS BISCAYNE NATURE CENTER (see above) Kids seem to enjoy touching slimy marine animals and spotting unusual creatures out at sea. This brand-new exhibit and tour center offers lots of educational and fun programs.

MIAMI METROZOO (see p. 152) This completely cageless zoo offers such star attractions as a monorail "safari" and a petting zoo. Kids can take a ride on an elephant.

MIAMI MUSEUM OF SCIENCE & SPACE TRANSIT PLANETARIUM (see p. 156) At the Planetarium, kids can learn about space and science by watching entertaining films and cosmic shows. The space museum also offers child-friendly explanations for natural occurrences.

MIAMI SEAQUARIUM (see p. 152) Kids can touch, swim with, or kiss a dolphin and watch exciting performances.

8 Video Arcades & Entertainment Centers

✪ **Game Works.** 5701 Sunset Dr. South Miami. ☎ **305/740-9091.** Mon–Fri 11am–2am, Sat 10am–2am, Sun 10am–midnight. Games 50¢–$5.

The biggest thing to hit Miami in years, Steven Spielberg's SEGA Gameworks in the Shops of Sunset Place has become the hottest place for young adults to play. You'll see kids, gen-Xers, and baby boomers fighting off dinosaurs from *Jurassic Park,* racing in the Indy 500, swooshing down a snowy ski trail, throwing darts, and shooting pool in this sleek, multilevel playground. The young at heart will find the perfect combination of vintage arcade games, high-tech videos, virtual reality arenas, pool tables, food, and cocktails in this playground occupying more than 33,000 square feet. The Gameworks Grill serves up everything from gourmet salads to pizzas and burgers.

IMAX Theatre at Sunset Place. 5701 Sunset Dr. South Miami. ☎ **305/663-4629.** www.imax.com. IMAX Adults $7.50 seniors and students $6.50, children under 12 $5.50. 3-D theater adults $9, seniors and students $8, children under 12 $7. Shows daily from 11am–11pm. Call for exact schedule and prices.

Utilizing high-tech film techniques, six-story-high screens, and wraparound digital sound, this unique movie experience really makes you feel like you're part of the action. At press time, the incredible story of Everest was showing. This 50-minute documentary style film captured the terrifying experience of the mountain climbers in the Himalayas in all its frigid, blinding wonder. Also available is a 3-D theater that really tempts you to reach out and touch the images.

For other nearby arcades and game parks see chapter 12.

9 Sightseeing Cruises & Organized Tours

BOAT & CRUISE-SHIP TOURS

Gondola Adventures. Docked at Biscayne Bay Marina, 1633 N. Bayshore Dr. (behind the Marriott Hotel), Miami. ☎ **305/358-6400.** Rates from $5 per person (minimum 4 people).

A real gondola in Miami? Well, it may not be the canals of Venice, but with a little imagination, the Biscayne Bay will do. You can go on a simple ride around Bayside, or splurge on your own private champagne cruise for $99.

Heritage Miami II Topsail Schooner. Bayside Marketplace Marina, 401 Biscayne Blvd., Downtown. ☎ **305/442-9697.** Fax 305/442-0119. Tickets $15 adults, $10 children 12 and under. Sept–May only. Tours leave daily at 1:30, 4, and 6:30pm, and Fri–Sun also at 9, 10, and 11pm.

More adventure than tour, this relaxing ride aboard Miami's only tall ship is a fun way to see the city. The 2-hour cruises pass by Villa Vizcaya, Coconut Grove, and Key Biscayne and put you in sight of Miami's spectacular skyline. Call to make sure the ship is running on schedule. On Friday, Saturday, and Sunday evenings, there are 1-hour tours to see the lights of the city.

A SIGHTSEEING TOUR

There are literally hundreds of tour operators in Miami and the Beaches. Check with your hotel's concierge to see which they recommend, or try the following company.

Miami Nice Excursion Travel and Service. 18430 Collins Ave., Miami Beach. ☎ **305/ 949-9180.** Admission $29–$55 adults, $25 children. Daily 7am–10pm. Call ahead for directions to various pickup areas.

Pick your destination. The Miami Nice tours will take you to the Everglades, Fort Lauderdale, the Seaquarium, Key West, Cape Canaveral, or wherever you desire. Included in most Miami trips is a fairly comprehensive city tour narrated by a knowledgeable guide. The company is one of the oldest in town.

SPECIALIZED TOURS

Besides those listed below, a great option for seeing the city is to take a tour led by **Dr. Paul George.** Dr. George is a history teacher at Miami-Dade Community College and a historian at the Historical Museum of Southern Florida—he also happens to be "Mr. Miami." There's a set calendar of tours, but all of them are fascinating to South Florida buffs. Tours focus on neighborhoods, such as Little Havana, Brickell Avenue, or Key Biscayne, and on themes, such as Miami cemeteries. The often long-winded discussions can be a bit much for those who just want a quick look-around, but Dr. George certainly knows his stuff. The cost is $15 to $25; reservations are required (☎ 305/375-1492). Tours leave from the Historical Museum at 101 W. Flagler St., Downtown.

Miami Design Preservation League. The Art Deco Welcome Center, 1001 Ocean Dr., South Beach. ☎ **305/672-2014.** Walking tours $10 per person. Tours leave Sat at 10:30am and Thurs at 6:30pm. Self-guided audio tours also available 7 days a week for $5. Call ahead for updated schedules.

On Thursday evenings and Saturday mornings, the Design Preservation League sponsors walking tours that offer a fascinating inside look at the city's historic Art Deco District. Tour-goers meet for a 1½-hour walk through some of America's most exuberantly "architectured" buildings. The league led the fight to designate this area a National Historic District and is proud to share the splendid locale with visitors.

Art Deco Cycling Tour. 601 5th St., South Beach. ☎ **305/674-0150.** $10 per person, plus $6 for bike rental. Tours depart every other Sun at 10am from the Miami Beach Bicycle Center.

If you'd rather bike or in-line skate than walk, catch this fun and interesting Sunday morning tour. The bicycle is the most efficient mode of transportation through the streets of South Beach, and one of the best ways to see the historic Art Deco District. Call to reserve a spot.

Biltmore Hotel Tour. 1200 Anastasia Ave., Coral Gables. ☎ **305/445-1926.** Free admission. Tours depart on Sun at 1:30, 2:30, and 3:30pm.

Take advantage of these free walking tours offered on Sunday to enjoy the hotel's beautiful grounds. The Biltmore is chock-full of history and mystery, including a few ghosts; go out there and see for yourself.

Coral Gables Art and Gallery Tour. Various locations in Coral Gables. Free. For more information, call Elite Fine Art (☎ **305/448-3800**) or stop by any of the galleries in the area. First Fri of the month from 7–10pm.

On this tour, art lovers are shuttled to more than 20 galleries that participate in Gables Night in the gallery section of Coral Gables. Viewers can sip wine as they gaze at American folk art; African, Native American, and Latin art; and photography. Most galleries are on Ponce de León Boulevard, between SW 40th and SW 24th streets. The vans run continuously from 7 to 10pm.

Lincoln Road Gallery Walk at the Art Center. 800, 810, 924 Lincoln Rd. (at the corner of Meridian Ave.). ☎ **305/674-8278.** www.artcentersofla.com. Free. Self-guided tours of artists studios and two galleries. Call for days and hours of tours.

Feel free to wander through the more than 50 studios housed in this cooperative art complex on your own. You can also walk through the pedestrian mall to catch a look at the works on display in other galleries (if you're lucky, you'll wander into one that serves wine and appetizers).

10 Water Sports

BOATING

Private rental outfits include **Beach Boat Rentals,** 2400 Collins Ave., Miami Beach (☎ **305/534-4307**), where 50-horsepower, 18-foot powerboats rent for some of the best prices on the beach. Rates are $61.25 for an hour, $165.15 for 4 hours, and $225.70 for 8 hours. All rates include taxes and gas. A $250 cash or credit-card deposit is required. Cruising is permitted only in and around Biscayne Bay—ocean access is prohibited. Renters must be over 21. The rental office is at 23rd Street, on the inland waterway in Miami Beach. It's open from 9am to 6pm (weather permitting) during the high season and 9am to 8pm during the summer.

Club Nautico of Coconut Grove, 2560 S. Bayshore Dr., Coconut Grove (☎ **305/858-6258**), rents high-quality powerboats for fishing, waterskiing, diving, and cruising in the bay or ocean. All boats are Coast Guard equipped, with VHF radios and safety gear. Rates range from $199 for 4 hours and $299 for 8 hours, to as much as $419 on weekends. Club Nautico is open daily from 9am to 5pm (weather permitting). Other locations include the Crandon Park Marina, 4000 Crandon Blvd., Key Biscayne (☎ **305/361-9217**), with the same rates and hours as the Coconut Grove location; and the Miami Beach Marina, Pier E, 300 Alton Rd., South Beach (☎ **305/673-2502**), where rates are $229 for 4 hours and $299 for 8 hours for a 20-foot boat; and $259 for 4 hours and $359 for 8 hours for a 24-footer. Nautico on Miami Beach is open daily from 9am to 5pm.

JET-SKIS/WAVE RUNNERS

Don't miss a chance to tour the islands on the back of your own powerful watercraft. Many beachfront concessionaires rent a variety of these popular (and loud) water scooters. The latest models are fast and smooth. Try **Tony's Jet Ski Rentals,** 3601 Rickenbacker Causeway, Key Biscayne (☎ **305/361-8280**), one of the city's largest rental shops, located on a private beach in the Miami Marine Stadium lagoon. Jet-skis rent for about $38 for a half hour and $64 for an hour. Wave Runners for two rent for $45 for a half hour and $70 for an hour. Tony's is open daily from 10:30am to 6:30pm.

KAYAKING

The laid-back **Urban Trails Kayak Company** rents boats at 10800 Collins Ave. (☎ **305/947-1302**). It offers scenic routes through rivers with mangroves and islands as your destination. Most of the kayaks are sit-on-tops, and most are plastic, although there are some fiberglass models available. Rates are $8 an hour, $20 for up to 4 hours, and $25 for over 4 hours. Tandems are $12 an hour, $30 for up to 4 hours, and $35 for the day. Open daily from 9am to 5pm.

The outfitters here give interested explorers a map to take with them and quick instructions on how to work the paddles and boats. If you have at least four people, you can get a guided half-day tour for $35 per person. This is a fun way to experience some of Miami's unspoiled wildlife, and it's good exercise, too.

SAILING

You can rent sailboats and catamarans through the beachfront concessions desk of several top resorts, such as the Doral Golf Resort, Sheraton Bal Harbour Beach Resort, and Dezerland Beach Resort Hotel (see chapter 5, "Miami Accommodations").

Sailboats of **Key Biscayne Rentals and Sailing School,** in the Crandon Marina (next to Sundays on the Bay), 4000 Crandon Blvd., Key Biscayne (☎ **305/361-0328** days, 305/279-7424 evenings), can also get you out on the water. A 22-foot sailboat rents for $27 an hour, or $81 for a half-day. A Cat-25 or J24 is available for $35 an hour or $110 for a half day. If you've always had a dream to win the America's Cup but can't sail, the able teachers at Sailboats will get you started. It offers a 10-hour course over 5 days for $250 for one person or $350 for you and a buddy, $50 for each additional person.

Shake-a-Leg, 2600 Bayshore Dr., Coconut Grove (☎ **305/858-5550**), is a unique sailing program for disabled and able-bodied people alike. The program pairs up sailors for day and evening cruises and offers sailing lessons as well. Consider a moonlight cruise (offered monthly) or a race clinic. Shake-a-Leg members also welcome able-bodied volunteers for activities on and off the water. It costs $60 for nonmembers to rent a boat for 3 hours; free for volunteers. Open on Wednesday through Sunday from 9am to 5pm.

SCUBA DIVING

In 1981, the government began a wide-scale project designed to increase the number of habitats available to marine organisms. One of the program's major accomplishments has been the creation of nearby artificial reefs, which have attracted all kinds of tropical plants, fish, and animals. In addition, Biscayne National Park (see "Biscayne National Park," in chapter10) offers a protected marine environment just south of Downtown.

Several dive shops around the city offer organized weekend outings, either to the reefs or to one of over a dozen old shipwrecks around Miami's shores. Check "Divers" in the Yellow Pages for rental equipment and for a full list of undersea tour operators.

Divers Paradise of Key Biscayne, 4000 Crandon Blvd. (☎ **305/361-3483**), offers two dive expeditions daily to the more than 30 wrecks and artificial reefs off the coast of Miami Beach and Key Biscayne. You can take a 3-day certification course for $399, which includes all the dives and gear. If you already have your C-card, a dive trip costs about $90 if you need equipment and only $35 if you bring your own gear. It's open Monday to Friday from 10am to 6pm and Saturday and Sunday from 8am to 6pm. Call ahead for times and locations of dives.

WINDSURFING

Many hotels rent Windsurfers to their guests, but if yours doesn't have a water-sports concession stand, head for Key Biscayne.

Sailboards Miami, Rickenbacker Causeway, Key Biscayne (☎ **305/361-SAIL**), operates out of big yellow trucks on Hobie Beach, the most popular windsurfing spot in the city. For those who've never ridden a board but want to try it, they offer a 2-hour lesson for $39 that's guaranteed to turn you into a wave warrior or you get your money back. After that, you can rent a board for $20 an hour or $37 for 2 hours. If you want to make a day of it, a 10-hour card costs $130. Open daily from 10am to 5:30pm. Make your first right after the tollbooth to find the outfitters.

11 More Ways to Play, Both Indoors & Out

CYCLING

The cement promenade on the southern tip of the island is a great place to ride. Cycling up the beach is great for surf, sun, sand, exercise, and people watching. Most of the big beach hotels rent bicycles, as does the **Miami Beach Bicycle Center,** 601 5th St., South Beach (☎ **305/674-0150**), which charges $5 per hour or $14 per day. It's open Monday to Saturday from 10am to 7pm, Sunday from 10am to 5pm.

Cyclists can also enjoy more than 130 miles of paved paths throughout Miami. The beautiful and quiet streets of Coral Gables and Coconut Grove are great for bicyclists. Old trees form canopies over wide, flat roads lined with grand homes and quaint street markers. Several bicycle trails are spread throughout these neighborhoods, including one that begins at the doorstep of **Grove Cycle,** 3216 Grand Ave., Coconut Grove (☎ **305/444-5415**). Open Tuesday to Saturday from 11am to 5:30pm; Sunday from 11am to 6pm; closed Monday.

The terrain in Key Biscayne is perfect for cycling, especially along the park and beach roads. If you don't mind the sound of cars whooshing by, **Rickenbacker Causeway** is also fantastic since it is one of the only bikeable inclines in Miami from which you get fantastic elevated views of the city and waterways. **Key Cycling,** 61 Harbor Dr., Key Biscayne (☎ **305/361-0061**), rents mountain bikes for $5 an hour or $15 a day. It's open Monday through Friday from 10am to 7pm, Saturday from 10am to 6pm, Sunday from 11am to 4pm.

Intra Mark, off the Rickenbacker Bridge across from the Rusty Pelican, Hobie Beach (☎ **305/365-0502**), rents scooters for $20 an hour or $35 for 2 hours, and bicycles for $5 an hour or $10 for 4 hours. The ecominded staff directs cyclists to the best paths for nature watching.

If you want to avoid the traffic altogether, head out to **Shark Valley** in the Everglades National Park—one of South Florida's most scenic bicycle trails and a favorite haunt of city-weary locals. See chapter 10, "Side Trips from Miami," for more details.

Biking note: Children under the age of 16 are required by Florida law to wear a helmet, which can be purchased at any bike store or retail outlet selling cycling supplies.

FISHING

Some of the best surf casting in the city can be had at **Haulover Beach Park** at Collins Avenue and 105th Street, where there's a bait-and-tackle shop right on the pier. **South Pointe Park,** at the southern tip of Miami Beach, is another popular fishing spot and features a long pier, comfortable benches, and a great view of the ships passing through Government Cut.

You can also do some deep-sea fishing. One bargain outfitter, the **Kelley Fishing Fleet,** at the Haulover Marina, 10800 Collins Ave. (at 108th Street), Miami Beach (☎ **305/945-3801**), has half-day, full-day, and night fishing aboard diesel-powered "party boats." The fleet's emphasis on drifting is geared toward trolling and bottom fishing for snapper, sailfish, and mackerel, but it also schedules 2- and 3-day trips to The Bahamas. Half-day and night fishing trips are $21 for adults and $14.50 for children; full-day trips are $33 for adults and $26.50 for children; rod and reel rental is

A Berry Good Time

South Florida's farming region has been steadily shrinking in the face of industrial expansion, but you'll still find several spots where you can get back to nature while indulging in a local gastronomic delight—picking your own produce at the "U-Pic-'Em" Farms that dot South Dade's landscape. Depending on what's in season, you can get everything from fresh herbs and vegetables to a mélange of citrus and berries. During berry season—January to April—it's not uncommon to see hardy pickers leaving the groves with hands and faces that are stained a taletelling crimson and garnished with happy smiles. On your way through South Dade, keep an eye out for the bright red "U-Pic" signs.

There are also a number of fantastic fruit stands in the region.

Burr's Berry Farms 12741 SW 216th St. (**305/235-0513**), located in the township of Goulds, has created a sensation with their fabulous fruit milk shakes. To get to Burr's go south on U.S. 1 and turn right on SW 216th Street. The fruit stand is about 1 mile west and on the same road as Monkey Jungle and is open from 9am to 5:30pm seven days a week.

If you like your fresh fruit in a scrumptious pastry or tart, head over to **Knaus Berry Farm** at 15980 SW 248th Street (**305/247-0668**), in an area known as the Redlands. The stand offers items ranging from fresh flowers to ice cream but be sure to indulge in one of their famous homemade cinnamon buns. To get there, head south on U.S. 1 and turn right on 248th Street, the stand is 2$^{1}/_{2}$ miles farther on the left-hand side and they are open Monday through Saturday from 8am to 5:30pm.

$5. Daily departures are scheduled at 9am, 1:45pm, and 8pm; reservations are recommended.

Also at the Haulover Marina is the charter boat *Helen C,* 10800 Collins Ave., Haulover (**305/947-4081**). Although there's no shortage of private charter boats here, Capt. Dawn Mergelsberg is a good pick, since she puts individuals together to get a full boat. Her *Helen* is a twin-engine 55-footer, equipped for big-game "monster" fish like marlin, tuna, dolphin, shark, and sailfish. The cost is $70 per person. Sailings are scheduled for 8am to noon and 1 to 5pm daily; call for reservations. Private charters and transportation are also available. Children are welcome.

Key Biscayne offers deep-sea fishing to those willing to get their hands dirty and pay a bundle. The competition among the boats is fierce, but the prices are basically the same no matter which you choose. The going rate is about $400 to $450 for a half day and $600 to $700 for a full day of fishing. These rates are usually for a party of up to six, and the boats supply you with rods and bait as well as instruction for first-timers. Some will take you out to Key Biscayne and even out to the Upper Keys if the fish aren't biting in Miami.

You might consider the following boats, all of which sail out of the Key Biscayne marina: *Sunny Boy III* (**305/361-2217**), *Queen B* (**305/361-2528**), and *L & H* (**305/361-9318**). Call them for reservations.

Bridge fishing is also popular in Miami; you'll see people with poles over almost every waterway. The Biscayne Bay area is prime tarpon fishing country and a pretty good spot for a lot of other trophy sportfish: snook, bonefish, dolphin, and sailfish.

> **Fishing Tip**
>
> The Biscayne Bay area is prime tarpon fishing country and a pretty good spot for a lot of other trophy sportfish: snook, bonefish, dolphin, and sailfish. For a fee, local guides are happy to show you the hot spots and make sure you hook up. One such guide is **Capt. David Parsons** (☎ **305/264-8346**), who owns a 28-foot boat *Hakuna Matada*. He will take you from Biscayne Bay to the Atlantic Ocean in search of the best catch of the day.

If you don't want to cast your pole alone, local guides are happy to show you the hot spots and make sure you hook up.

GAMBLING

Although gambling is technically illegal in Miami, there are plenty of loopholes that allow all kinds of wagering. Gamblers can try their luck at offshore casinos, bingo, jai alai, card rooms, horse tracks, and dog races.

Especially popular is **Miccosukee Indian Gaming,** 500 SW 177th Ave. (off S.R. 41), (☎ **800/741-4600** or 305/222-4600), a huge outpost west of Miami. This glitzy casino isn't Vegas, but you can play slots, high-speed bingo, and even poker (with a $10 maximum pot). With more than 85,000 square feet of playing space, the complex even offers overnight accommodations for those who can't get enough of the thrill.

One of the most popular gambling "cruises to nowhere" is the **Europa Sea Kruz.** It departs every afternoon and evening from Dock A at 1280 5th St., South Beach (☎ **800/688-PLAY** or 305/538-8300). Tickets cost $10 to $15. A reasonably priced à la carte menu offers basic American fare, from hamburgers to grilled chicken and salads. Most evenings, you'll hear live music on board. You and a few hundred other passengers can play blackjack or the slots. The biggest drawback—if you're losing big or just get bored, you're stuck at sea for 4^1/$_2$ hours.

A newer and more elegant option is the *Casino Princesa,* which docks behind the Hard Rock Cafe in Bayside Marketplace. This 200-foot, $15-million yacht has more than 200 slot machines, 32 tables, a restaurant and four lounges in 10,000 square-feet of gaming space on two decks. Prices range from $13 to $18 and includes meals. Ships sail twice daily on weekdays and three times on weekends. Call ☎ **305/379-5825** for updated schedules.

GOLF

There are more than 50 private and public golf courses in the Greater Miami area. Contact the **Greater Miami Convention and Visitors Bureau** (☎ **800/283-2707** or 305/539-3063) for a list of more courses and costs. Some of the area's best and most expensive are at the big resorts (many of which allow nonguests to play), such as the Doral Blue Course at the Doral Golf Resort and Spa in West Miami; Don Shula's Hotel and Golf Club, also in West Miami; and the Biltmore Hotel in Coral Gables. See chapter 5, "Miami Accommodations," for more details.

Otherwise, the following represent some of the area's best public courses. **Crandon Park Golf Course,** formerly known as The Links, 6700 Crandon Blvd., Key Biscayne (☎ **305/361-9129**), is the number-one ranked municipal course in the state and one of the top five in the country. The park is situated on 200 bay-front acres and offers a pro shop, rentals, lessons, carts, and a lighted driving range. The course is open daily from dawn to dusk; greens fees (including cart) are $86 per person during the winter and $45 per person during the summer. Special twilight rates are available.

One of the most popular courses among real enthusiasts is the **Doral Park Golf and Country Club,** 5001 NW 104th Ave., West Miami (☎ **305/591-8800**); it's not related to the Doral Hotel or spa. Call to book in advance since this challenging 18-holer is so popular with locals. The course is open from 6:30am to 6pm during the winter and until 7pm during the summer. Cart and green fees vary, so call ☎ **305/594-0954** for information.

Known as one of the best in the city, the **Golf Club of Miami,** 6801 Miami Gardens Dr., at NW 68th Avenue (☎ **305/829-8456**), has three 18-hole courses of varying degrees of difficulty. You'll encounter lush fairways, rolling greens, and some history to boot. The west course, designed in 1961 by Robert Trent Jones and updated in the 1990s by the PGA, was where Jack Nicklaus played his first professional tournament and Lee Trevino won his first professional championship. The course is open daily from 6:30am to sunset. Cart and greens fees are $45 to $75 per person during the winter, and $20 to $34 per person during the summer. Special twilight rates are available.

Golfers looking for some cheap practice time will appreciate **Haulover Park,** 10800 Collins Ave., Miami Beach (☎ **305/940-6719**), in a pretty bay-side location. The longest hole on this par-27 course is 125 yards. It's open daily from 7:30am to 5:30pm during the winter, and to 7:30pm during the summer. Greens fees are $5 per person during the winter, and $4 per person during the summer. Hand carts cost $1.40.

HEALTH CLUBS

Although many of Miami's full-service hotels have fitness centers, you can't count on them in less upscale establishments or in the small Art Deco District hotels. Several health clubs around the city will take in nonmembers on a daily basis. If you're already a member at the megahealth club chain **Bally's Total Fitness,** dial ☎ **800/777-1117** to find the clubs in the area. There are no outlets on the beaches; most are in South Miami.

One of the most popular clubs, which welcomes walk-in guests, is **Crunch,** 1253 Washington Ave., South Beach (☎ **305/674-8222**), where you might work out with Cindy Crawford, Madonna, or any of a number of supermodels when they're in town. This club offers star appeal and top-of-the-line equipment. Use of the facility is $18 daily or $65 weekly. It keeps late hours, especially in season, when it's often open until midnight.

IN-LINE SKATING

Miami's consistently flat terrain makes in-line skating easy. The heavy traffic and construction, however, make it tough to find long routes. Remember to keep a pair of

> **Fore!**
>
> You can get information about most Florida courses, including current greens fees, and reserve tee times through **Tee Times USA,** P.O. Box 641, Flagler Beach, FL 32136 (☎ **800/374-8633,** 888/465-3567, or 904/439-0001; fax 904/439-0099). This company also publishes a vacation guide that includes many stay-and-play golf packages.

sandals or sneakers with you, since many area shops won't allow you inside with skates on.

Because of the popularity of blading and skateboarding, the city has passed a law prohibiting skating on the west side (the cafe-lined strip) of Ocean Drive in the evenings. In addition, the city has passed a law that all bladers must skate slowly and safely. You wouldn't want to mow down an elderly stroller. You can still have fun, though, and the following rental outfit can help chart an interesting course for you and supply you with all the necessary gear.

In South Beach, **Fritz's Skate Shop,** 726 Lincoln Rd. Mall (☎ **305/532-1954**), rents top-quality skates, including safety pads, for $8 per hour, $24 per day, and $34 overnight. If you're an in-line skate newbie, an instructor will hold your hand for $25 an hour. The shop also stocks lots of gear and clothing.

SWIMMING

There is no shortage of water here. See "Best Beaches" and also the Venetian Pool under "Worldly Wonders," above, for descriptions of good swimming options.

TENNIS

Hundreds of tennis courts in South Florida are open to the public for a minimal fee. Most courts operate on a first-come, first-served basis, and are open from sunrise to sunset. For information and directions, call the **City of Miami Beach Recreation, Culture, and Parks Department** (☎ **305/673-7730**), or the **City of Miami Parks and Recreation Department** (☎ **305/575-5256**).

The three hard courts and seven clay courts at the **Key Biscayne Tennis Association,** 6702 Crandon Blvd. (☎ **305/361-5263**), get crowded on weekends since they're some of Miami's most beautiful. You'll play on the same courts as Lendl, Graf, Evert, McEnroe, and other greats; this is the venue for one of the world's biggest annual tennis events, the Ericsson Open (see "South Florida Calendar of Events," in chapter 2). There's a pleasant, if limited, pro shop, plus many good pros. Only four courts are lit at night, but if you reserve at least 48 hours in advance, you can usually take your pick. They cost $5 per person per hour. The courts are open daily from 8am to 9pm.

12 Spectator Sports

Check the *Miami Herald's* sports section for a daily listing of local events and the paper's Friday "Weekend" section for comprehensive coverage and in-depth reports. For last-minute tickets, call the venue directly, since many season ticket holders sell singles and return unused tickets. Expensive tickets are available from brokers or individuals, listed in the classified sections of the local papers. Some tickets are also available through **Ticketmaster** (☎ **305/358-5885**).

BASEBALL

The **Florida Marlins** shocked the sports world in 1997 when they became the youngest expansion team to win a World Series, but then floundered as their star players were sold off by former owner Wayne Huizenga. If you're interested in catching a game, be warned the summer heat in Miami can be unbearable, even in the evenings. As long as the rebuilding process continues and the Marlins continue to struggle, tickets are easy to come by.

Home games are held at the **Pro Player Stadium,** 2267 NW 199th St., North Miami Beach (☎ **305/626-7426**). Tickets are $4 to $30. Box office hours are Monday to Friday from 8:30am to 6pm, Saturday from 8:30am to 4pm, and before games; tickets are also available through Ticketmaster. The team currently holds spring training in Melbourne, Florida.

BASKETBALL
The **Miami Heat** (☎ **305/577-HEAT** or 305/835-7000), now led by celebrity coach Pat Riley, made its NBA debut in November 1988 and their games remain one of Miami's hottest tickets. The season lasts from October to April, with most games beginning at 7:30pm. They'll now play in the brand-new waterfront **American Airlines Arena** located downtown on Biscayne Blvd. Tickets are $14 to $50. Box office hours are Monday to Friday from 10am to 4pm (until 8pm on game nights); tickets are also available through Ticketmaster.

FOOTBALL
Miami's golden boys are the **Miami Dolphins,** the city's most recognizable team, followed by thousands of "dolfans." Coached by Jimmy Johnson, the team plays at least eight home games during the season, between September and December, at **Pro Player Stadium,** 2267 NW 199th St., North Miami Beach (☎ **305/620-2578**). Tickets cost between $20 and $40. The box office is open Monday to Friday from 8:30am to 5:30pm; tickets are also available through **Ticketmaster** (☎ **305/350-5050**).

HORSE RACING
Wrapped around an artificial lake, **Gulfstream Park,** at U.S. 1 and Hallandale Beach Boulevard, Hallandale (☎ **305/931-7223**), is both pretty and popular. Large purses and important races are commonplace at this suburban course, and the track is often crowded. Call for schedules. Admission is $3 to the grandstand, and $3 to the clubhouse; free parking. From January through March, post times are Wednesday to Monday at 1pm. Many weekends feature live concerts by well-known musicians.

You might remember the pink flamingos at **Hialeah Park,** 2200 E. 4th Ave., Hialeah (☎ **305/885-8000**), from *Miami Vice.* This famous colony is the largest of its kind. The track, listed on the National Register of Historic Places, is one of the most beautiful in the world, featuring old-fashioned stands and acres of immaculately manicured grounds. Admission is $1 to the grandstand and $2 to the clubhouse on weekdays, and $2 and $4, respectively, on weekends. Children 17 and under enter free with an adult. Parking starts at $2. Races are held mid-March to mid-May, but the course is open year-round for sightseeing Monday to Saturday from 9am to 5pm. Call for post times.

ICE HOCKEY
The young **Florida Panthers** (☎ **954/835-7000**) have already made history. In the 1994–95 season, they played in the Stanley Cup finals, and they have amassed a legion of fans who love them. Much to the disappointment of Miamians, they moved to a new venue in Sunrise, the next county north of Miami-Dade. Call for directions and ticket information.

JAI ALAI
Jai alai, sort of a Spanish-style indoor lacrosse, was introduced to Miami in 1924 and is regularly played in two Miami-area frontons. Although the sport has roots stemming from ancient Egypt, the game as it's now played was invented by Basque peasants in the Pyrenees mountains during the 17th century.

Players use woven baskets, called *cestas,* to hurl balls, called pelotas, at speeds that sometimes exceed 170 miles per hour. Spectators, who are protected behind a wall of glass, place bets on the evening's players.

The **Miami Jai Alai Fronton,** 3500 NW 37th Ave., at NW 35th Street (☎ **305/ 633-6400**), is America's oldest fronton, dating from 1926. It schedules 13 games per night. Admission is $1 to the grandstand, $5 to the clubhouse. It's open year-round. There are games Monday and Wednesday to Saturday at 7pm and matinees on Monday, Wednesday, and Saturday at noon.

Miami Shopping   8

There is no question that Miami is one of the world's premier shopping cities; more than 14 million visitors came here last year and they spent in excess of $12 billion. Visitors come to Miami from all over—from Latin America to Hong Kong—in search of something all-American. And they find a lot to choose from. Miami is home to a host of strip malls, chain stores, and boutiques (almost every few miles it seems). And then there are the megamalls, from the upscale Shops at Sunset to the mammoth Aventura to the ritzy Shops at Bal Harbour (just to name a few), you'll be hard-pressed to walk home empty-handed. Miami also offers more unique shopping spots, such as Bayside's Marketplace, where you can buy such eclectic items as handcrafted tropical birds or jewelry made of precious stones. In Little Havana, you can buy hand-rolled cigars, and in Little Haiti, you'll find one-of-a-kind paintings by young artists starving to get their names and work recognized. The city truly has something for everyone.

You may want to order the Greater Miami Convention and Visitors Bureau's "Shop Miami: A Guide to a Tropical Shopping Adventure." Although it is limited to details on the bureau's paying members, it provides some good advice and otherwise unpublished discount offers. The glossy little pamphlet is printed in English, Spanish, and Portuguese and provides information about transportation from hotels, translation services, and shipping. Call ☎ **800/283-2707** or 305/539-3034.

1 The Shopping Scene

Below, you'll find descriptions of some of the more popular retail areas, where many stores are conveniently clustered together to make browsing easier.

As a general rule, shop hours are Monday through Saturday from 10am to 6pm and Sunday from noon to 5pm. Many stores stay open late (until 9pm or so) 1 night of the week (usually Thursday). Shops in trendy Coconut Grove are open until 9pm Sunday through Thursday, and even later on Friday and Saturday nights. Department stores and shopping malls also keep longer hours, with most staying open from 10am to 9 or 10pm Monday to Saturday, and noon to 6pm on Sunday.

The 6.5% state and local sales tax is added to the price of all non-food purchases.

> **Impressions**
>
> Someday . . . Miami will become the great center of South American trade.
> —Julia Tuttle, Miami's founder, 1896

Most Miami stores can wrap your purchase and ship it anywhere in the world via the United Parcel Service (UPS). If they can't, you can send it yourself, either through UPS (☎ **800/742-5877**) or through the U.S. Mail (see "Fast Facts: Miami," in chapter 4).

SHOPPING AREAS

Most of Miami's shopping happens at the many megamalls scattered from one end of the county to the other; however, there is also some excellent boutique shopping and browsing to be done in the following areas: See "City Layout," in chapter 4, for more information about these areas.

AVENTURA Biscayne Blvd between Miami Gardens Drive and the county line is a 2-mile stretch of major retail stores including Best Buys, Borders, Circuit City, Linens N' Things, Marshall's, Sports Authority, and more. Also here is the mammoth Aventura Mall, housing a fabulous collection of shops and restaurants; and Loehmann's Plaza, a small shopping village anchored around Loehmann's, the discount clothing store (see "Fashion," below).

CALLE OCHO For a taste of "Little Havana," take a walk down 8th Street between SW 27th Avenue and 12th Avenue where you'll find some lively street life and many shops selling cigars, baked goods, shoes, furniture, and record stores specializing in Latin music. Be sure to take your Spanish dictionary if you need it.

COCONUT GROVE Downtown Coconut Grove, centered on Main Highway and Grand Avenue and branching onto the adjoining streets, is one of Miami's most pedestrian-friendly zones. The Grove's wide sidewalks, lined with cafes and boutiques, provide hours of browsing pleasure. Coconut Grove is best known for its dozens of avant-garde clothing stores, funky import shops, and excellent sidewalk cafes centered around Cocowalk and The Streets of Mayfair.

CORAL GABLES—MIRACLE MILE Actually only a half-mile long, this central shopping street was an integral part of George Merrick's original city plan. Today, the strip still enjoys popularity especially for its bridal stores, ladies' shops, haberdashers, and gift shops. Recently, newer "chain" stores, like Barnes and Noble, Old Navy, and Starbucks, have been appearing on the Mile. It also features several excellent restaurants before it terminates at the City Hall rotunda (see chapter 6).

DOWNTOWN MIAMI If you're looking for discounts on all types of goods—especially watches, fabric, buttons, lace, shoes, luggage, and leather—Flagler Street just west of Biscayne Boulevard is the best place to start. Be prepared for some hustling and haggling. Most signs are printed in English, Spanish, and Portuguese; however, many shopkeepers may not be entirely fluent in English.

✪ **SOUTH BEACH—LINCOLN ROAD** This luxurious pedestrian mall, originally designed in 1957 by Morris Lapidus, recently underwent a multimillion-dollar renovation restoring it to its former glory. Here, shoppers can find an array of clothing and art and a menagerie of South Beach's finest sidewalk cafes flanked on one end by a multiplex movie theater and at the other, the Atlantic Ocean. Monthly gallery tours, periodic jazz concerts, and a weekly farmer's market are just a few of the offerings on "The Road."

COLLINS & WASHINGTON AVENUES (between 6th Street & 9th Street) For the hippest clothing boutiques including Armani, Versace, Benneton, The Gap, Todd Oldham, Kenneth Cole, and Nicole Miller, stroll along this pretty strip of the deco district.

2 Shopping A to Z

ANTIQUES/COLLECTIBLES

Miami's antique shops are scattered in small pockets around the city. Many that feature lower-priced furniture can be found in North Miami, in the 1600 block of Northeast 123rd Street near West Dixie Highway. About a dozen shops sell china, silver, glass, furniture, and paintings. But you'll find the bulk of the better antiques in Coral Gables and in Southwest Miami along Bird Road between 64th and 66th avenues and between 72nd and 74th avenues. There are dozens of shops with eclectic offerings. For international collections from Bali to France, check out the burgeoning scene in the Design District centered on Northeast 40th Street west of 1st Avenue. Miami also hosts several large antique shows each year. In October and November are the most prestigious ones at the **Miami Beach Convention Center** (☎ **305/754-4931**). Exhibitors from all over come to display their wares, including jewelry. There's also a decent monthly show at the **Coconut Grove Convention Center** (☎ **305/444-8454**). Miami's huge concentration of deco buildings from the '20s and '30s makes this the place to find the best selections of deco furnishings and decorations.

✪ **Architectural Antiques.** 2500 SW 28th Lane (just west of U.S. 1), Miami. ☎ **305/285-1330**. Fax 305/285-7801.

A great place to browse—if you don't mind a little dust—this huge warehouse has an impressive stash of ironwork, bronzes, paintings, lamps, furniture, and sculptures, which have been salvaged from estates worldwide. Don't be surprised to find odd items too, like an old British phone booth or a pair of gargoyles off an ancient church.

Dietel's Antiques. 6572 Bird Rd., South Miami. ☎ **305/666-0724**.

An active trade business here means lots of different styles are revolving constantly. You'll find baubles of every assortment in this stocked shop located near Coral Gables' quaint antiques district.

Modernism. 1622 Ponce de León Blvd., Coral Gables. ☎ **305/442-8743**.

Specializing in 20th-century furnishings, this gorgeous shop has some of the most beautiful examples of deco goods from France and the United States.

Miami Twice. 6562 SW 40th St., South Miami. ☎ **305/666-0127**. Fax 305/661-1142. www.miamitwice.com.

While they are not technically antiques yet, the Old Florida furniture and decorations from the '30s, '40s, and '50s are great fun (and collectible). In addition to loads of deco memorabilia, there are vintage clothes, shoes, and jewelry.

ART GALLERIES

Miami's finest art galleries are located within walking distance of one another in Coral Gables along Ponce de León Boulevard, extending from U.S. 1 to Bird Road.

Still others are clustered in Bal Harbour's ritzy shopping district. And finally, South Beach's Lincoln Road, which once had dozens of galleries, now has only a few—a result of soaring rents.

Also, check out the burgeoning art scene in the design district north of downtown just west of Biscayne Boulevard around 40th Street. Listed below is a selection of galleries both in and out of these areas.

If you happen to be in town on the first Friday of the month, you should take the free trolley tour of the Coral Gables art district. The tour runs from 7 to 10pm; meet at Elite (listed below) or at any of the other participating galleries in the area.

On the second Saturday of the month, you can actually meet artists and see them working during the **Lincoln Road Gallery Walk at the Art Center,** 924 and 1035 Lincoln Rd. (☎ **305/674-8278**), from 7 until 11pm. Join a knowledgeable guide for a tour of more than 50 artists' studios.

See chapter 7, "What to See & Do in Miami," for more details on these walking tours and others.

Ambrosino Gallery. 3095 SW 39th Ave. Miami (Bird Rd.). ☎ **305/445-2211.** Fax 305/444-0101. www.ambrosino@earthlink.net.

This well-respected gallery shows works by contemporary artists and stages performance art and installations. Closed for Christmas holidays.

Elite Fine Art. 3140 Ponce de León Blvd., Coral Gables. ☎ **305/448-3800.** Fax 305/448-8147.

Touted as one of the finest galleries in Miami, Elite features modern and contemporary Latin American painters and sculptors.

✪ **Evelyn S. Poole Ltd.** 3925 N. Miami Ave., Miami. ☎ **305/573-7463.**

Known as the finest of the fine antiques collections, the Poole assortment of European 17th-, 18th-, and 19th-century decorative furniture and accessories is housed in 5,000 square feet of space in the newly revived Decorator's Row. Celebrity clients shop for that special "statement piece" in these vast museum-like galleries.

Gallery Antigua. 5130 Biscayne Blvd. (in the Boulevard Plaza Building), Miami. ☎ **305/759-5355.**

This frame shop and gallery in one is dedicated to showing works by African American and Caribbean artists. Gallery Antigua boasts a vast collection of prints and reproductions, as well as masks and sculptures.

Meza Fine Art. 275 Giralda Ave., Coral Gables. ☎ **305/461-2723.**

This gallery specializes in Latin American artists, including Carlos Betancourt, Javier Marin, and Gloria Lorenzo.

COSMETICS, FRAGRANCES & BEAUTY PRODUCTS

✪ **Browne's & Co.** 841 Lincoln Rd., South Beach. ☎ **305-532-8703.**

Designed to look like an old-fashioned apothecary, this beauty emporium combines the city's best selection of makeup and hair products—MAC, Shu Uemura, Kiehl's, Stila, and Dr. Hauschka, just to name a few—with lots of delicious smelling bath and body stuff, plus a full-service beauty salon.

Perfumania. 332 Lincoln Rd., South Beach. ☎ **305/538-8553.**

This huge chain has many popular fragrances for men and women at discount prices. They also sell makeup and skin-care products. It's a great place to pick up a gift basket. There are more than a dozen locations in Miami.

BOOKS

Barnes and Noble Booksellers. 152 Miracle Mile, Coral Gables. ☎ **305/446-4152.**

With half a dozen outlets in the area and more on the way, this huge chain offers anything readers could ask for, including a comfortable cafe, a large children's section, and tons of magazines. Plus, you'll get a 10% discount on all best-sellers and incredible close-out specials. They often schedule readings with noted authors, too. There are more than six locations in Miami.

✪ **Books & Books.** 296 Aragon Ave., Coral Gables. ☎ **305/442-4408.**

A dedicated following turns out to browse at this warm and wonderful little independent shop. Enjoy the upstairs antiquarian room, which specializes in art books and first editions. If that's not enough intellectual stimulation for you, the shop hosts free lectures from noted authors and experts almost nightly.

At another location at 933 Lincoln Rd., South Beach (☎ **305/532-3222**), you'll rub elbows with tanned and buffed South Beach bookworms sipping cappuccinos at the Russian Bear Cafe inside the store. They stock a large selection of gay literature.

Kafka's Cyberkafe. 1464 Washington Ave., South Beach. ☎ **305/673-9669.**

Check your e-mail and surf the Web while you sip a latte or snack on a sandwich or pastry with friendly neighborhood regulars. This popular used bookstore also stocks a wide range of foreign and domestic magazines.

CIGARS & CIGARETTES

Although it is illegal to bring Cuban cigars into this country, somehow Cohibas show up at every dinner party and nightclub in town. Not that I condone it, but if you hang around the cigar smokers in town, no doubt one will be able to tell you where you can get some of the highly prized contraband. Be careful, however, of counterfeits.

The stores listed below sell excellent hand-rolled cigars made with domestic and foreign-grown tobacco. Many of the *viejos* (old men) got their training in Cuba working for the government-owned factories in the heyday of Cuban cigars.

✪ **La Gloria Cubana.** 1106 SW 8th St., Little Havana. ☎ **305/858-4162.** Fax 305/858-3810.

This tiny storefront shop employs about 45 veteran Cuban rollers who sit all day rolling the very popular torpedoes and other critically acclaimed blends. They've got backorders until next Christmas, but it's worth stopping in. They will sell you a box and show you around.

Miccosukee Tobacco Shop. 850 SW 177th Ave. (Krome Ave. and Tamiami Trail), Miami. ☎ **305/226-2701.**

At this remote Native American–owned outpost, you are spared the state cigarette tax—national brands are available for $14 a carton, generics from $8 to $13.

Mike's Cigars. 1030 Kane Concourse (at 96th St.), Bay Harbor Island. ☎ **305/866-2277.**

Mike's recently moved to this location, but it's one of the oldest smoke shops in town. Since 1950, Mike's has been selling the best from Honduras, the Dominican Republic, and Jamaica, as well as the very hot local brand, La Gloria Cubana. Many say it has the best prices, too.

ELECTRONICS

The Sharper Image. 401 Biscayne Blvd. (in the Bayside Marketplace). ☎ **305/374-8539.**

Electronics nuts will love this store. It tends to be high-end, both in merchandise and in price, but it's free just to look and touch (yes, you're allowed), so even if you're not buying, visit the store to see what's new in the high-tech world. Another location is in the Dadeland Mall, at 7507 N. Kendall Dr., South Miami (☎ **305/667-9970**).

Sound Advice. 12200 N. Kendall Dr., Kendall. ☎ **305/273-1225.**

An audio junkie's candy store, Sound Advice features the latest in high-end stereo equipment, as well as TVs, VCRs, and telephone equipment. Techno-minded, but sometimes pushy, salespeople are on hand to help. Other locations are at 17641 Biscayne Blvd., Aventura (☎ **305/933-4434**), and 1222 S. Dixie Hwy., Coral Gables (☎ **305/665-4434**).

Spy Shops International Inc. 280 NE 4th St. ☎ **305/374-4779.**

This store is perfect for James Bond wannabes looking to buy electronic-surveillance equipment, day and night optical devices, stun guns, minisafes, doorknob alarms, and other anticrime gadgets.

FASHION

For the best quality designer clothes, Bal Harbour Shops is your best bet. See "Malls," below.

On the other end of the spectrum, you may want to try the popular Loehmann's (see below) for designer clothing, shoes, and accessories at deeply discounted prices. Or, consider hunting the thrift stores and resale shops (see below).

Island Trading. 1332 Ocean Dr., South Beach. ☎ **305/673-6300.**

One more part of music mogul Chris Blackwell's empire, Island sells everything you'll need to wear in a tropical resort town: batik sarongs, sandals, sundresses, bathing suits, cropped tops, and more. Many of the unique styles are created on the premises by a team of young and innovative designers.

✪ **Loehmann's.** 18701 Biscayne Blvd. (Fashion Island), North Miami Beach. ☎ **305/932-4207.**

Loehmann's has added men's clothing and shoes to its huge stock of women's wear. This discount mecca is the place to find designer clothes at bargain prices. But, you've got to hunt. If you don't mind communal dressing rooms and hordes of zealous shoppers, look here for great deals on everything from bathing suits to evening wear.

MEN'S

Brooks Brothers. 9700 Collins Ave. (in the Bal Harbour Shops), Miami Beach. ☎ **305/865-8686.**

If you need a new navy blazer or some khaki trousers to roll up for an oceanfront stroll, shop here for the classics. Other location at 8888 Howard Dr. (in The Falls shopping complex), Kendall (☎ **305/259-7870**).

Giorgio's. 208 Miracle Mile, Coral Gables. ☎ **305/448-4302.**

One of the finest custom men's stores, Giorgio's features an extensive line of Italian suits and all the latest by Canelli.

Hugo Boss. 9700 Collins Ave., Miami Beach. ☎ **305/864-7753.**

One of many men's stores in Bal Harbour, this one appeals to hipsters and businessmen alike who are willing to pay big money for the latest styles.

WOMEN'S

Alice's Day Off. 5900 SW 72nd St., South Miami. ☎ **305/284-0301.**

For beachwear, Alice's is the place. Season after season, you'll find pretty and flattering floral patterns and many flashy bikinis. If an itsy-bitsy bikini is not your style, Alice's has a range of more modest cuts for women not shaped like a *Baywatch* babe. Also at the Miami International Mall, 1455 NW 107th Ave, Miami (☎ **305/477-0393**), and Dadeland Mall, 7223 SW 88th St. Miami.☎ **305/663-7299.**

Betsey Johnson. 805 Washington Ave., South Beach. ☎ **305/673-0023.**

This New York–based shop sells slightly wild, faddish clothes for the young and young at heart, made of stretchy materials, velvet, knits, and more.

Therapy. 1065 Kane Concourse, Bay Harbor Islands. ☎ **305/861-6900.**

Opened by Ellen Lansburgh, who ran successful shops in Aspen and New York that catered to a famous clientele, including Cher and Goldie Hawn, this intimate boutique offers one-of-a-kind pieces. The clothes, made of luxurious fabrics such as silk, taffeta, and tulle, are elegant and comfortable.

CHILDREN'S

Most department stores have extensive children's sections. But if you can't find what you are looking for, consider one of the many Baby Gaps or Gap Kids outlets around town or try one of the specialty boutiques listed here.

French Kids Inc. 5829 Sunset Dr., South Miami. ☎ **305/667-5880.**

This fashionable boutique imports beautiful (and expensive) clothes for newborns to teenagers.

Roland Children's Wear. 450 41st St., Miami Beach. ☎ **305/531-0130.**

You'll find a unique assortment of kid's clothes for dress-up or for playtime. They specialize in cute, funky stuff.

LINGERIE

Belinda's. 827 Washington Ave., South Beach. ☎ **305/532-0068.**

This German designer makes some of the most beautiful and intricate teddies, nightgowns, and wedding dresses. The styles are a little too Stevie Nicks for me to actually consider wearing in public, but the creations are absolutely worth admiring. The prices are appropriately up there.

Corset Corner. 300 Miracle Mile, Coral Gables. ☎ **305/444-6643.**

As the name suggests, this little old store on Miracle Mile sells the basic, good old-fashioned gear.

La Perla. 9700 Collins Ave. (in the Bal Harbour Shops), Bal Harbour. ☎ **305/864-2070.**

The only store in Florida that specializes in this superluxurious Italian intimate apparel. Of course, you could fly to Milan for the price of a few bras and a nightgown, but you can't find better quality. Also in Bal Harbour, see Flash Lingerie (☎ **305/ 868-7732**), which carries a diverse selection of imports.

Victoria's Secret. 3015 Grand Ave., Coconut Grove. ☎ **305/443-2365.**

You've seen the sexy catalogs—now see the goods up close. The many shops in town stock the basic undergarments in shimmery rayons and polys as well as a few Chinese silk robes and undies. You'll find one of the largest selections of thongs anywhere. Other locations at 401 Biscayne Blvd., Miami (☎ **305/374-8030**), and Aventura Mall (☎ **305/932-0150**).

FOOD

There are dozens of ethnic markets in Miami, from Cuban bodegas to Jamaican import shops and Guyanese produce stands. Check the phone book under grocers for listings. I've listed a few of the biggest and best markets in town that sell prepared foods as well as staple items. On Saturday mornings, vendors set up stands loaded with papayas, melons, tomatoes, and citrus, as well as cookies, ice creams, and sandwiches on South Beach's Lincoln Road. Also on Saturday is the Green Market in Coconut Grove along Grand Avenue specializing in organic fruits, vegetables, and homemade treats.

Biga Bakery. 1080 Alton Rd., South Beach. ☎ **305/535-1008.**

You'll be happy to pay upwards of $6 a loaf when you sink your teeth into these inimitable Old-World–style breads. Also, most of the locations have a to-die-for prepared food counter serving up everything from chicken curry salad to hummus and pot pies. Pastries and cakes are as gorgeous as they are delicious. Also at 305 Alcazar, Coral Gables (☎ **305/446-2111**). Check directory for other locations.

East Coast Fisheries. 330 W. Flagler St., Downtown. ☎ **305/577-3000.**

This retail market and restaurant (see the review in chapter 6, "Dining"), has shipped millions of pounds of seafood worldwide from its own fishing fleet. Order 5- or 10-pound packages of stone-crab claws, Florida lobsters, Florida Bay pompano, fresh Key West shrimp, and a variety of other local delicacies to be shipped via overnight delivery.

Epicure. 1656 Alton Rd., Miami Beach. ☎ **305/672-1861.**

Here, you'll find not only fine wines, cheeses, meats, fish, and juices, but some of the best produce, such as portobello mushrooms the size of a yarmulke. This neighborhood landmark is best known for supplying the Jewish residents of the Beach with all the Jewish favorites, such as matzo ball soup, gefilte fish, and deli items. Prices are steep, but generally worth it.

Gardner's Market. 7301 Red Rd., South Miami. ☎ **305/667-9953.**

Anything a gourmet or novice cook could desire can be found here. One of the oldest and best grocery stores in Miami, Gardner's now has three locations, all of which offer great take-out and the freshest produce.

Joe's Stone Crab. 227 Biscayne St., South Beach. ☎ **800/780-CRAB** or 305/673-0365.

If you've never tasted Florida's favorite seafood, you must. And once you do, you'll want more. Or you may want to send some to very dear friends at home (they are pricier than lobster). Joe's, Miami's most famous restaurant (see the review in chapter 6), ships stone crabs anywhere in the country, but only during the season, which runs from mid-October through mid-May.

La Brioche Doree. 4017 Prairie Ave., Miami Beach. ☎ **305/538-4770.**

This tiny storefront off of 41st Street is packed most mornings with French expatriates and visitors who crave the real thing. There are luscious pastries and breads, plus soup and sandwiches at lunch. No one makes a better croissant anywhere. Period.

Laurenzo's Italian Supermarket and Farmer's Market. 16385 and 16445 W. Dixie Hwy. North Miami Beach. ☎ **305/945-6381** and 305/944-5052.

Anything Italian you want—from homemade ravioli to hand-cut imported Romano cheese to smoked salmon to fresh fish and ground pork—can be found here. Be sure to see the neighboring store full of just-picked herbs, salad greens, and every type of vegetable from around the world. Incredible daily specials, such as 10 Indian River pink grapefruits for 99¢, lure thrifty shoppers from all over the city (see review of cafe in chapter 6).

A Taste of Old Florida

Old-fashioned smokehouses used to dot U.S. 1 and Biscayne Boulevard, but as Miami grew, they were driven out of business. As popular as they were, the old shacks couldn't generate enough money from smoked fish to compete with condominiums and shopping centers.

One that remains is **Jimbo's** on Virginia Key. There's no real street address, since as Dan, an employee, likes to say: "We're out in the boonies."

Most days—depending on the seasons, the tides, and who feels like shopping—Jimbo's sells marlin and salmon. Really, its primary business is selling bait shrimp to fishermen, but there is always some odoriferous fish splayed out for the pungent smoke.

If you can find your way there, you'll see the old crew of Italians playing bocce, smoking, and drinking out on the bay, in a tiny sliver of backwater life tucked away from civilization. It's worth it. They're there most days if the sun is shining, and they stay until it sets.

To get to Jimbo's, drive over the Rickenbacker Causeway en route to Key Biscayne. After you've passed the second light on Crandon Boulevard, just past the MAST Academy, turn left. Drive about a mile until you see some old wooden fishing shacks (they're used as movie props). To ask about what kind of fish they're smoking, call ☎ **305/361-7026**.

Publix. 1045 Dade Blvd., South Beach. ☎ **305/534-4621**.

The largest supermarket chain in Florida keeps getting bigger. There are already more than 50 in Miami-Dade County. This branch on South Beach is worth at least driving by. Designed by well-known architect Carlos Zapata, it boasts 47,000 square feet, plus a moving walkway to whisk shoppers and their carts to and from the aboveground parking lot. In addition to valet parking, take-out sushi, a bakery, deli, cafe, and pharmacy, there is a large selection of exotic fruits.

Todd's Fruit Shippers. ☎ **305/448-5215**.

Order grapefruits, oranges, or other local produce by the bushel or basket. This longtime Florida shipper takes phone orders only.

HOUSEWARES/HARDWARE

Farrey's Decorative Hardware & Lighting. 1850 NE 146th St. (2 blocks west of US 1). North Miami. ☎ **305/947-5451**.

Open since 1924, this huge warehouse stocks elegant lighting, bathroom fixtures, and furnishings. From drawer pulls to chandeliers, plus a collection of eclectic furniture, you'll find something you absolutely must have. Another location at 4101 Ponce de León Blvd., Coral Gables (☎ **305/445-2244**).

Linge de Maison Veronique. 305 Alcazar Ave., Coral Gables. ☎ **305/461-3466**.

Fussy Coral Gables housewives flock here for beautiful wares, including custom and hand-embroidered linens, layettes, bed and bath accessories, and tableware to match their china patterns. There's also custom-made children's line of clothing, crib bedding, wallpaper, and accessories.

Pratesi Linens Inc. 9700 Collins Ave. (in the Bal Harbour Shops), Bal Harbour. ☎ **305/861-5677.**

The quality of the Italian linen here is unmatchable, but you could buy a car with what you'll pay for a full set of king-size hand-embroidered sheets.

real.life.basic. 643 Lincoln Rd., South Beach. ☎ **305/604-1984.**

Offering cool stuff for the kitchen and cooking demonstrations too, this ultrasleek split-level shop has become a hangout for foodies. Those who work in the industry get discounts, too.

JEWELRY

For the name designers like Gucci and Tiffany & Co., go to the Bal Harbour Shops (see "Malls," below).

The International Jeweler's Exchange. 18861 Biscayne Blvd. (in the Fashion Island), North Miami Beach. ☎ **305/931-7032.**

At least 50 jewelers hustle their wares from individual counters at one of the city's most active jewelry centers. Haggle your brains out for excellent prices on timeless antiques from Tiffany's, Cartier, or Bulgari, or on unique designs you can create yourself.

The Seybold Building. 36 NE 1st St., Downtown. ☎ **305/374-7922.**

Jewelers of every assortment gather here daily to sell their diamonds and gold. The glare is blinding as you enter this multilevel retail marketplace. You'll see handsome and up-to-date designs, but note that there aren't too many bargains to be had here.

MALLS

There are so many malls in Miami and more being built that it would be impossible to mention them all. What follows is a list of the biggest and most popular.

You can find any number of nationally known department stores including Saks Fifth Avenue, Macy's, Lord & Taylor, Sears, and JCPenney in the Miami malls listed below, but Miami's own is **Burdines,** at 22 E. Flagler St., Downtown (☎ **305/835-5151**), and 1675 Meridian Ave. (just off Lincoln Rd.) in South Beach (☎ **305/674-6311**). One of the oldest and largest department stores in Florida, Burdines specializes in good quality home furnishings and fashions.

✪ **Aventura Mall.** 19501 Biscayne Blvd. (at 197th St. near the Dade–Broward County line), Aventura. ☎ **305/935-1110.** www.shopaventuramall.com.

A multimillion-dollar makeover has made this spot one of the premier places to shop in South Florida. With more than 2.3 million square feet of space, this airy, Mediterranean-style mall has a 24-screen movie theater and more than 250 stores, including megastores JCPenney, Lord & Taylor, Macy's, Bloomingdale's, Sears, and Burdines. The mall offers moderate to high-priced merchandise and is extremely popular with families. A large indoor playground, "Adventurer's Cove," is a great spot for kids, and the mall frequently offers activities and entertainment for children. There are numerous theme restaurants, including a RainForest Café, and a food court that eschews the usual suspects in favor of local operations. The mall provides free shuttle service to and from the top downtown and Miami Beach hotels.

✪ **Bal Harbour Shops.** 9700 Collins Ave. (on 97th St., opposite the Sheraton Bal Harbour Hotel), Bal Harbour. ☎ **305/866-0311.** www.balharbourshops.com.

One of the most prestigious fashion meccas in the country, Bal Harbour offers the best-quality goods from the finest names. Giorgio Armani, Dolce & Gabbana, Christian Dior, Fendi, Joan & David, Krizia, Rodier, Gucci, Brooks Brothers, Waterford,

Cartier, H. Stern, Tourneau—the list goes on and on. With Neiman Marcus at one end and a newly expanded Saks Fifth Avenue at the other, this mall hardly deserves to be called by such a pedestrian title. It's like Rodeo Drive with elevators. Well-dressed shoppers stroll in a pleasant open-air emporium, featuring several good cafes, covered walkways, and lush greenery. Parking costs $1 an hour with a validated ticket. You can stamp your own at the entrance to Saks Fifth Avenue even if you don't make a purchase.

Bayside Marketplace. 401 Biscayne Blvd., Downtown. ☎ **305/577-3344.** www.baysidemarketplace.com.

A popular stop for cruise-ship passengers, this gorgeous waterfront marketplace is filled with lively and exciting shops in the heart of downtown Miami. Downstairs, about 100 shops and carts sell everything from Caribbean trinkets to high-tech electronics (some of the specialty shops are listed separately below). The upstairs eating arcade is stocked with dozens of fast-food choices and some fun bars. Most of the restaurants and bars stay open later than the stores. There's Lomardi's Conga Bar, Dick's Last Resort, Hard Rock Cafe, Fat Tuesday, Sharkey's, and Let's Make a Daiquiri. Parking is $1 per hour. You can watch the Opsail show in June and the Miami Sailboat Show in February.

Dadeland Mall. 7535 N. Kendall Dr. (intersection of U.S. 1 and SW 88th St., 15 minutes south of Downtown), Kendall. ☎ **305/665-6226.** Fax 665-5012.

One of the county's first malls, Dadeland features more than 175 specialty shops, anchored by four large department stores—Burdines, JCPenney, Lord & Taylor, and Saks Fifth Avenue. Sixteen restaurants serve from the adjacent Treats Food Court. New retail stores are constantly springing up around this granddaddy of Miami's suburban malls.

Dolphin Mall. Florida Turnpike at S.R. 836, West Miami. ☎ **305/365-7446.**

Still under construction at press time, this $250 million megamall and amusement park rivals Sawgrass Mills in Broward County. The 1.4 million-square-foot mall features outlets such as Off Sax Fifth Avenue, plus shops, a 28-screen movie theater, and a roller coaster. Opens March 1, 2001.

Falls Shopping Center. 8888 Howard Dr. (at the intersection of U.S. 1 and 136th St., about 3 miles south of Dadeland Mall), Kendall. ☎ **305/255-4570.**

Tropical waterfalls are the setting for this outdoor shopping center with dozens of moderately priced, slightly upscale shops. Miami's first Bloomingdale's is here, as are Polo, Ralph Lauren, Caswell-Massey, and more than 60 other specialty shops. After a recent renovation, A recent renovation added a number of new stores, including Macy's, Crate & Barrel, Brooks Brothers, and Pottery Barn. If you are planning to visit any of the nearby attractions, which include Metro Zoo and Monkey Jungle, check with customer service for information on discount packages. Parking is free.

Miami International Mall. 1455 NW 107th Ave., Miami. ☎ **305/593-1775.**

Housing more than 150 specialty stores and several well-known department stores, including a Burdines, JCPenney, and Sears, this popular mall is close to Miami International airport and filled with foreign shoppers.

Sawgrass Mills. 12801 W. Sunrise Blvd., Sunrise (west of Fort Lauderdale). ☎ **954/846-2300.**

Although this mammoth mall—the largest outlet mall in the country—is actually located in Broward County, it is a phenomenon worth mentioning, since thousands of tourists and locals trek there for bargains and fun. (See chapter 13, "The Treasure Coast," for more details.)

From Miami, buses run three times daily; the trip takes just under an hour. Call **Coach USA** (☎ **305/887-6223**) for exact pick-up points at major hotels. The price is $10 for a round-trip ticket. If you are driving, take I-95 north to 595 west until Flamingo Road. Exit and turn right, driving 2 miles to Sunrise Boulevard. You can't miss this monster on the left. Parking is free, but don't forget where you parked your car or you might spend a day looking for it.

The Shops of Sunset Place. 5701 Sunset Dr. (at 57th Ave. and U.S. 1, near Red Rd.), South Miami. ☎ **305/663-0482.**

Completed in early 1999 at a cost of over $140 million, this sprawling "mall of the future" offers more than just shopping. Visitors experience high-tech special effects, such as daily tropical storms (minus the rain) and the electronic chatter of birds and crickets. In addition to a 24-screen movie complex and an IMAX theater, there's a Gameworks—Steven Spielberg's Disney-esque playground for adults—a Virgin Records store, and a NikeTown.

The Streets of Mayfair. 2911 Grand Ave. (just east of Commodore Plaza), Coconut Grove. ☎ **305/448-1700.**

Recently revamped, this small and labyrinthine complex conceals a movie theater, several top-quality shops, restaurants, art galleries, and nightclubs. The emphasis is on boutiques and entertainment.

MUSIC & MUSICAL EQUIPMENT

Blue Note Records. 16401 NE 15th Ave., North Miami Beach. ☎ **305/940-3394.** Fax 305/948-3583 www.bluenoterecords.com.

Here for more than 15 years, Blue Note has hard-to-find progressive and underground music. There are new, used, and discounted CDs and old vinyl, too. Call to find out about performances. Some great names show up occasionally.

Casino Records Inc. 1208 SW 8th St., Little Havana. ☎ **305/856-6888.**

The young, hip salespeople here speak English and tend to be music buffs. You'll find the largest selection of Latin music in Miami, including pop icons such as Willy Chirino, Gloria Estefan, Albita, and local boy Nil Lara. Their slogan translates to, "If we don't have it, forget it." Believe me, they've got it.

CD Warehouse. 13150 Biscayne Blvd., North Miami. ☎ **305/892-1048.**

Buy, sell, or trade your old CDs at this eclectic music hut. Also at 1590 S. Dixie Hwy., Coral Gables (☎ **305/662-7100**).

Mars (Music and Recording Superstore). 12115 Biscayne Blvd., North Miami. ☎ **305/893-0191.** www.marsmusic.com.

You could spend a week here. With 35,000 square feet of space, MARS offers everything from musical instruments to sheet music, plus a recording studio, live stage, and repair center.

Revolution Records and CDs. 1620 Alton Rd., Miami Beach. ☎ **305/673-6464.**

Here you'll find a quaint and fairly well-organized collection of CDs, from hard-to-find jazz to original recordings of Buddy Rich. They'll search for anything and let you hear whatever you like.

Specs Music. 501 Collins Ave., South Beach. ☎ **305/534-6533.**

In addition to a great collection of multicultural sounds, you'll find a lively scene most weekends at this multilevel music mall. Other stores carry an impressive collection of all types of music. Another location is at 12451 Biscayne Blvd., North Miami Beach (☎ **305/899-0994**).

Virgin Records. 5701 Sunset Place (at the Shops of Sunset), South Miami. ☎ **305/665-4445.**

This enormous music store (33,000 square feet) indulges shoppers with listening booths and an "in-store radio station." They stock a huge collection of CDs, cassettes, and videos.

SPORTS EQUIPMENT

From golf to tennis, scuba to fishing, South Florida is a virtual playground. And, of course, you can find all the toys to outfit yourself nearby. One of the area's largest chains is the Sports Authority, with at least six locations throughout the county. Check the white pages for details.

Alf's Golf Shop. 524 Arthur Godfrey Rd., Miami Beach. ☎ **305/673-6568.**

The best pro shop around, Alf's can sell you balls, clubs, gloves, and instructional videos. The knowledgeable staff has equipment for golfers of every level, and the neighboring golf course offers discounts to Alf's clients. Also at 15369 S. Dixie Hwy., Miami (☎ **305/378-6086**).

Bass Pro Shops Outdoor World. 200 Gulf Stream Way, Dania. ☎ **954/929-7710.**

Fishing enthusiasts and sports enthusiasts must head north to Broward County to see this huge retail complex, which offers demonstrations in fly-fishing, archery, and pistol ranges, classes in marine safety, and every conceivable gadget you could ask for. (See "The Treasure Coast," chapter 13, for more details.)

Bird's Surf Shop. 250 Sunny Isles Blvd., North Miami Beach. ☎ **305/940-0929.**

If you're a hard-core surfer or just want to look like one, head to Bird's Surf Shop. Although Miami doesn't regularly get huge swells, if you're here during the winter and one should happen to hit, you'll be ready. The shop carries more than 150 boards. Call its surf line (☎ **305/947-7170**) to find the best waves from South Beach to Cape Hatteras and even The Bahamas and Florida's West Coast.

Edwin Watts Golf Shops. 15100 N. Biscayne Blvd., North Miami Beach. ☎ **305/944-2925.**

One of 30 Edwin Watts shops throughout the Southeast, this full-service golf retail shop is one of the most popular in Miami. You can find it all, including clothing, pro-line equipment, gloves, bags, balls, videos, and books. Plus, you can get coupons for discounted greens fees on many courses.

Island Water Sports. 16231 Biscayne Blvd. North Miami, Fl. ☎ **305/944-0104.** Fax 305/944-0194.

You'll find everything from booties to gloves to baggies and tanks. Check in here before you rent that WaveRunner or Windsurfer.

Nevada Bob's. 7930 NW 36th Ave. (near the airport), Miami. ☎ **305/593-2999.**

This chain store guarantees the lowest prices on golf equipment and accessories. There's more than 6,000 square feet of store here; you can even practice your swing at an indoor driving range, where a radar gun will clock your speed.

X-Isle Surf Shop. 437 Washington Ave., South Beach. ☎ 305/673-5900.

Prices are slightly higher at this beach location, but you'll find the hottest styles and equipment. They also offer surfboard rental. Free surf report at ☎ 305/534-7873.

THRIFT STORES/RESALE SHOPS

The Children's Exchange. 1415 Sunset Dr., Coral Gables. ☎ 305/666-6235. Fax 305/666-4860.

Selling everything from layettes to overalls, this pleasant little shop is chock-full of good Florida-style stuff for kids to wear to the beach and in the heat.

Douglas Gardens Jewish Home and Hospital Thrift Shops. 5713 NW 27th Ave., North Miami Beach. ☎ 305/638-1900.

Prices here are no longer the major bargain they once were, but for housewares and books, you can do all right. Call to see if they are offering any specials for seniors or students.

Rags to Riches. 12577 Biscayne Blvd., North Miami, Fl. ☎ 305/891-8981.

This is an old-time consignment shop in the thrift-store row. You might find some decent rags, and maybe even some riches. Not as upscale as it used to be, this place is still a good spot for costume jewelry and shoes.

Red White & Blue. 12640 NE 6th Ave., North Miami. ☎ 305/893-1104.

Miami's best-kept secret is this mammoth thrift store that is meticulously organized and well stocked. You've got to search for great stuff but it is there. There are especially good deals on children's clothes and housewares.

WINES & SPIRITS

Most gourmet stores carry wines and beers. See "Food," above.

Crown Liquors. 6751 Red Rd., Coral Gables. ☎ 305/669-0225.

This liquor store offers one of the most diverse selections in Miami. Its ever-rotating stock comes from estate sales around the country and worldwide distributors. And since there are several stores in the chain, the owners get to buy in bulk, which results in lower prices for oenophiles. If you want one of the tastiest and most affordable champagnes ever, try its exclusive import, Billecarte Salmon. Another location at 1255 Biscayne Blvd., North Miami (☎ 305/892-WINE).

The Estate Wines & Gourmet Foods. 92 Miracle Mile (at Douglas and Galiano), Coral Gables. ☎ 305/442-9915.

This exceedingly friendly storefront in the middle of Coral Gables' main shopping street offers a small but well-chosen selection of vintages from around the world. It also sells a great array of gourmet cheeses, pâtés, salads, and sandwiches.

Laurenzo's. 16385 and 16445 W. Dixie Hwy., North Miami Beach. ☎ 305/945-6381 or 305/944-5052.

Laurenzo's dedicates a few small aisles to its superb wine collection. A full-time expert can help you choose a bottle. *A word of warning:* You'll get an attitude if you're a novice.

Sunny Isles Liquors. 18180 Collins Ave., Sunny Isles Beach. ☎ 305/932-5782.

This well-located store has hundreds of brands of imported beer and hard-to-find liquor on hand. It will also search and find decanters and minis for your collection. There's also a fine selection of imported cigarettes and cigars.

Miami After Dark   9

You can't mention Miami and its magic without focusing on the momentous nightlife that rocks the city from the beach to the Grove and back again. With a world-class ballet under the aegis of Edward Villela, a recognized symphony, and a talented opera company, the city also has the clout and class expected of an upscale American metropolis.

Miami offers not only a fun-filled day of frolicking in the sun, but a full night of evening entertainment, where movie festivals, boat shows, and art galleries all compete for your attention. Outdoor concerts are staged periodically at Bayside and on the beach, and have been graciously hosted by the likes of Lauryn Hill and the Marley clan.

It is only after the sun goes down, that Miami's biggest attraction, its club scene, begins to sizzle, with most of the action taking place in South Beach. Unfortunately, the city seems to have trouble sustaining clubs that consistently offer good live music. In the past few years, Miami has watched more than a dozen music clubs shut their doors. That said, there are still some excellent venues for live music, and some especially popular spots for jazz and Latin music. Some of the hottest clubs feature Cuban and Caribbean bands playing rhythms that beat on until the break of dawn.

While the primary action still lies in South Beach and Coconut Grove, there is a burgeoning nightlife of a different sort in the staid restaurant capital of Coral Gables and in the more bohemian hoods of the Biscayne Corridor and North Beach. Coral Gables has added live jazz and blues to its tony eateries with the addition of Satchmo's. The Biscayne Corridor has exploded with activity thanks to Soyka's arrival as a trendy eatery and the whirlwind of activity surrounding Power Studios near the design district.

For real out-of-control party animals, however, nothing can replace the wild and wanton world of South Beach's clubs and bistros. Miami is making headlines as the rightful capital of Latin music, so expect even your most average American discos to mix and match Top 40 hits with sizzling salsa and hip-swaying calypso rhythms. The city's nightlife is indeed a mix of passionate sounds and a fusion of international dance beats. World-renowned divas, from Madonna to Donna Summer, have swung by Miami's wild clubs to have the world-class DJs here remix their songs to a techno-disco perfection.

Because Miami's nightlife is so important to its tourist trade, you'll find ample information on where to go and what to do. Check the

Miami Herald's "Weekend" section, which runs on Fridays, or the more comprehensive listings in *New Times,* Miami's free alternative weekly, available each Wednesday. There's also *Miamigo, Minigo* and *Scoop,* as well as *EgoTrip, Sun Post,* and the *Herald's* recent edition of *The Street.*

There are a number of Web sites that offer pertinent club information—Miami didn't earn the nickname "Silicon Beach" for nothing. If you're looking for event schedules, two very useful Web sites are **www.ClubMiami.com** and **www.scenetrack.com**. Another good site, and one of the most influential, is a spinoff from a popular local magazine, **www.oceandrive.com**. For those who don't have their data port connections handy (although Internet cafes are quite the rage on the beach), you can call the **Planet Radio Stuff To Do Hotline** (☎ **305/770-2513**), the **Zeta Concert Hotline** (☎ **305/770-2515**), and the **UM Concert Hotline** (☎ **305/284-6477**). There's always **TicketMaster;** call ☎ **305/358-5885** if you need to charge tickets. For hard-to-get seats, try a ticket broker. Fran at **Sold-Out Events** (☎ **305/534-2021**) can usually find what you need. Otherwise, call **Ultimate Travel & Entertainment** (☎ **305/444-8499**).

1 Bars

There are countless bars in and around Miami with the highest concentration on trendy South Beach. Keeping track of them all would be a full-time job—and not a bad one at that! The selection listed below is a mere sample. Keep in mind that many of the popular bars are in hotels. On the beach, you'd do best to walk along Ocean Drive and Washington Avenue to see what's hot. In Coconut Grove, check out CocoWalk and Mayfair next door. Unless mentioned, the bars listed below generally don't charge a cover. Most require proof that you are over 21 to enter, though some allow patrons over 18 to enter but not drink.

The Clevelander. 1020 Ocean Dr., South Beach. ☎ **305/531-3485.** Fax 305/531-3953. www.clevelanderhotel.com.

This old standby on one of Ocean Drive's busiest and most spacious corners is always crowded. You'll find mostly preppy types gathered around the large outdoor pool area up until 5am. Cheap drinks in plastic cups complete the beachy atmosphere in this casual, spring-breaky bar.

The Delano. 1685 Collins Ave., South Beach. ☎ **305/672-2000.**

I'm surprised they haven't started charging admission to this spectacular attraction. In the lobby, the Rose Bar is one of the best spots in South Beach to see beautiful people decked out in trendy splendor. Lounge on any of the cushy sofas casually arranged throughout the lobby and backyard, and grab an expensive drink.

Firehouse Four. 1000 S, Miami Ave. Downtown. ☎ **305/371-3473.** Cover varies from none to $10.

Renowned for its raucous weekday happy hours, this old favorite closed down for several years only to resurface in late 1998 to the delight of its former downtown corporate patrons. The ties here come off after 5pm, and nobody works as hard as the deejays, who keep the place rocking. Each night attracts a slightly different crowd, depending on the music. Thursday night is old Havana night. Call for a schedule.

The Forge. 432 41st St., Miami Beach. ☎ **305/538-8533.**

Step back in time at this ultraelegant restaurant and bar, where Wednesday night is the night to hang with dolled-up Eurosingles and New Yorkers. Call well in advance if you

South Beach After Dark

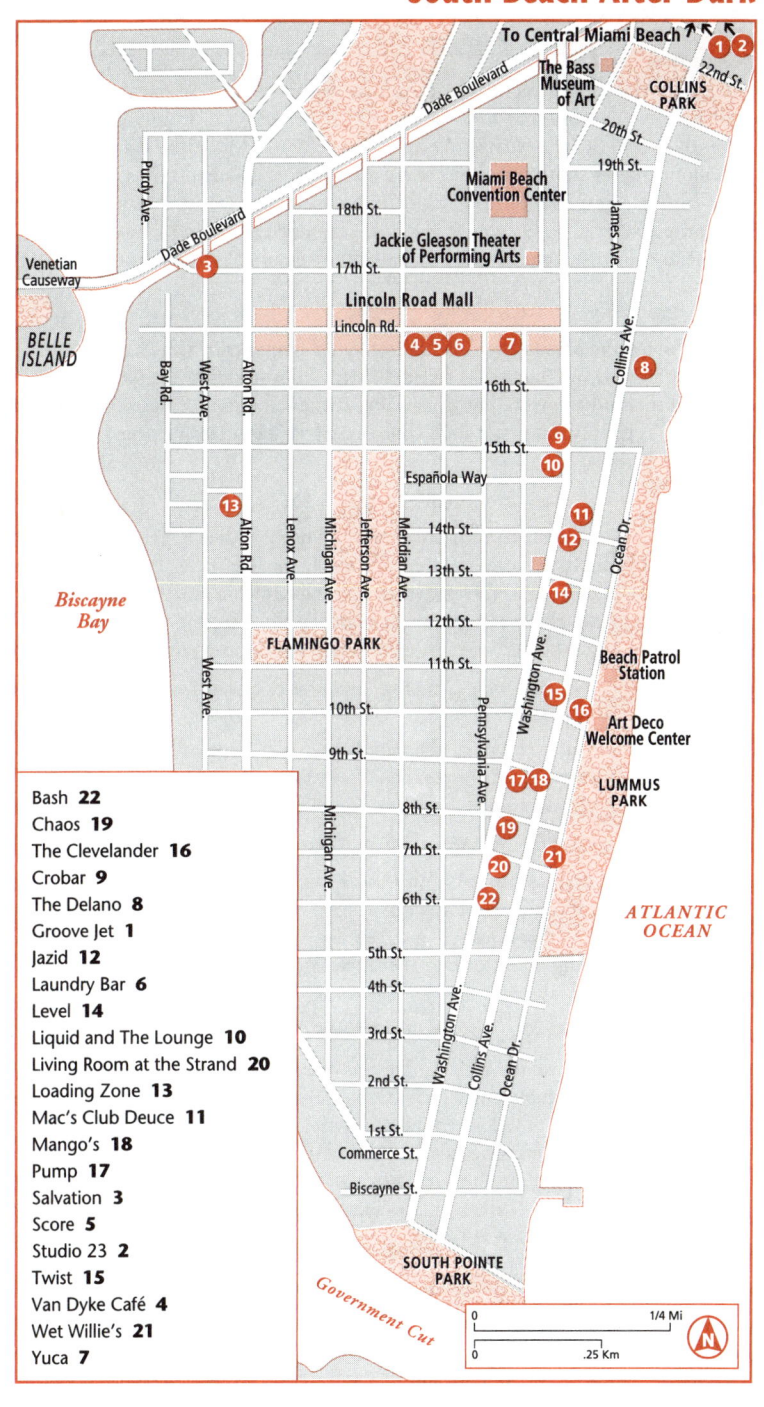

Bash **22**
Chaos **19**
The Clevelander **16**
Crobar **9**
The Delano **8**
Groove Jet **1**
Jazid **12**
Laundry Bar **6**
Level **14**
Liquid and The Lounge **10**
Living Room at the Strand **20**
Loading Zone **13**
Mac's Club Deuce **11**
Mango's **18**
Pump **17**
Salvation **3**
Score **5**
Studio 23 **2**
Twist **15**
Van Dyke Café **4**
Wet Willie's **21**
Yuca **7**

189

Star Gazing

Even on the clearest night, you're likely to see more stars on the streets of Miami than in the sky. You may find Cameron Diaz sitting across from you at Bambu on South Beach; Spike Lee cheering for the Knicks at a Miami Heat Game; Sylvester Stallone pulling up to your hotel in a convertible; or Leonardo Dicaprio celebrating his birthday at a club on the beach. If you do manage to catch a glimpse of your favorite celebrity while cruising the town, try not to gaze too long—the stars also want to enjoy the city, and the locals are pretty good about respecting their privacy.

---

want to watch the parade of characters from your dinner table (see chapter 6, "Miami Dining"). An elegant nightclub called Jimmy'z, a spin-off of Regine's, is adjacent. They say it's a private club, but if you dine at the restaurant or know someone, you can get in. A popular Latin hot spot, Club Nostalgia, has recently opened there to rave reviews.

Mac's Club Deuce. 222 14th St., South Beach. ☎ **305/673-9537.**

Housed in a squat, neon-covered art deco building, this dive is popular with bikers, barflies, and pool players who love the dark and smoky scene. It's a real local's favorite for those who like to slum it. Here, you'll no doubt catch a great conversation, some old tunes on the jukebox, or a good scene out the front picture window that faces a busy all-night tattoo parlor. Mac's is open daily from 8am to 5am. Yes, that's 5*am!*

Ebeel's Bar & Grill. 166 Sunny Isles Blvd. (just west of Collins Ave.), Sunny Isles Beach. ☎ **305/948-3512.**

Open all day and into the next, the American bar is popular with young and old drinkers alike. There's a pool table and darts, occasional Irish Rock or acoustic music, and of course, a selection of good ales and lagers.

Murphy's Law Irish Pub. 2977 McFarlane Dr., Coconut Grove. ☎ **305/446-9956.**

This wood- and brass-decorated Irish pub is a great choice for those who want to escape the more antiseptic night scene at CocoWalk down the road. Weekends offer live music, Irish or otherwise. A big-screen TV shows sports events, but this place is really about sharing a pint or two at the bar with old-timers, grungers, and young professionals.

Wet Willie's. 760 Ocean Dr., South Beach. ☎ **305/532-5650.**

The upstairs deck overlooking Ocean Drive is one of the prime spots for watching the hectic crowds that define South Beach craziness. From up here, you can see the ocean as well as the spectacle of folks who walk the strip night and day. *Watch out:* After just one of Wet Willie's frozen concoctions, you may not be able to see much of anything; they taste like soda pop but bite like a mad dog.

There's another Wet Willie's in Coconut Grove at 3390 Mary St. (☎ **305/443-5060**), on the third level of Mayfair.

2 The Club & Music Scene

LIVE MUSIC

Despite the spotty success of local music, Latin musicians such as Cuban diva Albita, Nil Lara, Willy Chirino, and, of course, Gloria Estefan got their start here. Julio Iglesias plays occasionally and Arturo Sandoval just moved here after defecting from Cuba.

South Florida's jazz scene is also very much alive with traditional and contemporary performers. Keep an eye out for guitarist Randy Bernsen, vibraphonist Tom Toyama, Melton Mustafah, and the flutist Nestor Torres, and the many young performers who lead local ensembles. Many come out of the **University of Miami's** well-respected jazz studies program (☎ **305/284-6477**), which often schedules low- and no-cost recitals. Additionally, many area hotels feature live music of every description. Schedules are listed in the newspaper entertainment sections.

The Globe. 377 Alhambra Circle (at LeJeune), Coral Gables. ☎ **305/445-3555.**

This odd little cafe is attached to a travel agency. On weekends, a red curtain transforms a corner into a stage, where a decent jazz band performs. There's good food, too. (See chapter 6.)

Satchmo Blues. 60 Merrick Way, Coral Gables (1 block from Coral Way and Douglas Rd). ☎ **305/774-1883.** Cover $5 after 8pm.

This is by far, the best happy-hour spot on Friday nights in Miami. In fact, it's a restaurant, club, and a bar all rolled into one. Every Friday night it's packed by locals and plenty of tourists—spilling over the sidewalks and into the streets—looking for an exciting night out. If you're lucky enough to get inside, you can listen to a live jazz, blues, or rock band playing everything from Chuck Berry to Miles Davis. Black and white photos of the great ones—Dizzie Gillespie, Louis Armstrong, Billie Holiday, Duke Ellington, John Coltrane, and Sam Cooke—adorn the walls. There's an American menu with Cajun fare and a full-service bar. The bartenders will gladly mix anything you ask them to. The happy-hour crowd dies down after 9pm, but another nightly crowd strolls right in its place. You can park in a huge lot next door for $1.50 an hour.

Jazid. 1342 Washington Ave., South Beach. ☎ **305/673-9372.** No cover.

This split-level jazz club is an unlikely spot to find on South Beach. It's warm, welcoming, cheap, and even has a pool table. Music ranges from classic jazz to blues and is often performed by talented locals.

Power Studios. 3701 NE 2nd Ave., Miami. ☎ **305/573-8042.** Cover varies.

Opened in the up-and-coming Design District (it's still a little seedy) area just north of downtown, this large warehousey club features live music on Fridays and Saturdays—mostly jazz and blues. There's plenty of room to dance.

✪ **Tobacco Road.** 626 S. Miami Ave. (over the Miami Ave. Bridge near Brickell Ave.), Downtown. ☎ **305/374-1198.** Cover none to $8.

This Miami institution is a must-see. It's been around since 1912, doing more in the back room than just dancing. These days, you'll find a good bar menu along with the best live music anywhere—blues, zydeco, brass, jazz, and more. Regular performers include Bill Warton and the Ingredients, who make a pot of gumbo while up on stage; Monkey Meet; Iko Iko; Chubby Carrier and his band; and many more. Famous recent performers include George Clinton and the P-Funk, and Koko Taylor and the Radiators. Escape the smoke and sweat in the backyard patio, where air is a welcome commodity. The downright cheap nightly specials, such as the $10 lobster on Tuesday, are quite good and served until 2am.

Van Dyke Cafe. 846 Lincoln Rd., Miami Beach. ☎ **305/534-3600.** Cover varies from $3–$6.

Enjoy live jazz until midnight, 7 nights a week, in an elegant upstairs lounge that features the likes of Eddie Higgins, Mike Renzi, and locals such as Don Wilner who play

Rock 'n' Bowl

The latest fad to hit Miami is "Rave" bowling. **Cloverleaf Lanes,** at 17601 NW 2nd Ave., North Dade (☎ **305/652-4197**), sets up glow-in-the-dark pins, turns the lights low and the music high every Friday and Saturday night from 8:30pm until 3am. Games are $4.50 each. Shoes and balls are an extra $2. It's become especially popular with teens, who are too young to get into the clubs.

---

strictly jazz for a well-dressed crowd of enthusiasts. You can have a drink or two at the pristine oak bar or enjoy some snacks from the bustling patio seats below.

DANCE CLUBS

In addition to quiet cafes and progressive poolside bars, Miami Beach pulsates with one of the liveliest night scenes in the city. Also check out "Latin Clubs" listings, later in this chapter for more places to dance.

A popular trend in Miami's club scene are "one-off" nights—events organized by a promoter and held in established venues on irregular schedules. Word of mouth, local advertising, and listings in the free weekly *New Times* are the best ways to find out about these hot events. You can also try asking a cool-looking waiter or waitress at a South Beach eatery.

And just for the record: No, Madonna, the original Material Girl, does not own a nightclub in South Beach. The club that uses her name on its oversized billboard on Washington Avenue is a strip joint, one of a handful in South Beach.

Bash. 655 Washington Ave., South Beach. ☎ **305/538-2274.** Cover $10 weeknights and $20 weekends.

This place has been around longer than most and is still pretty hot. Bash gets going late and features an eclectic mix of music, including Euro-dance, disco, and funk as well as special events, such as occasional funky fashion shows. The crowd is incredibly Eurohip and supertrendy. On weekends, the back patio is open and plays World Beat music. It's open nightly from 10pm to 5am except on Monday.

Bermuda Bar and Grill. 3509 NE 163rd St., North Miami. ☎ **305/945-0196.** Cover none to $10. No cover before 9pm.

This huge suburban danceteria specializes in ladies' nights (Wednesday and Thursday). Plus, it hosts cash-prize contests for women who wear the skimpiest outfits. Still, everybody loves the high-energy music that packs the dance floor. Thursday is Latin night and Friday features happy hour from 5 to 8pm. Saturday is the biggest night, when all the goings-on are broadcast live on a local radio station. Good pizzas and grilled foods are available, too. It's usually open until the sun comes up. Closed Monday, Tuesday, and Sunday.

Cafe Iguana. 8505 Mills Dr. (Town & Country Mall on the corner of 88th St. and 117th Ave.), Kendall. ☎ **305/274-4948.** Cover none to $10.

This tropical-themed bar and dance club is a bit much for low-key club-goers, but for those looking for a high-energy party, it's the place to be. Everything from male and female hot-body contests to a raging Latin night is incorporated into this nightspot. There's also Iguana Cantina at Streets of Mayfair on the third level (☎ **305/444-6606**).

Breaking Through the Velvet Ropes

In Miami, there are certain clued-in people who seem to know everyone on the club scene—they always look fabulous and never fret when they spy a mob at the door of the hippest spot in town. You've seen them kissing each other on both cheeks. Unless you're one of them, you may want to check out these basic rules regarding club admission etiquette:

- Never ever wear blue jeans, shorts, or sneakers. Most clubs with a discretionary door policy see only black or shades of gray—the hipper the better.
- Bring women. At the risk of sounding sexist, there is a direct mathematical relationship between the number of attractive females in your group and likelihood of getting into a hot club. Half a dozen guys without dates might as well look for the nearest frat party or pool hall.
- Call ahead to request a VIP table. You'll spend more than a couple of hundred dollars for overpriced bottles of Dom Perignon or Absolut, but at least you're guaranteed to get in.
- Call a day or two in advance and get phone-friendly with someone whose name you can drop at the door.
- Fax a guest list early in the day and wait for a confirmation number.
- Don't ever flash cash at a doorman. You're better off tipping the concierge at your hotel who can make arrangements to get on a guest list.
- Check your attitude at the sidewalk. "Don't you know who I am?" doesn't work. Be polite and positive; screaming and yelling doesn't work.
- Arrive before midnight. The later it gets, the less likely you'll get in—no matter who you are. When a club gets too full, the fire marshals show up and even Donald Trump gets the cold shoulder.
- Know when to give up. If you've been hanging out for more than 20 or 30 minutes and have been looked over by the dude with the clipboard, you have probably already been pegged as a "no-way." There are plenty of other hot spots in town, so try elsewhere.
- As a last resort, tag on to a hip crowd (this only works for one or two). When you see a good-looking crew get the nod, grab the hand of the last one in line and follow along as if you know what you're doing.

Chaos. 743 Washington Ave., South Beach ☎ **305/674-7350.** Cover usually $20.

Miami's club of the moment, this is where Oliver Stone, Harrison Ford, and other celebs spend their nights when on the beach. Don't expect easy entry, since the number of people waiting on the sidewalk often outnumbers the truly fabulous inside. Music in this intimate enclave ranges from Eurohouse to retro, but is always danceable. Open Wednesday through Saturday from 11pm to 5am.

crobar. 1445 Washington Ave., Miami Beach. ☎ **305/531-5027.** Cover varies. Reservations necessary.

South Beach continues to personify the exception to the rule with the hottest installment to its nightlife scene—a "hip with the heart" addition to the club scene born out of Midwestern vitality and hospitality. Transplanted from Chicago, owners **Cal Fortis** and **Ken Smith** (who have turned that city out with their clubs *glow* and *watusi*) have given the large art deco theater, formerly known as **Cameo,** a much-needed facelift both inside and out. This wonderful new incarnation is a hi-fi miracle of science and technology, with a good amount of wealth and wizardry spent on lighting, sculpted monuments, and a procession of catwalks that appear to wed the mysteries of universe to the planet earth. You won't forget a night spent at the primeval party house. On Sunday nights, the club is renamed Federation and caters to the gay crowd. (See "The Gay & Lesbian Scene," below.)

Groove Jet. 323 23rd St. (1 block west of Collins Ave.), South Beach. ☎ **305/532-5150.** Cover $10–$20.

This fantastic hidden spot north of the South Beach scene has been through many incarnations. Its most recent, Groove Jet, has three distinct areas playing totally different music. Deep house, jungle, and trance tunes are usually heard in the front room with more experimental music in the back rooms. A very hip young crowd hangs in this out-of-the-way scene, which doesn't really get going until after hours (usually after 2am), Thursday to Sunday 11pm to 5am.

Laundry Bar. 721 Lincoln Lane. South Beach ☎ **305/531-7700.** No cover.

If you haven't taken your clothes for a spin while ordering a draft beer or a well drink then you're in for a cultural treat at Laundry Bar, where no-nonsense big city-get-two-things-done-at-once professionals revel in this new concept that matches drinks and dryers. You'll find videos, Internet access, and pool tables too!

Level 1235 Washington. 1235 Washington, South Beach. ☎ **305/532-1525.** Cover $20–$30.

There aren't enough adjectives to describe the party space that is 1235 Washington, which in its latest incarnation has now dubbed "Level" by owners Gerry Kelley, and Rick and Noah Lazes. Mobs have rushed to in to sneak a peek of this thrilling nightclub's style. The club owners told us they didn't want to give out phone numbers to tourists, because if you knew how to get on a list you would already have access to the right channels. Snobbery aside, if you don't mind waiting a bit in line (my advice—arrive early, which in Miami means before midnight), it is well worth the anticipation. Fridays belong to the alternative/gay scene (see "The Gay & Lesbian Scene," below), and while Saturday and Sunday are dubbed "straight" nights, in a club this size—filled with adorable balconies, balustrades, nooks, and crannies—you can expect an "anything goes" atmosphere. Open Thursday to Sunday; check for special nights.

Liquid and The Lounge. 1439 Washington Ave., South Beach. ☎ **305/532-9154** for information, or 305/532-8899 for table reservations. Cover $10–$20.

Liquid is reminiscent of the 1980s New York club scene, so you can expect to wait at the ropes until a disdainful bouncer chooses you. Don't dare to wear the usual casual South Beach attire; they are looking for "casual chic." Once inside, you'll find a pulsing, cavernous space with up-to-the-minute dance music and half-a-dozen packed bars, VIP seating in a cozy back area, a hip-hop side room, and a downstairs lounge playing jazz and funk. Sunday night is gay. The club opens doors at 11pm but the action starts late (around 2am).

Living Room at the Strand. 671 Washington Ave., South Beach. ☎ **305/532-2340.** www.livingroom2000.com. Cover $15–$20.

This very Euro hot spot is the place to mix and mingle with South Beach's beautiful crowd. An ordinary person might have some trouble getting past the velvet-rope treatment out front, but once inside, the ambience alone will impress. Luscious cushions on velvet sofas greet you immediately. The lavishness here reminds one of Napoléon's living room quarters in the Louvre museum in Paris. Models and moguls alike converge here to drink and relive the art of conversation, until the music gets loud after about midnight. It's open 11pm to 5am.

THE GAY & LESBIAN SCENE

Miami and the beaches have long been host to what is called a "first-tier" gay community. Similar to the Big Apple, the Bay Area, or LaLa land, Miami has had a large alternative community since the days when Anita Bryant used her citrus power to boycott the rise in political activism in the early '70s. Well, things have changed and Miami-Dade now has a gay rights ordinance.

Along with this sense of fashionista hype comes the same-sex couples and coupling that might be de rigueur in Amsterdam or London but is sure to shock the more insular tourist. Newcomers intending to party in any bar, whether downtown or certainly on the beach, will want to check ahead for the schedule, as all clubs must have a gay or lesbian night to pay their rent. Miami Beach, in fact, is the capital of the gay circuit party scene, rivaling San Francisco, Palm Springs, and even the mighty Sydney, Australia for tourist dollars—because in the end, it's not about the pink–it's all about the green!

Cactus Bar & Grill. 2401 Biscayne Blvd. Downtown. ☎ **305/438-0662.** No cover charge.

This now famous local bar and restaurant (with the newly renovated Prickly Pear restaurant) has dance floors, show rooms, pool tables, and a great Friday happy hour. It's popular amongst the burgeoning crowds now calling the Biscayne Corridor home.

Club 5922. 5922 S. Dixie Hwy. South Miami ☎ **305/662-8779.** Cover $10-$20

This is an indoor-outdoor dance club that creates both a cool and steamy atmosphere. Almost exclusively Latin, it hosts several lesbian nights. It's called Bliss on Friday.

crobar @ the Cameo. 1445 Washington Ave. South Beach ☎ **877/CRO-SOBE** or ☎ **305/531-5027.** Cover $25.

Chicago's award-winning crobar offers something new with their South Beach megaclub inside the historic Cameo Theater. Gay night is slated for Sundays, and features Miami's own superstar DJ Abel.

The Eagle. 1252 Coral Way. South Miami ☎ **305/860-0056.** Cover $15.

Miami's Levi-leather emporium features beer and handcuffs. It's not for first-timers or the faint of heart.

Friends. 17032 Collins Ave., Sunny Isles/Aventura. ☎ **305/949-4112.** Cover $10-$15.

This is Miami's only boy strip club. It's open every night with video monitors screening movies and all kinds of other stuff.

Level @ 1235. 1235 Washington. South Beach ☎ **305/532-1525.** Cover $20–$30

One of Miami's most notorious gay venues has reawakened and, on Friday nights, it hosts probably the largest gay gathering on the East Coast. Gay night goes by the moniker "Federation," and when things get going, the colossal dance floor rocks. Many club hoppers find that nearly every night at Level turns into a fifty-fifty mix of straight and gay.

Loading Zone. 1426 Alton Rd. South Beach ☎ **305/531-5623.** Cover $15-$20

A leather and Levi bar known for its cruisability, pool tables, movies, and pitchers of beer. There's an in-house leather store for the kinky shopper.

O-Zone. 6620 SW 57 Ave.(Red Road), South Miami. ☎ **305/667-2888.** No cover for men on Saturdays. Cover ranges $10–$20 other nights.

Conveniently located near the University of Miami, this hip spot is the city's proof that, like the Beach, it too, can host a boy bar with plenty of bumptious bods. The crowd here is heavily Latin and collegiate.

Pump. 841 Washington Ave. South Beach ☎ **305/538-PUMP.** Cover $10-$15. Doors open at 4am.

South Florida's only 100% gay after-hours bar, it doesn't get going till 4:30am on Fridays and Saturdays—don't even ask when they close. Resident DJs Eddie X and Kiokio keep it packed to the pecs. Bring sunglasses.

Salvation. 1771 West Ave. Miami Beach ☎ **305/673-6508.** Cover $20.

This is the king (queen?) of the party circuit, as every Saturday night sees this colossal warehouse space transform into a jam-packed interior of literally thousands of shirtless men and scantily clad women gyrating to jungle beats. Because the rotating list of world-class DJs can usually be found remixing the hits of the stars, don't be surprised to find a diva or two (from Bette Midler to Madonna) sashaying through the crowds.

Score. 727 Lincoln Rd. South Beach ☎ **305/535-1111.** No cover.

Open 7 nights a week, this splashy extravaganza is smack in the middle of the pricey restaurant scene of Lincoln Road, so watching the watchers is worth the sideline view. A 16-screen video bar, five open bars, and a nice dance floor ensure that this place is always packed. Sundays host the infamous T-dance, where less is always more with the boyz.

Twist. 1057 Washington Ave. South Beach ☎ **305/538-9478.** No cover.

One of the of the most popular bars (and hideaways) on South Beach (and literally across the street from the police station—which actually used to ensure no bashing at a time when the gay scene was developing), this recently expanded bar has a relaxed local atmosphere. It's open daily from 1pm to 5am.

LATIN CLUBS

Considering that Hispanics make up a large part of Miami's population and that there's a huge influx of Spanish-speaking visitors, it's no surprise that there are some great Latin nightclubs in the city.

Plus, with the meteoric rise of the international music scene based in Miami, many international stars come through the offices of MTV Latino, SONY International, and a multitude of Latin TV studios based in Miami—and they're all looking for a good club scene on weekends. Most of the Anglo clubs reserve at least 1 night a week for Latin rhythms.

✪ **Cafe Nostalgia.** 2212 SW 8th St. (Calle Ocho), Miami. ☎ **305/541-2631.** Cover $10 on Thurs–Sun nights.

As the name implies, Cafe Nostalgia is dedicated to reminiscing about old Cuba. After watching a Celia Cruz film, you can dance to the hot sounds of Afro-Cuban jazz. With pictures of old and young Cuban stars smiling down on you and a live band celebrating Cuban heritage, Cafe Nostalgia sounds like a bit much; it's more than that. Be prepared—it's packed after midnight and dance space is mostly between the tables. Open Thursday to Sunday from 9pm to 4am. Films are shown from 10pm to midnight, followed by live music. Another location is on Miami Beach next to The Forge restaurant.

Where to Learn to Salsa

Are you feeling shy about hitting a Latin club because you fear your two left feet will stand out? Then take a few lessons before tripping the light fantastic. Here are the names of several dance companies and dance teachers around the city who offer individual and group lessons to dancers of any origin who are willing to learn. These folks have made it their mission to teach merengue and flamenco to non-Latinos and Latino left-foots.

You'll have a blast at **Starfish** (1427 West Ave., South Beach; ☎ **305/673-1717**), on Friday nights when it's "Strictly Salsa."

The cover is $5 and is well worth it for a chance to see some of the best (and worst) dancers in town. Learn the moves on Monday and Wednesday nights when group lessons cost only $8.

At Ballet **Flamenco La Rosa** (in the PAN building, 555 17th St., South Beach; ☎ **305/672-0552**), you can learn to flamenco, salsa, or merengue with the best of them. They are the only professional flamenco company in the area, so you'll hear those castanets going. If you're feeling shy, $50 will buy you a private lesson; otherwise, $10 an hour will allow you to learn the art of the dance with a group of other beginners.

Nobody salsas like **Luz Pinto** (☎ **305/868-9418**), and she also knows how to teach the basics with patience and humor. She charges between $40 and $55 for a private lesson for up to four people and $10 per person for a group lesson. A good introduction is her multilevel group class at 7pm Sunday evenings at the PAN building. Although she teaches everything from ballroom to merengue, her specialty is Casino-style salsa, popularized in the 1950s in Cuba, Luz's homeland. A mix between disco and country square dancing, Casino-style salsa is all the rage in Latin clubs in town. Good students may be able to talk Luz into chaperoning a trip to a nightclub to show off their moves. She'll work out a fee based on the number of participants and their ability.

Angel Arroya has been teaching salsa to the clueless out of his home at 16467 NE 27th Ave., North Miami Beach (☎ **305/949-7799**), for the past 10 years. Just $10 will buy you an hour's time in his "school." He traditionally teaches Monday and Wednesday nights, but call ahead to check for any schedule changes.

Casa Panza. 1620 SW 8th St. (Calle Ocho), Miami. ☎ **305/643-5343.** No cover.

Clap your hands or your castanets if you have them. Every Tuesday, Thursday, and Saturday night, Casa Panza, in the heart of Little Havana, becomes the House of Flamenco, with shows at 8 and 11pm. You can either enjoy a flamenco show or strap on your own dancing shoes and participate in the celebration. Enjoy a fantastic Spanish meal before the show, or just have a drink or two before you start stomping.

Mango's Tropical Cafe. 900 Ocean Dr., South Beach. ☎ **305/673-4422.** Cover $5–$15; varies by performer.

If you want to dance to a funky, loud Brazilian beat till you drop, check out Mango's on the beach. It features nightly live Brazilian and other Latin music on a little patio bar. There are also sexy male and female dancers drawing crowds in from the sidewalk. When you need refreshment, you can choose from a wildly eclectic menu of

Caribbean, Mexican, vegetarian, and Cuban specialties. The former hotel has also expanded its rooms to include two contemporary art galleries. It's open daily from 11:30am to 5:30am.

Studio 23. 247 23rd St. (1 block west of Collins Ave.), South Beach. ☎ **305/538-1196.** Cover $5–$10.

You've heard of *son?* Hear it here—along with salsa, cumbia, merengue, vallenato, and house music. This neighborhood Latin disco and nightclub gets going after hours with a wild strobe-lit atmosphere. If you don't know how to do it, just wait. You'll have plenty of willing teachers on hand. Open Friday to Sunday from 8pm to 4am.

Yuca. 501 Lincoln Rd., South Beach. ☎ **305/532-9822.** Cover $25, plus a 2-drink minimum for the Albita performance Fri–Sat nights at 11pm.

One of the city's best restaurants (see chapter 6) also serves up hot music in an upstairs club. If Albita is playing, don't miss her. The prices are ridiculous and you'll be squeezed into a table no bigger than a cocktail napkin, but it's worth it for the high-energy dance music, including traditional sol, salsa, and son from the old country. If you don't speak Spanish, sign language works here, too.

3 The Performing Arts

THEATER

In Miami, an active and varied selection of dramas and musicals are presented throughout the year. Thanks to the support of many loyal theater aficionados, especially an older crowd of New York transplants, season subscriptions are common and allow the theaters to survive, even when every show is not a hit. Some traveling Broadway shows make it to town, as well as revivals by big-name playwrights, such as Tennessee Williams, David Mamet, and Neil Simon. The best way to find out what's playing is to check the local paper or call the theaters directly.

The **Actors' Playhouse,** at the newly restored Miracle Theater in Coral Gables (☎ **305/444-9293**), is a grand 1948 art deco movie palace with a 600-seat main theater, as well as a smaller theater/rehearsal hall where a number of excellent musicals for children are put on throughout the year. In addition to these two rooms, the Playhouse recently added a 300-seat children's balcony theater. Tickets run from $26 to $50.

The **Coconut Grove Playhouse,** 3500 Main Highway in Coconut Grove (☎ **305/442-4000**), was also a former movie house, built in 1927 in an ornate Spanish rococo style. Today, this respected venue is known for its original and innovative staging of both international and local dramas and musicals. The house's second, more intimate Encore Room is well suited to alternative and experimental productions. Tickets run from $37 to $42.

The **Gables Stage,** on Anastasia Avenue in Coral Gables at the Biltmore Hotel (☎ **305/445-1119**), stages at least one Shakespeare play, one classic, and one contemporary piece a year. This well-regarded theater usually tries to secure the rights to a national or local premiere as well. Tickets cost $22 and $28; $10 and $17 for students and seniors.

The **Jerry Herman Ring Theatre** is on the main campus of the University of Miami in Coral Gables (☎ **305/284-3355**). The University's Department of Theater Arts uses this stage for advanced-student productions of comedies, dramas, and musicals. Faculty and guest actors are regularly featured, as are contemporary works by local playwrights. Performances are usually scheduled Tuesday through Saturday during the academic year. In the summer, don't miss "Summer Shorts," a selection of superb one-acts. Tickets sell for $5 to $20.

Acting Out

So you want to be a star? If you would rather get up on a stage than watch others perform, the Panaro Workshop & Theatre Co. at 421 Washington Ave., South Beach (☎ **305/532-9422**), offers several courses for the aspiring actor. There's a TV and commercial course; private coaching for TV and commercials; acting courses using the Stanislavski method; speech classes; screenwriting workshops (three levels); improvisational theater games, and 1-week intensive courses—advance TV, improvisation, and acting.

The **New Theater,** 65 Almeria Ave., in Coral Gables (☎ **305/443-5909**), prides itself on showing world-renowned works from America and Europe. As the name implies, you'll find mostly contemporary plays, with a few classics thrown in for variety. Performances are staged Thursday to Sunday year-round. Tickets are $20 on weekdays, and $25 weekends. If tickets are available, students pay half price.

CLASSICAL MUSIC

In addition to a number of local orchestras and operas, which regularly offer quality music and world-renowned guest artists, each year brings a slew of special events and touring artists. One of the most important and longest-running series is produced by the **Concert Association of Florida (CAF),** 555 17th St., South Beach (☎ **305/532-3491**). Known for more than a quarter of a century for its high-caliber, star-packed schedules, CAF regularly arranges the best "serious" music concerts for the city. Season after season, the schedules are punctuated by world-renowned dance companies and seasoned virtuosi like Itzhak Perlman, Andre Watts, and Kathleen Battle. Since CAF does not have its own space, performances are usually scheduled in either the Dade County Auditorium or the Jackie Gleason Theater of the Performing Arts (see below). The season lasts from October through April, and ticket prices range from $20 to $70.

Florida Philharmonic Orchestra. 1243 University Dr., Miami. ☎ **800/226-1812** or 305/476-1234. Tickets $15–$60. When extra tickets are available, students are admitted free on day of performance.

South Florida's premier symphony orchestra, under the direction of James Judd, presents a full season of classical and pops programs interspersed with several children's and contemporary popular music performances. The Philharmonic performs downtown in the Gusman Center for the Performing Arts and at the Dade County Auditorium.

Miami Chamber Symphony. 5690 N. Kendall Dr., Kendall. ☎ **305/858-3500.** Tickets $12–$30.

This professional orchestra is an inexpensive alternative to the high-priced classical venues. Renowned international soloists perform regularly. The season runs October to May, and most concerts are held in the Gusman Concert Hall, on the University of Miami campus.

✪ **The New World Symphony.** 541 Lincoln Rd., South Beach. ☎ **305/673-3331.** www.nws.org. E-mail: ticketsnws.org. Tickets $0–$58. Rush tickets $20. Students $10 (1 hour before concerts limited seating).

This organization, led by artistic director Michael Tilson Thomas, is a stepping stone for gifted young musicians seeking professional careers. The orchestra specializes in ambitious, innovative, energetic performances and often features renowned guest soloists and conductors. The symphony's season lasts from October to May during which time there are many free concerts.

OPERA

✪ **Florida Grand Opera.** 1200 Coral Way, Miami. ☎ **800/741-1010** or 305/854-1643; 305/854-7890 box office. Tickets $18–$100. Student discounts available.

Nearing its 60th birthday, this company regularly features singers from top houses in both America and Europe. All productions are sung in their original language and staged with projected English supertitles. Tickets become scarce when Placido Domingo or Luciano Pavarotti (who made his American debut here in 1965) come to town. The opera's season runs roughly from November to April, with five performances each week. A new $13.5 million headquarters for the opera is scheduled to open in late 2001.

DANCE

Several local dance companies train and perform in the Greater Miami area. In addition, top traveling troupes regularly stop at the venues listed above. Keep your eyes open for special events and guest artists.

✪ **Ballet Flamenco La Rosa.** ☎ **305/672-0552** or 305/757-8475. Tickets $25 at door, $20 in advance, $18 for students and seniors.

For a taste of local Latin flavor, see this lively troupe perform impressive flamenco and other styles of dance on Miami stages.

✪ **Miami City Ballet.** Ophelia and Juan Jr. Roca Center (on Collins and 22nd Street Ave.), Miami Beach. ☎ **305/532-4880,** or 305/532-7713 box office. Tickets $17–$50.

This artistically acclaimed and innovative company, directed by Edward Villella, features a repertoire of more than 60 ballets, many by George Balanchine, and more than 20 world premieres. The company moved into a new $7.5 million headquarters in January 2000—the Ophelia and Juan Jr. Roca Center at the Collins Park Cultural Center in Miami Beach. The three-story center features eight rehearsal rooms, a ballet school, a boutique, and ticket offices. The City Ballet season runs from September to April.

MAJOR VENUES

After a much-needed $1 million facelift, the **Colony Theater,** on Lincoln Road, South Beach (☎ **305/674-1026**), has become an architectural showpiece of the Art Deco District. This multipurpose 465-seat theater stages performances by the Miami City Ballet and the Ballet Flamenco La Rosa, as well as Off-Broadway shows and other special events.

At the **Dade County Auditorium,** West Flagler Street at 29th Avenue, Miami (☎ **305/547-5414**), performers gripe about the lack of space, but for patrons, this 2,430-seat auditorium is comfortable and intimate. It's home to the city's Greater Miami Opera and also stages productions by the Concert Association of Florida, many Spanish programs, and a variety of other shows.

At the 1,700-seat **Gusman Center for the Performing Arts,** 174 E. Flagler Street in Downtown Miami (☎ **305/372-0925**), seating is tight, and so is funding, but the sound is superb. In addition to producing a regular stage for the Philharmonic Orchestra of Florida and The Miami Film Festival, the elegant Gusman Center features pop concerts, plays, film-festival screenings, and special events. The auditorium was built as the Olympia Theater in 1926, and its ornate palace interior is typical of that era, complete with fancy columns, a huge pipe organ, and twinkling "stars" on the ceiling.

Not to be confused with the Gusman Center (above), the **Gusman Concert Hall,** 1314 Miller Dr., at 14th Street in Coral Gables (☎ **305/284-6477**), is a roomy 600-seat hall that gives a stage to the Miami Chamber Symphony and a varied program of university recitals.

The elegant **Jackie Gleason Theater of the Performing Arts (TOPA),** Washington Avenue at 17th Street, South Beach (☎ **305/673-7300**), is the home of the Miami Beach Broadway Series, which recently presented Rent, Phantom of the Opera, and Les Misérables. This 2,705-seat hall also hosts other big-budget Broadway shows, classical music concerts, opera, and dance performances.

4 Movies & More

CINEMAS

In addition to the annual Miami Film Festival in February and other, smaller film events (See "Miami Calendar of Events," in chapter 2), Miami is lucky to have some wonderful art cinemas showing a range of films from *Fresa y Chocolate* to *Crumb*.

The **Alliance Cinema** (☎ **305/531-8504**) is tucked behind a little tropical walkway just next to Books & Books at 927 Lincoln Rd., Suite 119, in South Beach. This old hideaway shows art films, Latin American features, and lots of gay films, too. You may want to bring a pillow; the seats are old and rickety. Tickets cost $6.

Astor Art Cinema, 4120 Laguna St. (☎ **305/443-6777**), is an oasis in the midst of a desert of Cineplex Odeons and AMCs in Coral Gables. This quaint double theater hosts foreign, classic, independent, and art films and serves decent popcorn, too. Tickets are $5, $3 for seniors.

Absinthe Cinemateque, 235 Alcazar Ave., Coral Gables (☎ **305/446-7144**), is a small one-screen theater, which shows good movies, often Spanish-language films, without the hustle and bustle of the crowded multiplexes. The Alcazar shows the more artsy of the major films as well as some obscure independents. Tickets are $6.

The **Bill Cosford Cinema** at the University of Miami, on the second floor of the memorial building off Campo Sano Avenue (☎ **305/284-4861**), is named after the deceased *Herald* film critic. This well-endowed little theater was recently revamped and boasts high-tech projectors, new air-conditioning, and new decor. It sponsors independent films as well as lectures by visiting filmmakers and movie stars. Andy Garcia and Antonio Banderas are a few of the big names this theater has attracted. It also hosts the African American Film Festival and a Student Film Festival, plus collaborations with the Fort Lauderdale Festival. Admission is $5.

THE LITERARY SCENE

Books & Books, in Coral Gables at 296 Aragon Ave., and in Miami Beach at 933 Lincoln Rd., hosts readings almost every night and is known for attracting such top authors as Colleen McCullough, Jamaica Kincaid, and Paul Levine. For details on the free readings, call ☎ **305/442-4408.**

To hear more about what's happening on Miami's literary scene, tune into the "Cover to Cover" show, broadcast at 8pm on Monday on public radio station WLRN (91.3 FM).

5 Late-Night Bites

Although some dining spots in Miami stop serving at 10pm, many are open very late or even around the clock—especially on weekends. So, if it's 4am and you need a quick bite after clubbing, don't fret. There are a vast number of pizza places lining Washington Avenue in South Beach that are open past 6am. Especially good is **Pucci's,** with several locations, including one at 651 Washington Ave. **La Sandwicherie,** 229 14th St. (behind the Amoco station; ☎ **305/532-8934**), serves up a great late-night sandwich until 5am. Another place of note for night owls is the **News Café,** 800 Ocean Dr. (☎ **305/538-6397**), a trendy and well-priced cafe that has an enormous menu offering great all-day breakfasts, Middle Eastern platters, fruit bowls, or steak and potatoes—and everything served 24 hours a day. In Coconut Grove, there's another crowded News Cafe, 2901 Florida Ave. (behind Mayfair; ☎ **305/774-6397**), serving up the same fresh food around the clock.

If your night out was at one of the Latin clubs around town, stop in at **Versailles,** 3555 SW 8th St. (☎ **305/444-0240**), in Little Havana. What else but a Cuban *medianoche* (midnight sandwich) will do? It's not open all night, but its hours extend well past midnight—usually until 3 or 4am on weekends—to cater to gangs of revelers, both young and old.

Side Trips from Miami   10

Miami has been called the "gateway to the world," because its port leads the pack in passengers heading to the Caribbean and Latin America. But many tourists also take some time out to see the wild plant and animal life in the swampy Everglades, and the underwater treasures of Biscayne National Park. Also convenient to Miami by boat or plane are the islands of The Bahamas, which are highlighted below.

1 A Glimpse of Everglades National Park— The Southeast Portion

35 miles SW of Miami

Marjory Stoneman Douglas, who fought tirelessly to save this fragile resource until her death in 1998 at the age of 108, might well be called the Mother of the Everglades. This vast and unusual ecosystem is actually a shallow, 40-mile-wide, slow-moving river. Rarely more than knee-deep, the water is the lifeblood of this wilderness. Subtle shifts in water level dictate the life cycle of the native plants and animals. Most folks viewed it as a worthless swamp until Douglas focused attention on the area with her moving and insightful book *The Everglades: River of Grass,* published in 1947.

It was that same year that 1.5 million acres—less than 20% of Everglades wilderness—were established as Everglades National Park. At that time, few lawmakers understood how neighboring ecosystems relate to each other: You can't just chop off a chunk of a much larger wilderness and expect it to survive. The park is heavily affected by surrounding territories, and is at the butt end of every environmental insult that occurs upstream in Miami.

Recently, environmental activists have succeeded in persuading politicians to enact some legislation to clean up the pollution that has threatened this unusual ecosystem ever since the days when heavy industry—most notably the sugar industry—first moved into the area. There has been a marked decrease in the indigenous wildlife here, but it remains one of the few places where you can see dozens of endangered species in their natural habitat, including the swallowtail butterfly, American crocodile, leatherback turtle, southern bald eagle, West Indian manatee, and Florida panther.

It takes a month for 1 gallon of water to move through the park, and I recommend a similar pace for you to fully experience the Everglades' grandeur. Take your time on the trails, and a hypnotic beauty begins

Everglades National Park

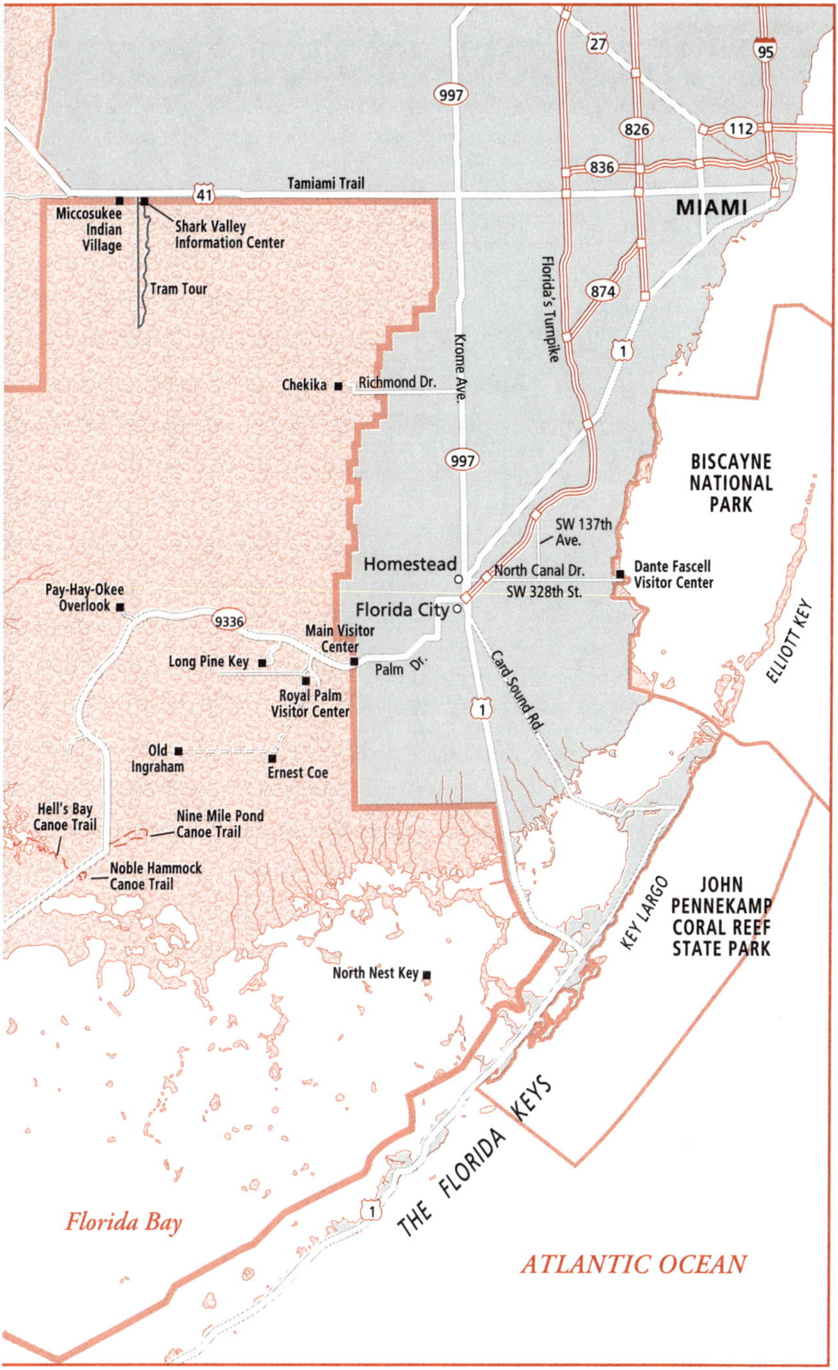

27
95
997
826
112
836
Tamiami Trail
41
MIAMI
Miccosukee Indian Village
Shark Valley Information Center
Tram Tour
874
Florida's Turnpike
Krome Ave.
1
Chekika
Richmond Dr.
997
BISCAYNE NATIONAL PARK
SW 137th Ave.
Homestead
North Canal Dr.
Dante Fascell Visitor Center
SW 328th St.
Pay-Hay-Okee Overlook
Florida City
9336
Main Visitor Center
Long Pine Key
Palm Dr.
Card Sound Rd.
ELLIOTT KEY
Royal Palm Visitor Center
1
Old Ingraham
Ernest Coe
Hell's Bay Canoe Trail
Nine Mile Pond Canoe Trail
Noble Hammock Canoe Trail
KEY LARGO
JOHN PENNEKAMP CORAL REEF STATE PARK
North Nest Key
THE FLORIDA KEYS
1
Florida Bay
ATLANTIC OCEAN

Impressions

There are no other Everglades in the world. They are, they have always been, one of the unique regions of the earth, remote, never wholly known. Nothing anywhere else is like them: their vast glittering openness, wider than the enormous visible round of the horizon, the racing free saltiness and sweetness of their massive winds, under the dazzling blue heights of space.
　　　　　—Marjory Stoneman Douglas, *The Everglades: River of Grass*, 1947

to unfold. Follow the rustling of a bush, and you might see a small green tree frog or tiny brown anole lizard, with its bright-red spotted throat. Crane your head around a bend and discover a delicate, brightly painted mule-ear orchid.

The slow and subtle splendor of this exotic land may not be immediately appealing to kids raised on video games and rapid-fire commercials, but they'll certainly remember the experience and no doubt thank you for it later. Meanwhile, you'll find plenty of dramatic fun around the park, like airboat rides, alligator wrestling, and biking to keep the kids satisfied for at least a day.

In the 1800s, before the southern Everglades were designated a national park, the only inhabited piece of this wilderness was a quiet fishing village called Flamingo. Accessible only by boat and leveled every few years by hurricanes, the mosquito-infested town never grew very popular. When the 38-mile road from Florida City was completed in 1922, many of those who did live here fled to someplace either more or less remote. Today, Flamingo is a center for visitor activities and the main jumping-off point for backcountry camping and exploration. Flamingo is now home to National Park Service and concessionaire employees and their families.

Some 1,400 residents still live in the small enclave in the eastern section of the park although the local agency governing the area has recently begun a buy out program to remove them so that the area can be returned to its original state.

Everglades National Park's northern Shark Valley entrance and the eastern approaches described below are the most accessible from Miami and the rest of Florida's east coast. You'll find great amenities along the way, like Indian villages, alligator farms, and boat rides. An excellent tram tour goes deep into the park along a trail that's also terrific for biking. This is also the best way to reach the park's only accommodation (and full-service outfitters), the Flamingo Lodge.

JUST THE FACTS

GETTING THERE & ACCESS POINTS Everglades National Park has four entrances. The following three are the most popular and the ones most convenient to visitors from Florida's east coast, including Miami. No matter which part of Miami you are starting in, the drive should take no longer than an hour (unless of course you are traveling during rush hour: between 8 and 9:30am or from 4 until 6pm. Then, the roads, especially S.R. 836, will be backed up, and your driving time could be doubled).

The main entrance, in Homestead on the park's east side, is located 10 miles southwest of Florida City. From Miami, take S.R. 836 west to the Florida Turnpike south until it ends in Florida City. Signs will point you southwest onto the road that leads into the park, S.R. 9336. The main entrance's Park Ranger Station is open 24 hours.

The Shark Valley entrance, on the park's north side, is located on the Tamiami Trail (U.S. 41), about 35 miles west of downtown Miami. From Miami, take S.R. 836 west to the Florida Turnpike south; exit on Tamiami Trail (U.S. 41), and go west for approximately 30 miles. The park will be on your left side. Shark Valley is known for its 15-mile trail loop that's used for an excellent interpretive tram tour, bicycling, and walking. This entrance is open daily from 8:30am to 5:30pm, with some seasonal variation. Call ahead.

Chekika, popular with day visitors, picnickers, and campers, is located halfway between the two entrances above in the northeast section of the park. Chekika can be reached from Miami as if going to Shark Valley (see above). After exiting on Tamiami Trail (Highway 41), head west 5 miles to Krome Avenue (177th Avenue); turn left, then proceed to SW 168th Street (Richmond Avenue) and head west (left) until you reach a stop sign. Turn right; the entrance will be on the left side. There are picnic facilities and a 20-site campground. You can enter Chekika from 8:30am until sundown.

VISITOR CENTERS & INFORMATION General inquiries and specific questions should be directed to **Everglades National Park Headquarters,** 40001 S.R. 9336, Homestead, FL 33034 (☎ **305/242-7700**). Ask for a copy of *Parks and Preserves,* a free newspaper that's filled with up-to-date information on goings-on in the Everglades. Headquarters is staffed by helpful phone operators daily from 8:30am until 4:30pm. You can also try the park's Web site at **www.nps.gov/ever/**.

Note that all hours listed are for the high season, generally November through May. During the slow summer months, many offices and outfitters keep abbreviated hours.

The **Flamingo Lodge, Marina and Outpost Resort,** in Flamingo (☎ **800/600-3813** or 941/695-3101), is the one-stop clearinghouse—and the only option—for in-park accommodations, equipment rentals, and tours.

Especially since its recent expansion, the **Ernest F. Coe Visitor Center,** located at the park's main entrance, is the best place to stop to gather information for your trip. In addition to free brochures outlining trails, wildlife and activities, and information on tours and boat rentals, you will also find state-of-the-art educational displays, films, and interactive exhibits. A gift shop sells postcards, film, unusual gift items, the best selection of books about the Everglades, and a selection of your most important gear: insect repellent. It is open from 8am until 5pm daily.

The **Royal Palm Visitor Center,** a small nature museum located 3 miles past the park's main entrance, is a smaller information center at the head of the popular Anhinga and Gumbo-Limbo trails and is open daily from 8am until 4pm.

The Shark Valley Information Center at the park's northern entrance and the Flamingo Visitor Center are also staffed by knowledgeable rangers who provide brochures and personal insight into the goings-on in the park. They are open from 8:30am until 5pm.

ENTRANCE FEES, PERMITS & REGULATIONS Permits and passes can be purchased either at the main park entrance, the Chekika entrance, or the Shark Valley entrance stations only.

Even if you are just visiting the park for an afternoon, you'll need to buy a 7-day permit, which costs $10 per vehicle. Pedestrians and cyclists are charged $5 each and $4 at Shark Valley.

An Everglades Park Pass, valid for a year's worth of unlimited entrances, is available for $20. U.S. citizens may purchase a 12-month Golden Eagle Passport for $65, which is valid for entrance into any U.S. national park. U.S. citizens aged 62 and older pay only $10 for a Golden Age Passport—that's valid for life. A Golden Access Passport is available free to U.S. citizens with disabilities.

Permits are required for campers to stay overnight either in the backcountry or in primitive campsites. See Camping, in "Where to Stay," below.

Those who want to fish without a charter captain must obtain a standard State of Florida saltwater fishing license. These are available in the park at Flamingo Lodge or any tackle shop or sporting goods store nearby. Nonresidents will pay $17 for a 7-day license or $7 for 3 days. Florida residents can get a fishing license good for the whole year for $14. Snook and crawfish licenses must be purchased separately at a cost of $2.

Charter captains carry vessel licenses that cover all paying passengers, but ask to be sure. Freshwater fishing licenses are available at various bait and tackle shops outside the park at the same rates. A good one nearby is **Don's Bait & Tackle** located at 30710 S. Federal Hwy. in Homestead right on U.S. 1 (☎ **305/247-6616**). Most of the area's freshwater fishing, limited to murky canals and artificial lakes near housing developments, is hardly worth the trouble when so much good saltwater fishing is available.

Firearms are not allowed anywhere in the park.

SEASONS There are two distinct seasons in the Everglades: high season and mosquito season. High season is also dry season, and lasts from late November to May. Despite the bizarre cold and wet weather patterns that El Niño brought in 1998, most winters here are warm, sunny, and breezy—a good combination for keeping the bugs away. This is the best time to visit, as low water levels attract the largest variety of wading birds and their predators. As the dry season wanes, wildlife follows the receding water, and by the end of May, the only living things you are sure to spot will cause you to itch. The worst, called "no-see-ums," are not even swattable. If you choose to visit during the buggy season, be sure to be vigilant in applying bug spray.

Also, realize that many establishments and operators either close or curtail offerings in the summer, so always call ahead to check schedules.

RANGER PROGRAMS More than 50 ranger programs, free with admission, are offered each month during high season and give visitors an opportunity to gain an expert's perspective. Some programs occur regularly, such as Glade Glimpses, a walking tour during which rangers point out flora and fauna and discuss issues affecting the Everglade's survival. These tours are scheduled at 10:15am, noon, and 3:30pm daily. The Anhinga Ambles, a similar program that takes place on the Anhinga Trail, starts at 10:30am, 1:30pm, and 4pm.

Park rangers tend to be helpful, well informed, good-humored, and happy to answer questions. Since times, programs, and locations vary from month to month, check a schedule, available at any of the visitor centers (see above).

SAFETY There are dangers inherent in this vast wilderness area. Always let someone know your itinerary before you set out on an extended hike. It's mandatory that you file an itinerary when camping overnight in the backcountry. When on the water, watch for weather changes; severe thunderstorms and high winds often develop rapidly. Swimming is not recommended because of the presence of alligators, sharks, and barracudas. Watch out for the region's four indigenous poisonous snakes: diamondback and pygmy rattlesnakes, coral snakes (identifiable by their colorful rings), and water moccasins (which swim on the surface of the water). Again, bring insect repellent to ward off mosquitoes and biting flies.

First aid is available from park rangers. The nearest hospital is in Homestead, 10 miles from the park's main entrance.

SEEING THE HIGHLIGHTS

Shark Valley provides a fine introduction to the wonder of the Everglades, but don't plan on spending more than a few hours here. Bicycling or taking a guided tram tour can be a satisfying experience, but neither fully captures the wonders of the park.

If you want to see a greater array of plant and animal life, make sure that you venture into the park through the main entrance, pick up a trail map, and dedicate at least a day to exploring from there.

Stop first along the Anhinga and Gumbo-Limbo trails, which start right next to one another, 3 miles from the park's main entrance. These trails provide a thorough introduction to Everglades flora and fauna and are highly recommended to first-time visitors. There's more water and wildlife here than in most parts of the Everglades, especially during dry season. Alligators, turtles, river otters, herons, egrets, and other animals abound, making this one of the best trails for seeing wildlife. Arrive early to spot the widest selection of exotic birds; like the Anhinga Trail's namesake, a large black fishing bird that is so used to humans, many of these birds build their nests in plain view. Others travel deeper into the park during daylight hours. Take your time—at least an hour is recommended. If you treat the trails and modern boardwalk as pathways to get through quickly, rather than destinations to experience and savor slowly, you'll miss out on the still beauty and hidden treasures that await.

Also, it's worth climbing the observation tower at the end of the quarter-mile-long Pa-hay-okee Trail. The panoramic view of undulating grass and seemingly endless vistas gives the impression of a semiaquatic Serengeti. Flocks of tropical and semitropical birds traverse the landscape, alligators and fish stir the surface of the water, small grottoes of trees thrust up from the sea of grass marking higher ground, and the vastness of the hidden world you've entered seems unparalleled.

If you want to get closer to nature, a few hours in a canoe along any of the trails allows paddlers the chance to sense the park's fluid motion, and to become a part of the ecosphere. Visitors who choose this option end up feeling more like explorers than merely observers. (See "Sports & Outdoor Activities," below.)

No matter which option you choose (and there are many), I strongly recommend staying for the 7pm program, available during high season at the Long Pine Key Amphitheater. This talk and slide show given by one of the park's rangers will give you a detailed overview of the park's history, natural resources, wildlife, and threats to its survival.

SPORTS & OUTDOOR ACTIVITIES

BIKING The relatively flat 38-mile paved Main Park Road is excellent for bicycling, as are many park trails, including Long Pine Key. Expect to spend 2 to 3 hours along the path.

If the park isn't flooded from excess rain (which it often is, especially in spring), Shark Valley in Everglades National Park is South Florida's most scenic bicycle trail. Many locals haul their bikes out to the Glades for a relaxing day of wilderness-trail riding. You can ride the 17-mile loop with no other traffic in sight. Instead, you'll share the flat paved road only with other bikers and a menagerie of wildlife. Don't be surprised to see a gator lounging in the sun or a deer munching on some grass. Otters, turtles, alligators, and snakes are common companions in the Shark Valley area.

Those who love to mountain bike, and who prefer solitude, might check out the **Southern Glades Trail,** a 14-mile unpaved trail opened in late 1998 that is lined with native trees and teeming with wildlife like deer, alligators, and the occasional snake. The remote trail runs along the C-111 canal, off S.R. 9336 and SW 217th Street.

You can rent bikes at the Flamingo Lodge, Marina and Outpost Resort (see "Where to Stay," below) for $17 per 24 hours, $14 per full day, $8.50 per half day (any 4-hour period), and $3 per hour. A $50 deposit is required for each rental. **Bicycles are also available from Shark Valley Tram Tours,** at the park's Shark Valley entrance

(☎ **305/221-8455**), for $3.25 per hour; rentals can be picked up any time after 8:30am and must be returned by 4pm.

BIRD WATCHING More than 350 species of birds make their home in the Everglades. Tropical birds from the Caribbean and temperate species from North America can be found here, along with exotics that have blown in from more distant regions. Eco and Mrazek ponds, located near Flamingo, are two of the best places for birding, especially in early morning or late afternoon in the dry winter months. Pick up a free birding checklist from a visitor center (see "Just the Facts," above), and ask a park ranger what's been spotted in recent days.

BOATING Motorboating around the Everglades seems like a great way to see plants and animals in remote habitats. However, environmentalists are taking stock of the damage motorboats (especially airboats) inflict on the delicate ecosystem. If you choose to motor, remember that most of the areas near land are "no wake" zones, and for the protection of nesting birds, landing is prohibited on most of the little mangrove islands. There's a long list of restrictions and restricted areas, so get a copy of the park's boating rules from National Park Headquarters before setting out (see "Just the Facts," above).

The Everglades' only marina—accommodating about 50 boats with electric and water hookups—is the Flamingo Lodge Marina and Outpost Resort, located in Flamingo. The well-marked channel to the Flamingo is accessible to boats with a maximum 4-foot draft and is open year-round. Reservations can be made through the marina store (☎ **941/695-3101, ext. 304**). Skiffs with 15-horsepower motors are available for rent. These low-power boats cost $90 per day, $65 per half day (any 5-hour period), and $22 per hour. A $125 deposit is required.

CANOEING The most intimate view of the Everglades comes from the humble perspective of a simple low boat. From a canoe, you'll get a closer look into the park's shallow estuaries where water birds, sea turtles, and endangered manatees make their homes.

Everglades National Park's longest "trails" are designed for boat and canoe travel, and many are marked as clearly as walking trails. The Noble Hammock Trail, a 2-mile loop, takes 1 to 2 hours, and is recommended for beginning canoers. The Hell's Bay Trail, a 3- to 6-mile course for hardier paddlers, takes 2 to 6 hours, depending on how far you choose to go. Park rangers can recommend other trails that best suit your abilities, time limitations, and interests.

You can rent a canoe at the Flamingo Lodge, Marina and Outpost Resort (see "Where to Stay," below) for $40 for 24 hours, $32 per full day, $22 per half day (any 4-hour period), and $8 per hour. They also have family canoes that rent for $12, $30, $40, and $50, respectively. A deposit is required. Skiffs, kayaks, and tandem kayaks are also available. The concessionaire will shuttle your party to the trailhead of your choice and pick you up afterward. Rental facilities are open daily from 6am to 8pm.

FISHING About one-third of Everglades National Park is open water. Freshwater fishing is popular in brackish Nine-Mile Pond (25 miles from the main entrance) and other spots along the Main Park Road, but because of the high mercury levels found in the Everglades, freshwater fishers are warned not to eat their catch. Before casting, check in at a visitor center, as many of the park's lakes are preserved for observation only. Fishing licenses are required. See "Just the Facts," above.

Saltwater anglers will find snapper and sea trout plentiful. Charter boats and guides are available at Flamingo Lodge, Marina and Outpost Resort (see "Where to Stay," below). Phone for information and reservations.

ORGANIZED TOURS

AIRBOAT TOURS Shallow-draft, fan-powered airboats were invented in the Everglades by frog hunters who were tired of poling through the brushes. And though it is the most efficient way to get around, airboats are not permitted in the park. Just outside the boundaries, however, you'll find a number of outfitters offering rides. These shallow-bottom runabouts tend to inflict severe damage on the animals and plants there. If you choose to ride on one, you should consider bringing earplugs; these high-speed boats are loud. Airboat rides are offered at the **Miccosukee Indian Village,** just west of the Shark Valley entrance on U.S. 41, the Tamiami Trail (☎ **305/223-8380**). Native American guides will take you through the reserve's rushes at high speed and stop along the way to point out alligators, native plants, and exotic birds. The price is just $7.

The **Everglades Alligator Farm,** 4 miles south of Palm Drive/S.R. 9336 and on SW 192 Ave. (☎ **305/247-2628**), offers half-hour guided airboat tours from 9am until 6pm daily. The price, which includes admission to the park, is $12 for adults, $6 for children.

MOTORBOAT TOURS Both Florida Bay and backcountry tours are offered at the **Flamingo Lodge, Marina and Outpost Resort** (see "Where to Stay," below). Both are available in 1^1/$_2$- and 2-hour versions that cost an average of $16 adults, $8 children, under 6 free. There are also charter-fishing and sightseeing boats that can be booked through the main reservation number (☎ **941/695-3101**). Florida Bay tours cruise nearby estuaries and sandbars, while six-passenger backcountry boats visit smaller sloughs. Tours depart throughout the day, and reservations are recommended.

TRAM TOURS At the park's Shark Valley entrance, open-air tram buses take visitors on 2-hour naturalist-led tours that delve 7^1/$_2$ miles into the wilderness. At the trail's midsection, passengers can disembark and climb a 65-foot observation tower that offers good views of the Glades. Visitors will see plenty of wildlife and endless acres of sawgrass. Tours run November to April only, daily from 9am to 4pm, and are sometimes stalled by flooding or particularly heavy mosquito infestation. Reservations are recommended from December to March. The cost is $9.30 for adults, $5.15 for children 12 and under, and $8.25 for seniors. For further information, contact the **Shark Valley Tram Tours** at ☎ **305/221-8455.**

SHOPPING

You won't find big malls or lots of boutiques in this area, although there is an outlet center nearby, the **Keys Factory Shops** (☎ **305/248-4727**), at 250 E. Palm Dr. (where the Florida Turnpike meets U.S. 1), in Florida City, with more than 60 stores including Nike Factory Store, Bass Co. Store, Levi's, OshKosh, and Izod. You can pick up a free coupon booklet from the Customer Service Center called the Come Back Pack, which includes coupons good for discounts in the outlet. It's open Monday to Saturday until 9pm, Sunday until 6pm.

A necessary stop and good place for a refreshment is one of Florida's best-known fruit stands, **Robert Is Here** (☎ **305/246-1592**). Robert has been selling home-grown treats for nearly 40 years at the corner of SW 344th Street (Palm Drive) and SW 192nd Avenue. You'll find the freshest pineapples, bananas, papayas, mangos, and melons anywhere as well as his famous shakes in unusual flavors like key lime, coconut, orange, and cantaloupe. Exotic fruits, bottled jellies, hot sauces, and salad dressings are also available. This is a great place to pick up culinary souvenirs and sample otherwise unavailable goodies. Open daily 8am until 7pm.

Along Tamiami Trail, there are several roadside shops hawking Indian handicrafts including one at the **Miccosukee Indian Village** (☎ **305/223-8380**), just west of the Shark Valley entrance. At nearly every one you'll find the same stock of feathered dreamcatchers, stuffed alligator heads and claws, turquoise jewelry, and other trinkets. *Tip:* Be sure to take note of the unique, colorful handmade cloth Miccosukee dolls.

WHERE TO STAY

The only lodging in the park proper is the Flamingo Lodge, a fairly priced and very recommendable option. However, here are a few hotels just outside the park that are even cheaper. A $45 million casino hotel was recently built adjacent to the Miccosukee bingo and gaming hall on the northern edge of the park.

Though bugs can be a major nuisance, especially in the warm months, camping is really the way to go in this very primitive environment. There are dozens of campsites and chickee platforms (see below for details) for tenters.

IN & AROUND EVERGLADES NATIONAL PARK

✪ **Flamingo Lodge, Marina and Outpost Resort.** 1 Flamingo Lodge Hwy., Flamingo, FL 33034. ☎ **800/600-3813** or 941/695-3101. Fax 941/695-3921. www.flamingolodge.com. E-mail: evergladesinfo@amfacpnr.com. 127 units A/C TV TEL. Winter from $95 double; from $135 cottage; $135–$150 suite. Off-season $65–$80 double; $89–$100 cottage; $99–$110 suite. Rates for cottages or suites are for 1 to 4 people. Children under 18 stay free. AE, DC, DISC, MC. Take Florida Turnpike South to Florida City; exit on U.S. 1; at 4-way intersection turn right onto Palm Dr.; continue for 3 miles and turn left at Robert Is Here fruit stand; turn right at the 3-way intersection. The park entrance is 3 miles ahead. Continue for about 38 more miles to reach lodge.

The Flamingo Lodge is the only lodging actually located within the boundaries of Everglades National Park. This woodsy, sprawling complex offers rooms overlooking the Florida Bay in either a two-story simple motel or the lodge. Either option feels very much like being at summer camp, with a few more amenities.

VCRs and videos are available for guests in the regular rooms or in the suite, but not in more primitively outfitted cottages. Still, the cottages are an especially good choice if you plan to stay more than a night or two since they come with small kitchens, equipped with dishes and flatware, but no television. They are also larger, more private, and almost romantic.

Facilities on the premises include a waterside bar and restaurant; a freshwater swimming pool; convenience store, and a gift shop; coin laundry; bike, canoe, and kayak rental; and a marina with boat tours, boat rentals, houseboats, and fishing charters. The hotel is open year-round although the restaurant (see "Where to Dine," below) closes in the summer. Reservations are accepted daily from 8am to 5pm. Guests are treated to free coffee in the lobby.

CAMPING & HOUSEBOATING IN THE EVERGLADES

Campgrounds are available in Flamingo and Long Pine Key, where there are more than 300 sites designed for tents and RVs. They have level parking pads, tables, and charcoal grills. There are no electrical hookups, and showers are cold water. Private ground fires are not permitted, but supervised campfire programs are conducted during winter months. Reservations may be made in advance through The National Park Reservations Service at ☎ **800/365-CAMP**. Campsites are $14 per night with a 14-day consecutive stay limit, 30 days a year maximum.

Camping is also available in the backcountry year-round on a first-come, first-served basis and is only accessible by boat, on foot, or by bicycle. Campers must register in person or by telephone no more than 24 hours before the start of their trip.

Permits must be obtained at ranger stations in either Flamingo or Everglades City. Campers can use only designated campsites, which are plentiful and well marked on visitor maps.

Many backcountry sites are chickee huts—covered wooden platforms on stilts. They're accessible only by canoe and can accommodate freestanding tents (without stakes). Ground sites are located along interior bays and rivers, and beach camping is also popular. In summer especially, mosquito repellent is necessary gear.

Houseboat rentals are one of the park's best-kept secrets. Available through the Flamingo Lodge, Marina and Outpost Resort, motorized houseboats make it possible to explore some of the park's more remote regions without having to worry about being back by nightfall. You can choose from two different types of houseboats. The first, a 40-foot pontoon boat, sleeps six to eight people in a single large room that's separated by a central head (bathroom) and shower. There's a small galley (kitchen) that contains a stove, oven, and charcoal grill. Prices aren't cheap unless you are with a good-sized group. It rents for between $340 and $475 for 2 nights (there's a 2-night minimum in high season).

The newer, sleeker Gibson fiberglass boats sleep six, have a head and shower, air-conditioning, and electric stove. There's also a full rooftop sundeck. These rent for $575 for 2 nights (with a 2-night minimum). With either boat, the seventh night is free when renting for a full week.

Boating experience is helpful but not mandatory, as the boats only cruise up to 6 miles per hour and are surprisingly easy to use. In-season, reservations should be made months in advance; call ☎ **800/600-3813** or 941/695-3101.

Nearby in Homestead & Florida City

Homestead and Florida City, two adjacent towns that were almost blown off the map by Hurricane Andrew in 1992, have come back better than before. Located about 10 miles from the park's main entrance, along U.S. 1, 35 miles south of Miami, these somewhat rural towns offer several budget lodging options, including a handful of chain hotels. There is a very recommendable **Days Inn** (☎ **305/245-1260**) in Homestead and a **Hampton Inn** (☎ **800/426-7866** or 305/247-8833) right off the turnpike in Florida City. The best option is the Best Western Gateway to the Keys.

○ **Best Western Gateway to the Keys.** 411 S. Krome Ave. (U.S. 1), Florida City, FL 33034. ☎ **800/528-1234** or 305/246-5100. Fax 305/242-0056. www.bestwestern.com. 114 units. A/C TV TEL. Winter from $89 double; from $109 suite. Off-season from $80 double; from $99 suite. Rates include continental breakfast. During races and very high season, there may be a 3-night minimum. AE, DC, DISC, MC, V.

Opened in late 1994, this two-story, pink-and-white Best Western offers contemporary style and comfort about 10 miles from the park's main entrance. A decent sized pool and a small spa are especially attractive. Each identical standard room has bright, tropical bedspreads and oversize picture windows. The suites offer convenient extras like a microwave, coffeemaker, an extra sink, and a small fridge. Overall, this business-oriented hotel is well priced and well maintained, and is the best choice in the area. The only drawback is that in season, there is often a 3-day minimum stay requirement. You'd do best to call the local reservation line (**305-246-5100**) instead of the toll-free number—on several occasions, the hotel made an exception to the rule while the central reservation line was not able to.

Everglades Motel. 605 S. Krome Ave., Homestead, FL 33030. ☎ **305/247-4117.** 14 units. A/C TV TEL. Winter $43 double. Off-season from $32 double. Additional person $5 extra. AE, DISC, MC, V.

This one-story hotel is probably the cheapest option you'll find in Homestead, but certainly not the greatest. There is a small swimming pool, coin laundry, and free coffee in the lobby. Though not thoroughly fluent in English, the East Indian staff is accommodating and friendly. Rooms are modest in size and decor, but could use a good scrub. Nonetheless, the place is safe, superaffordable, and perfectly fine for 1 or 2 nights. Make your local calls from here, since they are free.

WHERE TO DINE IN & AROUND THE PARK

You won't find fancy nouvelle cuisine in this suburbanized farm country, but there are plenty of fast-food chains along U.S. 1 and a few old favorites worth a taste.

Here for nearly a quarter of a century, **El Toro Taco** at 1 S. Krome Ave. (near Mowry Drive and Campbell Drive; ☎ 305/245-8182) opens daily at 9:30am and stays crowded until at least 9pm most days. The fresh grilled meats, tacos, burritos, salsas, guacamole, and stews are mild and delicious. No matter how big your appetite, it's hard to spend more than $12 per person at this Mexican outpost. You'll have to bring your own beer or wine.

Housed in a squat, one-story, windowless stone building that looks something like a medieval fort, the **Capri Restaurant,** 935 N. Krome Ave., Florida City (☎ 305/247-1542), has been serving hearty Italian American fare since 1958. Great pastas and salads complement a full menu of meat and fish dishes. Portions are big. They serve lunch and dinner every day (except Sunday) until 11pm.

The **Miccosukee Restaurant** (☎ 305/223-8380), just west of the Shark Valley entrance on the Tamiami Trail (U.S. 41), serves authentic pumpkin bread, fry bread, fish, and not-so-authentic Native American interpretations of tacos and fried chicken. This interesting spot is worth a stop for brunch, lunch, or dinner.

Once inside the Everglades, you'll want to eat at the only restaurant within the boundaries of this huge park, **The Flamingo Restaurant** (☎ 941/695-3101). Located in the Flamingo Lodge (See "Where to Stay," above), this is a very civilized and affordable restaurant. Besides the spectacular view of Florida Bay and numerous Keys from the large, airy dining room, you'll also find fresh fish, including my very favorite, mahimahi. All fish are prepared grilled, blackened, or deep-fried; and dinner entrees come with salad or conch chowder, and steamed vegetables, black beans, and rice or baked potato. The large menu has something for everyone, including basic and very tasty sandwiches, pastas, burgers, and salads. A kids menu offers standard choices like hot dogs, grilled cheese, or fried shrimp for less than $6. Prices are surprisingly moderate, with full meals starting at about $11 and going no higher than $22. You may need reservations for dinner, especially in season.

2 Biscayne National Park

35 miles S of Miami, 21 miles E of Everglades National Park

This unusual and underappreciated park celebrated its 30th birthday in 1998 when park rangers offered many free programs in order to entice more locals to visit. With only about 500,000 visitors each year (mostly boaters and divers), it is one of the least crowded parks in the country. Biscayne National Park is a little more difficult than most to access—more than 95% of its 182,00 acres are underwater.

Its significance was first formally acknowledged in 1968 when, in an unprecedented move and against intense pressure from developers, Pres. Lyndon Johnson signed a bill to conserve the barrier islands off South Florida's east coast as a national monument, a protected status that's a rung below national park. After being twice enlarged, once in 1974 and again in 1980, the waters and land surrounding the northernmost coral reef in North America became a full-fledged national park—the largest of its kind in the country.

To be fully appreciated, it should be thought of more as a preserve than a destination. I suggest using your time here to explore underwater life—but most of all, to relax.

The park's greatest dry attraction is the 29-acre island known as **Boca Chita Key,** once an exclusive haven for wealthy yachters. It was closed for years after the devastating hurricane of 1992 wiped out much of the tiny park. It took six years and nearly $2 million to restore the quaint island, which is an especially popular stopping point for boaters. Visitors can tour the island's restored historic buildings, including the county's second-largest lighthouse and a tiny chapel.

Also popular is Elliott Key, one of the park's 44 little islands, which contains a visitor center, hiking trails, and a campground. It's located about 9 miles from Convoy Point.

The park's small mainland mangrove shoreline and keys are best explored by boat. Its extensive reef system is renowned with divers and snorkelers from all over the world.

JUST THE FACTS

GETTING THERE & ACCESS POINTS The park's mainland entrance is Convoy Point, located 9 miles east of Homestead. To reach the park from Miami, take the Florida Turnpike to the Speedway Boulevard (Exit 6). Turn left, heading south $4^{1}/_{2}$ miles, then left again at North Canal Drive (SW 328th Street), and follow signs to the park. If you're coming from U.S. 1, whether you're heading north or south, turn east at North Canal Drive (SW 328th Street).

As I mentioned earlier, most of Biscayne National Park is accessible only to boaters. Mooring buoys abound, since it's illegal to anchor on coral. When no buoys are available, boaters must anchor on sand or on the new docks surrounding the small harbor off Boca Chita. Boats can dock overnight for $15. Even the most experienced boaters should carry updated nautical charts of the area, which are available at Convoy Point. The waters are often murky, making the abundant reefs and sandbars difficult to detect—and there are more interesting ways to spend a day than waiting for the tide to rise. There's a boat launch at adjacent Homestead Bayfront Park, and 66 slips on Elliott Key, available free on a first-come, first-served basis.

Transportation to and from the visitor center to the island costs $21 per person. Call for seasonal schedule (☎ **305/230-1100**).

VISITOR CENTERS & INFORMATION The **Convoy Point Visitor Center,** 9700 SW 328th St., at the park's main entrance (☎ **305/230-7275;** fax 305/230-1190), is the natural starting point for any venture into the park without a boat. In addition to providing comprehensive information on the park, rangers will show you a short video on request. Open Monday to Friday from 8:30am to 4:30pm and Saturday and Sunday from 8:30am to 5pm.

For information on transportation, glass bottom boat tours, and snorkeling and scuba diving expeditions, contact the park concessionaire, **Biscayne National Underwater Park, Inc.,** P.O. Box 1270, Homestead, FL 33030 (☎ **305/230-1100;** fax 305/230-1120; e-mail: captsaw@bellsouth.net). The company is open daily from 8:30am to 5pm and later in winter.

For more information contact **Biscayne National Park,** 9700 SW 328th St., Homestead, FL 33033-5634 (☎ **305/230-7275;** www.nps.gov/bisc).

ENTRANCE FEES & PERMITS Entrance to Biscayne National Park is free. There is a $15.00 per night overnight docking fee at Boca Chita Key Harbor and Elliott Key Harbor ($7.50 per night for holders of Golden Age or Golden Access Passports).

SEEING THE HIGHLIGHTS

Since Biscayne National Park is primarily underwater, the only way to truly experience it is with snorkel or scuba gear. You can rent a speedboat in Miami and cruise south for about an hour and a half, but a better idea would be to take one of the organized tours offered every day from the main visitor center. (See "Organized Tours," below). Beneath the surface, the aquatic universe pulses with multicolored life: Bright parrot and angelfish, gently rocking sea fans, and coral labyrinths abound. Before entering the water, be sure to apply waterproof sunblock—once you begin to explore, it's easy to lose track of time, and the Florida sun is brutal, even during winter.

Afterward, take a picnic out to Elliott Key and taste the crisp salt air blowing off the Atlantic. Or, head to Boca Chita, an intriguing island that was once the private playground of wealthy yachters.

SPORTS & OUTDOOR ACTIVITIES

CANOEING & KAYAKING Biscayne National Park offers excellent canoeing, both along the coast and across open water to nearby mangroves and artificial islands that dot the longest uninterrupted shoreline in the state of Florida. Since tides can be strong, only experienced canoeists should attempt to paddle far from shore. If you plan to go far, first obtain a tide table from the visitor center (see "Just the Facts," above) and paddle with the current. Free ranger-led canoe tours are scheduled for most weekend mornings; phone for information. You can rent a canoe at the park; rates are $8 an hour or $22 for 4 hours. Kayakers will have to bring their own boats but are welcome to explore the same quiet routes.

FISHING Ocean fishing is excellent year-round; many people cast their lines right from the breakwater jetty at Convoy Point. A fishing license is required (see "Entrance Fees, Permits & Regulations," under "Just the Facts," in section 1, for complete information). Bait is not available in Biscayne, but is sold in adjacent Homestead Bayfront Park. Stone crabs and Florida lobsters can be found here, but you're only allowed to catch these on the ocean side when they're in season. There are strict limitations on size, season, number, and method of take (including spear fishing) for both fresh- and saltwater fishing. The latest regulations are available at most marinas, bait and tackle shops, and at the park's visitor centers. Or you can contact the **Florida Game and Fresh Water Fish Commission,** Bryant Building, 620 S. Meridian St., Tallahassee, FL 32399-1600 (☎ **904/488-1960**).

HIKING & EXPLORING Since the majority of this park is underwater, hiking is not the main attraction here, but there are some interesting sights and trails. At Convoy Point you can walk along the 370-foot boardwalk, and along the half-mile jetty that serves as a breakwater for the park's harbor. From there you can usually see brown pelicans, little blue herons, snowy egrets, and a few exotic fish.

Elliott Key is accessible only by boat, but once you're there, you have two good trail options. True to its name, the Loop Trail makes a 1¹/₂-mile circle from the bay-side visitor center, through a hardwood hammock and mangroves, to an elevated ocean-side boardwalk. It's likely that you'll see purple and orange land crabs scurrying around the mangrove roots.

Reopened in 1998, Boca Chita Key was once the playground for wealthy tycoons; it still offers the peaceful beauty that attracted elite fishermen from cold climates.

Many of the historical buildings are still intact, including an ornamental lighthouse, which was thankfully never put into use. Since it was built on the western side of the island in the path of shallow reefs, boaters would have followed the beacon only to go aground.

Take advantage of the tours, usually led by an interpretative park ranger and available every Sunday at 1pm. The tour, including the boat trip, takes about 3 hours. The price for adults is $19.95 and $9.95 for children. However, call in advance to see if the sea is calm enough for the boat trip—boats won't run in rough seas.

SNORKELING & SCUBA DIVING   The clear, warm waters of Biscayne National Park are packed with colorful tropical fish that swim in the offshore reefs. If you don't have your own, or don't want to lug it the park, you can rent or buy snorkeling and scuba gear at the full service dive shop at Convoy Point. Rates are in line with dive shops on the mainland.

The best way to see the park from underwater is to take a snorkeling or scuba diving tour operated by **Biscayne National Underwater Park, Inc.** (☎ **305/230-1100**). Tours depart at 1:30pm daily, and last about 4 hours, and cost $27.95 per person including equipment. They also run two-tank dives for certified divers and provide instruction for beginners. The price is $35.50 per person. Dives depart at 9am Monday to Friday, at 8:30am weekends. Make your reservations in advance. The shop is open daily from 9am to 5pm.

SWIMMING   You can swim at the protected beaches of Elliott Key, Boca Chita Key, and adjacent Homestead Bayfront Park, but none of these beaches match the width or softness of other South Florida beaches. Check the water conditions before heading into the sea. Strong currents that make this a popular destination for windsurfers and sailors, can be dangerous even for strong swimmers.

WINDSURFING & SURFING   Strong and steady winds provide an excellent venue for windsurfers. Feel free to bring your own board and take on some of South Florida's most beautiful surf.

GLASS-BOTTOM BOAT TOURS

The best way to see the sites without getting wet is on the glass-bottom boat tour. **Biscayne National Underwater Park, Inc.** (☎ **305/230-1100**) offers daily trips to view some of the country's most beautiful coral reefs and tropical fish. Boats depart year-round from Convoy Point at 10am and stay out for about 3 hours. At $19.95 for adults, $17.95 for seniors, and $9.95 for children 12 and under, the scenic and informative tours are well worth the price. Boats carry fewer than 50 passengers; therefore, reservations are almost always necessary. The company also offers guided canoe, scuba, and snorkeling reef trips led by underwater naturalists.

WHERE TO STAY

There are no facilities available for overnight guests to this watery park. Most non-camping visitors come for an afternoon on their way to the Keys and stay overnight in nearby Homestead where there are many national chain hotels and other affordable lodgings. See "Where to Stay" in section 1 of this chapter.

CAMPING

Although you won't find hotels or lodges in Biscayne National Park, there are some of the state's most pristine campsites. Since they are completely inaccessible by motor vehicle, you'll be sure to avoid the mass of RVs so prevalent in so many of the state's other campgrounds. Sites are on Elliott Key and Boca Chita, and can only be reached by boat. If you don't have your own, call ☎ **305/230-1100** to arrange a drop-off. Transportation to and from the visitor center costs $21 per person. The best facilities are on the northeast side of newly reopened Boca Chita where there are brand-new showers, solar-powered rest rooms, and drinking fountains, as well as barbecue grills, and picnic tables. With a backcountry permit, available from the ranger station, you can pitch your tent somewhere even more private. Ask for a map at the visitor center, and be sure to bring plenty of bug spray. Sites cost $10 a night for up six persons staying in one or two tents. Reservations are not accepted.

3 Cruises & Other Caribbean Getaways

Many Miami visitors, seeking even more tropical wonders, often head out to sea on cruises, which run the gamut from gambling and fishing day trips to weeklong Caribbean adventures. A number of major cruising lines call the city home. Some of the most popular destinations from Miami are the Bahamian islands, where gambling is a big draw, or any of the dozens of nearby Caribbean islands.

If you want to catch a weekend in the Caribbean while you're in South Florida, but aren't enthralled with the idea of boat travel, there are a number of air packages available as well. Travel to Cuba is strictly prohibited from Miami (or anywhere in the United States) for all but those who have obtained licenses from the U.S. State Department, although many people choose to go there from Mexico, Jamaica, or The Bahamas.

The following sections aren't intended to be detailed descriptions of the cruising and package options available out of Miami and the Keys—that would fill up an entire book on its own—but they will give you a good overview of the cruising and package picture.

CRUISES

The Port of Miami is the world's busiest cruise-ship port, with a passenger load of close to three million annually. The popularity of these cruises shows no sign of tapering off, and the trend in ships is toward bigger, more luxurious liners. Usually all-inclusive, cruises offer value and simplicity compared to other vacation options. Most of the Caribbean-bound cruise ships sail weekly out of the Port of Miami. They are relatively inexpensive, can be booked without advance notice, and make for an excellent excursion.

All the shorter cruises are well equipped for gambling. Their casinos open as soon as the ship clears U.S. waters—typically 45 minutes after leaving port. Usually, four full-size meals are served daily, with portions so huge they're impossible to finish. Games, movies, and other onboard activities ensure you're always busy. Passengers can board up to 2 hours before departure for meals, games, and cocktails.

There are dozens of cruises from which to choose—from a 1-day excursion to a trip around the world. You can get a full list of options from the **Metro-Dade Seaport Department,** 1015 North America Way, Miami, FL 33132 (☎ **305/371-7678**). It's open Monday through Friday from 8am to 5pm.

The cruise lines and ships listed below offer 2- and 3-day excursions to the Caribbean, Key West, and other longer itineraries that change often. If you want more information, contact the individual line or, for Bahamas cruises, call the **Bahamas Tourist Office,** 19495 Biscayne Blvd., Suite 809, Aventura, FL 33180 (☎ **305/ 932-0051**). All passengers must travel with a passport or proof of citizenship for reentry into the United States.

Cruises & Other Caribbean Getaways

For detailed information on Caribbean cruises, pick up copies of *Frommer's Caribbean Cruises* and *Frommer's Caribbean Ports of Call.*

Carnival Cruise Lines (☎ 800/327-9501 or 305/599-2200; www.carnival.com) has 3- and 4-day cruises to Key West and the Caribbean as well as 7-day excursions that include stops in Mexico and Latin America. At press time, Carnival had four ships based at the Port of Miami, including *Destiny,* the world's largest. Cruises usually depart from Miami every Friday, Saturday, Sunday, and Monday. Prices range from $400 to $3,000, not including port charges, which can be as high as $100 per person.

Cunard (☎ 800/528-6273 or 305/463-3000; www.cunardline.com), which moved here in late 1997, is the most luxurious of Miami's lines, launching some of the most elegant ships ever to take to the seas. Its Miami ships include the *Queen Elizabeth 2,* the *Royal Viking Sun,* and the *Vistafjord.* Itineraries are usually at least 10 days long. Prices start at $1,300 per person.

Norwegian Cruise Line (☎ 800/327-7030 or 305/436-0866; www.ncl.com) has four ships based in Miami during the winter months and usually one in the summer. Ships go to Key West, The Bahamas, and the Western Caribbean. Its shortest cruises are 3 days; the longest—from Miami to France—is 15 days. Rates range from $349 per person for an inside cabin on the shortest cruises, to $4,500 per person for the very best cabin on the transcontinental journey.

Royal Caribbean Cruise Line (☎ 800/327-6700 or 305/539-6000; www.rccl.com), one of the premier lines in Miami, has about half a dozen ships departing Miami at any given time. The Port of Miami actually had to renovate three cruise terminals in 1999—at a price of $60 million—to accommodate Royal Caribbean's 142,000-ton ship *Voyager of the Seas.* The line mostly offers Caribbean cruises and some Bahamas destinations. The *Legend of the Seas* and the *Splendor of the Seas* offer 3- and 4-night Bahamas trips starting at $400. Longer trips can range from $1,600 per person to $7,500 for an 11-night cruise through the Caribbean.

FLIGHTS & WEEKEND PACKAGES

For those who want a quick getaway to the Caribbean without the experience of cruising, many airlines and hotels team up to offer extremely affordable weekend packages.

For example, one of The Bahamas' most elegant and family friendly resorts, The Atlantis on Paradise Island, hosts guests who like water sports or like to try their luck in its active casinos. Reasonably priced 3-day packages start at about $390, depending on departure date. It's generally cheaper to fly midweek. Flights on **Continental Airlines** (☎ 800/786-7202) or **Paradise Airlines** (☎ 800/231-0856) depart at least twice daily from Miami International. You can also choose to stay in the company's other luxurious resorts, The Paradise Beach Resort or the Ocean Club. Book package deals through **Paradise Island Vacations** (☎ 800/722-7466).

Other groups that arrange competitively priced packages include **American Flyaway Vacations,** operated by American Airlines (☎ 800/321-2121); **Bahamas Air** (☎ 800/222-4262 or 305/593-1910); **Chalks Ocean Airways** (☎ 305/371-8628); and the slightly rundown **Princess Casino** in Freeport (☎ 305/359-9898). Call for rates, since they vary dramatically throughout the year and also depend on what type of accommodations you choose.

11 The Keys

The drive from Miami to the Keys is the most scenic, relaxing drive imaginable. On either side of you, for miles ahead, lies nothing but emerald waters. The more than 400 islands that make up this 150-mile chain of the Keys are strung out across the Atlantic Ocean like loose strands of cultured pearls. Of course you want to go for the peaceful waters and the all-year-round warmth, but don't forget to explore the amazing sea life. Almost every species of fish in the most vibrant colors can be found swimming above the ocean's floor. You'll also discover the most abundant tropical and exotic plants, birds and reptiles known to man.

Despite the usually calm landscape, these rocky islands can be treacherous as the series of tropical storms, hurricanes, and tornadoes reminded residents in the summer and fall of 1998 when millions of dollars of damage was inflicted. The exposed coast has always posed dangers to those on land as well as at sea.

When Spanish explorers Juan Ponce de León and Antonio de Herrera sailed amid these craggy, dangerous rocks in 1513, they and their men dubbed the string of islands "Los Martires" (The Martyrs) because they thought the rocks looked like men suffering in the surf. It wasn't until the early 1800s that the larger islands were settled by rugged and ambitious pioneers, who amassed great wealth by salvaging cargo from ships sunk nearby. Actually, legend has it that these shipwrecks were sometimes caused by the "wreckers," who occasionally removed navigational markers from the shallows to lure unwitting captains aground. At the height of the salvaging mania (in the 1830s), Key West boasted the highest per capita income in the country.

However, wars, fires, hurricanes, mosquitoes, and the Depression took their toll on these resilient islands in the early part of this century, causing wild swings between fortune and poverty. In 1938, the spectacular Overseas Highway (U.S. 1) was finally completed atop the ruins of Henry Flagler's railroad, opening the region to tourists, who had never before been able to drive to this seabound destination.

These days, the highway connects more than 30 of the populated islands in the Keys. The hundreds of small, undeveloped islands that surround these "mainline" keys are known locally as the "backcountry" and are home to dozens of exotic animals and plants. To get to them, you must take to the water—a vital part of any trip to the Keys. Whether you fish, snorkel, dive, or just cruise, include some time on a boat in your itinerary; otherwise, you really haven't truly seen the Keys.

The Florida Keys

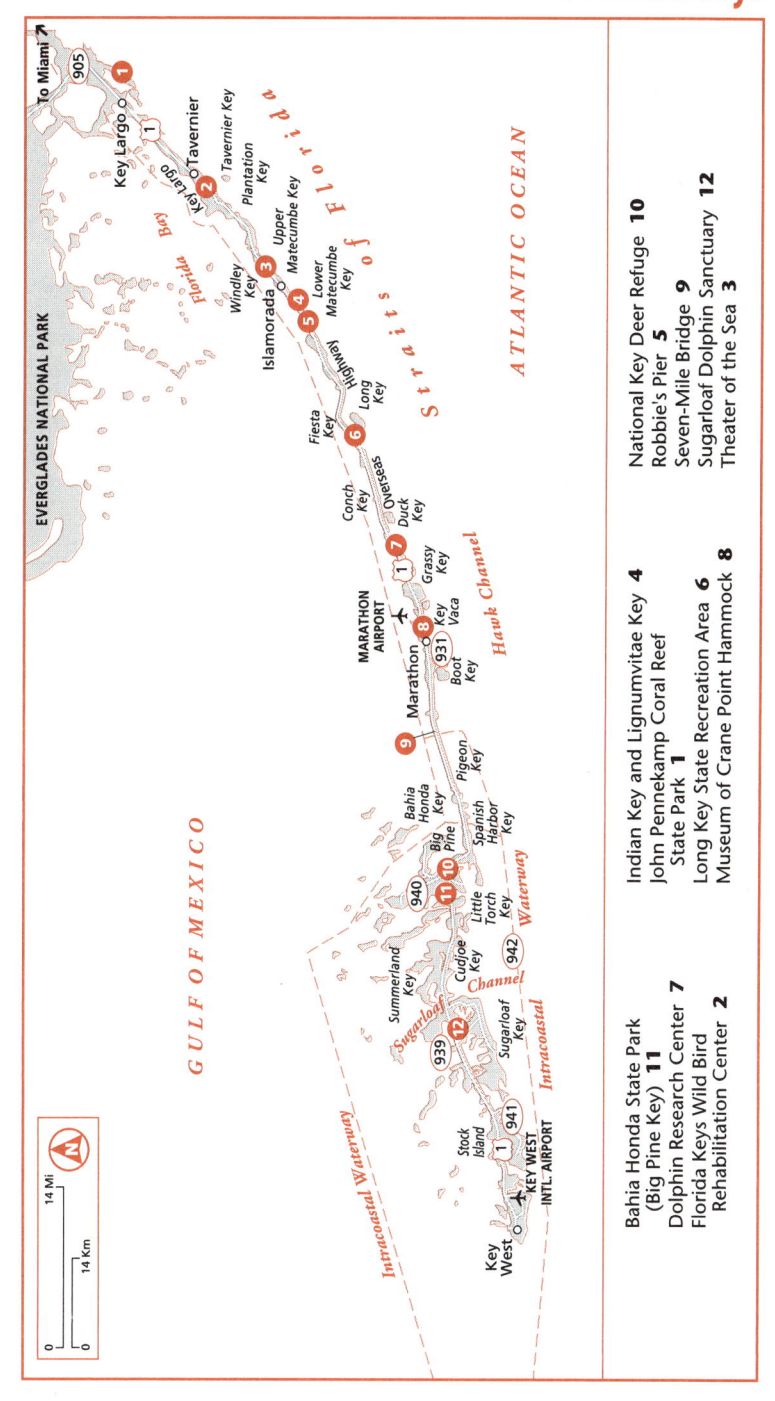

Bahia Honda State Park (Big Pine Key) **11**
Dolphin Research Center **7**
Florida Keys Wild Bird Rehabilitation Center **2**
Indian Key and Lignumvitae Key **4**
John Pennekamp Coral Reef State Park **1**
Long Key State Recreation Area **6**
Museum of Crane Point Hammock **8**
National Key Deer Refuge **10**
Robbie's Pier **5**
Seven-Mile Bridge **9**
Sugarloaf Dolphin Sanctuary **12**
Theater of the Sea **3**

221

The sea and the teeming life beneath it are the main attractions here. Warm, shallow waters nurture living coral that supports a complex delicate ecosystem of plants and animals—sponges, anemones, jellyfish, crabs, rays, sharks, turtles, snails, lobsters, and thousands of types of fish. This vibrant underwater habitat thrives on one of only two living tropical reefs in the entire North American continent (the other is off the coast of Belize). As a result, anglers, divers, snorkelers, and water-sports enthusiasts of all kinds come to explore. The heavy traffic has taken its toll on this fragile ecoscape, but efforts are underway to protect it.

Although the atmosphere throughout the Keys is that of a low-key beach town, don't expect to find many impressive beaches here. Especially since the tropical storms and hurricanes in 1998, there aren't any great beaches. Beaches are mostly found in a few private resorts and some small, sandy beaches in Bahia Honda State Park and in Key West (see "The Lower Keys," below). One great exception is Sombrero Beach in Marathon (see "Beaches" in "The Upper and Middle Keys," below).

The Keys are divided into three sections, both geographically and in this chapter. The Upper and Middle Keys are closest to the Florida mainland, so they are popular with weekend warriors who come by boat or car to fish, drink, or relax in towns like Key Largo, Islamorada, and Marathon. Further on, just beyond the impressive 7-mile bridge (which actually measures only 6.4 miles), are the Lower Keys, a small, unspoiled swath of islands teeming with wildlife. Here, in the protected regions of the Lower Keys is where you're most likely to catch sight of the area's many endangered animals. With patience, you may spot the rare eagle, egret, or Key deer. Also, keep an eye out for alligators, turtles, rabbits, and a huge variety of birds.

The last section of this chapter is devoted to the renowned island called Key West, literally at the end of the road. Made famous by the Nobel Prize–winning rogue Ernest Hemingway, this tiny island is the most popular destination in the Florida Keys, overrun with cruise-ship passengers and day-trippers, as well as franchises and T-shirt shops. More than 1.6 million visitors pass through each year. Still, you'll find in this "Conch Republic" a tightly knit community of permanent residents who cling fiercely to their live-and-let-live attitude—an atmosphere that has made Key West famously popular with painters, writers, and free spirited individuals.

EXPLORING THE KEYS BY CAR

After you have gotten off the Florida Turnpike and landed on U.S. 1, which is also known as the Overseas Highway (see "Getting There," under "Essentials," below), you'll have no trouble negotiating these narrow islands.

The Overseas Highway is the only main road connecting the Keys. The scenic, lazy drive from Miami to Key West is very enjoyable if you linger and explore the diverse towns and islands along the way. If you have the time, I recommend allowing at least 3 days to work your way down to Key West and 2 or more days once there.

Most of U.S. 1 is a narrow, two-lane highway, with some wider passing zones along the way. The speed limit is usually 55 miles per hour (35 to 45 miles per hour on Big Pine Key and in some commercial areas). Despite the protestations of island residents, there has been talk of expanding the highway, but by publication date, plans had not been finalized. Even on the narrow road, you can usually get from downtown Miami to Key Largo in just over an hour. If you're determined to drive straight through to Key West, allow at least 3^1/$_2$ hours. No matter what, avoid driving anywhere in the Keys on Friday afternoons or Sunday evenings, when the roads are jammed with weekenders from the mainland.

To find an address in the Keys, don't bother looking for building numbers; most addresses (except in Key West and parts of Marathon) are delineated by mile markers

(MM), small green signs on the roadside, which announce the distance from Key West. The markers start at number 127, just south of the Florida mainland. The zero marker is in Key West, at the corner of Whitehead and Fleming streets. Addresses in this chapter are accompanied by a mile marker (MM) designation when appropriate.

1 The Upper & Middle Keys: Key Largo to Marathon

58 miles SW of Miami

The Upper Keys are a popular, year-round refuge for South Floridians who take advantage of the islands' proximity to the mainland. This is the fishing and diving capital of America, and the swarms of outfitters and billboards never let you forget it.

Key Largo, once called "Rock Harbor" but renamed to capitalize on the success of the 1948 Humphrey Bogart film (which wasn't actually filmed there), is the largest Key and is more developed than its neighbors to the south. Dozens of chain hotels, restaurants, and tourist information centers service the many water enthusiasts who come to explore the nation's first underwater state park, John Pennekamp Coral Reef State Park, and its adjacent marine sanctuary. **Islamorada,** the unofficial capital of the Upper Keys, offers the area's best atmosphere, food, fishing, entertainment, and lodging. In these "purple isles," nature-lovers can enjoy nature trails, historic explorations, and big-purse fishing tournaments. **Marathon,** smack in the middle of the chain of islands, is one of the most populated Keys. It is part fishing village, part tourist center, and part nature preserve. This area's highly developed infrastructure includes resort hotels, a commercial airport, and a highway that expands to four lanes. Thankfully, high-rises have yet to arrive.

ESSENTIALS

GETTING THERE If you're coming from the Miami airport, take Le Jeune Road (NW 42nd Avenue) to Route 836 west. Follow signs to the Florida Turnpike South (about 7 miles). The turnpike extension connects with U.S. 1 in Florida City. Continue south on U.S. 1.

If you're coming from Florida's west coast, take Alligator Alley to the Miami exit and then turn south onto the turnpike extension. Have plenty of quarters for the tolls.

American Eagle (☎ 800/433-7300) has daily nonstop flights from Miami to Marathon, which is near the midpoint of the chain of Keys and at the very southern end of the area referred to here as the Upper and Middle Keys. Fares range depending on the season, from $88 to $336 round-trip.

Greyhound (☎ 800/231-2222; www.greyhound.com) has buses leaving Miami for Key Largo every day. At press time, the price was $13 one way. Seats fill up in season, so come early. It's first come, first served.

VISITOR INFORMATION Avoid the many "Tourist Information Centers" that dot the main highway. Most are private companies hired to lure visitors to specific lodgings or outfitters. You're better off sticking with the official, not-for-profit centers that are extremely well located and staffed. In particular, the **Key Largo Chamber of Commerce,** U.S. 1 at MM 106, Key Largo, FL 33037 (☎ 800/822-1088 or 305/451-1414; fax 305/451-4726; www.floridakeys.org) runs an excellent facility, with free direct-dial phones and plenty of brochures. Now headquartered in a handsome clapboard house, the chamber operates as an information clearinghouse for all of the Keys. It's open daily from 9am to 6pm.

The **Islamorada Chamber of Commerce,** in the Little Red Caboose, U.S. 1 at MM 82.5, P.O. Box 915, Islamorada, FL 33036 (☎ 800/322-5397 or 305/

664-4503; fax 305/664-4289; e-mail: islacc@ix.netcom.com), also offers maps and literature on the Upper Keys.

You can't miss the big blue visitors center at MM 53.5, the **Greater Marathon Chamber of Commerce,** 12222 Overseas Hwy., Marathon, FL 33050 (☎ **800/ 842-9580** or 305/743-5417; fax 305/289-0183; www.flakeys.com).

OUTDOOR SIGHTS & ACTIVITIES
BEACHES
Anne's Beach (at MM 73.5) is really more of a picnic spot than a full-fledged beach, but die-hard suntanners still congregate on this tiny strip of coarse sand which unfortunately was damaged beyond recognition during the series of storms in 1998. There are plans to reconstruct the boardwalk and huts, but at press time, work had not yet started.

A better choice for real beaching is **Sombrero Beach** in Marathon at the end of Sombrero Beach Road (near MM 50). This wide swath of uncluttered beachfront actually benefited from hurricane George in September 1998 with generous deposits of extra sand and a facelift courtesy of the Monroe County Tourist Development Council. More than 90 feet of sand is dotted with stands of palms, Australian Pines, and Royal Poncianas. There are some barbecue grills and clean bathrooms. A project is currently underway to add tiki huts, a pavilion, and a pier. Admission and parking at this little-known gem is free.

Indian Key and Lignumvitae Key. Off Indian Key Fill, Overseas Hwy., MM 79. ☎ **305/ 664-4815.**

If you are interested in seeing the Keys in their natural state, before modern development, you must venture off the highway and take to the water. Two backcountry islands that offer a glimpse of the "real" Keys are Indian Key and Lignumvitae Key. Visitors come to relax and enjoy the islands' colorful birds and lush hammocks (elevated pieces of land above a marsh).

Named for the lignum vitae ("wood of life") trees found there, **Lignumvitae Key** supports a virgin tropical forest, the kind that once thrived on most of the Upper Keys. Over the years, human settlers have imported "exotic" plants and animals to the Keys, irrevocably changing the botanical makeup of many backcountry islands and threatening much of the indigenous wildlife. Over the past 25 years, the Florida Department of Natural Resources has successfully removed most of the exotic vegetation, leaving this 280-acre site much as it existed in the 18th century. The island also holds a historic house built in 1919 that has survived numerous hurricanes.

Indian Key, a much smaller island on the Atlantic side of Islamorada, was occupied by Native Americans for thousands of years before European settlers arrived. The 10-acre historic site was also the original seat of Dade County before the Civil War. You can see the ruins of the previous settlement and tour the lush grounds on well-marked trails.

If you want to see both islands, plan to spend at least half a day. To get there, you can rent your own boat at **Robbie's Rent-A-Boat** (U.S. 1 at MM 77.5 on the bay side). Rates range from $60 for a 14-foot boat for half a day to $155 for an 18-foot boat for a full day. It's then a $1 admission fee to each island, which includes an informative hour-long guided tour by park rangers. This is a good option if you are a confident boater.

However, I also recommend taking Robbie's **ferry service** for $15, which includes the $1 park admission. Trips to both islands cost $25 per person. (If you are planning to visit only one island, make it Lignumvitae.) Not only is the ferry more economical, but it's easier to enjoy the natural beauty of the islands when you aren't negotiating the shallow reefs along the way. The runabouts, which carry up to six people, depart from Robbie's Pier Thursday to Monday at 9am and 1pm for Indian Key, and at 10am and 2pm for Lignumvitae Key. In the busy season, you may need to book as early as 2 days before departure. Call ☎ **305/664-4815** for information from the park service or ☎ **305/664-9814** for Robbie's.

Pigeon Key. East end of the 7-Mile Bridge near MM 47, Marathon. ☎ **305/743-5999.** Open 9am–5pm; shuttle tours run every hour from 10am–3pm. Admission $7.50; $5 for children under 13. Price includes shuttle transportation from the Visitor's Center.

Now open to the public, Pigeon Key, at the curve of the old bridge, is an intriguing historical site that has been under renovation since late 1993. This 5-mile island was once the camp for the crew that built the old railway in the early part of the century and later served as housing for the bridge builders. From here, your vista includes both bridges, many old wooden cottages, and a truly tranquil stretch of lush foliage and sea.

If you miss the shuttle tour or would rather walk or bike to the key, it's about 2.5 miles. Either way, you may want to bring a picnic to enjoy after a brief self-guided walking tour and museum visit. There is also an informative 28-minute video of the island's history offered every hour starting at 11:15am. Parking is available at the Knight's Key end of the bridge, at MM 48, or at the Visitor's Center at the old train car across the highway on the ocean side.

✪ **Seven-Mile Bridge.** Between MM 40 and 47 on U.S. 1. ☎ **305/289-0025.**

A stop at the Seven-Mile Bridge is a rewarding and relaxing break from the drive south. Built alongside the ruins of oil magnate Henry Flagler's incredible Overseas Railroad, the "new" bridge (between MM 40 and 47) is still considered an architectural feat. The wide arched span, completed in 1982 at a cost of more than $45 million, is impressive, its apex being the highest point in the Keys. The new bridge and its now-defunct neighbor provide an excellent vantage point from which to view the stunning waters of the Keys.

In the daytime, you may want to jog, walk, or bike along the scenic 4-mile stretch of old bridge, or join local fishermen, who catch barracuda, yellowtail, and dolphin on what is known as "the longest fishing pier in the world."

✪ **Tropical Crane Point Hammock.** 5550 Overseas Hwy. (MM 50), Marathon. ☎ **305/743-9100.** Admission $7.50 for adults; $6 for seniors over 64; $4 for students and free for children under 6. Mon–Sat 9am–5pm; Sun noon–5pm.

Crane Point Hammock is a little-known but very worthwhile stop, especially for those interested in the rich botanical and archaeological history of the Keys. This privately owned 64-acre nature area is considered one of the most important historical sites in the Keys. It contains what is probably the last virgin thatch palm hammock in North America. It also has an archaeological dig site with pre-Columbian and prehistoric Bahamian artifacts.

Now headquarters for the Florida Keys Land and Sea Trust, the hammock's impressive nature museum has simple, informative displays of the Keys' wildlife, including a walk-through replica of a coral-reef cave and life-size dioramas with tropical birds and Key deer. Kids can participate in art projects, see 6-foot-long iguanas, climb through a scaled-down pirate ship, and touch a variety of indigenous aquatic and landlubbing creatures.

The 10 "Keymandments"

The Keys have always attracted independent spirits, from Ernest Hemingway and Tennessee Williams to Jimmy Buffett, Mel Fisher, and Zane Grey. Writers, artists, and free thinkers have long drifted down here to escape.

Although you'll generally find a very laid-back and tolerant code of behavior in the Keys, some rules do exist. Be sure to respect the 10 "Keymandments" while you're here, or suffer the consequences.

- Don't anchor on a reef. (Reefs are alive.)
- Don't feed the animals. (They'll want to follow you home, and you can't keep them.)
- Don't trash our place (or we'll send Bubba to trash yours).
- Don't touch the coral. (After all, you don't even know them.)
- Don't speed (especially on Big Pine Key, where deer reside and tar-and-feathering is still practiced).
- Don't catch more fish than you can eat. (Better yet, let them go. Some of them support schools.)
- Don't collect conch. (This species is protected by Bubba.)
- Don't disturb the bird nests. (They find it very annoying.)
- Don't damage the sea grass. (And don't even think about making a skirt out of it.)
- Don't drink and drive on land or sea. (There's absolutely nothing funny about it.)

VISITING WITH THE ANIMALS

Dolphin Research Center. U.S. 1 at MM 59 (on the bay side), Marathon. ☎ **305/289-1121.** Swim with the Dolphins, $110 per person. Call on the first day of the month to book for the following month. Educational walking tours 5 times every day: 10am, 11am, 12:30pm, 2pm, and 3:30pm. Admission $12.50 adults; $10 seniors; $7.50 children 4–12; free for children 3 and under. (Prices are scheduled to increase.) MC, V. Daily 9:30am–4pm.

Don't miss this experience. If you've always wanted to touch, swim, or play with dolphins, this is the place to do it. Of the three such centers in the continental United States (all located in the Keys), the Dolphin Research Center is the most organized and informative. Although some people argue that training dolphins is cruel and selfish, the knowledgeable trainers at the Dolphin Research Center will tell you that the dolphins need stimulation and enjoy human contact. They certainly seem to. They nuzzle and seem to smile and kiss the lucky few that get to swim with them in the daily program. The "family" of 15 dolphins swims in a 90,000-square-foot natural saltwater pool carved out of the shoreline. If you can't get into the swim program, you can still take a walking tour of the facilities or sign up for a class in hand signals or feed the dolphins from docks. Children must be at least 12 years old to participate.

Florida Keys Wild Bird Rehabilitation Center. U.S. 1 at MM 93.6 Bayside, Tavernier. ☎ **305/852-4486.** Fax 305/852-3186 E-mail:fkwbc@reefnet.com. Donations suggested. Daily 8:30am–6pm.

Wander through lush canopies of mangroves on narrow wooden walkways to see some of the Keys' most famous residents—the large variety of native birds, including broadwing hawks, great blue and white herons, roseate spoonbills, white ibis, cattle egrets, and a number of pelicans. This not-for-profit center operates as a hospital for the many birds that have been injured. Come at feeding time, usually about 2pm, when you can watch the dedicated staff feed the hundreds of hungry beaks.

✪ **Robbie's Pier.** U.S. 1 at MM 77.5, Islamorada. ☎ **305/664-9814.** Admission $1. Bucket of fish $2. Daily 8am–5pm. Look for the Hungry Tarpon restaurant sign on the right after the Indian Key channel.

One of the best and definitely one of the cheapest attractions in the Upper Keys is the famed Robbie's Pier. Here, the fierce steely tarpons, a prized catch for backcountry anglers, have been gathering for the past 20 years. You may recognize these prehistoric-looking giants that grow up to 200 pounds; many are displayed as trophies and mounted on local restaurant walls. To see them live, head to Robbie's Pier, where tens and sometimes hundreds of these behemoths circle the shallow waters waiting for you to feed them. New kayak tours promise an even closer glimpse.

Theater of the Sea. U.S. 1 at MM 84.5, Islamorada. ☎ **305/664-2431.** Fax 305/664-8162. www.theaterofthesea.com. Admission $16.75 adults; $10.25 children 3–12. Dolphin swim $95; sea lion swim $65; stingray swim $40.00 per person. Must make a reservation. Daily 9:30am–4pm.

Established in 1946, the Theater of the Sea is one of the world's oldest marine zoos. Although the facilities could use some sprucing up, the dolphin and sea lion shows are entertaining and informative, especially for children who can also see sharks, sea turtles, and tropical fish. If you want to swim with dolphins and you haven't booked well in advance, this is the place you may be able to get in with just a few hours, or days, notice as opposed to the more rigid Dolphin Research Center in Marathon (see above). A recently introduced program allows visitors to swim with the sea lions or with the stingrays for $65 per person. Cat lovers will be thrilled to learn that the facility also serves as a haven for dozens of stray cats that have free run of the grounds and gift shop.

TWO EXCEPTIONAL STATE PARKS

One of the best places to discover the diverse ecosystem of the Upper Keys is in its most famous park, ✪ **John Pennekamp Coral Reef State Park,** located on U.S. 1 at MM 102.5, in Key Largo (☎ **305/451-1202**). Named for a former *Miami Herald* editor and conservationist, the 188-square-mile park is the nation's first undersea preserve. It's a sanctuary for part of the only living coral reef in the continental United States. The original plans for Everglades National Park included this part of the reef within its boundaries, but opposition from local homeowners made its inclusion politically impossible.

Because the water is extremely shallow, the 40 species of coral and more than 650 species of fish here are particularly accessible to divers, snorkelers, and glass-bottomed-boat passengers. You can't see the reef from the shore. To experience this park, visitors must get in the water. Your first stop should be the visitor center, which is full of educational fish tanks and a mammoth 30,000-gallon saltwater aquarium that re-creates a reef ecosystem. At the adjacent dive shop, you can rent snorkeling and diving equipment and join one of the boat trips that depart for the reef throughout the day. Visitors can also rent motorboats, sailboats, windsurfers, and canoes. The 2-hour glass-bottomed-boat tour is the best way to see the coral reefs if you refuse to get wet.

Canoeing around the park's narrow mangrove channels and tidal creeks is also popular. You can go on your own in a rented canoe, or in winter, sign up for a tour led by a local naturalist. Hikers have two short trails from which to choose: a boardwalk through the mangroves and a dirt trail through a tropical hardwood hammock.

Ranger-led walks are usually scheduled daily from the end of November to April. Phone for schedule information and reservations.

Park admission is $2.50 per vehicle for one occupant; for two or more, it is $4 per vehicle, plus 50¢ per passenger; $1.50 per pedestrian or bicyclist. Call ☎ **305/451-1621** for information. On your way into the park, ask the ranger for a map. Glass-bottomed-boat tours cost $13 for adults and $8.50 for children 11 and under. Snorkeling tours are $23.95 for adults and $18.95 for children 17 and under, including equipment. Sailing and snorkeling tours are $28.95 for adults, $23.95 for children 17 and under, including equipment but not tax. Canoes rent for $8 per hour or $28 for 4 hours. Reef boats (powerboats) rent for $25 to $45 per hour; call ☎ **305/451-6325**. Open daily from 8am to 5pm; phone for tour and dive times. Also, see below for more options on diving, fishing, and snorkeling these reefs.

Long Key State Recreation Area, U.S. 1 at MM 68, Long Key (☎ **305/664-4815**), is one of the best places in the Middle Keys for hiking, camping, and canoeing. This 965-acre site is situated atop the remains of an ancient coral reef. At the entrance gate, ask for a free flyer describing the local trails and wildlife.

There are two nature trails here perfect for hiking. The Golden Orb Trail is a 1-mile loop around a lagoon that attracts a large variety of birds. Rich in West Indian vegetation, this trail leads to an observation tower that offers good views of the mangroves. Layton Trail, the only part of the park that doesn't require an admission fee, is a quarter-mile shaded loop that goes through tropical hammocks before opening onto Florida Bay. The trail is well marked with interpretive signs; you can easily walk it in about 20 minutes.

The park's excellent 1 1/2-mile canoe trail is also short and sweet, allowing visitors to loop around the mangroves in about an hour—it couldn't be easier. You can rent canoes at the trailhead for about $4 per hour. Long Key is also a great spot to stop for a picnic if you get hungry on your way to Key West.

Railroad builder Henry Flagler created the Long Key Fishing Club here in 1906, and the waters surrounding the park are still popular with game fishers. In summer, sea turtles lumber onto the protected coast to lay their eggs.

Admission is $3.25 per car plus 50¢ per person (except for the Layton Trail, which is free). Open daily from 8am to sunset.

WATER SPORTS FROM A TO Z

There are literally hundreds of outfitters in the Keys who will set up all kinds of water activities, from cave dives to parasailing. If those recommended below are booked up or unreachable, ask the local chamber of commerce for a list of qualified members.

BOATING   In addition to the rental shops in the state parks, you will find dozens of outfitters along U.S. 1 offering a range of runabouts and skiffs for boaters of any experience level. **Captain Pip's,** U.S. 1 at MM 47.5, Marathon (☎ **800/707-1692** or 305/743-4403), rents 18.5- to 24-foot motorboats with 90 to 225 horsepower engines for $110 to $170 per day.

Robbie's Rent-a-Boat, U.S. 1 at MM 77.5, Islamorada (☎ **305/664-9814**), rents 14- to 27-foot motorboats with engines ranging from 15 to 200 horsepower. Boats cost $60 to $205 for a half day and $80 to $295 for a whole day.

CANOEING & KAYAKING   I can think of no better way to explore the uninhabited, shallow backcountry than by kayak or canoe. You can reach places big boats just can't get to because of their large draft. Sometimes manatees will cuddle up to the boats, thinking them another friendly species.

For a more enjoyable time, ask for a sit-inside boat—you'll stay drier. Also, a fiberglass (as opposed to plastic) boat with a rudder is generally more stable and easier to maneuver. Many area hotels rent kayaks and canoes to guests, as do the outfitters listed here. **Florida Bay Outfitters,** U.S. 1 at MM 104, Key Largo (☎ **305/451-3018**), rents canoes and sea kayaks for use in and around John Pennekamp Coral Reef State Park for $20 to $30 for a half day and $35 to $50 for a whole day. Canoes cost $25 for a half day and $35 for a whole day. At **Coral Reef Park Co.,** on U.S. 1 at MM 102.5, Key Largo (☎ **305/451-1621**), you can rent canoes and kayaks for $8 per hour, $28 for a half day; most canoes are sit-on-tops.

DIVING & SNORKELING The **Florida Keys Dive Center,** on U.S. 1 at MM 90.5, Tavernier (☎ **305/852-4599;** fax 305/852-1293), takes snorkelers and divers to the reefs of **John Pennekamp Coral Reef State Park** and environs every day. PADI training courses are also available for the uninitiated. Tours leave at 8am and 12:30pm and cost $25 per person to snorkel (including mask, snorkels, and fins) and $40 per person to dive (plus an extra $30 if you need to rent all the gear).

At **Hall's Dive Center & Career Institute,** U.S. 1 at MM 48.5, Marathon (☎ **305/743-5929;** fax 305/743-8168), snorkelers and divers can choose to dive at Looe Key, Sombrero Reef, Delta Shoal, Content Key, and Coffins Patch. Tours are scheduled daily at 9am and 1pm. If you mention this guide, you will get a special discounted rate of $30 per person to snorkel (including equipment) and $40 per person to dive. Choose from a wide and impressive array of equipment. Rental is extra.

With **Scuba Tours of Key Largo** (☎ **305/451-6391**), you can dive down to 20 feet attached to a comfortable breathing apparatus that really gives you the feeling of scuba diving without having to be certified. You can tour shallow coral reefs teeming with hundreds of colorful fish and plant life, from sea turtles to moray eels. Reservations are required; call to find out where and when to meet. A 2- to 3-hour underwater tour costs $70, including all equipment. If you have never dived before, you may require a 1-hour lesson in the pool, which costs an additional $40.

FISHING **Robbie's Partyboats & Charters,** on U.S. 1 at MM 84.5, Islamorada (☎ **305/664-8070** or 305/664-4196), located at the south end of the Holiday Isle Docks (see the Holiday Isle Resort in "Where to Stay," below), offers day and night deep-sea and reef fishing trips aboard a 65-foot party boat. Big-game–fishing charters are also available, and "splits" are arranged for solo fishers. Party-boat fishing costs $25 for a half day, $40 for a full day, and $30 at night. Charters run $400 for a half day, $600 for a full day; splits begin at $65 per person. Phone for information and reservations.

Bud n' Mary's Fishing Marina, on U.S. 1 at MM 79.8, Islamorada (☎ **800/742-7945** or 305/664-2461; fax 305/664-5592), one of the largest marinas between Miami and Key West, is packed with sailors offering guided backcountry fishing charters. This is the place to go if you want to stalk tarpon, bonefish, and snapper. If the seas are not too rough, deep-sea and coral fishing trips can be arranged. Charters cost $400 to $500 for a half-day, $600 to $800 for a full day, and splits begin at $125 per person.

The Bounty Hunter, 15th Street, Marathon (☎ **305/743-2446**), offers full- and half-day outings. For years, Capt. Brock Hook's huge sign has boasted no fish, no pay. You're guaranteed to catch something. Choose your prey from shark, barracuda, sailfish, or whatever else is running. Prices are $350 for a half-day, $375 for three-fourths day, and $450 for a full day. Rates are for groups of no more than six people.

SHOPPING

On your way to the Keys, you'll find an outlet center, the **Keys Factory Shops** (☎ **305/248-4727**), at 250 E. Palm Dr. (where the Florida Turnpike meets U.S. Hwy. 1), in Florida City. The center holds more than 60 stores, including Nike Factory Store, Bass Co. Store, Levi's, OshKosh, and Izod. Travelers can pick up a free discount coupon booklet called the Come Back Pack from the Customer Service Center. The outlet is open daily until 9pm, except Sunday when it closes at 6pm.

The Upper and Middle Keys have no shortage of tacky tourist shops selling shells and T-shirts and other hokey souvenirs, but for real Keys-style shopping, check out the **weekend flea markets.** One of the best is held every Saturday and Sunday bayside at MM 103.5 (☎ **305/451-0677**). Dozens of vendors open their stalls from 9am until 4 or 5pm, selling every imaginable sort of antiques, T-shirts, plants, shoes, books, toys, and games, as well as a hearty dose of good old-fashioned junk.

A mecca for fishing and sports enthusiasts, **The World Wide Sportsman** (☎ **305/664-4615**) opened in late 1997 at MM 81.5. It's not only the largest fishing store in the Keys, but also a meeting place for anglers from all over the world. Every possible gizmo and gadget, plus hundreds of T-shirts, hats, books, and gift items are displayed in its more than 25,000 square feet. The salespeople are knowledgeable and eager to help. Travel specialists can even arrange for charter trips and backcountry tours. The store is open daily from 7am until 8:30pm.

WHERE TO STAY

U.S. 1 is lined with chain hotels in all price ranges. In the Upper Keys, the best moderately priced options are the **Holiday Inn Key Largo Resort & Marina,** U.S. 1 at MM 99.7 (☎ **800/THE-KEYS** or 305/451-2121), and right next door, at MM 100, the **Ramada Limited Resort & Casino** (☎ **800/THE-KEYS** or 305/451-3939). Both hotels share three pools and a casino boat; however, the Ramada is cozier and offers slightly cheaper rates. Also, the **Best Western Suites at Key Largo,** 201 Ocean Dr., MM 100 (☎ **800/462-6079** or 305/451-5081), is just 3 miles from John Pennekamp Coral Reef State Park. Another good option in the Upper Keys is **Islamorada Days Inn,** U.S. 1 at MM 82.5 (☎ **800/DAYS-INN** or 305/664-3681). In the Middle Keys, the **Howard Johnson** at 13351 Overseas Hwy., MM 54 in Marathon (☎ **800/321-3496** or 305/743-8550), also offers reasonably priced ocean-side rooms.

Since the real beauty of the Keys lies mostly beyond the highways, there is no better way to see this area than by boat. Why not stay in a floating hotel? Especially if traveling with a group, houseboats can be economical. To rent a houseboat, call Ruth and Michael Sullivan at **Smilin' Island Houseboat Rentals** (MM 99.5), Key Largo, FL (☎ **305/451-1930**). Rates are from $750 to $1,350 for 3 nights. Boats accommodate up to six people.

For land options, consider these recommendations, grouped first by price, and then geographically from north to south.

VERY EXPENSIVE

Cheeca Lodge. U.S. 1 at MM 82 (P.O. Box 527), Islamorada, FL 33036. ☎ **800/327-2888** or 305/664-4651. Fax 305/664-2893. www.cheeca.com. 203 units. A/C MINIBAR TV TEL. Winter $295–$650 double; $400 suite. Off-season $195–$430 double; $285 suite. AE, CB, DC, DISC, MC, V.

One of the better places to stay in the Upper Keys, Cheeca has been hosting celebrities, royalty, and politicians since its opening in 1949. Guests now enjoy the luxury of the Cheeca's freshly renovated and remodeled rooms. All of the 203 units offer all the amenities of a world-class resort in a very laid-back setting. You may not feel compelled to leave the sprawling grounds, but it's good to know the hotel is conveniently situated near the best restaurants and nightlife. Located on 27 acres of beachfront property, this rambling resort is known for its excellent sports facilities, including one of the only golf courses in the Upper Keys.

All rooms are spacious and have small balconies. The nicer ones overlook the ocean and have large marble bathrooms.

Dining/Diversions: The Atlantic's Edge restaurant is one of the best in the Upper Keys (see "Where to Dine," below). A pool bar and comfortable lounge offer more casual options throughout the day and evening.

Amenities: Concierge, room service, dry-cleaning and laundry services, in-room massage, newspaper delivery, baby-sitting, express checkout, valet parking, free coffee and refreshments in lobby. Kitchenettes, VCRs and video rentals, three outdoor heated pools, kids' pool, five hot tubs, beach, access to nearby health club, Jacuzzi, bicycle rental, 9-hole, par-3 golf course, children's nature programs, conference rooms, car-rental desk, sundeck, six lighted tennis courts, water-sports equipment rental, tour desk, nature trail, boutiques.

✪ **Hawk's Cay Resort.** 61 Hawk's Cay Blvd. at MM 61, Duck Key, Fl 33050. ☎ **888/ 814-9104** or 305/743-7000. Fax 305/743-5215. www.hawkscay.com. 176 units A/C TV TEL. Winter $230–$385 double; $435–$875 suite. Off-season $190–$260 double; $335–$775 suite. AE, DC, DISC, MC, V.

Located on its own 60-acre island in the Middle Keys, this resort has a relaxed and casual island atmosphere. It offers an impressive array of recreational activities—sailing, fishing, snorkeling, and waterskiing to name a few—and the unique opportunity to have your own dolphin encounter in a special pool. (You'll need to reserve a spot well in advance for the dolphins—there's a waiting list.) The rooms are large and newly renovated with island-style furniture and bright tropical bedspreads and curtains. Every room opens onto a private balcony with ocean or tropical views. The rooms are similar and price varies with the view. The large bathrooms are well appointed and have granite counter tops. A newly built clubhouse has an exercise room, whirlpool, and steam room. In addition to a lagoon and several pools for families, the resort boasts a secluded pool for adults only. There's an extensive program of organized children's activities to keep your little ones busy while you relax.

Dining/Diversions: Three good restaurants and a lounge offer a wide range of food, from Italian to seafood. The marina Ship's Store is stocked with snacks and basic groceries. A lively lounge features live music every evening and most weekend afternoons.

Amenities: Concierge, room service, overnight laundry, in-room massage, express checkout, transportation to airport and golf course, free refreshments in lobby. Outdoor heated pool, a new adults-only private pool, beach, small fitness room, Jacuzzi, nearby golf course, sundeck, eight tennis courts (two lighted), water-sports equipment, bicycle rental, game room, children's center or programs, self-service laundry, marina store and gift shop, conference rooms, car-rental desk.

Westin Beach Resort. U.S. 1 at MM 97, Key Largo, FL 33037. ☎ **800/728-2738,** 800/539-5274, or 305/852-5553. Fax 305/852-8669. 200 units. A/C MINIBAR TV TEL. Winter $159–$339 double; from $389 Jacuzzi suite. Off-season $139–$299 double; from $289 Jacuzzi suite. AE, CB, DC, DISC, MC, V.

Under new ownership since 1996, this resort has benefited from an extensive $3 million renovation. In addition to an overall rehab, the resort distinguishes itself by its secluded yet convenient location—it's set back on 12 private acres of gumbo-limbo and hardwood trees, making it invisible from the busy highway. Despite its hideaway location, the sprawling pink-and-blue four-story complex is surprisingly large. A three-story atrium lobby is flanked by two wings that face 1,200 feet of the Florida Bay. The large guest rooms have tasteful tropical decor and private balconies. The suites are twice the size of standard rooms and have better-quality wicker furnishings and double-size balconies. Ten suites feature private spa tubs and particularly luxurious bathrooms with adjustable showerheads, bidets, and lots of room for toiletries.

Dining/Diversions: The hotel restaurant offers terrific views of the bay and surf-and-turf dinners nightly. A casual cafe serves breakfast, lunch, and dinner both inside and outdoors. A poolside snack bar serves sandwiches, salads, and refreshments. The top-floor lounge has a dance floor and a pool table.

Amenities: Concierge, 24-hour room service, newspaper delivery, dry-cleaning and laundry service, in-room massage, twice-daily maid service, baby-sitting, secretarial services, express checkout, free morning coffee in lobby, valet parking. Two outdoor heated swimming pools, beach, small but modern fitness room with Universal equipment, Jacuzzi, nature trails, two lighted tennis courts, water-sports equipment rental, children's programs, conference rooms, hair salon.

Expensive

Jules' Undersea Lodge. 51 Shoreland Dr., Key Largo, FL 33037. ☎ **305/451-2353.** Fax 305/451-4789. www.Jul.com. 1 unit. A/C TV TEL. $225–$325 per person. Rates include breakfast and dinner as well as all equipment and unlimited scuba diving in the lagoon. AE, DISC, MC, V. From U.S. 1 south, at MM 103.2, turn left onto Transylvania Ave., across from the Central Plaza shopping mall.

Originally built as a research lab in the 1970s, this small underwater compartment now operates as a single-room hotel. As expensive as it is unusual, Jules' is most popular with diving honeymooners. The lodge rests on pillars on the ocean floor. To get inside, guests swim under the structure and pop up into the unit through a 4-by-6-foot "moon pool" that gurgles soothingly all night long. The 30-foot-deep underwater suite consists of a bedroom and galley and sleeps up to six. There is a television and VCR. Also, room service will bring breakfast, lunch, and daily newspapers in waterproof containers at no extra charge. Needless to say, this novelty is not for everyone.

Marriott Key Largo Bay Beach Resort. 103800 Overseas Hwy. at MM 103, Key Largo, FL 33037. ☎ **800/932-9332** or 305/453-0000. Fax 305/453-0093. www.baybeach@reefnet.com. 150 units. A/C MINIBAR TV TEL. Winter $209–$269 double; $500 suite. Off-season $139–$179 double; $250 suite. AE, DC, CB, MC, V.

When this mammoth chain resort was built in 1993, many thought the sleepy little island town would be forever spoiled. On the contrary, this pristine, two-story Marriott created some major competition for the area's older resorts and the run-down 1950s motels, resulting in an overall upgrade of the neighboring accommodations. While it is hardly quaint, the amenities-laden, 17-acre complex has everything an active or resting traveler could want, including a decent-sized beach. Guests can now enjoy the new European health spa, a nine-hole minigolf course, and new tennis courts. All guests are welcome to sail for free on a gambling cruise ship that anchors in international waters from 2pm until 2am daily. Rooms are decorated in a pleasant (if generic) tropical style and include extras such as coffeemakers, hair dryers, and safes. Most rooms (all but 22) also offer balconies overlooking the stunning Florida bay. For real pampering, consider the enormous suites, which can easily sleep a family of five. All have large wraparound terraces and large sitting areas. With its rates being slightly cheaper than the nearby Westin and Checca Lodge, you'll find it a good value.

Dining/Diversions: A bay-side grill offers casually elegant dining, and an outdoor tiki bar has snacks and cocktails throughout the afternoon and evening.

Amenities: Concierge, room service, dry-cleaning and laundry services, in-room massage, newspaper delivery, baby-sitting, express checkout. Large outdoor pool, Jacuzzi, three small beaches, VCRs on request, gym, bicycle rental, conference rooms, sundeck, access to nearby tennis and racquetball courts, water-sports equipment rental, business center, tour desk, children's programs, game room, nature trail, boutiques.

✪ **The Moorings.** 123 Beach Rd. near MM 81.5 on the ocean side, Islamorada, FL 33036. ☎ **305/664-4708.** Fax 305/664-4242. 17 cottages. A/C TV TEL. Winter $165–$350 oceanfront cottages; $2,450–$6,300 weekly. Off-season $150–$275 oceanfront cottages; $1,900–$4,500 weekly. 2-night minimum for smaller cottages; 1-week minimum for larger cottages. MC, V.

Staying at The Moorings is more like staying at your second home than at a hotel. You'll never see another soul on this 18-acre resort if you choose not to. There isn't even maid service unless you request it. The romantic whitewashed houses are spacious and modestly decorated with funky island prints, bamboo, and tropical motifs. All have full kitchens and most have washers and dryers. Some have CD players and VCRs; ask when you book. The real reason to come to this cool resort is to relax on the more than 1,000-foot beach (one of the only real beaches around). There is a simple hard tennis court, a few kayaks and windsurfers, but absolutely no motorized water vehicles. There is no room service or restaurant (although Morada Bay across the street is excellent). This is a place for people who like each other a lot. Leave the kids at home unless they are extremely well behaved and not easily bored.

Amenities include laundry and dryers, full kitchens, some VCRs, large sandy beach, sundeck, large pool, boats, and jogging trails.

MODERATE

Banana Bay Resort & Marina. U.S. 1 at MM 49.5, Marathon, FL 33050. ☎ **800/BANANA-1** or 305/743-3500. Fax 305/743-2670. www.bananabay.com. 60 units. A/C TV TEL. Winter $115–$210 double. Off-season $85–$160 double. Rates include continental breakfast. Weekend and 3- and 7-night packages available. AE, DC, DISC, MC, V.

It doesn't look like much from the sign-cluttered Overseas Highway, but when you enter the lush grounds of Banana Bay, you will realize you're in one of the most bucolic and best-run properties in the Upper Keys. Built in the early 1950s as a fishing camp, the resort is a maze of pink-and-white two-story buildings hidden among banyans and palms. Guest rooms are very similar, but those with better views are more expensive. The rooms are moderately sized, and many have private balconies where you can enjoy your complimentary coffee and newspaper every morning.

The restaurant serves breakfast, lunch, and dinner by the pool or in a kitschy old dining room. A waterfront tiki bar offers great sunset views. Head down to the marina to sign up for charter fishing, sailing, and diving. Kids will enjoy the small game room and free use of bicycles.

✪ **Conch Key Cottages.** Near U.S. 1 at MM 62.3, Marathon, FL 33050. ☎ **800/330-1577** or 305/289-1377. Fax 305/743-8207. www.floridakeys.net/conchkeycottages. 12 cottages. A/C TV. Dec 15–Sept 8 $105–$246. Sept 9–Dec 14 $74–$215. DISC, MC, V.

Occupying its own private microisland just off U.S. 1, Conch Key Cottages is a unique and comfortable hideaway run by live-in owners Ron Wilson and Wayne Byrnes, who are constantly fixing and adding to their unique property. This is a place to get away from it all; the cottages aren't close to much, except maybe one or two interesting eateries. The cabins, which were built at different times over the past 40 years, overlook their own stretch of natural, but very small, private beach and have screened-in porches and cozy bedrooms and bathrooms. Each has a hammock and barbecue grill. Request one of the new two-bedroom cottages, completed in 1997—especially if you are traveling with the family. They are the most spacious and well designed, practically tailor-made for couples or families. On the other side of the pool are a handful of efficiency apartments that are similarly outfitted, but enjoy no beach frontage. All have fully equipped kitchens. There's also a small heated freshwater pool.

Faro Blanco Marine Resort. 1996 Overseas Hwy., U.S. 1 at MM 48.5, Marathon, FL 33050. ☎ **800/759-3276** or 305/743-9018. Fax 305/866-5235. 123 units, 31 houseboats with 4 units each. A/C TV TEL. Winter $89–$150 cottage; $109–$200 houseboat; $185 lighthouse; $267–$327 condo. Off-season $79–$119 cottage; $99–$178 houseboat; $145 lighthouse; $215–$263 condo. AE, DISC, MC, V.

Spanning both sides of the Overseas Highway and all on waterfront property, this huge, two-shore marina and hotel complex offers something for every taste. Freestanding, camp-style cottages with a small bedroom are the resort's least expensive accommodations, but are in dire need of rehabilitation. Old appliances and a musty odor also make them the least desirable units on the property.

The houseboats are the best choice and value. Permanently tethered in a tranquil marina, these white rectangular boats look like floating mobile homes and are uniformly clean, fresh, and recommendable. They have colonial American-style furnishings, fully equipped kitchenettes, front and back porches, and water, water everywhere. The boats are so tightly moored, you hardly move at all, even in the roughest weather.

Finally, there are two unusual rental units located in a lighthouse on the pier. Circular staircases, unusually shaped rooms and showers, and nautical decor make it a unique place to stay, but some guests might find it claustrophobic. Guests in any of the accommodations can enjoy the Olympic-size pool, any of the four casual restaurants, a fully equipped dive shop, barbecue and picnic areas, and a playground.

Holiday Isle Resort. U.S. 1 at MM 84, Islamorada, FL 33036. ☎ **800/327-7070** or 305/664-2321. Fax 305/664-2703. www.holidayisle.com. 199 units. A/C TV TEL. Winter $85–$425 double. Off-season $65–$350 double. AE, CB, DISC, MC, V.

A huge resort complex encompassing five restaurants, several lounges, tiki huts, a large marina, many retail shops, and four distinct (if not distinctive) hotels, the Holiday Isle is one of the biggest resorts in the Keys. It attracts a spring-break kind of crowd year-round. Its Tiki Bar claims to have invented the rum runner drink (151-proof rum, blackberry brandy, banana liqueur, grenadine, and lime juice), and there's no reason to doubt it. Hordes of partiers are attracted to the resort's nonstop merrymaking, live music, and beachfront bars. As a result, some of the accommodations can be noisy.

Rooms can be bare-bones budget to oceanfront luxury, as the broad range of prices reflect. Even the nicest rooms could use a good cleaning. El Captain and Harbor Lights, two of the least expensive hotels on the property, are both austere. Like the other hotels here, rooms could use a thorough rehab. Howard Johnson's, another Holiday Isle property, is a little farther from the action and a tad more civilized. If you plan to be here for a few days, choose an efficiency or a suite; both have kitchenettes. Guests can choose among two outdoor heated pools and a kids' pool. They also offer water-sports equipment rental, gift boutiques, and a shopping arcade.

✪ **Kona Kai Resort & Gallery.** 97802 Overseas Hwy. (U.S. 1 at MM 97.8), Key Largo, FL 33037. ☎ **800/365-7829** or 305/852-7200. Fax 305/852-4629. www.konakairesort.com.

11 units. A/C TV TEL Winter $179–$220 double; $216–$566 suite. Off-season $105–$119 double; $135–$315 suite. 3- to 4-night minimum stay usually required. AE, DISC, MC, V.

Unique in the Upper Keys, this little haven is both casual and elegant—thanks to a 3-year overhaul completed under the supervision of owners, Joe Harris an his wife, Ronnie, former executives with NBC television. The quaint, simply furnished rooms dot the lushly landscaped 2-acre property, which boasts a large variety of native vegetation like palms, bougainvillea, and ferns, plus an impressive collection of fruit-bearing trees, such as carambola, passion fruit, banana, key lime, guava, and coconut. Lounge chairs, hammocks, a Jacuzzi, and compact artificial beach are available for those who just want to relax, while a small lighted tennis court, heated pool, Ping-Pong table, volleyball court, and all kinds of water sports are available for those who are more active. For the adventurous, Joe and Ronnie will organize excursions to the Everglades, the backcountry, or wherever. No phones in the rooms and a 4-day minimum stay requirement in the winter make relaxing imperative. All the rooms are very private and simply furnished—you won't find anything like hair dryers or stereos. Smoking is not permitted on the property. An art gallery featuring work of local painters, photographers, and sculptors doubles as the property's office and lobby. Even if you are not staying here, stop in to see the artwork.

Lime Tree Bay Resort Motel. U.S. 1 at MM 68.5 in Layton, Long Key, FL 33001. ☎ **800/ 723-4519** or 305/664-4740. Fax 305/664-0750. 30 units. A/C TV TEL. Winter $102–$235 double. Off-season $80–$180 double. AE, DC, DISC, MC, V.

The Lime Tree Bay Resort is the only hotel in the tiny town of Layton (pop. 183). Midway between Islamorada and Marathon, the hotel is only steps from Long Key State Recreation Area. Motel rooms and efficiencies have tiny bathrooms with standing showers, but are clean and well maintained. The best deal is the two-bedroom bayview apartment. The large living area with new fixtures and furnishings leads out to a large private deck where you can enjoy a view of the gulf from your hammock. A full kitchen and two full bathrooms make it a comfortable space for six people.

This affordable little hideaway has all the amenities you could want, including shuffleboard, tennis, a small pool, water sports, and a little cafe with a small but decent menu. It's situated on a very pretty piece of waterfront graced with hundreds of mature palm trees and lots of other tropical foliage.

INEXPENSIVE

Bay Harbor Lodge. 97702 Overseas Highway; U.S. 1 at MM 97.7 (off the southbound lane of U.S. 1), Key Largo, FL 33037. ☎ **305/852-5695.** 16 units. A/C TV TEL. Winter $65–$145 double. Off-season $78–$98 efficiency; $85–$125 double. MC, V.

A small, simple retreat that's big on charm, the Bay Harbor Lodge is an extraordinarily welcoming place. The lodge is far from fancy, and the wide range of accommodations are not created equal. The motel rooms are small and ordinary in decor, but even the least expensive is recommendable. The efficiencies are larger motel rooms with fully equipped kitchenettes. The oceanfront cottages are larger still, have full kitchens, and represent one of the best values in the Keys. The vinyl-covered furnishings and old-fashioned wallpapers won't win any design awards, but elegance isn't what the "real" Keys are about. The 1^1/$_2$ lush acres of grounds are planted with banana trees and have an outdoor heated pool and several small barbecue grills. Guests are free to use the rowboats, paddleboats, canoes, kayaks, and snorkeling equipment. Bring your own beach towels.

✪ **Ragged Edge Resort.** 243 Treasure Harbor Rd. (near MM 86.5) Islamorada, FL 33036. ☎ **800/436-2023** or 305/852-5389. 11 units. A/C TV TEL. Winter $69–$99 motel rooms or efficiencies; $115 studio apt; $179 2-bed/2-bathroom apt. Off-season $48–$70 motel rooms or efficiency; $81 studio apt; $125 2-bed/2-bathroom apt. AE, MC, V.

This small property's 11 units are spread out along more than half a dozen gorgeous, grassy waterfront acres. All are immaculately clean and comfortable, and most are outfitted with full kitchens and tasteful furnishings. There's no bar, restaurant, or staff to speak of, but the retreat's affable owner, Jackie Barnes, is happy to lend you bicycles or good advice on the area's offerings. A large dock attracts boaters and a large variety of local and migratory birds.

CAMPING

John Pennekamp Coral Reef State Park. U.S. 1 at MM 102.5 (P.O. Box 487), Key Largo, FL 33037. ☎ **305/451-1202.** 47 campsites. Reservations can be made in advance. $24–$26 per site for camping. $4 per vehicle. (50¢ for each additional person.) Yearly permits and passes available. DISC, MC, V.

One of Florida's best parks (see above), Pennekamp offers 47 well-separated campsites, half of which are available by advance reservation, the rest distributed on a first-come, first-served basis. The car-camping sites are small but well equipped with bathrooms and showers. A small lagoon nearby attracts many large wading birds. Reservations are held until 5pm, and the park must be notified of late arrival by phone on the check-in date. Pennekamp opens at 8am and closes around sundown. No pets.

Long Key State Park. U.S. 1 at MM 67.5 (P.O. Box 776), Long Key, FL 33001. ☎ **305/664-4815.** 60 oceanfront sites. $24–$26 per site for 1 to 4 people. $3.25 per vehicle. Special permits and passes available. DISC, MC, V.

The Upper Keys' other main state park is more secluded than its northern neighbor—and more popular. All sites are located ocean-side and surrounded by narrow rows of trees and nearby toilet and bathroom facilities. Reserve well in advance, especially in winter.

WHERE TO DINE

Although not known as a culinary hot spot, the Upper and Middle Keys do offer some excellent restaurants, most of which specialize in seafood. Often, visitors (especially those who fish) take advantage of accommodations that have kitchen facilities and cook their own meals. Also, most restaurants will clean and cook your catch for a nominal charge.

VERY EXPENSIVE

✪ **Atlantic's Edge.** In the Cheeca Lodge, U.S. 1 at MM 82, Islamorada. ☎ **305/664-4651.** Fax 305/664-5427. Reservations recommended. Main courses $20–$36. AE, CB, DC, DISC, MC, V. Daily 5:30–10pm. SEAFOOD/REGIONAL.

Ask for a table by the oceanfront window to feel really privileged at this, the most elegant restaurant in the Keys. Although the service and food are first class, don't get dressed up—a sport coat for men will be fine, but isn't necessary. You can choose from an innovative, varied menu, which offers several choices of fresh fish, steak, chicken, and pastas. The crab cakes, made with stone crab when in season, are the very best in the Keys; served on a warm salad of baby greens with a mild sauce of red peppers, they're the stuff cravings are made of. Other excellent dishes include a Thai-spiced fresh baby snapper and the vegetarian angel-hair pasta with mushrooms, asparagus, and peppers in a rich broth. Service can sometimes be less than efficient, but is always courteous and professional.

Expensive

Barracuda Grill. U.S. 1 at MM 49.5 (bay side), Marathon. ☎ **305/743-3314.** Reservations not accepted. Main courses $15–$37. AE, MC, V. Mon–Sat 6–10pm. BISTRO/SEAFOOD.

Owned by Lance Hill and his wife, Jan (who used to be a sous chef at Little Palm Island), this casual spot serves excellent seafood, steaks, and chops. It's too bad it's open only for dinner. Some of the favorite dishes are old-fashioned meat loaf, classic beef Stroganoff, rack of lamb, and seafood stew. In addition, this small barracuda-decorated restaurant features a well-priced American wine list with a vast sampling of California vintages.

✪ **Marker 88.** U.S. 1 at MM 88 (bay side), Islamorada. ☎ **305/852-9315.** Reservations suggested. Main courses $14–$33. AE, DC, DISC, MC, V. Tues–Sun 5–11pm. SEAFOOD/REGIONAL.

An institution in the Upper Keys, Marker 88 has been pleasing locals and visitors since it opened in the early 1970s. Chef-owner Andre Mueller fuses tropical fruit and fish with such interesting items as crabmeat stuffing, asparagus, tomatoes, lemons, olives, capers, and mushrooms to make the most delectable and innovative seafood dishes imaginable. He has truly created a "gourmet" restaurant using a wide range of standard fare, tinged with his take on nouvelle cuisine. Taking full advantage of his island location, Andre offers dozens of seafood selections, including Keys lobster, Bahamas conch, Everglades frogs' legs, Florida Bay stone crabs, Gulf Coast shrimp, and an impressive variety of fish from around the country. After you've figured out what kind of seafood to have, you can choose from a dozen styles of preparation. The Keys' standard is meunière, which is a subtle, tasty sauce of lemon and parsley. Although everything looks tempting, don't overorder—portions are huge. The waitresses, who are pleasant enough, require a bit of patience, but the food is worth it.

✪ **Morada Bay.** U.S. 1 at MM 81.6, Islamorada. ☎ **305/664-0604.** Reservations recommended for large groups. Main courses $17–$28; appetizers $7–$16. AE, MC, V. Mon–Thurs 11:30am–10pm; Fri–Sun 11am–11pm. CARIBBEAN/AMERICAN.

This lovely bayside bistro offers superfresh, innovative seafood as well as more basic offerings, such as chicken fajitas, hamburgers, and salads. Salads such as the Sunshine Salad are large and generously lavished with slices of avocado, mango, and tomato. When in season, delicious raw oysters are imported from Long Island. Fish dishes are always fresh and served in a number of styles; I like mine jerked with a peppery coating and nearly black finish. If you can't decide, share a few items from the tapas menu: jumbo shrimp cocktails, fried calamari, conch fritters, smoked fish dip, or a charcuterie of sausages and hams on country bread.

Moderate

Lazy Days Oceanfront Bar and Seafood Grill. U.S. 1 at MM 79.9, Islamorada. ☎ **305/664-5256.** Main courses $11–$24. AE, DISC, MC, V. Tues–Sun 11:30am–10pm. SEAFOOD/AMERICAN.

Opened in 1992, the Lazy Days quickly became one of the most popular restaurants around, mostly because of its large portions and lively atmosphere. Meals are pricier than the casual dining room would suggest, but the food is good enough and the menu varied. Steamed clams with garlic and bell peppers make a tempting appetizer. The menu focuses on—what else?—seafood, but you can also find Italian dishes. Most main courses come with baked potato, vegetables, a tossed salad, and French bread, making appetizers redundant.

⭐ **Lorelei Restaurant and Cabana Bar.** U.S. 1 at MM 82, Islamorada. ☎ **305/664-4656.** Reservations not usually required. Main courses $12–$24; appetizers $4–$7. AE, MC, DC, DISC, V. Daily 7am–10pm. Outside bar serves breakfast 7–11am; lunch/appetizer menu 11am–9pm. Bar closes at midnight. SEAFOOD/BAR FOOD.

Don't resist the siren call of the enormous, sparkling, roadside mermaid—you won't be dashed into the rocks. This big old fish house and bar is a great place for a snack, a meal, or a beer. Inside, a good-value menu focuses mainly on seafood. When in season, lobsters are the way to go. For $20, you can get a good-sized tail—at least a 1-pounder—prepared any way you like. Other fare includes the standard clam chowder, fried shrimp, and doughy conch fritters. Salads and soups are hearty and satisfying. For those tired of fish, the menu also offers a few beef selections. The outside bar has live music every evening, and you can order snacks and light meals from a limited menu that is satisfying and well priced. Enjoy the live entertainment every night.

INEXPENSIVE

Calypso's. 1 Seagate Blvd. (near MM 99.5), Key Largo. ☎ **305/451-0600.** Main courses $8–$16. MC, V. Wed–Mon 11:30am–10pm; Fri until 11pm. SEAFOOD/PASTA.

The awning still bears the name of the former restaurant "Demar's" but the food here is all Todd Lollis's. Though he looks like he might be more comfortable at a Grateful Dead concert than in a kitchen, this inspired young chef turns out inventive seafood dishes in a casual and rustic waterside setting. If it's available, try the butter pecan sauce over whatever fish is freshest. Don't miss the white wine sangria, full of tangy oranges and limes and topped with a dash of cinnamon. The prices are surprisingly reasonable, but the service can be a little more laid back than you're used to. The toughest part is finding the place. From south, turn right at the blinking yellow lights near MM 99.5 to Ocean Bay Drive; turn right. Look for the blue vinyl-sided building on the left.

⭐ **Henry's Bakery and Gourmet Pizza Shop.** U.S. 1 at MM 82.5 (adjacent to Days Inn), 82700 Overseas Highway, Islamorada, FL ☎ **305/664-4030.** Pastas $5–$12; pizzas $7–$18; sandwiches and salads $4.50–$8. No credit cards. Mon–Sat 6am–10pm (sometimes later on weekends). BAKERY/PIZZERIA.

This recently expanded storefront bakery serves the best pizzas and sandwiches in town. My favorite is freshly sliced turkey on homemade warm French bread, with a splash of superbly tangy vinaigrette. Most days Henry bakes fresh multi-grain, semolina, and Italian bread, too. Stop by early for delicious pastries and croissants. If you want pizza, consider the decadent Sublime Pie with lobster tail, roasted bell peppers, and sun-dried tomatoes. The crust has the perfect texture—just a bit chewy, but not too doughy.

⭐ **Islamorada Fish Company.** U.S. 1 at MM 81.5 (up the street from Cheeca Lodge), Islamorada. ☎ **800/258-2559** or 305/664-9271. Reservations not accepted. Main courses $8–$27; appetizers $4–$7. DISC, MC, V. Mon–Sat 8am–9pm; Sun 9am–9pm. SEAFOOD.

The original Islamorada Fish Company has been selling seafood out of its roadside shack since 1948. It's still the best place to pick up a cooler of stone crab claws in season (mid-October through April). Also great are the fried fish sandwiches, served with melted American cheese, fried onions, and coleslaw. A few hundred yards up the road is Islamorada Fish Company Restaurant & Bakery, the newer establishment, which looks like an average diner, but has a selection of fantastic seafood and pastas. It's also the place for breakfast. Locals gather for politics and gossip as well as delicious grits, oatmeal, omelettes, and homemade pastries. It's at MM 81.6. (☎ **305/664-8363**);

open Thursday to Tuesday 6am to 9pm, Wednesday 6am to 2pm. Discover, MasterCard, and Visa are accepted.

Key Largo's Crack'd Conch. U.S. 1 at MM 105.5 (ocean side). ☎ **305/451-0732.** Reservations not accepted. Main courses $9–$15; sandwiches $3.25–$7. AE, DC, DISC, MC, V. Thurs–Tues noon–10pm. Closed Wed. SEAFOOD.

This colorful little shack looks appealing from the road and isn't a bad place to stop, especially if you like beer. More than 100 imported and domestic lagers, porters, stouts, and ales are available. Food choices, on the other hand, are not as varied or as predictable. The Crack'd Conch serves decent baskets of fried clams, shrimp, chicken, and, of course, conch. Prices are higher than they ought to be, considering the quality and atmosphere, but it won't bust your budget.

Time Out Barbecue. U.S. 1 at MM 81.5 (ocean side). ☎ **305/664-8911.** Sandwiches $4.25–$6; rib and chicken platters to share $7–$15. MC, V. Daily 11am–10pm. BARBECUE.

This barbecue joint serves up hot and hearty old-fashioned barbecue that is among the best around. The secret, Steve says, is in the slow-cooking—more than 10 hours for the melt-in-your-mouth soft pork sandwich. Topped off with delicious, not too-creamy coleslaw and sweet baked beans, any of the many offerings are worth a stop. You can grab a seat at the picnic table on the grassy lawn next to the Trading Post.

THE UPPER & MIDDLE KEYS AFTER DARK

Nightlife in the Upper Keys tends to start before the sun goes down, often at noon, since most people—visitors and locals alike—are on vacation. Also, many anglers and sports-minded folk go to bed early.

Opened in the early 1990s by some young locals tired of tourist traps, **Hog Heaven,** at MM 85.3 just off the main road on the ocean side in Islamorada (☎ **305/664-9669**), is a welcome respite from the neon-colored cocktail circuit. This whitewashed biker bar offers a waterside view and diversions that include big-screen TVs and video games. The food isn't bad, either. The atmosphere is cliquish since most patrons are regulars, so start up a game of pool or skeet to break the ice.

No trip is complete without a stop at the **Tiki Bar at the Holiday Isle Resort,** U.S. 1 at MM 84, Islamorada (☎ **800/327-7070** or 305/664-2321). Hundreds of revelers visit this ocean-side spot for drinks and dancing at any time of day, but the live rock music starts at 8:30pm. (See "Where to Stay," above.)

In the afternoon and early evening (when everyone is either sunburned, drunk, or just happy to be alive and dancing to live reggae), head for **Kokomo's,** just next door to the thatched-roof Tiki Bar. Kokomo's often closes at 7:30pm on weekends, so get there early. For information, call the Holiday Isle Resort.

Locals and tourists mingle at the outdoor cabana bar at **Lorelei** (see "Where to Dine," above). Most evenings after 5pm, you'll find local bands playing on a thatched roof stage—mainly rock and roll, reggae, and sometimes blues.

Woody's Saloon and Restaurant, on U.S. 1 at MM 82, Islamorada (☎ **305/664-4335**), is a lively, wacky, raunchy place serving up mediocre pizzas and live bands almost every night. The house band, Big Dick and the Extenders, showcases a 300-pound Native American who does a lewd, rude, and crude routine of jokes and songs starting at 9pm, Tuesday through Sunday. He is a legend. By the way, don't think you're lucky if you are offered the front table: It's the target seat for Big Dick's haranguing. Avoid the lame karaoke performance on Sunday and Monday evenings. There's a small cover charge most nights. Drink specials, contests, and the legendary Big Dick keep this place packed until 4am almost every night.

For a more subdued atmosphere, try the handsome wood bar at **Zane Grey's** (on the second floor of World Wide Sportsman at MM 81.5). Outside, enjoy a view of the calm waters of the bay, or inside, soak up the history of some real old anglers. You feel like a real swell in this stained-glass, mahogany-decked club. It is open from 11am to 11pm, and later on weekends. Call to find out who is playing on weekends (☎ **305/664-4244**), when there is live entertainment and no cover charge.

2 The Lower Keys: Big Pine Key to Coppitt Key

128 miles SW of Miami

Big Pine, Sugarloaf, Summerland, and the other Lower Keys are less developed and more tranquil than the Upper Keys. If you're looking for haute cuisine and a happening nightlife, look elsewhere. If you're looking to commune with nature or for an adventure in solitude, you've come to the right place. Unlike their neighbors to the north and south, the Lower Keys are devoid of rowdy spring-break crowds, boast few T-shirt and trinket shops, and have almost no late-night bars. What they do offer are the very best opportunities to enjoy the vast natural resources on land and water that make the area so rich. Stay overnight in the Lower Keys, rent a boat, and explore the reefs—it might be the most memorable part of your trip.

ESSENTIALS

GETTING THERE See "Essentials" for the Upper and Middle Keys. Continue south on U.S. 1. The Lower Keys start at the end of the Seven-Mile Bridge.

VISITOR INFORMATION The **Lower Keys Chamber of Commerce,** ocean side of U.S. 1 at MM 31 (P.O. Box 430511), Big Pine Key, FL 33043 (☎ **800/872-3722** or 305/872-2411; fax 305/872-0752; e-mail: lkchamber@aol.com), is open Monday through Friday from 9am to 5pm and Saturday from 9am to 3pm. The pleasant staff will help with anything a traveler may need. Call, write, or stop in for a comprehensive, detailed information packet.

WHAT TO SEE & DO

Once the centerpiece of the Lower Keys and still a great asset is **Bahia Honda State Park,** U.S. 1 at MM 37.5, Big Pine Key (☎ **305/872-2353**), which, even after the violent storms of 1998, has one of the most beautiful coastlines in South Florida. Bahia Honda (pronounced *Bah*-ya) is a great place for hiking, bird watching, swimming, snorkeling, and fishing. The 524-acre park encompasses a wide variety of ecosystems, including coastal mangroves, beach dunes, and tropical hammocks. There are miles of trails packed with unusual plants and animals and a small white beach. Shaded seaside picnic areas are fitted with tables and grills. Although the beach is never wider than 5 feet even at low tide, this is the Lower Keys' best beach area.

True to its name (Spanish for "deep bay"), the park has relatively deep waters close to shore and they are perfect for snorkeling and diving. Head to the stunning reefs at Looe Key where the coral and fish are more vibrant than anywhere else in the United States. Snorkeling trips depart daily from March through September and cost $22 for adults, $18 for youths 6 to 14, and free for children 5 and under. Call ☎ **305/872-3210** for a schedule.

Admission to the park is $4 per vehicle (plus 50¢ per person), $1.50 per pedestrian or bicyclist, free for children 5 and under. If you are alone in a car, you'll only pay $2.50. Open daily from 8am to sunset.

The most famous residents of the Lower Keys are the tiny Key deer. Of the estimated 300 existing in the world, two thirds live on Big Pine Key's **National Key Deer Refuge.** To get your bearings, stop by the rangers' office at the Winn-Dixie Shopping Plaza near MM 30.5 off U.S. 1. They'll give you an informative brochure and map of the area. It is open Monday through Friday from 8am to 5pm.

If the office is closed, head out to the Blue Hole, a former rock quarry now filled with the fresh water that's vital to the deer's survival. To get there, turn right at Big Pine Key's only traffic light onto Key Deer Boulevard (take the left fork immediately after the turn), and continue 1 1/2 miles to the observation site parking lot, on your left. The half-mile Watson Hammock Trail, about a third of a mile past the Blue Hole, is the refuge's only marked footpath. Try coming out here in the early morning or late evening to catch a glimpse of these gentle, dog-sized deer. Refuge lands are open daily from half an hour before sunrise to half an hour after sunset. Whatever you do, do not feed the deer—it will threaten their survival. Call the **park office** (☎ **305/872-2239**) to find out about the infrequent free tours of the refuge, scheduled at different times throughout the year.

The only human-made attraction in the Lower Keys is the **Sugarloaf Bat Tower,** off U.S. 1 at MM 17 (next to Sugarloaf Airport on the bay side). In a vain effort to battle the ubiquitous troublesome mosquitoes in the Lower Keys, developer Clyde Perkey built this odd structure to lure bug-eating bats. Despite his alluring design and a pungent bat aphrodisiac, his guests never showed. Since 1929, this wooden, flat-topped, 45-foot-high pyramid has stood empty and deserted, except for the occasional tourist who stops to wonder what it is. There is no sign or marker to commemorate this odd remnant of ingenuity. It's worth a 5-minute detour to see it. To get there, turn right at the Sugarloaf Airport sign, and then right again onto the dirt road that begins just before the airport gate; the tower is about 100 yards ahead.

OUTDOOR PURSUITS

BICYCLING If you have your own bike, or your lodging offers rental (many do), the Lower Keys is a great place to get off busy U.S. 1 to explore the beautiful back roads. On Big Pine Key, cruise along Key Deer Boulevard (at MM 30). Those with fat tires can ride into the National Key Deer Refuge.

BIRD WATCHING Bring your birding books. A stopping point for migratory birds on the Eastern Flyway, the Lower Keys are populated with many West Indian bird species, especially during spring and fall. The small vegetated islands of the Keys are the only nesting sites in the United States for the great white heron and the white-crowned pigeon. They're also some of the very few breeding places for the reddish egret, the roseate spoonbill, the mangrove cuckoo, and the black-whiskered vireo. Look for them on Bahia Honda and the many uninhabited islands nearby.

BOATING Dozens of shops rent powerboats for fishing and reef exploring. Most also rent tackle, sell bait, and have charter captains available. **Bud Boats,** at the Old Wooden Bride Fishing Camp and Marina, MM 30 in Big Pine Key (☎ **305/872-9165**), has a wide selection of well-maintained boats. Depending on the size, rentals cost between $70 and $250 for a day, between $50 and $130 for a half day. Another good option is **Jaybird's Powerboats,** U.S. 1 at MM 33, Big Pine Key (☎ **305/872-8500**). They rent for full days only. Prices start at $127 for a 19-footer.

CANOEING & KAYAKING The Overseas Highway (U.S. 1) touches on only a few dozen of the many hundreds of islands that make up the Keys. To really see the Lower Keys, rent a kayak or canoe—perfect for these shallow waters. **Reflections**

Kayak Nature Tours, operating out of Parmer's Place Resort Motel, on U.S. 1 at MM 28.5, Little Torch Key (☎ 305/872-2896), offers fully outfitted backcountry wildlife tours, either on your own or with an expert. A former U.S. Forest Service guide, Mike Wedeking, keeps up an engaging discussion describing the area's fish, sponges, coral, osprey, hawks, eagles, alligators, raccoons, and deer. The 3-hour tours cost $45 per person and include spring water, fresh fruit, granola bars, and use of binoculars. Bring a towel and sea sandals or sneakers.

DIVING & FISHING   A day spent fishing, either in the shallow backcountry or in the deep sea, is a great way to ensure yourself a fresh fish dinner, or you can release your catch and just appreciate the challenge. Especially since the Adolphus Busch was sunk off Looe Key in 100 feet of water, the lower Keys also offers some prime diving. Whichever you choose, **Larry Threlkeld's Strike Zone Charters,** U.S. 1 at MM 29.5, Big Pine Key (☎ 305/872-9863), is the charter service to call. Prices for fishing boats start at $250 to $400 for a half-day. If you have enough anglers to share the price, it isn't too steep. They may be able to match you with other interested visitors.

To get to the Adolphus Busch Sr., a 210-foot island freighter, on your own boat, head to coordinates: 24.31.819 N, 81.27.643W, between Looe Key and American Shoals. Strike Zone will take you for $50 without equipment.

HIKING   You can hike throughout the flat marshy Keys, on both marked trails and meandering coastlines. The best places to trek through nature are **Bahia Honda State Park** at MM 29.5 and **National Key Deer Refuge** at MM 30 (for more information on both, see "What to See & Do," above). Bahia Honda Park has a free brochure describing an excellent self-guided tour along the Silver Palm Nature Trail. You'll traverse hammocks, mangroves, and sand dunes and cross a lagoon. You can do the walk (which is less than a mile) in under half an hour, and can explore a great cross-section of the natural habitat in the Lower Keys.

SNORKELING & DIVING   Snorkelers and divers should not miss the Keys' most dramatic reefs at the **Looe Key National Marine Sanctuary.** Here, you'll see more than 150 varieties of hard and soft coral, some centuries old, as well as every type of tropical fish, including the gold and blue parrot fish, moray eels, barracudas, French angels, and tarpon. **Looe Key Dive Center,** U.S. 1 at MM 27.5, Ramrod Key (☎ 305/872-2215), offers a mind-blowing 2½-hour tour aboard a 45-foot catamaran with two shallow 1-hour dives for snorkelers and scuba divers. Snorkelers pay $30, and divers with their own equipment pay $65. Good-quality rentals are available. (See "What to See & Do," above, for other diving options.)

SHOPPING

Certainly not known for great shopping, the Lower Keys do happen to be home to many talented visual artists, particularly those who specialize in depicting their natural surroundings. The **Artists in Paradise Gallery,** on Big Pine Key in the Winn-Dixie Shopping Plaza, near MM 30.5, 1 block north of U.S. 1 at the traffic light (☎ 305/872-1828), displays an ever-changing selection of watercolors, oils, photos, and sculptures. This cooperative gallery displays the work of more than a dozen artists who share the task of watching the store. Usually hours are daily from 10am to 6pm.

WHERE TO STAY

There are a number of cheap fish shacks along the highway for those who want bare-bones accommodations, but so far, there are no national hotel chains in the Lower Keys. For information on lodging in cabins or trailers at local campgrounds, see "Camping," below.

Very Expensive

○ **Little Palm Island.** Launch is at the ocean side of U.S. 1 at MM 28.5, Little Torch Key, FL 33042. ☎ **800/343-8567** or 305/872-2524. Fax 305/872-4843. www.littlepalmisland.com. 28 bungalows, 2 deluxe suites. A/C MINIBAR. Winter $850–$1,600 per couple. Off-season $750–$1,500. Summer $550–$1,300 including transportation to and from the island and unlimited (nonmotorized) water sports. Meal plans include 2 meals daily for $125 per person per day. 3 meals are $140 per person. AE, CB, DC, DISC, MC, V. No children under 16.

Over the years this exclusive island escape—host to presidents and royalty—is not just a place to stay while in the Lower Keys; it is a resort destination all its own. Built on a private 5-acre island, it's accessible only by boat. Guests stay in thatched-roof duplexes amid lush foliage and flowering tropical plants. Many villas have ocean views and private sundecks with rope hammocks. Inside, the romantic suites have all the comforts and conveniences of a luxurious contemporary beach cottage, but without telephones, TVs, or alarm clocks. Note that on the breezeless south side of the island, you may get invaded by mosquitoes, even in the winter. Bring spray and lightweight long-sleeved clothing. Known for its innovative and pricey food, Little Palm also hosts visitors just for dinner or lunch. If you are staying on the island, opt for the full American plan, which includes three meals a day for about $140 per person. If you pay à la carte, you could spend that much just on dinner. At these prices, Little Palm appeals to those who aren't keeping track.

Dining/Diversions: The Little Palm Restaurant offers fine dining either indoors or alfresco at inflated prices. A pool bar offers refreshments and light snacks all day.

Amenities: Concierge, room service, dry cleaning, laundry, newspaper delivery, twice-daily maid service, in-room massage, courtesy van from Key West or Marathon airport, ferry service to and from the mainland. Outdoor pool with small waterfall, wide beach, in-room Jacuzzi tubs, sauna, sundeck, water-sports equipment, jogging trail, boutique.

Moderate

Deer Run Bed and Breakfast. Long Beach Dr. (P.O. Box 431), Big Pine Key, FL 33043. ☎ **305/872-2015.** Fax 305/872-2842. E-mail: deerrunbb@aol.com. 3 units. Winter from $125 double. Off-season from $95 double. Rates include full American breakfast. No credit cards. From U.S. 1 south, turn left at the Big Pine Fishing Lodge (MM 33); continue for about 2 miles. No children under 16.

Located directly on the beach, Sue Abbott's small, homey, smoke-free B&B is a real find. One upstairs and two downstairs guest rooms are comfortably furnished with queen-size beds, good closets, and touch-sensitive lamps. Rattan and 1970s-style chairs and couches furnish the living room, along with 13 birds and 3 cats. Breakfast, which is served on a pretty, fenced-in porch, is cooked to order by Sue herself. The wooded area around the property is full of deer, which are often spotted on the beach as well. Ask to use one of the bikes to explore nearby nature trails. The owner prefers adults and mature children only.

Inexpensive

○ **Parmer's Place Cottages.** Barry Ave. (P.O. Box 430665), near MM 28.5, Little Torch Key, FL 33043. ☎ **305/872-2157.** Fax 305/872-2014. www.palmersplace.com. 41 units. Winter and during festivals, from $77 double; from $93.50 efficiency. Off-season $55–$65 double; from $75 efficiency. AE, DISC, MC, V. Turn right onto Barry Ave. Resort is a $1/2$ mile down on the right.

Parmer's, a fixture here for more than 20 years, is well known for its charming hospitality and helpful staff. This downscale resort offers modest but comfortable cottages.

Every unit is different. Some face the water, some are a few steps away from the water, some have small kitchenettes, and others are just a bedroom. Room 26, a one-bedroom efficiency, is especially nice, with a small sitting area that faces the water. Room 6, a small efficiency, has a little kitchenette and an especially large bathroom. The rooms all have linoleum floors, dated 1970s-style painted rattan furnishings, fake flowers, and thrift-store art. They're very clean. Many can be combined to accommodate large families. Facilities include a horseshoes court, boat ramp, and a heated swimming pool.

CAMPING

Bahia Honda State Park (☎ **305/872-2353**) offers some of the best camping in the Keys, even after the devastating storms of 1998. It is as loaded with facilities and activities as it is with campers. However, don't be discouraged by its popularity—this park encompasses more than 500 acres of land. There are 80 campsites and six spacious and comfortable cabin units though some are still under reconstruction. Cabins hold up to eight guests and come complete with linens, kitchenettes, and utensils. You'll enjoy the wraparound terrace, barbecue pit, and rocking chairs.

Camping here costs about $25 per site for one to four people without electricity and $26 with electricity. Depending on the season, cabin prices change: From December 15 to September 14, it's about $125 per cabin for one to four people; from September 15 to December 14, it's $97.30 per cabin. Additional people (over four) cost $6. MasterCard and Visa are accepted.

Another excellent value can be found at the **KOA Sugarloaf Key Resort,** near MM 20. This ocean-side facility has 200 fully equipped sites that rent for about $53 a night (no-hookup sites cost about $38). Or pitch a tent on the 5 acres of lush waterfront property. The resort also rents out travel trailers. The 22-foot Dutchman sleeps six and is equipped with eating and cooking utensils. It costs about $100 a day. More luxurious trailers go for $160 a day. All major credit cards are accepted. For details, contact P.O. Box 420469, Summerland Key, FL 33042 (☎ **800/562-7731** or 305/745-3549; fax 305/745-9889; e-mail: sugarloaf@koa.net).

WHERE TO DINE

There aren't many fine dining options in the Lower Keys, but the following are worth a stop for those passing through.

MODERATE

✪ **Mangrove Mama's Restaurant.** U.S. 1 at MM 20, Sugarloaf Key. ☎ **305/745-3030.** Main courses $10–$20; lunch $6–$9; brunch $5–$7. MC, V. Daily 11:30am–10pm (11am in season). SEAFOOD/CARIBBEAN.

As the dedicated locals who come daily for happy hour will tell you, Mangrove Mama's is a true Lower Keys institution and a dive in the best sense of the word. The restaurant is a shack that used to have a gas pump as well as a grill. Now, guests share the property with some miniature horses (out back) and stray cats. A handful of simple tables, inside and out, are shaded by banana trees and palm fronds. Fish is, not surprisingly, the menu's mainstay, although soups, salads, sandwiches, and omelettes are also good. Grilled teriyaki chicken and club sandwiches are tasty alternatives to fish, as are meatless chef's salads and spicy barbecued baby back ribs.

✪ **Monte's.** U.S. 1 at MM 25, Summerland Key. ☎ **305/745-3731.** Main courses $13–$17; lunch $6–$10. No credit cards. Mon–Sat 9am–10pm; Sun 11am–9pm. SEAFOOD.

Monte's has survived for more than 20 years because the food is very good and incredibly fresh. Certainly nobody goes to this restaurant/fish market for its atmosphere:

The Truth About Keys Cuisine

There are few world-class chefs in the Florida Keys, but that's not to say the food isn't great. Restaurants here serve very fresh fish and a few local specialties—most notably conch fritters and chowder, key lime pie, and stone crab claws and lobster when they're in season.

Although a commercial net-fishing ban has diminished the stock of once abundant fish in these parts, even the humblest of restaurants can be counted on to take full advantage of the gastronomic treasures of their own backyard. The Keys have everything a cook could want: the Atlantic and the Gulf of Mexico for impeccably fresh seafood; a tropical climate for year-round farm stand produce, including great tomatoes, beans, berries, and citrus fruit; and a freshwater swamp for rustic delicacies such as alligator, frog's legs, and hearts of palm.

Conch fritters and chowder are mainstays on most tourist-oriented menus. Because the queen conch was listed as an endangered species by the U.S. government in 1985, however, the conch in your dish was most likely shipped fresh-frozen from The Bahamas or the Caribbean.

Key lime pie consists of the juice of tiny yellow key limes (a fruit unique to South Florida), along with condensed milk, all in a graham cracker crust. Experts debate whether the true key lime pie should have a whipped cream or a meringue topping, but all agree that the filling should be yellow, never green.

Another unique offering, the **Florida lobster** is an entirely different species from the more common Maine variety, and has a sweeter meat. It's also known as the "Spiney" lobster because of all the bumps on its shell. You'll see only the tails on the menu because the Florida lobster has no claws.

Stone crabs are even **better**—succulent, sweet, tender, and very meaty. They've been written about and talked about by kings, presidents, and poets. Although you'll find them on nearly every menu in season (from October until May), consider buying a few pounds of jumbos at the fish store to take to the beach in a cooler. Don't forget to ask them to crack them for you and to get a cup of creamy mustard sauce. Topped off with a cold bottle of champagne, there is no better meal. You'll be glad to know that after their claws are harvested the crabs grow new ones, thus ensuring a long-lasting supply of these unique delicacies.

Plastic place settings rest on plastic-covered picnic-style tables in a screen-enclosed dining patio. The day's catch may include shark, tuna, lobster, stone crabs, or shrimp.

INEXPENSIVE

✪ **Coco's Kitchen.** 283 Key Deer Blvd. (in the Winn-Dixie Shopping Center), Big Pine Key. ☎ **305/872-4495.** Main courses $5.50–$12; breakfast $2–$4.50. No credit cards. Mon–Sat 7am–7:30pm. Turn right at the traffic light near MM 30.5. Stay in the left lane. CUBAN/NICARAGUAN.

This tiny storefront has been dishing out black beans, rice, and shredded beef to fans of Cuban cuisine for more than 10 years. The owners, who are actually from Nicaragua, cook not only superior Cuban food but also some local specialties, Italian food, and Caribbean food. The best bet is the daily special, which may be roasted pork or fresh grouper, served with rice and beans or salad and crispy fries. Top off the huge, cheap meal with a rich caramel-soaked flan.

No Name Pub. ¹/₄ mile south of No Name Bridge on N. Watson Blvd., Big Pine Key. ☎ 305/872-9115. Pizzas $6–$18; subs $5. MC, V. 11am–11pm. Turn right at Big Pine's only traffic light (near MM 30.5) onto Key Deer Blvd. Turn right on Watson Blvd. At stop sign, turn left. Look for a small wooden sign on the left marking the spot. PUB FOOD/PIZZA.

This funky old bar out in the boonies serves snacks and sandwiches until 11pm on most nights and drinks until midnight. Pizzas are tasty—thick-crusted and supercheesy. Try one topped with local shrimps, or consider a bowl of chili with all the fixings—hearty and cheap. Also decent is the smoked fish dip. Everything is served on paper plates. Locals hang out at the rustic bar, one of the Florida Keys' oldest, drinking beer and listening to a jukebox heavy with 1980s selections. The decor, if you can call it that, is basic—the walls and ceilings are plastered with thousands of autographed dollar bills.

THE LOWER KEYS AFTER DARK

Although the mellow islands of the lower Keys aren't exactly known for wild nightlife, there are some friendly bars and restaurants where locals and tourists gather to hang out and drink.

One of the most scenic is **Sandbar** (☎ **305/872-9989**), a wide-open breezy wooden house built on slender stilts and overlooking a wide channel on Barry Avenue (near MM 28.5). It attracts an odd mix of bikers and blue-hairs daily from 11am until 10pm. Pool tables are the main attraction, but there's also live music some nights. The drinks are reasonably priced and the food isn't too bad, either. For another fun bar scene, see **No Name Pub,** listed above in "Where to Dine."

3 Key West

159 miles SW of Miami

The locals, or "conchs" (pronounced *conks*), and the developers here have been at odds for years. This once low-key island has been thoroughly commercialized—there's a Hard Rock Cafe smack in the middle of Duval Street and thousands of cruise-ship passengers descending on Mallory Square each day. It's definitely not the seedy town Hemingway and his cronies once called their own.

Laid-back Key West still exists, but it's now found in different places: the backyard of a popular guest house, for example, or an art gallery, or a secret garden, or the hip hangouts of Bahama Village. And, of course, there's always the calm waters of the Atlantic and the Gulf of Mexico all around.

The heart of town offers party people a good time. Here, you'll find good restaurants, fun bars, live music, rickshaw rides, and lots of shopping. Don't bother with a watch or tie—this is the home of the perennial vacation.

ESSENTIALS

GETTING THERE For directions by car, see "Essentials" for the Upper and Middle Keys, above. Continue south on U.S. 1. When entering Key West, stay in the far-right lane onto North Roosevelt Boulevard, which becomes Truman Avenue in Old Town. Continue for a few blocks, and you will find yourself on Duval Street, in the heart of the city. If you stay to the left, you'll also reach the city center after passing the airport and the remnants of historic houseboat row, where a motley collection of boats once made up one of Key West's most interesting neighborhoods.

Several regional airlines fly nonstop from Miami to Key West; fares are about $120 to $300 round-trip. **American Eagle** (☎ **800/443-7300**) and **US Airways Express**

Key West

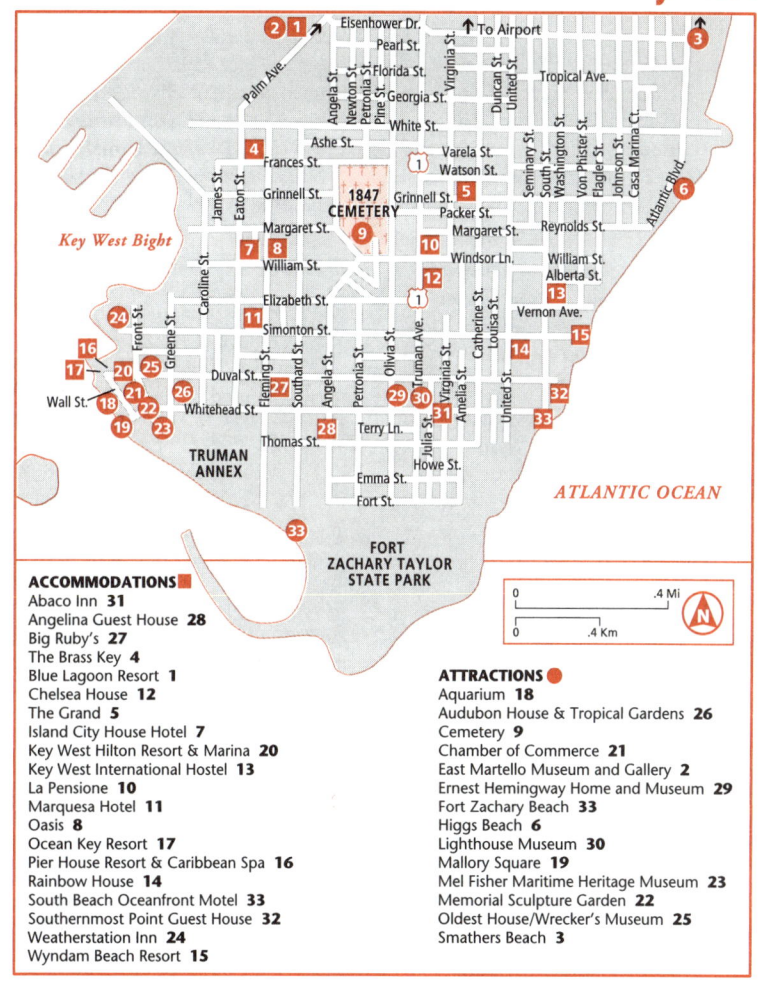

ACCOMMODATIONS
Abaco Inn **31**
Angelina Guest House **28**
Big Ruby's **27**
The Brass Key **4**
Blue Lagoon Resort **1**
Chelsea House **12**
The Grand **5**
Island City House Hotel **7**
Key West Hilton Resort & Marina **20**
Key West International Hostel **13**
La Pensione **10**
Marquesa Hotel **11**
Oasis **8**
Ocean Key Resort **17**
Pier House Resort & Caribbean Spa **16**
Rainbow House **14**
South Beach Oceanfront Motel **33**
Southernmost Point Guest House **32**
Weatherstation Inn **24**
Wyndam Beach Resort **15**

ATTRACTIONS
Aquarium **18**
Audubon House & Tropical Gardens **26**
Cemetery **9**
Chamber of Commerce **21**
East Martello Museum and Gallery **2**
Ernest Hemingway Home and Museum **29**
Fort Zachary Beach **33**
Higgs Beach **6**
Lighthouse Museum **30**
Mallory Square **19**
Mel Fisher Maritime Heritage Museum **23**
Memorial Sculpture Garden **22**
Oldest House/Wrecker's Museum **25**
Smathers Beach **3**

(☎ **800/428-4322**) land at **Key West International Airport,** South Roosevelt Boulevard (☎ **305/296-5439**), on the southeastern corner of the island.

Greyhound (☎ **800/231-2222;** www.greyhound.com) has buses leaving Miami for Key West every day. At press time, prices were $30 to $32 one-way and $57 to $60 round-trip. Seats fill up in season, so come early. The ride takes about 4½ hours.

GETTING AROUND With limited parking, narrow streets, and congested traffic, driving in Old Town Key West is more of a pain than a convenience. Unless you're staying in one of the more remote accommodations, consider trading in the car for a bicycle. The island is small and as flat as a board, which makes it easy to negotiate, especially away from the crowded downtown. Many tourists also choose to cruise by moped, an option that can make navigating the streets risky, especially since there are no helmet laws in Key West. Spend the extra few bucks and rent a helmet; hundreds of visitors are seriously injured each year.

Rates for simple one-speed cruisers start at about $8 per day (from $40 per week). Mopeds start at about $12 for two hours, $25 per day and $100 per week. The best shops include **The Bicycle Center** at 523 Truman Ave. (☎ **305/294-4556**); the **Moped Hospital,** 601 Truman Ave. (☎ **305/296-3344**); and **Tropical Bicycles & Scooter Rentals** at 1300 Duval St. (☎ **305/294-8136**). **The Bike Shop,** 1110 Truman Ave. (☎ **305/294-1073**), rents mountain bikes for $15 per day ($75 per week). Cruisers go for $8 per day and $40 per week.

PARKING Note that parking in Key West's Old Town is particularly limited. There is a well-placed **municipal parking lot** at Simonton and Angela streets just behind the firehouse and police station. If you have brought a car, you may want to stash it here while you enjoy the very walkable downtown section of Key West.

VISITOR INFORMATION The **Florida Keys and Key West Visitors Bureau,** P.O. Box 1147, Key West, FL 33041 (☎ **800/FLA-KEYS;** www.keywest.com), offers a free vacation kit packed with visitor information. The **Key West Chamber of Commerce,** 402 Wall St., Key West, FL 33040 (☎ **800/527-8539** or 305/294-2587), also offers both general and specialized information. The lobby is open daily from 8:30am to 6pm; phones are answered from 8am to 8pm. The **Key West Visitors Center** also provides information on accommodations, goings-on, and restaurants; the number is ☎ **800/LAST-KEY.** It's open weekdays from 8am to 5:30pm and weekends from 8:30am to 5pm. Gay travelers will want to call the **Key West Business Guild** (☎ **305/294-4603**), which represents more than 50 guest houses and B&Bs in town, as well as many other gay-owned businesses. Ask for its color brochure. Or try **Good Times Travel** (☎ **305/294-0980**), which will set up lodging and package tours on the island.

ORIENTATION A mere 2-by-4-mile island, Key West is simple to navigate, even though there is no real order to the arrangement of streets and avenues. As you enter town on U.S. 1 (also called Roosevelt Boulevard), you will see most of the moderately priced chain hotels and fast-food restaurants. The better restaurants, shops, and outfitters are crammed onto Duval Street, the main thoroughfare of Key West's Old Town. On surrounding streets are the many inns and lodges in picturesque Victorian/Bahamian homes. On the southern side of the island is the coral beach area and some of the larger resort hotels.

The area called Bahama Village has only recently become known to tourists. With several cool restaurants and guesthouses opened over the years, this hippie-ish neighborhood, complete with street-roaming chickens and cats, is the most urban and rough you'll find in the Keys. You might see a few seedy drug dealings on street corners, but it's nothing to be overly concerned with. Resident business owners tend to keep a vigilant eye on the neighborhood. It looks worse than it is.

SEEING THE SIGHTS

Before shelling out big bucks for any of the dozens of worthwhile attractions in Key West, I recommend getting an overview on either of the two comprehensive island tours, **The Conch Tour Train** or the **Old Town Trolley** (See "Organized Tours," below). There are simply too many attractions to list (including a Ripley's Believe it or Not! on Duval Street) and a number of historic houses. I've highlighted my favorites below but encourage you to seek out others.

✪ **Audubon House & Tropical Gardens.** 205 Whitehead St. (between Greene and Caroline sts.). ☎ **305/294-2116.** Admission $7.50 adults; $3.50 children 6–12. Daily 9:30am–5pm (last admission at 4:45pm). Discounts for students and AAA and AARP members.

This well-preserved home, dating from the early 19th century, stands as a prime example of early Key West architecture. Named after the renowned painter and bird expert, John James Audubon, who was said to have visited the house in 1832, the graceful two-story home is a peaceful retreat from the bustle of Old Town. Included in the price of admission is a self-guided audiotape tour that lasts about half an hour. With voices of several characters from the house's past, the tour never gets boring—although it is at times a bit hokey. See rare Audubon prints, gorgeous antiques, historical photos, and lush tropical gardens. Even if you don't want to spend the time and money to explore the grounds and home, check out the impressive gift shop, which sells a variety of fine mementos at reasonable prices.

Ernest Hemingway Home and Museum. 907 Whitehead St. (between Truman Ave. and Olivia St.). ☎ **305/294-1575** or 305/294-1136. Fax 305/294-2755 www.hemingwayhome.com. Admission $7.50 adults; $4.50 children. Daily 9am–5pm. Limited parking.

Hemingway's particularly handsome stone Spanish Colonial house, built in 1851, was one of the first on the island to be fitted with indoor plumbing and a built-in fireplace. The author owned the home from 1931 until his passing in 1961, and lived with about 50 six-toed cats, whose descendants still roam the premises. It was during those years that the Nobel Prize winner wrote some of his most famous works, including *For Whom the Bell Tolls, A Farewell to Arms,* and *The Snows of Kilimanjaro.* Fans may want to take the optional half-hour tour. It's interesting and included in the price of admission.

Key West Cemetery. Entrance at Margaret and Angela sts. ☎ **305/294-WALK** for tour reservations. Free admission. Daily dawn to dusk.

This funky picturesque cemetery is the epitome of the quirky Key West image, as irreverent as it is humorous. Many tombs are stacked several high, condominium style—the rocky soil made digging 6 feet under nearly impossible for early settlers. Headstones reflect residents' lighthearted attitudes toward life and death. I TOLD YOU I WAS SICK is one of the more famous epitaphs, as is the tongue-in-cheek widow's inscription AT LEAST I KNOW WHERE HE'S SLEEPING TONIGHT.

East Martello Museum and Gallery. 3501 S. Roosevelt Blvd. ☎ **305/296-3913.** Admission $6 adults; $2 children 8–12; free for children 7 and under. Daily 9:30am–5pm (last admission is at 4pm).

Adjacent to the airport, the East Martello Museum is located in a Civil War–era brick fort that itself is worth a visit. The museum contains a bizarre variety of exhibits that collectively do a thorough job interpreting the city's intriguing past. Historical artifacts include model ships, a deep-sea diver's wooden air pump, a crude raft from a Cuban "boat lift," a supposedly haunted doll, a Key West–style children's playhouse from 1918, and a horse-drawn hearse. Exhibits illustrate the Keys' history of salvaging, sponging, and cigar making. After seeing the galleries, climb a steep spiral staircase to the top of a lookout tower for good views over the island and ocean.

✪ **Key West Aquarium.** 1 Whitehead St. (at Mallory Square). ☎ **305/296-2051.** Admission $8 adults; $4 children 4–12; free for children under 4. Tickets are good for 2 consecutive days. Look for discount coupons from local hotels, at Duval St. kiosks, and from trolley and train tours. Daily 10am–6pm.

The oldest attraction on the island, the Key West Aquarium is a modest but fascinating exhibit. A long hallway of eye-level displays showcase dozens of varieties of fish and crustaceans. See delicate sea horses swaying in the backlit tanks. Kids can touch sea cucumbers and sea anemones in a shallow touch tank in the entryway. If you can, catch one of the free guided tours offered daily at 11am, 1pm, 3pm, and 4pm, when you can witness the dramatic feeding frenzy of the sharks, tarpon, barracudas, stingrays, and turtles. Tickets are good for 2 consecutive days, a bonus for kids with short attention spans.

Key West Lighthouse Museum. 938 Whitehead St. ☎ **305/294-0012.** Admission $6 adults; $2 children 7–12; free for children 6 and under. Daily 9:30am–5pm (last admission at 4:30pm).

When the Key West Lighthouse was opened in 1848, many locals mourned. Its bright warning to ships signaled the end of a profitable era for wreckers, pirate salvagers who looted reef-stricken ships. The story of this, and other Keys lighthouses, is illustrated in a small museum that was formerly the keeper's quarters. When radar and sonar made the lighthouse obsolete, it was opened to visitors as a tourist attraction. It's worth mustering the energy to climb the 88 claustrophobic steps to the top, where you'll be rewarded with magnificent panoramic views of Key West and the ocean.

Key West's Shipwreck Historeum. 1 Whitehead St. (at Mallory Square). ☎ **305/292-8990.** Fax 305/292-5536 www.historictours.com. Admission $8 adults; $4 children 4–12. Shows daily every half hour from 9:45am–4:45pm.

You'll see more impressive artifacts at nearby Mel Fisher's museum, but the dramatic reenactments of the old shipwrecking days at this place are unique and entertaining. The interactive show is best for teens and adults and includes scenes starring Key West's wealthiest wrecker Asa Tift, plus lots of intriguing video clips and stories of the area's heyday.

✪ **Mel Fisher Maritime Heritage Museum.** 200 Greene St. ☎ **305/294-2633.** Admission $6.50 adults; $2 children 6–12; free for children 5 and under. Daily 9:30am–5pm.

This museum honors local hero Mel Fisher, whose death in 1998 was mourned throughout South Florida, and who, along with a crew of other salvagers, found a multimillion-dollar treasure trove in 1985 aboard the wreck of the Spanish galleon *Nuestra Señora de Atocha*. The admission price is somewhat steep, but if you're into diving, pirates, and the mystery of sunken treasures, check out this small informative museum, full of doubloons, pieces of eight, emeralds, and solid-gold bars. A dated but informative film provides a good background of Fisher's incredible story.

Memorial Sculpture Garden. Mallory Square between Whitehead and Wall sts. Free admission.

Installed in 1997, this impressive sculpture garden contains a large monument to the wreckers who made Key West rich more than a century ago. Also on display are 36 bronze busts of the island's most colorful leaders and characters. There's Pres. Harry Truman, Henry Flagler, and of course, Ernest Hemingway, all mounted on elegant coral columns.

Oldest House/Wrecker's Museum. 322 Duval St. ☎ **305/294-9502.** Admission $5 adults; $1 children 6–12; free for children 5 and under. Daily 10am–4pm.

Dating from 1829, this old New England Bahama House has survived pirates, hurricanes, fires, warfare, and economic ups and downs and gives witness to a slower more easy time in the island's life. This 1$^1/_2$-story home was designed by a ship's carpenter and incorporates many features from maritime architecture including portholes and a ship's hatch designed for ventilation before the advent of air-conditioning. Especially interesting is the detached kitchen building outfitted with a brick "beehive" oven and vintage cooking utensils. Though not a must-see on the Key West tour, history and architecture buffs will appreciate the finely preserved details.

> ## Going, Going, Gone:
> ## Where to Catch the Famous Key West Sunset
>
> A tradition in Key West, the Sunset Celebration can be relaxing or overwhelming, depending on your vantage point. If you're in town, you must check this ritual out at least once. Every evening, locals and visitors gather at the docks behind Mallory Square (at the westernmost end of Whitehead Street) to celebrate the day gone by. Secure a spot on the docks early to experience the carnival of portrait artists, acrobats, food vendors, and animal acts. In season, the crowd can be overwhelming, especially when the cruise ships are in port.
>
> Better yet, get a seat at the Hilton's **Sunset Deck** (☎ **305/294-4000**), a luxurious bar on top of its restaurant at the intersection of Front and Greene streets. From the civilized calm of a casual bar, you can look down on the mayhem with a drink in hand.
>
> Also near the Mallory-madness is the **Ocean Key House's bar.** This long open-air pier serves up drinks and okay bar food against a dramatic pink and yellow streaked sky. It's located at the very tip of Duval Street (☎ **800/328-9815** or 305/296-7701).
>
> For the very best potent cocktails and great bar food on an outside patio or enclosed lounge, try **Pier House's Havana Docks** at 1 Duval St. (☎ **305/296-4600**). There's usually live music and a lively gathering of visitors enjoying this island's bounty.

ORGANIZED TOURS

BY TROLLEY-BUS & TRAM Yes, it's more than a bit hokey to sit on this 60-foot tram of yellow cars, but it's worth it. The city's whole story is packed into a neat, 90-minute package on the **Conch Tour Train,** which covers the island and all its rich, raunchy history. Operating since 1958, the trains are open-air, which can make it uncomfortable in bad weather. The "train's" engine is a propane-powered Jeep disguised as a locomotive. Tours depart from both Mallory Square and the Welcome Center, near where U.S. 1 becomes North Roosevelt Boulevard, on the other side of the island. For more information, contact the **Conch** at (☎ **305/294-5161**). The cost is $18 for adults, $9 for children 4 to 12, and free for children 3 and under. Daily departures are every half-hour from 9am to 4:30pm.

The **Old Town Trolley** is the choice in bad weather or if you are staying at one of the many hotels on its route. Humorous drivers maintain a running commentary as the enclosed tram loops around the island's streets past all the major sights. Trolleys depart from Mallory Square and other points around the island including many area hotels. For details, call (☎ **305/296-6688**). Tours are $18 for adults, $9 for children 4 to 12, and free for children 3 and under. Departures are daily every half-hour (though not always on the hour or half hour) from 9am to 4:45pm. One or the other, these historic trivia-packed tours are well worth the price of admission.

BY AIR Proclaimed by the mayor as "the official air force of the Conch Republic," **Island Airplane Tours,** at Key West Airport, 3469 S. Roosevelt Blvd. (☎ **305/294-8687** for reservations), offers windy rides in its open-cockpit 1940 Waco biplanes over the reefs and around the islands. Thrill seekers—and only they—will also enjoy a spin in the company's S2-B aerobatics airplane that does loops, rolls, and sideways figure-eights. Company owner Fred Cabanas was "decorated" in 1991, after he spotted a Cuban airman defecting to the United States in a Russian-built MiG fighter. Sightseeing flights cost $50 to $200, depending on the duration.

BY BOAT The Pride of Key West, *Fireball*, at Zero Duval St. (☎ **305/296-6293**; fax 305/294-8704), is a 58-foot glass-bottomed catamaran that goes on both day and evening coral-reef tours and sunset cruises. Reef trips cost $20 per person; sunset cruises are $25 per person and include snacks, sodas, and a glass of champagne.

The Wolf, at Schooner Wharf, Key West Seaport (☎ **305/296-9653**; fax 305/294-8388), is a 44-passenger topsail schooner, equipped with a cannon, that sets sail daily for daytime and sunset cruises around the Keys. Key West Seaport is located at the end of Greene Street. Day tours cost $25 per person; sunset sails cost $30 per person and include champagne, wine, beer, soda, and live music.

OTHER TOURS For a lively look at Key West, try a 2-hour tour of the island's five **most famous pubs.** It starts daily at 2:30pm, lasts 1½ hours, costs $21, and includes four drinks. Another fun tour, for those interested in the paranormal, is the **nightly ghost tour.** Cost is $18 for adults and $10 for children. This spooky and interesting tour gives participants insight into the many old island legends. Both tours are offered by the Key West Tour Association. And finally, there's a cemetery tour, which leaves daily at 10:30am (☎ **305/294-WALK**).

OUTDOOR PURSUITS

BICYCLING & MOPEDING A popular mode of transportation for locals and visitors, bikes and mopeds are available at many rental outlets in the city (see "Getting Around," above). Escape the hectic downtown scene and explore the island's scenic side streets. Head away from Duval Street to South Roosevelt Boulevard and the beachside enclaves along the way.

BEACHES Unlike the rest of the Keys, you'll actually find a few small beaches here, although they don't compare to the state's wide natural wonders up the coast. Here are your options: **Smathers Beach,** off South Roosevelt Boulevard west of the airport; **Higgs Beach,** along Atlantic Boulevard between White Street and Reynolds Road; and **Fort Zachary Beach,** located off the western end of Southard Boulevard.

Although there is an entrance fee ($3.75 per car, plus more for each passenger), I recommend Fort Zachary, since it also includes a great historical fort, a Civil War museum, and a large picnic area with tables, barbecue grills, bathrooms, and showers. Plus, large trees scattered across 87 acres provide shade for those who are reluctant to bake in the sun. The vulnerable point was damaged in Hurricane George in 1998, but replanting of native vegetation has made it even better than before. A narrow rocky beach is typical of the Key's beaches.

DIVING One of the area's largest scuba schools, **Dive Key West Inc.,** 3128 N. Roosevelt Blvd. (☎ **800/426-0707** or 305/296-3823; fax 305/296-0609; www.divekeywest.com; e-mail: divekeywest@flakeysol.com;), offers instruction on all levels. Its dive boats take participants to scuba and snorkel sites on nearby reefs.

Wreck dives and night dives are two of the special offerings of **Lost Reef Adventures,** 261 Margaret St. (☎ **800/952-2749** or 305/296-9737). Regularly scheduled runs and private charters can be arranged. Phone for departure information.

FISHING As any angler will tell you, there's no fishing like Keys fishing. Key West has it all: bonefish, tarpon, dolphin, tuna, grouper, cobia, and more. Sharks, too. When it comes to fishing, this is it.

Step aboard a small exposed skiff for an incredibly diverse day of fishing. In the morning, you can head offshore for sailfish or dolphin (the fish, not the mammal), and then by afternoon, get closer to land for a shot at tarpon, permit, grouper, or snapper. Here in Key West, you can probably pick up more cobia—one of the best fighting and eating fishes around—than anywhere else in the world. For a real fight, ask your skipper to go for the tarpon—the greatest fighting fish there is, famous for its dramatic "tail walk" on the water after it's hooked. Shark fishing is also popular.

You'll find plenty of competition among the charter fishing boats in and around Mallory Square. However, you should know that the bookers from the kiosks in town generally take 20% of a captain's fee in addition to an extra monthly fee. So you can usually save yourself money by booking directly with a captain or going straight to one of the docks. You can negotiate a good deal at **Charter Boat Row,** 1801 N. Roosevelt Ave. (across from the Shell station), home to more than 30 charter fishing and party boats. Just show up to arrange your outing, or call **Garrison Bite Marina** (☎ **305/292-8167**) for details.

The advantage of the smaller, more expensive charter boats is that you can call the shots. They'll take you where you want to go, to fish for what you want to catch. These "light tackles" are also easier to maneuver, which means you can go to backcountry spots for tarpon and bonefish, as well as out to the open ocean for tuna and dolphin. You'll really be able to feel the fish, and you'll get some good fights. Larger boats, for up to six or seven people, are cheaper and best for kingfish, billfish, and sailfish. Consider Jim Brienza's 27-foot *Sea Breeze,* docked at 25 Arbutus Dr. (☎ **305/294-6027**), if you want a light tackle experience. For a larger boat, try Capt. Henry Otto's 44-foot *Sunday,* docked at the Hyatt in Key West (☎ **305/294-7052**).

The huge commercial party boats are more for sightseeing than serious angling, though you can get lucky and get a few bites at one of the fishing holes. One especially good deal is the *Gulfstream III* (☎ **305/296-8494**), an all-day charter that goes out daily from 9:30am until 4pm. You'll pay $30, plus $3 for a rod and reel. This 65-foot party boat usually has at least 30 other anglers. Bring your own cooler or buy snacks on the boat. Beer and wine are allowed.

For serious anglers, nothing compares to the light tackle boats that leave from **Oceanside Marina** (☎ **305/294-4676**) on Stock Island, at 5950 Peninsula Avenue, 1¹/₂ miles off U.S. 1. It's a 20-minute drive from Old Town on the Atlantic side. There are more than 30 light tackle guides, which range from flatbed, backcountry skiffs to 28-foot open boats. There are also a few larger charters and a head or party boat that goes to the Dry Tortugas. Call the dockmaster for details.

For the light tackle experience of your life, call **Captain Bruce Cronin** at ☎ **305/294-4929** or **Captain Kenny Harris** at ☎ **305/294-8843,** two of the more famous (and pricey) captains still working these docks. You'll pay from $550 for a full day, usually about 8am until 4pm, and from $400 for half a day.

GOLF One of the area's only courses is **Key West Golf Club** (☎ **305/294-5232**), an 18-hole course located just north of the island of Key West at MM 4.5 (turn onto College Road to the course entrance). Designed by Rees Jones, the course has plenty of mangroves and water hazards on its 6,526 yards. It's open to the public and has a new pro shop. Call ahead for tee-time reservations.

KAYAKING **Mosquito Coast Outfitters,** housed in a woodsy wine bar at 1017 Duval St. (☎ **305/294-7178**), operates a first-rate kayaking and snorkeling tour every day as long as the weather is mild. The tours depart at 9am sharp and cost $45 per person. Included in the price are snacks, soft drinks, and a guided tour of the mangrove-studded islands of Sugar Key or Geiger Key just north of Key West. You'll be back by about 3pm.

SHOPPING

You'll find all kinds of unique gifts and souvenirs in Key West, from coconut postcards to key lime pies. On Duval Street, T-shirt shops outnumber almost any other business. If you must get a wearable memento, be careful of unscrupulous salespeople. Despite efforts to curtail the practice, many shops have been known to rip off unwitting shoppers. It pays to check the prices and the exchange rate before signing any sales slips. You are entitled to a written estimate of any T-shirt work before you pay for it.

At Mallory Square is the **Clinton Street Market,** an overair-conditioned mall of kiosks and stalls designed for the many cruise-ship passengers who never venture beyond this super-commercial zone. Amid the dreck are some delicious coffee and candy shops and some high-priced hats and shoes. There's also a free and clean rest room.

Once the main industry of Key West, cigar making is enjoying renewed success at the handful of factories that survived the slow years. Stroll through **"Cigar Alley,"** between Front and Greene streets, where you will find *viejitos* (little old men) rolling fat stogies just as they used to do in their homeland across the Florida Straits. Stop at the **Key West Cigar Factory,** at 308 Front St. (☎ 305/294-3470), for an excellent selection of imported and locally rolled smokes, including the famous El Hemingway. Remember, buying or selling Cuban-made cigars is illegal. Shops advertising "Cuban Cigars" are usually referring to domestic cigars made from tobacco grown from seeds that were brought from Cuba decades ago.

If you are looking for local or Caribbean art, you will find nearly a dozen galleries and shops clustered on Duval Street between Catherine and Fleming streets. You'll also find some excellent shops scattered on the side streets. One worth seeking out is the ✪ **Haitian Art Co.,** 600 Frances St. (☎ 305/296-8932), where you can browse through room upon room of original paintings from well-known and obscure Haitian artists in a range of prices from a few dollars to a few thousand. Also, check out **Cuba, Cuba!** at 814 Duval St. (☎ 305/295-9442). Here, you will find paintings, sculpture, and photos by Cuban artists and books and art from the island.

A favorite stop in the Keys is the deliciously fragrant **Key West Aloe** at 524 Front St., between Simonton and Duval streets (☎ 305/294-5592). Since 1971, this shop has been selling a simple line of bath products, including lotions, shampoos, and soothing balms for those who want a reminder of the tropical breezes once home. At the main shop (open until 8pm), you can find great gift baskets, tropical perfumes, and candies and cookies, too. In addition to frangipani, vanilla, and hibiscus scents, sample Key West for Men, a unique and alluringly musky best-seller.

Literature and music buffs will appreciate the many bookshops and record stores on the island. **Key West Island Bookstore** (☎ 305/294-2904) at 513 Fleming St. carries new, used, and rare books and specializes in fiction by residents of the Keys, including Hemingway, Tennessee Williams, Shel Silverstein, Ann Beattie, Richard Wilbur, and John Hersey. **Flaming Maggie's** (☎ 305/294-3931) at 830 Fleming St. carries a wide selection of gay books. Both shops are open daily.

New in 2000 is the combination museum and gift shop called **Reworx** just behind Pandemonium and the mosaic car at 825 Duval St. (☎ 305/295-0325 or 305/294-0351). Mammoth functional art made from salvaged metal parts is on display and smaller works from recycled material are on sale. Admission to the adjacent museum is $7 for adults, $5 for children aged 5 to 12 and well worth it.

Also worth checking out in the newly revitalized Bahama Village section of town are the shops along Petronia Street between Thomas and Whitehead streets. Especially interesting is **Maskerville** (☎ 305/293-6937), which sells a variety of feather-laden art work from masks to lampshades. Just next door is **Hello Gorgeous,** at 315 Petronia (☎ **305/294-1770**), which carries unique clothing, shoes, and jewelry for women and impersonators.

Off the beaten track at 814 Fleming St. (☎ **305/294-7901**) is the **Helio Gallery Store,** featuring locally made crafts and fine art.

For anything else, from bed linens to candlesticks to clothing, go to downtown's oldest and most renowned department store, **Fast Buck Freddie's,** at 500 Duval St. (☎ **305/294-2007**). For the same merchandise at reduced prices, try ✪ **Half Buck Freddie's,** 726 Caroline St. (☎ **305/294-6799**). Here you can shop for out-of-season bargains and "rejects" from the main store.

WHERE TO STAY

You'll find a wide variety of places to stay in Key West, from resorts with all the amenities to seaside motels, quaint bed-and-breakfasts, and clothing-optional guest houses. Unless you're in town during Key West's most popular holidays—Fantasy Fest (around Halloween), Hemingway Days (in July), and Christmas and New Year's—or for a big fishing tournament (many are held from October to December), you can almost always find a place to stay at the last minute. However, you may want to book early, especially in the winter, when prime properties fill up and many require 2- or 3-night minimums. Prices at these times are also extremely high. Finding a decent room for under $100 a night is a real trick.

Another suggestion is to call **Vacation Key West** (☎ **800/595-5397** or 305/295-9500; www.flakeysol.com/vkw). The phones are answered weekdays from 9am to 6pm and Saturday from 11am to 2pm. This wholesaler offers discounts of 20% to 30% and can usually find last-minute deals. They represent mostly larger hotels and motels but also can place visitors in guest houses. The **Key West Innkeepers Association,** P.O. Box 6172, Key West, FL 33041 (☎ **800/492-1911** or 305/292-3600), can also help find lodging in any price range from its dozens of members and affiliates.

Most major hotel chains have at least one location in Key West; most are clustered on North Roosevelt Boulevard (U.S. 1). Moderately priced options include **Howard Johnson,** 3031 N. Roosevelt Blvd. (☎ **800/942-0913** or 305/296-6595); the **Ramada Inn,** 3420 N. Roosevelt Blvd. (☎ **800/330-5541** or 305/294-5541); the **Econo Lodge,** 3820 N. Roosevelt Blvd. (☎ **800/553-2666** or 305294-5511); the **Holiday Inn Beachside,** 3841 N. Roosevelt Blvd. (☎ **800/292-7706** or 305/294-2571); and the **Quality Inn,** 3850 N. Roosevelt Blvd. (☎ **800/228-5151** or 305/294-6681). The Howard Johnson and the Holiday Inn are the only hotels with gulf-view rooms; the other hotels listed are just across the street. Duval Street is less than 5 minutes away by car or taxi.

A last resort should be the **Holiday Inn La Concha Hotel** at 430 Duval St. (☎ **800/745-2191**). It is centrally located, but there are few amenities for the price.

Gay travelers will want to call the **Key West Business Guild** (☎ **305/294-4603**), which represents more than 50 guest houses and B&Bs in town, as well as many other gay-owned businesses. Be advised that most gay guest houses have a clothing-optional policy. One of the most elegant and popular ones is **Big Ruby's** (☎ **800/477-7829** or 305/296-2323) at 409 Applerouth Lane (a little alley just off Duval Street). A low cluster of buildings surrounds a lushly landscaped courtyard where a hearty breakfast is served each morning and wine is poured at dusk. The mostly male guests hang out by a good-sized pool tanning in the buff. Also popular is **Oasis** at 823 Fleming St. (☎ **305/296-2131**), which is superclean and friendly, and you can enjoy the central location and a 14-seat hot tub.

Another luxurious property is **The Brass Key** at 412 Frances St. (☎ **305/ 296-4719**), which is more romantic and traditionally decorated and welcomes many lesbian travelers as well. *Out and About* gave it a five-star rating. For women only, the **Rainbow House,** 525 United St. (☎ **800/74-WOMYN** or 305/292-1450) is a large, fairly well-maintained guest house with lots of privacy and amenities, including two pools and two hot tubs. Rates in season range from $109 to $229.

Very Expensive

✪ **Key West Hilton Resort and Marina.** 245 Front St. (at the end of Duval St.), Key West, FL 33040. ☎ **800/221-2424** or 305/294-4000. Fax 305/294-4086. www.keywestresort. hilton.com. 215 units. A/C MINIBAR TV TEL. Winter $299–$525 double; $375–$800 suite. Off-season $195–$425 double; $300–$800 suite. 37 Sunset Key Cottages, up to 5 people: Winter $900–$1,495. Off-season $700–$1,000. AE, DC, CB, DISC, MC, V.

Completed in fall 1996, this Hilton is a truly luxurious addition to downtown's hotel scene. Key West's only full-service AAA four-diamond resort is situated at the very end of Duval Street in the middle of all of Old Town's action. The sparkling new rooms are large and well appointed, with tropical decor and all the modern conveniences. Choose a suite in the main building if you want a large Jacuzzi in your living room. Otherwise, the marina building has great views. This giant will no doubt be very popular with corporate and convention visitors.

Dining/Diversions: Flagler's, the elegant indoor dining room offers ample breakfasts and a huge Sunday brunch. Lunches and dinners focus on steak and seafood. The more casual beachside tiki hut specializes in frozen drinks but also serves sandwiches, fish-and-chips, and hearty snacks.

Amenities: Concierge, room service, laundry and dry-cleaning services, newspaper delivery, in-room massage, nightly turndown, twice-daily maid service, express checkout, valet parking, complimentary in-room coffee, secretarial services. Outdoor heated pool, offshore secluded beach, health club, Jacuzzi, sundeck, water-sports equipment, full-service marina, bicycle rental, game room, business center, self-service laundry, conference rooms, gift shops, and boutiques.

Wyndham Reach Resort. 1435 Simonton St., Key West, FL 33040. ☎ **800/626-0777.** For reservations ☎ 800/996-3426. Fax 305/296-4633. 150 units. www.casamarinakeywest. com. A/C MINIBAR TV TEL. Winter $259–$709 single or double. Off-season $149–$589 single or double. AE, CB, DC, DISC, MC, V. Valet parking $9.50

The Reach is one of the few hotels on the island with its own strip of sandy beach. The location here can be either a highlight or a drawback; it's a 5-minute walk away from the center of the Duval Street action. Supported by stilts that leave the entire ground floor for car parking, the hotel offers four floors of rooms designed around atriums. The wonderful guest rooms are large and feature tile floors, sturdy wicker furnishings, and tropical colors. Each contains a small service bar with a sink, fridge, and tea/coffeemaker, and has a vanity area separate from the bathroom. The rooms are so nice you can easily forgive the small closets and diminutive dressers. All have sliding glass doors that open onto balconies, and some have ocean views.

Ample palm-planted grounds surround a small pool area. There's also a private pier for fishing and suntanning. The protected waters are tame and shallow.

Amenities: Concierge, room service, dry cleaning, newspaper delivery, in-room massage, baby-sitting, express checkout. Outdoor heated swimming pool, beach, health spa, Jacuzzi, sauna, bicycle rental, business center, tour desk, conference rooms, sailboats, windsurfers, beauty salon.

◯ **Pier House Resort and Caribbean Spa.** 1 Duval St. (near Mallory Docks), Key West, FL 33040. ☎ **800/327-8340** or 305/296-4600. Fax 305/296-9085. 142 units. A/C MINI-BAR TV TEL. Winter $290–$460 double. Off-season $200–$355 double. AE, CB, DC, DISC, MC, V.

Pier House is one of the area's best resort choices, offering luxurious rooms, top-notch service, and a full-service spa. Its excellent location—at the foot of Duval Street and just steps from Mallory Docks—is the envy of every hotel on the island. Set back from the busy street, on a short strip of beach, this hotel is a welcome oasis of calm. The accommodations here vary tremendously, from relatively simple business-style rooms to romantic guest quarters complete with integrated stereo systems and whirlpool tubs. Their best waterfront suites and rooms have recently been renovated. Although every accommodation has either a balcony or a patio, not all overlook the water. My favorites, in the two-story spa building, don't have any view at all. But what they lack in scenery, they make up for in opulence; each well-appointed spa room has a sitting area and a huge Jacuzzi bathroom.

Dining/Diversions: The restaurant serves very respectable meals in a dark dining room or on an umbrella-covered patio overlooking the docks. Old Havana Docks is a good waterfront bar, especially at sunset.

Amenities: Concierge, room service, laundry services, newspaper delivery, in-room massage, express checkout. Heated swimming pool, beach, health club, spa treatments, two Jacuzzis, sauna, sundeck, water-sports equipment rentals, bicycle rental, tour desk, conference rooms, beauty salon.

Expensive

Island City House Hotel. 411 William St., Key West, FL 33040. ☎ **800/634-8230** or 305/294-5702. Fax 305/294-1289. 24 units. A/C TV TEL. Winter $175–$315. Off-season $115–$210. Rates include breakfast. AE, CB, DC, DISC, MC, V.

A small resort unto itself, the Island City House consists of three separate and unique buildings that share a common junglelike patio and pool. The first building, unimaginatively called the Island City House building, is a historic three-story wooden structure with wraparound verandas that allow guests to walk around the entire edifice on any floor. The warmly dressed old-fashioned interiors here include wood floors and many antique furnishings. Many rooms have full-size kitchens, queen-size beds, and sumptuous floral window treatments. The tile bathrooms could use more counter space, and the room lighting isn't always perfect, but eccentricities are part of this hotel's charm.

The unpainted wooden Cigar House has particularly large bedrooms, similar in ambience to those in the Island City House. Most rooms are furnished with wicker chairs and king-size beds and have big bathrooms (although lacking in counter space). As with the Island City House, rooms facing the property's interior courtyard are best. The Arch House is the least appealing of the three buildings, but still very recommendable. Built of Dade County pine, the Arch House's cozy bedrooms are furnished in wicker and rattan and come with small kitchens and bathrooms.

Amenities: Newspaper delivery, free coffee in lobby, dry cleaning, laundry service, in-room massage, baby-sitting. Kitchenettes, VCR rental and complimentary videos, outdoor heated pool, Jacuzzi, bicycle rental, sundeck, self-service Laundromat.

◯ **Marquesa Hotel.** 600 Fleming St. (at Simonton St.), Key West, FL 33040. ☎ **800/869-4631** or 305/292-1919. Fax 305/294-2121. www.marquesa.com. 27 units. A/C MINIBAR TV TEL. Winter $245–$380 double. Off-season $155–$265 double. AE, DC, MC, V. No children under 12 allowed.

The Marquesa offers the charm of a small historic hotel coupled with the amenities of a large resort. It encompasses four different buildings, two adjacent swimming pools, and a three-stage waterfall that cascades into a lily pond. Two of the hotel's houses are luxuriously restored Victorian homes whose rooms are outfitted with extraplush antiques and oversize contemporary furniture. The rooms in the two other, newly constructed buildings are even richer; many have four-poster wrought-iron beds with bright floral spreads. The green marble bathrooms are lush and spacious. The decor is simple, elegant, and spotless. These are the only hotel rooms I have ever seen that I would love to have in my own home.

Dining: One of Key West's most elegant restaurants, The Cafe Marquesa, serves only dinner. You can, however, order breakfast in your room or at poolside.

Amenities: Concierge, valet, newspaper delivery, twice-daily maid service, valet parking. Two outdoor swimming pools (one is heated), access to nearby health club.

Ocean Key Resort. Zero Duval St., Key West, FL 33040. ☎ **800/328-9745** or 305/296-7701. Fax 305/292-7685. www.oceankeyhouse.com. 99 units. A/C MINIBAR TV TEL. Winter from $289–$549 two-bedroom suite. Off-season $199–$449 two-bedroom suite. AE, DC, DISC, MC, V.

You can't get much more central than this modern hotel, located across from the Pier House at the foot of Duval Street. Most of the guest rooms here are suites, ample-sized accommodations fitted with built-in couches. Many rooms have sliding glass doors that open onto small balconies, some of which enjoy unobstructed water views. All suites have Jacuzzi tubs in either the master bedroom or living room.

Dining: A casual dockside grill serves lunch and dinner. Breakfast is served at an indoor/outdoor cafe.

Amenities: Concierge, room service, dry-cleaning and laundry services. VCRs and video rentals, outdoor heated pool, access to nearby health club, Jacuzzi in every suite, conference rooms, sundeck, water-sports concession, tour desk.

✪ **Weatherstation Inn.** 57 Front St., Key West FL, 33040. ☎ **800/815-2707** or 305/294-7277. Fax 305/294-0544. www.weatherstationinn.com. 8 units. A/C TV TEL. Winter $195–$315 double. Off-season $150–$215 double. Rates include continental breakfast. AE, MC, V.

Originally built in 1912 as a weather station, this beautifully restored and meticulously maintained two-story, renaissance-style inn is located just 2 blocks from Duval Street. It's situated on the tropical grounds of the former Old Navy Yard, now an exclusive and very private gated community. Harry Truman, Eisenhower, and J.F.K. have all visited the station. Spacious and uncluttered, each room is uniquely furnished to complement the interior architecture: hardwood floors, tall sash windows, and high ceilings. The large modern bathrooms are especially appealing. Breakfast is continental, an assortment of bakery breads, pastries, fresh fruit, coffee, tea, and juices. Enjoy breakfast by the pool among the flowers. The staff is friendly and accommodating. A full concierge service is available.

MODERATE

Chelsea House. 707 Truman Ave., Key West, FL 33040. ☎ **800/845-8859** or 305/296-2211. Fax 305/296-4822. www.chelseahousekw.com. 20 units. A/C TV TEL. Winter $130–$229 double. Off-season $85–$135 double. Rates include breakfast. Pets $10 extra. AE, CB, DC, DISC, MC, V. Private parking. Children 14 and under not accepted.

Despite its decidedly English name, the Chelsea House is "all American," a term that in Key West isn't code for "conservative." Chelsea House caters to a mixed gay/straight clientele and displays its liberal philosophy most prominently on the clothing-optional sundeck. One of only a few guest houses in Key West that offer TVs, VCRs, private bathrooms, and kitchenettes in each guest room, Chelsea House has a large number of repeat visitors. The apartments come with full kitchens and separate living areas, as well as palm-shaded balconies in back. The bathrooms and closets could be bigger, but both are adequate and serviceable.

When weather permits, which is almost always, breakfast is served outside by the pool.

✪ **La Pensione.** 809 Truman Ave. (between Windsor and Margaret sts.), Key West, FL 33040. ☎ **800/893-1193** or 305/292-9923. Fax 305/296-6509. www.lapensione.com. 9 units. A/C TEL. Winter from $168 double. Off-season from $98 double. Rates include breakfast. There's a 10% discount for readers who mention this guide. AE, DC, DISC, JCB, MC, V.

This classic bed-and-breakfast, located in the 1891 home of a former cigar executive, distinguishes itself from other similar inns by its extreme attention to details. The friendly and knowledgeable staff treats the stunning home and its guests with extraordinary care. The comfortable rooms all have air-conditioning, ceiling fans, king-size beds, and private bathrooms. Many have French doors opening onto spacious verandas. Although the rooms have no phones or televisions, the distractions of Duval Street, only steps away, should keep you adequately occupied during your visit. Breakfast, which includes made-to-order Belgian waffles, fresh fruit, and a variety of breads or muffins, can be taken on the wraparound porch or at the communal dining table. No children are allowed.

South Beach Oceanfront Motel. 508 South St. (at the Atlantic Ocean), Key West, FL 33040. ☎ **800/354-4455** or 305/296-5611. Fax 305/294-8272. www.oldtownresorts.com. 50 units. A/C TV TEL. Winter $135–$230 double. Off-season $85–$149 double. AE, MC, V.

This standard two-story motel is located directly on the ocean, within walking distance of Duval Street. Because the structure is perpendicular to the water, most of the rooms overlook a pretty Olympic-size swimming pool rather than a wide swath of beach. The best, and by far most expensive, are the lucky pair of beachfront rooms on the end (nos. 115 and 215).

All rooms share similar aging decor and include standard furnishings. The smallish bathrooms could use a makeover, and include showers but no tubs. There's a private pier, an on-site water-sports concession, and a laundry room available for guest use. When making reservations, ask for a room that's as close to the beach (and as far from the road) as possible. If you'll be there a while, ask for one of the rooms with a kitchenette; there is no restaurant on the premises.

Southernmost Point Guest House. 1327 Duval St., Key West, FL 33040. ☎ **305/294-0715.** Fax 305/296-0641. 6 units. A/C TV TEL. Winter $95–$200 double; $150 suite. Off-season $55–$135 double; $95 suite. Rates include breakfast. AE, MC, V.

One of the only inns that actually welcomes children and pets, this romantic and historic guest house is a real find. The antiseptically clean rooms are not as fancy as the house's ornate 1885 exterior. Each room has basic beds and couches and a hodgepodge of furnishings, including futon couches, high-back wicker chairs, and plenty of mismatched throw rugs. Each room is different. Room 5 is best; situated upstairs, it has a private porch, an ocean view, and windows that let in lots of light. Every room has a refrigerator and a full decanter of sherry. Mona Santiago, the hotel's kind, laid-back owner, provides chairs and towels that can be brought to the beach, which is just a block away. Plus, guests can help themselves to wine as they soak in the new 14-seat hot tub. Kids will enjoy the swings in the backyard and the pet rabbits.

Inexpensive

Abaco Inn. 415 Julia St. (between Truman Ave. and Virginia St.), Key West, FL 33040. ☎ **800/358-6307** or 305/296-2212. Fax 305/295-0349. www.abaco-inn.com. 3 units. A/C TV TEL. Winter from $99 double. Off-season from $69 double. 3-day minimum stay in season. Additional person $15 extra. AE, DISC, MC, V.

This tidy little guest house is situated on a secluded lane just off Duval Street. Though there is no pool or view, you'll find a hair dryer, iron and ironing board, small refrigerator, microwave, and coffeemaker in each of the three simple rooms. Once the home of a cigar maker, the house dates from the early 1900s. Now, it is owned and operated by George Fontana, a friendly and knowledgeable tour guide and writer. Look for his column on local characters in the *Key West Citizen*. You can't beat the price in this superconvenient location. No smoking is allowed on the property.

Angelina Guest House. 302 Angela St. (at the corner of Thomas St.) Key West, FL 33040. ☎ **305/294-4480.** Fax 305/294-0621. E-mail: theangelina@aol.com. 13 units. Winter $60–$175. Off-season $40–$120. DISC, MC, V.

This youth hostel–looking guest house is about the cheapest in town and conveniently located near a hot, hippie restaurant called Blue Heaven (see "Where to Dine," below). It is generally safe and full of character. The rooms are all furnished differently in a modest style. There are no televisions or telephones, so guests are compelled to spend more time exploring Key West rather than sitting in their rooms. Plans are now underway to add air-conditioning units in all guest rooms, as well as a new pool out back, a real consideration in the sweltering summer days. A good cross breeze and ceiling fans do cool the rooms considerably. Though sparse, the Angelina is a good place to crash if you are on the cheap.

Blue Lagoon Motel. 3101 N. Roosevelt Blvd., Key West, FL 33040-4118. ☎ **305/296-1043.** Fax 305/296-6499. 72 units. A/C TV TEL. Winter $80–$240 double. Off-season $50–$110 double. MC, V.

More than half of the rooms at this funky ocean-side resort rent for less than $100 year-round—an all-too-unusual occurrence in Key West, especially for full-service resorts. The rooms, furnished in heavy cedar wood, are basic and a bit run-down but still decent—along the lines of a Howard Johnson or other budget accommodation. Second-floor rooms are generally quieter. The pricier waterfront rooms aren't really worth the extra money (although some include a jet-ski ride). Guests tend to be young college-aged kids out for a wild time. Although pretty far from Old Town, the resort is convenient by scooter and car, and it is literally surrounded by Wave Runners, boats, parasailing, and diving fun.

✪ **The Grand.** 1116 Grinnell St. (between Virginia and Catherine sts.), Key West, FL 33040. ☎ **888/947-2630** or 305/294-0590. E-mail: thegrand@flakeysol.com. 10 units. A/C TV TEL. Winter $88–$138 double; $121 suite. Off-season $48–$98 double; $79 suite. AE, DISC, MC, V.

Don't expect cabbies or locals to know about this gem, located in a modest residential section of Old Town, about 5 blocks from Duval Street. It's got almost everything you could want, including a very moderate price tag. It's run by another one of those happy-to-be-alive Northeastern transplants, Elizabeth Rose, who goes out of her way to provide any and all services for her appreciative guests. All rooms have private bathrooms, air-conditioning, telephones, and private entrances. The floors are painted in bright colors, and beds are dressed in light tropical prints. Room no. 2 on the back side of the house is the best deal; it's small, but it has a porch and the most privacy. Suites are a real steal, too. The large two-room units come with a complete kitchen. This place is undoubtedly the best bargain in town.

Key West International Hostel. 718 South St., Key West, FL 33040. ☎ **800/51-HOSTEL** or 305/296-5719. Fax 305/296-0672. 100 units. A/C TV. Winter $17 for IYHF members, $20 for nonmembers dorm beds; $75–$105 motel units. Off-season from $15 for IYHF members, from $18 for nonmembers dorm beds; $50–$85 motel units. MC, V.

This well-run hostel is a 3-minute walk to the beach and to Old Town. It's not the Ritz, but it's affordable. Very busy with European backpackers, this is a great place to meet people. The dorm rooms are dark and sparse, but clean enough. The higher-priced motel rooms are a good deal, especially those equipped with full kitchens. Amenities include a pool table under a tiki-hut roof, and bicycle rentals for $6 per day. There are minisafes in each room. There's also cheap food available for breakfast, lunch, and dinner. They also have discounted prices for snorkeling, diving, and sunset cruises.

WHERE TO DINE

Key West offers a vast, tempting array of food. You'll find many cuisines represented: Thai, Cuban, Bahamian, Japanese, and barbecue. Plus, there are the usual drive-through fast-food franchises (mostly up on Roosevelt Boulevard). Duval Street even succumbed to the lure of a Hard Rock Cafe. Wander Old Town or the newly spruced up Bahama Village and browse menus after you have exhausted the list of my picks below.

If you don't feel like venturing out, call **We Deliver** (☎ **305/293-0078**), a service that for a small fee (between $3 and $6) will bring you anything you want from any of the area's restaurants or stores. We Deliver operates between 3 and 11pm. If you are staying in a condo or efficiency you may want to stock your fridge with groceries, beer, wine, and snacks from the area's oldest grocer, **Fausto's Food Palace.** Open since 1926, there are now two locations: 1105 White St. and 522 Fleming St. The Fleming Street location will deliver (☎ **305/294-5221** or 305/296-5663). Fausto's has a $25 minimum.

VERY EXPENSIVE

Cafe des Artistes. 1007 Simonton St. (near Truman Ave.). ☎ **305/294-7100.** Reservations recommended. Main courses $25–$38. AE, MC, V. Daily 6–11pm. FRENCH.

Open for nearly 2 decades, the Cafe des Artistes's impressive longevity is the result of its winning combination of food and atmosphere. Traditional French meals benefit from a subtle tropical twist. The food is served by uniformed waiters well versed in the virtues of fine food. Start with the duck-liver pâté made with fresh truffles and old cognac, or Maryland crabmeat served with an artichoke heart and herbed tomato confit. Nouvelle and traditional French entrees include lobster flambé with mango and basil and wine-basted lamb chops rubbed with rosemary and ginger.

Louie's Backyard. 700 Waddell Ave. ☎ **305/294-1061.** Reservations highly recommended. Main courses $25–$30; lunch $8–$15. AE, CB, DC, MC, V. Daily 11:30am–3pm and 6–10:30pm. CARIBBEAN.

Louie's, nestled amid blooming bougainvillea on a lush slice of the Gulf, remains one of the most romantic restaurants on earth. Famed chef Norman Van Aiken of Norman's in Miami brought his talents further south and started what has become one of the finest dining spots in the Keys. After dinner, sit at the dockside bar and watch the waves crash, almost touching your feet while enjoying a cocktail at sunset. You can't go wrong with the fresh catch of the day or any seafood dish for that matter. The weekend brunches are also great. Even if you can't stay for dinner, go for lunch; this is one dining experience you won't want to miss.

Expensive

Antonia's. 615 Duval St. ☎ **305/294-6565.** Fax 305/294-2743. Reservations suggested. Main courses $18–$26; pastas $12–$15. AE, DC, MC, V. Daily 6–11pm. REGIONAL ITALIAN.

The food is great but the atmosphere a bit fussy for Key West. If you don't have a reservation in season, don't bother. Still, if you are organized and don't mind paying high prices for dishes that go for much less elsewhere, try this old favorite. From the perfectly seasoned homemade focaccia to an exemplary crème brûlée, this elegant little standout is amazingly consistent. The menu includes a small selection of classics, such as *zuppa di pesce,* rack of lamb in a rosemary sauce, and veal Marsala. However, the way to go is with the nightly specials. You can't go wrong with any of the handmade pastas.

✪ **Bagatelle.** 115 Duval St. ☎ **305/296-6609.** Reservations recommended. Main courses $14–$21; lunch $5–$10. AE, DISC, MC, V. Daily 11am–11pm SEAFOOD/TROPICAL.

Reserve a seat at the elegant second-floor veranda overlooking Duval Street's mayhem. From the calm above, enjoy any of the selections from a large eclectic menu. You may want to start your meal with the excellent herb-and-garlic stuffed whole artichoke or the sashimi-like seared tuna rolled in black peppercorns. Also recommended is a lightly creamy garlic-herb pasta topped with Gulf shrimp, Florida lobster, and mushrooms. The best chicken and beef dishes are given a tropical treatment: grilled with papaya, ginger, and soy.

La Trattoria. 524 Duval St. ☎ **305/296-1075.** Appetizers $7–$9; pasta $10–$17; main courses $17–$22. AE, DC, DISC, MC, V. Daily 5:30–11pm ITALIAN.

Have a true Italian feast in a relaxed atmosphere. Each dish here is prepared and presented according to old, Italian tradition and is cooked to order. The antipasti are scrumptious. Try the delicious bread-crumb-stuffed, baked mushroom caps, they're firm yet tender. The stuffed eggplant with ricotta and roasted peppers is light and flavorful. Or have the seafood salad of shrimp, calamari, and mussels, fish market fresh and tasty. The pasta dishes here are also great. Try the *penne Venezia,* with mushrooms, sun-dried tomatoes, and crabmeat, or the cannelloni stuffed with veal and spinach. For dessert, don't skip the homemade tiramisu; it's light but full-flavored. The dining room is spacious yet intimate and the waiters are friendly and informative. Before you leave be sure to visit Virgilio's, the restaurant's very own cocktail lounge with live jazz until 2 am.

✪ **Mangoes.** 700 Duval St. (at Angela St.). ☎ **305/292-4606.** Fax 305/292-7291 www.mangoes.keywest.com. Reservations recommended for parties of 6 or more. Main courses $12–$24; pizzas $10–$12; lunch $7–$14. AE, CB, DC, DISC, MC, V. Daily 11am–midnight; pizza until 1am. FLORIBBEAN.

This restaurant's large brick patio, shaded by overgrown banyan trees, is so seductive to passersby that it's packed almost every night of the week. Appetizers include conch chowder laced with sherry, lobster dumplings with tangy key lime sauce, and grilled shrimp cocktail with spicy mango chutney. Spicy sausage with black beans and rice, crispy curried chicken, and local snapper with passion fruit sauce are typical among the entrees, but Mangoes' outstanding individual-size designer pizzas are the best menu items by far. They're baked in a Neapolitan-style oven fired by buttonwood. Even though it is right on tourist-laden Duval Street, Mangoes enjoys a good reputation among locals.

Moderate

Alonzo's Oyster Bar. 231 Margaret St. ☎ **305/294-7496.** Fax 305/296-4650. Appetizers $5–$8; main courses $11–$17. MC, V. Daily 11am–11pm. SEAFOOD.

Alonzo's Oyster Bar offers good seafood in a Key West casual setting. It's located on the ground floor of the A&B Lobster House at the end of Front Street in the marina. To start your meal off, try the Steamed Beer Shrimp—tantalizingly fresh jumbo shrimp in a garlic, Old Bay, beer, and cayenne pepper sauce. Don't forget to dunk your bread. A house specialty is white clam chili, a delicious mix of tender clams, white beans, and potatoes served with a dollop of sour cream. An excellent entree is the pan-fried lobster cakes, served with sweet corn mashed potatoes, chipotle gravy, and roasted corn salsa. Alonzo's is the casual section of the A&B Lobster House; if you want to dress up, go upstairs for their "fine dining." The staff is cheerful and informative and the service is very good.

✪ **Blue Heaven.** 729 Thomas St. (at the corner of Petronia St.). ☎ **305/296-8666.** Main courses $9–$24; lunch $5–$13; breakfast $3–$8.50. DISC, MC, V. Mon–Sat 8am–3pm and 6–10:30pm; Sun brunch 8am–1pm and 6–10:30pm. Mon–Tues closed for breakfast/lunch. SEAFOOD/AMERICAN/NATURAL.

This little hippie-run gallery and restaurant has become the place to be in Key West—and with good reason. Be prepared to wait in line. The food here is some of the best in town, especially for breakfast. You can enjoy homemade granola, huge tropical fruit pancakes, and seafood Benedict. Dinners are just as good and run the gamut from just-caught fish dishes to Jamaican-style jerk chicken, curried soups, and vegetarian stews. But if you're a neat freak, don't bother. Some people are put off by the dirt floors and roaming cats and birds. The building used to be a bordello, where Hemingway was said to hang out watching cockfights.

Mangia, Mangia. 900 Southard St. (at Margaret St.). ☎ **305/294-2469.** Reservations not accepted. Main courses $9–$15. AE, MC, V. Daily 5:30–10pm. ITALIAN/AMERICAN.

Mangia, Mangia is one of Key West's best values. Locals appreciate that they can get good, inexpensive food here in a town filled with many tourist traps. Off the beaten track, in a little corner storefront, this great Chicago-style pasta place serves some of the best Italian food in the Keys. The family-run restaurant offers superb homemade pastas of every description, including one of the tastiest marinaras around. The simple grilled chicken breast brushed with olive oil and sprinkled with pepper is another good choice. You wouldn't know it from the glossy glass front room, but there's a fantastic little outdoor patio dotted with twinkling pepper lights and lots of plants. You can relax out back with a glass of one of their excellent wines—they're said to have the largest selection in the Keys—or homemade beer while you wait for your table.

✪ **Pepe's.** 806 Caroline St. (between Margaret and Williams sts.). ☎ **305/294-7192.** Main courses $13–$22; breakfast $2–$9; lunch $5–$9. DISC, MC, V. Daily 6:30am–10:30pm. AMERICAN.

This old dive has been serving good, basic food for nearly a century. Steaks and Apalachicola Bay oysters are the big draw for regulars who appreciate the rustic bar-room setting and historic photos on the walls. Look for original scenes of Key West in 1909, when Pepe's first opened. If the weather is nice, choose a seat on the patio under a stunning mahogany tree. Burgers, fish sandwiches, and standard chili satisfy hearty eaters. Buttery sautéed mushrooms and rich mashed potatoes are the best comfort food in Key West. Stop by early for breakfast when you can get old-fashioned chipped beef on toast and all the usual egg dishes. In the evening, there are reasonably priced cocktails on the deck.

Turtle Kraals Wildlife Grill. 213 Margaret St. (corner of Caroline St.). ☎ **305/294-2640.** Main courses $10–$20. DISC, MC, V. Mon–Thurs 11am–10:30pm; Fri–Sat 11am–11pm; Sun noon–10:30pm. Bar closes at midnight. SOUTHWESTERN/SEAFOOD.

You'll join lots of locals in this out-of-the-way converted warehouse with indoor and dockside seating that serves innovative seafood at great prices. Try the twin lobster tails stuffed with mango and crabmeat or any of the big quesadillas or fajitas. Kids will like the wildlife exhibits and the very cheesy menu. Blues bands play most nights.

INEXPENSIVE

✪ **Anthony's Cafe.** 1111 Duval St. (at Amelia St.). ☎ **305/296-8899.** Breakfast $2–$5; sandwiches and salads $5.50–$7 with a side; hot plates $8–$13. Cash only. Daily 8am–10pm. ITALIAN DELI/ROTISSERIE

Though owned and operated by a Greek import, this rustic Italian-style trattoria is a welcome addition to an area crowded with more expensive and less delicious options. Fragrant roasted chicken and overstuffed sandwiches on fresh baked bread are the best choices. Also good are the many salads and daily specials.

Bahama Mama's Kitchen. 324 Petronia St. ☎ **305/294-3355.** Appetizers $4–$7; main courses $9–$13. MC, V. Daily 11am–10pm. BAHAMIAN.

Sit outside under an umbrella and enjoy the authentic Bahamian dishes from recipes that have been handed down through the owner, Corey's, family for the past 150 years. Made from scratch and prepared fresh daily, all dishes are created with their special "Bahamian" seasonings. Try the coconut shrimp butterfried, soaked in coconut oil, battered with egg, and then rolled in fresh shredded coconut and deep-fried. The fresh catch of the day comes blackened, broiled or fried and is served with island plantains, shrimp hash cakes and crab rice. The service is good and the staff is friendly. Bahama Mama's Kitchen is located in the Bahama Village Market.

The Deli. 531 Truman Ave. (corner of Truman Ave. and Simonton St.). ☎ **305/294-1464.** Full meals $7–$23; sandwiches $3–$8. DISC, MC, V. Daily 7:30am–10pm. DINER/AMERICAN.

In operation since 1950, this family-owned, corner eatery has kept up with the times. It's really more of a diner than a deli and has a vast menu with all kinds of hearty options, from meat loaf to yellowtail snapper. The seafood options are pretty good. A daily selection of more than a dozen vegetables includes the usual diner choices of beets, corn, and coleslaw with some distinctly Caribbean additions, such as rice and beans and fried plantains. Most dinners include a choice of two vegetables and homemade biscuits or corn bread. Breakfasts are made to order and attract a loyal following of locals. The Deli also offers ice cream sundaes and gourmet coffees.

✪ **El Siboney Restaurant.** 900 Catherine St. (at Margaret St.). ☎ **305/296-4184.** Main courses $5–$13. No credit cards. Mon–Sat 11am–9:30pm. CUBAN.

For good, cheap Cuban food, stop at this corner dive that looks more like a gas station than a diner. Be prepared however, to wait like the locals for succulent roast pork, Cuban sandwiches, grilled chicken, and ropa vieja, all served with heaps of rice and beans. This tiny storefront is a worthwhile, very affordable choice in a town with lots of glossy tourist traps.

PT's Late Night. 920 Caroline St. (at the corner of Margaret St.). ☎ **305/296-4245.** Main courses $5–$14; DISC, MC, V. Daily 11am–4am. AMERICAN.

This place is worth knowing about not only because it's one of the only places in town serving food past 10pm, but it also happens to serve good food at extremely reasonable prices. Let's say it's 1am, you're starving, and you've just parked your bike outside: You'll be ecstatic when your heaping plate of nachos arrives. Fajitas are served sizzling hot with a huge platter of fixings, including beans, rice, lettuce, jalapeños, and tomatoes. Superfresh salads are so big they can be a meal in themselves. PT's is more like a sports bar than a restaurant and service can be a bit slow and brusque.

KEY WEST AFTER DARK

Duval Street is the Bourbon Street of Florida. Amid the T-shirt shops and clothing boutiques, you'll find bar after bar serving neon-colored frozen drinks to revelers who bounce from one to the next from noon till dawn. Bands and crowds vary from night to night and season to season. Your best bet is to start at Truman Avenue and head up Duval to check them out for yourself. Cover charges are rare, so stop into a dozen and see which you like.

Captain Tony's Saloon. 428 Greene St. ☎ **305/294-1838.**

Just around the corner from Duval's beaten path, this smoky old wooden bar is about as authentic as you'll find. It comes complete with old-time regulars who remember the island before cruise ships docked here; they say Hemingway drank, caroused, and even wrote here. The owner, Capt. Tony Tarracino, a former controversial Key West mayor, has recently capitalized on the success of this once-quaint tavern by franchising the place.

Durty Harry's. 208 Duval St. ☎ **305/296-4890.**

This large entertainment complex features live rock bands almost every night. You can wander to one of the many outdoor bars or head up to Upstairs at Rick's, an indoor/outdoor dance club that gets going late. For the more racy singles or couples, there is the Red Garter, a pocket-sized strip club popular with bachelor and divorce parties. The hawker outside reminds couples that "The family that strips together sticks together."

Epoch. 623 Duval St. ☎ **305/296-8521.**

Until an arsonist put an end to the former legend in 1995, this former gay club was the place to dance to everything from techno to house and disco to reggae. Now expanded to include seven bars, an even bigger dance floor, a huge outside deck overlooking Duval Street, and a new state-of-the-art sound system, this is a better-than-ever choice for people of any orientation who can appreciate a good time.

Jimmy Buffett's Margaritaville Cafe. 500 Duval St. ☎ **305/292-1435.**

This cafe, named after another Key West legend, is a worthwhile stop. Although Mr. Buffett moved to glitzy Palm Beach years ago, his name is still attracting large crowds. This kitschy restaurant/bar/gift shop features live bands every night—from rock to blues to reggae and everything in between. The touristy cafe is furnished with plenty of Buffett memorabilia, including gold records, photos, and drawings. The margaritas are high-priced but tasty. The cheeseburgers aren't worth singing about.

Sloppy Joe's. 201 Duval St. ☎ **305/294-5717,** ext. 10. Daily 9am–4am

You'll have to stop in here just to say you did. Scholars and drunks debate whether this is the same Sloppy Joe's that Hemingway wrote about, but there's no argument that this classic bar's turn-of-the-century wooden ceiling and cracked tile floors are Key West originals. There's live music nightly as well as a cigar room and martini bar.

THE GAY SCENE

In Key West, the best music and dancing can be found at the predominantly gay clubs. While many of the area's other hot spots are geared toward tourists who like to imbibe, the gay clubs are for those who want to rave—mostly locals (or at least, recent transplants). None of the spots mentioned here discriminate—anyone open-minded and fun is welcome. Cover varies, but is rarely more than $10.

A popular late-night spot is **One Saloon,** 524 Duval St. (☎ **305/296-8118**), featuring great drag and lots more disco. A mostly male clientele frequents this hot spot from 9pm until 4am. Another Duval Street favorite is **Diva's** at 711 Duval St. (☎ **305/292-8500**), where you might catch drag queens belting out torch songs or judges voting on the best package in the wet jockey shorts contest.

Sunday nights are fun at two local spots. **Tea by the Sea,** on the pier at the Atlantic Shores Motel, 510 South St. (☎ **305/296-2491**), attracts a faithful following of regulars and visitors alike. Show up after 7:30pm. Better known around town as La-Te-Da, **La Terraza,** at 1125 Duval St. (☎ **305/296-6703**), is a great spot to gather poolside for the best martini in town—but don't bother with the food.

4 The Dry Tortugas

70 miles W of Key West

Few people realize that the Florida Keys don't end at Key West. About 70 miles west are a chain of seven small islands known as the Dry Tortugas. As long as you have come this far, you might as well take a trip to the Dry Tortugas, especially if you're into bird watching, which is the primary draw of these seven small islands.

Ponce de León, who discovered this far-flung cluster of coral keys in 1513, named them "Las Tortugas" because of the many sea turtles, which still flock to the area during the nesting season in the warm summer months. Oceanic charts later carried the preface "dry" to warn mariners that fresh water was unavailable here. Modern intervention has made drinking water available, but little else.

These underdeveloped islands make a great day trip for travelers interested in seeing the truly natural anomalies of the Florida Keys—especially the birds. The Dry Tortugas are nesting grounds and roosting sites for thousands of tropical and subtropical oceanic birds. Visitors will also find a historical fort, good fishing, and terrific snorkeling around shallow reefs.

GETTING THERE

BY BOAT The **Yankee Fleet,** based in Key West (☎ **800/634-0939** or 305/294-7009), offers day trips from Key West for sightseeing, snorkeling, or both. Cruises leave daily at 7:30am from the Land's End Marina, at Margaret Street. Breakfast is served on board. The journey takes 3 hours. Once on the island, called Garden Key, you can join a guided tour or explore it on your own. Boats return to Key West by 7pm. Tours cost $85 per person, including breakfast; $50 for children 16 and under; $75 for seniors, students, and military personnel. Snorkeling equipment rental is free. Phone for reservations.

The **Sunny Days Catamaran's "Fast Cat"** is faster than the loud Yankee fleet (☎ **800/236-7937**; 305/292-6100) and a better value. Included in the $85 round-trip adult fare is a continental breakfast and a buffet lunch with cold cuts, fresh veggies, fruits, and salads and a snorkeling excursion to a wreck in 5 to 20 feet of water. The high-speed power cat leaves Key West at 8am and returns by 6pm.

BY PLANE **Seaplanes of Key West,** based at Key West Airport (☎ **800/950-2-FLY** or 305/294-0709), offers daily excursions. Weather permitting, flights depart at 8am, 10am, noon, and 2pm. The 40-minute trip at about 500 feet offers a great introduction to these little-known islets. Fares, which include snorkeling equipment and a cooler for use on the island, start at $159 for adults for a half-day and $275 for a full day. Rates for kids under 12 are discounted by about 30%. Bring a bathing suit, snorkeling equipment, and some snacks to enjoy on these remote and beautiful islands.

EXPLORING THE DRY TORTUGAS

Fort Jefferson, a huge six-sided 19th-century fortress, is built almost at the water's edge of Garden Key, giving the appearance that it floats in the middle of the sea. The monumental structure is surrounded by formidable 8-foot-thick walls that rise up from the sand to a height of nearly 50 feet. Impressive archways, stonework, and parapets make this 150-year-old monument a grand sight. With the invention of the rifled cannon, the fort's masonry construction became obsolete, and the building was never completed. For 10 years, from 1863 to 1873, Fort Jefferson served as a prison, a kind of "Alcatraz East." Among its prisoners were four of the "Lincoln Conspirators," including Samuel A. Mudd, the doctor who set the broken leg of fugitive assassin John Wilkes Booth. In 1935, Fort Jefferson became a national monument administered by the National Park Service. For more information about Fort Jefferson and the Dry Tortugas, call the **Everglades National Park Service** at ☎ **305/242-7700.**

OUTDOOR PURSUITS

BIRD WATCHING Bring your binoculars and your bird books. Bird watching is the reason to visit this little cluster of tropical islands. The islands, uniquely situated in the middle of the migration flyway between North and South America, serve as an important rest stop for the more than 200 winged varieties that pass through here annually. The season peaks from mid-March to mid-May, when thousands of birds—including thrushes, orioles, boobies, swallows, black noddys, and snooty terns—show up. Many other species from the West Indies can be found year-round.

DIVING & SNORKELING The warm, clear, shallow waters of the Dry Tortugas combine to produce optimum conditions for snorkeling and scuba diving. Four endangered species of sea turtles—the green, leatherback, Atlantic ridley, and hawksbill—can be found here, along with a myriad of marine species. The region just outside the seawall of Garden Key's Fort Jefferson is excellent for underwater touring; an abundant variety of fish, corals, and more live in just 3 or 4 feet of water.

FISHING Fishing for snapper, tarpon, grouper, and other fish is popular. The mandatory saltwater fishing permit costs $7 for 3 days and $17 for 7 days. No bait or boating services are available in the Tortugas, but there are day docks on Garden Key as well as a cleaning table. The water is roughest in winter, but the fishing is excellent year-round. Outfitters from Key West can arrange day charters (see "Sports & Outdoor Activities," above).

CAMPING

The rustic beauty of tiny Garden Key is a camper's dream. Don't worry about sharing your site with noisy RVs or motor homes; they can't get here. The abundance of birds doesn't make it quiet, but camping here—literally a stone's throw from the water—is as picturesque as it gets. Campers are allowed to pitch tents only on Garden Key. Picnic tables, cooking grills, and toilets are provided, but there are no showers. All supplies must be packed in and out. Sites are $3 per person per night and are available on a first-come, first-served basis. With only 10 sites, they book up fast. For more information, call the **National Park Service** (☎ **305/242-7700**).

12 The Gold Coast

If you haven't visited the cities along Florida's southeastern coast in the last few years, you'll be amazed at how much has changed. Miles of sprawling grassland and empty lots have been replaced with luxurious resorts and high-rise condominiums. Taking advantage of their close proximity to Miami, the cities that make up the Gold Coast have attracted millions looking to escape crowded sidewalks, traffic jams and the everyday routines of life.

There is so much to see and do that one weekend, even one week, is hardly enough to take it all in. Those in love with nature and wildlife will enjoy exploring the 500-acre drive through Lion Country Safari, the nation's first cageless zoo in West Palm Beach. Catch the Montreal Expos and the St. Louis Cardinals during spring training in Jupiter's Roger Dean Stadium. Rent a bicycle and ride along a paved trail basking in the shade of 100-year-old Banyan trees. Shop in the exclusive shops in Boca Raton. Wander through museums and galleries containing collections ranging in everything from Buddhist sculptures to cartoon books. Discover new worlds at Delray Beach's Morikami Museum and Japanese Gardens or indulge in the history of Henry Flager's estate, "Whitehall," at The Flagler Museum, called the "Taj Mahal of North America."

But tourists aren't the only people coming here; thousands of transplants, fleeing the increasing population influx in Miami and the frigid winters up North, have made this area their home. As a result, there has been a construction boom in the existing cities and westward in the swampy areas of the Everglades. More than 20 homes per day are being built in Broward County alone. There has also been a great revitalization of several downtown areas, including Hollywood, Fort Lauderdale, and West Palm Beach. These once desolate urban centers have been spruced up and now attract more young travelers and families than ever before.

Unfortunately, like its neighbors to the south, the Gold Coast can be prohibitively hot and buggy in the summer. The good news is that bargains are plentiful in the summer months (between May and October), when many locals take advantage of package deals and uncrowded resorts.

For the purposes of this chapter, the Gold Coast will consist of the towns of Hallandale, Hollywood, Pompano Beach, Fort Lauderdale, Dania, Deerfield, Boca Raton, Delray Beach, Boyton Beach, and the Palm Beaches.

EXPLORING THE GOLD COAST BY CAR

Like most of the rest of South Florida, the Gold Coast consists of a mainland and an adjacent strip of barrier islands. You'll have to check the maps to keep track of the many bridges that allow access to the islands where most of the tourist activity is centered. Interstate 95, which runs north-south, is the area's main highway. Farther west is the Florida Turnpike, a toll road that can be worth the expense since the speed limit is higher and it is often less congested than I-95. Also on the mainland is U.S. 1, which generally runs parallel to I-95 (to the east) and is a narrower thoroughfare mostly crowded with strip malls and seedy hotels.

I recommend taking Fla. A1A, a slow ocean-side road that connects the long, thin islands of Florida's whole east coast. Though the road is narrow, it is the most scenic and forces you into the relaxed atmosphere of these resort towns.

1 Broward County: Hallandale & Hollywood to Fort Lauderdale

23 miles N of Miami

With more than 23 miles of beachfront and 300 miles of navigable waterways, Broward County is a great destination for outdoor lovers. Scattered amid the tacky shopping malls, gaudy condos, and glitzy tourist areas are some impressive natural wonders, including hundreds of parks, golf courses, and tennis courts, too. With year-round temperatures averaging 77° and a growing industrial base, the area attracts more than six million visitors each year. Some 1.5 million residents call the more than 28 cities and dozens of towns that make up Broward County home.

Like many other small American towns, the quaint city of Hollywood has been working on redeveloping its downtown area for years. Finally, in the late 1990s, the efforts seemed to start paying off. A spate of redevelopment has made the pedestrian-friendly center along Hollywood Boulevard and Harrison Street east of Dixie Highway a popular destination for travelers and locals alike. Some predict Hollywood will be South Florida's next big destination—South Beach without the attitude, traffic jams, and parking nightmares. Prices are a fraction of other tourist areas, and a true artsy image is apparent in the galleries, clubs, and restaurants that dot the new "strip." Its gritty undercurrent, however, still makes it more popular with bohemians and backpackers than society-page regulars.

Fort Lauderdale and its well-known strip of beaches, restaurants, bars, and souvenir shops has also undergone a major transformation. Once famous (or infamous) for the annual mayhem it hosted each spring when hedonism-bent college students descended from all over the country, this area is now attracting a more affluent crowd.

In addition to beautiful wide beaches, the city includes more than 300 miles of navigable waterways and innumerable canals that permit thousands of residents to anchor boats in their backyards. Boating is not just a hobby here; it's a lifestyle. It's the reason many choose to live in this area known as the "yachting capital of the world," or the "Venice of America." Visitors can easily get on the water, too, by renting a boat, or simply by hailing a moderately priced water taxi.

Huge cruise ships also take advantage of Florida's deepest harbor, Port Everglades. It is the second-busiest cruise-ship base in Florida (after Miami) and one of the top five in the world. For further information on cruises, consult *Frommer's Caribbean Cruises* or *Frommer's Caribbean Ports of Call.*

ESSENTIALS

GETTING THERE If you're driving up from Miami, it's a straight shot to Hollywood or Fort Lauderdale. Visitors on their way to or from Orlando should take the Florida Turnpike to Exit 53, 54, 58, or 62, depending on the location of your accommodations.

The Fort Lauderdale/Hollywood International Airport is small, easy to negotiate, and located just 15 minutes from both of the downtown areas it services.

Amtrak (☎ 800/USA-RAIL) stations are at 200 SW 21st Terrace (Broward Boulevard and I-95), Fort Lauderdale (☎ 954/587-6692), and 3001 Hollywood Blvd., Hollywood (☎ 954/921-4517).

VISITOR INFORMATION The **Greater Fort Lauderdale Convention & Visitors Bureau**, 1850 Eller Dr., Suite 303 (off I-95 and I-595 east), Fort Lauderdale, FL 33316 (☎ 954/765-4466; fax 954/765-4467; www.sunny.org), is an excellent resource in Spanish, French, or English. I highly recommend calling them in advance to request a free comprehensive guide with just about everything you could want to know about events, accommodations, and sightseeing in Broward County. In addition, once you are in town, you can call an **information line** (☎ 954/527-5600) to get easy-to-follow directions, travel advice, and assistance from multilingual operators who staff a round-the-clock help line. Also available 24 hours a day are operators who can book discount scuba, cruise, or cultural packages. Call ☎ 800/22-SUNNY for information.

The **Greater Hollywood Chamber of Commerce**, 330 N. Federal Hwy. (on the corner of U.S. 1 and Taylor Street), Hollywood, FL 33020 (☎ 954/923-4000; fax 954/923-8737), is open Monday through Friday from 8:30am to 5pm.

HITTING THE BEACH

The southern part of the Gold Coast, Broward County, has the region's most popular and amenities-laden beaches, which stretch for more than 23 miles. Most do not charge for access, though all are well maintained. Here's a selection of some of the county's best from south to north.

Hollywood Beach, stretching from Sheridan Street to Georgia Street, is a real carnival with an odd assortment of young hipsters, big families, and sunburned French Canadians who dodge bicyclers and skaters along the rows of tacky souvenir shops, T-shirt shops, game rooms, snack bars, beer stands, hotels, and even miniature golf courses. The 3-mile-long Hollywood Beach **Broadwalk** is notable as one of the area's only beach paths where the diversions are right on the beach separated from the sand and sea by only a thin paved strip instead of a busy highway and tall buildings. Popular with runners, skaters, and cruisers, the Broadwalk is also renowned as a hangout for thousands of retirement-age snowbirds, who get together for frequent dances and shows at a faded outdoor amphitheater. Despite efforts to clear out a seedy element, the area remains a haven for drunks and scammers, so keep alert.

If you tire of the hectic diversity that defines Hollywood's Broadwalk, enjoy the natural beauty of the beach itself, which is wide and clean. There are lifeguards, showers, bathroom facilities, and public areas for picnics and parties.

The **Fort Lauderdale Beach Promenade** recently underwent a $26 million renovation, and it looks fantastic. Note, however, that the beach is hardly pristine; it is across the street from an uninterrupted stretch of hotels, bars, and retail outlets. Also nearby is a megaretail and dining complex, Beach Place, on Fla. A1A, midway between Las Olas and Sunrise boulevards (see "Shopping & Browsing," below).

Fort Lauderdale Attractions & Accommodations

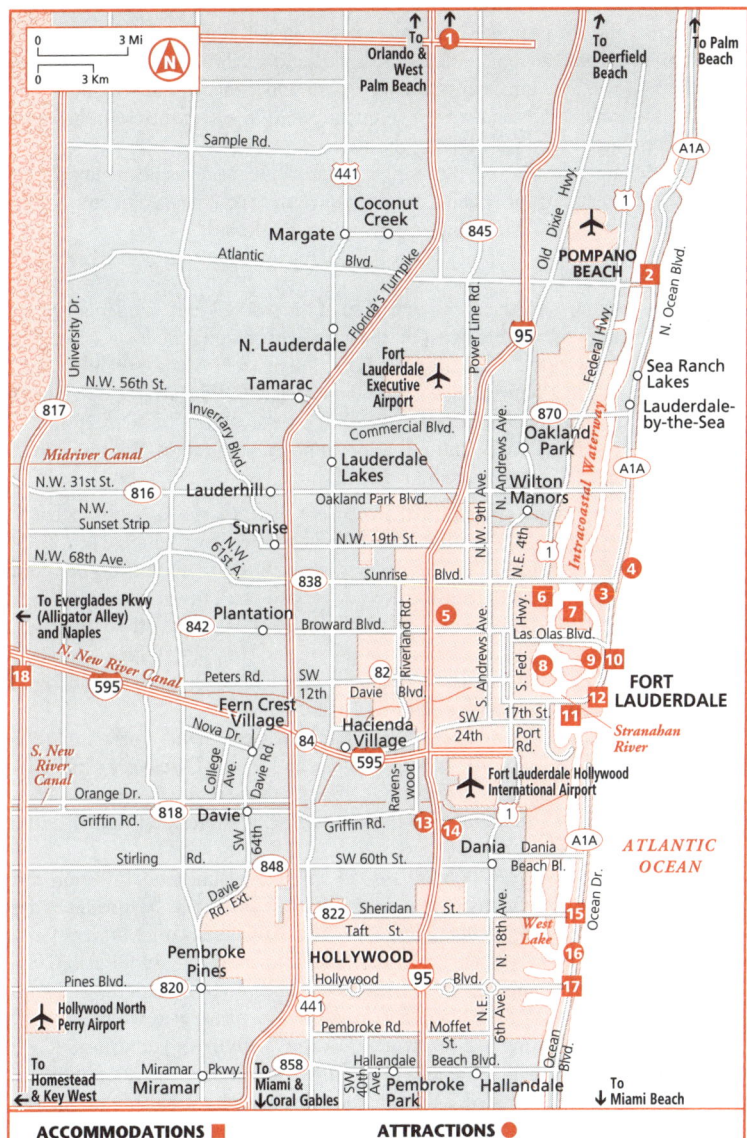

ACCOMMODATIONS ■
Banyan Marina Apartments 7
Hollywood Beach Resort 17
Hyatt Regency Fort Lauderdale
  at Pier 66 Marina 11
Lago Mar Resort and Club 12
Marriot's Harbor Beach Resort 10
Riverside Hotel 6
The Ronny Dee Resort Motel 2
Sea Downs (and the Bougainvillea) 15
Wyndham Resort and Spa 18

ATTRACTIONS ●
Bonnet House 3
Butterfly World 1
Grand Prix Race-O-Rama 14
Fort Lauderdale Beach Promenade 4
Hollywood Beach Boardwalk 16
IGFA World Fishing Center & Museum 13
Jungle Queen 9
Museum of Discovery and Science 5
Stranahan House 8

271

Just across the road, on the sand, most days you will find hard-core volleyballers, who always welcome anyone with a good spike, and a calm ocean welcoming swimmers of any level. The unusually clear waters are under the careful watch of some of Florida's best-looking lifeguards. Freshen up afterward in any of the clean showers and restrooms conveniently located along the strip.

Especially on weekends, parking along the ocean-side meters is nearly impossible to find. Try biking, skating, or hitching a ride on the water taxi instead. The strip is located on Fla. A1A, between SE 17th Street and Sunrise Boulevard.

ACTIVE PURSUITS

BOATING Known as "the yachting capital of the world," Fort Lauderdale provides ample opportunity for visitors to get on the water, either along the Intracoastal Waterway or out on the open ocean. If your hotel doesn't rent boats, try **Bill's Sunrise Watersports,** 2025 E. Sunrise Blvd., Fort Lauderdale (☎ 954/462-8963). They will outfit you with a variety of watercraft, including jet-skis, Wave Runners, 13-foot Cigarette boats, 15-foot jet boats, and 8-foot powerboats, year-round. Bill's is open daily from 9am to 6pm. Rates start at about $45 an hour.

CRUISES The **Jungle Queen,** 801 Sea Breeze Blvd. (3 blocks south of Las Olas Boulevard on Fla. A1A), in the Bahia Mar Yacht Center, Fort Lauderdale (☎ 954/462-5596), a Mississippi River–style steamer, is one of Fort Lauderdale's best-known attractions cruising up and down the New River. All-you-can-eat dinner cruises and 3-hour sightseeing tours take visitors past Millionaires' Row, Old Fort Lauderdale, and the new downtown. Cruises depart nightly at 7pm and cost $24.50 for adults and $12 for children 12 and under. Sightseeing tours are scheduled daily at 10am and 2pm and cost $11.50 for adults and $8 for children 10 and under.

If you're interested in gambling, several casino boat companies operate day cruises out of Port Everglades and offer blackjack, slots, and poker. **Discovery Cruise Lines** (☎ 800/937-4477) has daily cruises to The Bahamas where you can gamble, eat, and party for 5 to 6 hours for about $120. The price includes breakfast, lunch, and dinner, but drinks cost extra.

Sea Escape (☎ 800/327-2005 or 954/453-3333) also launches daily casino cruises. But theirs don't travel more than a few miles offshore. These trips "to nowhere" depart every day except Monday at 10am until 4pm. The party cruises offer buffet meals and full casinos for about $35 a person. I'd recommend spending an additional $20 for a cabin so you can stretch out and relax in between hands. Even though the cruises don't go far from the coast, 5 or 6 hours is a long time to spend at sea, especially if the weather is rough. Evening cruises, which leave at 7:30pm and return at 12:30 or 1:30am, cost a few dollars more and offer full buffet dinners and a Las Vegas–style show. Port charges are included, although you must pay a $3 departure tax and $2.65 passenger charge. This is one of the best deals you'll find. Sea Escape also has a new 2- and 3-night cruise option, where visitors can go to Nassau, The Bahamas, for as little as $199 per person with all meals included.

Also, see the box "One if by Land, Taxi if by Sea," below, for details on the water taxi.

FISHING Completed in 1999 at a cost of more than $32 million, the **IGFA World Fishing Center** at 300 Gulf Stream Way (☎ 954/922-4212) in Dania Beach is an anglers paradise. One of the highlights of this museum, library, and park is the virtual reality fishing simulator, which allows visitors to actually reel in their own computer generated catch. Also included in the 3-acre park are displays of antique fishing gear, record catches, famous anglers, various vessels, and a wetlands lab. To get a list of local captains and guides call **IGFA headquarters** and ask for the librarian (☎ 954/927-2628). Admission is $9 for adults, $5 for children between 3 and 12 and free for children under 3. On the grounds is also **Bass Pro Outdoor World Store,** a huge multi-floor retail complex situated on a 3-acre lake.

GAME PARKS This area seems to be the home of more mega-entertainment complexes than any other region in Southeast Florida. The **Grand Prix Race-O-Rama,** at 1801 NW 1st St., east of I-95 between Griffin and Sterling road exits, in Dania, is one of the originals and still the best for kids. With a massive video arcade, which is open 24 hours; five challenging miniature golf greens; go-carts for those over 4 feet 6 inches; and NASCAR racing for those over 5 feet tall; batting cages; and a huge sky coaster, this place is as exciting as it is exhausting. Plan to spend all day or night—or both. Call for prices and hours (☎ 954/921-1411).

One of the newest additions to the scene is **Dave & Busters** at 3000 Oakwood Blvd. in Hollywood, just off the Sheridan Street exit of I-95 (☎ **954/923-5505**). This 50,000-square-foot complex caters primarily to adults; it features a full liquor bar and sit-down restaurant, as well as a more casual spot with table service. On weekends this place is packed with young adults on dates and rowdy groups of guys of all ages. An admission of $5 is charged only on Friday and Saturday after 10pm. D&B's opens weekdays at 11am and at 11:30am on weekends and usually closes by 1am.

Gameworks, the huge, high-tech creation of Hollywood movie mogul Steven Spielberg is located in the mammoth Sawgrass Mills outlet center (See "Shopping & Browsing," below for more information on Sawgrass Mills.)

GOLF More than 50 golf courses in all price ranges compete for players. Some of the best include **Emerald Hills** at 4100 North Hills Dr., Hollywood, just west of I-95 between Sterling Road and Sheridan Street. This beauty consistently lands on "best of" lists of golf writers throughout the country. The 18th hole on a two-tier green is the challenging course's signature; it's surrounded by water and is more than a bit rough. Greens fees start at $80. Call ☎ **954/961-4000** for tee times. For one of Broward's best municipal challenges, try the 18-holer at the **Orangebrook Golf Course** at 400 Entrada Dr. in Hollywood (☎ **954/967-GOLF**). Built in 1937, this is one of the state's oldest courses and one of the area's best bargains. Morning and noon rates range from $21 to $26. After 2pm, you can play for less than $20, including a cart.

SCUBA DIVING In Broward County, the best wreck dive is the *Mercedes I,* a 197-foot freighter that washed up in the backyard of a Palm Beach socialite in 1984 and was sunk for divers the following year off Pompano Beach. The artificial reef, filled with colorful sponges, spiny lobsters, and barracudas, is located 97 feet below the surface, a mile offshore between Oakland Park and Sunrise boulevards. Dozens of reputable dive shops line the beach. Ask at your hotel for a nearby recommendation or contact **Lauderdale Undersea Adventures,** 2150 SE 17th St., Fort Lauderdale (☎ 954/527-0187).

SPECTATOR SPORTS Baseball fans can get their fix at the **Fort Lauderdale Stadium,** 5301 NW 12th Ave. (☎ **954/938-4980**), where the Baltimore Orioles play exhibition games starting in early March; call ☎ **954/776-1921** for tickets. They cost $6 for general admission, $9 for a spot in the grandstand, and $12 for box seats. During the season, the Florida Marlins play just south of Hallandale at the Pro Player Stadium near the Dade-Broward County line. Call Ticketmaster for tickets (☎ **305/358-5885**), which range from $2 to $40.

The **Pompano Harness Track,** 1800 SW 3rd St., Pompano Beach (☎ 954/972-2000), the only one in Florida, features horse racing and betting from October to early August. Grandstand admission is free; clubhouse admission is $2. They, like many other pari-mutuel outlets in the area, opened poker rooms in 1997.

A sort of Spanish-style indoor lacrosse, jai-alai was introduced to Florida in 1924 and still draws big crowds who bet on the fast-paced action. Broward's only fronton, **Dania Jai-Alai,** 301 E. Dania Beach Blvd. at the intersection of Fla. A1A and U.S. 1 (☎ **954/920-1511** or 954/426-4330), is a great place to spend an afternoon or evening.

Wrapped around an artificial lake, **Gulfstream Park,** at U.S. 1 and Hallandale Beach Boulevard, Hallandale (☎ **305/931-7223**), is both pretty and popular. Large purses and important races are commonplace at this recently refurbished suburban course, and the track is often crowded. It hosts the Florida Derby each year. Call for schedules. Admission is $3 to the grandstand, and $3 to the clubhouse. Parking is free. From January 3 to March 15, post times are Wednesday to Monday at 1pm and the doors open at 11am. Many weekends feature live concerts by well-known musicians.

In the sport of ice hockey, the young Florida Panthers (☎ **954/835-7000**) have already made history. In the 1994–95 season, they played in the Stanley Cup finals, and the fans love them. They play in Sunrise at 2555 NW 137th Way. Call for directions and ticket information.

TENNIS There are literally hundreds of courts in Broward County and plenty are accessible to the public. Many are at resorts and hotels. If not at yours, try one of these.

Famous as the spot where Chris Evert got in her early serves, **Holiday Park,** 701 NE 12th Ave. (off Sunrise Boulevard), Fort Lauderdale (☎ **954/761-5378**), has 18 clay and 3 hard courts (15 lighted). Her coach and father, James Evert, still teaches young players here, although he is very picky about who he'll accept. Nonresidents of Fort Lauderdale pay $3.50 to $4.50 per hour. Reservations are accepted after 2pm for the following day, but cost an extra $3. Lights are also an extra $3 per hour and are only available for the clay courts.

At the **Marina Bay Resort,** 2175 S.R. 84, west of I-95 and just behind the Ramada Inn, Fort Lauderdale (☎ **954/791-7600**), visitors can play free on any one of nine hard courts on a first-come, first-served basis. Three are lighted at night.

SEEING THE SIGHTS

For an overview of Fort Lauderdale, you may want to take an informative spin around the downtown area with **South Florida Trolley Tours** (☎ **954/946-7320**). Drivers narrate the history of the area as they loop around the city's streets past all the major (and many minor) sights. The charge for the 90-minute tour is $12 for adults, free for children 11 and under. The trolleys pick up passengers from most major hotels for six tours daily, starting at 9am. Call for current schedule.

For a tour by water, see the box below.

Museum of Discovery & Science. 401 SW 2nd St., Fort Lauderdale. ☎ **954/467-6637.** Fax 954/467-0046 www.mods.org. Museum admission $6 adults, $5 seniors, $5 children 3–12, free for children 2 and under; exhibit and IMAX combo prices $12.50 adults, $11.50 seniors, $10.50 children 3–12. Mon–Sat 10am–5pm, Sun noon–6pm. From I-95, exit on Broward Blvd. E.; continue to SW 5th Ave.; turn right, garage on right.

Children and teenagers especially love this interactive science museum that is a model of high-tech "infotainment." During the week, school groups meander through the cavernous two-story modern building. Younger kids 7 and under enjoy navigating their way through the wonderful explorations in the "Discovery Center." However,

One If by Land, Taxi If by Sea

Plan to spend at least an afternoon or evening cruising Fort Lauderdale's 300 miles of waterways the only way you can: by boat. The **Water Taxi of Fort Lauderdale** (☎ 954/467-6677) is one of the greatest innovations for water lovers since those cool Velcro sandals. A trusty fleet of old-port boats serves the dual purpose of transporting and entertaining visitors as they cruise through "The Venice of America."

Taxis operate on demand and also along a fairly regular route carrying up to 48 passengers. Choose a hotel on the route so you can be picked up at your hotel, usually within 15 minutes of calling, and then be shuttled to any of the dozens of restaurants, bars, and attractions on or near the waterfront. If you aren't sure where you want to go, ask one of the personable captains who can point out historic and fun spots along the way.

For a day cruise with the kids, make a stop at the Museum of Discovery and Science where you can catch an IMAX film or just enjoy the current educational exhibits. Then, if you are up for a walk, head across the 3-mile Riverwalk, a scenic palm-lined walkway along the New River where you can enjoy your picnic lunch, or try one of the restaurants dotting the way to Las Olas Boulevard and The Las Olas Riverfront. When you are ready for some shopping or a sit-down meal, reboard and head to Beach Place at Las Olas Boulevard and Cortez Street in the heart of Fort Lauderdale's most famous "strip." Stop for refreshments at Casablanca Cafe and then hit the beach.

In the evening, the water taxi is ideal for bar-hopping—no worrying about parking or choosing a designated driver. Make your first stop at Shooters where professionals, boaters, and tourists share the large lively patio for a popular happy hour from 5 to 7pm on weekdays. Right next door is Bootlegger's, featuring more than 70 beers at an outside bar. Later debark at O'hara's, in the downtown section of Las Olas Boulevard (see "The Hollywood & For Lauderdale Area After Dark") where you'll hear a great mix of live jazz and blues.

Starting daily from 10am, boats usually run until midnight, and until 2am on weekends, depending on the weather. The cost is $7 per person per trip, $13 round-trip, and $15 for a full day. Children under 12 ride for half price and free on Sunday. Opt for the all-day pass; it's worth it.

---

most weekend nights you'll find a diverse crowd ranging from hip high school kids to 30-somethings enjoying a rock film in the Blockbuster IMAX 3-D theater, which also shows short, science-related, supersize films daily. Out front, see a 52-foot-tall "Great Gravity Clock," located in the museum's atrium, the largest kinetic-energy sculpture in the state. Exhibits vary, so call for the latest details.

Billie Swamp Safari. Big Cypress Reservation, 1 1/2-hour drive west of Fort Lauderdale. ☎ 800/949-6101. No admission. Boat tours $10–$20. Daily 8am–8pm. Last airboat ride 4:30pm.

Here you can catch a glimpse of how Florida looked before developers went wild. Skimming across the shallow swamps in an airboat with Native American guides you may spot alligators and rare birds. Kids especially enjoy the swamp buggy rides, which leave every hour on the hour until 5pm.

Bonnet House. 900 N. Birch Rd. (1 block west of the ocean, south of Sunrise Blvd.), Fort Lauderdale. ☎ **954/563-5393.** Fax 954/561-4174. www.bonnethouse.com. Admission $9 adults, $8 seniors, $7 students under 18, free for children 6 and under. Tours Wed–Fri 10am–1:30pm, Sat–Sun noon–2:30pm.

This historic 35-acre plantation home and estate survives in the middle of an otherwise highly developed beachfront condominium area and is only open by guided tour.

Built in 1921, the sprawling two-story waterfront home surrounded with formal tropical gardens is really the backdrop of a love story, which the very chatty volunteer guides will share with you if you ask. Some have actually lunched with the former resident of the house, the late Evelyn Bartlett, the wife of world-acclaimed artist Frederic Clay Bartlett. If you like quirky people, whimsical artwork, lush grounds, and very interesting details of design, you'll love this tour, which takes about $1^{1}/_{2}$ hours. Inquire about literary walks and science workshops offered regularly on the grounds.

Butterfly World. Tradewinds Park South, 3600 W. Sample Rd., Coconut Creek (west of the Florida Turnpike). ☎ **954/977-4400.** Fax 954/977-4501. www.butterflyworld.com. Admission $11.95 adults, $6.95 children 4–12, free for children 3 and under. Mon–Sat 9am–5pm, Sun 1–5pm; last admission at 4pm.

One of the world's largest butterfly breeders, Butterfly World cultivates more than 150 species of these colorful and delicate insects. In the park's walk-through, screened-in aviary, visitors can see thousands of caterpillars and watch newborn butterflies emerge from their cocoons and flutter around as they learn to fly. Depending on how interested you are in these winged beauties, you may want to allow from 1 to 2 hours to tour the gardens and the well-stocked gift shop. There's a new lorikeet aviary that offers visitors the opportunity to hand-feed these birds.

Stranahan House. 335 SE 6th Ave. (Las Olas Blvd. at the New River Tunnel), Fort Lauderdale. ☎ **954/524-4736.** Fax 954/525-2838. www.stranahanhouse.com. Admission $5 adults, $2 students and children. Wed–Sat 10am–4pm, Sun 1–4pm; last tour begins at 3pm. Also accessible by water taxi.

In a town whose history isn't even as old as many of its residents, visitors may want to take a minute to see Fort Lauderdale's very oldest standing structure and a prime example of classic "Florida Frontier" architecture. Built in 1901 by "the father of Fort Lauderdale," this house once served as a trading post for Seminole trappers who came here to sell pelts. It's been a post office, town hall, and general store and now is a worthwhile little museum of South Florida pioneer life, containing turn-of-the-century furnishings and historical photos of the area. It is also the site of occasional concerts and social functions. Call for details.

SHOPPING & BROWSING

Broward County has some of Florida's best malls and some fantastic boutique areas, too.

Dania is known for its antique district where hundreds of shops are clustered along U.S. 1 just south of the airport. Known as **"Antique Row,"** this area has some of South Florida's best old treasures. Although many of the more upscale shops are overpriced, many of the smaller dealers offer bargains to hagglers.

Also for bargain mavens is a strip of "fashion" stores on **Hallandale Beach Boulevard's "Schmatta Row,"** east of Dixie Highway and the railroad tracks, where off-brand shoes, bags, and jewelry are sold at deep discounts. Funky Hollywood Boulevard also offers some wild shops with everything from Indonesian artifacts to used and rare books to leather bustiers to handmade hats. Dozens of shops line the pedestrian-friendly strip just west of Young Circle. The art galleries are clustered along Harrison Street just east of Dixie Highway.

The area's only beachfront mall, **Beach Place,** is in Ft. Lauderdale on Fla. A1A just north of Las Olas Boulevard. Completed in 1997 at a cost of $23 million, this 100,000-square-foot giant sports the usual chains like Sunglass Hut, Limited Express, Banana Republic, and The Gap as well as lots of popular bars and restaurants.

Other more traditional malls include the upscale **Galleria** at Sunrise Boulevard near the Fort Lauderdale Beach, and Broward Mall, west of I-95 on Broward Boulevard, in Plantation.

If you are looking for unusual boutiques, especially art galleries, head to trendy ✪ **Las Olas Boulevard,** where there are literally hundreds of shops with alluring window decorations and intriguing merchandise. You may find kitchen utensils posing as modern art sculptures or mural-size oil paintings.

On the edge of the Arts and Science District is a new retail complex known as **Las Olas Riverfront** with 260,000 square feet of restaurants, clothing stores, arcades, and a multiplex movie theater.

The well-known department store **Lord & Taylor** has a little-known clearance center where discounts on new clothing for women, kids, and men can be as much as 75%. If you can handle open dressing rooms, overstuffed racks, and surly sales help, it's a great find at 6820 N. University Dr. in Tamarac. You may want to call (☎ **954/720-1915**) to find out about specials.

The Fort Lauderdale Swap Shop, 3291 W. Sunrise Blvd. (☎ **954/791-SWAP**), is one of the world's largest flea markets. In addition to endless acres of vendors, there's a miniature amusement park, a 13-screen drive-in movie theater, weekend concerts, and even a free circus complete with elephants, horse shows, high-wire acts, and clowns.

The monster of all outlet malls is **Sawgrass Mills,** 12801 W. Sunrise Blvd., Sunrise (☎ **800-FL-MILLS** or 954/846-2350; fax 954/846-2312). Since the most recent expansion completed in mid-1999, which added more than 30 new designer outlet stores, this behemoth (shaped like a Florida alligator) now holds more than 300 shops, kiosks, a 24-screen movie theater, and many restaurants and bars including a Hard Rock Cafe. The enclosed area covers nearly 2.5 million square feet over 50 acres. There's no way to see it all in a day. Wear your most comfortable shoes or buy an extra pair while you're there. Stores include Donna Karan Company Store, Levi's Outlet, Sunglass Hut, Ann Taylor Loft, and Barney's New York, all selling goods at between 20% and 80% below retail. Label-conscious shoppers are especially impressed with Off Fifth, the Saks Fifth Avenue outlet store and Last Call, the Neiman-Marcus clearance center. You may want to invest in a coupon booklet ($5), which entitles you to even greater discounts at many of the mall's stores and restaurants as well as area attractions. Books are good for up to a year and can be turned in for updated books at no charge. To get there, take I-95 to I-595 west to the Flamingo Road exit, turn right, and drive 2 miles to Sunrise Boulevard; you will see the large complex on the left. From the Florida Turnpike, exit Sunrise Boulevard west. Parking is free, but don't forget where you parked; the lot holds more than 11,000 cars.

Fishing enthusiasts won't want to miss **Bass Pro Outdoor World** (☎ **954/929-7710**), a sprawling retail complex at Griffin Road and I-95 in Dania where you can buy anything from yachts to lures (see "Sports & Other Activities," above.)

WHERE TO STAY

The Fort Lauderdale beach has a hotel or motel on nearly every block, and they range from the run down to the luxurious. Both the **Howard Johnson** (☎ **800/327-8578** or 954/563-2451), at 700 N. Atlantic Blvd. (on Fla. A1A, south of Sunrise Blvd.), and the **Days Inn** (☎ **800/329-7466** or 954/462-0444), at 435 N. Atlantic Blvd. (Fla. A1A), offer clean ocean-side rooms starting at about $150.

In Hollywood, where prices are generally cheaper, the **Holiday Inn** at 101 N. Ocean Blvd. (☎ **954/921-0990**) operates a full-service hotel right on the ocean. With prices starting at around $110 in season and discounts for AAA, it's a great deal. **Howard Johnson** (☎ **800/423-9867** or 954/925-1411) has a great location right on the beach at 2501 N. Ocean Dr. (I-95 to Sheridan Street east to Fla. A1A south).

✪ **Extended Stay America/Crossland Economy Studios** (☎ **800/398-7829**) has four super-clean properties in Fort Lauderdale and offers year-round rates as low as $49 a night and $159 per week. The studios are designed with business travelers in mind, Each includes free local calls, a data port, a kitchenette, a recliner, and a well-lit desk.

Especially for rentals for a few weeks or months, call **Florida Sunbreak** (☎ **800/SUNBREAK**). Or call the **South Florida Hotel Network** (☎ **800/538-3616**) for help finding small inns and lodges in any price range. Also, check out the annual list of small lodgings compiled by the **Ft. Lauderdale Convention & Visitors Bureau** (☎ **954/765-4466**). It is especially helpful for those looking for privately owned, charming, and affordable lodgings.

New hotels are going up all the time. One notable addition to the Hallandale area is the 1,000-room **Diplomat Resort & Country Club;** the $500 million project had just opened its doors at press time.

VERY EXPENSIVE

Hyatt Regency Pier 66. 2301 SE 17th St. Causeway, Fort Lauderdale, FL 33316. ☎ **800/233-1234** or 954/525-6666. Fax 954/728-3541. www.hyatt.com. 380 units. A/C MINIBAR TV TEL. Winter $259 double. Off-season $219 double. Year-round from $1,000 suite. AE, CB, DC, DISC, MC, V. Valet parking $8.

The Pier 66 hotel and 142-slip marina has been hosting guests, especially boaters, since 1954. The luxurious resort attracts megayachts from all over the world, in addition to large groups and business travelers. Despite the emphasis on groups, for services and amenities this Hyatt is hard to beat.

The hotel's atrium-style lobby impresses with high ceilings and marble floors. The lushly landscaped grounds add to the exotic feel of this superconvenient locale, situated across from the beach, and within walking distance of the best shopping and dining. Every room has a balcony; the priciest have expansive panoramas of the marina, the beach across the street, and all of Fort Lauderdale beyond. The hotel is serviced by the convenient water taxi (see box, above). All rooms were renovated recently.

Dining: Best known for its revolving rooftop lounge, the hotel also offers an American grill and a very popular waterfront cafe for dinner and lunch.

Amenities: Concierge, room service (24 hours), dry-cleaning and laundry services, newspaper delivery, twice-daily maid service, baby-sitting, secretarial services, express checkout, courtesy car or limo. Spectravision movie channels, two swimming pools, beach, a fully equipped spa, Jacuzzi, sauna, 40-person whirlpool, jogging track, children's center or programs, business center, conference rooms, self-service Laundromat, sundeck, two lighted clay tennis courts, water-sports equipment and boat rentals, 142-slip marina, tour desk, beauty salon, boutiques, shopping arcade.

Marriott's Harbor Beach Resort. 3030 Holiday Dr., Fort Lauderdale, FL 33316. ☎ **800/222-6543** or 954/525-4000. Fax 954/766-6193. 659 units. A/C TV TEL. Winter $259–$429 double. Off-season $99–$279 double. Year-round from $600 suite. AE, CB, DC, DISC, MC, V. Valet parking $10. From I-95, exit on I-595 east to U.S. 1 north; proceed to SE 17th St.; make a right and go over the intracoastal bridge past three traffic lights to Holiday Dr.; turn right.

Recent renovations to the tune of $15 million gave this Marriott, situated on 16 oceanfront acres just south of Fort Lauderdale's "strip," a complete face-lift. From the spacious rooms and suites to the 8,000-square-foot swimming pool, everything in this very well run hotel is huge. All rooms open onto private balconies overlooking either the ocean or the Intracoastal Waterway. Return guests include many convention groups and families who enjoy the space and the great location.

Dining/Diversions: A formal restaurant serves one of Fort Lauderdale's most elegant dinners and a less formal Japanese restaurant serves hibachi dinners that are prepared at your table. Three other casual restaurants serve breakfast, lunch, dinner, and late-night drinks.

Amenities: Concierge, room service, in-room massage, laundry services, newspaper delivery, baby-sitting, twice-daily maid service, express checkout, secretarial services, courtesy car for shopping and golf, free coffee in lobby. Outdoor heated pool, beach, health club, Jacuzzi, sauna, sundeck, five clay tennis courts, water-sports equipment, bicycle rental, game room, children's center and programs, business center, self-service Laundromat, tour desk, boutiques, conference rooms, car-rental desk, beauty salon.

✪ **Wyndham Resort and Spa.** 250 Racquet Club Rd., Fort Lauderdale, FL 33326. ☎ **800/996-3426** or 954/389-3300. Fax 954/384-6878. www.wyndham.com. 496 units. A/C TV TEL. Winter from $245 double. Off-season from $175 double. Golf and spa packages (with or without meals) $265–$305 per person based on double occupancy. AE, CB, DC, DISC, MC, V. Valet parking $8. From I-95, exit at I-595 west to 136th Ave., S.R. 84; turn left to Bonaventure Blvd. Make a right to Racquet Club Rd.

From the West I-75, exit 12 (Arvida Parkway); continue west to Weston Blvd.; turn right and proceed to Saddle Club Rd.; turn left to Bonaventure Blvd. Make a right to Racquet Club Rd.

Having changed hands frequently, this unusual spa and golf resort is a bit difficult to peg down. Built in 1981 on 23 acres, this active resort quickly earned a great reputation for its world-class facilities. Unfortunately, years of mismanagement resulted in its deterioration. A $10 million renovation begun in 1996 improved things, but then the resort was sold again to Wyndham resorts, which has big plans. The continued renovation, under the new owner, has this resort looking fantastic once again.

The rooms, scattered throughout nine four-story buildings, have been thoroughly gutted and re-outfitted in a bright tropical style, with conveniences like telephone voice mail and data ports, irons, ironing boards, coffeemakers, clock radios, and hair dryers. Also, suites and deluxe rooms offer wet bars and small refrigerators.

Although it is a lengthy trek to the nearest beach, this first-class property has plenty of opportunities to sun and swim, with five pools, including separate lap pools for men and women, and a private lake.

Dining/Diversions: With four restaurants, including one serving superb Tuscan food in a formal setting and another with real spa cuisine, you'll find plenty of delicious choices. You may even want to request recipes to take home. Also on the premises are four lounges for afternoon and evening entertainment and cocktails.

Amenities: Concierge, 24-hour room service, dry-cleaning and laundry service, newspaper delivery, in-room massage, twice-daily maid service, express checkout, secretarial services, shopping transportation. Limited kitchenettes in some suites, Spectravision movie channels, five swimming pools, full-service spa, Jacuzzi, sauna, two championship golf courses, sundeck, 15 night-lit tennis courts, children's programs, business center, tour desk, boutiques, conference rooms, car-rental desk, beauty salon, boutique, and gift shop.

EXPENSIVE

✪ **Lago Mar Resort and Club.** 1700 S. Ocean Lane, Fort Lauderdale, FL 33316. ☎ **800/524-6627** or 954/523-6511. Fax 954/524-6627. E-mail: reservations@lagomar.com. 212 units.

A/C TV TEL. Winter $195 double; from $295 suite. Off-season $100–$135 double; from $135 suite. AE, DC, MC, V. Free valet parking. From Federal Hwy. (U.S. 1), turn east onto SE 17th St. Causeway; turn right onto Mayan Dr.; turn right again onto S. Ocean Dr.; turn left onto Grace Dr.; then left again onto S. Ocean Lane to the hotel.

After extensive renovations, this sprawling family-owned resort is even better than before. Lago Mar, a casually elegant resort, occupies its own little island between Lake Mayan and the Atlantic, and is very family oriented, with lots of facilities and supervised activities for children, especially during spring break and Christmas vacations. It's also good for business travelers looking for value. Unfortunately, the word has gotten out and it has become difficult to get reservations during the season. Chess fanatics should be sure to check out the life-size, custom-made chess set.

Most accommodations here are suites, available in a variety of configurations. The smallest suites, called "executive," are decorated in contemporary prints and are simple and comfortable. The executive suites are very large, with a king-size bed, separate dressing area, pullout sofa, and separate tub and shower in an extralarge bathroom. Each has a private balcony and full kitchen, or at least a microwave and a refrigerator. Ask for one of the newer units since they are generally larger and have more closet space. Definitely take advantage of the hotel's waterfront location to use the convenient water taxi (see box above).

Dining/Diversions: Two full-service restaurants, a grill, soda shop, and a lounge may tempt you to never leave this top-rated resort. An outdoor cafe overlooking the sea serves grilled chicken and fish, sandwiches and salads; another more formal indoor dining room features standards like Caesar salads and filet mignon. (Note that men are required to wear jackets.) Also, in addition to a casual poolside grill, there is an old-fashioned soda shop that serves up hot dogs and milkshakes. In season, the hotel lounge features live music.

Amenities: Concierge, room service, dry-cleaning and laundry service, secretarial services, newspaper delivery. Kitchenettes in most suites, outdoor pool and lagoon, beach, small fitness center, game rooms, children's playground, supervised children's programs during holiday periods, business center, conference rooms, sundeck, four tennis courts, miniature golf course, volleyball courts, shuffleboard, water-sports concession, men's and women's apparel shops, Laundromat, tour desk.

Riverside Hotel. 620 E. Las Olas Blvd., Fort Lauderdale, FL 33301. ☎ **800/325-3280** or 954/467-0671. Fax 954/462-2148. www.riversidehotel.com. 116 units. A/C TV TEL. Winter $179–$369 suite. Off-season $124–$339 suite. AE, DC, MC, V. Valet parking $6. From I-95, exit onto Broward Blvd.; turn right onto Federal Hwy. (U.S. 1), then left onto Las Olas Blvd.

Right in the thick of Ft. Lauderdale's hottest downtown area, the six-story Riverside Hotel is one of the oldest in South Florida. Built in 1936, it looks like a Wild West movie set, complete with a second-floor wooden terrace and an enormous mural on the front facade. You are in the middle of trendy Las Olas Boulevard and on the route of the popular water taxi. On weekends the hotel is often packed with wedding guests attending ceremonies that are held outside by the small heated swimming pool. A bit nicer than the public areas, which are outfitted in Mexican tile and wicker furnishings, the guest rooms upstairs are spacious and well maintained. Details like intricately tiled bathrooms and old-style furniture enhance the charm of the otherwise stark building. The best rooms face the New River, but it's hard to see the water past the parking lot and trees. The hotel does not have an abundance of services or facilities, but the central downtown location makes almost anything you could desire just steps away.

Dining/Diversions: Do sample Indigo, a fantastic Asian/Indonesian restaurant in the hotel lobby (see "Where to Dine," below). Also on the premises is a more standard grill restaurant and a lounge.

Amenities: Room service, dry-cleaning and laundry service, secretarial services, refrigerators, outdoor pool, nearby health club, conference rooms, sundeck.

MODERATE

○ **Banyan Marina Apartments.** 111 Isle of Venice, Fort Lauderdale, FL 33301. ☎ **954/ 524-4430.** Fax 954/764-4870. www.banyanmarina.com. 10 units. A/C TV TEL. Winter $90–$215 apt. Off-season $60–$150 apt. Weekly and monthly rates available. EURO, MC, V. To get there from I-95, exit Broward Blvd. E.; cross U.S. 1 and turn right on SE 15th Ave.; at the first traffic light (Las Olas Blvd.), turn left. Turn left at the third island (Isle of Venice).

One of the best accommodation values in South Florida, this hidden treasure is built around a dramatic 75-year-old banyan tree and is located directly on the active canals halfway between Fort Lauderdale's downtown and the beach. When available, you'll choose between one- and two-bedroom apartments. All are comfortable and spacious, with full kitchens and living rooms. The best part of staying here, besides your gracious and knowledgeable hosts, Peter and Dagmar Neufeldt, is that the water taxi will find you here and take you anywhere you want to be day or night. There is also a small outdoor heated pool and a marina for those with boats in tow. In 1998, the Neufeldts were honored by a local campaign to enhance the area, Broward Beautiful, winning First Place in the category of small multifamily dwellings.

Caribbean Quarters Bed and Breakfast Inn. 3012 Granada St., Ft. Lauderdale, FL 33304. ☎ **888/414-3226** or 954/523-3226. Fax 954/523-7541. www.caribbeanquarters.com. E-mail: CQBandB@aol.com. 12 units. A/C TV TEL Winter $95–$220 double. Off-season $75–$175 double. Rates include continental breakfast. AE, MC, V, DISC.

Originally built as an apartment/lodging house in the 1930s, this appealing hotel is now a bed and breakfast. New Orleans–style balconies overlook a lush tropical courtyard. Most rooms have a private bedroom and a pullout couch in the living room, accommodating up to four people. The original cypress wood floors set off the plantation-style white wicker furniture and the colorful bedspreads. All have private baths and most come with a well-stocked kitchenette, making this place especially good for long stays and families. All rooms also come with a VCR. The inn is located a half block from the beach, and a number of shops and restaurants.

Courtyard Villa. 4312 El Mar Dr., Lauderdale-by-the-Sea, FL 33308. ☎ **800/291-3560** or 954/776-1164. Fax 954/491-0768. www.courtyardvilla.com. 8 units. A/C TV TEL. Winter $150 double. Off-season $105 double. AE, MC, V, DC.

Nestled between a bunch of larger hotels, this small, eight-room historic hotel offers a romantic getaway right on the beach. It recently underwent a complete renovation. The upstairs rooms face the ocean and offer stunning beach views from their balconies. Spacious and comfortable, all the rooms feature traditional Florida decor, with a rattan table and chairs, carved four-poster beds with white chenille spreads, and white curtains. The fully equipped kitchenettes include a service for four. The tiled bathrooms have good, strong hot showers to wash the beach sand off. Relax in the hotel's unique heated pool/spa or swim off the beach to a living reef just 50 feet offshore. Scuba diving instruction is available on premises.

○ **Hollywood Beach Resort.** 101 N. Ocean Dr. (at Fla. A1A and Hollywood Blvd.), Hollywood, FL 33019. ☎ **954/921-0990.** Fax 954/920-9480. 400 units (approximately 200 on rental program). A/C TV TEL. Winter from $119–$245. Off-season from $89–$189. AE, DC, DISC, MC, V.

There is nothing cozy or quaint about this sprawling 1920s beachfront hotel, but it couldn't be better located or better priced. Its two best features are the rooms' full kitchens and the hotel's location directly on the ocean. This eight-story building actually operates as a privately held condominium where owners can elect to put their units on a rental program. So there is no telling how rooms may be furnished or outfitted (management does maintain certain standards). All the units I have seen are clean and modest. Larger units and those with views are significantly more expensive than studios. If the weather is bad, consider shopping at the adjacent Ocean Walk Mall or hit a movie at the on-site, multiplex movie theater. Also on the premises is a large outdoor pool and Jacuzzi. The many conveniences of this well-situated property make it especially popular with tour groups from Europe, South America, and Canada.

INEXPENSIVE

Ronny Dee Resort Motel. 717 S. Ocean Blvd., Pompano Beach, FL 33062. ☎ **954/943-3020.** Fax 954/783-5112. 35 units. A/C TV. Winter from $49–$72 double; from $390 efficiency. Off-season from $35–$41 double; from $249 efficiency. AE, MC, V. From I-95, exit Atlantic Blvd. E. to Fla. A1A N.

The bad news is that this family owned motel is located on busy Fla. A1A; the good news is that it's just 100 yards from the beach and amazingly inexpensive. Popular with European guests, this two-story yellow motel, wrapped around a central swimming pool, contains almost three dozen suburban-style wood-paneled guest rooms filled with an eclectic mix of furniture. All contain a small refrigerator, but none have a telephone; pay phones are located in a public area, near a large game room that contains a pool table, VCR, books, and other games. Ping-Pong and shuffleboard are also available.

Sea Downs (and the Bougainvillea). 2900 N. Surf Rd., Hollywood, FL 33019. ☎ **954/923-4968.** Fax 954/923-8747. www.seadowns.com or www.bougainvilleahollywood.com. 14 units. A/C TV TEL. Winter $70–$93 efficiency; $102–$120 one-bedroom apt; $128 penthouse. Off-season $45–$74 efficiency; $68–$99 one-bedroom apt; $90–$108 penthouse. Special weekly and monthly rates also available. No credit cards accepted. From I-95, exit Sheridan St. E. to Fla. A1A south; drive $1/2$ mile to Coolidge St.; turn left.

This bargain accommodation is often booked months in advance by returning guests who want to be directly on the beach without paying a fortune. The hosts of this superclean '50s motel, Claudia and Karl Herzog, live on the premises and keep things running smoothly. Renovations completed in 1997 have replaced bathroom fixtures, and many rooms have been redecorated here and at the Herzogs' other even less expensive property next door, the Bougainvillea. Guests at either spot can use the heated pool, barbecue grills, picnic area, laundry facilities, and sundeck.

A HOSTEL

Floyd's Youth Hostel/Crew House. Please call for address and directions in Fort Lauderdale. ☎ **954/462-0631.** Fax 954/462-6881. E-mail: FECreamer@aol.com. 20-plus beds. $17 per person for a dorm bed. 4 nights for $64.60. No credit cards. Free daytime pickup.

Although there are a number of cheap hostels operating near Fort Lauderdale's renowned strip, the best place to crash is Floyd's. While it is a few miles inland from the beach, this well-kept lodging offers what every backpacker and international traveler wants—safety and good, warm fellow travelers. Floyd himself takes care of the guests, many of whom have come looking for work on the area's yachts. In fact, we have agreed not to list the address since Floyd insists on interviewing each prospective guest by phone before booking. Rest assured, you've found one of the area's best and safest hostels with extras like a cupboard full of complimentary staples—milk, cereal, and generic-brand macaroni and cheese.

WHERE TO DINE

Having hosted visitors for so long, Fort Lauderdale, and to some extent Hollywood as well, have some of South Florida's finest restaurants. Increasingly, ethnic options are joining the legions of surf-and-turf options that dominated the area for so long. **Las Olas Boulevard** has dozens of eateries (so many, in fact, that the city has disallowed any new restaurants to open on the overcrowded 2-mile street). In addition to those reviewed below, consider **Jackson's 450,** 450 E. Las Olas Blvd. (☎ **954/522-4450**), and **ZAN(Z)BAR,** a romantic South African restaurant decked out in zebra and leopard skin at 602 E. Las Olas Blvd. (☎ **954/767-3377**).

Very Expensive

✪ **Cafe Maxx.** 2601 E. Atlantic Blvd., Pompano Beach. ☎ **954/782-0606.** Fax 954/782-0648. Reservations recommended. Main courses $18–$37; appetizers $8.25–$12.95. AE, CB, DC, DISC, MC, V. Mon–Thurs 5:30–10:30pm, Fri–Sat 5:30–11pm, Sun 5:30–10pm. From I-95, exit at Atlantic Blvd. E. The restaurant is three lights east of Federal Hwy. FLORIDIAN/NEW WORLD.

Every one of chef/owner Oliver Saucy's restaurants has received accolades from all who bestow them in the culinary arena. This is his best. An oak-burning grill fills the contemporary and casually formal space with enticing aromas from around the globe. The pricey à la carte offerings borrow from Italian, Asian, Creole, Cuban, and Caribbean kitchens to create exotic and delicious mixes like potato-encrusted soft-shell crab, barbecued chicken quesadilla, and pistachio-fried oysters, as well as a host of other exciting but not overwrought dishes. Reserve early on weekends when the most coveted seats, the cozy booths, book well in advance.

Expensive

East City Grill. 505 N. Ft. Lauderdale Beach Blvd. (Fla. A1A between Las Olas and Sunrise blvds.), Fort Lauderdale. ☎ **954/565-5569.** Fax 954/565-5582. Reservations recommended well in advance. Main courses $17–$28. AE, DC, DISC, MC, V. Mon–Fri 6pm–midnight; lunch only on Fri 11:30am–3pm; Sat brunch 11:30am–3pm; Sun brunch 8am–3pm; dinner 5:30–10:30pm. AMERICAN/SEAFOOD.

This happening spot on the beach offers an ocean-side location and a killer nouvelle-style menu; it's yet another hit by the mega-Maxx group (see Cafe Maxx, above). For starters consider steamed crab and goat-cheese dumplings, lots of innovative sushi dishes, or Jamaican beer-steamed prawns. A steamer bar allows you to create your own dinner with a choice of steaming broths, sauces, and sides. You must be creative to dine here. If you are, and you love fresh, interesting seafood, you won't mind the wait at the stunning oak bar, where you can look into the open kitchen. Otherwise, stick to the old-fashioned steak-and-fish houses in town.

Moderate

✪ **Casablanca Cafe.** On the ocean at the corner of Fla. A1A and Alahambra St., Fort Lauderdale. ☎ **954/764-3500.** Reservations not accepted. Main courses $15–$25; appetizers $5–$8. AE, DISC, DC, MC, V. Daily 11am–11:30pm. CONTINENTAL/AMERICAN.

Although it may seem odd to sit next to a roaring fire while listening to live music in the warm South Florida climate, at Casablanca it's a perfect complement to the stunning architecture and stupendous cooking. Everything from the warm macadamia nut–encrusted goat-cheese salad to a filet mignon in a cognac-and-mushroom sauce served with perfectly al dente pasta is immaculately prepared and served by a friendly staff. Six or seven specials are included daily on the menu; the best are seafood creations with superfresh local fish or lobster.

Conca'D'Oro. 1833 Tyler St. (on Young Circle), Hollywood. ☎ **954/927-6704.** Reservations not accepted. Pizzas $7–$12.50; main courses $10–$28. MC, V. Mon–Thurs 11am–11pm, Fri–Sat 11am–midnight, Sun 4–11pm. ITALIAN.

This bustling Italian restaurant is always busy. It's not that the food is so extraordinary, but that the portions are large, service is quick, and the attitude is straight from Brooklyn. The pizzas, served Neapolitan (thin crust) or Sicilian style, are large and topped with lots of cheese and a good tangy tomato sauce. Don't expect more than iceberg lettuce in the salads, but do take advantage of the huge heroes and tasty house wines. If you are with a group, order one or two entrees to share. You will have leftovers. Although they are not always on the menu, ask for fresh mussels if they are in season. While other appetizers are battered and fried, the young black mussels are done to perfection in a red or white sauce. Also good is the hearty lasagna that is full of chunks of garlicky meatballs and mild sausage.

Creolina's. 209 S.W. 2nd St., Fort Lauderdale. ☎ **954/524-2003.** Appetizers $4–$9; main courses $13–$18. AE, MC, V. Mon–Fri 11am–2:30pm and 5pm–10pm; Fri–Sat 5pm–11pm. Sun brunch 11am–2:30pm. CREOLE.

You'll find authentic Louisiana Creole cuisine at this restaurant, situated along the River Walk in old town. Try the Shrimp Jambalaya with shrimp sausage and vegetables in a rich brown Cajun sauce served over rice, or the Crayfish Etouffe with crayfish tail meat simmered in a mellow Cajun sauce served over rice. The mashed potatoes are homemade, and the delicious fresh-squeezed lemonade is made daily. There is also have a delicious New Orleans Sunday brunch.

✪ **Indigo.** In the Riverside Hotel, 620 E. Las Olas Blvd., Fort Lauderdale. ☎ **954/467-0671.** Reservations only for groups of 6 or more. Main courses $12–$22. AE, DISC, DC, MC, V. Mon–Thurs 7am–10:30pm, Fri–Sat 7am–11:30pm, Sun 7am–10:30pm. SOUTHEAST ASIAN/ECLECTIC.

This not-so-traditional Southeast Asian meal begins with a basket of pappadoms, nan, and shrimp puff bread. All are delicious and easy to fill up on, especially when spread with the tangy pineapple chutney or cucumber pickle. An impressive appetizer is a lightly peppered, dusted, seared tuna served in a crispy basket of udon noodles. Look underneath for a hidden dab of sweet apricot puree. It's fantastically rich and a good complement to the spicy fish. Entrees run the gamut from a lean though somewhat dry Balinese lamb to a musky smoked duckling to a rosemary-skewered shrimp. As to be expected in Asian cuisine, vegetarians have plenty of choices, too. In addition to a superrich grilled vegetable cassoulet au gratin and a fried rice dish with shallots, corn, and asparagus, there are pizzas baked on top of puffy nan bread covered with such toppings as onions, shiitake mushrooms, goat cheese, spinach, eggplant, garlic, curried tomato, and pine nuts. Particularly good is a meaty soy and portobello mushroom combination wrapped in fluffy puff pastry and served with a delicate broccoli sauce. Ask servers for suggestions, though. Even if they are a bit harried on weekends, they tend to be knowledgeable and honest.

✪ **Sugar Reef.** 600 N. Surf Rd. (on the Boardwalk just north of Hollywood Blvd.), Hollywood. ☎ **954/922-1119.** Reservations only for groups over 6. Main courses $10–$24; sandwiches and salads $4–$9. AE, DISC, MC, V. Mon 4–10:30pm, Tues–Thurs 11am–10:30pm, Fri–Sun 11am–11pm (sometimes later in winter). TROPICAL FRENCH.

A welcome addition to a strip of greasy fish joints, hot-dog stands, and bars, Sugar Reef has captured the attention of visitors and locals who appreciate superior and imaginative meals served for very reasonable prices. Chef/owner Patrick Farnault left a successful and formal restaurant in Fort Lauderdale to open this ocean-side bistro.

Simple offerings might include a salmon BLT with dill mayonnaise or Jamaican-style pork loin or a burger and fries. Portions are generous but not huge. Escargot in a green curry sauce with lemongrass is a delicious twist on an old favorite, evoking memories of subtle and spicy Vietnamese dishes. More than half a dozen salads, some with cheese, chicken, or fish, are a perfect meal for beach-goers looking for something light and healthful as they enjoy the view. As is fitting for a beachside eatery, service is laid back but still professional.

Sushi Blues Cafe. 1836 S. Young Circle (east on Hollywood Blvd.), Hollywood. ☎ **954/929-9560.** Reservations recommended on weekends. Main courses $11–$20; sushi $1.75–$2.75 per piece. AE, MC, V. Mon–Thurs 6pm–midnight, Fri–Sat 6pm–2am. JAPANESE.

Live loud blues and jazz combine with pretty good sushi to make an unusual pair at this small storefront eatery located on Hollywood's largest traffic circle. There are about 12 tables and a dozen counter stools in this relatively straightforward and unadorned sushi room. In addition to raw fish, the cafe offers some inventive specials like salmon carpaccio with caper sauce, fried soft-shell crab drizzled with a spicy sesame sauce, miso-broiled eggplant, and grilled smoked sausage with Japanese mustard. The restaurant is popular with a 20-something crowd and is packed Friday and Saturday nights, when there's live music.

Tarpon Bend. 200 SW 2nd St., Fort Lauderdale. ☎ **954/523-3233.** Reservations available for parties of 6 or more. Main courses $12–$15. AE, M, V. Mon–Thurs 11:30am–1am, Fri–Sat 11:30am–3am. SEAFOOD/AMERICAN.

This restaurant is a real seafood-lover's delight. It's one of the few places where the fishermen still bring the fish to the back door. The oysters from the raw bar are shucked to order and out of sight. Try the house specialty "smoked fish dip"—a king fish smoked on premises. The steamed clambake, with half a Maine lobster, clams, potatoes, mussels, and corn on the cob is scrumptious and served in its own pot. It's a real fish fest. Also try some of their homemade side dishes. For chocolate lovers, the chocolate brownie sundae is a must. There's live entertainment Wednesday through Saturday, and a full bar.

Topanga! 5001 N. Federal Hwy. (at Commercial Blvd.), Fort Lauderdale. ☎ **954/771-8555.** Reservations for 5 or more suggested. Main courses $9–$18; pastas $9–$14. AE, DC, DISC, MC, V. Mon–Thurs 11:30am–10pm, Fri 11:30am–11pm, Sat noon–11pm, Sun 10:30–10pm. CALIFORNIA-STYLE GRILL AND PIZZA BISTRO.

This bright and bustling restaurant is a perfect choice for a quick healthful lunch or dinner. Local businesspeople favor it in the afternoons since they can get in and out within 45 minutes or linger for hours in the pleasant sun-drenched eatery. There is even an outside terrace for those who don't mind the busy highway as a backdrop. With a large but not overwhelming menu featuring Italian favorites like chicken Marsala, pizzas, and more than a dozen pastas, this is a place that appeals to everyone (including the kids). Salads are large (like most other entrees) and can easily be shared by three. Or, ask for a half portion, which is plenty big for one or two. My favorite is a mix of fresh baby greens with large slabs of moist and spicy dolphin (mahimahi) and chunks of feta cheese, briny Greek olives, and a slightly sweet champagne vinaigrette dressing. Pizzas, too, are fresh and filling. Try the goat cheese and basil or the unusual Acapulco chicken with tequila, lime, herbs, and a side of guacamole and salsa. The daily specials like beef and veal meat loaf, seafood quesadilla, or lemon and dill salmon are usually a good bet. An impressive selection of wines and beers, plus lots of decadent desserts make this place a great find in the middle of a fast-food-glutted highway.

Inexpensive

✪ **Deli Den.** 2889 Stirling Rd. (west of I-95), Hollywood. ☎ **954/961-4070.** Lunch $4.95–$6.95; main courses $9–$13; bagel sandwiches $1–$7.50. AE, MC, V. Daily 8am–10pm. JEWISH-STYLE DELI.

Catering to Broward's New York crowd for nearly 3 decades, this warehouse-sized deli serves the area's finest cheese blintzes, red cabbage soup, and matzo balls. Breakfast selections include superthick French toast with bacon, sausage, or ham, plus dozens of egg specialties like minced lox, eggs and onions, or corned beef hash and eggs. All baking is done on the premises. And owners are proud to say that absolutely everything else, from coleslaw to blintzes, is also homemade. The best news is that kids under 12 eat free every Monday and Thursday.

East Coast Burrito Factory. 261 E. Commercial Blvd., Fort Lauderdale. ☎ **954/772-8007.** Tacos and burritos $3.85–$9.15; salads $4–$6.50. AE, CB, DC, DISC, MC, V. Mon–Sat 11am–9:45pm, Sun noon–7:45pm. FLORIDA/MEXICAN.

Just off of I-95 is an oasis. A dozen wooden benches line the counter at this super Mexican diner, which serves made-to-order soft tacos, burritos, hot dogs, and salads. For a healthier spin on a burrito, try the Florito, made with black beans instead of refried beans—a uniquely Florida invention. My favorite is the "Super Veggie," stuffed with corn, salsa, mushrooms, black olives, carrots, peppers, and hearts of palm, then doused with the restaurant's own superhot chile pepper sauce. The guacamole and various huge salads are also fantastic, especially on a sunny day on the back patio. To finish it off, try a Latin flan or an honest slice of key lime pie. There are four other locations throughout Broward and Palm Beach counties.

✪ **The Floridian Restaurant.** 1410 E Las Olas Blvd., Fort Lauderdale. ☎ **954/463-4041.** Fax 954/761-3930. Sandwiches $3–$7; breakfast combos $3.50–$8; hot platters $7–$14. Daily 24 hours. No credit cards. AMERICAN/DINER.

A landmark on Las Olas, this popular spot turns out excellent diner fare around the clock. It's especially busy on weekend mornings when locals and tourists come in for huge omelettes, fresh oatmeal, sausage, muffins, and biscuits. Service can be a bit brusque, but it's worth it.

Thai Spice. 1514 E. Commercial Blvd. (east of I-95), Fort Lauderdale. ☎ **954/771-4535.** Fax 954/771-5678. Reservations recommended. Main courses $9.95–$26. AE, DC, DISC, MC, V. Lunch Mon–Fri 11am–3pm, dinner Sun–Thurs 5–10pm; Fri–Sat 5–11pm. THAI.

The tacky and typical decor of Thai Spice belies the authentic and delicious food turned out here. Soft-shell crab in a light and subtle chile sauce and tender shrimp cakes are fantastic and frequent specials. Regular menu items include a slightly sweet and almost buttery pad Thai with a generous serving of shrimp, chicken chunks, and scallion. Lunch specials are obscenely cheap and include all the favorites.

✪ **Yellow Moon.** 201 S.W. 2nd St., Fort Lauderdale. ☎ **954/522-1253.** Fax 954/522-0975. Main courses $8–$25. AE, MC ,V. Sun–Fri 4pm–4am; Sat noon–4am. BAR/AMERICAN FOOD.

If you're in the mood for a light meal and rock, pop, blues, or jazz, head down to this friendly bar in Fort Lauderdale's old town. Enjoy a full bar or a great selection of wines and imported and domestic bottled beers. There is live music Thursday through Sunday, and Happy Hour runs from 5 to 7pm, Monday through Friday. The Japanese chef here creates great specials throughout the week. Try the fresh sushi or chicken teriyaki. Salads are fresh and large, served with the signature house dressing, a Balsamic Ginger Vinaigrette. The fresh mahimahi sandwich is a good pick, too.

THE HOLLYWOOD & FORT LAUDERDALE AREA AFTER DARK

The newly hip downtown area of Hollywood is centered around **Harrison Street and Young Circle** (east of Dixie Highway at Hollywood Boulevard). A funky menagerie of bookstores, coffee shops, galleries, and a couple of live music joints are worth exploring. One of the latest and most welcome additions is **O'Hara's Pub and Jazz Cafe** at 1905 Hollywood Blvd. (☎ 954/925-2555). Kitty Ryan, who operates another club with the same name in Fort Lauderdale, has duplicated her success here with a smoking jazz club, which attracts superior acts from all over.

A funkier set hangs out at **Warehaus 57** just across the street (☎ 954/926-6633), where longhairs converse over killer frozen coffee drinks or glasses of jug wine. This used bookstore, clothing store, and acoustic music venue is an inviting and happening little spot. During the week, come for a game of backgammon or a cup of joe. Folky local bands play on weekends to the delight of an eclectic crowd that comes at the generous invitation of owner Lauren Tellman (who also designs the racy and strappy leather clothing in the back). During the week she closes at 6pm. Friday and Saturday, she's there until at least midnight.

Sushi Blues was one of the first spots to offer live music in this neighborhood (see "Where to Dine," above). Live bands play jazz, blues, or world music on Friday and Saturday, and if you have dinner there you can skip the cover (usually $10).

Also in Hollywood, just west of Young Circle at Federal Highway, is **Club M** (☎ 954/925-8396), a small local blues showcase with a bit of good jazz and electric thrown in. On busy Friday and Saturday nights when live bands perform, you'll pay a small cover.

Fort Lauderdale has hundreds of bars and clubs for every taste. There are essentially four main areas that have clusters of happening scenes you can check out for yourself. To get you started, I have highlighted the best in each neighborhood. Plus, I have listed a few out-of-the-way spots for the more adventurous.

The waterfront bars and restaurants on the Intracoastal just south of Oakland Park Boulevard are especially recommendable for their outdoor patio bar scenes at all hours. Accessible by boat or car, **Bootlegger's**, at 3003 NE 32nd Ave. (☎ 954/563-4337), features more than 70 kinds of beers, with a featured draft of the day going for only $1. Here and next door at **Shooters**, 3033 NE 32nd Ave. (☎ 954/566-2855), you'll find nautical types, families, and young professionals mixed in with a good dose of sunburned tourists enjoying the live reggae, jazz, or Jimmy Buffett–style tunes with the gorgeous backdrop of the bay and marinas all around. If you don't have your own boat, take the water taxi to really get the feel (see box above). Both are open until 2am.

The once-famous "Strip" on the waterfront just north of Las Olas was overrun with spring-breakers. Now, it's been replaced with a mellower (and unfortunately more generic) scene. A newish shopping and entertainment complex called **Beach Place** is a sort of outdoor megamall modeled after Miami's hugely successful Bayside and Cocowalk. This block-long monster is the new home to a number of franchised bars and restaurants, like **Sloppy Joe's** (of Key West fame), **Howl at the Moon,** and **Hooters,** amid the requisite Gap and Banana Republic. The view, overlooking the ocean, makes it worth a stop for a drink.

Some of the college kids' old standbys remain in the neighborhood, including the **Elbo Room** at 241 S. Atlantic Blvd., on the corner of Las Olas Boulevard and Fla. A1A (☎ 954/463-4615). It's maintained its rowdy and divey reputation by serving up frequent drink specials and live bands. A dedicated beer-drinking, football-watching crowd mingles with young tourists. This area is also accessible by water taxi.

An older crowd hangs out after dark on Las Olas Boulevard, where there are blocks and blocks of good restaurants and music clubs. One of the most happening is **O'Hara's Pub and Jazz Cafe,** at 722 E. Las Olas Blvd. (☎ **954/524-1764**). They pack 'em in until they spill onto the sidewalk of this smoky little club. Best known for presenting original jazz performers, O'Hara's also has blues and big-band music some Sunday afternoons. Call their jazz hot line (☎ **954/524-2801**) to hear the lineup for this and the newer **Hollywood Cafe.**

Most of the alternative music scene is centered in the downtown area of Fort Lauderdale. One good choice is the **Chili Pepper** (☎ **954/525-0094**) at 200 W. Broward Blvd., east of I-95. With big-name concerts as well as local band showcases, this place captures the heart and soul of the young and supercharged Wednesday through Sunday.

To find the heart of Fort Lauderdale's gay scene, head to **The Copa,** at 2800 S. Federal Hwy., east on I-595, near the airport (☎ **954/463-1507**). This big '80s-style black box has been the cornerstone of Fort Lauderdale's gay nightlife forever. Popular and updated shows are common on the many elevated stages surrounding a large and loud dance floor. **Club Cathode Ray** at 1105 E. Las Olas Blvd. (☎ **954/462-8611**) caters to a good-looking crowd and plays hot dance music daily from 4pm until 2am.

2 Boca Raton & Delray Beach

26 miles S of Palm Beach, 40 miles N of Miami

With its many mansions and waterfront condominiums, Boca Raton is winter home to many of society's wealthy industrialists and retirees. Increasingly, the area is also attracting young families from other areas in the state who have tired of crime, corruption, and overcrowding. This planned city, known simply as "Boca," is a bit overmanicured and glitzy for my taste, although there are certainly some great restaurants and resorts worth exploring.

Delray, named after a suburb of Detroit, grew up completely separate from its southern neighbor. This community was founded in 1894 by a Midwestern postmaster who sold off 5-acre lots through Michigan newspaper ads. Because of their close proximity, Boca and Delray can easily be explored together. Budget-conscious travelers would do well to eat and sleep in Delray and dip into Boca for sightseeing and beaching only.

ESSENTIALS

GETTING THERE Like the rest of the cities on the Gold Coast, Boca Raton and Delray are easily reached from I-95 or the turnpike. Both the Fort Lauderdale/Hollywood International Airport and the Palm Beach International Airport (at Congress Avenue and Belvedere Road) are convenient. Amtrak (☎ **800/USA-RAIL;** www.amtrak.com) trains make stops in Delray Beach at an unattended station at 345 S. Congress Ave.

VISITOR INFORMATION Before your trip, call or write the **Palm Beach County Convention and Visitors Bureau,** 1555 Palm Beach Lakes Blvd., Suite 204, West Palm Beach, FL 33401 (☎ **800/554-PALM** or 561/471-3995; fax 561/471-3990). On weekdays from 8:30am until at least 4pm, stop by the **Boca Raton Chamber of Commerce** at 1800 N. Dixie Hwy., 4 blocks north of Glades Road (☎ **561/395-4433;** fax 561/392-3780; www.bocaratonchamber.com), Boca Raton, FL 33432, for information on attractions, accommodations, and events in the area. Also, try the **Delray Beach Chamber of Commerce** (☎ **561/278-0424;** fax 561/278-0555; e-mail: chamber@delraybeach.com), at 64 SE 5th Ave., half a block south of Atlantic Avenue on U.S. 1, Delray Beach, FL 33483.

WHERE TO PLAY, ON & OFF THE BEACH

BEACHES Thankfully, Florida had the foresight to set aside some of its most beautiful coastal areas for the public's enjoyment. Many of the area's best beaches are located in state parks and are free to pedestrians and bikers. Most do charge for parking.

The **Delray Beach Public Beach**, on Ocean Boulevard at the east end of Atlantic Avenue, is one of the area's most popular hangouts. Weekends especially attract a young and good-looking crowd of active locals and tourists. Regular volleyball, Frisbee, and paddleball games make for good entertainment. For refreshments, a number of snack shops, bars, and restaurants are just across the street. Families enjoy the protection of lifeguards on the clean, wide beach. Gentle waters make it a good swimming beach, too. There's limited parking at meters along Ocean Boulevard.

Spanish River Park, on North Ocean Boulevard (Fla. A1A), 2 miles north of Palmetto Park Road in Boca Raton, is a huge oceanfront park with a large grassy area, making it one of the best choices for picnicking. Facilities include picnic tables, grills, rest rooms, and a bilevel 40-foot observation tower. You can walk through tunnels under the highway to nature trails that wind through fertile grasslands. Volleyball nets are ocean-side and always have at least one serious game going on. The park is open from 8am until 8pm. Also, read below about Red Reef Park.

GOLF This area has plenty of good courses. Unfortunately, most of the best are private or are in the very expensive resorts. However, from May to October or November, about a dozen private courses open their greens to visitors staying in Palm Beach County hotels. This "Golf-A-Round" program is free or severely discounted (carts are additional), and reservations can be made through most major hotels. Ask at your hotel, or contact the **Palm Beach County Convention and Visitors Bureau** (☎ **561/471-3995**) for information on which clubs are available for play.

The semiprivate, 18-hole, par-61 course at the **Boca Raton Executive Country Club**, 7601 E. Country Club Blvd. (☎ **561/997-9510**), is usually open to the public. A driving range is also on the property as well as a pro shop and a restaurant. A PGA professional gives lessons, and rental clubs are available. From Yamato Road East, turn left onto Old Dixie Highway; after about a mile, turn left onto Hidden Valley Boulevard and continue straight to the club. Greens fees are $11 to $27.

The **Boca Raton Municipal Golf Course**, 8111 Golf Course Rd. (☎ **561/ 483-6100**), is located just north of Glades Road, half a mile west of the Florida Turnpike. This public 18-hole, par-72 course covers approximately 6,200 yards. There's a snack bar and a pro shop where clubs can be rented. Greens fees are $11 to $14 for 9 holes and $19 to $25 for 18 holes. Ask for special summer discount fees.

SCUBA DIVING & SNORKELING **Moray Bend**, a 58-foot dive spot located about 3/4 mile off Boca Inlet, is the area's most popular. It's home to three moray eels that are used to being fed by scuba divers. The reef is accessible by boat from **Force E Dive Center**, 877 E. Palmetto Park Rd., Boca Raton (☎ **561/368-0555**). Phone for dive times. Dives cost $38 to $45 per person.

Red Reef Park, 1400 N. Ocean Park Blvd. (☎ **561/393-7974**), a fully developed 67-acre oceanfront park in Boca Raton, has year-round lifeguard protection. There's good snorkeling for beginners around the rocks and reefs that lie just off the beach in 2 to 6 feet of water. There's also good swimming and a small picnic area with grills, tables, and rest rooms. The park, located a half mile north of Palmetto Park Road, is open daily from 8am to 10pm. You only pay if you drive in. It's $8 per car during the week or $10 on weekends.

TENNIS The snazzy **Delray Beach Tennis Center,** 201 W. Atlantic Ave. (☎ 561/243-7360), has 14 lighted clay courts and 5 hard courts available by the hour. Phone for rates and reservations.

The 17 public lighted hard courts at **Patch Reef Park,** 2000 NW 51st St. (☎ 561/997-0881), are available by reservation. The fee for nonresidents is $5.75 per person per hour. Courts are available Monday to Saturday from 7:30am to10pm and Sunday from 7:30am to dusk; you can phone ahead to see if a court is available. To reach the park from I-95, exit at Yamato Road West and continue past Military Trail to the park.

SEEING THE SIGHTS

Boca Raton Museum of Art. 801 W. Palmetto Park Rd. (1 mile east of I-95), Boca Raton. ☎ **561/392-2500.** Admission $3 adults, $2 seniors, $1 students, children under 12 free. Tues–Thurs, Fri 10am–4pm; Wed 10–8pm; Sat–Sun noon–4pm; closed Mon. Free admission Wed.

In addition to a relatively small but well-chosen permanent collection that's strongest in 19th-century European oils, the museum stages a wide variety of temporary exhibitions by local and international artists. Lectures and films are offered on a fairly regular basis, so call ahead for details. Special exhibits and performances may be cost more than regular admission.

Gumbo Limbo Environmental Complex. 1801 N. Ocean Blvd. (on Fla. A1A between Spanish River Blvd. and Palmetto Park), Boca Raton. ☎ **561/338-1473.** Fax 561/338-1483. Free admission. Mon–Sat 9am–4pm, Sun noon–4pm.

Named for an indigenous hardwood tree with continuously shedding bronze bark, the 20-acre complex protects one of the few surviving coastal hammocks, or forest islands, in South Florida. Visitors can walk through the hammock, on a ¹/₂-mile-long elevated boardwalk that ends at a 40-foot observation tower, from which you can see the Atlantic Ocean, the Intracoastal Waterway, and much of Boca Raton. From mid-April to September, sea turtles come ashore here to lay their eggs. During this time, the center conducts turtle-watching tours and sea turtle lectures. If you haven't seen turtles doing their thing, definitely stop in for a memorable experience.

In the museum is an impressive array of local flora and fauna, including live snakes, fish, crabs, sea turtles, and scorpions. Even city kids seem to like touching all the strange creatures here.

International Museum of Cartoon Art. 201 Plaza Real at Mizner Park, Boca Raton. ☎ **561/391-2200.** www.cartoon.org. Admission $6 adults, $5 seniors, $4 students, $3 children 6–12 years old, under 5 free as well as members. Tues–Sat 10am–6pm, Sun noon–6pm. Closed Mon.

Reborn and hugely expanded after nearly 20 years of life in New York City, this extensive collection of cartoon art spans the decades and styles in its glitzy home in Mizner Park. In a gorgeous 52,000-square-foot gallery space, cartoon fans can see prints, frames, moving pictures, and books by some of the world's greatest cartoonists, including many by the museum's founder, Mort Walker (of *Beetle Bailey* fame). A fantastic gift shop offers posters, books, and lots of memorabilia.

✪ **Morikami Museum and Japanese Gardens.** 4000 Morikami Park Rd. Delray Beach. ☎ **561/495-0233.** Museum $5.25 adults, $4.75 seniors, $3 children 6–18, free for members and children 5 and under. Museum Tues–Sun 10am–5pm; gardens Tues–Sat 10am–5pm. Closed major holidays.

Slip off your shoes and into a serene Japanese garden community that dates from 1905, when an entrepreneurial farmer, Jo Sakai, came to Boca Raton to build a tropical agricultural community. The Yamato Colony, as it was known, was short-lived; by the 1920s only one tenacious colonist remained: George Sukeji Morikami. But Morikami was quite successful, eventually holding one of the largest pineapple plantations in the area. The 200-acre Morikami Museum and Japanese Gardens, which opened to the public in 1977, was Morikami's gift to Palm Beach County and the State of Florida. The park section, dedicated to the preservation of Japanese culture, is constructed to appeal to all the senses. An artificial waterfall that cascades into a koi- and carp-filled moat, a small rock garden for meditation, and a large bonsai collection that includes miniature maple, buttonwood, juniper, and Australian pine trees are all worth contemplation—and it's free. The Gardens have been expanded and there's also a cafe with a Japanese and Asian-inspired menu if you want to stay for lunch.

SHOPPING & BROWSING

Famous in New York City for its upscale antiques and gorgeous rugs, **ABC Carpet & Home** also has an outlet store in Delray Beach just off I-95 at 777 S. Congress (between Linton and Atlantic). Look for deep discounts (usually at least 30%) on very high-priced furnishings and flooring.

Mizner Park, on Federal Highway (between Palmetto Park and Glades roads) in Boca Raton (☎ **561/362-0606**), is the town square of this tiny enclave, complete with clothing shops, shoe stores, restaurants, live performances, and lots of beautiful landscaping. It's really an outdoor mall, with 45 specialty shops, seven good restaurants, and a multiplex. Each shop front faces a grassy island with blue and green gazebos, potted plants, and garden benches. It's extremely popular with folks who come here just to stroll, often until late in the evening.

Town Center Mall of Boca Raton has six huge department stores including Bloomingdale's, Burdines, Lord & Taylor, and Saks Fifth Avenue. Add to that the hundreds of specialty shops, an extensive food court, and a range of other restaurants, and you have the area's most comprehensive and beautiful shopping opportunity. The mall is located on the south side of Glades Road just west of I-95.

Another great area for a stroll is in the more artsy community of **Delray Beach,** known by many as Pineapple Grove. Here, along Atlantic Avenue, especially east of Swinton Avenue, you'll find a fantastic array of antique shops, clothing stores, and art galleries shaded by palm trees and colorful awnings. A lively cafe culture and many celebrations take place on this quaint old-style main street. Pick up the "Downtown Delray Beach" map and guide at almost any of the stores on this strip, or call ☎ **561/278-0424** for more information.

WHERE TO STAY

If you choose to stay in Boca or the surrounding areas, you will find some very luxurious lodgings, epitomized by the famous and often photographed pink **Boca Raton Hotel and Country Club,** where deluxe suites have gone for up to $6,000 per night. But don't worry, there are plenty of other choices on and near the beach.

A number of national chain hotels worth considering include a moderately priced **Holiday Inn Highland Beach Oceanside** at 2809 S. Ocean Blvd., on Fla. A1A southeast of Linton Boulevard (☎ **800/234-6835** or 561/278-6241). **The Radisson Bridge Resort,** at 999 E. Camino Real (☎ **800/333-3333** or 561/368-9500), operates a particularly popular and affordable resort on the Intracoastal Waterway just a few blocks from the Boca Raton Resort. *Beware:* It books up well in advance.

Although you won't find the rows and rows of cheap hotels as in Fort Lauderdale and Hollywood, a handful of mom-and-pop motels have survived along Fla. A1A between the towering condos of Delray Beach. Look along the beach just south of Atlantic Boulevard. Especially noteworthy is a pleasant little two-story, shingle-roofed **Bermuda Inn** at 64 S. Ocean Blvd. (☎ **561/276-5288**).

Even more economical options can be found in Deerfield Beach, Boca's neighbor, south of the county line. A number of beachfront efficiencies offer great deals, even in the winter months. Try the **Panther Motel and Apartments,** at 715 S. A1A (☎ **954/ 427-0700**). This clean and convenient motel has rates starting as low as $40. Although in season, you may find you have to book for a week at a time. Weekly rates in season start at $457.

If you are looking for something more private or for longer than just a few days, you may want to call a reservations service for help. Especially for rentals for a few weeks or months, call **Palm Beach Accommodations** (☎ **800/543-SWIM**).

Very Expensive

✪ **Boca Raton Resort and Club.** 501 E. Camino Real (P.O. Box 5025), Boca Raton, FL 33431. ☎ **800/327-0101** or 561/395-3000. Fax 561/447-3183. 963 units, 120 golf villas. A/C MINIBAR TV TEL. Winter $315–$500 double. Off-season $155–$275 double. Very reasonable seasonal packages available. AE, DC, DISC, MC, V. From I-95 N., exit onto Palmetto Park Rd. E.; turn right onto Federal Hwy. (U.S. 1), and then left onto Camino Real to the resort.

Boca's most historical and romantic resort straddles both sides of the Intracoastal Waterway and encompasses more than 350 acres of land, with extensive and outstanding facilities for tennis, golf, and anything else an active family or individual could want, including three fitness centers with brand-new equipment, more than 30 tennis courts, and two 18-hole golf courses. Since 1926, this palatial hotel has been hosting the most discriminating international guests. Now, with a sizable population of local sports enthusiasts who have joined the country club, and lots of conferences going on, the place is still pleasing demanding visitors. Don't worry: The huge proportions of the Spanish-Moorish architecture and the sprawling grounds will ensure that you will never feel crowded or processed. And yearly renovations guarantee that you won't feel as if you are staying in a musty museum.

Compared to other destination resorts on Florida's east coast, this superior facility is a great value, with all the amenities and elegance but none of the stuffiness. Everything is easy once you have decided which type of room you'll stay in. There are several options. Those in the original Cloisters building have exquisite architectural details, like arched doorways, high-beamed ceilings, a mix of reproduction antiques, and the most charm. The best part is that, although they are more modest in size than newer rooms, they are also the least expensive. The Boca Beach Club building, just a 5-minute drive and accessible by free shuttle or your own car, offers spacious cabana-style rooms on the ocean with sliding glass doors that open to beach breezes. Dressed with dark woods and rich colors, the rooms in the modern 27-story tower adjacent to the Cloisters are the most formal and enjoy sweeping views of this idyllic coast. Golf villas overlook the perfectly manicured greens. All are outfitted with two phones, large bathrooms, fluffy robes, and first-class furnishings.

Dining/Diversions: There are nine restaurants and three lounges to satisfy all tastes and budgets. A formal Italian restaurant on the top floor of the main building offers extraordinary views over Boca Raton. A seafood restaurant at the Boca Beach Club is known for its excellent and diverse menu. A coffee bar in the Cloister building is particularly popular in mornings and afternoons.

Amenities: Concierge, room service (24 hours), fitness classes, laundry, overnight shoe shine. An impressive array of children's programs. Three fitness centers, five swimming pools, two golf courses, 34 tennis courts (nine lighted), water-sports and bicycle rentals, snorkeling and scuba instruction, croquet, volleyball, basketball court, 2-mile jogging course, business center, well-priced boutiques and gift shops, racquetball.

Palm Beach & Boca Raton

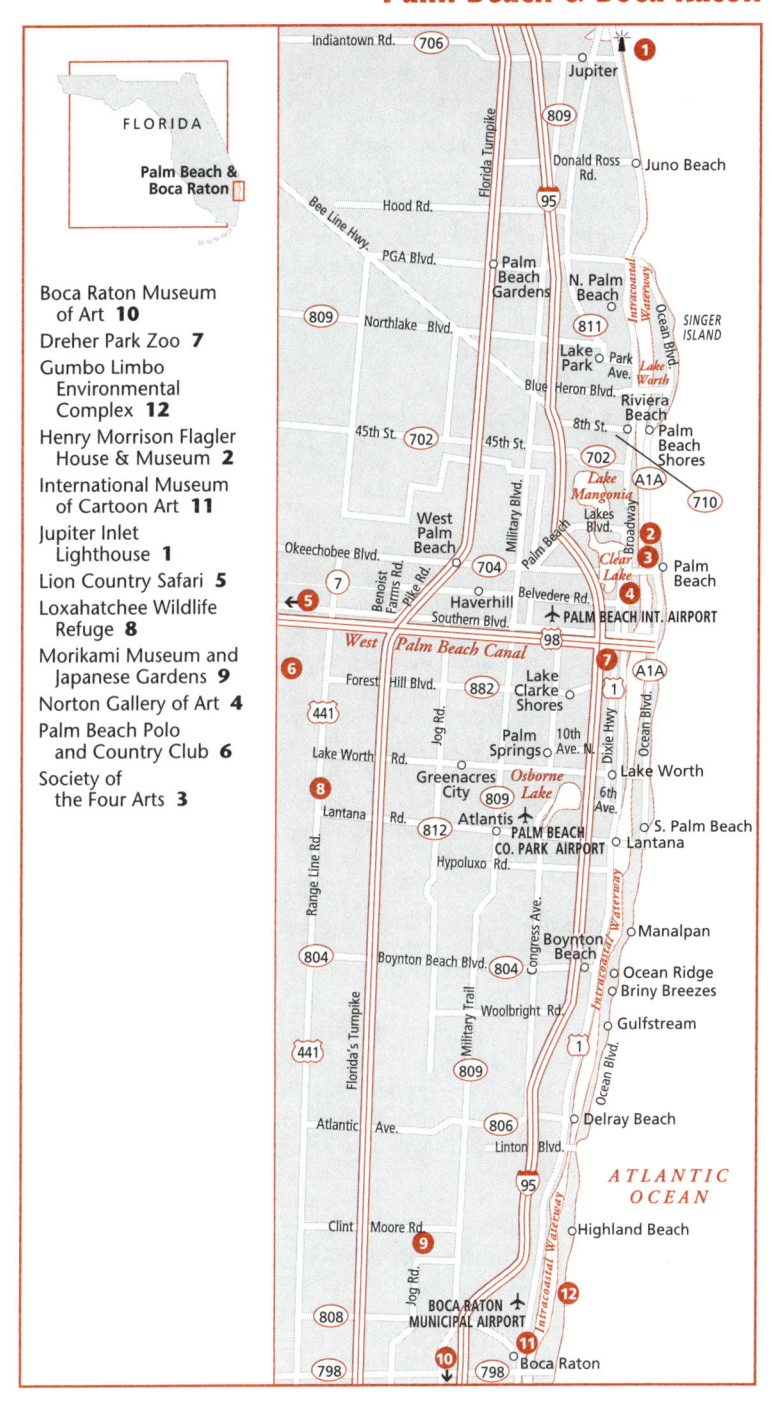

Boca Raton Museum of Art **10**
Dreher Park Zoo **7**
Gumbo Limbo Environmental Complex **12**
Henry Morrison Flagler House & Museum **2**
International Museum of Cartoon Art **11**
Jupiter Inlet Lighthouse **1**
Lion Country Safari **5**
Loxahatchee Wildlife Refuge **8**
Morikami Museum and Japanese Gardens **9**
Norton Gallery of Art **4**
Palm Beach Polo and Country Club **6**
Society of the Four Arts **3**

293

Moderate

Colony Hotel & Cabana Club. 525 E. Atlantic Ave. (P.O. Box 970), Delray Beach, FL 33483. ☎ **800/552-2363** or 561/276-4123. Fax 561/276-0123. www.thecolonyhotel.com/florida/. E-mail: info-fla@thecolonyhotel.com. 66 units. A/C TV TEL. Winter $160–$210 double. Off-season $125–$150 double. AE, MC, V.

This lovely three-story hotel is located right on Delray's main commercial thoroughfare about a mile from the hotel's private beach and club. The Colony benefited from a 1996 refurbishment that brought back some of its original 1926 details, including hardwood floors and authentic furnishings. Still, the rooms are modest in size and style but comfortable and clean. The hotel is popular with families who appreciate the many planned activities at the hotel's beachfront club 1 mile away, which offers a heated saltwater swimming pool, a private beach, as well as putting and shuffleboard tournaments. All facilities are free for guests.

Seagate Hotel & Beach Club. 400 S. Ocean Blvd., Delray Beach, FL 33483. ☎ **800/233-3581** or 561/276-2421. Fax 561/243-4714. www.seagate@hudsonhotels.com. 70 units. A/C TV TEL. Winter $194–$349 suite; $398–$419 two-bedroom suite. Off-season $74–$305 suite; $136–$375 two-bedroom suite. AE, CB, DC, MC, V. From I-95, exit onto Atlantic Ave. E., turn right onto Ocean Blvd. (Fla. A1A), and continue $^1/_2$ mile to the hotel.

This modest, well-located hotel features generously sized rooms located in two buildings directly across the street from the beach. To make your stay more affordable and convenient, the hotel furnishes coffeemakers, fully stocked kitchens or kitchenettes, irons, large closets, and safes in each room. A recent redecorating replaced the quaint Old Florida furnishings with industrial Formica, plain blond wood, and commercial-grade carpeting. Also regrettable are the tiny bathrooms with little or no counter space.

The Beach Club is located across the street, directly on the sand, where you can relax on a chaise lounge or dip into one of the heated pools. A moderately priced restaurant and bar will deliver snacks and cocktails to the beach. There's 400 feet of private beach, and special children's programs are offered during the high season. Overall, the resort is pleasant and extremely practical, especially for families. Little extras like newspapers and refreshments in the lobby make this an especially appealing option.

Spanish River Resort. 1111 E. Atlantic Ave., Delray Beach, FL 33483. ☎ **800/543-SWIM** or 561/243-7946. Fax 561/276-9634. www.pbai.com. 75 units. A/C TV TEL. Winter $150 studio; $350 two bedroom. Off-season from $98 studio; $228 two bedroom. Free 6th and 7th nights with weekly booking. DISC, MC, V.

An especially good value for those staying longer than a few days, this pleasant family-oriented property offers fully furnished condominiums half a block from a popular beach and walking distance to Delray's best shops, restaurants, and galleries. The 11-story Mediterranean-style building has free lighted tennis courts, a large outdoor pool, and lovely ocean-view balconies. Apartments are spacious and outfitted with fully equipped kitchens. All units also have pullout queen-size sofa beds. The best part is there is no additional charge for extra guests. A one-bedroom unit can comfortably fit four or five people; a two-bedroom unit can easily accommodate six. Cots and roll-away beds are available at a minimum charge. Compared with many of the run-down 1950s motels in the area, this moderately priced, well-maintained tower is a real find.

Inexpensive

Ocean Lodge. 531 N. Ocean Blvd. (just north of Palmetto Park Rd. on Fla. A1A), Boca Raton, FL 33432. ☎ **800/STAY-BOCA** or 561/395-7772. Fax 561/395-0554. 18 units. A/C TV TEL. Winter $99–$125 double. Off-season $75–$99 double. AE, MC, V.

Situated around a small heated pool and sundeck, this two-story motel is a particularly well-kept accommodation in an area of run-down or overpriced options. The large rooms offer furnishings and decor that are clean but a bit impersonal. A recent do-over that added modern Formica and floral wallpaper lifts this a notch above a basic motel. Ask for a room in the back since the street noise can be a bit loud, especially in season. The bonus is that you are across the street from the ocean and in one of Florida's most upscale resort towns.

Shore Edge Motel. 425 N. Ocean Blvd. (on Fla. A1A, north of Palmetto Park Rd.), Boca Raton, FL 33432. ☎ **561/395-4491.** Fax 561/347-8759. 16 units. A/C TV TEL. Winter $85–$99 double. Off-season $55–$65 double. AE, MC, V.

Another relic of the '50s recently spiffed up with new landscaping and some redecorating, this motel is a good choice, especially because of its location—across the street from a public beach, just north of downtown Boca Raton. It's the quintessential South Florida motel: a small, pink, single-story structure surrounding a modest swimming pool and courtyard. Although the rooms are a bit on the small side, they're very neat and clean. The higher-priced accommodations are larger and come with full kitchens.

WHERE TO DINE

The Boca Raton and Delray areas have more than their fair share of expensive fish and steak houses. Thankfully, too, there are more and more innovative and health-conscious places moving in. Mizner Park has nearly a dozen eateries including a fantastic oyster bar, serving microbrew beers, called **Gigi's** (☎ **561/368-4488**). The area's other great options are highlighted below.

VERY EXPENSIVE

La Vieille Maison. 770 E. Palmetto Park Rd., Boca Raton. ☎ **561/391-6701** or 561/737-5677. Reservations recommended. Main courses $18–$50; fixed-price dinners $42 and $68. AE, CB, DC, DISC, MC, V. Daily 6–9:30pm (call for seating times). FRENCH.

The luxurious setting, a Mediterranean-inspired home filled with a variety of antique French furnishings and paintings, gives you the feeling of walking into a friend's country manor. Begin with lobster bisque, gratin of escargots with fennel and pistachio nuts, or pan-seared foie gras—each is equally delectable. It's difficult to choose from the many enticing entrees, which range from red snapper in black- and green-olive potato crust to medallions of beef, lamb, and venison over three sauces. You'll surely have to try at least a few of the gorgeous cheeses the server offers after your main course—the most extensive selection I've ever seen in this country. The lemon crepe soufflé with raspberry sauce is the dessert of choice—remember to order it early.

EXPENSIVE

Fifth Avenue Grill. 821 S. Federal Hwy., Delray Beach. ☎ **561/265-0122.** Reservations accepted only for large parties. Main courses $16–$29. AE, DC, MC, V. Sun–Mon 11:30am–4pm and 5–11pm. STEAK HOUSE.

The Old-World Fifth Avenue Grill is very popular with well-dressed seniors who come for the superb steaks, reliable service, and classic selections—onion soup, shrimp scampi, London broil, Caesar salad, and broiled local fish. This is the kind of place where they still remember to offer a touch of sherry for your conch chowder. Every main course includes unlimited house salad and is accompanied by a cheese-stuffed baked potato, fried shoestrings, or brown rice. Add to that a huge and varied wine list, and you've got a perfect night out in Delray. Everything on the predictable menu is well prepared and presented by professional servers in a dark and woodsy dining room.

An additional location is at 4650 N. Federal Hwy., Lighthouse Point (☎ 954/782-4433).

Max's Grille. 404 Plaza Real, in Mizner Park, Boca Raton. ☎ **561/368-0080.** Reservations accepted only for 6 or more. Main courses $14–$26; pastas $10.95–$16.95. AE, CB, DC, DISC, MC, V. Daily lunch 11:30am–3pm, Mon–Thurs 5–10:30pm, Fri–Sat 5–11pm, brunch/dinner Sun 11:30am–10pm. AMERICAN.

One of the most popular choices in restaurant-crowded Mizner Park, Max's Grille is part of the growing chain of Unique Restaurants that have been wowing critics for years. With a large exhibition kitchen that occupies the entire back wall of the restaurant, patrons can watch as their yellowfin tuna steak or filet mignon is seared on a flaming oak grill. A large selection of chicken, meat loaf, pastas, and main-course salads provide healthful and delicious choices for sophisticated palates. A stunning bar serves trendy martinis in more than 15 varieties. For a more economical option, try Max's coffee shop next door for good old-fashioned comfort food in a real diner atmosphere.

MODERATE

Splendid Blendeds. 432 E. Atlantic Ave., Delray. ☎ **561/265-1035.** Reservations recommended. Main courses $10.95–$21.95; sandwiches and salads $3.50–$8.95. AE, DC, MC, V. Mon–Fri 11:30am–2:30pm; Mon–Sat 5:30–10pm. Closed Sun and Aug. ECLECTIC.

Loyal regulars would like to keep this storefront bistro a secret so that the lines won't get even longer on weekends. The draw here is fresh, uncomplicated seafood and pastas that are interesting without being overly ambitious. The Southwestern-inspired chicken Santa Cruz is tender and juicy, served with a black-bean sauce and tangy *pico de gallo*. Many seafood specialties, like tuna, snapper, and shrimp dishes, are slight departures from classic recipes and seem to work most of the time. The drawback of this otherwise superb spot is the staff; they're well meaning but easily flustered.

INEXPENSIVE

The Tin Muffin Cafe. 364 E. Palmetto Park Rd. (between Federal Hwy. and the Intercoastal Bridge), Boca Raton. ☎ **561/392-9446.** Sandwiches and salads $6.50–$10.95. No credit cards. Mon–Fri 11am–5pm, Sat 11am–4pm. BAKERY/SANDWICH SHOP.

Popular with the downtown lunch crowd, this excellent storefront bakery keeps them lining up for big fresh sandwiches on fresh bread, muffins, quiches, and good homemade soups like split pea or lentil. The curried chicken sandwich is stuffed with oversized chunks of only white meat doused in a creamy curry dressing and fruit. There are a few cafe tables inside and even one outside on a tiny patio. Be warned, however, that service is forgivably slow and parking is a nightmare. Try parking a few blocks away at a meter on the street.

Tom's Place. 7251 N. Federal Hwy., Boca Raton. ☎ **561/997-0920.** Reservations not accepted. Main courses $8–$15; sandwiches $5–$6; early-bird special $7.95. AE, MC, V. Tues–Fri 11:30am–10pm, Sat noon–10pm. Closed Sun–Mon. BARBECUE.

There are two important factors in a successful barbecue: the cooking and the sauce. Tom and Helen Wright's no-nonsense shack wins on both counts, offering flawlessly grilled meats paired with well-spiced sauces. Beef, chicken, pork, and fish are served soul-food style, with your choice of two sides like rice with gravy, collard greens, black-eyed peas, coleslaw, or mashed potatoes. Signed celebrity photographs decorate the walls. There's also full bar serving beer, wine, and liquor.

BOCA RATON & DELRAY AFTER DARK
THE BAR, CLUB & MUSIC SCENE

The best variety of entertainment is offered in Delray Beach, where a younger and funkier set makes its home. Atlantic Avenue now boasts several venues for live music, including **The Back Room,** 909 W. Atlantic Ave. near the corner of Swinton Avenue (☎ **561/243-9110**). A reasonable cover, usually between $2 and $6, depends on who is playing. A funky decor, eclectic crowd, and excellent music almost every night make this old standby another good option for live music from jazz to big band to classic rock. Only beer and wine are served (in plastic glasses). It's open Tuesday to Saturday until 3am.

Boston's on the Beach, at 40 S. Ocean Blvd. (☎ **561/278-3364**), is always a good choice for happy hour, Monday to Friday from 4 to 8pm, or for live reggae on Monday. A lively bar scene and good seafood on a deck overlooking the beach keep this place packed almost every night.

Boca Raton's most famous dance spot, **Club Boca** at 7000 W. Palmetto Park Rd. (☎ **561/368-3333**), which you'll hear advertised on obnoxious radio commercials, is a big, noisy warehouse out west of the highway that attracts a range of big-haired girls and macho guys. It's a fun diversion in otherwise sterile Boca and is open Thursday to Sunday until 5am.

True to her word, Gloria Gaynor has survived, and she is in Boca at **Polly Esther's,** 99 SE 1st Ave. (☎ **561/447-8955**). She and other disco divas can be heard blasting from the enormous sound system as the mixed young and 30-something set dances like it's Saturday night and they have the fever. Open Wednesday to Saturday. Take Palmetto Park Road East to Federal Highway; turn left onto SE 1st Avenue, where you'll see the club on the left.

THE PERFORMING ARTS

For details on upcoming events, check the *Boca News, Sun-Sentinel,* or call the **Palm Beach County Cultural Council** information line at ☎ **800/882-ARTS.** During business hours, a staffer can give details on current performances. After hours, a recorded message describes the week's events. The *Sun-Sentinel* also hosts a comprehensive "Source Line" for information on everything from weather to garage sales. Detailed arts information is included.

The **Florida Symphonic Pops,** a 70-piece professional orchestra, performs jazz, swing, rock, big band, and classical music throughout Boca Raton. For nearly 50 years, this ever-growing musical force has entertained audiences of every age. Call ☎ **561/393-7677** for a schedule of concerts.

Boca's best theater company is the **Caldwell Theatre,** and it's worth checking out. Located in a strip shopping center at 7873 N. Federal Hwy., this equity showcase does well-known dramas, comedies, classics, Off-Broadway hits, and new works throughout the year. Prices are reasonable (usually between $29 and $38). Full-time students will be especially interested in the little-advertised "Student Rush." When available, tickets are sold for $5 to those who arrive at least an hour in advance. Call ☎ **561/241-7432** for details.

3 Palm Beach & West Palm Beach

65 miles N of Miami, 193 miles E of Tampa

Palm Beach County encompasses cities including Boca Raton in the south to Jupiter and Tequesta in the north. But it is Palm Beach, the small island town across the Intracoastal Waterway, that has been the traditional winter home of America's aristocracy—the Kennedys, the Rockefellers, the Pulitzers, the Trumps, and plenty of CEOs.

The island holds the distinction of being the only continental destination with three resorts that have earned the prestigious AAA five-diamonds rating. And beyond the upscale resorts and chic boutiques, it holds some surprises too, from a world-class art museum to one of the top bird-watching areas in the state.

By contrast, West Palm Beach is a grittier workaday city. Recent renovations have made the metropolitan area a lively and affordable place to dine, shop, and hang out.

In addition to good beaching, boating, and diving, you'll find great golf and tennis throughout the county.

Note: For a general map of Palm Beach and West Palm Beach, see the map on page 293.

ESSENTIALS

GETTING THERE   If you're driving up or down the Florida coast, you'll probably reach the Palm Beach area by I-95. Exit at Belvedere Road or Okeechobee Boulevard and head east to reach the most central part of Palm Beach.

Visitors on their way to or from Orlando or Miami should take the Florida Turnpike, a toll road with a speed limit of 65 miles per hour. If you are watching your budget, avoid the turnpike—tolls are high. You may pay upward of $9 from Orlando and $4 from Miami. Finally, if you're coming from Florida's west coast, you can take either S.R. 70, which runs north of Lake Okeechobee to Fort Pierce, or S.R. 80, which runs south of the lake to Palm Beach.

Among the airlines serving Palm Beach International Airport, at Congress Avenue and Belvedere Road (☎ 561/471-7400), are **American** (☎ 800/433-7300), **Continental** (☎ 800/525-0280), **Delta** (☎ 800/221-1212), **Kiwi** (☎ 800/538-5494), **Northwest** (☎ 800/225-2525), **TWA** (☎ 800/221-2000), **United** (☎ 800/241-6522), and **US Airways** (☎ 800/428-4322).

Amtrak (☎ 800/USA-RAIL; www.amtrak.com) has a terminal in West Palm Beach, at 201 S. Tamarind Ave. (☎ 561/832-6169).

GETTING AROUND   Although a car is almost a necessity in this area, a recently revamped public transportation system is extremely convenient for getting to some attractions. Palm Tran underwent a major expansion in late 1996, increasing service to 32 routes and more than 140 buses. The fare is $1 for adults, 50¢ for children ages 3 to 18, as well as for the elderly and disabled. Free route maps are available by calling ☎ 561/233-4-BUS. Information operators are available from 6am to 7pm, except Sunday.

In downtown West Palm, free shuttles operate Monday through Friday from 9am until 4pm with plans to expand operations to evenings and weekends too. Look for the bubble-gum-pink minibuses throughout downtown. Call ☎ 561/833-8873 for more details.

For a more nostalgic route, consider the stately wicker chariots that run in the downtown area especially on weekends and during special events. Rates vary according to the time of day but average $1 to $2 per block, plus a per person charge of $1. Call ☎ 561/835-8922 for pickup or information.

VISITOR INFORMATION   The **Palm Beach County Convention and Visitors Bureau**, 1555 Palm Beach Lakes Blvd., Suite 204, West Palm Beach, FL 33401 (☎ 800/554-PALM or 561/471-3995; www.palmbeach.com), distributes an informative brochure and will answer questions about visiting the Palm Beaches. Ask for a map as well as a copy of its Arts and Attractions Calendar, a day-to-day guide to art, music, stage, and other events in the county.

FUN ON & OFF THE BEACH

BEACHES Public beaches are a rare commodity here in Palm Beach. Most of the island's best beaches are fronted by private estates and inaccessible to the general public. However, there are a few notable exceptions, including Midtown Beach on Ocean Boulevard, between Royal Palm Way and Gulfstream Road, which boasts more than 100 feet of undeveloped beach. There are no rest rooms or concessions here, although a lifeguard is on duty until sundown. This newly widened sandy coast is now a centerpiece and a natural oasis in a town dominated by commercial glitz. Also, about $1^1/_2$ miles north near Dunbar Street is a popular hangout for locals who enjoy the relaxed atmosphere. Parking is available at meters along Fla. A1A. To the south is a less popular but better equipped beach at Phipps Ocean Park. On Ocean Boulevard, between the Southern Boulevard and Lake Avenue causeways, is a large and lively public beach encompassing more than 1,300 feet of groomed and guarded oceanfront. With picnic and recreation areas as well as plenty of parking, the area is especially good for families.

BICYCLING Rent anything from an English single-speed to a full-tilt mountain bike at the **Palm Beach Bicycle Trail Shop**, 223 Sunrise Ave. (☎ **561/659-4583**). The rates—$7 an hour, $18 a half day (9am to 5pm), or $24 for 24 hours—include a basket and lock (not that it's necessary in this fortress of a town). The most scenic route is called the Lake Trail, running the length of the island along the Intracoastal Waterway. On it you'll see some of the most magnificent mansions and grounds. Enjoy the views of downtown West Palm Beach and some great wildlife.

CRUISES **Atlantic Coastal Cruises,** 900 E. Blue Heron Blvd., Singer Island (☎ **561/848-7827**), runs regularly scheduled tours along the Intracoastal Waterway, offering visitors unobstructed views of the area's grand mansions. Daily sightseeing as well as lunch, dinner, and theme cruises are offered, some feature live entertainment. They cost $14 to $38. Phone for more information and reservations.

The *Palm Beach Princess* (☎ **800/841-7447** or 561/845-7447), a small cruise ship (421 feet), offers reasonably priced casino gambling cruises out of the Port of Palm Beach (U.S. 1 between 45th Street and Blue Heron Boulevard) every day and evening. Evening cruises usually leave at 7pm and cost $20 to $25; they include a large buffet with average food like spaghetti and meatballs, chicken, shrimp, Greek salad, and vegetables. Best is the prime rib at the carving board. Day trips cost the same and offer slightly less food. Sunday brunch trips cost $25. A popular monthly Bahamas voyage costs $95. Call during business hours for details. Choose from craps, roulette, poker, blackjack, and slots.

GOLF There's good golfing here, but many of the private club courses are maintained exclusively for the use of their members. Ask at your hotel, or contact the **Palm Beach County Convention and Visitors Bureau** (☎ **561/471-3995**) for information on which clubs are currently available for play. In the off-season, some private courses open their greens to visitors staying in a Palm Beach County hotel. This "Golf-A-Round" program offers free greens fees (carts are additional); reservations can be made through most major hotels.

One of the state's best courses that is open to the public is ✪ **Emerald Dunes Golf Course,** 2100 Emerald Dunes Dr. in West Palm Beach (☎ **561/687-1700**). Designed by Tom Fazio, this dramatic 7,006-yard, par-72 course was voted "One of the Best 10 You Can Play" by *Golf* magazine. It is located just off the Florida Turnpike at Okeechobee Boulevard. Bookings are taken up to 30 days ahead. Fees start at $125.

The **Palm Beach Public Golf Course,** 2345 S. Ocean Blvd. (☎ **561/547-0598**), a popular public 18-hole course, is a par-54 and is open at 8am; the course is run on a first-come, first-served basis. Club rentals are available. Greens fees start at $19 per person.

POLO   What's Palm Beach without polo? See the "Sport of Kings," below, for details.

SCUBA DIVING   Year-round warm waters, barrier reefs, and plenty of wrecks make South Florida one of the world's most popular places for diving. One of the best-known artificial reefs in this area is a vintage Rolls-Royce Silver Shadow, which was sunk offshore in 1985. Mother Nature has taken her toll, however, and divers can no longer sit in the car ravaged by time and saltwater.

Call any of the following outfitters for gear and excursions: **Dixie Divers,** 1401 S. Military Trail, West Palm Beach (☎ **561/969-6688**); and **Ocean Sports Scuba Center,** 1736 S. Congress Ave., West Palm Beach (☎ **561/641-1144**).

TENNIS   There are literally hundreds of tennis courts in Palm Beach County. Wherever you are staying, you are bound to be within walking distance of one. In addition to the many hotel tennis courts (see "Where to Stay," below), you can play at **Currie Park,** 2400 N. Flagler Dr., West Palm Beach (☎ **561/835-7025**), a public park with three lighted hard courts. They are free and available on a first-come, first-served basis.

WATER SPORTS   Call the **Seaside Activities Station** (☎ **561/835-8922**) to arrange sailboat, jet-ski, bicycle, kayak, water ski, and parasail rentals.

SEEING THE SIGHTS

Flagler Museum. 1 Whitehall Way (at Cocoanut Row and Whitehall Way), Palm Beach. ☎ **561/655-2833.** www.flagler.org. Admission $7 adults, $3 children, ages 6–12. Tues–Sat 10am–5pm, Sun noon–5pm.

Known as the "Taj Mahal of North America," this luxurious mansion was commissioned as a gift to his third wife by the renowned Henry Flagler, a cofounder of the Standard Oil Company and builder of the Florida East Coast Railroad. The classically columned Edwardian-style mansion contains 55 rooms, including a Louis XIV music room and art gallery, a Louis XV ballroom, and 14 guest suites outfitted with original antique European furnishings. Out back, climb aboard "The Rambler," Mr. Flagler's recently revamped railroad car. Allow at least 1 1/2 hours to tour the stunning grounds and interior.

Norton Museum of Art. 1451 S. Olive Ave., West Palm Beach. ☎ **561/832-5196.** Fax 561/659-4689. www.norton.org. Admission $6 adults, $2 students, free for children 12 and under. Mon 10am–5pm (Dec–Apr), Tues–Sat 10am–5pm, Sun 1–5pm. From I-95, take Belvedere Rd. (Exit 51) east to the end; then, turn left onto S. Olive Ave. to the museum.

Since a 1997 expansion doubled the Norton's space, the museum has gained even more prominence in the art world. It is world famous for its prestigious permanent collection and top temporary exhibitions. The museum's major collections are divided geographically. The American galleries contain major works by Edward Hopper, Georgia O'Keefe, and Jackson Pollack. The French collection contains Impressionist and post-Impressionist paintings by Cézanne, Degas, Gauguin, Matisse, Monet, Picasso, Pissarro, and Renoir. And the Chinese collection contains more then 200 bronzes, jades, and ceramics as well as a collection of monumental Buddhist sculptures.

The Sport of Kings

The annual ritual of the ponies is played out each season at the posh Palm Beach Polo and Country Club. It is one of the world's premier polo grounds and hosts some of the sport's top-rated players.

Even if you're not a sports fan, you absolutely must attend a match. Although the field is actually on the mainland in an area called Wellington, rest assured, the spectators, and many of the players, are pure Palm Beach. After all, a day at the pony grounds is one of the only good reasons to leave Palm Beach proper.

Don't worry, though—you need not be a Vanderbilt or a Kennedy to attend. Matches are open to the public and are surprisingly affordable.

Even if you haven't a clue how the game is played, you can spend your time people-watching. Stargazers have spotted Prince Charles, the duchess of York, Sylvester Stallone, and Ivana Trump in recent years, among others. Dozens of lesser-known royalty, and just plain old characters, keep box seats or chalets right on the grounds.

Incidentally, the point of polo is to keep the other team from getting the ball through your goal. The fast-paced game is divided into six chukkers—like an inning in baseball—each 7 minutes long. There are 3-minute breaks between chukkers except at half-time, which lasts 10 minutes. The whole thing is narrated by a British chap who sounds as though he has walked off a Monty Python set.

Dress is casual; a navy or tweed blazer over jeans or khakis is a standard for men, while neat-looking jeans or a pantsuit is the norm for women. On warmer days, shorts and, of course, a polo shirt are fine, too.

General admission is $6 to $10; box seats cost $10 to $36. Matches are held throughout the week. Schedules vary, but the big names usually compete on Sunday at 3:30pm from January to April.

The fields are located at 11809 Polo Club Rd., Wellington, 10 miles west of the Forest Hill Boulevard exit of I-95. Call ☎ **561/798-7000** for a detailed schedule of events.

✪ **Playmobil Fun Park.** 8031 N. Military Trail, Palm Beach Gardens. ☎ **800/351/8697** or 561/691-9880. Fax 561/691-9517. www.playmobil.com. Free admission. Mon–Sun 10am–6pm. I-95 North to Palm Beach Lakes Blvd west to Military Trail. Turn left, and the park is about a mile down on the right side.

This monstrous retail outlet and play park is one of only two such parks in the world (the other one is in Germany, the company's headquarters). Housed in a replica of a castle, this indoor fantasy world is even better than FAO Schwarz. You could spend hours here and not spend a penny. The 17,000-square-foot play floor is divided into age-specific play areas and theme areas, including a water zone for kids to play with boats and a Victorian area with elaborately constructed doll houses.

NATURE PRESERVES & ATTRACTIONS

Lion Country Safari. Southern Blvd. W. at S.R. 80, West Palm Beach. ☎ **561/793-1084,** or 561/793-9797 for camping reservations. Admission $15.50 adults, $10.50 seniors and $10.50 children 3–9, and free for children under 3. Daily 9:30am–5:30pm (last vehicle admitted at 4:30pm). From I-95, exit on Southern Blvd. Go west for about 18 miles.

More than 1,300 animals are divided into their indigenous regions, from the East African preserve of the Serengeti to the American West. On this 500-acre preserve you can see elephants, wildebeest, ostriches, American bison, buffalo, watusi, pink flamingos, and many other more unusual species. Even the lions and elephants roam the huge grassy landscape without a cage in sight. In fact, you're the one who's confined, in your own car without an escort (no convertibles allowed). You're given a detailed informational pamphlet with photos and descriptions and are instructed to obey the 15-mile-per-hour speed limit—unless you see the rhinos charge, in which case you're encouraged to floor it. To drive the loop takes just over an hour, though you could make a day of just watching the chimpanzees play on their secluded islands. Included in the admission price is Safari World, an amusement park with paddleboats, a carousel, and a nursery for baby animals born in the preserve. Picnics are encouraged and camping is available (call for reservations). Don't miss this incredible experience.

Palm Beach Zoo at Dreher Park. 1301 Summit Blvd. (east of I-95 between Southern and Forest Hill blvds.). ☎ **561/547-WILD.** Fax 561/585-6085. www.palmbeachzoo.org. Admission $6, $5 senior citizens, $4 children 3–12, children under 3 free. Daily 9am–5pm.

Unlike big-city zoos, this intimate 23-acre park is more like a stroll in the park than an all-day excursion. It features about 500 animals representing more than 100 different species. A special monkey exhibit and petting zoo are favorites with kids. Stroller and wagon rental available.

SHOPPING & BROWSING

From thrift items to jewels, Palm Beach has it all. Known as "the Rodeo Drive of the south," Worth Avenue is a window-shopper's dream. No matter what your budget, don't miss the Worth Avenue experience. To look like you belong, you might want to dress as if you were going to an elegant luncheon, not to the mall down the street. The 4 blocks between South Ocean Boulevard and Coconut Row—a stretch of more than 200 boutiques, posh shops, art galleries, and upscale restaurants—are home to the stores of Armani, Louis Vuitton, Cartier, Polo Ralph Lauren, and Chanel, among like company.

Victoria's Secret, Limited Express, and several other chains have sneaked in here too, but so have a good number of unique boutiques. Stop into **Paper Treasures,** at 217 Worth Ave.; it's an autograph gallery with a priceless collection of John Hancocks, including those of Joe DiMaggio, Mickey Mantle, Andrew Jackson, Abe Lincoln, Howard Hughes, and hundreds more, all displayed in beautiful frames. At **Myer's Luggage,** 313 Worth Ave., Richard Myers is happy to demonstrate his impressive assortment of toys and gifts, including a vast collection of amusing alarm clocks, spy equipment, gorilla masks, and gag gifts, along with pricey leather bags and English picnic baskets. Just off Worth Avenue, at 374 S. County Rd., is the **Church Mouse** (☎ **561/659-2154**), a great consignment/thrift shop with antique furnishings and tableware. Lots of good castaway clothing and shoes are reasonably priced. This shop usually closes for 2 months during the summer. Call to be sure.

The **Palm Beach Outlet Center,** at 5700 Okeechobee Blvd. (3 miles west of I-95), West Palm Beach, is the most elegant outlet mall I have ever seen. Upscale clothing, luggage, and shoes are offered at bargain prices in lushly decorated surroundings. The fully enclosed mall also sports a food court.

Downtown West Palm Beach has a number of interesting boutiques along Clematis Street. In addition to a large and well-organized bookstore, Clematis Street Books, at 206 Clematis (☎ **561/832-2302**), there are used-record stores, clothing shops, and a few interesting art galleries.

WHERE TO STAY

The island of Palm Beach is perhaps the most exclusive destination in the country. Royalty and celebrities come to winter here, and there are plenty of royally priced options to accommodate them. It's no accident that the only three hotels in the state to receive five stars from AAA are all located in Palm Beach County. Happily, there exist a few special little inns that offer reasonably priced rooms in elegant settings. Surrounding the island are many more modest places to lay your straw hat.

A few of the larger hotel chains operating in Palm Beach include the **Howard Johnson Palm Beach,** at 2870 S. Ocean Blvd. (☎ **800/654-2000** or 561/582-2581), which is across the street from the beach. Also beachside is the pricey **Palm Beach Hilton,** at 2842 S. Ocean Blvd. (☎ **800/433-1718** or 561/586-6542).

An excellent and affordable alternative right in the middle of Palm Beach's commercial section is a condo that operates as a hotel, too: the **Palm Beach Hotel,** at 235 Sunrise Ave. (between County Road and Bradley Place, across the street from Publix; ☎ **561/659-7794**). With winter prices starting at about $105, this clean and comfortable accommodation is a great option for those looking for the rarely available bargain in Palm Beach.

In West Palm Beach, the chain hotels are mostly located on the main arteries close to the highways and a short drive to the activities in downtown. They include a **Best Western,** 1800 Palm Beach Lakes Blvd. (☎ **800/331-9569** or 561/683-8810), and, just down the road, a **Comfort Inn,** 1901 Palm Lakes Blvd. (☎ **800/221-2222** or 561/689-6100). Further south is the **Parkview Motor Lodge,** 4710 S. Dixie Hwy., just south of Southern Boulevard (☎ **561/833-4644**). This 28-room, single-story motel is the best of the many motels along Dixie Highway (U.S. 1). With rates starting at $50 for a room with television, air-conditioning, and telephone, you can't ask for more.

For other options, try Palm Beach Accommodations (☎ **800/543-SWIM**).

VERY EXPENSIVE

✪ **The Breakers.** 1 S. County Rd., Palm Beach, FL 33480. ☎ **800/833-3141,** 888/BREAKERS, or 561/655-6611. Fax 561/659-8403. www.thebreakers.com. 569 units. A/C MINIBAR TV TEL. Winter $380–$800 double; $610 club double; from $660 suite. Off-season $250–$510 double; $415 club double; from $485 suite. Special packages available. AE, CB, DC, DISC, MC, V. Valet parking $15. From I-95, exit Okeechobee Blvd. E., and head east to S. County Rd.; turn left.

The biggest and grandest of all of this area's resorts, this five-star historic beauty epitomizes Palm Beach luxury. It's one of only two Florida properties to win five stars from the Mobil guide and five diamonds from AAA. From the expansive manicured lawns to the elegant marble lobby, The Breakers is the place to be in Palm Beach if you want to be on the beach, but within walking distance from all the area's most exclusive shopping and dining. The lush 130-acre grounds also sport one of the island's only 18-hole golf courses.

Though this 1926 palace was built for the world's most elite, it now handles more corporate clients and families with ease. While the Gatsbyesque grounds of Palm Beach's first hotel reveal a sense of history, the newly reconstructed rooms are equipped with all the modern conveniences. Even the least expensive rooms are luxuriously appointed and include every amenity you could desire. Ask for one of the few corner rooms, which are a little larger for the same price.

Dining/Diversions: Five restaurants and three bars offer a delicious range of meals and snacks from an elegant European dining room to a beach bar with burgers and fries. A romantic oceanfront bar (Palm Beach's only) is reserved for hotel guests.

Amenities: Concierge, 24-hour room service, dry-cleaning and laundry service, overnight shoe shine, newspaper delivery, in-room massage, evening turndown, twice-daily maid service, baby-sitting, secretarial services, express checkout. VCR and video rentals, four outdoor pools, private beach, bicycle rental, two golf courses, putting green, game rooms, supervised children's activities, business center, car-rental desk, 14 tennis courts, water-sports (including scuba and sailing), croquet, shuffleboard, beach volleyball courts, beauty salon, boutiques and shopping arcade, full-service spa/fitness center.

○ **Four Seasons Resort Palm Beach.** 2800 S. Ocean Blvd., Palm Beach, FL 33480. ☎ **800/432-2335** or 561/582-2800. Fax 561/547-1557. www.fourseasons.com. 210 units. A/C MINIBAR TV TEL. Winter $365–$640 double; from $1,200 suite. Off-season $270–$490 double; $775 suite. AE, CB, DC, DISC, EURO, ER, JCB, MC, V. Valet parking $17. From I-95, take 6th Ave. exit east and turn left onto Dixie Hwy.; then, turn east onto Lake Ave. and north onto S. Ocean Blvd., and the hotel is just ahead on your right.

For over-the-top pampering in a perfect location, the Four Seasons is my favorite in an area filled with fantastic resorts. Built in 1989 at the edge of Palm Beach's downtown district, this elegant resort has quickly gained accolades from around the world. The incredibly hospitable staff works hard to be sure this beachfront gem lives up to its reputation. The elegant marble lobby is replete with hand-carved European furnishings, grand oil paintings, tapestries, and dramatic flower arrangements.

The ambience of the common areas extends to the guest rooms as well. All are exceptionally spacious and thoughtfully appointed with extras like a small color TV in the bathroom. Club-floor rooms include access to a special lounge where continental breakfast, afternoon refreshments, and evening cocktails are served gratis. One-bedroom suites include an additional sitting room, a CD/stereo, oversize balconies, and two bathrooms.

Dining/Diversions: The main dining room for dinner serves one of the best meals in Palm Beach. An impeccable menu of Southeastern regional cuisine includes daily fish, meat, and pasta specials served in white-glove elegance. Two other less formal restaurants, including a pool bar and grill, round out the dining options. The lobby lounge is one of the best places in town for an intimate cocktail. Weekend evenings promise excellent live jazz.

Amenities: Concierge, room service (24 hours), evening turndown, dry-cleaning and laundry services, shoe shine, newspaper delivery, in-room massage, twice-daily maid service, baby-sitting and child amenities, pet amenities secretarial services, express checkout. VCRs and video rental, movie channels and video games, outdoor heated pool, beach, whirlpool, jogging track, bicycle rentals, supervised activities for children 3 to 12, conference rooms, weekly cooking classes, sundeck, three tennis courts, water-sports rentals, beauty salon, gift shop, and a 6,000-square-foot spa.

○ **Ritz-Carlton Palm Beach.** 100 S. Ocean Blvd., Manalpan, FL 33462. ☎ **800/241-3333** or 561/533-6000. Fax 561/540-4999. E-mail: ritzpalmbch@earthlink.net. 270 units. A/C MINIBAR TV TEL. Winter $395–$695; $3,150 suite. Off-season $185–$325; $2,700 suite. AE, CB, DISC, MC, V, EURO, JCB. Valet parking $15. From I-95, take Exit 45 east; after a mile, turn left onto Federal Hwy. (U.S. 1), continue north for about a mile, and turn right onto Ocean Ave.; cross the Intracoastal Waterway, turn right onto Fla. A1A.

As is to be expected from any member of this upscale chain, the Palm Beach Ritz-Carlton is superluxurious. In this case, it is on a beautiful beach in a tiny town about 8 miles from Palm Beach's shopping and dining area—a plus for those who want privacy and a drawback for those interested in the activity of "town."

The hotel's elegant and dramatic lobby is dominated by a huge, double-sided pink-marble fireplace, and French 18th- and 19th-century antique furnishings give no hint that the property is not yet 10 years old. The ambience and attention to detail here is rivaled by no other hotel in the area.

Each room has a private balcony and at least a glimpse of the ocean below. All are spacious and decorated in lush contemporary design. Thoughtful details include plush bathrobes and telephones in the large marble bathrooms. Club-level accommodations come with dedicated concierge service and a private lounge where complimentary continental breakfasts, afternoon snacks, and evening cordials are served.

Dining/Diversions: The elegant dining room serves continental-style dinners in ornate surroundings. Other restaurants on the property include a grill, for dinner only; a casual restaurant, which serves all day; and a poolside cafe and bar. Cocktails are also served in the lobby lounge, where you can often find live entertainment. Afternoon tea is served daily, but is best Wednesday to Saturday when a jazz trio entertains.

Amenities: Concierge, 24-hour room service, dry-cleaning and laundry services, overnight shoe shine, newspaper delivery, in-room massage, evening turndown, twice-daily maid service, baby-sitting, secretarial services, express checkout, airport transportation, free coffee or refreshments in lobby. VCR rentals, Spectravision movie channels, outdoor pool, beach, health club, Jacuzzi, sauna, bicycle rental, children's center and programs, business center, conference rooms, car-rental desk, seven night-lit tennis courts, scuba and snorkeling concessions, beauty salon, gift shop.

EXPENSIVE

Chesterfield Hotel. 363 Cocoanut Row, Palm Beach, FL 33480. ☎ **800/243-7871** or 561/659-5800. Fax 561/659-6707. E-mail: chesterpb@aol.com. 65 units. A/C TV TEL. Winter $309–$350 single or double. Off-season $139–$539. single or double. Rollaway bed $15 extra. AE, CB, DC, DISC, MC, V. Free valet parking. From I-95, exit onto Okeechobee Blvd. E., cross the Intracoastal Waterway, and turn right onto Cocoanut Row.

With more charm than its more expensive rivals, the intimate Chesterfield, located just a block from Worth Avenue, has been popular with visitors in the know since the 1920s. Behind its light stucco facade, arched windows, and colorful flags is an overly designed interior with Laura Ashley prints battling Ralph Lauren. It all creates a wonderfully authentic country-manor feel.

Guest rooms also have formal chintz and taffeta prints. Heavy wooden furniture and plush carpets give each room a warm but dark feel. Although most rooms have no view to speak of, they are comfortable and attractive. A stunning lobby library provides a quiet nook for those who may want to read at the large oak desk or borrow a book for the beach. Afternoon tea completes the illusion of being in a well-run country inn across the Atlantic.

Dining/Diversions: The Leopard Room serves fantastic English, French, and continental favorites all day; reservations are essential for dinner and Sunday brunch. The Leopard Lounge is an area hangout in the evenings when there is usually live music and no cover charge (see "The Palm Beaches After Dark," below).

Amenities: Concierge, room service, newspaper delivery, in-room massage, dry cleaning, twice-daily maid service, baby-sitting, secretarial services, express checkout. Swimming pool, access to nearby health club, Jacuzzi, nature trails, bicycle rental, video rentals, conference rooms, business center, car-rental desk, tour desk.

Plaza Inn. 215 Brazilian Ave., Palm Beach, FL 33480. ☎ **800/233-2632** or 561/832-8666. Fax 561/835-8776. www.plazainnpalmbeach.com. 47 units. A/C TV TEL. Winter $205–$285 double; $325 suite. Off-season $105–$165 double; $195 suite. Rates include breakfast.

AE, MC, V. From I-95, exit onto Okeechobee Blvd. E., cross the Intracoastal Waterway, turn right onto Cocoanut Row, then left onto Brazilian Ave.

This ever-improving bed-and-breakfast–style inn is as understated and luxurious as the guests it hosts. Nothing is flashy here. From the simple and elegant flower arrangements in the marble lobby to the well-worn period antiques haphazardly strewn throughout, the Plaza Inn has the look of studied nonchalance. A small staff, including owner Ajit Asrani, is remarkably hospitable and knowledgeable about the island's inner workings.

Each uniquely decorated room is dressed with quality furnishings, several with carved four-poster beds, hand-crocheted spreads, and lace curtains. The bathrooms are lovely if quite small, and the wall-mounted air conditioners can be noisy when they are needed in the warm months. Choose a corner room or one overlooking the small pool deck for the best light.

In any room, you are sure to appreciate the convenient location: less than 2 blocks from the ocean and all of the best shopping. For those who appreciate the fine hospitality of a small lodging without the sometimes-invasive feel of a bed-and-breakfast, this is the island's number-one choice.

Dining/Diversions: A full cooked-to-order breakfast that includes fresh fruit, breakfast breads, and hot main dishes is served each morning in a charming, English country–style dining room. The cozy Stray Fox Pub, a comfortable little bar with mahogany tables, serves cocktails throughout the evening and sometimes has live piano music on the weekends.

Amenities: Concierge, dry-cleaning and laundry services, newspaper delivery, in-room massage, baby-sitting, secretarial services. VCRs, heated outdoor pool, Jacuzzi and small workout room, access to nearby health club.

MODERATE

Heart of Palm Beach Hotel. 160 Royal Palm Way, Palm Beach, FL 33480. ☎ **800/ 523-5377** or 561/655-5600. Fax 561/832-1201. 88 units. A/C TV TEL. Winter $149–$259 double; $275 suite. Off-season $69–$149 double; $175 suite. AE, DC, MC, V. Free parking. From I-95, exit onto Okeechobee Blvd. E. and continue over the Royal Palm Bridge onto Royal Palm Way.

The centrally located Heart of Palm Beach Hotel is within walking distance of Worth Avenue's shops and just half a block from the beach. Ongoing renovations since the 1990s have improved the patio space, as well as the rooms in the hotel's two buildings. Most are decorated with modest but new furnishings and fittings in a colorful contemporary style. The tiled bathrooms are small, clean, and functional. Besides the great location, another plus here is that each accommodation comes with a private balcony or patio. Choose a room on a higher floor, as those on the ground floor tend to be a bit dark. The staff is particularly outgoing and will help guests plan outings and itineraries.

There's a heated swimming pool. A clubby restaurant serves a selection of salads, sandwiches, pastas, and cocktails. Breakfast is served in a bright dining room overlooking the gardens.

Palm Beach Historic Inn. 365 S. County Rd., Palm Beach, FL 33480. ☎ **561/832-4009.** Fax 561/832-6255. www.palmbeachhistoricinn.com. 13 units. A/C TV TEL. Winter $150–$185 double; $250–$275 suite. Off-season $75–$95 double; $125–$150 suite. Rates include continental breakfast. Children stay free in parents' room. AE, MC, V.

Despite a rather abandoned look, this bed-and-breakfast is a cozy and comfortable place to stay in Palm Beach. Built in 1923, the Palm Beach Historic Inn is an area landmark located within walking distance of Worth Avenue, the beach, and several good restaurants. The small lobby is filled with antiques, books, magazines, and an old-fashioned umbrella stand, all of which add to the homey feel of this intimate bed-and-breakfast. All the rooms are on the second floor, and each is uniquely decorated and full of frills. Floral prints, sheer curtains, and the plethora of lace can sometimes be overwhelming, masking rather than complementing beautiful antique writing desks and dressers. Happily, there are also fluffy bathrobes, an abundance of towels, and plenty of good-smelling toiletries.

MODERATE/INEXPENSIVE

✪ **Beachcomber Apartment Motel.** 3024 S. Ocean Blvd., Palm Beach, FL 33480. ☎ **800/833-7122** or 561/585-4646. Fax 561/547-9438. 45 units. A/C TV TEL. Winter $85–$155 motel room; from $110–$210 apt. Off-season $45–$80 motel room; from $60–$125 apt. AE, DISC, MC, V. From I-95, exit 10th Ave. N., head east to Federal Hwy., and turn right. Continue to Lake Ave. and turn left. Go over bridge and turn right at first traffic light (S. Ocean Dr.).

It's not just the bright-pink building that makes this two-story motel stand out. For more than 35 years the Beachcomber has been bringing sanity to pricey Palm Beach by offering a good standard of accommodation at reasonable prices. Squeezed between beachfront high-rises, the motel is located oceanfront, adjacent to Lake Worth Beach and a short drive from Worth Avenue shops and local attractions. Every room has two double beds, large closets, and distinctive green-and-white tropical-style furnishings; some have kitchenettes. The most expensive have balconies overlooking the ocean. The bathrooms are basic, and amenities are limited to towels and soap. Facilities at the motel include a coin-operated laundry, shuffleboard, a large pool, and a sundeck overlooking the Atlantic.

Hibiscus House. 501 30th St., West Palm Beach, FL 33407. ☎ **800/203-4927** or 561/863-5633. Fax 561/863-5633. www.hibiscushouse.com. 8 units. A/C TV TEL. Winter $95–$240 double. Off-season $65–$150 double. Rates include breakfast. AE, MC, V. From I-95, exit onto Palm Beach Lakes Blvd. E. and continue 4 mi.; turn left onto Flagler Dr., continue for about 20 blocks, then turn left onto 30th St.

Inexpensive bed-and-breakfasts are rare in Southeast Florida, making the Hibiscus House one of the area's firsts—a true find. Located a few miles from the coast in a quiet residential neighborhood, this 1920s-era B&B is filled with handsome antiques and tapestried in luxurious fabrics. Every room has its own private terrace or balcony. The backyard, a peaceful retreat, has been transformed into a tropical garden, complete with heated swimming pool and lounge chairs. Also, there are plenty of pretty areas for guests to enjoy inside; one little sitting room is wrapped in glass and is stocked with playing cards and board games. *Beware:* Breakfast portions are enormous. The gourmet creations are as filling as they are beautiful. Ask for any special requests in advance; owners Raleigh Hill and Colin Rayer will be happy to oblige.

WHERE TO DINE

Palm Beach has some of the area's finest restaurants, with many classical and elegant options as well as a few more innovative choices. Dress here is slightly more formal than in most other areas of Florida: Men wear blazers, and women generally put on modest dresses when they dine out, even in the dog days of summer.

EXPENSIVE

✪ **Amici.** 288 S. County Rd. (at Royal Palm Way), Palm Beach. ☎ **561/832-0201.** Fax 561/659-3540. Reservations strongly recommended on weekends. Main courses $18–$27; pastas and pizzas $8–$19. AE, CB, DC, MC, V. Mon–Thurs 11:30am–3pm and 5:30–10:30pm, Fri–Sat 11:30am–3pm and 5:30–11pm, Sun 5:30–10:30pm. ITALIAN.

You'd think that there would be a dozen good Italian restaurants in Palm Beach. There are plenty of decent ones, but Amici tops them all, with homemade pastas, a vast array of innovative antipasti, and a variety of lighter fare. Diners come dressed in blazers and ties at lunch, though the atmosphere here is fairly casual, with simple decor and lots of window space to let in light. The food is nothing unusual—grilled sandwiches, pastas with rustic sauces, pizzas, grilled shrimp, and fish—but the execution is flawless. You could argue that the prices don't match the simple food, but where else in Palm Beach can you get broccoli rabe, fresh roasted peppers loaded with garlic, and pizzas with escarole, homemade sausage, and pine nuts?

Cafe l'Europe. 331 S. County Rd. (at the corner of Brazilian Ave.), Palm Beach. ☎ **561/655-4020.** Reservations recommended. Main courses $18–$34. AE, CB, DC, DISC, MC, V. Tues–Sat noon–2:30pm and 5:45–10:30pm, Fri–Sat open until 1am, Sun 6–10:30pm. FRENCH/CONTINENTAL.

One of Palm Beach's finest, this award-winning formal restaurant is located on the upper level of the Esplanade, a Spanish-style shopping arcade. The interior is made romantic and luxurious by the tapestried cafe chairs and linen-topped tables set with crystal and china. The enticing appetizers served by a superb staff might include Chinese spring rolls, baked goat-cheese salad with raspberry-walnut dressing, poached salmon, or chilled gazpacho with avocado. Main courses run the gamut from sautéed potato-crusted Florida snapper to lamb chops to roast Cornish game hen. Seafood dishes and steaks in sumptuous but light sauces are always exceptional.

Chuck & Harold's Cafe. 207 Royal Poinciana Way (corner of S. County Rd.), Palm Beach. ☎ **561/659-1440.** Fax 561/659-2197. www.chuckandharolds@muer.com. Reservations recommended. Main courses $13–$28. AE, DC, DISC, MC, V. Mon–Thurs 7:30am–midnight, Fri–Sat 7:30am–1am, Sun 8am–11pm. AMERICAN.

For predictable American fare, this old standby delivers. Chuck & Harold's serves good food at inflated prices. Remember, you are paying for one of the area's best people-watching perches. Sit outside and enjoy the view. Main dishes include fresh grilled or broiled fish, boiled lobster, and a small variety of straightforward homemade pasta and chicken dishes. If you happen to visit during stone crab season, order them here. The crab claws are steamed or chilled and served with a traditional honey-mustard sauce.

MODERATE

Rhythm Cafe. 3800 S. Dixie Hwy., West Palm Beach. ☎ **561/833-3406.** Reservations recommended on weekends. Main courses $10–$26. AE, DISC, MC, V. Tues–Sat 6–10pm; Sun brunch 10am–2pm and dinner 6–10pm during winter. Sometimes earlier on Sun. From I-95, exit east on Southern Blvd., 1 block north of Southern Blvd., on the right. ECLECTIC AMERICAN.

This hole-in-the-wall is where those in the know come to eat some of West Palm Beach's most laid-back gourmet food. On the handwritten, photocopied menu, you'll always find a fish specialty with a hefty dose of greens and garnishes. Also reliably outstanding is the sautéed medallion of beef tenderloin, served on a bed of arugula with a tangy rosemary vinaigrette. Salads and soups are a great bargain since portions are relatively large and the display usually spectacular. The kitschy decor of this tiny cafe comes complete with vinyl tablecloths and paintings by local amateurs. Young, handsome waiters are attentive but not solicitous. The old drugstore where the restaurant recently relocated features an original '50s lunch counter and stools.

Taboo. 221 Worth Ave., Palm Beach. ☎ **561/835-3500.** Reservations recommended. Main courses $10–$25. AE, DC, MC, V. Sun–Thurs 11:30am–11pm, Fri–Sat 11:30am–1am. AMERICAN BISTRO.

Taboo is a snazzy Worth Avenue eatery that successfully combines the classic and the trendy. Lots of greenery, a fireplace, and a contemporary Southwestern charm make it comfortable and inviting. Variety is always the chef's special, with extensive lunch and dinner offerings that are often calorie- and cholesterol-conscious. For lunch, the kitchen creates California-style individual-size pizzas topped with delicacies like barbecued chicken, goat and mozzarella cheeses, and sweet roasted red peppers. Other choices include a delicious sandwich of sweet peppers and goat cheese. The best dinner starter is fresh tuna marinated in ginger and lime. Dinner choices change nightly and may include grilled swordfish topped with olive-caper sauce or grilled veal served on the bone.

INEXPENSIVE

Green's Pharmacy. 151 N. County Rd., Palm Beach. ☎ **561/832-0304.** Fax 561/832-6502. Breakfast $2–$5; burgers and sandwiches $3–$6; soups and salads $2–$7 AE, MC, V. Mon–Sun 6am–4pm AMERICAN.

This neighborhood corner pharmacy offers one of the best meal deals in Palm Beach. Both breakfast and lunch are served coffee-shop style at either a Formica bar or plain tables above a black-and-white checkerboard floor. Breakfast specials include eggs and omelettes served with home fries and bacon, sausage, or corned-beef hash. At lunch, the grill serves burgers and sandwiches, as well as ice-cream sodas and milkshakes, to a loyal crowd of pastel-clad Palm Beachers.

✪ **John G's.** 10 S. Ocean Blvd., Lake Worth. ☎ **561/585-9860.** www.johngs.com. Reservations not accepted. Breakfast $3–$8.50; lunch $5–$14. No credit cards. Daily 7am–3pm. Off Florida Turnpike, take the Lake Worth exit and head toward the ocean. AMERICAN.

This coffee shop is the most popular in the county. For decades, John G's has been attracting huge breakfast crowds; lines run out the door (on weekends, all the way down the block). Stop in for some good, greasy-spoon–style food served in heaping portions right on the beachfront. This place is known for fresh and tasty fish-and-chips and its selection of creative omelettes and grill specials.

TooJay's. 313 Royal Poinciana Plaza (3 miles east of I-95 off Exit 52A), Palm Beach. ☎ **561/659-7232.** Reservations not accepted. Main courses $8–$13. CB, DC, MC, V. Daily 8am–9pm. GOURMET DELI.

This simple and predictable restaurant and take-out deli is a favorite with locals and out-of-towners that want good old-fashioned deli food. So popular, in fact, that TooJay's now has more than a dozen outlets. For good cover while people-watching, choose a booth surrounded by a jungle of potted plants. The food is excellent and could hardly be fresher. All the classic sandwiches are available: hot pastrami, roast beef, turkey, chicken, chopped liver, egg salad, and more. Comfort food in the form of huge portions of stuffed cabbage, chicken pot pie, beef brisket, and sautéed onions and chicken livers is sure to satisfy.

THE PALM BEACHES AFTER DARK
THE BAR, CAFE & MUSIC SCENE: DOWNTOWN WEST PALM BEACH

A decade-old project to revitalize downtown West Palm Beach has finally become a reality, with ✪ **Clematis Street** at its heart. Artist lofts, sidewalk cafes, bars, restaurants, consignment shops, and galleries dot the street from Flagler Drive to Rosemary Avenue, creating a hot spot for a night out, especially on weekends when yuppies mingle with stylish Euros and disheveled artists. Every Thursday night is a popular night out called *Clematis by Night.* Each week features a different rock, blues, or reggae band plus an art show. Vendors sell food and drinks and the street's bars and restaurants are packed. It is a bit raucous at times, but fun. Note that minors unaccompanied by their guardians are not permitted in the downtown area around Clematis Street after 10pm on weeknights and after 11pm on weekend nights.

Some highlights of the Strip include **Sforza**, at 223 Clematis St.—it's the only Italian restaurant I've seen that needs a bouncer at the door. On weekends this place draws crowds of yuppies and well-dressed Euros who wait to be picked to get in the elegant dining room to dance and sip expensive martinis (☎ **561/832-8819**).

If you are looking for a more casual scene, stop by **Ray's**, at 519 Clematis St. (☎ **561/835-1577**), on a Thursday, Friday, or Saturday for free blues and mediocre drinks. This dusty little bar hosts homegrown blues bands that give it all up for the few patrons who appreciate the rough stuff.

Across the street is a longtime favorite, **Respectable Street café**, at 518 Clematis St. (☎ **561/832-9999**). The cafe's plain storefront exterior belies its funky high-ceilinged interior decorated with large black booths, psychedelic wall murals, and a large checkerboard-tile dance floor where young hipsters dance to both live and recorded alternative music.

Over the bridge in Palm Beach is ✪ **E. R. Bradley's Saloon**, at 111 Bradley Place, between Royal Poinciana Way and Sunset Avenue (☎ **561/833-3520**). Bradley's, as it is known, is about as wild as the "island" allows. Most nights a crowd of young professionals share the old wooden tavern with hard-drinking regulars in blue blazers. Check out the happy-hour buffets in the late afternoon.

A more sophisticated crowd gathers nightly at the **Leopard Lounge** in the **Chesterfield Hotel** (see "Where to Stay," above). Live piano music, good conversation, and a comfortable sofa make this a perfect place to spend an evening.

THE PERFORMING ARTS

With a number of dedicated patrons and enthusiastic supporters of the arts, this area happily boasts many good venues for those craving culture. Check the *Palm Beach Post* or the *Palm Beach Daily News*, known as "the shiny sheet," for up-to-date listings and reviews. Call ☎ **800/882-ARTS** for a recorded announcement of the week's events.

The **Raymond F. Kravis Center for the Performing Arts**, 701 Okeechobee Blvd., West Palm Beach (☎ **561/832-7469**), is the area's largest and most active performance space. With a huge curved-glass facade and more than 2,500 seats in two lushly decorated indoor spaces, and a new outdoor amphitheater, The Kravis, as it is known, stages more than 300 performances each year. Phone for a current schedule of Palm Beach's best music, dance, and theater.

4 Jupiter & Northern Palm Beach County

20 miles N of Palm Beach, 81 miles N of Miami

Northern Palm Beach County and its main town, Jupiter, are known primarily for pristine beaches and expansive tracts of land. The surrounding towns of Tequesta, Jupiter, Juno Beach, North Palm Beach, Palm Beach Gardens, and Singer Island are inviting for tourists who want to enjoy the many outdoor activities that make this area so popular with retirees, snowbirds, and families. Beaches and parks are clean, large, and easily accessible to the public.

ESSENTIALS

GETTING THERE The quickest route from West Palm Beach to Jupiter is on the Florida Turnpike or the sometimes congested I-95. You can also take a slower but more scenic coastal route, U.S. 1 or Fla. A1A.

Since Jupiter is so close to Palm Beach, it's easy to fly into the **Palm Beach International Airport** (☎ 561/471-7420) and rent a car there. The drive should take less than half an hour.

VISITOR INFORMATION A **Visitor Information Center** is located between I-95 and the Florida Turnpike at 8020 Indiantown Rd. in Jupiter (☎ 561/575-4636; www.jupiterfloridausa.com) and is open from 9am to 6pm daily.

BEACHES & OUTDOOR PURSUITS

BASEBALL The **Roger Dean Stadium,** 4751 Main St. (☎ 561/775-1818), hosts spring training for both the St. Louis Cardinals and the Montreal Expos, along with minor-league action from Florida's state league, The Hammerheads. Tickets range in price from $5 to $15. Baseball aficionados should call for schedules and specific ticket information.

BEACHES The farther north you head from populated Palm Beach, the more peaceful and pristine the coast becomes. Just a few miles north of the bustle, castles and condominiums give way to wide open space and public parkland. There are dozens of recommendable spots. Following are a few of the best.

John D. MacArthur Beach, a state park, dominates a large portion of Singer Island, the barrier island just north of Palm Beach. Straddling the island from shore to shore, the park has lengthy frontage on both the Atlantic Ocean and Lake Worth Cove. The beach is great for hiking, swimming, and sunning. To reach the park from the mainland, cross the Intracoastal Waterway on Blue Heron Boulevard and turn north on Ocean Boulevard.

Jupiter Inlet meets the ocean at **Dubois Park,** a 29-acre beach that is popular with families. The shallow waters and sandy shore are perfect for kids, while adults can play in the rougher swells of the lifeguarded inlet. A footbridge leads to **Ocean Beach,** an area popular with windsurfers and surfers. There's a short fishing pier, and plenty of trees shading barbecue grills and picnic tables. Visitors can also explore the Dubois Pioneer Home, a small house situated atop a shell mound built by the Jaega Indians. The park entrance is on Dubois Road, about a mile south of the junction of U.S. 1 and Fla. A1A.

BICYCLING Bring your own, get one from your hotel, or rent one from **Raleigh Bicycles of Jupiter,** at 103 U.S. 1, Unit F1 (☎ 561/746-0585). Bicycle enthusiasts will enjoy exploring this flat and uncluttered area. North Palm Beach has hundreds of miles of smooth paved roads. Loggerhead Park in Juno Beach or Fla. A1A along the ocean has great trails for starters. You'll find many more scenic routes over the bridges and west of the highway.

BOATING & CANOEING You can rent a boat at several outlets throughout northern Palm Beach County, including **Canoe Outfitters,** 8900 W. Indiantown Rd. (west of I-95), North Jupiter (☎ 561/746-7053), which provides access to one of the area's most beautiful natural waterways. Canoers start at Riverbend Park along an 8-mile stretch of Intracoastal Waterway, where the lush foliage supports dozens of exotic birds and reptiles. Keep your eyes open for the gators who love to sunbathe on the shallow shores of the river. You'll end up tired and thoroughly wide-eyed at Jonathan Dickinson Park about 5 or 6 hours later. Eric Bailey, a local who runs the concession, will sell the environmentally minded a pamphlet for $1 that describes local flora and fauna. Trips run Wednesday to Sunday and cost $16 per person, including park charges.

CRUISES Several sightseeing cruises offer scenic tours of the magnificent waterways that make up northern Palm Beach County. Several water taxis conduct daily narrated tours through the scenic waters. One interesting excursion departs from **Panama Hatties** at PGA Boulevard and the Intracoastal Waterway. Prices are $15 per person for the 1½-hour ride. Call ☎ **561/775-2628.** The Manatee Queen, 1065 N. Ocean Blvd. (at the Crab House), Jupiter (☎ **561/744-2191**), a 40-foot catamaran with bench seating for up to 49 people, offers 2-hour tours of Jupiter Island departing daily at 2:30pm that pass Burt Reynolds's and Perry Como's mansions, among other historical and natural spots of interest. Reservations are highly recommended, especially in season; call for the current schedule of offerings. The cruise is wheelchair-accessible. Prices start at $14 for adults and $10 for children and can range up to $15 for special tours. Bring your own lunch or purchase chips and sodas at the minisnack bar.

FISHING Before you leave, send for an information-packed fishing kit with details on fish camps, charters, tournament, and tide schedules, distributed by the **West Palm Beach Fishing Club,** c/o Fish Finder, P.O. Box 468, West Palm Beach, FL 33402. The cost is $10 and is well worth it. Allow at least 4 weeks for delivery.

Once in town, several outfitters along U.S. 1 and Fla. A1A have vessels and equipment for rent if your hotel doesn't. One of the most complete facilities is the **Sailfish Marina & Resort,** 98 Lake Dr. (off Blue Heron Boulevard), Palm Beach Shores (☎ **561/844-1724**). Call for equipment, bait, guided trips, or boat rentals.

GOLF Even if you're not lucky enough to be staying at the PGA National Resort, you may still be able to play on their award-winning courses. If you or someone in your group is a member of another golf or country club, have the head pro write a note on club letterhead to **Jackie Rogers at PGA** (see "Where to Stay," below) to request a play date. Be sure the pro includes his PGA number and contact information. Allow at least 2 weeks for a response. Also, ask about the Golf-A-Round program, where selected private clubs open to nonmembers for free or discounted rates. Contact the **Palm Beach County Convention and Visitors Bureau** (☎ **561/471-3995**) for details.

Plenty of other great courses dot the area, including the **Golf Club of Jupiter,** 1800 Central Blvd., Jupiter (☎ **561/747-6262**). A well-respected 18-hole, par-70 course is situated on more than 6,200 yards featuring narrow fairways and fast greens. Fees are $27 to $60, depending on the season, and include a mandatory cart. The course borders I-95.

HIKING In an area that's not particularly known for extraordinary natural diversity, **Blowing Rocks Preserve** has a terrific hiking trail along a dramatic limestone outcropping. You won't find hills or scenic vistas, but you will see Florida's unique and varied tropical ecosystem. The well-marked mile-long trail passes oceanfront dunes, coastal strands, mangrove wetlands, and a coastal hammock. The preserve, owned and managed by the Nature Conservancy, also protects an important habitat for West Indian manatees and loggerhead turtles. The preserve is located along South Beach Drive (Fla. A1A), north of the Jupiter inlet, about a 10-minute drive from Jupiter. From U.S. 1, head east on S.R. 707 and cross the Intracoastal Waterway to the park. Admission is free, but a $3 per person donation is requested. For more information, contact the Preserve Manager, Blowing Rocks Preserve, P.O. Box 3795, Tequesta, FL 33469 (☎ **561/575-2297**).

SCUBA DIVING & SNORKELING Year-round, warm, clear waters make northern Palm Beach County great for both diving and snorkeling. The closest coral reef is located a quarter-mile from shore and can easily be reached by boat. Three popular wrecks are clustered near each other less than a mile off shore of the Lake Worth Inlet at about 90 feet. If your hotel doesn't offer dive trips, call the **South Florida Dive**

Discovering a Remarkable Natural World

North Palm Beach is well known for the giant sea turtles that lay their eggs on the county's beaches from May to August. These endangered marine animals return here annually, from as far as South America, to lay their clutch of about 115 eggs each. Nurtured by the warm sand, but preyed upon by birds and other predators, only about one or two babies from each nest survive to maturity.

Many environmentalists recommend that visitors take part in an organized turtle-watching program (rather than going on their own) to minimize disturbance to the turtles. The Jupiter Beach Resort (see "Where to Stay," below) and the Marinelife Center of Juno Beach (see below) both sponsor free guided expeditions to the egg-laying sites from May to August. Phone for times and reservations.

Just south of Jupiter, in Juno Beach, is the **Marinelife Center of Juno Beach,** in Loggerhead Park, 14200 U.S. 1, Juno Beach (☎ **561/627-8280**). Combining a science museum and nature trail, the small Marinelife Center is dedicated to the coastal ecology of northern Palm Beach County. Hands-on exhibits teach visitors about wetlands and beach areas, as well as offshore coral reefs and the local sea life. Visitors are encouraged to walk the center's sand dune nature trails, all of which are marked with interpretive signs. This is one place that you're guaranteed to see live sea turtles year-round, and during high breeding season (June and July) the center conducts narrative walks along a nearby beach. Reservations are a must. The book opens on May 1 and is usually full by midmonth. Admission to the center is free, though donations are accepted. Open Tuesday to Saturday from 10am to 4pm and Sunday from noon to 3pm.

Headquarters, 23141 Lyons Rd., Boca Raton (☎ **800/771-DIVE** or 561/627-9558); or **Seafari Dive and Surf,** 75 E. Indiantown Rd., Suite 603, Jupiter (☎ **561/747-6115**).

TENNIS In addition to the many hotel tennis courts (see "Where to Stay," below), you can swing a racquet at a number of local clubs. The **Jupiter Bay Tennis Club,** 353 U.S. 1, Jupiter (☎ **561/744-9424**), has seven clay courts (three lighted) and charges $12 per person per day. Reservations are highly recommended.

More economical options are available at relatively well-maintained municipal courts. Call for locations and hours (☎ **561/966-6600**). Many are available free on a first-come, first-served basis.

A HISTORIC LIGHTHOUSE

Jupiter Inlet Lighthouse. U.S. 1 and Alt. Fla. A1A, Jupiter. ☎ **561/747-8380.** Admission $5. Sun–Wed 10am–4pm (last tour departs at 3:15pm). Children must be 4 feet or taller to climb.

Completed in 1860, this redbrick structure is the oldest extant building in Palm Beach County. Still owned and maintained by the U.S. Coast Guard, the lighthouse is now home to a small historical museum, located at its base. The Florida History Museum sponsors tours of the lighthouse, enabling visitors to explore the cramped interior, which is filled with artifacts and photographs illustrating the rich history of the area. First, a 15-minute video explains the various shipwrecks, Indian wars, and other events that helped shape this region. Helpful volunteers are eager to tell colorful stories to highlight the 1-hour tour.

SHOPPING

Northern Palm Beach County may not have the glitzy boutiques of Worth Avenue, but it does have an impressive indoor mall, the **Gardens of the Palm Beaches,** at 3101 PGA Blvd., where you can find large department stores including Bloomingdale's, Burdines, Macy's, and Saks Fifth Avenue, as well as more than 100 specialty shops. A large and diverse food court and fine sit-down restaurants in this 1.3 million-square-foot facility make this shopping excursion an all-day affair. Call ☎ **561/775-7750** for store information.

WHERE TO STAY

The northern part of Palm Beach County is much more laid-back and less touristy than the rest of the Gold Coast. Here, there are relatively few fancy hotels or attractions. In addition to several Holiday Inns, there is a reasonably priced and recently renovated **Wellesley Inn,** at 34 Fisherman's Wharf (I-95, exit east on Indian Town Road; turn left before the bridge), in Jupiter (☎ **800/444-8888**). Suites include sofa beds, refrigerators, and microwave ovens. Though not within walking distance of the beach, the inn is located near shops and restaurants and Fla. A1A.

VERY EXPENSIVE

Jupiter Beach Resort. 5 N.A1A, Jupiter, FL 33477. ☎ **800/228-8810** or 561/746-2511. Fax 561/747-3304. 153 units. www.jupiterbeachresort.com. A/C MINIBAR TV TEL. Winter $200–$360 double; $310–$450 suite; $750–$1,000 penthouse. Off-season $140–$200 double; $160–$240 suite; $500–$750 penthouse. AE, DC, DISC, MC, V. Valet parking $5. From I-95, take Exit 59A east to the end of Indiantown Rd. at A1A. Jupiter Beach Resort is at this intersection on the ocean.

The only resort located directly on Jupiter's beach, this unpretentious retreat is a world away from the more luxurious resorts just a few miles to the south. The lobby and public areas have a formal Caribbean motif, accented with green marble, arched doorways, and chandeliers. The simple and elegant guest rooms are furnished in a comfortable island style, and every room has a private balcony with ocean or sunset views looking out over the uncluttered beachfront. A thorough refurbishing in the mid-1990s has made this resort very popular with conventions and large groups. In fact, it is so popular that it is being gradually converted into a time-share property. Excursions are available to top-rated golf courses in the area.

Dining/Diversions: A popular and well-run lobby restaurant serves an eclectic mix of continental, Southwestern, and Caribbean cuisine. Three other pool and beach bars serve snacks and refreshments throughout the day. The lounge features live music several nights a week.

Amenities: Concierge, room service, dry-cleaning and laundry services, overnight shoe shine, newspaper delivery, in-room massage, daily maid service, baby-sitting, express checkout, free coffee in room. Kitchenettes and VCRs in suites, VCR rentals, Spectravision movie channels, outdoor heated swimming pool, beach, exercise room, bicycle rental, supervised children's programs, conference rooms, self-service Laundromat, car-rental desk, night-lit tennis court, water-sports equipment rentals, boutique, dive shop, summer turtle-watch program.

✪ **PGA National Resort & Spa.** 400 Avenue of the Champions, Palm Beach Gardens, FL 33418. ☎ **800/633-9150** or 561/627-2000. Fax 561/622-0261. 339 units. A/C MINIBAR TV TEL. Winter $319–$389 double; from $489 suite. Off-season $129–$169 double; from $249 suite. Children 16 and under stay free in parents' room. Special packages available. AE, DC, DISC, MC, V. From I-95, take Exit 57B (PGA Blvd.) west and continue for approximately 2 miles to the resort entrance on the left.

This rambling resort, built in 1981, is known primarily as a golf destination. With five 18-hole courses on more than 2,300 acres, golfers and other sports-minded travelers will find plenty to keep them occupied—croquet, tennis, sailing, a health and fitness center, and a top-rated Mediterranean-style spa. Constant updating has kept the grounds and buildings in like-new condition. The par-72 Champion Course, redesigned in 1990 by Jack Nicklaus, is the resort's most valuable asset. More than 100 sand bunkers and plenty of water on 6,400-square-foot greens keep golfers of all levels alert. Watch out for hole 16.

When you are ready to rest, you will enjoy the comfortable and spacious accommodations and good food. Ample-size guest rooms are furnished with tasteful modern furnishings and tropical prints. Bathrooms are large and thoughtfully outfitted with cushy robes, good light, and magnifying mirrors. Although you are miles from the beach, the resort has nine pools and a private lake where you can ski or sail. As for views, the best you will get is the golf course or gardens.

Dining/Diversions: Six restaurants and lounges include Don Shula's award-winning steak house, a poolside grill, and an eatery featuring spa cuisine. In the "Hall of Fame" lounge there's live piano music Monday through Thursday, and on Friday and Saturday a guitarist plays everything from Jazz to light Rock & Roll.

Amenities: Concierge, room service, evening turndown, overnight shoe shine, laundry, baby-sitting. This is the national headquarters of the PGA, so it's no surprise that there are five 18-hole tournament courses, plus the PGA National's Academy of Golf. There are also 19 clay tennis courts (12 lighted), nine swimming pools, a private beach on a 26-acre lake, water-sports equipment rentals, five tournament croquet lawns, five indoor racquetball courts, a full-service Mediterranean spa, aerobics studio, salon, and car rental.

MODERATE/INEXPENSIVE

Baron's Landing Motel & Apartments. 18125 Ocean Blvd. (Fla. A1A at the corner of Love St.), Jupiter, FL 33477. ☎ **561/746-8757.** 8 units. A/C TV TEL. Winter $80–$125 double; $1,400–$1,700 monthly. Off-season $55–$75 double; $700–$1,000 monthly. No credit cards.

This charming family-run inn is a perfect little beach getaway. It's not elegant, but it's cozy. A single-story motel fronting the Intracoastal Waterway is often full in winter with snowbirds, who dock their boats at the hotel's marina for weeks or months at a time. Nearly all rooms, which are situated around a small pool, have small kitchenettes. Each unit has a hodgepodge of used furniture, and some have pullout sofas. Considering that you're a few blocks from some of the most expensive real estate in the country, this is a good deal. Dock rentals are available.

Cologne Motel. 220 U.S. 1, Tequesta/Jupiter, FL 33469. ☎ **561/746-0616.** 9 units. A/C TV. Winter $50–$85 double. Off-season $45 double. Weekly rates available. AE, DC, MC, V.

A pleasant Hungarian couple runs this modest roadside motel that is always busy. After they finish the landscaping and pool, they hope to add more rooms to this nine-room, one-story little gem. The small rooms were updated in 1999 with modest but bright bedspreads and curtains, and the retiled bathrooms are small but clean. The area is safe if not scenic and only about a 5-minute drive to the beach. A more direct route by foot gets you there in about 15 minutes.

WHERE TO DINE

In addition to all the national fast-food joints that line Indiantown Road and U.S. 1, you'll find a number of touristy fish restaurants serving battered and fried everything. There are only a few really exceptional eateries in North Palm Beach and Jupiter. Try these listed below for guaranteed good food at reasonable prices.

Athenian Cafe. In the Chasewood Shopping Center, 6350 Indiantown Rd., Suite 7, Jupiter. ☎ **561/744-8327.** Main courses $5–$16. AE, MC, V. Mon–Sat 11am–9pm, Sun 4–9pm during season. GREEK.

Peter Papadelis and his family have been running this pleasant storefront cafe for more than a decade. Tucked in the corner of a strip mall, this place is a favorite with businesspeople, who stop in for a heaping portion of rich and meaty moussaka or a flaky spinach pie made fresh by Peter himself. You could make a meal of the thick and lemony Greek soup and the large fresh antipasto. In a town replete with tourist-priced fish joints, this is a welcome alternative. Early bird specials, served until 7pm, include many Greek favorites and broiled local fish with soup or salad, rice, vegetables, pita, dessert, and coffee or tea.

✪ **Capt. Charlie's Reef Grill.** 12846 U.S. 1 (behind O'Brian's and French Connection), Juno Beach. ☎ **561/624-9924.** Reservations not accepted. Main courses $9.95–$18.95. MC, V. Sun–Thurs 11:30am–9:30pm, Fri–Sat 11:30am–10pm. SEAFOOD/CARIBBEAN.

The trick here is to arrive early, ahead of the crowd of local foodies who come for the more than dozen daily local-catch specials prepared in dozens of styles. Imaginative appetizers include Caribbean chili, a rich chunky stew filled with fresh seafood; or a tuna spring roll big enough for two. The enormous Cuban crab cake is moist and perfectly browned without tasting fried and is served with homemade mango chutney and black beans and rice. Sit at the bar to watch the hectic kitchen turn out perfect dishes on the 14-burner stove. Somehow, the pleasant waitresses keep their cool even when the place is packed. In addition to the terrific seafood, this little dive offers an extensive, affordable wine and beer selection—more than 30 of each from around the world.

Nick's Tomato Pie. 1697 W. Indiantown Rd. (1 mile east of I-95, Exit 59A), Jupiter. ☎ **561/744-8935.** Reservations accepted only for parties of 6 or more. Main courses $12–$20; pastas $10–$15. AE, CB, DC, DISC, MC, V. Mon–Thurs 5–10pm, Fri–Sat 5–11pm, Sun 5–10pm. ITALIAN.

A Bennigan's-style family restaurant, Nick's is a popular attraction in otherwise food-poor Jupiter. With a huge menu of pastas, pizzas, fish, chicken, and beef, this cheery (and noisy) spot has something for everyone. On Saturday night you'll see lots of couples on dates and some families leaving with take-out bags left over from the impossibly generous portions. The homemade sausage is a delicious treat, served with sautéed onions and peppers. The *pollo marsala*, too, is good and authentic.

No Anchovies! 2650 PGA Blvd., Palm Beach Gardens. ☎ **561/622-7855.** Pizza and pasta $7–$13; main courses $9–$22; appetizers $6–$10. AE, DC, MC, V. Mon–Thurs 11:30am–10:30pm, Fri–Sat 11:30am–11pm, Sun 4–10pm. ITALIAN.

This large and colorful restaurant is popular with families that appreciate the large portions and reasonably priced children's specials. An equally colorful menu offers a large variety of pastas, pizzas, salads, and meat and fish specials. Mix and match your pasta with half a dozen sauces. My favorite is the thick and simple *fillete de tomato* over fusilli. You may also want to try some of the delicious chicken or meats prepared on the oak-burning grill.

JUPITER & NORTHERN PALM BEACH COUNTY AFTER DARK

With one notable exception, there just isn't much going on here after dark. **Club Safari,** 4000 PGA Blvd. (just east of I-95), in Palm Beach Garden's Marriott Hotel (☎ **561/622-8888**), is more hip than any hotel dance club I have ever seen, although the safari theme is a bit much. The huge, sunken dance floor is surrounded by vines and lanky, potted trees. Nearby, a large Buddha statue blows steam and smoke while waving its burly arms in front of a young gyrating crowd. There is deejay music, a large video screen, and a modest cover charge on the weekends.

The Treasure Coast 13

The Treasure Coast is truly an undiscovered paradise. Miles of uninterrupted beaches and aquamarine waters attract swimmers, boaters, divers, fishermen, and sun worshippers who love to dip, dive, and surf in these emerald waters. If you love nature and the great outdoors, you'll enjoy the Treasure Coast, which prides itself on preserving natural and historic landmarks.

For hundreds of years, Florida's east coast was a popular stopover for European explorers, many of whom arrived from Spain to fill coffers with gold and silver. Rough weather and poor navigation often took a toll on their ships, but in 1715, a violent hurricane stunned the northeast coast and sank an entire fleet of Spanish ships laden with gold. Though Spanish salvagers worked for years to collect the lost treasure, much of it remained buried beneath the shifting sand. Builders hired to excavate the area in the 1950s and 1960s discovered centuries-old coins under their tractors. The McLarty Treasure Museum at Sebastian Inlet State Recreation Area in Melbourne Beach highlights the history of the 1715 Treasure Fleet. There are also incredible barrier reefs and shipwrecks in St. Lucie County that can be reached from the beaches of Fort Pierce and Hutchinson Island.

Today, on these same beaches you'll find an occasional treasure hunter trolling the sand with a metal detector, and swimmers and sunbathers who come to enjoy the stretches of beach that extend into the horizon. The sea, especially around Sebastian Inlet, is a mecca for surfers, who find some of the largest swells in the state.

The array of wildlife you'll find here is extraordinarily impressive. The endangered West Indian Manatee can be spotted along the Treasure Coast's inland waterways. You can learn more about this mammal at The Manatee Observation and Education Center in Fort Pierce. St. Lucie Inlet State Preserve has a wonderful nestling area for loggerhead and leatherback turtles. Take a boat tour through the Loxahatchee Everglades, home to tropical fish, alligators, deer, and exotic birds. Go fishing in Lake Okeechobee, for the best freshwater fish around.

If you're a sports enthusiast you'll enjoy the boundless sporting opportunities here—from golf and tennis to polo and motorcar racing. If you tire from playing yourself, take time and watch the pros play hard. Catch the New York Mets practicing at the St. Lucie City Stadium (☎ **561/871-2115**) in Port St. Lucie during spring training.

Away from the talcum powder sands, of course there's great shopping, entertainment, clubbing, boating, golfing, tennis, and a reprieve from the hubbub of the rat race.

Over the past few years, the Treasure Coast has been attracting unprecedented numbers of new residents, but this area still retains its small-town feel. The growth is happening at a reasonable pace, and the influx has brought with it a renewed interest in renovating once-abandoned downtown areas. The result is a batch of freshly spruced-up accommodations, shops, and restaurants from Stuart to Sebastian.

The Treasure Coast, for the purposes of this chapter, runs roughly from Hobe Sound in the south to the Sebastian Inlet in the north, encompassing some of Martin, St. Lucie, and Indian River counties and all of Hutchinson Island.

TREASURE COAST ESSENTIALS
GETTING THERE

Since virtually every town described in this chapter runs along a straight route, along the Atlantic Ocean, I've given all directions below.

BY PLANE The **Palm Beach International Airport** (☎ **561/471-7420**), located about 35 miles south of Stuart, is the closest gateway to this region if you're flying. See the "Getting Around" section on Palm Beach in chapter 12 for complete information. If you are traveling to the northern part of the Treasure Coast, **Melbourne International Airport,** off U.S. 1 in Melbourne (☎ **407/723-6227**), is less than 25 miles north of Sebastian and about 35 miles north of Vero Beach.

BY CAR If you're driving up or down the Florida coast, you'll probably reach the Treasure Coast via I-95. If you are heading to Stuart or Jensen Beach, take Exit 61 (Route 76/Tanner Highway) or 62 (Route 714); to Port St. Lucie or Fort Pierce, take Exit 63 or 64 (Okeechobee Road); to Vero Beach, take Exit 68 (S.R. 60); to Sebastian, take Exit 69 (County Road).

You can also take the Florida Turnpike; this toll road is the fastest (but not the most scenic) route, especially if you're coming from Orlando. If you are heading to Stuart or Jensen Beach, take Exit 133; to Fort Pierce, take Exit 152 (Okeechobee Road); to Port St. Lucie, take Exit 142 or 152; to Vero Beach, take Exit 193 (S.R. 60); to Sebastian, take Exit 193 to S.R. 60 east and connect to I-95 north.

If you are staying in Hutchinson Island, which runs almost the entire length of the Treasure Coast, you should check with your hotel, or see the listings below, to find the best route to take.

Finally, if you're coming directly from the west coast, you'll probably take S.R. 70, which runs north of Lake Okeechobee to Fort Pierce, located just up the road from Stuart.

BY RAIL Amtrak (☎ **800/USA-RAIL;** www.amtrak.com) stops in West Palm Beach at 201 S. Tamarind Ave., and in Okeechobee at 801 N. Parrot Ave., off U.S. 441 north.

BY BUS Greyhound buses (☎ **800/231-2222;** www.greyhound.com) service the area with terminals in Stuart, at 1308 S. Federal Hwy.; in Fort Pierce, at 7005 Okeechobee Rd. (☎ **561/461-3299**); and in Vero Beach, at U.S. 1 and S.R. 60 (☎ **561/562-6588**).

GETTING AROUND

A car is a necessity in this large and rural region. Although heavy traffic is not usually a problem here, on the smaller coastal roads, like Fla. A1A, expect to travel at a slow pace, usually between 25 and 40 miles an hour.

The Treasure Coast

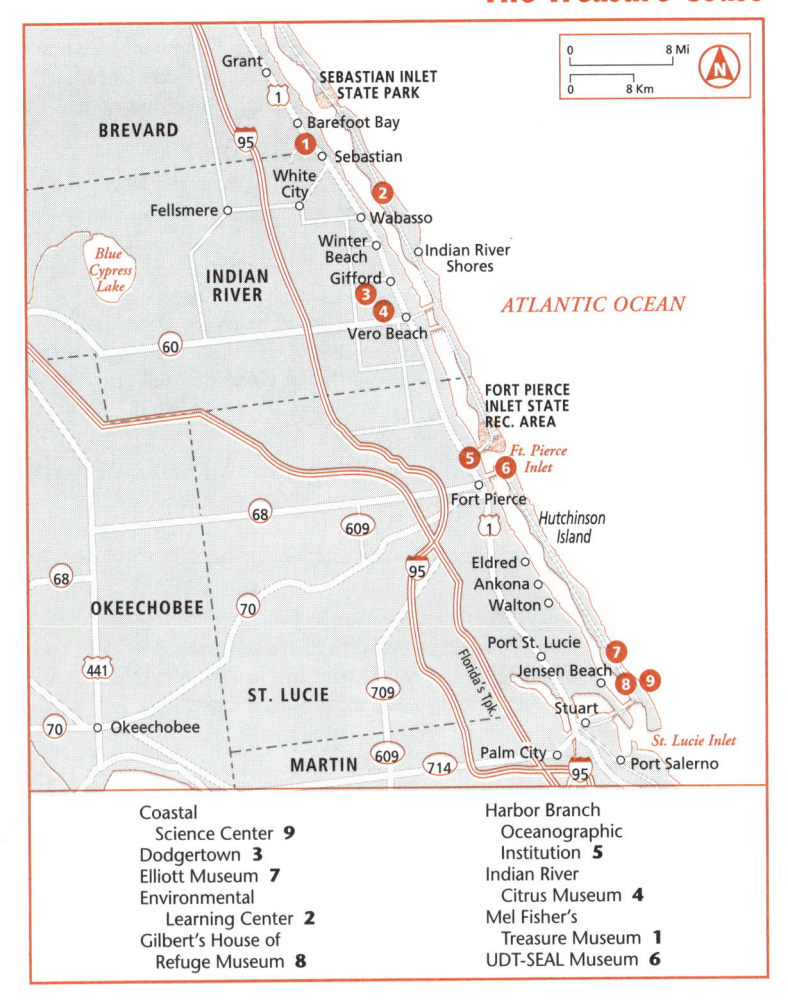

Coastal Science Center **9**	Harbor Branch Oceanographic Institution **5**
Dodgertown **3**	Indian River Citrus Museum **4**
Elliott Museum **7**	Mel Fisher's Treasure Museum **1**
Environmental Learning Center **2**	UDT-SEAL Museum **6**
Gilbert's House of Refuge Museum **8**	

1 Hobe Sound, Stuart & Jensen Beach

130 miles SE of Orlando, 98 miles N of Miami

Once just a stretch of pineapple plantations, the towns of Martin County, which include Stuart, Jensen Beach, Port Salerno, and Hobe Sound, still retain much of their rural character. Dotted between citrus groves and mangroves are modest homes and an occasional high-rise condominium. Though the area is definitely still seasonal (with a distinct rise in street and pedestrian traffic beginning after the Christmas holidays), the atmosphere is pure small town. Even in historic downtown Stuart, the result of a successful, ongoing restoration, expect the storefronts to be dark and the streets abandoned after 10pm.

ESSENTIALS

The **Stuart/Martin County Chamber of Commerce,** 1650 S. Kanner Hwy., Stuart, FL 34994 (☎ **800/524-9704** in Florida, or 561/287-1088; fax 561/220-3437), is the region's main source for information. The **Jensen Beach Chamber of Commerce,** 1901 NE Jensen Beach Blvd., Jensen Beach, FL 34957 (☎ **561/334-3444;** fax 561/334-0817), also offers visitors information about its simple beachfront town.

OUTDOOR PURSUITS: THE BEACHES & BEYOND

BEACHES Beaches are easily accessible throughout Hutchinson Island, the long, thin barrier island that stretches north and south from Stuart. Look for "coastal access" signs pointing the way to the public beach areas.

The best of them is **Bathtub Beach,** on North Hutchinson Island. Here, the calm waters are protected by coral reefs, and visitors can explore the region on dune and river trails. Pick a secluded spot on the wide stretch of beach or enjoy marked nature trails across the street. Facilities include showers and toilets open during the day. To reach the park, head east on Ocean Boulevard (Stuart Causeway) and turn right onto MacArthur Boulevard. The beach is about a mile ahead on your left, just north of the Indian River Plantation. Parking is plentiful.

CANOEING **Jonathan Dickinson State Park** (see the "Wildlife Exploration" box) is the area's most popular for canoeing. The route winds through a variety of botanical habitats. You'll see lots of birds and, of course, the occasional manatee. Canoes cost $6 per hour. The concession is open Monday to Friday from 9am to 5pm and Saturday and Sunday from 8am to 5pm.

FISHING Several independent charter captains operate on Hutchinson Island and Jensen Beach. One of the largest operators is the **Sailfish Marina,** 3565 SE St. Lucie Blvd., in Stuart (☎ **561/221-9456**), which maintains half a dozen charter boats for fishing excursions year-round. Also on-site is a bait-and-tackle shop and a knowledgeable, helpful staff.

GOLF The pricey **Indian River Plantation Beach Resort** is a terrific destination for golfers, but unless you're a guest at the resort or are playing with a member, you cannot play these courses. Instead, try the **Champions Club at Summerfield,** on U.S. 1, south of Cove Road in Stuart (☎ **561/283-1500**), a somewhat challenging championship course designed by Tom Fazio. This rural course, the best in the area, was built in 1994 and offers great glimpses of wildlife amid the wetlands. In winter, greens fees are around $60, and carts are mandatory. Reservations are a must and are taken 4 days in advance.

SCUBA DIVING & SNORKELING Three popular artificial reefs off Hutchinson Island provide excellent scenery for both novice and experienced divers. The **USS Rankin,** sunk in 120 feet of water in 1988, lies 7 miles east-northeast of the St. Lucie Inlet. The 58-foot-deep **Donaldson Reef** consists of a cluster of plumbing fixtures sunk in 58 feet of water. It's located due east of the Gilbert's House of Refuge Museum. The **Ernst Reef,** made from old tires, is a 60-foot dive located $4^1/_2$ miles east-southeast of the St. Lucie inlet.

Deep Divers Unlimited, 6083 SE Federal Hwy. (corner of Cove Road and U.S. 1), Stuart (☎ **561/286-0078**), arranges two-tank dive trips to these sites and others starting at about $37 a person. A full set of gear will cost you another $30 for the day. They will also rent gear to those wanting to explore the area's best snorkeling at Bathtub Beach (see "Beaches," above). There's a natural coral reef within swimming distance of shore.

SEEING THE SIGHTS

✪ Coastal Science Center. 890 NE Ocean Blvd. (across the street from the Elliott Museum), Hutchinson Island, Stuart. ☎ **561/225-0505.** www.fosuga.org. Admission $4 adults, $2.50 children 3–12, free for children under 3. Mon–Sat 10am–5pm.

Wildlife Exploration: From Gators to Manatees to Turtles

One of the most scenic areas on this stretch of the coast is ✪ **Jonathan Dickinson State Park,** at 16450 S. Federal Hwy. (U.S. 1), Hobe Sound (☎ **561/546-2771**). The park is intentionally low managed so that it will resemble the habitat of hundreds of years ago, before Europeans started chopping, dredging, and "improving" the area. Dozens of species of Florida's unique wildlife, including alligators and manatees, live on more than 11,300 acres. Bird watchers should bring their books and binoculars to spot the many ospreys, woodpeckers, ibises, herons, anhingas, egrets, and even some bald eagles. Deer, reptiles, tortoises, and snakes also call this area home. There are concession areas for daytime snacks and four different scenic nature and bike trails through the scrublands and flatwoods. You can also rent canoes from the concession stand to explore the Loxahatchee River on your own. Admission is $3.25 per car of up to eight adults. Day hikers, bikers, and walkers pay $1 each. The park is open from 8am until sundown. See "Where to Stay," below for details on camping.

Nearby is **Hobe Sound Wildlife Refuge,** on North Beach Road off S.R. 708, at the north end of Jupiter Island (☎ **561/546-6141**). This is one of the best places to see sea turtles that nest on the shore in the summer months, especially in June and July. Because it's home to a large variety of other plant and animal species, the park is worth visiting at other times of year as well. Admission is $4 per car, and the preserve is open daily from sunrise to sunset. Exact times are posted at each entrance and change seasonally.

Opened by the South Florida Oceanographic Society in late 1994, this 44-acre site surrounded by coastal hammock and mangroves is its own little ecosystem and serves as an outdoor classroom, teaching visitors about the region's flora and fauna. The modest building houses saltwater tanks and wet and dry "discovery tables" with small indigenous animals. The incredibly eager staff of volunteers encourages visitors to wander the lush, well-marked nature trails.

✪ **Elliott Museum.** 825 NE Ocean Blvd. (north of Indian River Plantation Resort), Hutchinson Island, Stuart. ☎ **561/225-1961.** Admission $6 adults, $2 children 6–13, free for children 5 and under. Daily 10am–4pm.

A treasure trove of early Americana, the Elliott Museum is a rich tribute to inventors, sports heroes, and collectors. A series of life-size dioramas depicts an apothecary, a barbershop, a blacksmith forge, a clock and watch shop, and other old-fashioned commercial enterprises. Sports fans will appreciate the baseball memorabilia—a half million dollars' worth—including an autographed item from every player in the Baseball Hall of Fame.

A gallery of patents and models of machines, invented by the museum's founder, Harmon Parker Elliott, and his son, provides an intriguing glimpse into the business of tinkering. Their collection of restored antique cars is also pretty impressive. Expect to spend at least an hour seeing the highlights.

Gilbert's House of Refuge Museum. 301 SE MacArthur Blvd. (south of Indian River Plantation resort), Hutchinson Island, Stuart. ☎ **561/225-1875.** Admission $4 adults, $2 children 6–13, free for children 5 and under. Daily 10am–4pm.

Gilbert's, the oldest structure in Martin County, dates from 1875, when it functioned as one of 10 such rescue centers for shipwrecked sailors. After undergoing a thorough rehabilitation to its original condition along the rocky shores, the house now displays marine artifacts and turn-of-the-century lifesaving equipment and photographs and is worth a quick visit to get a feel for the area's early days.

A BOAT TOUR

✪ The *Loxahatchee Queen,* a 35-foot pontoon boat (☎ 561/746-1466) in Jonathan Dickinson State Park in Hobe Sound, makes daily tours of the area's otherwise inaccessible backwater, where curious alligators, manatees, eagles, and tortoises often peek out to see who's in their yard. Try to catch the 2-hour tour, given Wednesday to Sunday as the tide permits, when it includes a stop at Trapper Nelson's home. Known as the "Wildman of Loxahatchee," Nelson lived in primitive conditions—on a remote stretch of the water in a log cabin fashioned from his own hand—which is preserved for visitors to see. Tours leave four times daily at 9am, 11am, 1pm, and 3pm and cost $10 for adults, $5 for children 6 to 12, and free for children 5 and under. See the "Wildlife Exploration" box for more information on the park.

SHOPPING

Downtown Stuart's historic district, along Flagler Avenue between Confusion Corner and St. Lucie Avenue, offers shoppers diversity and quality in a small old-town setting. Shops offer a range of goods: antique bric-a-brac, old lamps and fixtures, books, gourmet foods, furnishings, and souvenirs.

WHERE TO STAY

Although the area boasts some beautiful beaches, the bulk of the hotel scene is downtown, where the nicer (and more reasonably priced) accommodations can be found among the shops and restaurants. There are, however, a few excellent beachfront hotels and inns. One of the bigger hotel chains in the area is the **Holiday Inn.** Its recently renovated, stunning beachfront property is at 3793 NE Ocean Blvd., on Hutchinson Island in Jensen Beach (☎ 800/992-4747 or 561/225-3000). Rates in season range from $130 to $180. Holiday Inn also has a downtown location at 1209 S. Federal Hwy. (☎ 561/287-6200). This simple two-story building on a busy main road is kept in very good shape and is convenient to Stuart's downtown historic district. Rates range from $99 to $140.

VERY EXPENSIVE

✪ **Indian River Plantation Marriott Resort.** 555 NE Ocean Blvd., Hutchinson Island, Stuart, FL 34996. ☎ **800/775-5936** or 561/225-3700. Fax 561/225-0003. www.marriott.com/marriott/pbiir. 299 units. A/C TV TEL. Winter $189–$209 double; from $300 suite. Off-season $99–$139 double; from $149 suite. AE, CB, DC, DISC, MC, V. From downtown Stuart, take E. Ocean Blvd. over two bridges to NE Ocean Blvd.; turn right.

This sprawling 190-acre compound offers so many diversions for active (or not-so-active) vacationers that you won't want to leave. Having undergone more than $6 million worth of renovations in 1998, Indian River is now Hutchinson Island's best resort, occupying the lush grounds of a former pineapple plantation. Family oriented activities include tennis, golfing, and boating. Sportfishing (especially for sailfish) is a big draw here, as are scuba diving and other water sports.

The grand, white lattice-and-wicker lobby is filled with a jungle of plants, and large windows overlook the hotel's swimming pool and tiki bar. Generously sized rooms, some with fully equipped kitchens, are decorated with colorful spreads and draperies.

Some rooms could use a thorough renovation, since old fixtures have suffered from years of exposure to sea air and salt.

Be sure to sign up for a "turtle watch" in the summer months to watch the large turtles crawl onto the sand to lay their eggs.

Dining/Diversions: Scalawags, a seafood restaurant, is the resort's top dining room and is popular with locals. A less-formal restaurant serves continental breakfast, lunch, and all-day snacks. There's live music nightly in two bars.

Amenities: Room service, laundry and dry-cleaning services, newspaper delivery, baby-sitting, express checkout, on-property transportation, free juice in lobby. Four outdoor pools, beach, health club, Jacuzzi, 18-hole golf course, nature trails, some kitchenettes, sundeck, 13 tennis courts (five night-lit), nearby racquetball courts, water-sports equipment, jogging track, bicycle rental, game room, children's program, Spectravision movie channels, self-service Laundromat, conference rooms, car-rental desk, boutiques.

MODERATE

✪ **Harborfront Inn Bed & Breakfast.** 310 Atlanta Ave., Stuart, FL 34994. ☎ **561/ 288-7289.** Fax 561/221-0474. www.harborfrontinn.com. 6 units. A/C TV TEL. Winter $85–$175 double. Free dockage. Off-season discounts available. Rates include breakfast. DISC, MC, V. From I-95 take Exit 61 east to U.S. 1 north; turn left on W. Ocean Blvd. and then make the first right (Atlanta Ave.). No children.

The Harborfront Inn has the advantage of being right on the river, where you can sail, kayak, and ski. It consists of a series of little blue-trimmed shingled cottages within walking distance of the restaurants of downtown Stuart. Each room in this highly recommended B&B has its own private entrance, making it more like a rambling inn. Also, every accommodation has a sitting area and private bathroom. The two best rooms are the bright Garden Suite, which has a queen-size bed, rattan furnishings, and a deck with river and garden views; and the Guest House, which has an extra-large bathroom with two sinks and can be rented with an adjoining full kitchen. Smoking is not permitted.

The inn's cozy public areas are surrounded by an enclosed porch where breakfast is served. The morning meal usually includes fresh fruit from the trees that grow on the property. Amenities include kitchenettes in cottages, VCRs in suites, a Jacuzzi and sundeck, and water-sports equipment rentals.

Hutchinson Inn. 9750 S. Ocean Dr. (Fla. A1A), Jensen Beach, FL 34957. ☎ **561/ 229-2000.** 21 units. A/C TV TEL. Winter from $100 double; $150–$225 efficiency or suite. Off-season $80 double; from $110–$165 efficiency or suite. Rates include continental breakfast. MC, V. From I-95 take Exit 61 east to Monterey; turn right; cross U.S. 1; go to second light, turn right on East Ocean Blvd. Come onto the island. Inn is approx. 8 miles ahead.

It doesn't look like much from the road—only the tennis court is visible—but you'll soon happen upon striking white gazebos dotting thick green lawns. Located directly on the beach, the Hutchinson Inn is a quiet and charming two-story hideaway. Unfortunately, so many people know about it that it's usually booked a year in advance in high season.

The newly refurbished rooms have rattan furnishings; sofas convert into pull-out beds, and several rooms can be joined to accommodate large families.

Amenities include a good swimming beach, a large outdoor pool, one outdoor night-lit tennis court, water-sports equipment, bicycle rentals, and a self-service Laundromat. Freshly baked cookies are offered each evening before bedtime.

Camping

There are comfortable campsites in **Jonathan Dickinson State Park** in Hobe Sound (see the "Wildlife Exploration" box). You can stay overnight in rustic cabins or in your tent or camper in two different sections of the park. The River Camp area offers the benefit of the nearby Loxahatchee River, while the Pine Grove site has beautiful shade trees. There are concession areas for daytime snacks and 135 campsites with showers, clean rest rooms, water, optional electricity, and an open-fire pit for cooking. Overnight rates in the winter are $18 without electricity, $20 with electricity. In the summer, rates are about $14 for four people.

For a more cushy camping experience, reserve a wood-sided cabin with a furnished kitchen, a bathroom with shower, heat and air-conditioning, and an outside grill. Bring your own linens. Cabins rent for $65 and up a night and sleep four people comfortably, six if your group is really into togetherness. Call ☎ **561/546-2771** Monday to Friday from 9am to 5pm, well in advance to reserve a spot. A $50 key deposit is required.

Where to Dine
Expensive

Eleven Maple Street. 11 Maple St., Jensen Beach. ☎ **561/334-7714.** Reservations recommended. Main courses $16–$29. MC, V. Wed–Sun 6–10pm. Head east on Jensen Beach Blvd. and turn right after the railroad tracks. AMERICAN.

The most highly rated restaurant in Jensen Beach, Eleven Maple Street occupies a lovely little house with a white picket fence, French doors, lace curtains, and pink-clothed tables. Dining is both indoors and out, in any one of a series of cozy dining rooms or on a covered patio surrounded by gardens. Straightforward meat and fish dishes run the gamut from local seafood to game and poultry such as venison and duck. Maine lobster, filet mignon, and pastas are also available, and most everything is spiced with fresh-picked herbs from the restaurant's own organic garden.

Flagler Grill. 47 SW Flagler Ave. (just before the Roosevelt Bridge), downtown Stuart. ☎ **561/221-9517.** Reservations strongly suggested in season. Main courses $17–$25. AE, MC, V. Winter daily 5:30–10pm. Off-season Thurs–Sat 5:30–9:30pm. Lounge and bar open to 11:30pm. AMERICAN/FLORIDA REGIONAL.

In the heart of historic downtown, this Manhattan-style bistro serves up classics with a twist. The dishes are not so unusual as to alienate the conservative pink-shirted golfers who frequent the place, yet they're fresh and light enough to quench the appetites of the more adventurous—for example, the saffron and mushroom pasta with Cajun shrimp and roasted tomatoes. The menu changes every few weeks, so see what your server recommends. It's hard to go wrong with any of the many salads, pastas, fishes, or delectable beef choices. The desserts, too, are worth the calories. Note that the restaurant and bar are no smoking.

Moderate

Black Marlin. 53 W. Osceola St., downtown Stuart. ☎ **561/286-3126.** Reservations not accepted. Salads and sandwiches $4–$8; full meals $9–$24. AE, MC, V. Mon–Thurs 5–10pm, Fri–Sat 5–11pm (the bar is open later). FLORIDA REGIONAL.

Although it sports the look and feel of an English pub, the Black Marlin offers regional flavor. The salmon BLT is typical of the dishes here—grilled salmon on a toasted bun topped with bacon, lettuce, tomato, and coleslaw. Designer pizzas are topped with shrimp, roasted red peppers, and the like; and main dishes, all of which are served with vegetables and potatoes, include lobster tail with a honey-mustard sauce, and a charcoal-grilled chicken breast served on radicchio with caramelized onions.

Conchy Joe's Seafood. 3945 NE Indian River Dr. ($1/2$ mile from the Jensen Beach Causeway), Jensen Beach. ☎ **561/334-1130.** Main courses $12–$20. AE, DISC, MC, V. Daily 11:30am–2:30pm and 5–10pm (happy hour daily 3–6pm). SEAFOOD.

Known for fresh seafood and Old Florida hospitality, Conchy Joe's enjoys an excellent reputation that's far bigger than the restaurant itself. Dining is either indoors, at red-and-white cloth-covered tables, or on a covered patio overlooking the St. Lucie River. The restaurant features a wide variety of freshly shucked shellfish and daily-catch selections that are baked, broiled, or fried. Beer is the drink of choice here, though other beverages and a full bar are available. Conchy Joe's has been the most active place in Jensen Beach since it opened in 1983. The large bar is especially popular at night and during weekday happy hours.

INEXPENSIVE

✪ **Bubba's Fish Camp.** 421 S. Federal Hwy. (at south side of Roosevelt Bridge), Stuart. ☎ **561/220-3747.** Full meals $8–$10; seafood specials $8–$12. AE, MC, V. Daily 11am–10pm and later on weekends. Call for details on weekend breakfasts. SEAFOOD/SOUTHERN.

Run by the same family who created the lovely B&B Home Place, and just a stone's throw from there, is an ultracasual spot designed to resemble an old-Florida fish camp. Don't miss the great crawfish gumbo, corn bread, catfish, creamy spinach, hush puppies (fried cornmeal), and fried green tomatoes, too. After 4pm, you'll find bargain deals on hearty Southern classics like meat loaf, baked Virginia ham with red-eye gravy, fried chicken, and pork chops. Each includes a choice of delicious side dishes. Fresh and crispy onion rings are actually served on tiny bathroom plunger handles. Locals and highway travelers line up outside the screen porch to get into this rustic eatery just at the base of the new Roosevelt Bridge.

✪ **Nature's Way Cafe.** 25 SW Osceola St., in the Post Office Arcade, Stuart. ☎ **561/220-7306.** Sandwiches and salads $4–$7; juices and shakes $1–$3. No credit cards. Mon–Fri 10am–4pm, Sat 11am–3pm. HEALTH FOOD.

This lovely, clean and green dining room has dozens of little tables, a few barstools, and some sidewalk seating, too. A sort of health-food deli, Nature's Way excels in putting out quick and nutritious meals like huge salads, vegetarian sandwiches, and frozen yogurts. Try some of the homemade baked goods. Sit outside on quaint Osceola Street or ask them to pack your lunch for you to take to the beach.

STUART & JENSEN BEACH AFTER DARK

Local restaurants serve as the nightlife centers of Stuart and Jensen Beach. And "night" ends pretty early here, even on the weekends. The bar at the Black Marlin (see "Where to Dine," above) is popular with local professionals and tourists alike.

No list of Jensen nightlife would be complete without mention of Conchy Joe's Seafood (see "Where to Dine," above), one of the region's most active spots. Inside, locals chug beer and watch a large-screen TV, while outside on the waterfront patio, live bands perform a few nights a week for a raucous crowd of dancers. Happy hours, weekdays from 3 to 6pm, draw large crowds with low-priced drinks and snacks. No cover.

In a strip mall just outside of downtown, you'll find pickup trucks as far as the eye can see parked outside the **Rock 'n' Horse,** 1580 S. Federal Hwy. (U.S. 1), Stuart (☎ **561/286-1281**). It's a real locals' country-and-western spot that rocks, especially on Tuesday night, when women drink all night for $5. Bring your hat and boots for line dancing, beer drinking, and a good time in one of the only real late-night spots in town. Cover varies.

The centerpiece of Stuart's slowly expanding cultural offerings is the newly restored **Lyric Theater,** at 59 SW Flagler Ave. (☎ **561/286-7827**). This beautiful 1920s-era, 600-seat theater hosts a variety of shows and films throughout the year. Programs run the gamut from amateur plays to top-name theatrical shows, poetry readings, and concerts.

2 Port St. Lucie, Fort Pierce & North Hutchinson Island

7 miles N of Stuart

Port St. Lucie and Fort Pierce, two Old Florida towns, thrive on sportfishing. A seemingly endless row of piers juts out along the Intracoastal Waterway and the Fort Pierce Inlet for both river and ocean runs. Here visitors can also dive, snorkel, beachcomb, and sunbathe in an area that hasn't been visited by the overdevelopment that has altered its neighbors to the south and north.

Most sightseeing takes place along the main beach road. Driving along Fla. A1A on Hutchinson Island, you'll discover several secluded beach clubs interspersed with 1950s-style homes, a few small inns, grungy raw bars, and a few high-rise condominiums. Much of this island is government owned and kept undeveloped for the public's enjoyment.

ESSENTIALS

The **St. Lucie County Chamber of Commerce,** 2200 Virginia Ave., Fort Pierce, FL 34982 (☎ **561/595-9999**), is the region's main source of information. There's another branch at 1626 SE Port St. Lucie Blvd., in Port St. Lucie. Both spots are open Monday through Friday from 9am to 5pm.

BEACHES & NATURE PRESERVES

North Hutchinson Island's beaches are the most pristine in this area. You won't find restaurants, hotels, or shopping; instead, spend your time swimming, surfing, fishing, and diving. Most of the beaches are private along this stretch of the Atlantic Ocean. Thankfully, the state has set aside some of the best areas for the public.

Fort Pierce Inlet State Recreation Area (☎ **561/468-3985**) is a stunning 340-acre park with almost 4,000 feet of sandy shores that was once the training ground for the original navy frogmen. A short nature trail leads through a canopy of live oaks, cabbage palms, sea grapes, and strangler figs. The western side of the area has swamps of red mangroves that are home to fiddler crabs, osprey, and a multitude of wading birds. Jack Island State Preserve, in the State Recreation Area, is popular with bird watchers and offers hiking and nature trails. Jutting out into the Indian River, the mangrove-covered peninsula contains several marked trails, varying in distance from a half mile to over 4 miles. The trails go through mangrove forests and lead to a short observation tower.

The best beach here, called Jetty Park, lies in the northern part of the park. Families enjoy the large picnic areas and barbecue grills. There are rest rooms and outdoor showers, and swimmers are looked after by lifeguards.

The park is located at 905 Shorewinds Dr., north of Fort Pierce Inlet. To get there from I-95, take Exit 66 east (Route 68) and turn left onto U.S. 1 north; in about 2 miles, you will see signs to Fla. A1A and the North Bridge Causeway. Turn right on A1A and cross over to North Hutchinson Island. Admission is $3.25 per vehicle, and it's open daily from 8am to sunset.

SPECTATOR SPORTS & OUTDOOR PURSUITS

BASEBALL The **New York Mets** hold spring training in Port St. Lucie from late February through March at the **Thomas J. White Stadium,** 525 NW Peacock Blvd. (☎ **561/871-2115**). Tickets cost $9 to $12. From April through August, their farm team, the Port St. Lucie Mets, plays home games in the stadium.

FISHING The **Fort Pierce City Marina,** 1 Avenue A, Fort Pierce (☎ **561/464-1245**), has more than a dozen charter captains who keep their motors running for anglers anxious to catch a few. The price starts at $150 per person for half-day tours, depending on the season. Charters are organized on an as-desired basis. In general, plan to arrive very early in the morning (by 6am) before all the other early birds.

GOLF The most notable courses in Port St. Lucie are at the **PGA Golf Club at the Reserve** (☎ **561/467-1300**), at 1916 Perfect Dr. The club's first public golf course opened in January 1996 and was designed by Tom Fazio; it will soon complete its fourth 18-hole course. The South Course, a classic Old Florida–style course, is set on wetlands and offers views of native wildlife. It is the most popular. Greens fees are usually under $60.

SEEING THE SIGHTS

Harbor Branch Oceanographic Institution. 5600 U.S. 1 N., Fort Pierce. ☎ **800/333-4264** or 561/465-2400. www.hboi.com. Admission $10 adults, $6 children 6–12, free for children 5 and under. Mon–Sat 10am–4pm (tours scheduled at 10am, noon, and 2pm); Sun noon–5pm (tours scheduled at noon and 2pm). Arrive at least 20 min. before tour.

Harbor Branch is a working nonprofit scientific institute that studies oceanic resources and welcomes visitors on regularly scheduled tours. The first stop is the J. Seward Johnson Marine Education Center, which houses institute-built submersibles that are used to conduct marine research at depths of up to 3,000 feet. A video details current research projects, and several large aquariums simulate the environments of the Indian River Lagoon and a saltwater reef. Tourists are then shuttled by minibus to the Aqua-Culture Farming Center, a research facility containing shallow tanks growing seaweed and other oceanic plants. The new Lagoon Explorer Cruise, examining the Indian River Lagoon, departs at 10am, noon, and 2pm; the price is $15 adults, $12 children 3 to 13.

UDT-SEAL Museum. 3300 N. S.R. A1A, Fort Pierce. ☎ **561/595-5845.** Admission $4 adults, $1.25 children, free for children 6 and under. Mon–Sat 10am–4pm, Sun noon–4pm. Closed Mon in off-season.

Florida is full of unique museums, but none is more curious than the UDT-SEAL Museum, a most peculiar tribute to the secret forces of the U.S. Navy frogmen and their successors, the SEAL teams. Chronological displays trace the history of these clandestine divers and detail their most important achievements. The best exhibits are those of the intricately detailed equipment used by the navy's most elite members.

A BOAT TOUR

St. Lucie River Tours, 500 E. Prima Vista Blvd. (☎ **561/871-2817**), offers intriguing tours of the St. Lucie River twice daily (at 10:45am and again at 1pm). The 2-hour tours go through winding waterways that are home to hundreds of wading birds and reptiles. This historical and wildlife tour is well worth the $15 for adults and $7 for children under 12.

WHERE TO STAY

The Port St. Lucie mainland is pretty run-down, but there are a number of inexpensive hotel options on scenic Hutchinson Island that are both charming and well priced. Probably the best option is the **Hampton Inn** (☎ **800/426-7866** or 561/460-9855), 2831 Reynolds Dr., which is relatively new and beautifully maintained. However, if you want to be closer to the water, try the **Days Inn Hutchinson Island,** 1920 Seaway Dr. (☎ **800/325-2525** or 561/461-8737), a small motel that sits along the intracoastal inlet and is simple but very well kept.

Budget travelers will be glad to know about the **Edgewater Motel and Apartments,** 1160 Seaway Dr. (next door to and under the same ownership as the Harbor Light Inn), Fort Pierce (☎ **800/286-1745** or 561/468-3555). Motel rooms start at less than $60 in high season, and efficiencies are also available from $80. Guests can enjoy a private pool, shuffleboard courts, and a nearby fishing pier.

Expensive

Club Med—Sandpiper. 3500 SE Morningside Blvd., Port St. Lucie, FL 34952. ☎ **800/CLUB-MED** or 561/335-4400. Fax 561/398-5101. www.clubmed.com. 338 units. A/C TV TEL. Winter $170–$280 per person, based on double occupancy. Off-season $150–$275 per person, based on double occupancy. Rates include 3 meals per day. AE, MC, V. From U.S. 1 south, turn left onto Westmoreland Blvd.; turn left onto Pine Valley Rd.; the resort entrance is straight ahead.

The Sandpiper is not one of the French-owned company's flagship properties. It's a decent resort housed in buildings that could use a major overhaul. A former Hilton Hotel, the 400-acre resort was purchased by Club Med in 1985 and marketed to Europeans looking for a Florida getaway. They come in droves with all the kids and nannies for a sunny, active vacation with meals for a reasonable prepaid price. The drawback is that guests are 20 minutes from the nearest beach. On the grounds there are plenty of diversions, such as golf, tennis, and waterskiing, sailing, and boating on the Indian River. There's even a circus school.

As in most other Club Meds, the rooms are sparse and small, but pleasant enough. All come with in-room safes, large closets, tiled bathrooms, and minirefrigerators.

Dining/Diversions: All-you-can-eat buffets are served in the main dining room three times a day. In addition, La Fontana serves late breakfasts and Italian cuisine at dinner, and a French restaurant is open for dinner. Excellent live entertainment is provided in bars and a showroom nightly. Another bonus is free wine and beer at lunch and dinner.

Amenities: Laundry services, massage, baby-sitting. Five outdoor heated pools, kids' pool, fitness center, three golf courses (36-hole, 18-hole, and 9-hole), 19 tennis courts (9 of which are lighted), circus workshops, Ping-Pong and billiards, children's center and programs, water-sports equipment, self-service Laundromat, tour desk, boutique, conference rooms, car-rental desk, waterskiing, volleyball courts, basketball, softball, soccer, boccie, exercise classes, in-line skating.

Moderate

Dockside–Harbor Light Resort. 1160 Seaway Dr., Fort Pierce, Hutchinson Island, FL 34949. ☎ **800/286-1745** or 561/468-3555. Fax 561/489-9848. 64 units. www.docksideinn.com. A/C MINIBAR TV TEL. Winter $50–$95 guest rooms; $67–$95 efficiencies. Off-season $43–$84 guest rooms and efficiencies. AE, CB, DC, DISC, MC, V. From I-95, exit at 66A east to U.S. 1 north to Seaway Dr.

Fronting the Intracoastal Waterway, the Harbor Light is a great choice for boating and fishing enthusiasts, offering 15 boat slips and two private fishing piers. The hotel itself carries on the nautical theme with pierlike wooden stairs and rope railings. While not exactly captain's quarters, the rooms, simply decorated with pastel colors and small wall prints, are attractive, especially since a thorough renovation completed in 1999. Higher-priced rooms have either waterfront balconies or small kitchenettes that contain a coffeemaker, a refrigerator, an oven, and a toaster. Facilities include an outdoor heated pool with a large sundeck and a self-service Laundromat.

Mellon Patch Inn. 3601 N. Fla. A1A, North Hutchinson Island, FL 34949. ☎ **800/MLN-PTCH** or 561/461-5231. Fax 561/464-6346. www.sunet.net/mlnptch. 4 units. A/C TV TEL. $85–$150 double year-round. Rates include breakfast. AE, DISC, MC, V. Children not accepted.

Opened in mid-1994 by innkeepers Andrea and Arthur Mellon, the Mellon Patch offers just four bright rooms in what looks like a single-family house, each with a large bathroom and sturdy soundproof walls.

The public living room is nicer than any of the small guest rooms. It's designed with a two-story vaulted ceiling, a fireplace, and lots of windows that overlook the Indian River. A gourmet breakfast that might include waffles topped with strawberries and pecans, chocolate-chip pancakes, or spinach soufflé is served here each morning. The best part is there are free tennis courts and a public beach across the street. The inn is smoke-free.

✪ **Villa Nina Island Beach Bed & Breakfast.** 3851 North A1A, N. Hutchinson Island, FL 34949. ☎ and fax **561/467-8673.** www.villanina.com. 4 units. Winter $125–$195. Off-season $105–$165. DISC, MC, V.

A more private option just down the road from the Mellon Patch is Villa Nina, in another simple but brand-new home on the river's edge. Innkeepers Nina and Glenn live in the main house and have built rooms along the back, each with a private entrance and either a fully equipped kitchen or kitchenette. Enjoy breakfast delivered to your room or near the outdoor heated pool. Guests are free to use the laundry facilities, and there are canoes and rowboats for river rides on this stunning 8-acre property. Smoking is not allowed. The nearby casino cruise ship called the *Midnight Gambler* is also available to guests (☎ **561/464-7773**), which includes a 5-hour tour with food and drink.

The honeymoon suite in the back is the largest and brightest of all the pleasant rooms. Night-lit tennis and basketball courts, a public beach, and nature trails are just across the street.

WHERE TO DINE
There are a number of good seafood restaurants in the Fort Pierce and St. Lucie area, but it's also easy to drive to Stuart for more diverse dining options. See section 1 of this chapter for recommendations in Stuart.

MODERATE
✪ **Harbortown Fish House.** 1930 Harbortown Dr., Fort Pierce. ☎ **561/466-8732.** Reservations accepted. Main courses $14–$20. AE, DISC, MC, V. Sun–Thurs 11:30am–9pm, Fri–Sat 5–10pm. SEAFOOD.

You have to drive to the end of the harbor to reach this open-air waterfront fish house. It's a rustic place with outdoor tables overlooking the port, and you might be surprised to learn that it serves the area's best and freshest seafood. The menu is posted on white boards throughout the dining room and might include jumbo shrimp cocktail or New England clam chowder. The list of main courses is long and contains both fish and meat dishes. Dishes include angel-hair pasta with scallop- and anchovy-stuffed mushrooms, roast Muscovy duck with wild-mushroom risotto, and charcoal-grilled pepper-crusted tuna served over sautéed escarole.

★ **P.V. Martin's.** 5150 N. Fla. A1A (North Hutchinson Island), Fort Pierce. ☎ **561/569-0700.** Reservations recommended. Main courses $9–$20. AE, MC, V. Mon–Sat 11am–3:30pm and 5–9pm, Sun 10:30am–2:30pm and 5–8:30pm. SEAFOOD/AMERICAN.

This relatively elegant eatery with an eclectic American menu is tops in Fort Pierce. The wood floors, beamed ceilings, tiled-top tables, and rattan chairs would be nice anywhere, but here they look out, through floor-to-ceiling windows, onto sweeping ocean vistas. At night, the room is warmed by a huge central stone fireplace, and on weekends there's live entertainment in the adjacent bar.

Surf-and-turf dinners run the gamut from crab-stuffed shrimp and grouper baked with bananas and almonds to Brie- and asparagus-stuffed chicken breast and barbecued baby back ribs. An excellent selection of appetizers includes escargots in mushroom caps and a succulent fried soft-shell crab (available in season).

Theo Thudpucker's Raw Bar and Seafood Restaurant. 2025 Seaway Dr., Fort Pierce. ☎ **561/465-1078.** Reservations not accepted. Main courses $8–$24. MC, V. Mon–Thurs 11:30am–9:30pm, Fri–Sat 11:30am–11pm, Sun 1–9:30pm. SEAFOOD.

Located in a little building by the beach, wallpapered with maps and newspapers, Thudpucker's is a straightforward chowder bar. There's not much more to the dining room than one long bar and a few simple tables. Prominently placed signs attest to the food's purity: Both clams and oysters are packed with ice and are not opened until you place your order. Please be patient. Chowder and stews, often made with sherry and half-and-half, make excellent starters or light meals. The most recommendable (and filling) dinner dishes are sautéed scallops, deviled crabs, and deep-fried Okeechobee catfish.

PORT ST. LUCIE/FORT PIERCE AFTER DARK

Besides a few heavy-drinking bars, waterside restaurants (see P.V. Martin's, above), and hotel lounges, the nightlife of Port St. Lucie and Fort Pierce takes place in the neighboring towns north and south of here. See sections 1 and 3 of this chapter for nightspots in Stuart, Jensen Beach, Vero Beach, and Sebastian.

3 Vero Beach & Sebastian

85 miles SE of Orlando, 130 miles N of Miami

Vero Beach and Sebastian are located at the northern tip of the Treasure Coast region in Indian River County. These two beach towns are populated with folks who knew Miami and Fort Lauderdale in the days before massive high-rises and overcrowding. They appreciate the area's small-town feel, and that's exactly the area's appeal for visitors, as well: a laid-back, relaxed atmosphere, friendly people, and friendlier prices.

A crowd of well-tanned surfers from all over the state descend on the region, especially the Sebastian Inlet, to catch some of the state's biggest waves. Water-sports enthusiasts enjoy the area's fine diving, surfing, and windsurfing. Anglers are in heaven here. In spring, baseball buffs can catch some action from the L.A. Dodgers as they train in exhibition games.

ESSENTIALS

The **Indian River County Tourist Council,** 1216 21st St., Vero Beach, FL 32961 (☎ **561/567-3491;** fax 561/778-3181; www.vero-beach.fl.us/chamber), will send visitors an incredibly detailed information packet on the entire county, which includes Vero Beach and Sebastian and Fellsmere. You'll find a detailed full-color map of the area, a comprehensive listing of upcoming events, a hotel guide, and more.

BEACHES & OUTDOOR PURSUITS

BEACHES You'll find plenty of free and open beachfront along the coast. Most beaches are uncrowded and are open from 7am until 10pm.

South Beach Park, on South Ocean Drive, at the end of Marigold Lane, is a busy, developed, lifeguarded beach with picnic tables, rest rooms, and showers. It's known as one of the best swimming beaches and also attracts a young crowd that plays volleyball and Frisbee. A well-laid-out nature walk takes you into beautiful secluded trails.

At the very north tip of the island, ✪ **Sebastian Inlet** has flat sandy beaches with lots of facilities, including kayak, paddleboat, and canoe rentals; a well-stocked surf shop; picnic tables; and a snack shop. The winds seem to stir up the surf with no jetty to stop their swells, to the delight of surfers and boarders, who get here early to catch the big waves. Campers enjoy fully equipped sites in a woody area. Admission to the Sebastian Inlet State Recreation Area, 9700 S. A1A, Melbourne, is $3.25 per car and $1 for those who walk or bike in.

FISHING Capt. Jack Jackson works 7 days a week out of **Vero's Tackle and Sportshop,** 57–59 Royal Palm Point (☎ **561/567-6550**), taking anglers out on his 25-foot boat for private river excursions. Captain Jackson provides all the equipment. Half-day jaunts on the Indian River cost $175 for two people (the minimum required for a charter).

You can also head up to Sebastian, where **Capt. Hiram's,** 1606 Indian River Rd. (☎ **800/797-1582** or 561/589-5433), offers private sailboat charters on the Indian River. In addition, it runs a party boat, the *Capt. Kidd II,* which heads out daily for a full day of bottom fishing for grouper, snapper, and more (it's usually only a half day on Mon). The cost is $35 per person ($40 per person will get you your rod, reel, and bait). You can bring your own lunch and beer on board, and someone will be available to clean your fish for you. Call ahead to reserve your place.

Many other charters, guides, party boats, and tackle shops operate in this area. Ask at your hotel for suggestions, or call the chamber of commerce for a list of local operators.

GOLF Hard-core golfers insist that of the dozens of courses in the area, only a handful are worth their plot of grass.

Set on rolling hills with uncluttered views of sand dunes and sky, the **Sandridge Golf Club** (☎ **561/770-5000**), at 5300 73rd St., Vero Beach, offers two par-72 18-holers. The Dunes is a long course with rolling fairways, and the newer Lakes course has lots of water. Both charge less than $50, including a cart. There is a small snack bar selling beer and sandwiches. Reservations are recommended and are taken 2 days in advance.

Though less challenging, the **Sebastian Municipal Golf Course** (☎ **561/589-6800**), at 1010 E. Airport Dr., is a good 18-hole par-72. It's scenic, well maintained, and a great bargain. Greens fees are $33 with a cart and about half that if you want to play 9 holes after 1:30pm.

Also, see "Dodgertown," below.

SURFING See Sebastian Inlet details under "Beaches," above. Also, consider the beach north of the Barber Bridge (S.R. 70), where waves are slightly gentler and the scene less competitive, and Wabasso Beach, Fla. A1A and County Road 510, a secluded area near Disney's resort where lots of teenage locals congregate, especially when the weather gets rough.

TENNIS There are dozens of tennis courts around Vero Beach and Sebastian, many of which are at hotels and resorts. Check the phone book, or try **Riverside Park,** 350

Dahlia Lane, at Royal Palm Boulevard at the east end of Barber Bridge in Vero Beach (☎ 561/231-4787). This popular park has 10 hard courts (6 lighted) that can be rented for $3 per person per hour, and two racquetball courts with reasonable rates as well. Reservations are accepted up to 24 hours in advance. On the premises, you'll also find nature trails and other facilities.

SEEING THE SIGHTS

Environmental Learning Center. 255 Live Oak Dr. (just off the 510 Causeway), Wabasso Island. ☎ **561/589-5050.** www.elcweb.org. Free admission. Tues–Fri 10am–4pm, Sat 9am–noon, Sun 1–4pm.

The Indian River is not really a river at all, but a large brackish lagoon that's home to a greater variety of species than any other estuary in North America. The privately funded Environmental Learning Center was created to protect the local habitat and educate visitors about their environment. Situated on 51 island acres, the center features dozens of hands-on exhibits that are geared to both children and adults. There are live touch tanks, exhibits, and microscopes for viewing the smallest sea life close up. The best thing to do here is join one of the center's interpretive canoe trips, offered by reservation only. The cost for these is $10 for adults, $5 for children. Phone for details.

Indian River Citrus Museum. 2140 14th Ave., Vero Beach. ☎ **561/770-2263.** Admission $1 donation. Tues–Fri 10am–4pm.

The tiny Indian River Citrus Museum exhibits artifacts relating to the history of the citrus industry, from its initial boom in the late 1800s to the present. Also, a small grove has taped information on the varieties of fruits there. The gift shop sells unique citrus-themed gift items, along with, of course, ready-to-ship fruit.

McKee Botanical Garden. 350 U.S. 1, Vero Beach. ☎ **561/794-0601.** Fax 561/794-0602. www.mckeegarden.org.

This impressive attraction was originally opened in 1932 and featured a virtual jungle of orchids, exotic and native trees, monkeys, and birds. After years of neglect, it was placed on the National Register of Historic Places in 1998. It underwent a top-to-bottom overhaul that was completed in February 2000.

✪ **McLarty Treasure Museum.** 13180 N. A1A, Sebastian Inlet State Recreation Area, Vero Beach. ☎ **561/589-2147.** Admission $1, children under 6 free. Daily 10am–4:30pm.

Erected on the actual site of a salvaging camp from a wreck in 1715, this quaint little museum is full of interesting history. It may not have the vast treasures of the nearby Fisher museum, but it does offer a very engaging 45-minute video describing the many aspects of treasure hunting. You'll also see household items salvaged from the Spanish fleet and dioramas of life in the 18th century. For the price, you can't beat it.

Mel Fisher's Treasure Museum. 1322 U.S. 1, Sebastian. ☎ **561/589-9874.** www.melfisher.com. Admission $5 adults, $4 seniors over 55, $1.50 children 6–12, free for children 5 and under. Mon–Sat 10am–5pm, Sun noon–5pm.

Here's where you can see millions of dollars of treasures from the fateful fleet that went down in 1715. Though not as extensive as the museum in Key West, this exhibit includes gold coins, bars, and Spanish artifacts that are worth a look. Also, the preservation lab shows how the goods are extricated, cleaned, and preserved.

DODGERTOWN

Vero is the winter home of the **Los Angeles Dodgers** (at least for the time being; there's been talk of a move), and the town hosts the team in grand style. The 450-acre compound at 3901 26th St. (☎ 561/569-4900) encompasses two golf courses, a conference center, a country club, a movie theater, and a recreation room. You can watch afternoon exhibition games during the winter (usually between mid-February and the end of March) in the comfortable 6,500-seat outdoor stadium. Even if the game sells out, you can sprawl on the lawn for just $5. The stadium has never turned away an eager fan.

Even when spring training is over, you can still catch a game; the Dodgers's farm team, the Vero Beach Dodgers, has a full season of minor-league baseball in summer.

Admission to the complex is free; tickets to games are $5 to $9. The complex is open daily from 9am to 5pm; game time is usually 1pm. From I-95 take Exit S.R. 60 east to 43rd Avenue, and turn left; continue to 26th Street, and turn right.

SHOPPING

Ocean Boulevard and Cardinal Drive are Vero's two main shopping streets. Both are near the beach and lined with specialty boutiques, including antique and home-decorating shops.

If you want to send fruit back home, the local source is **Hale Indian River Groves,** 615 Beachland Blvd. (☎ **561/231-1752**), a shipper of local citrus and jams since 1947. Note that it is closed 2 to 3 months a year, usually from summer through early fall, depending on the year's crop; the season runs generally from November through Easter. There are four locations in Vero Beach.

The **Horizon Outlet Center,** at S.R. 60 and I-95, Vero Beach (☎ **877/GO-OUTLET** or 561/770-6171), contains more than 80 discount stores selling name-brand shoes, kitchenware, books, clothing, and anything else you could want. The mall is open Monday to Saturday from 9am to 8pm and Sunday from 11am to 6pm.

The **Indian River Mall** (☎ **561/770-6255**), 6200 20th St. (S.R. 60 about 5 miles east of I-95), which opened its doors in November 1996, is a big deal in Vero Beach. This monster mall has all the big national chains, like The Gap, Structure, and Victoria's Secret, as well as several large department stores, and is open Monday through Saturday from 10am to 9pm and Sunday from noon to 6pm.

WHERE TO STAY

You can stay on the mainland or at the beach. Although the beaches in many areas have eroded, leaving only narrow strips of sand, most areas offer pristine beachfronts where turtles lay eggs and sand crabs scurry around. As you might expect, the beachfront accommodations are a bit more expensive—but, I think, worth it. There are deals to be had in the chain hotels and some lovely privately owned properties, especially on weekdays and during off-season. Both **The Palm Court Inn** (☎ **800/245-3297** or 561/231-2800), at 3244 Ocean Dr., and the **Holiday Inn Oceanside** (☎ **800/465-4329** or 561/231-2300), at 3384 Ocean Dr., offer oceanfront rooms and suites at comparable prices (from around $80 for a standard room off-season to $185 for an oceanfront suite). The Holiday Inn may be a better choice since it offers discounts to AAA members and its restaurant and lounge directly face the ocean. The Palm Court (formerly a Days Inn) was thoroughly renovated in 1998. Also, a great spot to know, especially if you are planning to fish, is **Capt. Hiram's** (see "Fishing," above, and also "Vero Beach & Sebastian After Dark," below), where there are four clean and cozy rooms available adjacent to the restaurant and overlooking the water. Rates are between $80 and $110.

Comfortable and inexpensive chain options near the Vero Beach Outlet Center off S.R. 60 include a **Holiday Inn Express** (☎ **800/465-4329** or 561/567-2500), opened in June 1998, and a slightly older **Hampton Inn** (☎ **800/426-7866** or 561/770-4299). Rates for both run between $70 and $80 and include breakfast and free local phone calls.

EXPENSIVE

✪ **Disney's Vero Beach Resort.** 9250 Island Grove Terrace, Vero Beach, FL 32963. ☎ **800/359-8000** or 561/234-2000. Fax 561/234-2030. 112 units, 60 cottages. A/C TV TEL. Winter inn room from $170; ocean view from $190; one bedroom villa from $250; two bedroom villa from $325. Off season inn room from $145; inn-ocean view/studio from $165; one-bedroom villa from $230; two-bedroom villa from $300; three-bedroom beach cottage from $700 year-round (sleeps up to 12 persons). AE, MC, V. From I-95 take Exit 69 (512 east); turn right onto County Rd. 510 east; turn right onto S. Fla. A1A.

Situated on the tip of one of the most pristine beaches on the coast, this Disney timeshare resort takes advantage of its setting by offering truly exciting children's programs like canoe adventures, poolside miniature golf, stories around a campfire, a trip to a working cattle ranch, and stargazing from a powerful telescope. The best part is a large lagoonlike pool with a huge winding slide that elicits squeals of delight from kids and adults alike. And, for younger kids, a pirate ship that squirts water is a fun way to cool off. The resort offers reservation-only Disney character breakfasts on select days and is less than 2 hours away from Walt Disney World.

The sprawling complex, opened in 1995, is designed to resemble a turn-of-the-century Florida beach community, complete with sand-washed buildings and faux-worn furniture. The beachside cottages are huge and tasteful. The villas have fully equipped kitchens, with dishwashers and microwaves.

Dining/Diversions: The resort offers some of the best food in the region. An elegant steak house, Sonya's, serves dinner from an eclectic, Florida-inspired menu with superb steaks, pecan-crusted salmon, and salads. In addition, a casual restaurant for lunch and dinner serves interesting pizzas, sandwiches, salads, roasted vegetables, and pastas. A picturesque lounge, which overlooks the ocean and hosts live music most nights, is popular with guests, and locals occasionally stop in. A poolside snack bar rounds out this resort's food and drink options.

Amenities: Concierge, room service, laundry services for inn rooms, dry cleaning, newspapers in lobby, express checkout, secretarial services during business hours, baby-sitting, free morning coffee in lobby. Large theme-based pool with two-story pool slide, as well as a treasure-ship pool deck, beach, health club, Jacuzzi, sauna, sundeck, nature trails, kitchenettes, VCRs, video rentals, shuffleboard, croquet lawn, two night-lit tennis courts, water-sports equipment, jogging track, tee times available at local courses, nine-hole miniature golf, basketball half-court, volleyball, tetherball, game room, extensive children's programs, conference rooms, business center, self-service Laundromat, tour desk/guest services, gift shop, general store.

Doubletree Guest Suites. 3500 Ocean Dr., Vero Beach, FL 32963. ☎ **800/841-5666** or 561/231-5666. Fax 561/234-4866. 55 units. A/C TV TEL. Winter $235–$265 one-bedroom suite. Off-season $125–$185 one-bedroom suite. AE, CB, DC, DISC, MC, V.

Vero's best all-suite hotel, part of the Doubletree chain, is located directly on the beach and is close to local restaurants and shops. First-class accommodations are located in a modern four-story building. The guest rooms, renovated in late 1996, are unremarkable, but clean and attractive. What the nearly identical suites lack in character they make up for in content. The rooms are equipped with small refrigerators and coffeemakers, two phones, and modern bathrooms that include hair dryers.

Dining/Diversions: The Lanai Room is open for breakfast only, daily from 7am to 10pm. The Seabreeze pool bar is open daily for lunch, dinner, and cocktails.

MODERATE

Driftwood Resort. 3150 Ocean Dr., Vero Beach, FL 32963. ☎ 561/231-0550. Fax 561/234-1981. 100 units. A/C TV TEL. Winter $110–$250 double. Off-season $89–$130 double. AE, MC, V.

Originally planned in the 1930s as a private estate by local legend Waldo Sexton, the Driftwood was opened to the public after several travelers stopped to inquire about renting a room here. Today the hotel's rooms and public areas are filled with the nautical knickknacks collected by Sexton on his travels all over the world.

All the guest rooms are different. Some feature terra-cotta–tiled floors and lighter furniture, while others have a more rustic feel with hardwoods and antiques. Each accommodation has its own bathroom and few frills. The resort, which was recently listed on the National Register of Historic Places, offers two outdoor heated pools, a sometimes-narrow beach, a bicycle trail, dry-cleaning services, and VCR and video rentals.

✪ **Islander Motel.** 3101 Ocean Dr., Vero Beach, FL 32963. ☎ **800/952-5886** or 561/231-4431. 16 units. A/C TV TEL. Winter $95–$120 double. Off-season $69–$105 double. Efficiencies cost $10 extra. AE, MC, V.

Resident owner Tom Collins runs one of the most comfortable and welcoming inns in the area. Well located in downtown Vero Beach, this motel is just a short walk to the beach, restaurants, and shops. Every guest room has a small refrigerator and either a king-size bed or two double beds. The accommodations are designed in a Caribbean motif with bright fabrics and white rattan furniture. There is a pool and a barbecue area in the handsomely landscaped central courtyard, along with a small walk-up cafe.

INEXPENSIVE

Davis House Inn. 607 Davis St., Sebastian, FL 32958. ☎ **561/589-4114.** Fax 561/589-1722. 12 units. Winter $69–$79 double. Off-season $59–$79 double. A/C TV TEL. Rates include continental breakfast. Weekly and monthly rates available. AE, DISC, MC, V. From I-95, take Exit 69 east to Indian River Dr., turn left, go 1$^1/_4$ miles to Davis St., turn left.

Each of the dozen rooms in this contemporary, three-story, blue-and-white bed-and-breakfast on the mainland has a private entrance and door-front parking. The rooms are large and clean, although somewhat plain, and each has a king-size bed, a pull-out sofa, and a small kitchenette, making the rooms popular with long-term guests. The bathrooms are equally ample and have plenty of counter space. There are a large wooden deck for sunbathing, a sunny second-floor breakfast room, and a self-service Laundromat. It's a bit out of the way but is within walking distance to some nearby restaurants; the beach is a 10-minute drive.

✪ **Sea Turtle Inn & Azalea Lane Apartments.** 835 Azalea Lane, Vero Beach, FL 32963. ☎ **561/234-0788.** Fax 561/234-0717. www.vero-beach.fl.us/seaturtle@vero-beach.fl.us. 21 units. A/C TV. Winter $79–$89 double. Off-season $59–$79. Weekly and monthly rates available. MC, V. From I-95, go east on S.R. 60 (about 10 mi.) to Cardinal Dr.; turn right.

This two-part property offers the very best value on the beach (just 2 blocks from the ocean). The 1950s motel and an adjacent apartment building have been fully renovated by Joe Polce and outfitted with understated but efficient furnishings. You won't find any fancy amenities (or even a phone for that matter, unless you request one), but most units have a microwave, a coffeemaker, a toaster, cable TV, and a small refrigerator. The properties share a small pool and sundeck. Book early, especially in season, since it fills up quickly with long-term visitors.

Camping

This area is popular with campers, who can choose from nearly a dozen sites throughout Vero and Sebastian. If you aren't camping at the scenic and very popular Sebastian Inlet (see "Beaches," above), then try the **Vero Beach KOA RV Park,** 8850 U.S. 1, Wabasso (☎ **561/589-5665**). This 120-site campground is 2 miles from the ocean and the Intracoastal Waterway and one quarter of a mile from the Indian River, a big draw for the crowd of regular fishing fanatics. There are running water and electricity, as well as showers, a shop, and hookups for RVs. Rates range from $20 to $24 per site, and $19 for tents. To get there, take I-95 to Exit 69 east; at U.S. 1 turn left.

WHERE TO DINE
EXPENSIVE

⭐ **Chez Yannick.** 1605 S. Ocean Dr., Vero Beach. ☎ **561/234-4115.** Reservations recommended. Main courses $15–$30; fixed-price dinner $19–$21 is available in the off-season. AE, MC, V. Mon–Sat open at 6pm; closing time may vary based on last reservation. FRENCH/CONTINENTAL.

Excellent cooking, a comprehensive wine list, and white-glove service complement the crystal and gilded decor at this five-star–rated French standout. Excellent starters include a succulent sliced duckling breast, cream of lobster soup, and hearts-of-palm salad with a slightly spicy vinaigrette. Some items, like lobster and shrimp in a cognac-dill sauce, are available as either an appetizer or an entree. Other main courses include beef tenderloin stuffed with Gorgonzola cheese and sautéed soft-shell crabs. Desserts might include profiteroles with ice cream and chocolate or raspberry sauce, crème caramel, chocolate-mousse pie, or raspberry sorbet. When available, the fixed-price dinner includes soup or salad, entree, and dessert, and is a truly outstanding value.

MODERATE

⭐ **Black Pearl Brasserie and Grill.** 2855 Ocean Dr., Vero Beach. ☎ **561/234-4426.** Fax 561/234-9074. Reservations recommended. Main courses $12–$21. AE, CB, DC, DISC, MC, V. Mon–Sun 11:30am–10pm; Sun brunch 10:30am–2pm. CONTINENTAL.

The brasserie's small list of appetizers includes many salads, chilled sweet-potato vichyssoise, crispy fried chicken fingers with mango dipping sauce, and grilled oysters with tangy barbecue sauce. Equally creative main courses are uniformly good. Don't miss their signature dish, an onion-crusted mahimahi with caramel citrus glaze. Both this original unassuming restaurant and its newer counterpart, The Black Pearl Riverfront, at 4445 N. A1A (☎ 561/234-4426), serve fantastically fresh and inventive food. The riverfront location is more formal and serves only dinner from 5pm.

Ocean Grill. 1050 Sexton Plaza (by the ocean at the end of S.R. 60), Vero Beach. ☎ **561/231-5409.** Reservations accepted only for large parties. Main courses $17–$30. AE, DC, DISC, MC, V. Mon–Fri 11:30am–2:30pm and 5:30–10pm, Sat–Sun 5:30–10pm. AMERICAN.

The Ocean Grill is an institution that attracts tourists and locals alike with its simple but rich cooking and its stunning locale, right on the ocean's edge. For a dramatic experience, ask for a table along the wall of windows that open onto the sea. Dinners are uniformly good. Try stone crab claws when they are in season or any of the big servings of pasta or meats. This huge and handsome old-timer specializes in steaks and seafood. Try the house shrimp scampi baked in butter and herbs and served with a tangy mustard sauce. There is also a gift shop and a popular bar.

INEXPENSIVE

Beachside Restaurant. 3125 Ocean Dr., Vero Beach. ☎ **561/234-4477.** Breakfast combos $2–$5; full dinners $7–$15. AE, DC, DISC, MC, V. Mon–Sat 6:30–9pm and Sun 6:30am–3pm. AMERICAN/DINER.

For a great big, cheap American breakfast, this is the place to go. You can get omelets, home fries, cream chipped beef, corn beef hash, pancakes, Belgian waffles, and even grits. Friendly waitresses also serve lunch and dinner in the comfy wooden booths. The best dishes, like chili, fried chicken, and steaks, are hearty and delicious. Though it's just across the road from the beach, it attracts more locals than tourists.

Nino's Cafe. 1006 Easter Lily Lane (off Ocean Dr., next to Humiston Park), Vero Beach. ☎ **561/231-9311.** Main courses $8.50–$11.95; subs and burgers $4.50–$6.95; pastas $7–$10. No credit cards. Mon–Thurs 11am–9pm; Fri–Sat 11am–10pm; Sun 4pm–9pm. ITALIAN.

This little beachside cafe looks like a stereotypical pizza joint, complete with fake brick walls, murals of the Italian countryside, and red-and-white checked tablecloths. The atmosphere is pure cheese and so is much of the food. Pizza and parmigiana dishes are smothered in the stuff. Still, the thin crust and fresh toppings make this a step above your ordinary pizza. Entrees and pastas are tasty, especially thanks to a tangy and rich homemade sauce.

VERO BEACH & SEBASTIAN AFTER DARK

More than half the residents in this area are retirees, so it shouldn't be a surprise that even on weekends, this town retires relatively early. Still, there are a few popular spots, in addition to the many hotel lounges, that have live music and a good bar scene, especially in high season. For beachside drinks, go to the Driftwood Resort. See "Where to Stay," above.

A mostly 30-something and younger crowd goes to Vero's **Bombay Louie's**, at 398 21st St. (☎ **561/978-0209**), where a DJ spins dance music after 9pm from Wednesday to Saturday.

In Sebastian, you'll find live music every weekend (and daily in season) at **Capt. Hiram's**, 1606 N. Indian River Dr. (☎ **561/589-4345**), a salty outdoor restaurant and bar on the Intracoastal Waterway. The feel is tacky Key West, complete with a sand floor and thatched-roof bar that locals and tourists love at all hours of the day and night.

North of the inlet, head for the tried-and-true **Sebastian Beach Inn** (or SBI to locals), 7035 S. Fla. A1A (☎ **407/728-4311**), for live music on the weekends. Jazz, blues, or sometimes rock and roll starts at 9pm on Friday and Saturday. On Sunday, it's old-style reggae after 2pm. It's open daily for drinks from 11am until anywhere from midnight to 2am.

4 A Side Trip Inland: Fishing at Lake Okeechobee

60 miles SW of West Palm Beach

Many visitors to the Treasure Coast come to fish, and they certainly get their fill off the miles of Atlantic shore and on the inland rivers. But if you want to fish freshwater and nothing else, head for "The Lake"—✪ **Lake Okeechobee,** that is. The state's largest, it's chock-full of good eating fish. Only about a 1 1/2-hour drive from the coast, it makes a great day or weekend excursion.

Two things happen in the area surrounding Lake Okeechobee: sugar production and fishing. The area, which actually encompasses five counties, is known as the bass-fishing and winter-vegetable capital of the state.

Okeechobee comes from the Seminole Indian word for "big water"—and big it is. The lake covers more than 467,000 acres; that's more than 730 square miles. At one time, the lake supported an enormous commercial fishing industry. Due to a commercial fishing-net ban, much of that industry has died off, leaving the sportfishers all the rich bounty of the lake.

As you approach the lake area, you'll notice a large levy surrounding its circumference. This was built after two major hurricanes, including one in 1947 that killed hundreds of area residents and cattle. In an effort to control future flooding, the Army Corps of Engineers, which had already built a cross-state waterway, constructed a series of locks and dams. The region is now safe from the threat of floods, but the ecological results of the flood control have not been as positive. The bird and wildlife population suffered dramatically, as did the southern portion of the Everglades, which relied on the down flow of water from the lake to replenish and clean the entire ecosystem.

Another threat to the region is posed by the area's largest employer, U.S. Sugar, which owns most of the land around Belle Glade and Clewiston, "America's Sweetest Town."

Still, the area retains its rural charm and boasts the best bass fishing in the state.

ESSENTIALS

GETTING THERE The best route is to take I-95 south to Southern Boulevard (U.S. 98 west) in West Palm Beach, which merges with S.R. 80 and S.R. 441. Follow signs for S.R. 80 west through Belle Glade to South Bay. In South Bay, turn right onto U.S. 27 north, which leads directly to Clewiston.

VISITOR INFORMATION Contact the **Clewiston Chamber of Commerce,** 544 W. Sugarland Hwy., Clewiston, FL 33440 (☎ **941/983-7979;** www.clewiston.org), for maps, business directories, and the names of numerous fishing guides throughout the area. In addition, you might contact the **Pahokee Chamber of Commerce,** 115 E. Main St., Pahokee, FL 33476 (☎ **561/924-5579;** fax 561/924-8116; www.pelinet.net/Pahokee); they'll send a complete package of magazines, guides, and accommodations listings.

For an excellent map and a brief history of the area, contact the **U.S. Army Corps of Engineers,** Natural Resources Office, 525 Ridgelawn Rd., Clewiston, FL 33440 (☎ **941/983-8101;** fax 941/983-8579). It is open weekdays from 8am to 4:30pm.

OUTDOOR PURSUITS

BOAT TOURS **Captain JP's Boat Charters** (☎ **800/845-7411** or 561/924-2100) go out every day on a number of tour and dinner cruises on his 350-passenger *Viking Starliner* throughout the southern region of Lake Okeechobee. Most cruises leave from Pahokee or Moore Haven marina, though schedules change daily. Most cruises depart at 10am during the season and include breakfast and an all-you-can-eat buffet of salads, cheeses, and hot entrees. Prices start at $30. Call for seasonal schedules.

FISHING See the "Going After the Big One," box.

SKYDIVING Besides fishing, the biggest sport in Clewiston is jumping out of planes. Because of the limited air traffic and vast areas of flat undeveloped land, this area attracts novice and expert skydivers. **Air Adventures** (☎ **800/533-6151** or 941/983-6151) operates a year-round program from the Airglades Airport. If you've never jumped before, you can go on a tandem dive, which means, as the name implies, you'll be attached to a "jumpmaster." For the first 60 seconds, the two of you free-fall,

Going After the Big One

Fishing on the lake is a year-round affair, though the fish tend to bite a little better in the winter, perhaps for benefit of the many snowbirds that flock here, especially in February and March. RV camps are mobbed with fish-frenzied anglers who come down for weeks at a time for a decent catch.

You'll need a fishing license to go out with a rod and reel. It's a simple matter to apply. The chamber of commerce and most fishing shops can sign you up on the spot. The cost for non-Florida residents for 7 days is $16.50; $31.50 for the year.

You can rent, charter, or bring your own boat to Clewiston; just be sure to schedule your trip in advance. You don't want to show up during one of the frequent fishing tournaments, only to find you can't get a room, campsite, or fishing boat because hundreds of the country's most intense bass fishers are vying for the $100,000 prizes in the Redman Competition, which happens four times a year in the spring and winter.

There are, of course, more than a few marinas where you can rent or charter boats. If it's your first time on the lake, I suggest chartering a boat with a guide who can show you the lake's most fertile spots and handle your tackle while you drink a beer and get some sun. **Roland Martin,** 920 E. Del Monte (☎ **941/983-3151**), is the one-stop spot where you can find a guide, boat, tackle, rods, bait, coolers, picnic supplies, and choice of boats. Rates, including the boat, start at $175 for a half day. A full day costs $250 and includes all necessary equipment except bait. You'll need a license for this, too, which Roland Martin also sells. They also have boat rentals: A 16-foot john boat is $40 for half a day, $60 for a full day with a $40 deposit. A 26-foot pontoon is $125 for a full day and $85 for half a day with a $50 deposit.

Another reputable boat-rental spot is **Angler's Marina,** 910 Okeechobee Blvd. (☎ **800/741-3141** or 941/983-BASS). Rentals for a 14-footer start at $40 for a half day, with a maximum of four people. A full day is $60. I'd opt for the 22-foot pontoon, which comes with a 50-horsepower engine and fits a max of 10 people and some more space for supplies and fish. If you want a guide, rates start at $150 (for two people) for a half day, though in the summer (June to October), when it's slow, you can usually get a cheaper deal.

---

from about 12,500 feet. Then, a quick pull of the chute turns your rapid descent into a gentle, balletic cruise to the ground with time to see the whole majestic lake from a privileged perspective. Dive packages start at $150 on weekdays and $165 on weekends. Group rates are available.

WHERE TO STAY

If you aren't camping, book a room at the ✪ **Clewiston Inn,** 108 Royal Palm Ave., Clewiston (☎ **800/749-4466** or 941/983-8151). Built in 1938 by U.S. Sugar to house executives and visitors, this Southern plantation–inspired hotel is the oldest in the Lake Okeechobee region. It still hosts sugar executives and visiting sportfishers in its 52 simply decorated, nondescript, Holiday Inn–style rooms. The lounge area sports a 1945 mural depicting the animals of the region. Double rooms start at $89 a night; suites, from $109. All have air-conditioning, TVs, and telephones.

Another choice, especially if you're here to fish, is **Roland Martin,** 920 E. Del Monte (☎ **800/473-6766** or 941/983-3151), the "Disney of fishing." This RV park offers modest motel rooms, efficiencies, condominiums, apartments, or campsites, with two heated pools, gift and marina shops, and a restaurant. The modern complex, dotted with prefab buildings painted in sparse white and gray, is clean and well manicured. Rooms rent for $58 to $68 and efficiencies for $78 to $88. Condos are about $150 a night with a 3-night minimum. RV sites are about $25 with TV and cable hookup.

CAMPING

During the winter, campers own the Clewiston area. Campsites are jammed with regulars, who come year after year for the simple pleasures of the lake and, of course, the warm weather. Every manner of RV, from simple pop-top Volkswagens to Winnebagos to fully decked-out mobile homes, finds its way to the many campsites along the lake. Also, see Roland Martin, above.

Okeechobee Landings, U.S. 27 east (☎ **941/983-4144**), is one of the best; it has every conceivable amenity included in the price of a site. More than 250 sites are situated around a small lake, clubhouse, snack bar, pool, Jacuzzi, horseshoe pit, shuffleboard court, and tennis court. Full hookup includes sewer, which is not the case throughout the county. RV spots are sold to regulars. But there are usually some spots available for rental to one-time visitors. Rates start at $25 a day, $235 to $305 weekly or around $350 a month, including hookup. Year-round rates for trailer rentals, which sleep two people, start at $32 from Sunday to Thursday and from $37 on Friday and Saturday.

WHERE TO DINE

If you aren't frying up your own catch for dinner, you can find a number of good eating spots in town. At the **Clewiston Inn** (see "Where to Stay," above), you can get catfish, beef Stroganoff, ham hocks, fried chicken, and liver and onions in a setting as Southern as the food. The dining room is open daily from 6am to 2pm and 5 to 9pm, and entrees cost $9 to $18.

Not to be missed is the ✪ **Old South Barbecue Ranch,** 602 E. Sugarland Hwy. (☎ **941/983-7756**). You'll see signs from miles around, imploring you to come to this Lake Okeechobee landmark. Go ahead; they're known for their barbecued pork, meat, and chicken, but the catfish isn't bad either. You can also get good fried gator. The place looks like a movie set from an old Western. It's open Sunday through Thursday from 11am to 9pm and Friday and Saturday from 11am to 10pm.

Appendix: Useful Toll-Free Numbers & Web Sites

AIRLINES

Aer Lingus
☎ 800/474-7424 in the U.S.
☎ 01/886-8888 in Ireland
www.aerlingus.ie

Air Canada
☎ 800/776-3000
www.aircanada.ca

Air New Zealand
☎ 800/262-2468 in the U.S.
☎ 800/663-5494 in Canada
☎ 0800/737-767 in New Zealand

Alaska Airlines
☎ 800/426-0333
www.alaskaair.com

American Airlines
☎ 800/433-7300
www.americanair.com

American Trans Air
☎ 800/435-9282
www.ata.com

America West Airlines
☎ 800/235-9292
www.americawest.com

British Airways
☎ 800/247-9297
☎ 0345/222-111 in Britain
www.british-airways.com

Canadian Airlines International
☎ 800/426-7000
www.cdnair.ca

Continental Airlines
☎ 800/525-0280
www.continental.com

Delta Air Lines
☎ 800/221-1212
www.delta-air.com

Hawaiian Airlines
☎ 800/367-5320
www.hawaiianair.com

Midway Airlines
☎ 800/446-4392
www.midwayair.com

Midwest Express
☎ 800/452-2022
www.midwestexpress.com

Northwest Airlines
☎ 800/225-2525
www.nwa.com

Qantas
☎ 800/474-7424 in the U.S.
☎ 612/9691-3636 in Australia
www.qantas.com

Southwest Airlines
☎ 800/435-9792
www.iflyswa.com

Trans World Airlines (TWA)
☎ 800/221-2000
www.twa.com

United Airlines
☎ 800/241-6522
www.ual.com

US Airways
☎ 800/428-4322
www.usairways.com

Virgin Atlantic Airways
☎ 800/862-8621 in Continental U.S.
☎ 0293/747-747 in Britain
www.fly.virgin.com

CAR-RENTAL AGENCIES

Advantage
☎ 800/777-5500
www.arac.com

Alamo
☎ 800/327-9633
www.goalamo.com

Auto Europe
☎ 800/223-5555
www.autoeurope.com

Avis
☎ 800/331-1212 in Continental U.S.
☎ 800/TRY-AVIS in Canada
www.avis.com

Budget
☎ 800/527-0700
www.budgetrentacar.com

Dollar
☎ 800/800-4000
www.dollarcar.com

Enterprise
☎ 800/325-8007
www.pickenterprise.com

Hertz
☎ 800/654-3131
www.hertz.com

Kemwel Holiday Auto (KHA)
☎ 800/678-0678
www.kemwel.com

National
☎ 800/CAR-RENT
www.nationalcar.com

Payless
☎ 800/PAYLESS
www.paylesscar.com

Rent-A-Wreck
☎ 800/535-1391
rent-a-wreck.com

Thrifty
☎ 800/367-2277
www.thrifty.com

MAJOR HOTEL & MOTEL CHAINS

Baymont Inns & Suites
☎ 800/301-0200
www.baymontinns.com

Best Western International
☎ 800/528-1234
www.bestwestern.com

Clarion Hotels
☎ 800/CLARION
www.hotelchoice.com

Comfort Inns
☎ 800/228-5150
www.hotelchoice.com

Courtyard by Marriott
☎ 800/321-2211
www.courtyard.com

Days Inn
☎ 800/325-2525
www.daysinn.com

Doubletree Hotels
☎ 800/222-TREE
www.doubletreehotels.com

Econo Lodges
☎ 800/55-ECONO
www.hotelchoice.com

Fairfield Inn by Marriott
☎ 800/228-2800
www.fairfieldinn.com

Hampton Inn
☎ 800/HAMPTON
www.hampton-inn.com

Hilton Hotels
☎ 800/HILTONS
www.hilton.com

Holiday Inn
☎ 800/HOLIDAY
www.basshotels.com

Howard Johnson
☎ 800/654-2000
www.hojo.com

Hyatt Hotels & Resorts
☎ 800/228-9000
www.hyatt.com

ITT Sheraton
☎ 800/325-3535
www.sheraton.com

Knights Inn
☎ 800/843-5644
www.knghtsinn.com

La Quinta Motor Inns
☎ 800/531-5900
www.laquinta.com

Marriott Hotels
800/228-9290
www.marriott.com

Motel 6
☎ 800/4-MOTEL6
(800/466-8536)
www.motel6.com

Quality Inns
☎ 800/228-5151
www.hotelchoice.com

Radisson Hotels International
☎ 800/333-3333
www.radisson.com

Ramada Inns
☎ 800/2-RAMADA
www.ramada.com

Red Carpet Inns
☎ 800/251-1962
www.reservahost.com

Red Lion Hotels & Inns
☎ 800/547-8010
www.redlion.com

Red Roof Inns
☎ 800/843-7663
www.redroof.com

Residence Inn by Marriott
☎ 800/331-3131
www.residenceinn.com

Rodeway Inns
☎ 800/228-2000
www.hotelchoice.com

Sleep Inn
☎ 800/753-3746
www.sleepinn.com

Super 8 Motels
☎ 800/800-8000
www.super8motels.com

Travelodge
☎ 800/255-3050
www.travelodge.com

Vagabond Inns
☎ 800/522-1555
www.vagabondinns.com

Wyndham Hotels and Resorts
☎ 800/822-4200 in Continental U.S. and Canada
www.wyndham.com

Index

See also Accommodations and Restaurant indexes, below.

GENERAL INDEX
Accommodations. *See* Accommodations Index
Actors' Playhouse, 198
Adolphus Busch Sr. sunken boat, 242
Airboat tours of the Everglades, 211
Airlines, 24, 26, 46
Airport Lost and Found office in Miami, 61
Albita, 198
Alice's Day Off, 178
Ambrosino Gallery, 176
Amelia Earhart Park, 161
America's Riviera, 55
America's Sweetest Town, 338
American Airlines Arena, 171
American Eagle flights, 223, 246
American Police Hall of Fame and Museum, 156
Amtrak, 28, 46, 270, 298, 318
Angler's Marina at Lake Okeechobee, 339
Anhinga Ambles, 208
Anhinga trail, 209
Animal parks in Miami, 151, 152
Anne's Beach, 224
Antique Row in Dania, 276
Antique shops/shows, 175
Aquariums, 40, 152, 162, 249
Arabian Nights Festival, 17
Architectural Antiques, 175
Architecture sites, 157
Art Deco District, 4, 10, 55, 151, 163. *See also* South Beach
Art Deco Weekend, 15
Art galleries
    Coral Gables, 164
    Lower Keys, 242
    Miami, 153, 175

Art Miami fair, 15
Arthur Frommer's Budget Travel, 25
Artificial reefs, 320
Artists in Paradise Gallery, 242
Atlantic Coastal Cruises, 299
ATMs, 12, 44
Audobon House & Tropical Gardens, 249
Aura, 110
Auto Train, 28
Autograph gallery, 302
Aventura Mall, 173, 174, 182

Back Room in Delray Beach, 297
Backcountry in the Keys, 220
Bahamian bacchanalia, 18
Bahia Honda State Park, 240, 242, 244
Bal Harbour, 55. *See also* Miami Beach
Bal Harbour Beach, 150
Bal Harbour Shops, 182
Baleen's, 7, 99
Ballet Flamenco La Rosa, 200
Bambu, 105
Barnacle State Historic Site, 157
Bars. *See also* Nightlife
    Astor Hotel, 105
    best happy hours, 9
    Conga Bar/Lombardi's, 131
    Duval Street, 5
    Hog Heaven, 239
    John Martin's, 139
    Key West, 266
    Lower Keys, 246
    Miami, 188
    Nexxt Cafe, 116
    Palm Beach, 306
    Sundays on the Bay, 128

    Tiki Bar at the Holiday Isle Resort, 239
    West Palm Beach, 310
Baseball, 170, 273, 311, 327, 332
Bash, 192
Basketball in Miami, 171
Bass Museum of Art (South Beach), 153
Bass Pro Outdoor World Store (Dania), 185, 273, 277
Bathtub Beach, 320
Bay Harbor. *See* Miami Beach
Bayside Marketplace (Miami), 56, 173, 183
Beach House Bal Harbour, 82
Beach Place mall, 277, 287
Beaches
    Boca Raton, 289
    Delray Beach, 289
    Gold Coast, 270
    Key West, 252
    Keys, 222, 224, 233
    Miami, 147
    North Hutchinson Island, 326
    Northern Palm Beach County, 311
    Palm Beach, 299
    Treasure Coast, 320, 331
BED (Beverage.Entertainment.Dining), 105
Belinda's, 179
Belle Glade, 338
Bermuda Bar and Grill, 192
Betsey Johnson shop, 179
Bice, 141
Bicycling
    Everglades, 209
    Key West, 248, 252
    Lower Keys, 241
    Miami, 59, 166
    Northern Palm Beach County, 311
    Palm Beach, 299

Bid for Travel Web site, 33
Big Dick and the Extenders band, 239
Big Ruby's, 255
Biga Bakery, 180
Bill Baggs Cape Florida State Recreation Area, 161
Bill Baggs State Park, 56
Bird watching, 210, 226, 241, 267
Biscayne Corridor, 56
Biscayne National Park, 4, 39, 214, 216
Biscayne National Underwater Park, Inc., 215, 217
Black heritage festival, 18
Black Marlin, 324
Black Pearl Brasserie and Grill, 336
Black Pearl Riverfront, 336
Blowing Rocks Preserve, 312
Blue Hole in Bahia Honda State Park, 241
Boating. *See also* Canoeing; Houseboats; Kayaking
    Everglades, 210
    Gold Coast, 272
    Keys, 228
    Lake Okeechobee, 340
    Lower Keys, 241
    Miami, 164
    Northern Palm Beach County, 311
Boca Beach Club, 292
Boca Chita Key in Biscayne National Park, 215, 216
Boca Raton, 288-291, 295
Boca Raton Museum of Art, 290
Bombay Louie's, 337
Bonnet House, 276
Books & Books, 177, 201
Books, shopping for, 177
Bootlegger's, 275, 287
Boston's on the Beach, 297
Botanical garden, 158
Bougainvillea, 282
The Bounty Hunter, 229
Bradley's, 310
The Brass Key, 256
Breakers golf course, 7
Broadwalk on Hollywood Beach, 270
Broward County, 269
Broward Mall, 277
Browne's & Co. beauty emporium, 176
Bubba Gump Shrimp Co., 129, 137

Bubba's Fish Camp, 325
Buffett, Jimmy, 265
Bus travel, 47. *See also* Greyhound
Buses in Miami, 58
Business hours in Miami, 60
Butterfly World, 276

Cabs. *See* Taxis
Cactus Bar & Grill, 195
CAF (Concert Association of Florida), 199
Café cubano, 133, 134
Café Des Artes, 113
Cajun/Zydeco Crawfish Festival, 18
Calle Ocho. *See* Little Havana
Camarones, 101, 134, 115
Cameo. *See* crobar
Camping
    Biscayne National Park, 217
    Dry Tortugas, 267
    Everglades, 212
    Keys, 236
    Lower Keys, 244
    Treasure Coast, 324, 336, 340
Canoeing. *See also* Boating; Kayaking
    Biscayne National Park, 216
    Everglades, 5, 210
    John Pennekamp Coral Reef State Park, 227
    Keys, 228
    Lower Keys, 241
    Northern Palm Beach County, 311
    Treasure Coast, 320
Capital Grille, 8, 129
Capt. Hiram's, 331, 337
Capt. Kidd II party boat, 331
Captain JP's Boat Charters, 338
Captain Pip's, 228
Captain Tony's Saloon, 265
Car, travel by, 27, 58
Car rentals, 27, 47, 52, 58, 59
Caribbean, 218, 219
Carjackings, 45
Cartoon art, International Museum of, 290
Casa Panza, 197
Casa Salsa, 66, 110
Casino Princesa, 168
Casino Records Inc., 184

Catamarans, 252, 266
CD Warehouse, 184
Ceviche, 134
Champions Club at Summerfield, 320
Chaos, 193
Charter boats, 167, 253
Cheap Tickets, 24, 33
Cheeky Monkey, 111
Chekika, 207
Chez Yannick, 336
Chickee huts, 213
Children
    accommodations
        Colony Hotel & Cabana Club, 294
        Disney's Vero Beach Resort, 334
        Indian River Plantation Marriott Resort, 322
        Lago Mar Resort and Club, 6, 280
        Marriott's Harbor Beach Resort, 278
        Newport Beachside Hotel & Resort, 87
        Sonesta Beach Resort Key Biscayne, 6
        Spanish River Resort, 294
    animal parks
        Miami Metrozoo, 151
    aquariums
        Key West aquarium, 249
    beaches
        Palm Beach, 299
    Christmas theme park
        Santa's Enchanted Forest, 21
    clothes shopping
        French Kids Inc., 179
        Roland Children's Wear, 179
    family-friendly restaurants
        Bubba Gump Shrimp Co., 137
        Deli Den, 7
        GameWorks, 7
        No Anchovies!, 316
        Van Dyke Café, 137
        Wilderness Grill, 137, 145

345

General Index

General Index

Children (cont.)
  game parks
    Grand Prix Race-O-Rama, 273
  malls
    Aventura Mall, 182
  museums
    Gumbo Limbo Environmental Complex, 290
    Museum of Discovery and Science, 274
  nature areas
    Crane Point Hammock, 225
  nature preserves
    Lion Country Safari, 302
  New Year's celebration
    First Night, 21
  parks
    Amelia Earhart Park, 161
    in Miami, 161
    Playmobil Fun Park, 301
  planetarium
    Miami Museum of Science & Space Transit Planetarium, 162
  seafood festival, 16
  seaquarium
    Miami Seaquarium, 40, 152, 162
  swamp buggy rides, 275
  swimming pools
    Octopus pool, 83
    Venetian Pool, 158
  youth center
    Scott Rakow Youth Center, 161
  zoos
    Miami Metrozoo, 162, 151
The Children's Exchange, 186
Chili Pepper, alternative music in Fort Lauderdale, 288
Christmas theme park, 21
Chubby Carrier and his band, 191
Church Mouse consignment/thrift shop, 302
Cigar making in Key West, 254
Cigars and cigarettes, shopping for, 177

Cinemas in Miami, 201
Cirrus ATM network, 12
City Ballet. *See* Miami City Ballet
City guides for Miami, 37
Classical music, 19, 199
Clematis Street Books, 302
Clematis Street in West Palm Beach, 309
Clewiston, 338
Clinton Street Market, 254
Cloverleaf Lanes, 192
Club 5922, 195
Club Boca, 297
Club Cathode Ray, 288
Club M, 287
Club Safari, 316
Club scene. *See* Nightlife
ClubMiami.com, 188
Coastal Science Center, 321
Coco Pazzo, 145
Coconut Grove, 57
  Art Festival, 16
  Bed Race, 17
  Chamber of Commerce, 12
  cuisine, 141
  Goombay Festival, 18
  Playhouse, 198
  shopping in, 174
Coconuts Dolphin Tournament, 18
Coffee, Cuban, 133
Cohibas, 177
Collins Avenue, 54, 55, 175
Colony Theater (South Beach), 200
Columbus Day Regatta, 19
Concert Association of Florida (CAF), 199
Conch Republic, 222
Conch Tour Train, 248, 251
Conchs, 246
Condo Canyon in Miami Beach, 80
Conga Bar/Lombardi's, 131
Consolidators, 24
Convoy Point Visitor Center in Biscayne National Park, 215
The Copa, 288
Coral Castle, 158
Coral Gables, 57
  Art and Gallery Tour, 164
  Chamber of Commerce, 12
  shopping in, 174

Cover to Cover radio show, 201
Crack'd Conch, 239
Crandon Park Beach, 150
Crandon Park Golf Course, 168
Crane Point Hammock, 225
Crawfish Festival, 18
Crime, precautions against, 45
crobar, 193
crobar @ the Cameo, 195
Croissants, 180
Croquetas, 134
Crown Liquors, 186
Cruises, 218, 272, 299, 312
Cuba, Cuba! in Key West, 254
Cuban coffee, 133
Cuban cuisine, 7, 133
Currency, 35, 44, 47
Customs (U.S. Customs), 35, 43
Cycling in Miami, 59, 166
Cycling tour of the Art Deco District, 163

Dade County, 39, 57, 61, 200
Dade Human Rights Foundation, 16, 23
Dadeland Mall, 183
Dance clubs in Miami, 192
Dance companies in Miami, 200
Dania Jai-Alai, 274
Dave & Busters (Hollywood), 273
Deaf Services Bureau, 23
Deco Drive. *See* Ocean Drive
Deep Divers Unlimited, 320
Deep-sea fishing. *See* Fishing
Deerfield Beach, 292
Delray Beach, 288, 289, 290, 295
Demar's. *See* Calypso's
Dentists, 22, 60
Design District, 56
Design Preservation League. *See* Miami Design Preservation League
Diaspora Vibe Art Gallery, 154
Dietel's Antiques, 175
Digital City South Florida on AOL, 36

Dining. *See also* Pretheater Dinners; Restaurant Index
  Everglades National Park, 214
  Fort Lauderdale, 283
  Key West, 261
  Keys, 236
  Lower Keys, 244
  Miami, 101, 202
  Northern Palm Beach County, 315
  online guides to Miami, 38
  Palm Beach, 307
  Treasure Coast, 324, 336, 340
Diplomat Resort & Country Club, 278
Dirty Harry's, 265
Discover Key West Web site, 37
Disney of fishing, 340
District (Design District), 56
Diva's, 266
Dive Key West Inc., 252
Divers Paradise, 165
Diving
  Dry Tortugas, 267
  Key West, 252
  Keys, 229
  Lower Keys, 242
Dixie Divers, 300
Dockside–Harbor Light Resort, 328
Doctors, 60
Dolphin Mall, 183
Dolphins, swimming with, 152, 226, 227, 231
Don's Bait & Tackle in Homestead, 208
Donaldson Reef, 320
Donna's Bistro & Bar, 97
Doral Park Golf and Country Club, 169
Doral Ryder Golf Open, 16
Downtown Miami, 56, 128, 174
Drawbridges, 58
Drumming on a full moon, 5
Dry Tortugas, 266
Dubois Park, 311
Duval Street, 5, 265

Eagle, The, 195
East Coast Auto Train, 28
East Martello Museum and Gallery, 249
Ebeel's Bar & Grill, 190
Elbo Room, 287

Electronics, shopping for, 177
Elite Fine Art, 176
Elite Modeling Agency, 72
Elliott Key in Biscayne National Park, 215, 216
Elliott Museum, 321
Emerald Coast, 125
Emerald Dunes Golf Course, 299
Emerald Hills golf course, 273
Emergencies, 13, 21, 48, 60
Entry requirements for foreign visitors, 42
Environmental Learning Center, 332
Epicure gourmet market, 180
Epoch club, 265
Ericsson Open, 17, 170
Ernest F. Coe Visitor Center, 207
Ernest Hemingway Home and Museum, 249
Ernst Reef, 320
Esplanade, 308
The Estate Wines & Gourmet Foods, 186
Estefan, Gloria and Emilio, 71, 115
Evelyn S. Poole Ltd., 176
Events, calendar of, 14
Everglades Alligator Farm, 211
Everglades National Park, 5, 39, 203, 207, 212
Everglades Seafood Festival, 16
Evert, Chris, 274
Expedia, 30, 32

Fairchild Tropical Gardens, 20, 39, 158
Falls Shopping Center, 183
Families. *See* Children
Family Travel Forum (FTF), 32
Fantasy Fest in Key West, 20
Fashion, shopping for, 178
Fast Buck Freddie's, 255
Fazio, Tom, 299, 320, 327
Ferry service in the Keys, 224
Festival Miami, 19
Film Society of Miami, 16
Fireball catamaran, 252
Firehouse Four, 188
First Night, 21

First-tier gay community, 195
Fisher, Mel, 250
Fishing
  Biscayne National Park, 216
  Dry Tortugas, 267
  Everglades, 210
  Everglades National Park, 208
  Gold Coast, 272
  Key West, 252
  Keys, 229
  Lake Okeechobee, 339
  Lower Keys, 242
  Miami, 166
  Northern Palm Beach County, 312
  Treasure Coast, 320, 327, 331
FLA USA Web site, 36
Flager Museum in Palm Beach, 300
Flagler Grill, 324
Flagler Street, 174
Flagler, Henry, 228, 300
Flaming Maggie's, 254
Flea markets, 230, 277
Florida Association of Convention and Visitors Bureaus Web site, 36
Florida Bay Outfitters in Key Largo, 229
Florida City, 16, 213
Florida Frontier architecture, 276
Florida Grand Opera, 200
Florida History Museum, 313
Florida Keys. *See* Keys
Florida Marlins, 40, 170, 273
Florida Museum of Hispanic and Latin American Art, 154
Florida Panthers, 40, 171, 274
Florida Philharmonic Orchestra, 199
Florida State Parks Web site, 36
Florida Sunbreak, 278
Florida Symphonic Pops, 297
Florito, 286
Football in Miami, 171
Force E Dive Center, 289
Foreign visitors, entry requirements for, 42
Fort Jefferson (Garden Key), 267

347

General Index

Fort Lauderdale, 269
  accommodations, 270
  Beach Promenade, 270
  International Boat Show, 19
  nightlife, 287
  Stadium, 273
  Swap Shop, 277
Fort Pierce, 326-327. *See also* Hutchinson Island
Fort Zachary Beach, 252
The Four Ambassadors, 91
Fourth of July Festivities, 19
Franz & Joseph's in the Grove, 8, 142
French cuisine, 105, 112, 130, 143
French Kids Inc., 179
Friends boy strip club, 195
Fritz's Skate Shop, 170
Front Porch Café, 118
Frontons for jai alai, 171
Fruit stands, 211
FTF (Family Travel Forum), 32
Full moon drumming celebration, 5
Funjet, 32

Gables. *See* Coral Gables
Gables Stage, 198
Galleria in Fort Lauderdale, 277
Gallery Antigua, 176
Gambling in Miami, 168
Game parks on the Gold Coast, 273
Gameworks at Sawgrass Mills, 273
GameWorks at Shops of Sunset Place, 7, 162
Garden Key, 266
Gardens of the Palm Beaches, 314
Gardner's Market, 180
Garrison Bite Marina in Key West, 253
Gaucho Room, 111
Gay and lesbian travelers
  accommodations
    Kenmore hotel, 79
    Key West, 248, 255
    Nassau Suite Hotel, 77
    Park Washington Hotel, 79
    Taft House hotel, 79
  book stores
    Books & Books, 177

Flaming Maggie's in Key West, 254
cinemas, 201
dining
  Balan's, 113
  Jeffrey's, 115
events
  White Party Week, 20
  Winter Party, 16
Miami Gay & Lesbian Film Festival, 17
nightlife, 195
  Fort Lauderdale, 288
  Key West, 265
  Level 1235 Washington, 194
  Miami, 194
tips for Miami, 23
Web sites
  Gay Key West Travel Guide, 37
Gay circuit party scene, 195
Gay Key West Travel Guide Web site, 37
Gay Men's Health Crisis, 43
George Bush Cheeca Lodge Bonefish Tournament, 20
George Clinton and the P-Funk, 191
Gilbert's House of Refuge Museum, 322
Giorgio's, 178
Giralda bell tower, 5, 96
Glade Glimpses walking tour, 208
Glades. *See* Everglades National Park
Glass-bottom boat tours, 217
Go4less Web site, 33
goflorida.com, 12
Gold Coast, 12, 268, 269
Golden Passports, 207
Golden Orb Trail, 228
Golf, 6
  Boca Raton, 289
  Gold Coast, 273
  Jupiter, 312
  Key West, 253
  Miami, 168, 169
  Northern Palm Beach County, 312
  Palm Beach, 299
  Treasure Coast, 320, 327, 331
Golf-A-Round program, 289, 299, 312
Gondola Adventures, 162

Goombay Festival, 20, 57
Grand Prix of Miami, 17
Grand Prix Race-O-Rama, 273
Granny Feelgoods, 131
Great Gravity Clock, 275
Great Sunrise Balloon Race & Festival, 18
Great White Course, 93
The Greenview, 70
Greyhound, 47, 223, 247, 318
Groove Jet, 194
Guaraná Brazilian soda, 126
Gulfstream Park, 171
Gumbo Limbo Environmental Complex, 290
Gumbo-Limbo trail, 209

Haitian Art Co., 254
Hale Indian River Groves, 333
Half Buck Freddie's, 255
Hall's Dive Center & Career Institute in Marathon, 229
Hammerheads baseball team, 311
Hammocks (forest islands), 290
Hand-controlled cars, rental of, 23
Harbor Branch Oceanographic Institution, 327
Harbortown Fish House, 329
Harrison Street and Young Circle in Hollywood, 287
Hatusume Fair, 16
Haulover Beach, 151
Haulover Beach Park, 166
Haulover Park, 169
Health clubs in Miami, 169
Hearst Castle of the East, 157
Helio Gallery Store, 255
Hell's Bay Trail, 210
Hello Gorgeous, 255
Hemingway, Ernest, 222, 249
Hemingway Days Festival, 18
Heritage Miami II topsail schooner, 163
Hialeah, streets in, 54
Hialeah Park, 171
Higgs Beach, 252
High season in the Everglades, 208

Hiking
  Biscayne National Park, 216
  Long Key State Recreation Area, 228
  Lower Keys, 242
  Northern Palm Beach County, 312
Historical Museum of Southern Florida, 39, 156, 163
Hobe Sound Wildlife Refuge, 321
Hobie Beach, 56, 150
Hog Heaven, 239
Holidays, 48
Hollywood, 269, 287
Hollywood Beach, 270
Holocaust Memorial, 153
Homestead, 213
Homestead Rodeo, 15
Horizon Outlet Center, 333
Horse racing in Miami, 171
Hospitals, 48, 60
Hostels, 79, 261, 282
Houseboats, 213, 230, 234
Housewares, shopping for, 181
Howl at the Moon in Fort Lauderdale, 287
Hugo Boss, 178
Hurricane Andrew, 14
Hurricanes, 14, 63
Hurricanes (football team), 40
The Hut, 128
Hutchinson Island, 326. *See also* Fort Pierce

I-95, 27
Ice hockey in Miami, 171
IGFA World Fishing Center, 272
Iko Iko, 191
IMAX Theatre at Sunset Place, 162
In-line skating in Miami, 169
Independence Day, events in Miami, 18
Indian Key, 224
Indian River, 332
  Citrus Museum, 332
  County Tourist Council, 330
  Mall, 333
  Plantation Beach Resort, 320
  Plantation Marriott Resort, 322

Information sources. *See also* Web sites
  on the Everglades National Park, 207
  on the Gold Coast, 270
  on Key West, 248
  on the Lower Keys, 240
  in Palm Beach, 298
  on traveling in Florida, 10
  for visitors to Miami, 54
Intellicast Web site, 34
Interactive science museum, 274
International Jeweler's Exchange, 182
International Museum of Cartoon Art, 290
International Youth Hostel Federation (IYHF), 79
Internet cafes, 35
Islamorada, 223, 230
Italian Renaissance Festival, 16

Jack Island State Preserve, 326
Jackie Gleason Theater of the Performing Arts (TOPA), 201
Jai alai, 171, 274
Jamaica Awareness, 19
Japanese gardens, 291
Jazid club, 191
Jazz at Moca concerts, 156
Jazz hot line for O'Hara's, 288
Jensen Beach. *See* Martin County
Jerry Herman Ring Theatre, 198
Jet-skis, rental of, 164
Jetty Park, 326
Jewelry, shopping for, 182
Jiffy Lube Miami 300 Weekend of NASCAR, 20
Jimmy Buffett's Margaritaville Cafe, 265
Jimmy'z nightclub, 190
John D. MacArthur Beach, 311
John Pennekamp Coral Reef State Park, 223, 227, 236
Johnson & Wales University, 85, 101
Jonathan Dickinson State Park, 311, 320, 324
Jungle Queen, 39, 272

Jupiter. *See* Northern Palm Beach County and Palm Beach County
Jupiter Inlet Lighthouse, 313
Just Go South Florida Web site, 37

Kafka's Cyberkafe, 177
Kayaking. *See also* Boating; Canoeing; Houseboats
  Biscayne National Park, 216
  Key West, 253
  Keys, 228
  Lower Keys, 241
  Miami, 164
Key Biscayne, 15, 56, 150, 165, 170
Key deer, 241
Key Largo, 223
Key rats, 126
Key West, 222, 246
  Aloe, 254
  Aquarium, 249
  barhopping on Duval Street, 5
  Business Guild, 248, 255
  Cemetary, 249
  Chamber of Commerce, 248
  Cigar Factory, 254
  Golf Club, 253
  Innkeepers Association, 255
  International Airport, 247
  Island Bookstore, 254
  Lighthouse Museum, 250
  Literary Seminar, 15
  online guide to, 37
  Shipwreck Historeum, 250
  Visitors Center, 248
Keys, 220, 222. *See also* Lower Keys and Upper Keys
Keys Factory Shops, 211, 230
Kids. *See* Children
King Orange Jamboree Parade, 21
Kokomo's, 239
The Kravis, 310

La Brioche Doree, 180
La Esquina de Tejas, 7, 133
La Fontaine, 143
La Gloria Cubana, 177
La Perla, 179

349

General Index

La Terraza in Key West, 266
La Trattoria, 262
Lake Okeechobee, 317, 337
Las Olas Boulevard, 5, 277, 283
Last Minute Travel Bargains Web site, 26
LastMinuteTravel.com, 33
Late-Night Dining, 8, 202. *See also* Dining; Restaurant Index
Latin clubs in Miami, 196
Latin cuisine, 134
Laurenzo's Italian Supermarket and Farmer's Market, 180
Layton Trail, 228
Leather and Levi bars, 195
Le Bouchondu, 142
Leopard Lounge, 310
Level 1235 Washington, 194
Level @ 1235, 195
Lignumvitae Key, 224
Lily Guest House, 76
Lincoln Road
 area restaurants, 104
 Gallery Walk at the Art Center, 164, 176
 Mall, 174
 walking along, 151
Linge de Maison Veronique, 181
Lingerie, shopping for, 179
The Links, 168
Lion Country Safari, 268, 302
Lipton Championship. *See* Ericsson Open
Liquid and The Lounge, 194
Liquor stores, 61, 186
Literary scene in Miami, 201
Little Acorns Kite festival, 17
Little Haiti, 56, 173
Little Havana, 4, 56, 17
 cuisine of, 132
 shopping in, 173, 174
 Three King's Parade, 15
Live music in Miami, 190
Living Room at the Strand, 194
Loading Zone, 195
Loehmann's, 178
Lombardi's, 131
Long Key State Park, 236

Long Key State Recreation Area, 228
Looe Key Marine Sanctuary, 18, 242
Lorelei cabana bar, 239
Lorikeet aviary, 276
Los Angeles Dodgers, 332
Lost Reef Adventures, 252
Lower Keys, 222, 240
Lower Keys Underwater Music Fest, 18
Loxahatchee Everglades, 317
Loxahatchee Queen, 322
Lummus Park Beach, 150
Lyric Theater in Stuart, 326

Mac's Club Deuce, 190
Macaluso's, 116
Madonna, 68, 106, 169
Magazines, 38, 49, 61
MAM (Miami Art Museum), 154
Manatee Queen, 312
Manatees, 317, 321
Mapquest Web site, 35
Marathon, 223
Marine zoos, 227
Marinelife Center of Juno Beach, 313
Marjory Stoneman Douglas Biscayne Nature Center, 161
Marlin, 72
Mars (Music and Recording Superstore), 184
Martin County, 319
Martin Luther King Day Parade, 15
Maskerville, 254
McKee Botanical Garden, 332
McLarty Treasure Museum, 317, 332
Medianoches, 115, 133, 202
Mel Fisher Maritime Heritage Museum, 250
Mel Fisher's Treasure Museum, 332
Memorial Sculpture Garden, 250
Mercedes I wreck dive, 273
Merrick, George, 5, 57, 98
Metroguide Miami Web site, 37
Metrorail (Miami), 58
Metrozoo, 152, 162
Meza Fine Art, 176
Miami Art Museum (MAM), 154

Miami Beach, 55. *See also* Bal Harbour; South Beach; Surfside
 beaches, 150
 Convention Center, 55
 getting around in, 54
 information, 12
Miami Chamber Symphony, 199
Miami City Ballet, 200
Miami Dade County Online Web site, 39
Miami Dade Transit Web site, 41
Miami Design Preservation League, 10, 163
Miami Dolphins, 40, 171
Miami Film Festival, 16, 39, 201
Miami Gay & Lesbian Film Festival, 17
Miami Heat, 40, 171
Miami Herald, 38, 49, 54, 61, 188
Miami Hurricanes. *See* Hurricanes (football team)
Miami International Airport (MIA), 41, 52
Miami International Boat Show, 16, 39
Miami International Mall, 183
Miami Metrozoo, 152, 162
Miami Museum of Science, 40, 162
Miami New Times Web site, 38
Miami Reggae Festival, 19
Miami Seaquarium, 40, 152, 162
Miami Vice, 171
Miami-Dade Cultural Center, 156
Miami-Dade Public Library, 156
miami.citysearch.com, 54
Miamigo, 188
Miccosukee Everglades Festivals, 18
Miccosukee Indian Gaming, 168
Miccosukee Indian Village, 211, 212
Miccosukee Tobacco Shop, 177
Miccosukee tribe, 94
Midnight Gambler casino cruise ship, 329
Mile markers (MM) in the Keys, 223

Minigo, 188
Miracle Mile shopping street, 174
Miracle Theater in Coral Gables, 198
Mississippi River–style steamer, 272
Mizner Park (Boca Raton), 291, 295
MM (Mile markers), 223
MOCA (Museum of Contemporary Art), 156
Modernism, 175
Money. *See* Currency
Monkey Jungle, 152
Monkey Meet, 191
Moped Hospital, 248
Mopeding in Key West, 252
Morikami Japanese museum, 16
Morikami Museum and Japanese Gardens, 290
Murphy's Law Irish Pub, 190
Museum of Contemporary Art (MOCA), 156
Museum of Discovery & Science in Fort Lauderdale, 274
Museum of Science. *See* Miami Museum of Science
Museums
    Boca Raton, 290
    Delray Beach, 290
    Key West, 249, 250
    Miami, 153
    Palm Beach, 300
    Treasure Coast, 321, 327, 332
Music and musical equipment, shopping for, 184

National Hurricane Center, 14
National Key Deer Refuge, 241, 242
Neighborhoods in Miami, 55
Nevada Bob's, 185
New Theater in Coral Gables, 199
New Times, 54, 61
New World Cuisine, 4
New World symphony, 199
New York Mets, 317, 327
News Café, 119, 202
Newspapers, 38, 49, 61
Nexxt Cafe, 116

Nightlife. *See also* Bars
    Boca Raton, 297
    Delray Beach, 297
    Key West, 265
    Lower Keys, 246
    Miami, 187, 190
    Palm Beach, 309
    Treasure Coast, 325, 337
    Upper Keys, 239
Noble Hammock Trail, 210
North Miami Beach, 55
Northern Palm Beach County, 310, 314
Norton Museum of Art (West Palm Beach), 300
Nude beaches, 150

O'Hara's Pub and Jazz Café
    in Fort Lauderdale, 288
    in Hollywood, 287
O-Zone, 196
Ocean Beach, 311
Ocean Drive, 61, 65, 151
oceandrive.com, 188
Oceanside Marina on Stock Island, 253
Octopus pool at the Fontainebleau Hilton, 6, 83
Off season, 14, 64
Okeechobee Landings, 340
Oktoberfest, 19
Old South Barbecue Ranch, 340
Old Town Trolley tour of Key West, 248
Oldest House/Wrecker's Museum, 250
One Saloon, 266
One-off nights at Miami clubs, 192
1travel.com, 33
Online directory for trip planning, 28
Online tools for travelers, 34
Online travel agencies, 28, 30
Opera in Miami, 200
Orange Bowl, 14
Orangebrook Golf Course, 273
Ortanique on the Mile, 140
Outlet malls, 183, 291, 302
Overseas Highway (U.S. 1), 220, 222

P.V. Martin's, 330
Pa-hay-okee Trail, 209
Package tours, 25

Paella, 116, 134
Palm Beach, 292, 297, 299-303
Palm Beach Gardens. *See* Northern Palm Beach County
Palm Beach International Airport, 298, 318
Palomilla, 115, 134
Pan cubano, 134
Panama Hatties, 312
Panaro Workshop & Theatre Co., 199
Paper Treasures, 302
Parks and Preserves newspaper, 207
Parrot Jungle and Gardens, 40, 152
Pelican, 126
People-watching, 8, 119, 150, 308
Perfumania, 176
PGA Golf Club at the Reserve, 327
PGA National's Academy of Golf, 315
PGA Seniors Golf Championship, 17
Picadillo, 134
Pigeon Key (Marathon), 225
Pineapple Grove in Delray Beach, 291
Pink flamingos at Hialeah Park, 171
Planetarium, 156
Playmobil Fun Park, 301
Plátano, 134
Police in Miami, 62
Polly Esther's, 297
Polo, 301
Pompano Harness Track, 274
Port Everglades, 269
Port of Miami, 218
Port Salerno. *See* Martin County
Port St. Lucie, 326
Preston B. Bird and Mary Heinlein Fruit and Spice Park, 159
Pretheater Dinners, 8. *See also* Dining
Princess Casino, 219
Pro Player Stadium (Miami), 170
Publix, 181
Pucci's, 202
Pump, 196

Queen Elizabeth 2, 219
quesadillas, 108

351

General Index

General Index

Racetracks on the Gold Coast, 274
Rags to Riches, 186
Rail travel. *See* Train, travel by
Rainbow flag, 77
Rainbow House, 256
The Ramble, 20
Rave bowling, 192
Ray's bar, 310
Raymond F. Kravis Center for the Performing Arts, 310
Red Garter strip club, 265
Red Reef Park (Boca Raton), 289
Red White & Blue, 186
Reefs, artificial, 320
Reflections Kayak Nature Tours, 242
Religious services in Miami, 62
Reservation services, 65
Respectable Street Café, 310
Rest rooms, 62. *See also* Toilets
Restaurants. *See* Restaurants Index
Revolution Records and CDs, 184
Reworx in Key West, 254
Riande, 75
Rickenbacker Causeway, 166
Riverside Park tennis courts, 331
Robbie's Partyboats & Charters, 229
Robbie's Pier, 227
Robbie's Rent-A-Boat, 224, 228
Rock 'n' Horse country-and-western spot, 325
Rock Harbor. *See* Key Largo
Rodeo Drive of the south, 302
Roger Dean Stadium (Jupiter), 311
Roland Children's Wear, 179
Roland Martin at Lake Okeechobee, 339
Ropa vieja, 133, 134
Rose Bar in The Delano, 188
Royal Caribbean Cruise Line, 219
Royal Caribbean Golf Classic, 15

Royal Palm Visitor Center, 207
Royal Viking Sun, 219
Rubell family, 70, 82, 154

Sabor (taste), 145
Safari World, 302
Safety concerns, 45, 62, 208
Saffron Scented Bouillabaisse, 109
Sailboards Miami, 165
Sailing in Miami, 165
Salvation, 196
Sandbar, 246
Sandridge Golf Club, 331
Santa's Enchanted Forest, 21
Satchmo Blues, 191
Sawgrass Mills outlet mall, 183, 277
Schmatta Row, 276
Schooners, 163, 252
Science museum, 274
Scott Rakow Youth Center, 161
Scuba diving. *See also* Snorkeling
    Biscayne National Park, 217
    Boca Raton, 289
    Gold Coast, 273
    Miami, 165
    Northern Palm Beach County, 312
    Palm Beach, 300
    Treasure Coast, 320
Scuba Tours of Key Largo, 229
Sea Escape, 272
Sea lions, swimming with, 227
Sea turtles, 228, 267, 290, 313, 323
Seafari Dive and Surf, 313
Seafood, 8, 129, 130
SEAL teams museum, 327
Seasons in the Everglades, 208
Sebastian, 330, 331
SEGA Gameworks, 162
Seniors, 23
Serrucho en escabeche, 115
Seven-Mile Bridge, 225
The Seybold Building, 182
Sforza, 310
Shake-a-Leg sailing program, 165
Shark Valley, 166, 207, 208, 209, 211
Shell-hunting, 150

Shooters, 275, 287
Shopping
    Boca Raton, 291
    Broward County, 276
    business hours in Miami, 60
    Delray Beach, 291
    Key West, 254
    Keys, 230
    Lower Keys, 242
    Miami, 173, 174, 179
    Northern Palm Beach County, 314
    Palm Beach, 302
    Treasure Coast, 322, 333
Shops at Bal Harbour, 173
Shops at Sunset, 173
Shops of Sunset Place, 184
Shoulder season, 65
Shula, Don, 80
Singer Island. *See* Northern Palm Beach County
Singer, Issac Bashevis, 126
Skydiving on the Treasure Coast, 338
Sloppy Joe's in Fort Lauderdale, 287
Sloppy Joe's in Key West, 265
Smarter Living, 25, 34
Smathers Beach, 252
Snorkeling. *See also* Scuba diving
    Biscayne National Park, 4, 217
    Boca Raton, 289
    Dry Tortugas, 267
    Keys, 229
    Lower Keys, 242
    Northern Palm Beach County, 312
    Treasure Coast, 320
Sobe crowd, 114
Sombrero Beach, 222, 224
Sopa de pollo, 133, 134
Sound Advice, 178
South Beach, 55
    accommodations in, 65
    Art Deco District, 4
South Beach Park, 331
South Beach Studios, 72
South Florida International Auto Show, 20
South Florida Trolley Tours, 274
South Miami, 57, 144
South Pointe Park, 166
Southern Glades Trail, 209
Southern Miami–Dade County, 57

Spanish Monastery Cloisters (North Miami Beach), 158
Spanish River Park, 289
Spas, 7
Specs Music, 185
Spice park, 159
Sports equipment, shopping for, 185
Sports teams, Web sites for, 40
Spy Shops International Inc., 178
St. Lucie City, 317, 326, 327
Stallone, Sylvester, 190
Steakhouses, 8, 122, 137
Stingrays, swimming with, 227
Stone crabs, 106, 112, 144
Stranahan House, 276
Stray Fox Pub, 306
Streets of Mayfair, 184
Stuart. *See* Martin County
Students, discounts for, 23
Studio 23, 198
Sugarloaf Bat Tower, 241
Sun Sentinel Showtime Web site, 38
Sunfest, 17
Sunny Days Catamaran's Fast Cat, 266
Sunny Isles, 12, 55, 186. *See also* Palm Beach
SunTrust Sunday Jazz Brunch at Riverwalk, 19
Super Boat Racing Series, 18
Super Boat World Championship, 20
SuperShuttle, 41, 53
Surf casting. *See* Fishing
Surfing, 151, 217, 331
Surfside, 55. *See also* Miami Beach
Swimming, 150, 217
Symphonies, 199, 297

Taj Mahal of North America, 300
Tantra, 109
Tapas, 133, 134
Taquitos, 108
Tarpons, 227
Taste of the Grove Food and Music Festival, 15
Taxes, 49, 63
Taxis
   in Miami, 52, 59
   water, 275
Tea by the Sea, 266

Tee Times USA, 169
Telephone system, 50, 51
Television stations in Miami, 63
Tennis
   Delray Beach, 290
   Gold Coast, 274
   Miami, 170
   Northern Palm Beach County, 313
   packages, 26
   Palm Beach, 300
   Treasure Coast, 331
Tequesta. *See* Palm Beach County
Theater in Miami, 198
Theater of the Sea (Islamorada), 227
Therapy boutique, 179
Thomas J. White Stadium, 327
Three Kings Parade, 15
Thrift stores in Miami, 186
TicketMaster, 40, 170, 188
TicketWeb Web site, 41
Tiki Bar at the Holiday Isle Resort, 239
Time Out: Miami Web site, 37
Tobacco Road, 191
Tony's Jet Ski Rentals, 164
TOPA (Jackie Gleason Theater of the Performing Arts), 201
Tourist season, 14, 64
Tours. *See also* Package tours
   boat and cruiseship, 162
   boat tours on the Treasure Coast, 338
   Everglades, 211
   glass-bottom boat, 217
   Key West, 251
   scuba diving, 217
   sightseeing, 163
   snorkeling, 217
   South Florida Trolley Tours in Fort Lauderdale, 274
   specialized, 163
   Treasure Coast, 327
   walking tours of the Everglades, 208
Town Center Mall in Boca Raton, 291
Trailways. *See* Greyhound
Train, travel by, 28, 46. *See also* Amtrak
Tram tours of the Everglades, 211

Travelers
   online tools for, 34
   with disabilities, 22, 77
Travelers' Tales Web site, 35
Travelite FAQ, 35
Travelocity, 25, 30, 32
Travelzoo.com, 34
Treasure Coast, 317, 318
   accommodations, 322, 333, 339
   inexpensive hotel options, 328
Trip planning, online directory for, 28
TRIP.com, 31
Tropical Crane Point Hammock, 225
Tropical Everglades Visitor's Center, 12
Tropical Park (Miami), 161
Tropical reefs, 222
Tropical storms, 14
Tropicool Miami Web site, 38
Turtles. *See* Sea turtles
Twist bar, 196

U.S. 1. *See* Overseas Highway (U.S. 1)
U.S. Army Corps of Engineers, 338
U.S. Customs, 43
UDT SEAL Museum, 327
Underwater compartment hotel, 232
University of Miami, 23, 40, 191, 198
Upper and Middle Keys, 222
Upper Keys, 223, 230. *See also* Keys

Vacation Key West, 255
Vacation.com, 32
vacationpackager.com, 26
Vanderbilt Club at the Fisher Island Club, 69
Venetian Pool (Coral Gables), 40, 158
Venice of America, 269, 275
Vero Beach, 330
Vero Beach Dodgers, 333
Vero Beach KOA RV Park, 336
Vero's Tackle and Sport-shop, 331
Versace, Gianni, 72
Visa ATM locator Web site, 34
Visas, obtaining, 42

353

General Index

Warehaus 57, 287
Washington Avenue, shopping, 175
Water sports, 228, 300
Water Taxi of Fort Lauderdale, 275
Watson Hammock Trail, 241
Wave Runners, 164
Weather forecasts online, 34
Weather in Miami, 63
Web sites
    Miami club information, 188
    South Florida and Miami, 36
Web Travel Secrets Web site, 35
WebFlyer Web site, 34
Weeks Air Museum, 157
West Palm Beach, 298, 303, 309
West Palm Beach Fishing Club, 312
Western Hemisphere, oldest building in, 158
Wet Willie's, 190
Wheelchair Getaways, 22
White Party Week, 20
White Salon, 61
Wildman of Loxahatchee, 322
Windsurfing, 150, 165, 217
Wine and All That Jazz party, 19
Wines & spirits, shopping for, 186
Winter Antique Show, 15
Winter Party, 16
Winterfest Boat Parade, 21
Wish, 109
Wolf schooner, 252
The Wolfsonian, 153
World Cup Polo Tournament, 17
Worth Avenue in Palm Beach, 5, 302

X Isle Surf Shop, 186

Yamato Colony, 290
Yankee Fleet, 266
Yellow Moon, 286

Zagat Restaurant Survey Web site, 38
Zane Grey's, 240
Zeta Concert Hotline, 188
Zoos, 151, 152, 162, 227, 302

ACCOMMODATIONS

Abaco Inn (Key West), 260
Abbey Hotel, 73
Airport hotel in Miami, 94
Albion Hotel (South Beach), 70
Alexander All Suite Luxury Hotel (Miami Beach), 80
Angelina Guest (Key West), 260
Avalon Majestic Hotel (South Beach), 73
Azalea Lane Apartments, 335
Bahama Village (Key West), 248, 254
Banana Bay Resort & Marina (Marathon), 233
Banana Bungalow (Miami Beach), 78
Banyan Marian Apartments (Ft. Lauderdale), 281
Baron's Landing Motel & Apartments (Jupiter), 315
Bay Harbor Inn, 6, 85
Bay Harbor Lodge (Key Largo), 235
The Bayliss Guest House, 78
Baymar Ocean Resort (Miami Beach), 85
Beach Castle Hotel, 85
The Beachcomber Hotel, 78
Beachcomber Apartment Motel (Palm Beach), 307
Bentley Hotel, 66
Bermuda Inn, 291
Best Westerns, 86, 213, 230, 303
Biltmore Hotel (Coral Gables), 5, 6, 39, 96, 157, 163
Biscayne Bay Marriott Hotel and Marina, 91
Blue Lagoon Motel (Key West), 260
Blue Moon Hotel, 70
Boca Raton Resort and Club, 292
The Breakers (Palm Beach), 6, 303
Brigham Gardens (South Beach)
Cardozo Hotel, 6, 71
Caribbean Quarters Bed and Breakfast Inn, 281
Casa Grande Suite Hotel (South Beach), 66
Cavalier (South Beach), 74
Cheeca Lodge (Islamorada), 230

Chelsea House (Key West), 258
Chesterfield Hotel (Palm Beach), 74, 305
The Clarion Hotel & Suites, 93
Clay Hotel & International Hostel (South Beach), 79
The Clevelander, 188
Clewiston Inn, 339, 340
Club Med—Sandpiper, 328
Cologne Motel (Jupiter), 315
Colonnade, 98
Colony Hotel & Cabana Club (Delray Beach), 294
Comfort Inn (West Palm Beach), 303
Conch Key Cottages (Marathon), 233
Courtyard Villa (Lauderdale-by-the-Sea), 281
David William Hotel, 97
Davis House Inn, 335
Days Inns, 80, 87, 95, 213, 277, 328
Deer Run Bed and Breakfast (Big Pine Key), 243
The Delano (South Beach), 6, 68, 188
Dezerland Beach Resort Hotel (Surfside), 86
Disney's Vero Beach Resort, 334
Don Shula's Hotel and Golf Club (Miami Lakes), 94
Doral Golf Resort and Spa (West Miami), 7, 93
The Dorchester Hotel, 74
Doubletree Guest Suites, 334
Driftwood Resort, 335
Eden Roc Resort and Spa (Miami Beach), 82
Edgewater Motel and Apartments, 328
Essex House Hotel and Suites (South Beach), 74
Everglades Hotel (downtown Miami), 93
Everglades Motel (Homestead), 214
Extended Stay America/Crossland Economy Studios (Ft. Lauderdale), 5, 278
Faro Blanco Marine Resort (Marathon), 234
Fisher Island Club, 7, 68

Flamingo Lodge, 206, 207, 211, 212
Floyd's Youth Hostel/Crew House (Ft. Lauderdale), 282
Fontainebleau Hilton (Miami Beach), 6, 83
Four Points Sheraton Miami Beach, 86
Four Seasons Resort Palm Beach, 304
The Grand (Key West), 6, 260
Grand Bay. *See* Wyndham Grand Bay Hotel
Grand Bay Resort, 88
Grove Isle Club and Resort (Coconut Grove), 5, 99
Hampton Inns, 100, 213, 328, 334
Harbor Light Resort (Hutchinson Island), 328
Harborfront Inn Bed & Breakfast, 323
Hawk's Cay Resort (Duck Key), 231
Heart of Palm Beach Hotel, 306
Hibiscus House (West Palm Beach), 307
Holiday Inns, 96, 230, 255, 278, 291, 322, 333
Holiday Inn Express (Vero Beach), 333
Holiday Isle Resort (Islamorada), 234
Hollywood Beach Resort, 281
The Hotel, 71
Hotel Astor (South Beach), 71
Hotel Continental Riande (South Beach), 75
Hotel Franklin, 75
The Hotel Impala, 72
Hotel Inter-Continental Miami (downtown Miami), 5, 90
Hotel Leon (South Beach), 75
Hotel Ocean, 72
Hotel Place St. Michel (Coral Gables), 98
Hotel Shelley, 76
Howard Johnsons, 80, 96, 230, 277, 278, 303
Hutchinson Inn, 323
Hyatt Regency at Miami Convention Center, 91
Hyatt Regency Coral Gables, 97

Hyatt Regency Pier 66 (Ft. Lauderdale), 278
Indian Creek Hotel (Miami Beach), 86
Island City House Hotel (Key West), 257
Islander Motel, 335
Jules' Undersea Lodge (Key Largo), 232
Jupiter Beach Resort, 314
Kenmore hotel, 79
The Kent (South Beach), 76
Key West Hilton Resort and Marina, 256
Key West International Hostel, 261
KOA Sugarloaf Key Resort, 244
Kona Kai Resort & Gallery (Key Largo), 235
La Pensione (Key West), 259
Lago Mar Resort and Club (Ft. Lauderdale), 6, 280
Lime Tree Bay Resort (Long Key), 235
Little Palm Island (Little Torch Key), 6, 243
Loews Hotel (Miami Beach), 66
Marquesa Hotel (Key West), 258
Marriott Key Largo Bay Beach Resort, 232
Marriott's Harbor Beach Resort (Ft. Lauderdale), 278
Marseilles Hotel (South Beach), 76
Mayfair House Hotel (Coconut Grove), 99
Mellon Patch Inn, 329
The Mermaid Guesthouse (Miami Beach), 77
Miami Beach Ocean Resort, 84
Miami International Airport Hotel, 94
Miami River Inn, 6, 92
Miccosukee Resort and Convention Center, 94
The Moorings (Islamorada), 233
Mutiny Hotel, 100
The Nassau Suite Hotel, 77
The National Hotel (South Beach), 69
Newport Beachside Hotel & Resort, 87
Ocean Key Resort (Key West), 258

Ocean Lodge (Boca Raton), 295
Omni Colonnade Hotel (Coral Gables), 98
Palm Beach Hilton, 303
Palm Beach Historic Inn, 306
Palm Beach Hotel, 303
Palm Beach Ritz Carlton, 304
Palm Court Inn (Vero Beach), 333
Panther Motel and Apartments (Deerfield Beach), 292
Park Washington Hotel (South Beach), 79
Parkview Motor Lodge, 303
Parmer's Place Cottages (Little Torch Key), 243
PGA National Resort & Spa (Palm Beach Gardens), 315
Pier 66 hotel, 278
Pier House Resort and Caribbean Spa (Key West), 257
Plaza Inn (Palm Beach), 306
President Hotel, 78
Radisson Bridge Resort, 291
Ragged Edge Resort (Islamorada), 236
Ramada Limited Resort & Casino, 230
Ramada Miami Beach Resort, 87
Reach (Key West), 256
Riande Continental Bayside (downtown Miami), 92
Ritz Carlton Palm Beach (Manalpan), 6, 304
Riverside Hotel (Ft. Lauderdale), 280
Riviera Court Motel (Coral Gables), 98
Roney Palace Resort & Spa, 83
Ronny Dee Resort Motel (Pompano Beach), 282
Sailfish Marina & Resort, 312
Sandpiper Club Med (Port St. Lucie), 328
Sea Downs (Hollywood), 282
Sea Turtle Inn & Azalea Lane Apartments, 335

355

Accommodations Index

Seagate Hotel & Beach Club (Delray Beach), 294
Sebastian Beach Inn, 337
Sheraton Bal Harbour Beach Resort, 84
Sheraton Biscayne Bay Hotel (Key Biscayne), 92
Shore Edge Motel (Boca Raton), 295
Shorehaven Hotel (Miami Beach), 88
Silver Sands Beach Resort (Key Biscayne), 88
Sonesta Beach Resort Key Biscayne, 6, 90
South Beach Oceanfront Motel (Key West), 259
Southernmost Point Guest House (Key West), 259
Spanish River Resort (Delray Beach), 294
Suez Oceanfront Resort (Sunny Isles Beach), 88
Taft House hotel, 79
The Tides (South Beach), 69
The Tiffany Hotel, 71
Turnberry Isle Resort (Aventura), 7, 95
Villa Nina Island Beach Bed & Breakfast, 329
Villa Paradiso (Miami Beach), 79
Weatherstation Inn, 258
Wellesley Inn, 314
Westin Beach Resort (Key Largo), 231
Winterhaven Hotel, 73
Wyndham Grand Bay Hotel (Coconut Grove), 100
Wyndham near the Miami airport, 95
Wyndham Reach Resort, 256
Wyndham Resort and Spa (Ft. Lauderdale), 7, 279

RESTAURANTS

Alonzo's Oyster Bar, 263
Amici (Palm Beach), 8, 308
Amos' Juice Bar (North Miami Beach), 136
Anacapri (South Miami), 144
Anthony's Café (Key West), 264
Antonia's (Key West), 262
Astor Place (South Beach), 105
Athenian Café (Jupiter), 316
Atlantic Restaurant, 82
Atlantic's Edge restaurant (Islamorada), 231, 236
Bagatelle (Key West), 262
Bagel Factory (South Beach), 118
Bahama Mama's Kitchen, 264
Balan's (South Beach), 113
Barracuda Grill (Marathon), 237
Bayside Seafood Restaurant and Hidden Cove Bar (Key Biscayne), 128
Beachside Restaurant (Vero Beach), 337
Biscayne Miracle Mile Cafeteria (Coral Gables), 140
Blue Door (South Beach), 8, 68, 106
Blue Heaven (Key West), 263
Bocca di Rosa (Coconut Grove), 141
Brasserie Les Halles (Coral Gables), 139
Cafe des Artistes (Key West), 261
Cafe Hammock (South Miami), 144
Cafe Iguana, 192
Cafe l'Europe (Palm Beach), 308
Cafe Maxx (Pompano Beach), 283
Cafe Nostalgia, 196
Cafe Prima Pasta (Miami Beach), 123
Cafe Ragazzi (Surfside), 123
Café Tabac, 114
Cafe Tu Tu Tango (Coconut Grove), 144
Caffe Abbracci (Coral Gables), 138
Caffe Da Vinci, 124
Calypso's restaurant (Key Largo), 238
Capri Restaurant, 214
Capt. Charlie's Reef Grill (Jupiter), 316
Caribbean Delite (downtown Miami), 130
Carpaccio (Bal Harbour), 122
Casa Juancho (Little Havana), 8, 132
Casablanca Café (Ft. Lauderdale), 283
Chef Allen's (North Miami Beach), 135
Chinese Gourmet Buffet, 125
Chinese restaurant, kosher, 87
Christy's (Coral Gables), 137
Chrysanthemum Chinese restaurant (South Beach), 7, 114
Chuck & Harold's Café (Palm Beach), 308
Coco's Kitchen (Big Pine Key), 245
Conca'D'Oro restaurant (Hollywood), 284
Conchy Joe's Seafood, 325
Creolina's restaurant, 284
The Crepe Maker Café (South Miami), 145
Crystal Café (Miami Beach), 7, 122
Curry's (Miami Beach), 125
The Daily Bread Marketplace (Coral Gables), 140
The Deli (Key West), 264
Deli Den (Hollywood), 7, 286
E. R. Bradley's Saloon (Palm Beach), 9, 310
East City Grill (Ft. Lauderdale), 283
East Coast Burrito Factory (Ft. Lauderdale), 286
East Coast Fisheries (downtown Miami), 129, 180
El Siboney Restaurant (Key West), 264
El Toro Taco, 214
Eleven Maple Street restaurant, 324
Escopazzo (South Beach), 8, 106
Fausto's Food Palace, 261
Fifth Avenue Grill (Delray Beach), 295
Fishbone Grille (downtown Miami), 8, 130
Flamingo Restaurant (Everglades), 214
Floridian Restaurant, 8, 286
The Forge Restaurant, 7, 8, 122, 188
Gables Diner (Coral Gables), 139
The Globe (Coral Gables), 139
Globe cafe, 191
Gourmet Diner (North Miami Beach), 135

Greek Place (Surfside), 125
Green Street Café (Coconut Grove), 142
Green's Pharmacy (West Palm Beach), 309
Grillfish (South Beach), 114
Henry's Bakery and Gourmet Pizza Shop (Islamorada), 238
Here Comes the Sun (North Miami), 136
Hollywood Cafe, 288
House of India (Coral Gables), 140
Hy Vong (Little Havana), 134
Indigo restaurant (Ft. Lauderdale), 280, 284
Indigo Restaurant and Bar, 129
Islamorada Fish Company, 238
Jeffrey's (South Beach), 115
Joe Allen restaurant (South Beach), 115
Joe's Stone Crab Restaurant (South Beach), 106, 180
John G's coffee shop (Lake Worth), 309
John Martin's (Coral Gables), 139
Joia Restaurant and Bar, 111
Key Largo's Crack'd Conch, 239
Kosher Chinese restaurant, 87
L'Entrecote de Paris (South Beach), 115
La Carreta (Little Havana), 133
La Cibeles Café (downtown Miami), 131
La Sandwicherie (South Beach), 119, 202
La Vieille Maison (Boca Raton), 295
The Lagoon (North Miami Beach), 135
Larios on the Beach (South Beach), 115
Laurenzo's Café (North Miami Beach), 136, 186
Lazy Days Oceanfront Bar and Seafood Grill (Islamorada), 237
Le Festival (Coral Gables), 138
Lemon Twist (Miami Beach), 124

Lorelei Restaurant and Cabana Bar (Islamorada), 238
Louie's Backyard (Key West), 261
Lou's Philly Cheesesteak and South Street BBQ, 118
Macarena (South Beach), 116
Mama Vieja (South Beach), 124
Mangia, Mangia (Key West), 263
Mango's Tropical Cafe, 197
Mangoes (Key West), 262
Mangrove Mama's Restaurant (Sugarloaf Key), 244
Marker 88 (Islamorada), 237
Max's Grille (Boca Raton), 296
Mayya Restaurant & Cafe, 106
The Melting Pot (North Miami Beach), 136
Miami Beach Place, 126
Miccosukee Restaurant (Shark Valley), 214
Monte's restaurant (Summerland Key), 244
Monty's Stone Crab/Seafood House (South Beach), 112
Morada Bay bistro (Islamorada), 237
Mrs. Mendoza's Tacos al Carbon (South Beach), 8, 119
Nature's Way Cafe, 325
Nemo (South Beach), 112
New York Prime (Boca Raton), 8
News Cafe in the Grove (Coconut Grove), 144
Nick's Tomato Pie (Jupiter), 316
Nino's Cafe (Vero Beach), 337
No Anchovies! Restaurant (Palm Beach Gardens), 316
No Name Pub (Big Pine Key), 246
NOA (Noodles of Asia) in South Beach, 117
Norman's (Coral Gables), 8, 137
Oasis (Key Biscayne), 128, 255
Ocean Grill (Vero Beach), 336

Oggi Caffe (North Bay Village), 125
Osteria del Teatro (South Beach), 108
Pacific Time (South Beach), 108
The Palm (Bay Harbour Island), 123
Pauloluigi's Ristorante Italiana, 143
Pepe's (Key West), 263
Perricone's Marketplace (downtown Miami), 131
Pollo Tropical (South Miami), 9, 145
Provence Grill, 130
PT's Late Night (Key West), 264
Puerto Sagua (South Beach), 119
Raja's (downtown Miami), 132
The Red Lantern (Coconut Grove), 143
Rhythm Café (West Palm Beach), 308
Rusty Pelican (Key Biscayne), 126
Ruth's Chris Steak House, 138
S&S Restaurant (downtown Miami), 132
Scalawags restaurant, 323
Señor Frogs (Coconut Grove), 143
Sergio's (Coral Gables), 141
Sheldon's Drugs (Surfside), 126
Shorty's (South Miami), 146
Shula's Steak House (Miami), 8, 94
Shula's Steak House (Miami Beach), 8, 80, 123
Smith & Wollensky (South Beach), 109
Sonya's steak house, 334
Soyka Restaurant & Café, 130, 187
Splendid Blendeds (Delray), 296
Sports Café (South Beach), 120
Stefano's (Key Biscayne), 126
Stephan's Gourmet Market & Café (South Beach), 120
Strand Restaurant and Beach Grill, 112
Sugar Reef (Hollywood), 284

357

Restaurant Index

Restaurant Index

Sundays on the Bay (Key Biscayne), 128
Sushi Blues Café (Hollywood), 285, 287
Taboo (West Palm Beach), 309
Tap Tap (South Beach), 117
Tarpon Bend restaurant, 285
The Tea Room (South Miami), 146
Thai Spice (Ft. Lauderdale), 286
Theo Thudpucker's Raw Bar and Seafood Restaurant, 330
Thudpucker's chowder bar, 330
Time Out Barbecue (Islamorada), 239
Tin Muffin Café (Boca Raton), 296
Tom's Place (Boca Raton), 296
Toni's Sushi (South Beach), 117
TooJay's (Palm Beach), 309
Topango! Restaurant (Ft. Lauderdale), 285
Turtle Kraals Wildlife Grill (Key West), 264
Tuscan Steak (South Beach), 113
Van Dyke Café (South Beach), 118, 191
Van Dyke Café, 137
Versailles (Little Havana), 7, 134, 202
Wilderness Grill, 137, 145
Wolfie Cohen's Rascal House (Sunny Isles), 125
Woody's Saloon and Restaurant, 239
Wrapido (South Miami), 146
Yuca (South Beach), 7, 110, 198

FROMMER'S® COMPLETE TRAVEL GUIDES

Alaska
Amsterdam
Arizona
Atlanta
Australia
Austria
Bahamas
Barcelona, Madrid & Seville
Beijing
Belgium, Holland & Luxembourg
Bermuda
Boston
British Columbia & the Canadian Rockies
Budapest & the Best of Hungary
California
Canada
Cancún, Cozumel & the Yucatán
Cape Cod, Nantucket & Martha's Vineyard
Caribbean
Caribbean Cruises & Ports of Call
Caribbean Ports of Call
Carolinas & Georgia
Chicago
China
Colorado
Costa Rica
Denmark
Denver, Boulder & Colorado Springs
England
Europe
European Cruises & Ports of Call
Florida
France
Germany
Greece
Greek Islands
Hawaii
Hong Kong
Honolulu, Waikiki & Oahu
Ireland
Israel
Italy
Jamaica
Japan
Las Vegas
London
Los Angeles
Maryland & Delaware
Maui
Mexico
Miami & the Keys
Montana & Wyoming
Montréal & Québec City
Munich & the Bavarian Alps
Nashville & Memphis
Nepal
New England
New Mexico
New Orleans
New York City
New Zealand
Nova Scotia, New Brunswick & Prince Edward Island
Oregon
Paris
Philadelphia & the Amish Country
Portugal
Prague & the Best of the Czech Republic
Provence & the Riviera
Puerto Rico
Rome
San Antonio & Austin
San Diego
San Francisco
Santa Fe, Taos & Albuquerque
Scandinavia
Scotland
Seattle & Portland
Singapore & Malaysia
South Africa
Southeast Asia
South Pacific
Spain
Sweden
Switzerland
Thailand
Tokyo
Toronto
Tuscany & Umbria
USA
Utah
Vancouver & Victoria
Vermont, New Hampshire & Maine
Vienna & the Danube Valley
Virgin Islands
Virginia
Walt Disney World & Orlando
Washington, D.C.
Washington State

FROMMER'S® DOLLAR-A-DAY GUIDES

Australia from $50 a Day
California from $60 a Day
Caribbean from $70 a Day
England from $70 a Day
Europe from $60 a Day
Florida from $60 a Day
Hawaii from $70 a Day
Ireland from $60 a Day
Italy from $70 a Day
London from $85 a Day
New York from $80 a Day
Paris from $85 a Day
San Francisco from $60 a Day
Washington, D.C., from $60 a Day

FROMMER'S® PORTABLE GUIDES

Acapulco, Ixtapa & Zihuatanejo
Alaska Cruises & Ports of Call
Bahamas
Baja & Los Cabos
Berlin
California Wine Country
Charleston & Savannah
Chicago
Dublin
Hawaii: The Big Island
Las Vegas
London
Maine Coast
Maui
New Orleans
New York City
Paris
Puerto Vallarta, Manzanillo & Guadalajara
San Diego
San Francisco
Sydney
Tampa & St. Petersburg
Venice
Washington, D.C.

FROMMER'S® NATIONAL PARK GUIDES

Family Vacations in the
  National Parks
Grand Canyon

National Parks of the
  American West
Rocky Mountain

Yellowstone & Grand Teton
Yosemite & Sequoia/
  Kings Canyon
Zion & Bryce Canyon

FROMMER'S® MEMORABLE WALKS

Chicago
London

New York
Paris

San Francisco
Washington D.C.

FROMMER'S® GREAT OUTDOOR GUIDES

New England
Northern California

Southern California & Baja
Southern New England

Washington & Oregon

FROMMER'S® BORN TO SHOP GUIDES

Born to Shop: China
Born to Shop: France

Born to Shop: Italy
Born to Shop: London

Born to Shop: New York
Born to Shop: Paris

FROMMER'S® IRREVERENT GUIDES

Amsterdam
Boston
Chicago
Las Vegas

London
Los Angeles
Manhattan
New Orleans

Paris
San Francisco
Seattle & Portland
Vancouver

Walt Disney World
Washington, D.C.

FROMMER'S® BEST-LOVED DRIVING TOURS

America
Britain
California

Florida
France
Germany

Ireland
Italy
New England

Scotland
Spain
Western Europe

THE UNOFFICIAL GUIDES®

Bed & Breakfasts in
  California
Bed & Breakfasts in
  New England
Bed & Breakfasts in
  the Northwest
Beyond Disney
Branson, Missouri
California with Kids
Chicago

Cruises
Disneyland
Florida with Kids
Golf Vacations in the
  Eastern U.S.
The Great Smoky &
  Blue Ridge
  Mountains
Inside Disney

Hawaii
Las Vegas
London
Miami & the Keys
Mini Las Vegas
Mini-Mickey
New Orleans
New York City
Paris

Safaris
San Francisco
Skiing in the West
Walt Disney World
Walt Disney World
  for Grown-ups
Walt Disney World
  for Kids
Washington, D.C.

SPECIAL-INTEREST TITLES

Frommer's Britain's Best Bed & Breakfasts and
  Country Inns
Frommer's Britain's Best Bike Rides
The Civil War Trust's Official Guide
  to the Civil War Discovery Trail
Frommer's Caribbean Hideaways
Frommer's Food Lover's Companion to France
Frommer's Food Lover's Companion to Italy
Frommer's Gay & Lesbian Europe
Frommer's Exploring America by RV
Hanging Out in Europe
Israel Past & Present

Mad Monks' Guide to California
Mad Monks' Guide to New York City
Frommer's The Moon
Frommer's New York City with Kids
The New York Times' Unforgettable
  Weekends
Places Rated Almanac
Retirement Places Rated
Frommer's Road Atlas Britain
Frommer's Road Atlas Europe
Frommer's Washington, D.C., with Kids
Frommer's What the Airlines Never Tell You